For
reference

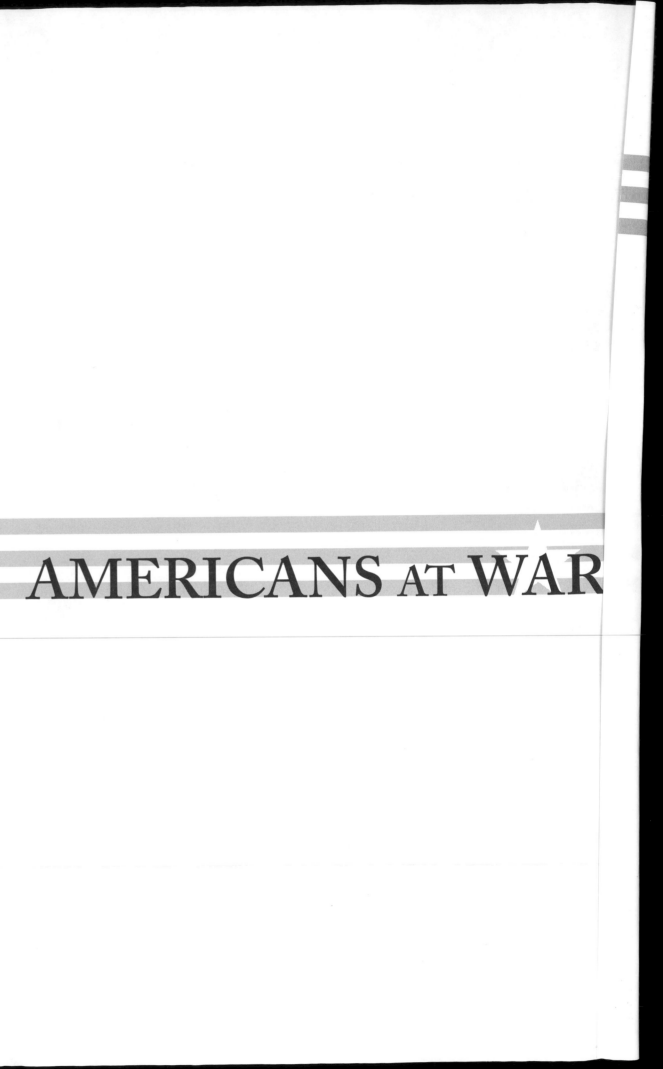

AMERICANS AT WAR

EDITORIAL & PRODUCTION STAFF

TABLE OF CONTENTS

VOLUME 1: 1500–1815

VOLUME 2: 1816–1900

VOLUME 4: 1946–PRESENT

Daniel W. Aldridge, III
Davidson College
African Americans (Freed People)
Douglass, Frederick

John K. Alexander
University of Cincinnati
Sons of Liberty

Donna Alvah
St. Lawrence University
Military Families
Vietnam Veterans
Women's Rights and Feminism, 1946–Present

Angelo T. Angelis
Hunter College
Revolution and Radical Reform

Janis Appier
University of Tennessee
Catt, Carrie Chapman

Marie L. Aquila
Ball State University's Indiana Academy of Science,
Mathematics, and Humanities
Music, World War II

Robert A. Arlt
Independent Scholar
Jefferson, Thomas

Stephen V. Ash
University of Tennessee at Knoxville
Occupation of the South

Jeanie Attie
Long Island University
United States Sanitary Commission

Allan W. Austin
College Misericordia
Japanese Americans, World War II
Tokyo Rose

Jean Harvey Baker
Goucher College
Lincoln, Mary Todd
Women's Suffrage Movement

James M. Banner, Jr.
Washington, D.C.
Federalist Party
Hartford Convention

Lance Banning
Independent Scholar
Jeffersonian Republican Party
Madison, James

J. L. Bell
Independent Scholar
Boston Massacre: Pamphlets and Propaganda
Boston Tea Party: Politicizing Ordinary People
Hewes, George Robert Twelves

Richard J. Bell
Harvard University
Republican Womanhood

Scott H. Bennett
Georgian Court University
Dissent in World War I and World War II

Chad Berry
Maryville College
Regional Migration, World War I and World War
    II

Michael E. Birdwell
Tennessee Technological University
York, Alvin Cullum

Mary W. Blanchard
Independent Scholar
Visual Arts, World War I

Larry I. Bland
Marshall Museum VMI
Marshall, George C.

Rose Blue
Independent Scholar
Age of Westward Expansion
Cochran, Jackie
Compromise of 1850
Confederate States of America
Davis, Angela
Ford, Henry
Hiroshima Guilt
Kirkpatrick, Jeanne
Madison, Dolley
New York City Draft Riots
Pirates and the Barbary War
United Nations

David Bogen
Emerson College
Iran-Contra Affair

Mark Boulton
University of Tennessee
Allies, Images of
Peace Movements, 1898–1945
Propaganda, 1898–1945
Wayne, John

Terry Bouton
University of Maryland
Civil Liberties: Kentucky and Virginia Resolutions

Charlene M. Boyer Lewis
Kalamazoo College
Recreation and Social Life

Patricia Bradley
Temple University
Slavery and the Homefront, 1775–1783

Stuart D. Brandes
Independent Scholar
Financing, World War I
Financing, World War II

Dewey A. Browder
Austin Peay State University
Berlin as Symbol

Margaret Lynn Brown
Brevard College
Civilian Conservation Corps (CCC)

Mary Lynn McCree Bryan
Duke University
Addams, Jane

Lisa M. Budreau
St. Anthony's College, Oxford University
Armistice Day
Gold Star Mothers Pilgrimage
Monuments, Cemeteries, Spanish American War
Monuments, Cemeteries, World War I

Stephanie M. H. Camp
University of Washington
Slavery

D'Ann Campbell
United States Coast Guard Academy
Equal Rights Amendment (ERA) and Drafting
    Women

Feminism
Women and World War I
Women and World War II
Women Integrated into the Military

Nicholas J. Capasso
DeCordova Museum and Sculpture Park
Vietnam Veterans Memorial

Lewis H. Carlson
Independent Scholar
Red Scare

John Whiteclay Chambers II
Rutgers University
Wilson, Woodrow

Paul A. Cimbala
Fordham University
Civil War Veterans
Freedmen's Bureau

J. Ransom Clark
Muskingum College
CIA and Espionage

John E. Clark, Jr.
Independent Scholar
Railroads

Craig T. Cobane
Culver-Stockton College
Atomic Energy Commission
Star Wars
Terrorism, Fears of
Think Tanks

David G. Coleman
Miller Center of Public Affairs, University of Virginia
Kennedy, John Fitzgerald

Susan G. Contente
Independent Scholar
Clothing, World War I and World War II

Conrad C. Crane
United States Army War College
Mitchell, Billy
Stewart, Jimmy

Robert E. Cray, Jr.
Montclair State University
Politics and Expressions of Patriotism

Lynda Lasswell Crist
Rice University
Davis, Jefferson

Wayne Cutler
University of Tennessee
Polk, James K.

Ginger R. Davis
Independent Scholar
Vietnamese and Hmong Refugees
Who Served in Vietnam?

Michael Davis
Independent Scholar
Adams, John
Common Sense
Olympics and Cold War

Mary A. DeCredico
United States Naval Academy
Chesnut, Mary Boykin

James X. Dempsey
Center for Democracy & Technology
Civil Liberties, 1945–Present

Victor G. Devinatz
Illinois State University
Labor, 1946–Present

Jose O. Diaz
Ohio State University
Davis, Varina Howell

Jonathan M. DiCicco
Rutgers, The State University of New Jersey
Disarmament and Arms Control, 1898–1945

Ricky Dobbs
Texas A & M - Commerce
Texas, Republic of

Michael B. Dougan
Arkansas State University
Black Codes
Civil Liberties, Civil War

Robert C. Doyle
Franciscan University of Steubenville
Prisons and Prisoners of War, 1815–1900

James D. Drake
Metropolitan State College
King Philip's War, Legacy of

Mara Drogan
University of Albany, SUNY
Arms Control Debate

Christopher M. Duncan
University of Dayton
Anti-Federalists

Sylvia Engdahl
Independent Scholar
Space Race

Thomas I. Faith
George Washington University
Roosevelt, Eleanor

Victoria A. Farrar-Myers
University of Texas at Arlington
Bush, George H.W.
Bush, George W.

Elizabeth Faue
Wayne State University
Veterans Benefits

Ilene Rose Feinman
California State University, Monterey Bay
Peace Movements, 1946–Present

Daniel Feller
University of Tennessee
Jackson, Andrew

Michael D. Fellman
Simon Fraser University
Lee, Robert E.

Phyllis F. Field
Ohio University
Political Parties

Gayle V. Fischer
Salem State College
Clothing

Thomas Fleming
Independent Scholar
Hamilton, Alexander

Justin Florence
Harvard University
Quasi-War and the Rise of Political Parties

Ernest Freeberg
University of Tennessee
Civil Liberties, World War I
Journalism, Spanish American War

Richard M. Fried
University of Illinois at Chicago
McCarthyism

Tim Alan Garrison
Portland State University
Indian Removal and Response

Edith B. Gelles
Stanford University
Adams, Abigail

Nancy Gentile Ford
Bloomsburg University of Pennsylvania
Americanization
Labor, World War I
Mobilization for War

Delia Gillis
Central Missouri State University
Education
Powell, Colin
Refugees

Andrew D. Glassberg
University of Missouri—St. Louis
Military Bases

David T. Gleeson
University of Charleston
Immigrants and Immigration
Lost Cause

Rebecca Goetz
Harvard University
Galloway, Grace: Diary of a Loyalist

Eliga H. Gould
University of New Hampshire
Peace of Paris, 1763

Lewis L. Gould
University of Texas, emeritus
Great Society
Johnson, Lyndon Baines
1968 Upheaval

Charles D. Grear
Texas Christian University
Blockade, Civil War

Emily Greenwald
Historical Research Associates, Inc. (Missoula, MT)
 Dawes Severalty Act

Beth Griech-Polelle
Bowling Green State University
 Holocaust, American Response to

David Grimsted
University of Maryland
 Violence

Ricardo Griswold del Castillo
San Diego State University
 Guadalupe Hidalgo, Treaty of

Michael J. Guasco
Davidson College
 Bacon's Rebellion

Allen C. Guelzo
Gettysburg College
 Lincoln, Abraham

Joan R. Gundersen
University of Pittsburgh
 Brown, Charlotte: Diary of a Nurse
 Camp Followers: War and Women
 Drinker, Elizabeth

Michael W. Hail
Morehead State University
 Poor Relief, 1815–1900
 States and Nation Building, 1775–1783

Jeremy L. Hall
Independent Scholar
 States and Nation Building, 1775–1783

John Earl Haynes
Library of Congress
 Rosenberg, Hiss, Oppenheimer Cases

Sam W. Haynes
University of Texas at Arlington
 Manifest Destiny

Kenneth J. Heineman
Ohio University
 Americanism vs. Godless Communism
 Communism and Anticommunism

Jan Kenneth Herman
Bureau of Medicine and Surgery, Wash DC
 Medicine, World War II

Donald R. Hickey
Wayne State College
 Embargo
 War of 1812

Sarah Hilgendorff List
Independent Historian
 Ku Klux Klan
 Segregation, Racial, 1815–1900
 Whitman, Walt

Sylvia D. Hoffert
University of North Carolina at Chapel Hill
 Woman's Rights Movement

Leonne M. Hudson
Kent State University
 Food Shortages

Darren Hughes
University of Tennessee
 Motion Pictures during World Wars I and II

Jean M. Humez
University of Massachusetts, Boston
 Tubman, Harriet

R. Douglas Hurt
Iowa State University
 Farming

Samuel C. Hyde, Jr.
Southeastern Louisiana University
 Sharecropping and Tenant Farming

Christina Jarvis
State University of New York at Fredonia
 Visual Arts, World War II
 World War II, Images of

Laura S. Jensen
University of Massachusetts
 Veterans' Benefits

Richard Jensen
Independent Scholar
 9–11

Herbert A. Johnson
University of South Carolina Law School
 Supreme Court
 Supreme Court and War Powers

Adam Jones
Center for Research and Teaching in Economics (CIDE), Mexico City
 Latinos in the Military, 1946–Present

Steven Jones
Brown University
Nuclear Freeze Movement
Weapons of Mass Destruction

John P. Kaminski
University of Wisconsin, Madison
Washington, George

Angela Frye Keaton
University of Tennessee
Civil Liberties, World War II

Jennifer D. Keene
Chapman University
American Legion
Bonus March
Demobilization
Profiteering

Richard Kirkendall
University of Washington
Truman, Harry S.
Truman Doctrine

Wendy Kozol
Oberlin College
Photojournalism

Gregory Kupsky
University of Tennessee
Prisoner of War Camps, United States

Stanford J. Layton
Weber State University
Homestead Act

Jama Lazerow
Wheelock College
Black Power/Black Panthers

James S. Leamon
Bates College
Armed Conflicts in America, 1587-1815
Loyalists
Shays's and Whiskey Rebellions

Daniel B. Lee
Pennsylvania State University
Television, 1946–Present

Edward Lengel
Independent Scholar
Memoirs, Autobiographies

Neil W. Lerner
Davidson College
Music, Civil War
Music, Musicians, and the War on Terrorism
Music, World War I

J. E. Lighter
University of Tennessee
Literature, World War I
Literature, World War II

Blanche M. G. Linden
Independent Scholar
Anthony, Susan B.
Friedan, Betty

Judy Barrett Litoff
Bryant College
Rosie the Riveter
Women, Employment of

Ellen M. Litwicki
State University of New York at Fredonia
Fourth of July
Memorial (Decoration) Day

M. Philip Lucas
Cornell College
Elections, Presidential: The Civil War

Ralph E. Luker
Independent Historian
Churches, Mainstream
Civil Rights Movement
Jackson, Jesse Louis
King, Martin Luther, Jr.
Nonviolence

Michael Lynch
Cornell University
Iran-Contra Affair

John Majewski
University of California
Financing the War

John W. Malsberger
Muhlenberg College
Cuban Missile Crisis
Kissinger, Henry
Nixon, Richard M.

Anthony Maravillas
Independent Scholar
Tet, Impact of

Rosemary Bryant Mariner
Center for the Study of War and Society
Conscription, World War II
National Guard

Norman Markowitz
Rutgers University
Higher Education
Labor, World War II

John F. Marszalek
Mississippi State University
Sherman's March to the Sea

James Marten
Marquette University
Children and the Civil War

Cathy Matson
University of Delaware
Continental Congresses

Holly A. Mayer
Duquesne University
Generals' Wives: Martha Washington, Catharine
Greene, Lucy Knox

Paul T. McCartney
University of Richmond
Neo-isolationism
Triumphalism
War Powers Act

Richard B. McCaslin
High Point University
Johnson, Andrew

Michael A. McDonnell
University of Sydney
Republicanism and War

Gordon B. McKinney
Berea College
Peace Movements

John R. McKivigan
Indiana University- Purdue University at Indianapolis
Abolitionists

Sally G. McMillen
Davidson College
Civil War and Industrial and Technological
Advances
Civil War and Its Impact on Sexual Attitudes on
the Homefront

Dix, Dorothea
Family Life
Stanton, Elizabeth Cady

Daniel T. Miller
Historical Solutions LLC, Indiana
Alien and Sedition Laws
Hamilton's Reports

Laura M. Miller
Vanderbilt University
Arnold, Benedict
Du Bois, W.E.B.
Grant, Ulysses S
Hemingway, Ernest
Jackson, Thomas J. (Stonewall)

Randall M. Miller
St. Joseph's University
Religion, Civil War

D. E. "Gene" Mills Jr.
Florida State University
Churches, Evangelical, 1946–Present

Curtis Miner
State Museum of Pennsylvania
Levittown

Susan Moeller
Philip Merrill College of Journalism
Photography, Civil War
Photography, World War I
Photography, World War II

Edwin E. Moise
Clemson University
Pentagon Papers

John Morello
DeVry University
Antiwar Movement
Drugs and Vietnam
Grunts
Music, Vietnam Era
My Lai
Selective Service

Michael A. Morrison
Purdue University
Kansas Nebraska Act

James C. Mott
Independent Scholar
Holocaust Guilt
Politics and Elections

Malcolm Muir, Jr.
Austin Peay State University
    MacArthur, Douglas

Brigitte L. Nacos
Columbia University
    Hostage Crisis, 1979–1981

Corinne J. Naden
Independent Scholar
    Age of Westward Expansion
    Cochran, Jackie
    Compromise of 1850
    Confederate States of America
    Davis, Angela
    Ford, Henry
    Hiroshima Guilt
    Kirkpatrick, Jeanne
    Madison, Dolley
    New York City Draft Riots
    Pirates and the Barbary War
    United Nations

June Namias
Independent Historian
    Rowlandson, Mary

Michael S. Neiberg
United States Air Force Academy
    ROTC
    Volunteer Army and Professionalism

John Nerone
University of Illinois, Urbana–Champaign
    Newspapers and Magazines

Thomas M. Nichols
Naval War College
    Preemptive War
    Preventive War

Travis Nygard
University of Pittsburgh
    Visual Arts, Civil War and the West

Greg O'Brien
University of Southern Mississippi
    Jamestown: Legacy of the Massacre of 1622
    Legacies of Indian Warfare
    Native Americans: Images in Popular Culture

Christopher J. Olsen
Indiana State University
    Secession

Russell Olwell
Eastern Michigan University
    Manhattan Project

William L. O'Neill
Rutgers University
    Roosevelt, Franklin Delano

Stephen R. Ortiz
University of Florida
    Hoover, Herbert
    Veterans of Foreign Wars

Victoria E. Ott
University of Tennessee
    Widows and Orphans
    Women on the Homefront

Matthew M. Oyos
Radford University
    Roosevelt, Theodore

Chester J. Pach, Jr.
Ohio University
    Eisenhower, Dwight D.
    Korea, Impact of
    Nitze, Paul
    Nonalignment
    Patriotism
    Reagan, Ronald

Richard Panchyk
Independent Historian
    Clinton, William Jefferson
    Conscription, World War I
    Flags
    Fort William Henry Massacre, Cultural Legacy
    Homeland Security
    Men on the Home Front, Civil War
    Monuments, Cemeteries, World War II
    Rationing
    War, Impact on Ethnic Groups
    Washington's Farewell Address

Melinda Lee Pash
Independent Historian
    African Americans, World War I
    American Indians, World War I and World War II
    National Anthem
    Sexual Behavior

Sidney L. Pash
Fayetteville State University
    Economy, World War I
    Economy, World War II

Isolationism
McKinley, William
New Deal
Pearl Harbor Investigation
Public Opinion

Edward Piacentino
High Point University
Humor, Political

Jim Piecuch
Clarion University
Commonwealth Men
Federalist Papers
Stamp Act Congress

S. W. Pope
University of Lincoln, UK
Sports, World War I
Sports, World War II

Charles B. Potter
Independent Scholar
Cooper, James Fenimore
The Spy: First American War Novel
Wyoming Valley Conflict

Caren Prommersberger
Independent Scholar
Conscription, World War I
Fort William Henry Massacre, Cultural Legacy
Monuments, Cemeteries, World War II

Luca Prono
ABC-Clio
Painters and Patriotism, Late 18th and Early 19th
Centuries
Popular Culture and Cold War
"Who Lost China" Debate

Sarah J. Purcell
Grinnell College
Battle of New Orleans
Bunker Hill Monument
Lafayette's Tour
Memory and Early Histories of the Revolution
Montgomery, Richard

Richard J. Regan
Fordham University
Just-War Debate

John P. Resch
University of New Hampshire—Manchester

Constitution: Creating a Republic
Paine, Thomas
Religion and Revolution
Revolutionary War Veterans

Jason S. Ridler
Royal Military College of Canada
H-Bomb, Decision to Build

Edward Rielly
Saint Joseph's College of Maine
Fiction and Memoirs, Vietnam

Stuart I. Rochester
Office of the Secretary of Defense
POW, MIA

John B. Romeiser
University of Tennessee
Journalism, World War II

Frank A. Salamone
Iona College
Civil War and Industrial and Technological
Advances
Civil War and Its Impact on Sexual Attitudes on
the Homefront
Gays, Civil Rights for, 1946–Present
Journalism, World War I
Multiculturalism and Cold War
Race and Military
Teenagers, 1946–Present

Walter L. Sargent
University of Minnesota
Association Test
Mobilization, War for Independence

Alfred Saucedo
University of Chicago
Enemy, Images of

Gregory L. Schneider
Emporia State University
Goldwater, Barry
John Birch Society

Nancy Schurr
University of Tennessee, Knoxville
Medicine and Health

Larry Schweikart
University of Dayton
Aerospace Industry

Ben H. Severance
University of Tennessee, Knoxville
Reconstruction

John Y. Simon
Southern Illinois University Carbondale
Gettysburg Address

Philip L. Simpson
Brevard Community College
Cold War Novels and Movies
Literature

Gerald L. Sittser
Whitworth College
Religion, World War II

Sheila L. Skemp
University of Mississippi
Franklin, Benjamin

David Sloan
Morehead State College
Poor Relief, 1816–1900

Fred H. Smith
Davidson College
Economic Change and Industrialization

John David Smith
North Carolina State
Emancipation Proclamation

Mark M. Smith
University of South Carolina
Stono Rebellion

André B. Sobocinski
Bureau of Medicine and Surgery, Washington, D.C.
Medicine, World War I

Richard C. Spicer
Boston University
Music and the Revolution

Kathryn St. Clair Ellis
University of Tennessee, Knoxville
GI Bill of Rights

Ian K. Steele
University of Western Ontario
European Invasion of Indian North America, 1513–1765

Stephen K. Stein
University of Memphis
Israel and the United States

Christopher H. Sterling
George Washington University
Radio and Power of Broadcasting

Margaret D. Stock
United States Military Academy
Al Qaida and Taliban
Supreme Court, 1815–1900

Brian D. Stokes
Camden County College
States' Rights, Theory of

Amy H. Sturgis
Belmont University
Monroe, James
Monroe's Tour of New England

Kirsten D. Sword
Georgetown University
Families at War

James Lance Taylor
University of San Francisco
Slavery in America

Athan Theoharis
Marquette University
Federal Bureau of Investigations (FBI)

Rod Timanus
Independent Scholar
Alamo

Lorett Treese
Bryn Mawr College Library
Valley Forge

A. Bowdoin Van Riper
Southern Polytechnic State University
Civil Defense, 1946–Present

John R. Vile
Middle Tennessee State University
Articles of Confederation
Constitution: Bill of Rights
Constitutional Amendments and Changes

Jonathan E. Vincent
University of Kentucky
Red Badge of Courage

Michael Wala
Ruhr-Universität Bochum, Historisches Institut
Containment and Détente

Matthew C. Ward
University of Dundee, Scotland
French and Indian War, Legacy of
Mobilization, French and Indian War

Matt Wasniewski
University of Maryland
Cold War Mobilization
Military-Industrial Complex
NSC #68

Cindy Weinstein
California Institute of Technology
Uncle Tom's Cabin

Patricia Weiss Fagen
Georgetown University
Human Rights

Douglas L. Wheeler
University of New Hampshire
Espionage and Spies

George White, Jr.
University of Tennessee, Knoxville
African Americans, World War II
Imperialism

Stephen J. Whitfield
Brandeis University
Arts as Weapon

Robert C. Williams
Davidson College
Greeley, Horace

Tony Williams
Southern Illinois University, Carbondale
Vietnam Films

Clyde N. Wilson
University of South Carolina
Calhoun, John Caldwell

Mark R. Wilson
University of North Carolina at Charlotte
Business and Finance
Labor and Labor Movements
Preparedness

Meghan Kate Winchell
Independent Scholar
USO

Mitchell Yockelson
*United States National Archives and Records
Administration*
Red Cross, American
Veterans of Foreign Wars

Ronald Young
Georgia Southern University
Declaration of Independence
Foreign Aid, 1946–Present
Latinos, World War I and World War II
Urbanization

Rosemarie Zagarri
George Mason University
Sampson, Deborah
Warren, Mercy Otis

Stephen Zunes
University of San Francisco
Muslims, Stereotypes and Fears of

Preparation for war, war itself, and the legacy of war are among the most important forces shaping American society and culture. Nevertheless, the study of war is often treated as if the only topics of importance were battles and campaigns, results measured in territory, and reputations gained or lost. This four-volume reference set, *Americans at War*, provides students with a different perspective by examining the profound effect of war upon American society, culture, and national identity. The 395 articles in this set, written by leading academic and independent scholars, cover a wide range of topics. We hope that these articles, focused on the effect of war upon society, will provide new insights into the nation's history and character, and will serve as a resource for further study of America's past and for charting the nation's future.

Volume 1 covers the longest period, 1500 to 1815, especially the era beginning in 1607 with the first permanent English settlement at Jamestown. Between 1607 and 1700, apart from frontier skirmishes, raids, and ambushes, colonists from South Carolina through New England were engaged in over a score of declared wars, rebellions, and insurrections. In the eighteenth century Americans were at war more than at peace. Between 1700 and 1800 Americans engaged in seventeen separate conflicts and rebellions, including the 1739 uprising of slaves at Stono, South Carolina, and the Revolutionary War, 1775–1783. Between 1798 and 1825 the United States was at war with Barbary pirates, Seminole Indians, and in the "Second War of Independence," 1812–1815, with Great Britain and Canada.

The articles in this volume examine how those wars, especially the Revolutionary War, influenced American literature, art, and music; affected the role of women; shaped the economy; and challenged the institution of slavery. Articles also examine how dissent and rebellion contributed to America's creed of liberty and the formation of its Constitution. Some articles focus on the effects of war in forming and reinforcing American racial attitudes towards Indians and blacks. Others discuss the effect of war upon civil liberties, such as freedom of speech and politics. The memory of America's wars helped to define the nation's culture and identity through patriotic celebrations, monuments, and memorials, and by honoring Revolutionary war veterans. Wars also reinforced the religious view that the nation was a beacon to the world's suffering and repressed.

The articles in Volume 2, 1816 to 1900, examine how wars in the nineteenth century shaped American society, culture, and identity while the United States changed from a small, nearly homogeneous, agricultural country into a continental, multicultural, industrial nation. American literature and art, the role of women, industry and technology, race relations, popular culture, political parties, and the Constitution were influenced by those wars, especially the Civil War (1861–1865) Protests against the institution of slavery and the spread of slavery affected the nation's expansion westward. The coming of the Civil War changed American politics through the formation of new parties.

In many ways, the Civil War was America's second revolution, fought to preserve and advance the founding principles of the nation. When Lincoln spoke of a "new birth of freedom" at Gettysburg, he addressed the meaning and vitality of America's most cherished ideals and values—values that were tested and refined by that war. Prior to the Civil War women sought equal rights and Abolitionists fought to end the institution of slavery. Whereas women did not secure their rights after the war, Constitutional amendments ended slavery and redefined the rights of citizenship that later generations struggled to achieve.

The Civil War also resolved the Constitutional issue of whether the states had the right to secede from the Union. The South clung to its image of the war as a "Lost Cause" that had impoverished the region and undermined its way of life. One legacy of defeat was the restoration of racial subjugation through "Black Codes," sharecropping, and the Ku Klux Klan. For both North and South, the Civil War became a source for literature, art, music, and public celebrations to memorialize their concepts of conflict and to honor their own veterans. Although the Civil War preserved the Union, society and culture remained divided.

The articles in Volume 3, 1901 to 1945, examine how America's rise as an imperial and then a world power shaped American society, culture, and identity. During this period the United States engaged in four significant overseas wars, the Spanish American War (1898), the Philippine Insurrection (1899–1902), the First World War (1917–1918), and the Second World War (1941–1945). American literature and art, the role of women, industry and technology, race and ethnic relations, popular culture, political parties, and the power of government were profoundly affected by those wars. The First World War produced a mass migration of blacks from the South to northern cities to work in defense industries. Hostility toward the enemy produced public discrimination against citizens with German ancestors. A "Red Scare," meaning the fear of Communist subversion and restriction of civil liberties by our government, followed the Russian Revolution in 1917. Americans became increasingly suspicious of aliens and dissenters. While seeking world peace through treaties promoting disarmament and renouncing war in the 1930s, America turned its back on the League of Nations and aggression in Asia and Europe.

When World War II began in Europe in 1939, the United States remained neutral. Nevertheless, the nation began to prepare for war, which was declared after Pearl Harbor was attacked by Japan. World War II reshaped American society. Massive defense spending and the mobilization of young men and women for military service ended the Great Depression, which had begun in 1929. As a result of defense orders, big business prospered and labor union membership soared during the war years. America achieved a full employment economy during this conflict and this required a large number of women to enter the work force to increase defense production. It also spurred the massive migration of many Americans, especially African Americans, to cities in the North and West. The war effort reinvigorated movements to end racial discrimination and gender inequity. Many of the articles examine the legacy of that war in a wide range of areas that include the expansion of the federal government over the economy and the life of the average citizen as well as fashion, sports, veterans' organizations, medicine, gender roles, race relations, movies, music, patriotic celebrations, veterans, civil liberties, and war widows and orphans.

Volume 4's articles cover 1946 to 2004 and examine how the Cold War (1946–1991) and the War on Terror have formed American society, culture, and identity. For nearly fifty years, United States and its allies contested the Communist Bloc led by the Soviet Union. The "cold" part of the Cold War involved an elaborate worldwide network of alliances and military bases, an arms race to produce nuclear weapons, and the means to deliver those weapons to destroy whole civilizations. The fall of the Berlin Wall in 1989 and collapse of the Soviet Union in 1991 left the United States as the only superpower on the globe. The years after 1991 appeared to begin a new era of peace as fear of a cataclysmic war began to fade. However, since September 11, 2001 a new threat, terrorism, has again led America to an unprecedented form of war that is both foreign and domestic. Homeland security has become a feature of war in the twenty-first century.

The articles in this volume reflect the new role of America after World War II. Unlike the generation following World War I, Americans could not return to isolationism. National Defense became the nation's priority. Safeguarding the nation against subversion and aggression affected all parts of American society, culture and identity. Anticommunism following World War II produced a second Red Scare that again tested the limits of civil liberties and introduced a new term, "McCarthyism." In 1954 Congress amended the Pledge of Allegiance, adding "under God" to the description of "one nation" to underscore the difference between "godless communism" and the religious foundation of American democracy.

An arms race with the Soviet Union contributed to the growth of the federal government, fueled spending on education, and created a significant defense industry. In his farewell address in 1961 President Eisenhower warned of a "military-industrial complex." Films and novels about experiences in World War II, the Korean War, and especially the Vietnam War revealed the traumatic effects of combat on soldiers and their families. During the Vietnam War television brought the images of combat into American homes.

Defeating Fascism and Nazi racialism in World War II energized efforts to close the gap between American ideals of equality and opportunity and social practices that involved racial, gender, and sexual discrimination. During the late 1950s, 1960s, and early 1970s, anti-war and anti-establishment protests as well as the civil rights, feminist, and black power movements, challenged cultural conventions and roiled American society. These conflicts changed American literature and art, gender and race relations, popular culture, the entertainment industry, political parties, and the Constitution. The articles in this volume examine those changes as legacies of the Cold War and America's conflicts since World War II. They also explore the impact of the War on Terror on American citizens through the Homeland Security Act, the implications of the concepts of "just wars" and "preemptive war" on American society, culture, and identity as a nation.

All of the articles in these four volumes are written for the general reader and are supplemented with aids to make the material accessible. A Topic Outline assists readers who wish to focus on a particular issue, such as civil liberties, that appears in all volumes. Additional text appears as sidebars to further illustrate or elaborate portions of articles. A select bibliography follows each article for readers who wish to study the subject further. A general chronology of events from 1500 to 2004 will assist readers in placing the articles they are reading in a larger historical context. An Index will lead readers to

specific subjects. A Glossary defines key terms that might not be clear to younger readers. The editors hope that *Americans at War* will not only assist students and researchers in obtaining information, but will also encourage additional reading about the effect of war upon American society, culture, and identity.

Americans at War is the product of 234 authors and the editorial board. I thank all of the contributors for their fine work and outstanding scholarship. In particular, I wish to express gratitude and admiration to my associate editors for their thoughtful, timely, and untiring work on this project. Sally G. McMillen, Babcock Professor of History at Davidson College, edited Volume 2. Professor G. Kurt Piehler, Director, Center for the Study of War and Society, University of Tennessee, edited Volume 3. Professor D'Ann Campbell, Dean of Academics, U.S. Coast Guard Academy, and Professor Richard Jensen, Independent Scholar, edited Volume 4. I wish to thank Hélène Potter, senior editor at Macmillan Library Reference. She brought this editorial team together early in the process and has provided support, guidance, and encouragement to transform a concept into reality.

I also thank Oona Schmid at Macmillan, who recognized the need for a reference set on the effects of war upon American society and initiated the project. I hope that she, although no longer at Macmillan, feels the satisfaction of seeing her vision come true. The editors thank Anthony Aiello, who was our first project editor and who is also a contributor to the set. Finally, we wish to extend our deep appreciation and thanks to Kristin Hart, our project editor, who assisted us through the final stages of producing the set. Her attention to detail, responsiveness, clarity, and helpfulness were invaluable in the completion of the project. Finally, I thank the Humanities Center at the University of New Hampshire–Durham for its grant of a Senior Faculty Research Fellowship which helped to provide the time for me to devote to this project, and for support from the University of New Hampshire–Manchester.

John P. Resch
Editor-In-Chief
Editor, Volume 1
Professor of History
University of New Hampshire–Manchester

SETTLEMENT AND THE CREATION OF THE UNITED STATES, 1607–1825

This volume covers the period of American history from 1607 to 1825, an era of dramatic change. The events of that era were set against the sixteenth-century background of Indian civilizations in Central and South America decimated by disease and conquest at the hands of Spain, and Indian culture throughout the New World changed by European trade and Christian missionaries. Beginning in the early seventeenth century, the "European Invasion" (the term used by modern historians to describe colonization), expanded in North America with increased migration of French, Dutch, Spanish, and English settlers. The eighteenth century was a period of fundamental change as a result of the rapid expansion of English provinces, the War for Independence, and the creation of the United States. Between 1789 and 1825 the United States launched an experiment in republican government; began to develop its own culture; doubled in size; and developed a market economy that produced a division between the emerging industrial north, which relied on wage labor, and the plantation south, which relied on slavery.

From colonial settlement through the early years of the nation, war was a powerful force shaping American society and culture. Between 1607 and 1700, apart from frontier skirmishes, raids, and ambushes, colonists from South Carolina through New England were engaged in over a score of declared wars, rebellions, and insurrections. In the eighteenth century Americans were at war more than at peace. Between 1700 and 1800 Americans engaged in seventeen separate conflicts and rebellions, including the 1739 uprising of slaves at Stono, South Carolina, and the Revolutionary War, 1775–1783. Between 1800 and 1825, the United States was at war with Barbary pirates, Seminole Indians, Great Britain in the "Second War of Independence" (1812–1815), and even with its own citizens in the Whiskey Rebellion in Western Pennsylvania.

The articles in this volume examine how colonial wars and especially the Revolutionary War shaped American society, culture, and identity. American literature and art, the role of women, the economy, race relations, popular culture, patriotic celebrations, national memory, political parties, and the Constitution were profoundly affected by those wars.

1607–1700

War fashioned the first permanent English settlement in North America. The English founders of Jamestown in

1607, following the example of the Spanish and Portuguese, sought wealth through conquest. The English expected to dominate local inhabitants and to take what they needed. Having first established a military outpost, the "adventurers" at Jamestown believed that they could subjugate local tribes through force of arms. The expansion of settlements around Jamestown increased friction between English and Indians. Jamestown became a fortified village. In 1622 warriors attacked the settlers, inflicting 347 deaths out of a population of nearly 1,400. For the next twenty-four years skirmishes, raids, and ambushes were part of the fabric of life of the struggling colony of Jamestown. These conflicts reinforced the racial and religious identity of the settlers, who viewed themselves as civilized Christians at war with savage pagans.

Jamestown illustrated a pattern found in other English settlements—frontier conflicts, social organization for self-defense, and use of race and religion to explain and justify warfare. In New England, during the Pequot War, 1636–1637, Connecticut settlers aided by Indian allies killed nearly 700 Pequot men, women, and children in their village on the Mystic River. The destruction of the tribe opened the Connecticut Valley to English settlement. Even more devastating was King Philip's War (also known as Metacom's War), 1675–1676. During this war the New England frontier was in flames. A dozen towns were destroyed in Indian raids, about 600 colonists were killed, and hundreds more were captured. Mary Rowlandson's account of her captivity became a benchmark in American romantic literature that portrayed divinely inspired feminine heroism overcoming satanic savagery. Nearly half of the 10,000 Indians in New England died in King Philip's War, including women and children, as well as some Indians who had converted to Christianity. Some survivors were sold into East Indian slavery.

As a result of the war, New England reorganized its militia to improve security. Puritan ministers, who interpreted Indian devastation as punishment from God, instructed their congregations to end their sinful ways to prevent future wars. The gun and Bible were the foundations of this society that believed its divine mission was to establish a kingdom guided by God, who was perceived both as benefactor and as avenger. In the nineteenth century, James Fenimore Cooper used colonial wars as a source for his stories, but muted the viciousness of frontier warfare to celebrate the American spirit and character.

By contrast to colonists in Virginia and New England, Quakers settlers who began arriving in Pennsylvania and New Jersey in 1675 practiced pacifism. Quakers believed that people of different religions and races could coexist peacefully. Sustaining friendly relations with Indians, Pennsylvanians did not experience the bloody conflicts that characterized Virginia and New England. Pennsylvania had no organized militia until 1740. By the mid-eighteenth century, however, imperial wars, a changing mix of European settlers, westward expansion, and decline of Quaker authority changed Pennsylvania's treatment of Indians to resemble that of its militant northern and southern neighbors.

1700–1791

A second period in American history began about 1700, after the English had taken the Dutch colony of New Amsterdam (now New York City) and the Hudson Valley and had consolidated their hold along the Atlantic seaboard from New England to Florida. Between 1700 and 1763 the American colonies were involved in a succession of imperial wars between England and its European rivals, Spain and France, as well as wars with Indian tribes. Queen Anne's War (1702–1713), the Tuscarora War (1711–1713), The War of Jenkins Ear, King George's War (1739–1748), and the French and Indian War, 1754–1763 affected the colonies' economies, politics, and identities. England's defeat of France in the French and Indian War brought to an end nearly fifty years of imperial wars, although conflict with Indians continued with Pontiac's War (1763–1766). The year 1765 marked the height of English power in North America with the expansion of its rule to Canada, formerly a French territory, and of the Indian lands east of the Mississippi River. That year also marked the beginning of a twenty-five year period that included a constitutional struggle that led to American independence, the creation of a new nation, and the breakup of the English empire in North America.

These eighteenth-century wars, in particular the French and Indian War and the Revolutionary War, contributed to a distinct American political culture and identity. The French and Indian War had a profound effect upon ordinary colonists who served under English officers and alongside British troops. Military service revealed a cultural gap between the English in America and those who resided in Great Britain. In 1765 that gap widened with the constitutional conflict over the right of Parliament to directly tax the colonists. The Stamp Act controversy (1765–1766) brought to the surface subtle, yet substantial differences in political philosophy that had evolved over nearly a century and half of colonial self-governance. It also united the colonies through committees of correspondence and the Stamp Act Congress. From 1765 to 1775, events leading to war against Britain forced the American colonists to assess their values, to clarify their identity, and to rethink the political principles that had guided them as English citizens in colonial America.

Rarely in history do people have an opportunity to remake their world by creating a new nation. The Revolutionary War, 1775–1783, and the creation of the Constitution and its Bill of Rights, 1787–1791, produced such an opportunity. During this period Americans established the principal features of their society, culture, and national identity. Most articles in this volume focus on this intense revolutionary period. Some examine the effect of war on American society. The war disrupted the institution of slavery. Thousands of blacks fled their masters to join the British who promised them freedom. Patriots responded by granting freedom to slaves who, with their master's permission, joined the Continental Army. The war affected the lives of women. Wives of soldiers and political leaders assumed new roles. The war exposed the vulnerability of loyalist families whose property had been confiscated, and of wives whose husbands had been forced to emigrate because they sided with Great Britain. The Revolution also created a legacy that affected the next generation of women through the concept of "Republican Motherhood," the idea that only women were fit to teach children civic values.

The Revolutionary Era had a profound effect upon political thinking and governmental institutions. The American meaning of republicanism was derived from a blend of classical Greek and Roman teachings; Enlightenment philosophy, especially the work of John Locke; and principles learned from the experiences of political protest, rebellion, and the formation of state governments. The transformation of English colonies into independent states permitted political leaders to experiment with new ideas of government—separating the executive, legislative and judicial branches, separating church and state, and limiting government through a bill of rights and written constitution.

More than a war, the Revolution was an era of nation-building. Necessity forced independent states to unite to win the war and to perpetuate their victory over England. In doing so revolutionaries struggled to create a central government that could unite and protect a diverse people and promote their prosperity, and yet not become tyrannical. Failing to achieve these goals as a loose confederation under the Articles of Confederation, Americans launched a new national experiment with the adoption of the Constitution in 1788. The Constitution created a novel form of government that incorporated features of democracy and republicanism, that made people citizens both of their state and of the national government, and that established a republic of unprecedented size.

The Revolutionary era produced symbols of national identity in art, music, and popular culture that celebrated American victories and heroes. "Yankee Doodle," Fourth of July celebrations, the national flag, Valley Forge, and portraits of military and political leaders helped to define American identity at a time when the nation's English heritage remained strong. Revolutionary leaders such as Washington, Jefferson, John and Abigail Adams, Franklin, and James and Dolley Madison became icons of American values and patriotism for later generations. The war also produced one the most famous symbols of betrayal, Benedict Arnold.

The Revolution was a source of ideals that Americans used to define themselves then and now. They spoke eloquently of liberty; they fought the war so as not to be enslaved by British tyranny. Embodied in documents such as the Declaration of Independence, the Constitution, and the Federalist Papers, the concepts of equality, human rights, and the rule of law were expressed by Americans even though they treated Indians as savages, owned slaves, and denied equal rights to women. These concepts had deep consequences for American society as the nation confronted the gap between its ideals and practices.

The Revolution began slavery's demise. Prior to the war slavery existed in all of the colonies. After the war, slavery was gradually abolished in the northern states and indentured servitude ended. By 1791, the nation had rejected the European world of kings, royalty, and rigid class structure. A new world of democracy, republican self-governance, individual liberty, and equality—although not enjoyed by all—emerged. The American experiment had begun.

1791–1825

During this early national period the United States pursued its republican experiment. A two-party system evolved—the Federalists led by Washington and Alexander Hamilton, and the Jeffersonian Republicans. The authors of the Constitution had not anticipated the formation of political parties, but the party system proved necessary to the peaceful transfer of power between opposing groups. The Supreme Court under Chief Justice John Marshall affirmed that the Constitution was the supreme law of the land and that laws must conform to it in order to be legitimate. The Supreme Court also ensured that the nation's economy would be built along capitalist principles and would extend beyond Jefferson's ideal of an agrarian nation to include industry and commerce.

America engaged in minor conflicts during this period, as well as a major war with England from 1812 to 1815. War tested the unity of the nation and helped to define its political culture. The Alien and Sedition Acts of 1798, passed to protect the nation against internal subversion during America's "quasi war" with France, suppressed the freedoms of speech and press. The acts first tested the authority of the federal government to curtail civil rights during war. That controversy reoccurred in subsequent wars and continues today in the "war against terror." War also tested the meaning of patriotism when New England threatened to secede from the Union as a result of Congress's declaration of war against England in 1812 and the economic disruption that followed.

The War of 1812 produced new heroes and patriots, such as Andrew Jackson, reinforcing the myth of American military prowess following his victory in New Orleans in 1815. An outburst of American nationalism followed. A new generation of Americans used past wars as a source in building the nation's identity and culture to unite a diverse people. Americans celebrated the idea that United States had a special, even divine, mission to play in the world. Histories of the Revolution and America's struggle of independence elevated its leaders as "Founding Fathers" who possessed both genius and virtue. Revolutionary War veterans who had been largely ignored after that war became national heroes who were rewarded with pensions approved in 1818. The nation held up men of the Revolutionary generation as models for later generations to follow. American writers, such as James Fenimore Cooper, captured the frontier spirit in his novels. Popular celebrations such as the Fourth of July, national tours of President James Monroe (1817) and Lafayette (1824–1825), efforts to save Revolutionary War sites, and the construction of monuments to im-

mortalize the war helped to build a common culture. Artists such as Benjamin West idealized the Revolution's leaders and America in their paintings.

By 1825 the first era of American history was drawing to a close. The nation had doubled in size with the Louisiana Purchase in 1803. The number of states had increased from eleven to twenty four. The population had doubled between 1790 and 1825 to about ten million. Slavery had been expanded in the South. Indians had been either subdued or forced to move west of the Mississippi. White migration had expanded into the new western territories, including Spanish lands in the southwest. The beginning of a transportation revolution with the construction of the Erie Canal and the introduction of manufacturing had increased commerce and created new wealth in the North and South. The nation had secured its revolution in the War of 1812. It had become more democratic by extending the right to vote to males without property.

After 1825 war would be a major means both of fulfilling the nation's "manifest destiny" to rule the continent, and of fulfilling what Lincoln called the "last best hope of freedom" by destroying slavery. Then and now, Americans have returned to their Colonial and Revolutionary eras for guidance in shaping their society, culture, and identity as a nation.

John P. Resch

VOLUME 1: 1500–1815

AMERICAN REVOLUTION
Association Test
Boston Massacre: Pamphlets and Propaganda
Boston Tea Party: Politicizing Ordinary People
Common Sense
Commonwealth Men
Continental Congresses
Declaration of Independence
Loyalists
Peace of Paris, 1763
Republicanism and War
Revolution and Radical Reform
Sons of Liberty
Stamp Act Congress
States and Nation Building, 1775–1783

BIOGRAPHY
Adams, Abigail
Adams, John
Arnold, Benedict
Cooper, James Fenimore
Drinker, Elizabeth
Franklin, Benjamin
Hamilton, Alexander
Hewes, George Robert Twelves
Jackson, Andrew
Jefferson, Thomas
Madison, Dolley
Madison, James
Monroe, James
Montgomery, Richard
Paine, Thomas
Rowlandson, Mary
Sampson, Deborah
Warren, Mercy Otis
Washington, George

CONSTITUTION
Alien and Sedition Laws
Anti-Federalists
Articles of Confederation
Civil Liberties: Kentucky and Virginia Resolutions
Constitution: Bill of Rights
Constitution: Creating a Republic
Federalist Papers
Hartford Convention
Shays and Whiskey Rebellions

This systematic outline provides a general overview of the conceptual scheme of *Americans at War,* listing the titles of each entry in each volume. Because the section headings are not mutually exclusive, certain entries in *Americans at War* are listed in more than one section.

VOLUME 2: 1816–1900

VETERANS
Civil War Veterans
Memorial (Decoration) Day
Prisons and Prisoners of War, 1815–1900

VISUAL ARTS
Photography, Civil War
Visual Arts, Civil War and the West

VOLUME 3: 1901–1945

BIOGRAPHY
Addams, Jane
Catt, Carrie Chapman
Cochran, Jackie
Ford, Henry
DuBois, W.E.B.
Hemingway, Ernest
Hoover, Herbert
McKinley, William
Mitchell, Billy
Roosevelt, Eleanor
Roosevelt, Franklin Delano
Roosevelt, Theodore
Stewart, Jimmy
Tokyo Rose
Wayne, John
Wilson, Woodrow
York, Alvin

CONSTITUTION
Civil Liberties, World War I
Civil Liberties, World War II
Conscription, World War I
Conscription, World War II
Dissent in World War I and World War II
Japanese Americans, World War II
Red Scare

CIVIL LIBERTIES
Civil Liberties, World War I
Civil Liberties, World War II
Dissent in World War I and World War II
Japanese Americans, World War II
Red Scare

DISSENT
Dissent in World War I and World War II
Peace Movements, 1898–1945

ECONOMY
Economy, World War I
Economy, World War II

Financing, World War I
Financing, World War II
GI Bill of Rights
Labor, World War I
Labor, World War II
Profiteering
Rationing
Rosie the Riveter
Women, Employment of

FAMILY AND COMMUNITY
Clothing, World War I and World War II
Gold Star Mothers Pilgrimage
Japanese Americans, World War II
Prisoner of War Camps, United States
Red Cross, American
Refugees
Regional Migration, World War I and World War II
Sexual Behavior
Sports, World War I
Sports, World War II
USO
Widows and Orphans

GENDER
Feminism
Gold Star Mothers Pilgrimage
Rosie the Riveter
Widows and Orphans
Women, Employment of
Women and World War I
Women and World War II
Women's Suffrage Movement

LITERATURE
Literature, World War I
Literature, World War II
Memoirs, Autobiographies

MEDIA
Allies, Images of
Enemy, Images of
Journalism, Spanish American War
Journalism, World War I
Journalism, World War II
Motion Pictures, World War I and World War II
Photography, World War I
Photography, World War II
Propaganda, 1898–1945
Public Opinion
Radio and Power of Broadcasting

MOBILIZATION
Conscription, World War I
Conscription, World War II

CHRONOLOGY

Subjects marked in **bold** can be found within *Americans at War*, either in the main body or in the Primary Source Documents in the appendix.

Date	President	Event
1434		Beginning of African Slave Trade by Portuguese.
1494		Line of Demarcation dividing North and South America between Spain and Portugal.
1500–1542		Spanish and Portuguese exploration and conquests in North and South America. Few Spanish and Portuguese migrate to America. Their officials, soldiers, and priests rule native tribes. Plantations established. **Beginning of the decline of the native population** from 20 million to about 2 million due largely to disease.
1517		Beginning of the Protestant Reformation. Martin Luther posts his ninety-five theses challenging the authority of the Roman Catholic Church.
1519–1522		Hernando Cortez conquers the Aztecs in Mexico.
1529		Henry VIII of England separates from the Roman Catholic Church to create the Church of England.
1520s		**Slaves imported from Africa** in large numbers to work on sugar plantations in the West Indies.
1530–1533		Francisco Pizarro and *Conquistadores* defeat Inca civilization on the Western coast of South America, now the countries of Peru and Chile.
1539–1542		Hernando de Soto expedition from Florida to the Mississippi.
1540		Silver deposits discovered in Peru and Mexico. Mined by Indians.
		The Society of Jesus, Jesuits, formed by Ignatius of Loyola. Missioners sent throughout the world to convert people to Christianity, including many sent among the Indian tribes of North America.

Date	President	Event
1540–1542		Francisco Vásquez de Coronado explores the Southwest of what would become the United States.
1541		John Calvin and his Protestant followers take control of Geneva, Switzerland
1542		Juan Rodriquez Cabrillo explores what would become the California coast.
1555		Peace of Augsburg ends religious wars in the Habsburg Empire and divides the land between Protestants and Catholics.
1564		French Calvinists known as Huguenots establish settlement at Fort Caroline in Florida. The fort is destroyed by Spanish in 1564 and most settlers killed.
1565		Queen Elizabeth I of England encourages colonization of Ireland by English Protestants.
August 24, 1572		St. Bartholomew's Day Massacre in Paris, which began a killing spree of Huguenots by Catholic mobs. Massacres and religious warfare in France follows, leaving 70,000 to 100,000 Huguenots dead.
1584		Richard Haklute publishes *A Discourse Concerning Western Planting,* a report on his voyage to America with Sir Walter Raleigh. Report encouraged English settlement to claim land for Protestantism, expand English trade, and to a find productive work for the unemployed.
1588		Founding of the English colony at Roanoke, Virginia by Sir Walter Raleigh. When the supply ship returns three years later the colony is found mysteriously abandoned and the whereabouts of the settlers unknown. All that is left is the message "Croatoan" on a post, the meaning of which is unclear.
		Defeat of the Spanish Armada by the English. End of Spanish effort to conquer England and restore the Catholic Church.
1598		Edict of Nantes ends religious persecution in France; Huguenots are granted religious rights, which are revoked in 1685.
1603		James I becomes King of England. Favors colonization in America.
1605		French colony established at Port Royal in what is now Nova Scotia, Canada.
1606		Virginia Company of Jamestown and Virginia Company of Plymouth created as joint-stock companies to finance and promote English colonization of America.
1607		**Jamestown** founded—first permanent English colony in North America.

Date	President	Event
1608		Quebec founded by Samuel de Champlain for fur trading. Becomes the capital of New France or Canada.
1608–1609		John Smith becomes head of **Jamestown** colony. Colony suffers from disease, starvation and attacks by Indians.
1609		Henry Hudson explores what is now the New York region and Hudson valley on behalf of the Dutch.
1610		Decision made to abandon **Jamestown**; colonists return when relief ships arrive bringing supplies and settlers.
1614		Lutheran refugees from Amsterdam, Holland, establish a trading post in what is now Albany, New York.
1616		John Rolf and Pocahontas visit England to promote tobacco sales and settlement.
1619		First African **slaves** arrive at **Jamestown.**
1620		Pilgrims land at Plymouth. The day before landing they sign the Mayflower Compact, often described as America' first constitution.
1622		**Massacre of 350 settlers at Jamestown** led by Opechancanough.
1624		Jamestown company disbanded. Virginia becomes a Royal Colony.
1626		Dutch purchase Manhattan Island from Indians; establish New Amsterdam.
1630		Puritans led by John Winthrop settle in what becomes Boston, Massachusetts.
1632		Maryland chartered by Charles I to be refuge for English Catholics.
1635		Roger Williams banished from the Massachusetts Bay Colony, establishes Rhode Island.
1636–1637		Pequot War, the first serious armed conflict between Native Americans and settlers, takes place in New England.
1637		Anne Hutchinson excommunicated.
1642		Beginning of English Civil War between supporters of Charles I and Parliament led by Oliver Cromwell.
1649		Charles I beheaded; England becomes a republic under Oliver Cromwell.
1660		Monarchy restored under Charles II. Navigation Act demands colonial tobacco shipped to England for tax.
1660–1688		England establishes six colonies, including Pennsylvania by Quakers and Carolina by Barbadian planters who receive charter in 1663.

Date	President	Event
1664		Dutch colony surrenders to English. New Amsterdam becomes New York.
1675–1676		**King Philip's War** in New England; 10,000 Indians die
1676		**Bacon's rebellion.** Uprising in Virginia by settlers to overthrow government that prevents them from seizing Indian land.
1688		Glorious Revolution in England. James II deposed and Parliament's power increased.
1688–1689		John Locke produces his *Second Treatise on Government* professing that individuals have inalienable rights of life, liberty and property.
1692		Salem Witch Trials. By the end, nineteen accused witches had been hung, one was crushed to death, and seventeen more died in prison.
1702–1713		Queen Anne's War—A series of raids by the French and their Indian allies upon New Englanders, including the raid on Deerfield, Massachusetts.
1711–1713		The Tuscarora War—War between Carolina settlers and Tuscarora Indians.
1715–1716		Yamasee War—War between Carolina settlers and Yamasee Indians and their allies in Florida.
1730s–1740s		The religious revival led by Jonathan Edwards and George Whitefield, called the Great Awakening, sweeps through the colonies.
1739		**Stono Rebellion,** slave uprising in Stono, South Carolina.
1739–1743		The War of Jenkins Ear—War between England and Spain on the Georgia-Florida border. Named after Robert Jenkins who lost his ear.
1744–1748		King George's War—War between England and France on American soil. Louisburg on Cape Breton is captured by New England troops, stiking a blow to the French.
1754–1763		**French and Indian War**—Conflict for empire. France is defeated and its lands, especially Canada, become part of the British empire.
1763		Pontiac's War—Indian attacks on English posts and settlers in the Great Lakes region.
1765		**Stamp Act** Passed by Parliament; American protest and resistance to the Stamp Act; **"Sons of Liberty"** formed in Boston.
October 1765		**Stamp Act Congress** approves Resolutions upholding rights as Englishmen.

Date	President	Event
1766		Protest against the **Stamp Act** is successful and the act is repealed.
		Parliament passes the Declaratory Act proclaiming full authority over the American colonies.
1767		Townshend duties passed by Parliament; protests result.
1768		Riots in Boston against the Townshend Duties; British Troops sent to Boston.
1770		**Boston Massacre.**
December 16, 1773		**Boston Tea Party.** English tea is destroyed in Boston harbor by the "Sons of Liberty" in reaction to Britain's Tea Act of 1773.
1774		Britain places Massachusetts under military rule—Parliament approves four laws to quell the Massachusetts rebellion. Laws branded by colonists as the Intolerable Acts.
September 5, 1774		First **Continental Congress** meets in Philadelphia to organize colonial protest and resistance.
October 25, 1774		Edenton, North Carolina tea party by local women protesting British imports. Fifty-one local women met and openly declared "We, the aforesaid Ladys will not promote ye wear of any manufacturer from England until such time that all acts which tend to enslave our Native country shall be repealed."
April 19, 1775		Battles of Lexington and Concord. Beginning of the War for Independence.
January 1776		**Thomas Paine** publishes *Common Sense.* Argues for American independence and formation of a republican form of government; rejected European style monarchy and aristocracy.
July 4, 1776		**Declaration of Independence.**
1776		Virginia creates the first state constitution. It includes a Bill of Rights. Other states follow by making their own constitutions.
1777		Vermont outlaws **slavery.**
November 15, 1777		**Articles of Confederation** agreed to by the **Continental Congress.** Creates the United States as an alliance of independent states.
1778		France allies with the United States after the Americans defeat the British at Saratoga in 1777.
1779		Spain declares war on Great Britain.
October 19, 1781		Cornwallis defeated at Yorktown; last major battle of the Revolutionary War and peace negotiations begin.
1783		**Peace of Paris.** American Independence recognized.

Date	President	Event
1787		**Shays's rebellion** in Massachusetts. National government under the **Articles of Confederation** shaken.
May 14, 1787		Constitutional convention gathers in Philadelphia. Proposes to replace the Articles of Confederation with a new constitution.
1788		**Constitution** adopted.
1789	**George Washington, 1789–1797**	French Revolution begins.
		French Assembly adopts the *Rights of Man* declaration written by **Thomas Paine.**
April 30, 1789		**George Washington** inaugurated as first president of the United States.
1790		First federal census undertaken.
1791		Bill of Rights—First Ten Amendments added to the **Constitution.**
1792		French Republic proclaimed.
1793		Eli Whitney invents cotton gin.
January 21, 1793		French King, Louis XVI tried and executed; French Revolution takes radical turn.
1794		United States and Great Britain agree to blockade France. Beginning of American **quasi-war** with France.
		Whiskey rebellion in western Pennsylvania. **George Washington** and **Alexander Hamilton** send the militia to put down the protesters against the tax on whiskey.
		"Mad" Anthony Wayne defeats Indians at "Fallen Timbers" near Detroit.
September 26, 1796		**Washington's Farewell Address.**
1797	**John Adams, 1797–1801**	
1798–1800		**Quasi-War** with England and France. Military mobilization proposed. **Alien and Sedition laws** passed to curtail freedom of speech because of threat of war and subversion. **James Madison** and **Thomas Jefferson** respond with the **Kentucky and Virginia Resolutions** proclaiming the right of states to void federal laws that violate individual or states' rights.
1801	**Thomas Jefferson, 1801–1809**	John Marshall appointed Chief Justice of the **Supreme Court** (1801–1835). Generally considered one of the principal architects of American government and cultural values.
1801		**Thomas Jefferson** inaugurated. Peaceful transfer of power between two opposing political parties, Federalists and Democratic Republicans. Beginning of wars with **Barbary pirates** (1801–1805; 1815).

Date	President	Event
		Great Revival begins, Cane Ridge, Kentucky.
1803–1815		Napoleonic Wars. War between France and England in Europe and the Western Hemisphere. American ships and men seized by both countries.
April 30, 1803		American purchase of Louisiana territory from France.
1804–1806		Lewis and Clark Expedition to Pacific.
1808		African Slave traded to the United States prohibited.
1809	James Madison, 1809–1817	
1812–1815		War with England. Washington, D.C. occupied by the British and burned.
September 14, 1814		Francis Scott Key composes poem, "Star-Spangled Banner."
1815		Andrew Jackson's victory at New Orleans.
		Hartford Convention. New England protest against the war with England. Demands changes in the Constitution to weaken Congress's power to declare war. Some New England states threaten to secede from the Union if federal power is not reduced.
1816–1826		Outburst of American nationalism and patriotism.
1817	James Monroe, 1817–1825	Monroe's tour of New England and beginning of Bunker Hill monument.
1818		Passage of the Revolutionary War Pension Act to honor and reward veterans.
1820s		Expansion of factory towns and creation of new mill cities in New England.
1820		Missouri Compromise.
1820–1861		Expansion of the market economy in the North and South. Northern manufacturing, commerce, and farming; Southern farming, plantations, and export of cotton. Wage labor in the North, Wage and slave labor in the South.
1822		Discovery of Denmark Vesey's slave conspiracy for a rebellion in Charleston, South Carolina.
1823		Monroe Doctrine proclaimed in 1823.
1824–1825		Lafayette's tour of the United States.
1825	John Adams, 1825–1829	Completion of the Erie Canal connecting Buffalo with New York City. Part of the "Transportation Revolution" that binds the nation by roads, canals, and later railroads.
1826		Second Bank chartered. National Road completed.

Date	President	Event
		James Fenimore Cooper publishes *The Last of the Mohicans*, a tale about the **French and Indian War**, 1754–1763. Beginning of an American literature.
July 4, 1826		Death of **John Adams** and **Thomas Jefferson**. Viewed as a time of reflection on the Revolution.
1828		First **railroad** completed, the Baltimore and Ohio.
1829	**Andrew Jackson, 1829–1837**	
1830		Religious revival, "Second Great Awakening," begins in western New York.
		Indian Removal Act; relocate Indians in Georgia.
1831		*Cherokee Nation v. Georgia Supreme Court* decision.
		Nat Turner slave uprising in Virginia.
1832		William Lloyd Garrison founds the abolitionist newspaper, *The Liberator.*
1833		Garrison and **Abolitionists** create the American Anti-Slavery society to end the institution of slavery.
		Nullification Crisis in South Carolina; South Carolina votes to nullify federal law on tariffs.
1834		Mobs attack **abolitionists** in New York City. Race riot in Philadelphia. Female mill workers at Lowell, Massachusetts strike and again in 1836.
1836		Ralph Waldo Emerson publishes *Nature*, first major work on transcendentalism. Part of the effort to create an American **literature.**
March 6, 1836		Defeat of Americans at **Alamo** by General Santa Anna.
1837	**Martin Van Buren, 1837–1841**	
1838		Cherokee Indians forcibly removed from Georgia to Oklahoma; thousands die along the "trail of tears" before arriving.
1840s		Famine in Ireland and failed revolution in Germany in 1848 result in surge of Irish and German immigrants to the United States.
1840		Liberty Party formed. Opposes the spread of **slavery** to the territories. Receives less than one percent of the popular vote.
1841	**William Henry Harrison, 1841; John Tyler, 1841–1845**	
1844		Margaret Fuller publishes *Woman in the Nineteenth Century*, which examines the role of women and argues for **equal rights for women.**

Date	President	Event
1845	James Polk, 1845–1849	Proclamation of **Manifest Destiny** by the United States. Americans feel it is their mission and part of God's plan to spread democracy throughout the continent.
		United States **annexes Texas,** which permits **slavery.**
		Frederick Douglass publishes *Narrative of the Life of Frederick Douglass,* a powerful autobiography that further inspires the **Abolitionist** movement.
1846		United States declares war with Mexico. Anti-war protests divide the nation.
		Wilmot Proviso. Proposal for popular sovereignty to prohibit **slavery** in territories won from Mexico approved by the House of Representatives but defeated in the Senate.
June 10, 1846		Bear Flag Revolt in California. "Bear Flaggers" raise the grizzly bear flag and officially declare the territory free from Mexican rule. The bear flag becomes the official flag of California.
June 15, 1846		U.S. and Great Britain settle Oregon border. The 49th parallel is determined to be the border between Great Britain and the United States, with the exception of Vancouver Island.
1847		Brigham Young leads Mormons to Great Salt Lake, Utah.
1848		**Treaty of Guadalupe Hidalgo** ends war with Mexico and results in the United States acquiring California and what is now the U.S. southwest.
		Free Soil Party formed; opposes the spread of the slave institution. Absorbs the Liberty Party.
		Gold discovered in California, leading to California gold rush of 1849.
July 19, 1848		Women's Rights Movement convenes in Seneca Falls, New York. Demands equal rights under the law, including the right to vote.
1849	Zachary Taylor, 1849–1850	Henry David Thoreau publishes *Walden,* an account of man and nature and part of the new American literary genre.
1850	Millard Fillmore, 1850–1853	**Compromise of 1850.** Intended to resolve the conflict over the spread of **slavery;** California admitted as a free state (prohibited slavery). Fugitive slave law strengthens recovery of runaway slaves in the North.
1851		Herman Melville publishes *Moby-Dick,* a novel that has become an American classic.

Date	President	Event
1852		Harriet Beecher Stowe publishes *Uncle Tom's Cabin.* The novel attacks the institution of **slavery** and increases tension between the North and South.
1853	Franklin Pierce, 1853–1857	American or "Know Nothing" party formed. The party is composed of nativists, people who oppose immigration, Catholics, and citizenship for blacks. Members, when asked about their organizations were suppose to reply they knew nothing, hence the name of the party.
		Gadsden Purchase adds territory in Southwest.
1854		**Kansas-Nebraska Act** opens the west to the possibility of slavery.
		Republican Party formed to oppose the **Kansas-Nebraska Act.** Absorbs the Free Soil Party.
1856		"Bleeding Kansas" erupts as northerners and southerners fight over future of **slavery** in territory.
1857	James Buchanan, 1857–1861	Dred Scott case. **Supreme court** declares that the **Constitution** does not apply to free blacks and that it allows slave owners to take their property (slaves) to any state or territory.
1858		**Lincoln**-Douglas debates in Illinois for Senate seat.
October 16, 1859		John Brown's raid on Harpers Ferry, Virginia. His intent is to arm slaves and to lead a slave uprising. He is captured and later hanged.
1860		**Abraham Lincoln** elected president with 40 percent of the popular vote. South Carolina votes to **secede** from the Union.
1861	Abraham Lincoln, 1861–1865	**Confederacy** formed by **seceded** states. Fort Sumter attacked and **Abraham Lincoln** calls out militia to end rebellion. Civil War begins.
		Harriet Jacob publishes *Incidents in the Life of a Slave Girl,* describing the life of a female under **slavery.**
1862		Bloody battles at Shiloh and Antietam.
		Homestead Act passed by Congress.
January 1, 1863		**Emancipation Proclamation** by Abraham Lincoln, ending **slavery** in territory conquered by northern troops.
July 1863		Battles at Gettysburg and Vicksburg turn the tide toward the Union.
September 2, 1864		Atlanta falls. After several weeks of preparation General **Sherman begins his march to the sea.**
1865	Andrew Johnson, 1865–1869	Congress establishes **Freedmen's Bureau** to assist former slaves. South enacts **Black Codes** to suppress blacks.
		Thirteenth Amendment to **Constitution** ratified, abolishing **slavery.**

Date	President	Event
April 9, 1865		End of Civil War at Appomattox Courthouse. Six days later **Abraham Lincoln** is assassinated.
1866		Founding of Equal Rights Association to seek woman's suffrage.
		Formation of the Grand Army of the Republic composed of veterans of the Union Army. To become an organization for **veterans' benefits**.
		Ku Klux Klan organized as the "Invisible Empire of the South."
1868		**Fourteenth Amendment** added to **Constitution**, ensuring all male citizens equal protection of the laws and due process of law.
1869	**Ulysses S. Grant, 1869–1877**	Woman's suffrage groups split in two over tactics and issue of black male suffrage; will reunite in 1890.
		Territory of Wyoming allows women to vote.
May 10, 1869		Completion of transcontinental **railroad** in Promontory, Utah.
1870		**Fifteenth Amendment** added to **Constitution**, guaranteeing the right to vote to males regardless of race or color.
1870–1871		Franco-Prussian War.
1876		Westward migration increases conflicts with Indians. Custer defeated at Little Bighorn.
1877	**Rutherford B. Hayes, 1877–1881**	Troops withdrawn from the South. Disputed election of 1876 resolved and Rutherford B. Hayes was determined to have won 185 electoral votes to Samuel Tilden's 184. **Reconstruction** ended.
1881	**James Garfield, 1881; Chester Arthur, 1881–1885**	Helen Hunt Jackson publishes *A Century of Dishonor*—documents the mistreatment of American Indians.
1882		Chinese Exclusion Act passed by Congress.
1885	**Grover Cleveland, 1885–1889**	
1887		**Dawes Severalty Act,** which dissolves Indian tribes and turns tribal lands into private property for Indians—an effort to Americanize Indians.
1888		Edward Bellamy publishes *Looking Backward*—a critical assessment of American capitalism and endorsement of more cooperative society.
1889	**Benjamin Harris, 1889–1893**	
1890		Formation of the National American Woman's Suffrage Association, uniting the two groups working for woman's suffrage.

Date	President	Event
		Jacob Riis publishes *How the Other Half Lives,* an exposé aided by photographs of squalor and exploitation of New York's **immigrants** and poor.
1890–1904		Ex-confederate states pass laws prohibiting Blacks from voting. "Jim Crow" laws enforce **racial segregation.**
December 29, 1890		Battle of Wounded Knee marking last major conflict between Native Americans and federal troops in West.
1893	**Grover Cleveland, 1893–1897**	
1895		Booker T. Washington's "Atlanta Compromise."
		Stephen Crane published *Red Badge of Courage,* a novel giving psychological insights into combat during the Civil War.
1896		*Plessy v. Ferguson* ruling by the **Supreme Court** that **segregation**—"separate but equal"—is constitutional.
1897	**William McKinley, 1897–1901**	
1898		Spanish-American War.
1899–1902		American-Filipino War. Insurrection against American rule.
1900		United States becoming one of the world's leading industrial powers.
1900–1914		**Immigration** averages one million people a year. Many from Eastern and Southern Europe, including Jews and Catholics.
1901	**Theodore Roosevelt, 1901–1909**	
1903		United States acquires the Panama Canal Zone. Construction on canal begins.
December 17, 1903		First powered flight. The age of air transportation and warfare begins.
1904		President **Theodore Roosevelt** issues his "corollary" to the **Monroe Doctrine.**
1904–1917		Progressives expand the regulatory powers of the national government.
1905		The Industrial Workers of the World (IWW) founded.
1908		**Henry Ford** produces the Model T.
		Race riot in Springfield, Illinois.
1909	**William H. Taft, 1909–1913**	National Association for the Advancement of Colored People (NAACP) founded to fight racial discrimination and to secure **civil rights.**

Date	President	Event
1913	Woodrow Wilson, 1913–1921	
1914–1918		World War I in Europe.
1914–1917		Unites States remains neutral about the war in Europe.
1917		Russian Revolution begins. Communists under Lenin seize power.
April 6, 1917		United States declares war on Germany in April. **Draft begins**. Security Espionage Act. President Wilson creates the Committee on Public Information (CPI). Over 400,000 blacks serve in armed forces.
1918		**Sedition Act**. Eugene V. Debs, head of the IWW, jailed.
November 11, 1918		World War I concludes. A total of 112,000 American soldiers killed.
1919		**Peace of Paris**. Congress rejects American membership in the League of Nations.
		Widespread labor strikes.
		Race riot in Chicago.
1919–1920		**Red Scare**. Campaign to suppress communists, radicals and socialists. Federal raids to round up aliens.
1920s		Rise of a consumer society; mass marketing and advertising; expansion of highways and automobile travel, and entertainment industry, particularly **movies**.
1920		Marcus Garvey, a Black Nationalist, calls for blacks to create a separate nation within the United States.
		Nineteenth Amendment to the **Constitution** ratified giving women the right to vote.
		Election of Warren G. Harding on the pledge to return America to "normalcy," meaning returning to the pre-World War I society.
		Census reports a majority of Americans live in cities.
1921	Warren Harding, 1921–1923	
1922		Benito Mussolini becomes Fascist dictator of Italy
		United States along with four other great powers agree to limit the size of their navies.
1923	Calvin Coolidge, 1923–1929	Adolf Hitler and his Nazi party attempt to overthrow the government in Bavaria. Hitler imprisoned and writes *Mein Kampf*
April 18, 1923		Yankee Stadium opens. Part of era of mass public **sports** in baseball and college football.
1924		**Ku Klux Klan** achieves a membership of nearly 4 million people.

Date	President	Event
		America **aids European recovery** with the Dawes Plan.
1924–1926		Joseph Stalin rises to power in the Soviet Union.
1925		Hitler rebuilds Nazi party.
		Scopes trial in Tennessee.
1926		**Ernest Hemingway** publishes *The Sun Also Rises* about the "Lost Generation."
1928		Kellogg-Briand Pact. International agreement not to use war as means to fulfill national policies.
1929	**Herbert Hoover, 1929–1933**	Eric Maria Remarque publishes *All Quiet on the West ern Front,* a powerful anti-war **novel.** Made into a popular **film** in 1930.
		Ernest Hemingway publishes *A Farewell to Arms,* another anti-war **novel.**
October 29, 1929		Stock Market crash.
1929–1932		Economic depression spreads through United States and Europe. Unemployment in the United States rises to 25 percent of the work force.
1931		Japan invades Manchuria.
1932		World War I veterans march on Washington. "Bonus Army" dispersed by troops.
		Franklin Roosevelt elected president.
1933	**Franklin D. Roosevelt, 1933–1945**	**Roosevelt's inaugural address** declares that Americans have "nothing to fear but fear itself."
		Adolf Hitler becomes Chancellor of Germany.
1933–1935		First **New Deal.** Prohibition repealed. "Alphabet" measures implemented such as the Agricultural Adjustment Act (AAA), **Civilian Conservation Corps (CCC),** and Tennessee Valley Authority (TVA). Banking and stock market regulated.
1935		Italy invades Ethiopia.
		Congress passes first of **Neutrality Acts** aimed at keeping the United States out of war.
1935–1937		Second **New Deal.** Social Security Act passed. National Labor Relations Acts (Wagner Act) strengthens unions. Rural Electrification Act brings power to rural America. Works Progress Administration (WPA) provides employment for workers, artists, and performers.
1936		Civil war in Spain. Germany and the Soviet Union aid combatants.
		Germany and Italy agree to form an alliance as "Axis Powers."
1937		Japan invades China.

Date	President	Event
		Neutrality Acts strengthened.
1937–1938		Recovery of the American economy halted. Unemployment approaches 1932 levels.
October 5, 1937		Roosevelt gives his "Quarantine Speech" urging peace-loving countries to unite against aggressors.
1938		Germany occupies part of Czechoslovakia following Munich agreement.
1939		Congress rejects Wagner-Rogers bill to increase **immigration** quotas to allow 20,000 Jewish children in Germany to enter the United States.
September 1, 1939		Germany invades Poland. World War II begins in Europe.
1940		Congress passes the **first peace-time draft**. American rearmament begins.
June 1940		Germany defeats France. Battle of Britain begins.
1941		**Franklin D. Roosevelt** announces the "Four Freedoms."
		Roosevelt proposes that America become the "arsenal for democracy." Congress passes **"Lend-Lease"** legislation to provide arms to Britain.
		Roosevelt creates the Fair Employment Practices Commission (FEPC) to ensure nondiscrimination in industries receiving federal contracts.
		Roosevelt and Winston Churchill agree on the "Atlantic Charter" to create a new world organization to ensure collective security.
December 7, 1941		Japans attacks **Pearl Harbor**. United States declares war. Germany and Italy, allies of Japan, declare war on the United States.
1942–1945		Economic depression begun in 1929 ends. About 15,000,000 people in the armed services. Military remains racially segregated.
1942		Roosevelt signs **Executive Order 9066** authorizing **internment of Japanese** on the west coast for reasons of national security.
		Roosevelt creates the Office of War Information (OWI) to oversee **propaganda** and censorship affecting the war.
		Congress of Racial Equality (CORE) formed to secure **civil rights** for blacks.
1943		Many blacks move north. Black employment in defense industries increases. Race riot in Detroit.
1944		Gunnar Myrdal publishes *The American Dilemma* analyzing the depth of racism in America.

Date	President	Event
		Bretton Woods agreement creates a new economic organization for the world.
		GI Bill passed.
June 0, 1944		D-Day. Allied forces land in Normandy.
December 18, 1944		**Supreme Court** declares **internment of Japanese** constitutional in *Korematsu v. United States.*
1945	**Harry Truman, 1945–1953**	Yalta and Potsdam agreements by allies to divide Germany and reestablish governments in Easter Europe. A source of conflict during the **Cold War.**
May 7, 1945		Germany surrenders unconditionally. One day later is V-E Day, Victory in Europe.
August 6 and 9, 1945		United States drops **atomic bombs** on Hiroshima and Nagasaki. Japan surrenders within days.
September 2, 1945		V-J Day, Victory over Japan.
November 1945		Nuremberg trial of Nazi leaders.
December 1945		**United Nations** established.
1946		Baruch plan for international control of atomic power approved by the **United Nations.**
		Atomic Energy Commission created. RAND (Research and Development) "think tank" established.
		Winston Churchill delivers his "iron curtain" speech in Fulton, Missouri.
1947		Beginning of "**Cold War.**" **Truman Doctrine** National Security Act passes creating the Defense Department, National Security Council, and **CIA.** George Kennan outlines the policy of "containment." President Truman issues **Executive Order 9835** to remove "security risks" from government.
		Marshall Plan approved.
		British colonialism ends in India. Pakistan created. New countries emerge as decolonization occurs elsewhere in the world.
		House Un-American Activities Committee conducts hearings to reveal communist influence in the movie and entertainment industry.
		Postwar baby boom peaks at nearly 27 million births. Suburbs expand. **Levittown,** the beginning of mass housing developments.
1948		Soviet Union blockades West Berlin. Berlin airlift begins.
		State of **Israel** created. **Israel** repels attacks.
		Truman issues Executive Order 9981 desegregating the armed forces.

Date	President	Event
1949		Communists under Mao Zedong take control of China.
		Soviet Union detonates its first atomic bomb.
		North Atlantic Treaty Organization (NATO) formed for mutual security against a Soviet invasion of Western Europe.
		George Orwell publishes *1984*—prophesizes the triumph of totalitarianism.
		Major League Baseball integrated.
1950s		Beginning in the late 1940s the "new look" return to women's fashion. Television replaces radio as the principal source of home entertainment.
		Employment of married mothers outside of the home increases.
1950		NSC #68, a top secret policy approved by the National Security Council, which approves use of covert force and encouraging "captive nations" to revolt against Soviet rule. Places the United States on a quasi-war footing.
		Julius and Ethel Rosenberg arrested for treason. Both executed in 1953.
		Passage of the McCarran Internal Security Act.
1950–1953		Korean War.
1950–1954		"McCarthyism." Civil liberties challenged. 1954 Senate censors Senator Joseph McCarthy.
1951		European Coal and Steel Community formed. Beginning of what would become the European Economic Community (known as the Common Market, and later the European Union.
April 1951		Truman removes General McArthur from command in Korea.
1952		Election of Dwight D. Eisenhower as president. First Republican in 20 years.
1953	Dwight D. Eisenhower, 1953–1961	East Germans rise up against Soviet rule. Suppressed by force.
March 5, 1953		Soviet dictator, Joseph Stalin, dies.
1954		French defeated at Dien Bien Phu. French Indochina divided into Laos, Cambodia and Vietnam.
		Historian David Potter publishes *People of Plenty*, describing the rise of American consumer economy and expansion of the middle class.
		Congress adds "under God" to the Pledge of Allegiance.
		Elvis Presley tops the music charts.

Date	President	Event
May 17, 1954		*Brown v. Board of Education.* **Supreme Court** rules that **segregation** in schools is unconstitutional.
1955		Movie *The Blackboard Jungle* warns of social decay caused by youth gangs and rock 'n roll **music.**
December 1, 1955		Rosa Parks refuses to give up her seat on a Montgomery bus. Boycott begins to end **segregation** on the city buses. **Civil rights movement** intensifies. **Martin Luther King, Jr.** and the Southern Christian Leadership Conference emerge as leaders.
1956		Passage of the Highway Act authorizing construction of the interstate highway system to improve American defense and promote commerce.
		Congress approves adding "In God We Trust" to the nation's motto.
		Supreme Court declares **segregation** on public buses unconstitutional.
		Hungarian uprising against **Communist** regime suppressed.
September 1957		Federal troops enforce integration of Little Rock, Arkansas, high school.
October 4, 1957		Soviet Union launches Sputnik, the **first space satellite.** Soviet leadership in missile technology and delivery of atomic weapons feared. Sales of bomb shelters increase in United States.
1958		National Defense Education Act passed to improve the teaching of mathematics and science.
1959		Fidel Castro leads revolution in Cuba. Establishes a **communist** regime.
1960		Young Americans for Freedom (YAF) formed—College activists favoring aggressive American actions to defeat **communism** and to reduce "big government" at home.
1960–1963		Increased **civil rights** activism—sit ins and "freedom rides."
1961	**John F. Kennedy, 1961–1963**	President **John F. Kennedy** increases American aid to South Vietnam against communist insurgents.
		Construction of the **Berlin Wall.**
January 7, 1961		**President Eisenhower's** farewell speech. Warns of the dangers of a **"military-industrial complex"** dominating American economy and society.
April 17, 1961		**CIA** supports attack on Cuba by exiles defeated at the "Bay of Pigs."

Date	President	Event
1962		Students for a Democratic Society (SDS) formed in response to YAF. Young activists against racial discrimination and social injustices. Becomes part of the "New Left." Beliefs expressed in its **Port Huron Statement.**
October 1962		Cuban missile crisis.
1963	**Lyndon B. Johnson, 1963–1969**	**Betty Friedan** publishes *The Feminine Mystique* expressing women's dissatisfaction with limitations of domestic life and wish for careers and more active public life.
August 28, 1963		March on Washington where **Martin Luther King, Jr.** gives his "I have a dream" speech.
September 15, 1963		Bombing of Birmingham, Alabama, church killing four children.
November 22, 1963		Assassination of **President Kennedy.**
1964		Congress approves Tonkin Gulf Resolution authorizing increased military force in South Vietnam.
		Movie, *Dr. Strangelove: Or How I Stopped Worrying and Learned to Love the Bomb* presents a critical parody of cold war fears and American policy of Mutual Assured Destruction (MAD).
		Passage of the **Civil Rights** Act. Prohibits racial discrimination in public facilities and discrimination against women.
1965		President **Lyndon Johnson** announces his **"Great Society"** program—Medicare, Medicaid, and a "war on poverty."
		Voting Rights Act removes barriers used to restrict Blacks from voting.
		President Johnson orders operation "Rolling Thunder," the limited bombing of North Vietnam. 50,000 more troops sent to South Vietnam.
1965–1970s		Counterculture. Associated with "hippies," "yippies," the **anti-war movement.** Woodstock Festival in New York.
February 21, 1965		Malcolm X murdered by enemies within his own movement.
1967		Anti-war march on the Pentagon.
1968		**Civil Rights** Act ending racial discrimination in housing.
		Tet Offensive in Vietnam. A majority of Americans turn against the Vietnam war.
April 4, 1968		Assassination of **Martin Luther King, Jr.**
June 6, 1968		Assassination of Robert F. Kennedy.
August 1968		Riots at the Chicago convention of the Democratic Party.

Date	President	Event
1969	Richard Nixon, 1969–1974	President **Richard Nixon** begins negotiations with the Soviet Union to reduce nuclear missiles. Strategic Arms Limitations Treaty (SALT) formalized two years later.
		American withdrawal from Vietnam begins.
July 20, 1969		**Americans land on the moon.**
1970		American incursion in Cambodia sets off campus riots and protests. Students killed at Kent State University in Ohio.
June 1971		Daniel Ellsberg leaks the so-called "**Pentagon Papers.**"
1972		**President Nixon** opens relations with Communist China.
1973		Paris Peace Agreement. American troops withdrawn from Vietnam. **POWs** returned.
1973		*Roe v. Wade.*
August 8, 1974	Gerald Ford, 1974–1977	**President Nixon** resigns from office as a result of the Watergate scandal.
1975		South Vietnam falls to the **communists.**
1977	Jimmy Carter, 1977–1981	**Feminist movement** becomes international. First meeting in Houston, Texas.
1980		Microsoft licenses its computer software, MS-DOS (Microsoft Disk Operating System).
1980s		Legal **immigration** of Asians and Hispanics increases social diversity.
		America becoming a "knowledge and service" economy.
		AIDs epidemic begins.
1980–1988		The so-called "Reagan Revolution." A massive build-up of the American military, a more aggressive policy to combat Soviet influence, efforts to restore more political power to the states, and federal tax cuts.
1981	Ronald Reagan, 1981–1989	
1985		Mikhail Gorbachev becomes head of the Soviet Union. Begins programs of reform *glasnost* (openness), and *perestroika* (restructuring) to revitalize the Soviet economy.
April 25–26, 1986		Nuclear power plant at Chernobyl explodes. World's worst nuclear accident.
June 3–4, 1989	George H. W. Bush, 1989–1993	Chinese students demonstrate in Tiananmen Square for more freedoms. Suppressed by military force.
November 19, 1989		Destruction of the **Berlin Wall.**
1990s		Internet moves from college and military use to public use. Contributes to the worldwide computer and digital information revolution.

Date	President	Event
1991		**First Gulf War.** Iraqi forces defeated. Sovereignty restored in Kuwait.
		Ethnic wars and ethnic cleansing begins in the former Yugoslavia.
December 21, 1991		The Soviet Union officially ceases to exist. **Cold War** ends.
February 26, 1993	**William J. Clinton, 1993–2001**	**Al-Qaida** detonates a truck bomb under the World Trade Center.
1995		The Dayton Accords. NATO forces enforce the peace in the Balkans.
2001	**George W. Bush, 2001—**	American-led forces defeat the **Taliban** in Afghanistan and destroy **al-Qaida** training bases.
September 11, 2001		**Al-Qaida Terrorists** destroy the two World Trade Center towers and damage the Pentagon. Nearly 3,000 people killed. President George W. Bush declares War on **Terror.**
October 26, 2001		USA PATRIOT Act passed.
2002		The Euro becomes the currency for many countries in the European Union.
March 19, 2003		United States-led forces invade Iraq.
2004		The European Union expands from fifteen to twenty-five members.
		An interim regime established in Iraq.
		American policy in Iraq and conduct of the War on **Terror** become key issues in the election campaign for president of the United States.

ADAMS, ABIGAIL

(b. November 11, 1744; d. October 24, 1818) Wife of President John Adams and mother of President John Quincy Adams, noted for her correspondence.

Abigail Smith Adams is best known for the letters she wrote for over a half century, but also she is historically visible because she was the wife of one president of the United States (John Adams, 1797–1801) and mother of another (John Quincy Adams, 1825–1829). The stream of her letters that began in the early 1760s and ended with her death in 1818 represents the most complete record that survives of a woman's experiences during the Revolutionary War era and subsequent decades in American history.

Abigail was born in Weymouth, Massachusetts. Her father was a Congregational minister and her mother descended from distinguished New England clergymen. Abigail's youth—indeed, most of her adult life—was spent in the countryside around Boston. As was typical for girls, she was educated at home. The great milestone in her young life was marriage to John Adams in 1764.

The Adams marriage coincided with the escalation of events that led to the Revolution, and during the next decade, while Abigail gave birth to four children (as well as others who did not survive to adulthood), John was lured into the politics that took him to distant places for the quarter of a century after 1774. This is significant, because Abigail remained at home in Braintree during the Revolutionary War, supporting her family and maintaining their farm. She also began to write the torrent of letters that have become the best surviving record of a New England woman's experience of the Revolutionary era.

For almost a decade Abigail took over John's role as breadwinner, supporting herself, her children, and her household. She managed their farm; she began a small business enterprise by selling locally items that John sent from Europe; she negotiated for and purchased property (in his name, since married women could not hold land in their own names); she speculated in currency and paid their taxes. She did all of this with the understanding that it was her patriotic duty in wartime. "The unfealing [sic] world may consider it in what light they please," she wrote to John in mid-1777. "I consider it as a sacrifice to my Country" (Butterfield, II, p. 301).

Abigail's experiences during the Revolution were typical of many women whose husbands served their country. She suffered many hardships. Soon after John

Abigail Adams.

departed for Philadelphia, a dysentery epidemic struck, and everyone in Abigail's household, herself included, was afflicted. Both her mother and her servant Patty, whom she nursed for many weeks, died, but her critically ill son Tommy survived. Then, after British troops occupied Boston, she feared she would have to abandon her own home just outside the city limits. Fortunately, the battle resumed farther to the south, and she did not have to move her family.

In her famous letter of March 31, 1776, when the Declaration of Independence was being drafted, Abigail reminded John to "Remember the Ladies" in the new "Code of Laws which I suppose it will be necessary for you to make." She specifically asked the Founding Fathers to remember women's rights when they wrote their laws. This was a bold statement for a woman to make, and her words have resonated for American women for more than two centuries. That same letter carried an indictment against the continuation of slavery in the new nation, as she reminded the Founders of the "principal [sic] of doing to others as we would that others should do unto us" (Butterfield, I, p. 329).

Abigail believed that another outcome of the Revolutionary War should be improved education for women.

In the summer of 1776, she waged another brief campaign in a letter to John: "I most sincerely wish that our new constitution may be distinguished for Learning and Virtue. If we mean to have Heroes, Statesmen and Philosophers, we should have learned women" (Butterfield, II, p. 94).

The war ended in 1783, and in 1784 Abigail traveled to Europe to join her husband, who became the first American minister to the Court of St. James. Following the Adamses' return in 1788, John was elected vice president (1789–1797) and then president, so Abigail played a public role at the nation's early capitals. All the while, she wrote letters to family and friends that captured the events, the spirit, and the consciousness of her times.

The final decades of her life were spent in her beloved Quincy, where she took care of her household and her family, gardened, attended worship, observed political developments, engaged in social activities, and recorded all in letters. She died after a long illness on October 24, 1818.

BIBLIOGRAPHY

Butterfield, L. H.; Garrett, Wendell D.; Sprague, Marjorie E., eds. *The Adams Family Correspondence*. 6 vols. Cambridge, MA: Belknap Press of Harvard University Press, 1963–1993.

Gelles, Edith B. *Portia: The World of Abigail Adams*. Bloomington: Indiana University Press, 1992.

Gelles, Edith B. *Abigail Adams: A Writing Life*. New York: Routledge, 2002.

McCullough, David. *John Adams*. New York: Simon and Schuster, 2001.

Withey, Lynne. *Dearest Friend: A Life of Abigail Adams*. New York: Macmillan, 1981.

Edith B. Gelles

See also: **Drinker, Elizabeth; Madison, Dolley; Republican Womanhood; Sampson, Deborah.**

ADAMS, JOHN

(b. October 30, 1735; d. July 4, 1826) Second president of the United States 1797–1801).

In the years between his birth in 1735 and death in 1826 John Adams became a member of an elite group of men who became universally praised as America's Founding Fathers—a title he richly deserved. And while Jefferson may have had a more subtle intellect, Franklin more popular appeal and Washington more stature, few could argue that any one person did more for the cause of American independence than John Adams. In addition to this contribution, he personified the ideals of republican virtue that have left a lasting imprint on American society, culture and identity.

SIMPLE BEGINNINGS

John Adams came from humble origins. Unlike Washington and Jefferson who came from wealth and had amassed vast land holdings by the time of the Revolutionary War, Adams was born into a more simple life. His father was a farmer and pastor in Braintree, Massachusetts, about ten miles south of Boston. A quick study who was reading the Greek classics at a young age, Adams gravitated to law, eventually graduating from Harvard and setting up a profitable law practice in the Boston area.

It was as a leading local lawyer that Adams first gained wide prominence. In 1770, with relations between England and the colonies deteriorating, Adams took the unpopular step of defending British soldiers accused of firing on and killing a number of Americans in what became known as the Boston Massacre. Adams was able to clear all these soldiers of the most serious charges. And whereas he was criticized in some quarters for taking the case, his own writing against unfair British policies and his conviction that the rule of law had to prevail, even against the enemy, showed that Adams was an honest man of strong principles.

When the first Continental Congress met in Philadelphia in 1774, Adams was sent as a delegate from Massachusetts. In 1775 he was instrumental in having George Washington named as the Commander in Chief of the fledgling Continental Army. By 1776 Adams had established himself as one of the preeminent leaders of the Independence movement. His *Thoughts on Government* was one of the most influential pamphlets produced during the era. While Thomas Paine's *Common Sense* was the literary shot heard round the colonies, Adams's reasoned document focused on the practical matter of what would happen after independence. Adams probed fundamental questions of sovereignty—what type of government would be formed and how would it operate.

When the Second Continental Congress met in June 1776 Adams was on a multitude of committees, not the least of which was that charged to draw up the Declaration of Independence. And while Jefferson rightly became known as the father of the Declaration, he had no more passionate advocate in Congress than Adams. Years later Jefferson would call Adams the "colossus of independence."

DIPLOMACY AND LEADERSHIP

With independence far from certain, Adams was sent to France in the hopes of securing an alliance and the badly needed armaments and aid that would come with it. Along with Benjamin Franklin and Arthur Lee, Adams

John Adams, in a lithograph after a painting by John Singleton Copley.

was able to secure the French support that ensured the success of the Revolution.

After his tenure in France, Adams served in the Netherlands and became the first American minister to England. With the Constitution written in his absence, Adams finally returned home in 1788 and was chosen to be vice president under Washington. In 1797 Adams became the second president of the United States, beating Thomas Jefferson.

Adams was a Federalist, and his one term was far less distinguished than his contribution during the Revolution, in part because of ongoing quarrels with Jefferson and other Democratic Republicans. The political squabbling of the newly-formed parties reached a fever pitch with the so-called XYZ Affair. With France and Britain at war, Adams fought to keep the young democracy neutral. But when France began demanding tribute, a wave of anti-France fervor swept the country. The crisis sparked a few naval engagements before cooler heads prevailed and both sides quietly backed down.

The first resident of the White House, Adams made way for rival Thomas Jefferson in 1801 and retired to Braintree with his beloved wife Abigail. In the years that followed, Jefferson and Adams mended fences and produced a voluminous series of letters that gives unique insight into the founding of the nation.

Adams lived to see his son, John Quincy Adams, become the sixth president in 1825. In 1826 Adams died, his last words being "Thomas Jefferson survives." Little did he know that his friend and fellow Founding Father had died just hours earlier. The date: July 4, 1826—exactly fifty years from the first Independence Day.

BIBLIOGRAPHY

Flexner, James Thomas. *Washington, the Indispensable Man.* New York: Little, Brown, 1974.

Isaacson, Walter. *Benjamin Franklin: An American Life.* New York: Simon & Schuster, 2003.

Liell, Scott. *46 Pages: Thomas Paine, Common Sense, and the Turning Point to Independence.* Philadelphia, PA: Running Press, 2003.

Mccullough, David. *John Adams.* New York: Simon & Schuster, 2001.

Randall, Willard Sterne. *Thomas Jefferson; A Life.* New York: Henry Holt, 1993.

Michael Davis

See also: **Constitution: Creating a Republic; Federalist Party; Jefferson, Thomas; Madison, James; Memory and Early Histories of the Revolution; Monroe, James.**

ALIEN AND SEDITION LAWS

Enacted in 1798, the Alien and Sedition Laws were the nation's first legislative acts designed to stifle political dissent in wartime. Congress enacted four laws to discourage domestic criticism and protest of the "Quasi-War" against France. The laws set a precedent for strengthening national and public security at the expense of civil liberties.

The Alien and Sedition Laws sprang from American responses to the French Revolution. On one side, led by Alexander Hamilton and including most of the Federalist Party, were shopkeepers, merchants, and tradesmen who viewed the French Revolution, with its execution of opponents, abolition of many religious laws and practices, and forcible seizure of property from the nobility and aristocracy, as horrifyingly radical. They sympathized more with England than France, maintaining that French aid in the War of American Independence was an act of naked self-interest. Not so, retorted a large number of farmers, small landowners, laborers, and newly arrived European immigrants. Articulated through the emerging Republican Party and the speeches and writings of Thomas Jefferson and James Madison—authors of the Kentucky and Virginia Resolutions that would denounce the Alien and Sedition Laws—they viewed the French as brethren in a global march of democracy against monarchy, class-based privilege, and centuries-old traditions. The French Revolution, as they saw it, continued the American Revolution, and the 1778 treaties between the two nations were morally binding on Americans to support the French.

The controversy over Edmund Genet typified the dispute. Genet, French ambassador to the United States, traveled the United States to raise money for the revolutionaries, sailors for service aboard French privateers, and troops for military expeditions. Genet also criticized George Washington's neutrality policy in harsh tones. Federalists accused him of being a spy and Republicans countered that the Federalists were involved in a conspiracy to ruin Genet.

This was the political climate when John Adams, a Federalist, became president in 1797. By July 1798 the Federalist-controlled Congress, with Adams's support, ordered U.S. naval operations to begin against France. In August Federalists enacted the Alien and Sedition Laws to prevent domestic violence and opposition they believed could result from the Quasi-War.

The program consisted of four laws. First, immigrants would have to wait fourteen years instead of the customary five to become naturalized citizens. Second, the president received powers to deport aliens in peace time. Third, a similar presidential power would be applied to enemy aliens located in the United States during a declared state of war. Adams did not exercise either of these powers, but several French officials fled for fear of deportation. Fourth, and most significantly, stiff fines and jail time awaited a person found guilty of writing, speaking, or publishing "false, scandalous, and malicious" content about the president or either house of Congress, or causing the American people to despise the federal government. This law produced federal prosecutions of seventeen writers, editors, and publishers. Only one of the accused was found not guilty. The laws expired with the defeat of Adams in the 1800 election. Adams's successor, Thomas Jefferson, pardoned all who had been punished under the controversial program.

The Alien and Sedition Laws illustrated the effect of public fear in wartime or, in the case of the late 1790s, "quasi-wartime." Federalists imagined Republicans would aid French infiltrators and saboteurs. Depictions of guillotines severing the heads of French citizens intensified the fears of people who recalled Genet's efforts only a few years before. What would stop more Genets from organizing cells to kill Federalists or launch slave revolts? In Federalist eyes, behind every Republican stood a potential French agent, and behind every immigrant stood a potential Republican voter. Federalists calmed themselves by crafting the Alien and Sedition Laws to strengthen internal security and weaken the opposing political party that appeared to foment domestic discord.

More fundamentally, these laws revealed a belief that an open, self-governing society is vulnerable in wartime to domestic attacks from its enemies, regardless of how distant they might be. The existence of peacetime liberties and freedoms, the argument went, must be reduced during periods of armed conflict or the openness that Americans cherish will be turned against them. The laws further showed an inherent tension in the life of the early republic between political disagreements—the signs of a healthy public discourse—and the waging of war. Republicans in the late 1790s maintained that Federalists wanted to control the levers of power and crush organized political opposition in the name of fighting a war.

The Federalists used the Alien and Sedition Laws to wage the Quasi-War of 1798 at home. The laws epitomized the divisive effects of the French Revolution among Americans in the 1790s, and foreshadowed tensions over civil liberties and war that characterized American life in succeeding generations.

BIBLIOGRAPHY

Miller, John Chester. *Crisis in Freedom: The Alien and Sedition Acts*. New York: Little Brown, 1951.

Smith, James Morton. *Freedom's Fetters: The Alien and Sedition Laws and American Civil Liberties*. Ithaca, NY: Cornell University Press, 1966.

Daniel T. Miller

See also: Civil Liberties; Kentucky and Virginia Resolutions; Federalist Party; Jeffersonian Republican Party.

ANTI-FEDERALISTS

The Anti-Federalists were a loosely associated group of men and women who opposed the ratification of the United States Constitution in the wake of the Constitutional Convention of 1787. Although the intensity of and reasons for their opposition varied by individual, state, and region, a common thread bound Anti-Federalists: fear that a powerful, distant, and centralized national government was a direct threat to democracy (defined as local self-government or states' rights) and individual rights and liberties. Anti-Federalists believed passionately that the U.S. Constitution with its Supremacy Clause (Article VI) and the Necessary and Proper Clause (Article I, sec. 8) would create a tyrannical central government and so they agitated vigorously against its adoption in newspapers, on the streets, and in state ratifying conventions.

To understand the Anti-Federalists as they understood themselves, it is important to know that they were ardent supporters (and many were veterans) of the American Revolution. For Anti-Federalists, the American Revolution was fought on behalf of the liberal principles of liberty, equality, and democracy as asserted in the Declaration of Independence and Thomas Paine's *Common Sense*. For them, the war was a sacred event representing a blood sacrifice on the part of American patriots to vanquish tyranny and give birth to liberty. They believed that the Revolutionary War was fought to diminish the power of government to prevent centralization of authority. It was their belief that men like Alexander Hamilton and other nationalists had constructed a constitution that would ultimately betray the principles of the Revolution and transform the fledgling democracy into an authoritarian aristocratic or monarchical nation in fairly short order. Their fears were based on the seemingly open-ended clauses noted above along with provisions like the lifetime tenure of Supreme Court Justices and the long length of Senatorial terms. They were alarmed by Hamilton's statements that he greatly admired Julius Caesar and by his proposition that the American president be elected for life.

BILL OF RIGHTS

Prominent Federalists like James Wilson and James Madison supported ratification and argued vehemently that the new constitution was a "limited document for limited ends" that should be read as only authorizing the grants of power and authority that were specifically outlined in the text itself. Leading Anti-Federalists like Patrick Henry, Luther Martin, Mercy Warren, Elbridge Gerry, George Clinton, and others were not convinced, and saw the seeds of political expansion and potential tyranny in the document. They pushed its supporters to add a Bill of Rights that would limit the power and scope of the new regime. These well-known provisions of the Constitution are stated with typical Anti-Federalist simplicity and parsimony. They begin with the well-known phrase "Congress shall make no law" and continue on to detail a number of important limits on national power, such as prohibiting Congress from abridging freedom of speech and freedom of press. They conclude with the much-debated and often-maligned Tenth Amendment which preserves to the states and the people respectively all powers not expressly prohibited to them nor delegated to the United States.

That final amendment is, indeed, the true heart and soul of Anti-Federalist political ideology. Embedded in that brief sentence is the whole of their hope that the Constitution would be strictly constructed to limit the power of the federal government. It is critical to note that the Bill of Rights as proposed was intended only to apply to the actions of the national government. Each state had its own constitution (often with its own bill of rights) that was designed to delineate the scope and limits of their power and authority within their own borders. As odd as it may seem to contemporary readers given the issues of slavery, civil rights, and women's rights, the Anti-Federalists believed that it was the states, not the national government, that could be trusted to defend the rights and liberties of the citizenry. To use the Second Amendment as an example, Anti-Federal proponents of states' rights thought that the "right to keep and bear arms" was necessary to physically defend themselves from a centralized government turned tyrannical. Beginning with the Fourteenth Amendment (1868), the federal government guaranteed equal protection under the Constitution. America gradually adopted the notion that all citizens possessed the same rights and that it was the responsibility of the national government to ensure those rights and liberties.

While the latter transformation was certainly not foreseen in the debates surrounding ratification, and perhaps not even desired by many who later passed the Fourteenth Amendment, the Anti-Federalists were responsible for forcing the adoption of the Bill of Rights. It is considered not only the hallmark of our own Constitution, but also the measuring stick by which other nations' own democratic legitimacy is gauged. So pervasive were their arguments and so persistent was their presence that in fairly short order after the Constitution was ratified, the remnants of the Anti-Federalists migrated toward Thomas Jefferson (the author of their beloved Declaration of Independence), and the emerging Republican Party (bringing James Madison along for good measure). While the Anti-Federalists ceased to exist as a party, they left an enduring legacy. Throughout the nineteenth and twentieth centuries, many Americans sustained the Anti-Federalist convictions that government is best that is closest to home and that "government governs best that governs least." In this way the Revolutionary War and the struggle over the Constitution continue to shape politics and social values.

BIBLIOGRAPHY

Cornell, Saul. *The Other Founders: Anti-Federalism & the Dissenting Tradition in America, 1788–1828.* Chapel Hill: University of North Carolina Press, 1999.

Duncan, Christopher M. *The Anti-Federalists and Early American Political Thought.* DeKalb: Northern Illinois University Press, 1995.

Siemers, David J. *Ratifying the Republic: Antifederalists and Federalists in Constitutional Time.* Stanford, CA: Stanford University Press, 2002.

Storing, Herbert J. *What the Anti-Federalists Were For.* Chicago: University of Chicago Press, 1981.

Wolin, Sheldon S. *The Presence of the Past: Essays on the State and the Constitution.* Baltimore, MD: Johns Hopkins University Press, 1989.

Christopher M. Duncan

See also: Articles of Confederation; Commonwealth Men; Constitution: Creating a Republic.

ARMED CONFLICTS IN AMERICA, 1587–1815

Four continuities, or themes, link the disparate wars, rebellions, and revolutions that characterize English North America during its colonial and early national periods. Conflicts between English colonists and the Native American peoples whose lands were being colonized constitute the first theme. By the late seventeenth century, a second continuity emerges in the European struggle for control of North America, which gradually absorbed the regional struggles between settlers and Indians. This triangular relationship between English American settlers, Native Americans, and European states persisted through this entire period. Warfare frequently aggravated pre-existing sectional hostilities leading to the third theme of armed conflict between English settlers and their eastern governments. Not only did war stimulate sectional violence among whites, but in the fourth theme offered America's African slaves the occasion and inspiration to assert their drive for freedom in armed insurrections. Altogether these four themes intertwine as recurring patterns through the armed conflicts that America experienced from the end of the sixteenth to the early nineteenth century.

CONFLICTS OF COLONIZATION

England's first effort to colonize the new world ended in disaster. After an initial voyage of discovery, Sir Walter Raleigh in 1587 sent an expedition of over one hundred men, women, and children to establish a permanent colony on Roanoke Island off the Carolina coast. Three years later, a long-delayed relief fleet returned only to find the place abandoned with obvious signs of a struggle.

Historians differ as to whether or not the Roanoke colonists moved to another location, but they generally agree that they fell victim to Indian attack. The same fate nearly befell the Jamestown colony which had been struggling for survival since its founding in 1607. Mutual co-existence with neighboring Indians came to a shocking end in 1622 when local tribes conducted a surprise attack that killed nearly one third of the Jamestown settlers. Yet, not only did the colony survive, it managed to weather yet another American Indian attack in 1644 and to retaliate with a ferocity that reduced the Indians to powerless tributaries.

The ever-expanding New Englanders also clashed with their Native American neighbors. In 1637–1638 English forces from Connecticut and Massachusetts combined to virtually destroy the Pequot of southern Connecticut in a dispute over land and trade. Forty years later Indians from southern New England, westward to the Connecticut River and northward in Maine, combined in a general movement to counter New England's imperialism. King Philip's War, named for a Wampanoag leader known as Philip by the English, broke out in 1675 and eventually rolled the frontier back to within twenty miles of Boston. But the Indians lacked the resources and organization to maintain their momentum. Philip was killed in 1676 as the war in southern New England came to a close; it dragged on for two years in northern New England. But like their counterparts in Virginia, New England's Indians were eventually reduced to subservience.

About the time of King Philip's War in New England, Virginia once more experienced Indian unrest along its western frontier. The disturbance provided Virginia's frontiersmen, led by the politically ambitious Nathaniel Bacon, the opportunity to vent their own frustrations and unleash a colony-wide rebellion against the royal governor and his ruling clique. Bacon, however, died in 1676 at the very moment of his success, and without his leadership, so did the movement. Governor Sir William Berkeley then reasserted his control over the colony with a heavy hand.

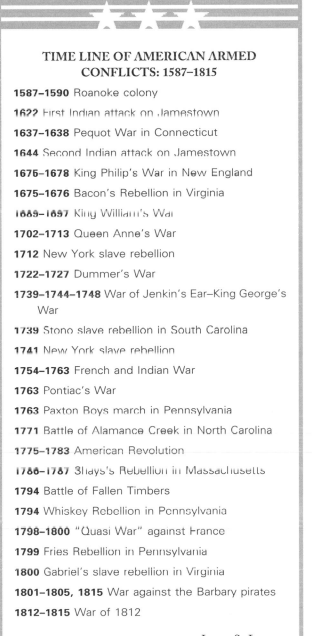

TIME LINE OF AMERICAN ARMED CONFLICTS: 1587–1815

1587–1590 Roanoke colony

1622 First Indian attack on Jamestown

1637–1638 Pequot War in Connecticut

1644 Second Indian attack on Jamestown

1676–1678 King Philip's War in New England

1675–1676 Bacon's Rebellion in Virginia

1689–1697 King William's War

1702–1713 Queen Anne's War

1712 New York slave rebellion

1722–1727 Dummer's War

1739–1744–1748 War of Jenkin's Ear–King George's War

1739 Stono slave rebellion in South Carolina

1741 New York slave rebellion

1754–1763 French and Indian War

1763 Pontiac's War

1763 Paxton Boys march in Pennsylvania

1771 Battle of Alamance Creek in North Carolina

1775–1783 American Revolution

1786–1787 Shays's Rebellion in Massachusetts

1794 Battle of Fallen Timbers

1794 Whiskey Rebellion in Pennsylvania

1798–1800 "Quasi War" against France

1799 Fries Rebellion in Pennsylvania

1800 Gabriel's slave rebellion in Virginia

1801–1805, 1815 War against the Barbary pirates

1812–1815 War of 1812

James S. Leamon

IMPERIAL RIVALRY AND REGIONAL CONFLICT

During the years from the end of the seventeenth to the middle of the eighteenth century, England, France, and Spain engaged in a series of wars for control of North America's native inhabitants. Most of these conflicts have European names and dates, but are known in America by the names of contemporary English sovereigns. Thus, the first is known as King William's War (1689–1697). An exception to the naming pattern is the brief conflict called Dummer's War (1722–1727), named after the acting governor of Massachusetts. But the pattern resumes with

Queen Anne's War (1702–1713). An exception to this naming pattern is the brief conflict called Drummer's War (1722–1727), named after the acting governor of Massachusetts. But the pattern resumes with King George's War (1739–1748)—which began as the War of Jenkin's Ear—and finally, the French and Indian War, (1754–1763), so-called because although George II sat on Britain's throne there already was a war named after George I.

Although these wars become increasingly global in scope, the American frontier continued to play a vital part. For example, King William's War in the colonies began as a series of Indian raids before authorities, English or French in North America, ever received news of the European war. In similar fashion, the French and Indian War opened in America as a contest between colonists and the French over access to the trans-Appalachian west a full two years prior to the official declarations of war in Europe—making it really a war of nine years in North America rather than the Seven Years' War to which Europeans refer. Great Britain defeated both the French and Spanish in the French and Indian War, and by the peace settlement in 1763 gained possession of all territory east of the Mississippi, but the conflict on the frontier did not cease. A loose confederation of western Indians led by the Ottawa chief Pontiac, resentful at being excluded from the settlement and apprehensive about their future under the British, continued the hostilities. "Pontiac's War" ended later in 1763 only when the British agreed to protect Indian territory by enforcing a Proclamation Line drawn down the divide of the Appalachian Mountains, beyond which white settlement was prohibited.

INTERNAL CONFLICT

Almost one hundred years of continuous conflict with Native American enemies aggravated tensions—political, regional, and racial—within early American society. A mere dozen years after Bacon's Rebellion in Virginia, King William's War broke out, during which similar uprisings erupted in Massachusetts, New York, and Maryland. In each case, wartime anxieties and local political rivalries in a power vacuum led to rebellions that overthrew existing colonial governments. Queen Anne's and King George's wars provided the environment for no less than three rebellions by African slaves, two of them in New York. In 1712 a handful of slaves in New York City conspired to set the town on fire and then to murder the white population as it responded to the emergency. The conspirators actually initiated their plan, setting fires and killing several townspeople before authorities acted quickly to reestablish control. In the aftermath, twenty-five slaves were executed by methods among which hanging was the most humane.

During King George's War rumors spread that English slaves who fled to the Spanish would be freed. In 1739 this news inspired a group of slaves near Stono Creek in South Carolina to murder their owners, seize arms, and begin a march toward Florida. The local militia quelled the movement with a terrible ferocity. But the news of the Stono uprising reached New York, inspiring anxiety among a population that vividly recalled the events of 1712 and was nervously conscious of its vulnerability to enemy attack by sea. In 1741 New York's townspeople responded to several unexplained fires with almost hysterical alarm over another conspiracy that embodied virtually all of New Yorkers' worst nightmares: arson and a slave rebellion led by Jesuit priests, coordinated with a Spanish invasion. In New York's search for revenge and stability, thirty-four persons were executed for conspiracy: thirty slaves and four whites, two of them women.

Frontier conflict had a particularly disruptive impact by intensifying the sense of discrimination and exploitation of which the backcountry repeatedly complained. Lacking political influence, western regions often resorted to armed violence against eastern governments. Pennsylvania's frontier had suffered severe losses during Pontiac's War in 1763. A group of westerners known as the "Paxton Boys" expressed their anger by slaughtering a group of peaceful Indians and then marching on the provincial capitol in Philadelphia. The government's hasty promise to redress grievances finally persuaded the angry frontiersmen to go home.

A similar situation provoked a similar response in the Carolina backcountry, where depredations during the French and Indian war had created anarchy. During the late 1760s, local vigilantes called "regulators" restored a semblance of order in both South and North Carolina, but demanded from their respective governments reforms such as more effective protection, lower taxes, better representation, and an effective judicial system. In South Carolina, the mere threat of violence won assurances of reform, but in North Carolina angry armed regulators exchanged fire with an eastern militia, commanded by the royal governor himself, in the "Battle" of Alamance Creek in 1771. After an initial volley that killed several on each side, the regulators turned and fled.

THE AMERICAN REVOLUTION

The most serious repercussions of the French and Indian War arose from the means of paying for it. This issue led directly to the American Revolution. Victory over the French and Spanish, and the subduing of Pontiac's confederacy, had left the British with a huge debt, plus the cost of administering an expanded empire. It seemed only reasonable to the British that Americans should bear some share of the burden since they were the obvious beneficiaries of the wars. Beginning in 1764, Parliament passed a series of measures imposing duties on sugar and molasses as well as taxes on stamps, paper, paint, lead, glass, and especially tea. Although many of these taxes were later repealed, they stimulated heated debate over whether Parliament had a constitutional right to tax or to legislate for those whom it did not represent. Debate led to protests, protests to riots, riots to armed rebellion in 1775, and to revolution in 1776 with the Declaration of Independence.

As a military conflict, the Revolution had several different theaters. The "frontiers" of the war included the high seas as well as the more traditional western frontier where Native Americans generally sided with the British as the lesser of the evils confronting them. The states, however, became the military focus of major campaigns that moved progressively from New England (1775–1777), to the middle states (1776–1778), to the south (1779–1781) until October 19, 1781, when the British surrender at Yorktown ended formal hostilities. Meanwhile the scope of the revolution had expanded from a mere civil war to an international conflict when, in 1778, France allied with the Americans, and in successive years the Spanish and even the Dutch joined in the expanding conflict against Great Britain. The war finally came to an end in the Treaty of Paris, September 3, 1783, which acknowledged the independence of the United States with boundaries extending from Florida to Canada and westward all the way to the Mississippi River. The Revolutionary War thus concluded the long sequence of imperial conflicts over the control of North America that had begun almost one hundred years earlier in 1689.

THE NEW NATION IN A CONFLICTED WORLD

The new United States now had to deal with the expectations and fears accompanying the end of the war. Freed from British restrictions, the western frontier surged into the Northwest Territory, creating a crisis with Native Americans similar to that of 1763. Already angry at being excluded from the peace negotiations and fearful of American intentions, Chief Little Turtle of Ohio's Miami tribe, like Pontiac before him, sought to build an Indian confederation. In 1790 and 1791 this confederacy soundly defeated two American military expeditions, but it broke apart in 1794 after the Indians were defeated in the Battle of Fallen Timbers. The collapse of Indian resistance opened most of the Ohio territory to white settlement.

Americans themselves clashed over their expectations and fears in the postwar world. A dislocated economy, debts, taxes, and unresponsive governments provoked widespread unrest, especially in western Massachusetts during the winter of 1786–1787. Led by Daniel Shays, among others, western farmers shut down courts and even attacked the armory at Springfield before being dispersed by the state militia. Not long after Shays's Rebellion, two more armed uprisings, the Whiskey and the Fries Rebellions, broke out in Pennsylvania. In 1794, farmers in the western counties challenged the authority of the new federal government by riotously nullifying a federal tax on whiskey, their chief export. Five years later in the eastern part of the state, Pennsylvania Dutch (German) farmers, led by John Fries, resisted a new federal tax on land and houses as an assault on their local autonomy. In both

episodes, popular opposition simply evaporated when federal troops arrived to restore order. The two rebellions soon assumed a significance more political than military as the two emerging political parties, Federalist and Democratic Republican, blamed each other for the disturbances.

Meanwhile, the United States was discovering the perils of being a weak neutral nation in a world engaged in war. Britain and France had once again resumed their hostilities. In an effort to weaken each other economically, each country interfered with the other's American trade. Britain was the worst offender, but when French officials brazenly demanded that American commissioners pay a large bribe simply to open negotiations, a powerful groundswell of popular hostility to France could easily have led to open war. Congress expanded the army and navy, and in fact, informal naval warfare, as a "Quasi War," did break out on the high seas in 1798. Already engaged in a war with Britain, the French government responded positively when President John Adams renewed the offer for negotiations. By 1800 outstanding differences were resolved.

As was frequently the case, the agitated wartime atmosphere again stirred unrest among America's African slave population, this time in Virginia. Talk of potential war with France and the heated political rhetoric between Federalists and Democratic Republicans convinced observant slaves that civil war was imminent. Providing inspiration was the apparently successful slave rebellion on the French-owned island of Santo Domingo (Haiti). In 1800, slave Gabriel Prosser devised a plan to seize Richmond, the state capital, taking hostage the governor, James Monroe. The occupation of Richmond was to be the signal for a general slave uprising which, with the aid of non-slaveholding whites, would destroy the institution of slavery throughout the South. So complex a scheme never had a chance. Authorities quelled the conspiracy as Gabriel and his followers were in the act of carrying it out. Interrogations and executions quickly followed, but the dream lived on in yet another abortive insurrection by one of Gabriel's followers in 1802.

The civil war that Gabriel had anticipated with hope, and many other Americans with dread, never materialized, even when Jefferson and the Democratic Republicans won the election of 1800. Indeed, Jefferson even rallied the country in a short naval war against the so-called Barbary Pirates. These petty North African pirate kingdoms had long exacted tribute, or protection money, to allow commercial vessels unmolested passage through the Mediterranean. Now independent, the United States had to pay for its own protection, but a dispute over the amount induced the pasha of Tripoli to commence plundering American vessels and holding their crews for ransom. Jefferson retaliated by sending the American navy to chastise the pasha, but despite moments of daring and even brilliance by American forces, the war dragged on from 1801 to 1805 when the United States and the pasha reached a compromise on how much protection money the Americans were willing to pay. For Jefferson, diplomatic tensions with Great Britain were taking precedence over the Barbary pirates, but late in 1815 President Madison dispatched a fleet to the Barbary Coast that ended payments of tribute once and for all.

THE WAR OF 1812

By 1805, Britain and France had resumed their almost perpetual warfare, which meant that American commerce was again subjected to interference by both powers. Jefferson tried to withhold American trade as a lever to exact concession from each belligerent, but Great Britain's powerful navy continued to confiscate cargos and impress crews from American vessels—even on one occasion firing upon an American warship. Discarding economic coercion as ineffective, President James Madison led the country into war on June 17, 1812. The chief push for war, however, came not from the commercial northeast, but from the American west, where settlers were again engaged in conflict with the Indians—in the north with a confederation led by Tecumseh, a Shawnee, and with the Creek Indian confederacy in the south. Behind Indian resistance westerners suspected British intrigue and they hoped for the opportunity to acquire more land, even Canada.

For the United States, the early fortunes of war on land varied from disappointing to disastrous, but Americans enjoyed brilliant success on the water, both on the Great Lakes and on the high seas. In the latter part of the war, the order was somewhat reversed. The British imposed a successful blockade of the American navy and burned Washington in 1814. But in the north, in 1813, American forces defeated the British and their Indian allies at the Battle of the Thames, where Tecumseh died, and continued to dominate the Great Lakes. In the southwest, Andrew Jackson crushed the Creek confederacy in 1814 then invaded Spanish Florida to pursue Indian renegades and to punish those who protected them. Jackson's demonstration of Spanish ineptitude laid the foundation for the 1819 purchase of Florida by the United States. But Jackson's greatest acclaim as a national hero came from his overwhelming victory against the British army in 1815 in the Battle of New Orleans.

The Treaty of Ghent that ended the war was signed before the Battle of New Orleans took place, and that the treaty resolved none of the issues that caused the war bothered almost no one except some grumpy New Englanders. A sense of national euphoria enveloped the country with the conviction that having defeated their enemies at home and abroad, Americans were now free to exploit the fruits of their success. As Thomas Jefferson had phrased it somewhat earlier, Americans were a "chosen nation" blessed "with destinies beyond the reach of mortal eye"—an exhilarating, but dangerous, self image.

James S. Leamon

See also: **Legacies of Indian Warfare; Shays's and Whiskey Rebellion; Slavery in America; War of 1812.**

ARNOLD, BENEDICT

(b. January 14, 1741; d. June 14, 1801) General of the American Revolution; traitor.

Benedict Arnold, born in Norwich, Connecticut, and who died in England, was one of America's most courageous generals during the Revolution. He became, however, a symbol of treachery, and his name has come to mean deceit and treason in American culture.

Arnold's early years were just a taste of the upheaval and difficulty that would mark much of the rest of his life. He was still a young man when his father managed to squander a great deal of the family fortune (much of it had come to Hannah Arnold, Benedict's mother, from a former marriage) on ill-advised business ventures. In despair, the elder Arnold drank himself to death. Soon after, young Arnold was removed from school and fell into the sort of trouble typical of boys who lack discipline and structure. He was adrift.

Rescue came in the form of an apothecary (the precursor to today's pharmacy) owned by two cousins who were willing to take Arnold in and make an apprentice of him. It was during these years, too, that Arnold made his first attempts at soldiering, in the colonial militia in New York and during the French and Indian Wars. In 1762 he opened his own apothecary in New Haven, Connecticut, and prospered. In 1767 he married Margaret Mansfield, and the couple would have three sons. In possession of his own ships, he became one of the wealthiest citizens in New Haven. Never one to shy away from trouble, Arnold even dabbled in smuggling.

Shortly after the start of the Revolution, Arnold was named colonel of the new patriot army. In 1775 he led American forces into Canada but failed in his attempt to occupy Quebec, in addition to taking a bullet in the leg. Nevertheless, his courage—some would say stubbornness—under impossible conditions led to his promotion to brigadier general.

More victories and defeats followed. Particularly useful to Arnold was a knowledge of ships acquired during his years as a merchant. His feats with the burgeoning American fleet at Valcour Island, New York, earned him widespread recognition and led some to predict that he would become the grandfather of American naval warfare.

He fought other, more personal battles as well, and it may have been these that proved Arnold's undoing. In 1777 Arnold watched as several junior officers were promoted ahead of him. It took the special pleas of Arnold's friend, George Washington, to persuade him not to resign his commission. Throughout his career, Arnold was often at odds with his fellow officers. Because he was at times openly hostile toward official opinions and orders, he faced several courts-martial.

In 1778 Arnold, now unable to fight because of injuries suffered in the fight against British General John Burgoyne during the Battle of Saratoga, was named commander of Philadelphia. Margaret had died some years earlier, leaving Arnold free to marry a young woman named Peggy Shippen, the daughter of a family with loyalist tendencies. By then, it may have been that Arnold's own tendencies had been irretrievably altered. In addition to his combative relationship with Congress and many of his fellow officers, the decision of the French to ally themselves with the patriots seems to have turned him against the Revolution.

In 1778 Arnold was court-martialed for misuse of government property and received a reprimand from Washington himself. Nevertheless, Arnold was given command of the fort at West Point, New York. Shortly thereafter, he agreed to hand it over to the British for 20,000 pounds sterling. His disloyal tendencies, long festering, now became an act of treason. Unfortunately for Arnold, the courier given the task of relaying his schemes to the British was apprehended in possession of incriminating documents, and Arnold was forced to abandon his plans and flee. For this service, though incomplete, the British Crown named Arnold brigadier general to command forces against his former compatriots.

In 1782 Arnold journeyed to England to hold court with an appreciative George III. But he was never trusted again, even among his new friends, who balked at giving him important or sensitive work. Returning to the merchant trade, Arnold split his exile between England and Canada, where the British government had rewarded him with a sizable estate. Over the years, he volunteered again for service, but no one would have him. In 1801, his merchant business in collapse, Benedict Arnold died.

It has often been said of Benedict Arnold that, had he died early on in the Revolution—during the doomed but courageous Canadian expedition or after being wounded (again, in the same leg) at Saratoga—his historical fortunes might have been better. As he did not,

Benedict Arnold.

his name has become a byword for treason and inconstancy of the worst order, a name reviled.

BIBLIOGRAPHY

Brandt, Clare. *The Man in the Mirror: A Life of Benedict Arnold.* New York: Random House, 1994.

Fritz, Jean. *Traitor: The Case of Benedict Arnold.* New York: Putnam, 1981.

Randall, Willard Sterne. *Benedict Arnold: Patriot and Traitor.* New York: Morrow, 1990.

Wilson, Barry. *Benedict Arnold: A Traitor in Our Midst.* Montreal: McGill-Queen's University Press, 2001.

Laura M. Miller

See also: **Association Test; Hewes, George Robert Twelves; Loyalists; Monroe, James.**

ARTICLES OF CONFEDERATION

The first postcolonial government of the colonies, the Articles of Confederation grew directly out of the exigencies of war. When the first shots of the Revolutionary War were fired at Lexington and Concord in April 1775, most Americans still considered themselves to be English citizens. Indeed, in responding negatively to various taxes enacted by the British Parliament, colonists thought they were upholding their rights as English citizens to "no taxation without representation." The First Continental Congress, which met in 1774, and the Second Continental Congress, which began meeting in 1775, were not intended as a new form of government but a way of collecting colonial grievances and sending them to the English king. As George III proved no more willing than the British Parliament to back down from British policies, and as Thomas Paine undermined the idea of kingly rule and hereditary succession in his *Common Sense* (published in January 1776), the colonies inched closer to Revolution. This step was ultimately taken with the proclamation of independence in July 1776.

THE WRITING AND ADOPTION OF THE ARTICLES OF CONFEDERATION

At the same time that the Second Continental Congress appointed a committee to write the Declaration of Independence, it also appointed committees to seek foreign allies and to draw up a form of government. Up to this point, colonies had been governed directly by Great Britain, which had, however, prior to the French and Indian War (1754–1763), often allowed for considerable colonial autonomy by exercising a policy now known as "salutary neglect." Given the separate histories and identities that the colonies had developed, it is not surprising that their first attempt at continental government, or at least government over that part of the continent represented by the thirteen former colonies, reflected relative jealousy of individual states' powers. This jealousy ultimately doomed the Articles to failure, but the Articles served a useful purpose during the period of transition between British rule and the inauguration of the new Constitution in 1789.

John Dickinson of Delaware was the primary author of the Articles of Confederation, but Congress was so preoccupied by war, that it took more than a year for the Second Continental Congress to send the proposal to the states (1777). During debates in Congress, Thomas Burke of North Carolina was particularly successful in seeing that the new government primarily embodied the principle of state sovereignty. Because of a running dispute between states like Maryland that did not have western land claims and those like Virginia that did, the Articles were not ratified by the final state (Maryland) until March 1, 1781, and, by 1787, states were meeting to reformulate the document.

THE STRUCTURE OF THE ARTICLES OF CONFEDERATION

The Articles of Confederation contained twelve articles, but Article II is the key. Introduced by Thomas Burke,

it specified that "Each state retains its sovereignty, freedom, and independence, and every Power, Jurisdiction and right, which is not by this confederation expressly delegated to the United States, in Congress assembled" (Solberg, p. 42). Similarly, Article III referred to the Articles as a "league of friendship" among the states, more along the order of a treaty than a common government.

As in such a league, although they could send from two to seven delegates, each state had only one vote in a unicameral Congress that had limited powers. For example, Congress did not have power, exercised by today's Congress, over interstate and foreign commerce. Moreover, Article IX provided that:

> The united states in congress assembled shall never engage in a war, nor grant letters of marque and reprisal in time of peace, nor enter into any treaties or alliances, nor coin money, nor regulate the value thereof, nor ascertain the sums and expences necessary for the defence and welfare of the united states, or any of them, nor emit bills, nor borrow money on the credit of the united states, nor appropriate money, nor agree upon the number of vessels of war, to be built or purchased, or on the number of land or sea forces to be raised, nor appoint a commander in chief of the army or navy, unless nine states assent to the same.

Congress was especially hampered in the area of finances and defense. In the former area, Congress had the power to requisition the states for money, but no power to act directly upon states or individuals to collect it. Similarly, Congress had to raise troops for national defense by relying on similar requisition measures from the states. States were even permitted to have their own navies during times of war. Added to the overall weakness of the Articles was the fact that, even when defects were widely recognized, the document could not be changed without the consent of Congress and the unanimous approval of the states. Although some amendments had wide support, none was adopted during the period in which the Articles were in effect.

STRENGTHS AND WEAKNESSES OF THE ARTICLES

During the war, states often competed with one another for volunteers to meet their troop requisitions. State residents were far more willing to defend their state's own frontiers than to march in defense of the nation. Those who served in the nation's defense (and who were often underpaid), however, appear generally to have developed a more continental view. The Congress under the Articles of Confederation largely financed the war through issuing currency, which quickly lost value, and through foreign borrowing. Although U.S. forces succeeded under George Washington and the French allies in beating the British, it was not altogether certain that the result-

Patrick Henry and the First Continental Congress. The First Continental Congress laid the groundwork for the Second Continental Congress, the Articles of Confederation, and ultimately the Declaration of Independence.
© BETTMANN/CORBIS

ing nation would long survive. The government under the Articles proved inadequate to enforce the treaty that had ended the Revolutionary War and was continually plagued by its inability to raise revenue. Had George Washington been more ambitious, and less republican-minded, he could have probably taken over the government by military force.

Weak as it was, the Articles had provided the structure for the colonies to unite against a common foe and win the Revolution. Although financing was desultory during the war, it became even more impaired once the war had ended and the nation no longer faced a common enemy. Generally known for its failure, the most striking accomplishment of the Articles other than its role in winning the Revolutionary War was the passage of the Northwest Ordinance during the meeting of the Constitutional Convention. This farsighted measure, which was reaffirmed by the new government, allowed for the eventual inclusion of the western states on an equal basis as the original thirteen, thus preventing the United States

from exercising colonial powers in the West. It also recognized congressional power to forbid slavery in the territories.

THE END OF THE ARTICLES
The Articles eventually fell prey to governmental weaknesses. The central government proved unable to raise adequate revenue, to enforce treaties of peace that it had entered into, or to compete on an equal basis on the world stage. The national government proved largely impotent in the wake of Shays's Rebellion in western Massachusetts and other populist and taxpayer revolts at the state level. States, which had written their constitutions fairly hurriedly, often emphasized popular sovereignty in the selection of their legislatures over the kinds of checks and balances needed for wise and stable governments. Such instability, in turn, threatened the liberty for which the Revolutionary War had been fought. Hope for increased strength and stability at both state and local levels eventually led to a conference of five states over commercial

matters known as the Annapolis Convention, held in 1786. This meeting in turn issued a call for the Constitutional Convention of 1787.

Although called to revise and enlarge the Articles of Confederation, the delegates instead embarked on a reworking of government that provided for three distinct branches of government and for a bicameral Congress (where states were represented according to population in the lower house) with power to act directly on individual citizens. Although the new government weakened state powers, it did not abolish the states as entities. Moreover, although the new Constitution invested Congress with increased powers to regulate commerce, to impose duties and excises, and the like, the structure of the new government, which emphasized separation of powers, checks and balances, and federalism, was still designed to secure both the rights of individuals and the rights of states. These concerns were reinforced by the early adoption of the Bill of Rights.

SUMMARY

Although it ultimately failed, the government under the Articles of Confederation made some notable achievements and gave the former colonists many important lessons in self-government. Today's Constitution would have been much different without such lessons. The U.S. Constitution strengthened the national authority while preserving significant roles for the states. Both systems of government preserved representative government, and both invested the national authority with limited powers. In sum, America's first constitution, known as the Articles of Confederation, was a product of war and colonial culture. The Articles reflected American fear of central authority and adherence to the principle of local self-rule. Both remain part of the nation's identity and political culture in the forms of federalism and states' rights.

BIBLIOGRAPHY

Edling, Max M. *A Revolution in Favor of Government: Origins of the U.S. Constitution and the Making of the American State.* New York: Oxford University Press, 2003.

Hendrickson, David C. *Peace Pact: The Lost World of the American Founding.* Lawrence: University Press of Kansas, 2003.

Jensen, Merrill. *The Articles of Confederation.* Madison: University of Wisconsin Press, 1976.

McLaughlin, Andrew C. *The Confederation and the Constitution, 1783–1789.* In *The American Nation, a History: From Original Sources by Associated Scholars,* edited by Albert Bushnell Hart. New York: Harper & Brothers Publishers, 1903.

Rakove, Jack. *The Beginnings of National Politics: An Interpretive History of the Continental Congress.* New York: Knopf, 1979.

Solberg, Winton, ed. *The Federal Convention and the Formation of the Union of the American States.* New York: Liberal Arts Press, 1958.

Wood, Gordon S. *The Creation of the American Republic, 1776–1787.* Chapel Hill: University of North Carolina Press, 1969.

John R. Vile

See also: **Constitution: Creating a Republic; Continental Congresses; States and Nation Building, 1775–1783.**

ASSOCIATION TEST

In September 1774, just prior to the outbreak of the American Revolution, the First Continental Congress passed a resolution called the Continental Association. The Association was essentially a boycott designed to place economic pressure on Britain and a political tool to prompt Americans to declare their loyalties. The "test" was simply whether or not a citizen agreed to join the Association in support of the American cause. The Association had a limited effect on British politics, but the test forced colonists to take a political stand, even when uncertainties made many reluctant.

The passage of the Association culminated a decade of deteriorating relations between Americans and Britain. Following defeat of the French in North America in 1763, the British Empire tightened imperial controls and introduced a series of new taxes on the American colonies. Colonists known as Whigs resisted British initiatives with riots and boycotts. When Whigs destroyed East India Company tea in Boston in December 1773, Parliament retaliated with a series of punitive measures, known as the Coercive Acts, that closed the Port of Boston, disallowed town meetings, removed judicial powers from the colony, and instituted a quartering act for British troops. American Whigs united in opposition to the British encroachments on traditional rights, but a significant number of colonists, some conservative in outlook, others with business ties to the Empire, and still others who held royal offices, felt their interest or duty was to Britain.

The first task for the Continental Congress in 1774 was to devise a response to the Coercive Acts that would persuade the British to alter their policy and simultaneously solidify domestic support for the American cause. Congressional deliberations produced the Continental Association. It called for colonists to "firmly agree and associate, under the sacred ties of virtue, honour and love of our country" in support of "a non-importation, non-consumption, and non-exportation agreement." Ameri-

EXCERPT FROM THE CONTINENTAL ASSOCIATION, OCTOBER 20, 1774

1. That from and after the first day of December next, we will not import, into British America, from Great-Britain or Ireland, any goods, wares, or merchandise whatsoever, or from any other place, any such goods, wares, or merchandise, as shall have been exported from Great-Britain or Ireland; nor will we, after that day, import any East-India tea from any part of the world; nor any molasses, syrups, paneles [brown unpurified sugar], coffee, or pimento, from the British plantations or from Dominica; nor wines from Madeira, or the Western Islands; nor foreign indigo.

2. We will neither import nor purchase, any slave imported after the first day of December next; after which time, we will wholly discontinue the slave trade, and will neither be concerned in it ourselves, nor will we hire our vessels, nor sell our commodities or manufactures to those who are concerned in it.

3. As a non-consumption agreement, strictly adhered to, will be an effectual security for the observation of the non-importation, we, as above, solemnly agree and associate, that, from this day, we will not purchase or use any tea, imported on account of the East-India company, or any on which a duty hath been or shall be paid; and from and after the first day of March next, we will not purchase or use any East-India tea whatever; nor will we, nor shall any person for or under us, purchase or use any of those goods, wares, or merchandise, we have agreed not to import . . . .

8. We will, in our several stations, encourage frugality, economy, and industry, and promote agriculture, arts and the manufactures of this country, especially that of wool; and will discountenance and discourage every species of extravagance and dissipation, especially all horse-racing, and all kinds of gaming, cock-fighting, exhibitions of shews, plays, and other expensive diversions and entertainments; and on the death of any relation or friend, none of us, or any of our families, will go into any further mourning-dress, than a black crape or ribbon on the arm or hat, for gentlemen, and a black ribbon and necklace for ladies, and we will discontinue the giving of gloves and scarves at funerals . . . .

11. That a committee be chosen in every county, city, and town, by those who are qualified to vote for representatives in the legislature, whose business it shall be attentively to observe the conduct of all persons touching this association; and when it shall be made to appear, to the satisfaction of a majority of any such committee, that any person within the limits of their appointment has violated this association, that such majority do forthwith cause the truth of the case to be published in the gazette; to the end, that all such foes to the rights of British-America may be publicly known, and universally contemned as the enemies of American liberty; and thenceforth we respectively will break off all dealings with him or her.

cans who signed the pledge agreed to halt imports of goods from Britain, agreed not to sell or buy British goods, agreed to discontinue the slave trade, agreed to curb exports, and agreed to "encourage frugality, economy, and industry."

Although the first portion of the Association intended to leverage America's economic clout to convince Parliament to rescind the Coercive Acts, a brief closing clause provided the authorization for local Whigs to encourage undecided citizens to join the Association and endorse the American cause. Congress empowered local committees "to establish such farther regulations as they may think proper, for carrying into execution this association" (*Journals of the American Congress* I: 22, 26.).

Committees inspected merchants' records and publicly published the names of transgressors. They also organized town meetings in defiance of the ban at which townspeople were asked to join the Association. Individuals who refused to sign or cooperate were ostracized, labeled Tories, and considered enemies of American liberty.

In Massachusetts, Israel Litchfield recorded in his diary, "We went to town meeting. They had the Association of the Continental Congress presented to the people to sign. Almost all of them that were there signed it, young and old, I for one" (Johnson, p. 162). The decision of whether or not to sign the Association was a public declaration of one's political loyalties. Signing the

Association was a public oath of support for the Whigs. Refusal to sign signaled open support for the British. The Association test forced reluctant patriots to take a stand, and the test identified non-signers as Tories who posed a potential danger to the movement.

ENFORCING PATRIOTISM

In nearly every colony associators confronted individuals who spoke for the royal government or denigrated the Whig movement. Groups of associators intimidated suspected Tories, demanding a recantation of British loyalties and public endorsement of the American cause. In 1775 a Philadelphian named Christopher Marshall wrote, "about thirty of our associators waited upon and conducted Isaac Hunt from his dwelling to the Coffee House, where having placed him in a cart, he very politely acknowledged he had said and acted wrong, for which he asked pardon of the public and committed himself under the protection of the associators" (Duane, p. 41).

In Northampton, Massachusetts, local Whigs embarked on a "tour of education" in which the mob went about forcing recantations of Tory sympathies from a number of eminent local citizens who held royal political appointments. In Virginia influential planters led the effort to require all the merchants to sign the Association or be branded as enemies. One man accused of writing a letter deemed "false and inimical" to America apologized in an open letter: "I implore the forgiveness of this country for so ungrateful a return made for the advantages I have received from it . . . and hope, from this contrition for my offence, I shall at least be admitted to subsist among the people I greatly esteem" (Middlekauff p. 258). Another Virginia man, shown the error of his ways by the local associators, publicly repented in the *Virginia Gazette* of July 20, 1775, for calling the Americans "an unlawful mob" among other things. He wrote, "I did not mean as much as I said . . . and in the most humble manner ask pardon. I most heartily wish success to this my native country in her present honest struggle for liberty." When given the Association test, these men, like many other hesitant patriots, chose to endorse the American cause rather than risk the consequences of being labeled Tory and ostracized by their neighbors.

BIBLIOGRAPHY

Duane, William, ed. *Extracts from the Diary of Christopher Marshall, 1774–1781* [1839, 1849]. New York: Arno Press, 1969.

Johnson, Richard Brigham, ed. "The Diary of Israel Litchfield." *The New England Historical and Genealogical Register* 129 (1975).

Journals of the American Congress: From 1774 to 1788. 4 vols. Washington, DC: Way and Gideon, 1823.

Middlekauff, Robert. *The Glorious Cause: The American Revolution, 1763–1789.* New York: Oxford University Press, 1982.

Walter L. Sargent

See also: **Boston Massacre: Pamphlets and Propaganda; Boston Tea Party: Politicizing Ordinary People; Families at War; Loyalists; Mobilization, War for Independence; Stamp Act Congress.**

BACON'S REBELLION

Bacon's Rebellion was the largest popular uprising prior to the American Revolution. The rebellion began as a dispute among English settlers in Virginia over American Indian policy. At its height, however, it erupted into a civil war pitting anti–American-Indian western settlers (including many servants and slaves) against Governor William Berkeley and his allies who encouraged more conciliatory policies toward indigenous peoples. Although the rebellion took the name of Nathaniel Bacon, who arrived as young man in Virginia in 1674 and was immediately welcomed into elite society, the causes and consequences of the rebellion, like all wars, were more profound than the ideas and leadership of a single man.

When Bacon migrated to Virginia in search of personal gain he entered a precarious world wherein American Indians, free and enslaved blacks, and English colonists (including many indentured servants) struggled to coexist. By the 1670s there were only four thousand American Indians, divided into twenty different tribes, who continued to live in close proximity to the European settlers. Many of these had long since accepted a dependent status as subjects of the English crown, but tensions between the natives and newcomers continued.

Governor Berkeley strove to treat American Indians equitably and to distinguish carefully between American Indian allies and foes. Regardless, many colonists, particularly those located on the western frontier, were deeply suspicious of all American Indians. The frontier situation was particularly complicated by the presence of more powerful native peoples, like the Susquehannocks, who resisted English encroachments on their lands. Anglo–American-Indian relations were further exacerbated by a depressed tobacco economy, anger over what were perceived to be excessive taxes, and displeasure with the restrictions on trade as a result of England's Navigation Acts. The larger economic and political issues, then, contributed to the volatile nature of colonial society and made American Indians convenient scapegoats for all manner of grievances.

REBELLION

The details of the rebellion are fairly straightforward. In July 1675 a violent dispute erupted over a misunderstanding between a band of Doegs and English settlers in the Potomac River Valley. In late August, Governor Berkeley's efforts to facilitate a peaceful resolution were hampered by angry colonists who chose to take matters

Nathaniel Bacon and Governor William Berkeley. Governor Berkeley attempted to balance to interests of Native Americans and the colonists. Bacon led an uprising against the governor and his allies, and against the Native Americans in the Chesapeake area. What began as an external conflict devolved to resemble class warfare. © BETTMANN/CORBIS

Governor Berkeley to lead his volunteers in military action against the American Indians. Berkeley soon insisted that he had granted the commission under duress, leading Bacon to attack the governor and his small band of allies, forcing a retreat across the Chesapeake from Jamestown to the Eastern Shore. By July the Old Dominion was firmly in Bacon's hands. His forces crushed a group of friendly Occaneechees and scattered a bedraggled band of Pamunkeys hiding out in a swamp, but they were never able to do anything about the Susquehannocks beyond their frontier. Berkeley temporarily regained control of Jamestown in early September, only to see Bacon's forces return and burn the capitol to the ground. In subsequent weeks, rebels looted and burned the homes of numerous loyalists. When Bacon died in late October, however, the rebellion collapsed. By January Berkeley was back in Jamestown, where he proceeded to hang a number of the remaining rebel leaders, but he was soon recalled to England and replaced by a more conciliatory administration.

LEGACY

Bacon's Rebellion redefined the domestic landscape of seventeenth-century Chesapeake. What began as an external conflict with American Indians rapidly developed into a domestic insurrection among predominantly western settlers who rejected the accommodationist policies of the eastern establishment. As it developed, however, Bacon's Rebellion took on a tenor of class warfare as his forces, increasingly composed of runaway servants and slaves, plundered the property of Berkeley's allies in the Tidewater. Some historians have argued that class conflict and racial egalitarianism among Bacon's rebels prompted tobacco planters to replace white indentured servants with African slaves, thus sowing the seeds of the racial divide that would define the South and much of America in the eighteenth and nineteenth centuries. The rebellion also decimated the remaining tribes in Virginia and forced many of the survivors to flee the colony. Bacon's Rebellion therefore illustrates the racism that would spill so much American Indian blood in the future, ultimately leading to the subjection of native peoples in the expanding United States.

BIBLIOGRAPHY

Morgan, Edmund S. *American Slavery, American Freedom: The Ordeal of Colonial Virginia.* New York: Norton & Co., 1975.

Washburn, Wilcomb E. *The Governor and the Rebel: A History of Bacon's Rebellion in Virginia.* Chapel Hill: University of North Carolina Press, 1957.

Webb, Stephen Saunders. *1676: The End of American Independence.* New York: Knopf, 1984.

Michael J. Guasco

into their own hands. By early 1676 (at precisely the same moment that word began to arrive in the colony about King Philip's War in New England), a full-scale war threatened to tear apart the colony.

Berkeley sought to contain the situation, but his attempt to balance the interests of both American Indians and Englishmen proved untenable. When frontiersmen began looking for a leader more willing to condone their virulent anti–American-Indian measures, Nathaniel Bacon embraced the opportunity to elevate his local standing and agreed to lead volunteer militia units. The governor, however, was suspicious of the young man's real intentions and refused to authorize his command.

Western settlers were undeterred and in June 1676 Bacon secured (by threat of force) a commission from

See also: European Invasion of Indian North America, 1513–1765; Jamestown, Legacy of the Massacre of 1622; King Philip's War, Legacy of; Slavery in America; Stono Rebellion.

BATTLE OF NEW ORLEANS

Although the Battle of New Orleans was fought after the peace treaty concluding the War of 1812 had been signed in Europe, it proved to be the most decisive battle of the war and the one that would live on longest in American memory. That memory and the political consequences of the Battle of New Orleans made it the seminal event of the War of 1812, a war that otherwise has been largely forgotten by the American public.

The battle itself was an impressive military victory for U.S. forces, and most especially for their commander, Andrew Jackson. Jackson arrived in New Orleans on December 1, 1814, fresh off a victory against Native Americans in the Creek War. American commanders had expected the British to attack the Gulf Coast near New Orleans for the entire duration of the War of 1812, and now that British Admiral Alexander Cochrane and Lieutenant General Edward Pakenham were massing troops in Jamaica, an invasion seemed imminent. After a series of skirmishes throughout the month of December, Jackson had successfully fortified positions in and around the city of New Orleans. Jackson assembled a mixed military force that included regular army soldiers, Southern militia forces, Creole and free African-American volunteers from New Orleans, and members of the Baratarian pirates led by the infamous Jean Lafitte. No one in North America had yet heard that the Treaty of Ghent had been signed on December 24, 1814, and the British advanced at the beginning of January.

Although Jackson commanded fewer troops than the British, he skillfully coordinated their positions, and Jackson's plans were further aided by a dense fog that confused the main British assault on January 8, 1815. After several days of nasty artillery exchanges, the main battle

General Andrew Jackson leading the American forces to victory over the British during the Battle of New Orleans in a painting by E. Percy Moran, ca. 1910.

action took place at the Rodriguez Canal, where the Americans cut down several advances of British troops when the fog lifted to reveal their movements. The lopsided casualty figures tell much of the tale of the battle. The British suffered over 1,500 casualties, and 484 were taken prisoner. The dead included Pakenham himself. The Americans took only seventy casualties during the entire month of January, and along Jackson's main line at the canal, only six men were killed.

The victory at New Orleans allowed Americans to claim victory in the War of 1812. Although the overall war had been, at best, a draw, and Americans had experienced severe disappointments, including the burning of their national capital, the Battle of New Orleans seemed to blot out all the dubious effects of the previous years and to promote a positive culture of victory. In his study *The War of 1812*, Donald Hickey quotes one congressman as declaring: "The terms of the treaty are yet unknown to us, but the victory at Orleans has rendered them glorious and honorable, be they what they may. . . . Who is not proud to feel himself an American—our wrongs revenged—our rights recognized!" (1989, p. 309).

By severely beating the British army, among the most impressive military forces in the world at the time, Andrew Jackson also catapulted himself into immediate fame. He had been known as an Indian fighter for some time, but now the former Revolutionary soldier from Tennessee became universally known as "the Hero of New Orleans." Jackson, and his victory, were celebrated throughout the country. American pride at having beaten Great Britain and shored up the national independence coalesced around the figure of Jackson, who was lauded in heroic poetry, biographies, and other forms of popular culture. Both the Battle of New Orleans and the martial heroism of Andrew Jackson boosted Americans' postwar sense of nationalism.

Andrew Jackson's subsequent political career was strongly influenced by the heroic reputation he won at New Orleans. He was immediately begged to run for several different political offices, and his renown helped him to dodge congressional censure for dubious actions taken during his command in the Seminole War in 1817–1818. Jackson served as territorial governor of Florida and was elected to the U.S. Senate in 1823, just as a Tennessee convention nominated him for president. Jackson's reputation as the "Hero of New Orleans" boosted his campaigns for president. In 1824 he lost, after the election was thrown into the House of Representatives; in 1828 he won, and in 1832 he was reelected. Pamphlets and handbills touting the political career of the "Hero of New Orleans" helped to usher in a new style of political campaigning.

The memory of the Battle of New Orleans continued to mark a high point in American national self-respect far after Jackson was elected to office. Jackson paid a return visit to the New Orleans battlefield in 1840, where he laid a cornerstone for a battle monument that would not be completed until the twentieth century. Residents of New Orleans celebrated the battle anniversary throughout the nineteenth century and have continued to do so ever since. The battle site is presently part of Chalmette National Historic Park, where it lies adjacent to Chalmette National Military Cemetery.

Andrew Jackson remains an icon in American history and his portrait appears on the twenty-dollar bill. He was among several presidents—George Washington, Ulysses S. Grant, Theodore Roosevelt, and Dwight Eisenhower—whose political careers were propelled by becoming military heroes in American eyes. American culture has sought such military heroes to affirm the nation's identity and to lead the country.

BIBLIOGRAPHY

Hickey, Donald R. *The War of 1812: A Forgotten Conflict*. Urbana: University of Illinois Press, 1989.

Owsley, Frank Lawrence, Jr. *Struggle for the Gulf Borderlands: The Creek War and the Battle of New Orleans, 1812–1815*. Tuscaloosa: University of Alabama Press, 2000.

Remini, Robert V. *The Battle of New Orleans*. New York: Viking, 1999.

Sarah J. Purcell

See also: **Jackson, Andrew.**

BOSTON MASSACRE: PAMPHLETS AND PROPAGANDA

On the night of March 5, 1770, British soldiers fired their muskets into a violent crowd in Boston. Five townspeople died, and the Sons of Liberty, opposing the growth of royal authority, proclaimed the event a "massacre." Condemned in the American press, the Boston Massacre became a major colonial grievance against the London government.

The gunshots in Boston followed seventeen months of friction between locals and British troops deployed to protect royal customs officials. In "A Journal of These Times," a series of one-sided reports sent to other colonies' newspapers in 1768–1769, Bostonians complained about British "redcoats" starting fights, insulting women, and encouraging slaves to revolt. To Whiggish colonists, such episodes reinforced their conviction that "standing armies"—troops maintained by kings in peacetime—were potential oppressors. These disputes coincided with Boston merchants' efforts to enforce a boycott on imports from Britain and thus pressure Parliament into repealing

English soldiers fire on American patriots on the night of March 5, 1770, in Boston. Although only five towns-people died, the Sons of Liberty declared it a "massacre," and the event became a major colonial grievance against the British government.

the Townshend duties (taxes) on glass, tea, and other goods.

More friction arose from workingmen and off-duty soldiers competing for jobs. On Friday, March 2, 1770, a ropemaker told a private that if he wanted work, he could clean an outhouse. That insult sparked two days of waterfront brawling between soldiers and ropemakers. Boston was quiet on Sunday, as Puritan tradition demanded, but fights resumed Monday evening.

What brought the violence to King Street was even more mundane. A barber's apprentice complained long and loud that an army captain was late in paying his bill. The private guarding the customs office whacked the youth's head with his musket. Soon apprentices were dashing around the center of town, yelling about this attack. Bostonians were quickly inflamed because only eleven days before a customs employee had shot into a mob around his house, killing an eleven-year-old.

A snowball-throwing crowd surrounded the sentry, who sent for reinforcements. Captain Thomas Preston brought a squad of seven grenadiers. Waterfront workers arrived, carrying clubs of cordwood, and backed the soldiers into an arc at the customs office door. Knocked down by a thrown stick, one grenadier shouted, "Damn you! Fire!" and pulled his trigger. His fellow privates responded with a ragged volley. Their seven shots hit eleven men. Three died immediately, two more over the next eight days.

Remarkably, that ended the night's violence. The crowd fell back. Captain Preston surrendered to civilian magistrates. The royal governor promised the townspeople justice and the next day, under immense public pressure, ordered all troops out of town. Wealthy Bostonians patrolled in their militia companies, determined to show that townspeople could keep the peace. The Sons of Liberty helped hire a special attorney to prosecute the soldiers but also, recognizing the value of a fair trial, encouraged two of their party (including future president John Adams) to join a Crown loyalist in defending the men.

Boston issued a report on the shootings titled *A Short Narrative of the Horrid Massacre*, marshaling ninety-six sworn depositions to blame the army and customs officials. The town sent copies to London Whigs and other American colonies but refused to let the printers sell it locally, lest it prejudice a jury. (After a reprint arrived from London, Boston printers reproduced the London title page at the front of their copies and sold them as imports.)

Friends of the royal government collected their own depositions, some printed in London as *A Fair Account of the Late Unhappy Disturbance at Boston*. Preston was quoted by both sides: Boston newspapers printed his statement that he had no complaints in jail, then London newspapers published a long letter blaming the crowd for the violence.

Propaganda also took visual form. The town's version of the shootings was illustrated by twenty-year-old Henry Pelham and then copied by activist Paul Revere when the young artist was slow to market his engraving. In this image, soldiers fire at their captain's command. Another shot comes from the customs office. Hand-colored prints were available, with blood added in red.

Preston came to trial in November 1770. His lawyers convinced the jury that he had never given an order to shoot. Then the same legal teams faced off over whether the soldiers had fired in self-defense. The second trial ended in a mixed verdict. Most of the soldiers were acquitted. The private who shouted "Fire!" and another seen brawling with ropemakers beforehand were convicted of manslaughter and punished by being branded on the thumb.

Ironically, on the same day as the massacre, Parliament moved to revoke all Townshend duties but the tea tax. When this news reached America, the boycott fizzled. The Sons of Liberty would have difficulty rousing most colonists until the crisis that led to the Boston Tea Party in 1773.

Nevertheless, the propaganda continued. Frustrated Sons of Liberty filled newspapers with complaints about corrupt judges. From 1771 to 1782 Boston commissioned an annual oration in memory of the victims. Broadsides appeared each March. In 1776 the Declaration of Independence referred to the Boston Massacre when it blamed the king "For quartering large bodies of armed troops among us; [and] For protecting them, by a mock trial, from punishment for any murders they should commit."

When the Revolutionary War began, Massachusetts Sons of Liberty applied what they had learned from publicizing the Boston Massacre. Within days of the shots on Lexington Green, patriots collected depositions, printed those that blamed the redcoats, and sped them to other colonies and to England. Artists produced battlefield engravings that, like the massacre prints, showed a line of British soldiers firing at unthreatening Americans.

In the following centuries Americans continued to invoke the Boston Massacre as an exemplar of political violence. Some authors described its victims as the first men killed for America's independence, whereas others argued that the real victims were the soldiers, threatened by an anarchic mob. Abolitionists emphasized the part-African roots of massacre victim Crispus Attucks, making him a symbol of black patriotism. After the shootings of Vietnam War protesters at Kent State University in Ohio on May 4, 1970, the demonstrators drew parallels to the Boston Massacre 200 years before.

During the years leading to the Revolutionary War, opponents of new British laws used what they called the "Boston Massacre" to arouse public hostility toward royal authorities. The use of the press to promote a political cause—playing up an event to inflame public opinion and portraying opponents as villainous—is a tactic that commonly appears before Americans enter a war and during wartime.

BIBLIOGRAPHY

A Short Narrative of the Horrid Massacre in Boston. Reprint. Williamstown, MA: Corner House, 1973.

Davidson, Philip. *Propaganda and the American Revolution, 1763–1783*. Chapel Hill: University of North Carolina Press, 1941.

Dickerson, Oliver M., ed. *Boston under Military Rule, 1768–1769: As Revealed in a Journal of These Times*. Boston: Mount Vernon Press, 1936.

Hoerder, Dirk. *Crowd Action in Revolutionary Massachusetts, 1765–1780*. New York: Academic Press, 1977.

Schlesinger, Arthur M. *Prelude to Independence: The Newspaper War on Britain, 1764–1776*. New York: Knopf, 1958.

Wroth, L. Kinvin, and Zobel, Hiller B., eds. *The Legal Papers of John Adams*, vol. 3. Cambridge, MA: Harvard University Press, 1965.

Zobel, Hiller B. *The Boston Massacre*. New York: Norton, 1970.

J. L. Bell

See also: **Boston Tea Party: Politicizing Ordinary People; Common Sense; Sons of Liberty.**

BOSTON TEA PARTY: POLITICIZING ORDINARY PEOPLE

On the evening of December 16, 1773, a few dozen of the Sons of Liberty, opposing new British laws in the colonies, systematically dumped three shiploads of tea

"The Destruction of Tea at Boston Harbor," by Sarony and Major, 1846.

into Boston harbor. They acted to prevent the royal authorities from collecting taxes on that import. The destruction of the tea was a political protest against one British tax, but it had the unintended effect of setting off a chain of events that would lead to war in April 1775.

Tea seems like an odd basis for such a bitter conflict, and a decade earlier Americans would probably have reacted tepidly to changes in imperial tea policy. But since the Stamp Act of 1765, colonial politicians had railed against taxation without representation, urging people to protest by buying fewer goods from Britain. The Sons of Liberty used "non-importation" campaigns to avoid the Townshend duties of 1767 and to pressure British merchants into lobbying for repeal. This strategy seemed to work: by 1770, Parliament had canceled the stamp tax and all but one of the Townshend duties—the tax on tea.

Boycotts pulled all consumers into the political arena—even women, who were otherwise shunted out of public affairs. In 1767 the *Boston Gazette* praised Mehitable May for wearing a locally woven wedding dress. In 1770 the Boston town meeting declared milliners Ame and Elizabeth Cumings "Enemies of their Country" because they continued to sell imports. The few political documents women were ever encouraged to sign were promises to boycott certain goods or shops. Duties

on a popular product like tea forced all free Americans to make a political choice.

Thus, though the new Tea Act of 1773 promised to lower the consumer price of East India Company tea by eliminating costs elsewhere, most Americans had come to view any tea tax as unfair. Furthermore, the law was obviously written to benefit well-connected interests: the East India Company and the few merchants granted a monopoly on importing tea into North America, called consignees. (In Massachusetts, two of those men were the royal governor's sons.) This seemed to confirm complaints of corruption in the London government.

News of the Tea Act incited widespread protests in America. Mass meetings pressured the consignees in Philadelphia, New York, and Charleston into resigning. Bostonians stormed one importer's office, driving local tea merchants to seek shelter in an army fort. In smaller towns, tea chests washed up from shipwrecks were publicly burned. Tea ships turned away from Philadelphia and New York, but on November 28 the *Dartmouth*, with 114 chests on board, arrived in Boston harbor.

Sons of Liberty urged that ship's owner not to unload the tea so as to avoid triggering the tax. Royal authorities in Massachusetts responded by applying trade regulations strictly. Governor Thomas Hutchinson invoked a law that forbade the *Dartmouth* and two later tea ships from leaving Boston harbor without unloading. Meanwhile, customs officials warned that if the *Dartmouth* was still unloaded on December 17, they could confiscate its cargo. (In Charleston the customs office carried out a similar threat.)

Boston radicals had summoned "the Body of the People," calling anyone interested in the tea issue to public meetings. Hundreds of men gathered in the Old South Meeting-House; by choosing a rural businessman to moderate the discussion, they signaled that Boston and the countryside were united. Eventually the crowd overflowed even that space, the largest in town. More than 5,000 people, equal to a third of all Bostonians, thronged the final meetings.

Both sides called on military resources. Governor Hutchinson ordered the Royal Navy and the cannons of the harbor fort to keep the three ships from leaving. The tea meetings recruited armed volunteers, mustering like militia units, to patrol Griffin's Wharf and ensure the ships were not unloaded secretly at night.

The son of the *Dartmouth*'s owner shuttled between Boston and the governor's country home, seeking a compromise. On the evening of December 16, he returned to the meeting-house and reported that Hutchinson still would not let the ship sail. Organizer Samuel Adams announced, "This meeting can do nothing more to save the country." Nonetheless, he and other prominent politicians remained at Old South, in view of the crowd.

Outside, in response to Adams's words, two or three dozen Sons of Liberty, mostly mechanics used to physical labor, moved swiftly toward Griffin's Wharf. They wore blankets and face paint to hide their identities, as New England rioters often did. Others spontaneously joined these "Mohawks," blacking their faces with soot. The group split into three squads and boarded the ships.

The Sons of Liberty were determined to harm only East India Company tea. There were customs employees on the ships, including one man a mob had tarred and feathered in 1770, but this night the crowd merely ordered them below deck. Searchers broke the padlock on one captain's trunk, but it was anonymously replaced the next day.

Working quickly, the "Mohawks" winched 342 tea chests from the holds, chopped them open, sliced through their canvas liners, and dumped the tea overboard. In an unusually low tide, leaves began to heap up beside the ships. A few apprentices were set to raking the tea into the salt water so nothing could be salvaged. By nine o'clock the men finished and marched away.

The result was no ordinary property damage. The tea had been worth £9,659, or over six times the governor's salary. Furthermore, the event was clearly an organized defiance of the law. Royal ministers sought individuals to prosecute, but could not link town leaders to the destruction. Hundreds of people had watched, yet no eyewitnesses appeared. On March 7 Bostonians destroyed tea on a fourth ship. The ministers decided to punish the town as a whole.

Parliament closed Boston harbor to transatlantic trade until locals repaid the East India Company, sending army regiments to enforce that closure. Parliament also overhauled the Massachusetts government to reduce the power of voters at every level, from town meetings to the governor's council. With the American populace already aroused, these laws produced a backlash that led to the Continental Congresses, and eventually to America's War for Independence.

Opposition to taxes mobilized ordinary people, believing they were exercising their rights as British citizens, to protest British authority. The Boston Tea Party of 1773 was among the most forceful and tightly organized of these protests. Colonists hoped that their action would force Parliament to repeal its tax on tea—not foreseeing that it would lead to revolution.

BIBLIOGRAPHY

Drake, Francis S. *Tea Leaves*. Boston: A. O. Crane, 1884.

Hoerder, Dirk. *Crowd Action in Revolutionary Massachusetts, 1765–1780*. New York: Academic Press, 1977.

Labaree, Benjamin Woods. *The Boston Tea Party*. New York: Oxford University Press, 1964.

Young, Alfred F. *The Shoemaker and the Tea Party: Memory and the American Revolution*. Boston: Beacon Press, 1999.

J. L. Bell

See also: **Boston Massacre: Pamphlets and Propaganda; Continental Congresses; Hewes, George Robert Twelves; Sons of Liberty; Stamp Act Congress.**

BROWN, CHARLOTTE: DIARY OF A NURSE

Charlotte Bristowe Brown's diary provides a rare firsthand perspective on the challenges facing women who traveled with the British forces, providing medical services to the military, in the Great War for Empire (1754–1763).

When the widowed Charlotte Brown was appointed Matron of the General Hospital for the Braddock expedition to America in 1754, she was already an experienced campaigner. Leaving her children in England in November, Brown and her brother, who was an apothecary with the expedition, sailed with other hospital staff and officers on the *London*, part of the fleet bringing the

EXCERPT FROM CHARLOTTE BROWN'S DIARY, 1756

April the 12. At 3 in the Afternoon we cast Anchor at Albany all the Gentlemen went on Shore but could get no Lodging the Town being full of Officers so returned at Night.

April the 13. Went on Shore with Mr. Cherr'n [Cherrington] who was so kind as to take me a Rome Went out to see the Town which is inhabited by the Dutch saw several Indians who were adorned with Beads in their Noses and Ears and black Blankets being in mourning for their Friend who were kill'd in the last Campaign.

April the 16. Went to the Fort to deliver a Letter from Dr. Bard at New York to Col'n Marshall [Col. Hubert Marshall, commander at the fort at Albany] and was receiv'd with great politeness but the Dutch had a very bad Opinion of me saying I could not be good to come so far without a Husband.

April the 26. Receiv'd an Invitation to dine at Col'n Marshalls Miss Miller an old Acquaintance of mine at Louisburg [on Cape Breton Island] came to see me she told me that the Dutch said I was Gen'l Braddocks Miss[tress] but she had convinced them that I was not for that her Father had known me Maid, Wife and Widow and that nobody could say any thing bad of me . . . .

May the 25. News came from Oswaga [Oswego, New York] that L't Blare and 40 Men were killed by the Indians.

May the 28. 6 Men were Hanged for Desertion.

June the 1. Captain Rogers came from Lake George with a french Prisoner and 1 Scalp.

June the 11. All the Town alarmed 2 Men taken by the Indians not half a Mile of.

June the 12. A Girl taken by the Indians just out of Town All the Fort Ladies came to see me . . . .

July 26. This Day War was proclaimed in America [The king's proclamation of war against France was read in Albany, July 28, 1756].

July 28. My Lord Louden [John Campbell, fourth Earl of Louden] arrived at Albany from Hallifax with his Troops.

August 10. This unhappy Day I recēd an Account of the Death of my dear Child Charlott in whom my Soul was center'd. God only knows what I suffer. when shall I die and be at rest! . . .

Oct'r 4. My Lord Louden march'd with all the Troops to Fort Henry [Fort William Henry, at the southern end of Lake George] and Fort Edward [on east side of the Hudson River, fifty miles north of Albany] to take a View of the Country.

Oct'r 23. Several People died of the small Pox All the New England men left Albany thro' fear.

Nov'r 20. My Lord Louden return'd from the Forts nothing to be done this Year.

Dec'r 1. Mr. Cherrington left Albany for England in whom I have lost all my Friends in one.

Dec'r 6. Extream cold, and I am reduced to my last Stick of Wood there being none to be bought for Mony . . . .

Jan'y 18, 1757. This is the coldest Day I think that I ever knew.

Jan'y 19. Recēd Orders to remove to the Hospital which was no better than a Shed and it was so excessive cold that my Face and Neck were frost bitten in moving.

SOURCE: *Colonial Captivities, Marches and Journeys,* edited by Isabel M. Calder, Port Washington, NY: Kennikat Press, 1967.

44th and 48th regiments to Virginia as part of General Braddock's command. The four-month voyage taxed the tempers of all on board.

The group disembarked in Bellhaven (Alexandria), Virginia, in late March 1755. Braddock and the main force left Bellhaven on April 22 in order to dislodge the French at Fort Duquesne. On June 1, Brown, her brother, her servant (the wife of an enlisted man), two nurses, two cooks, and about fifty sick soldiers in wagons left for Fort

Campbell under escort of one officer and forty men. On the second day, Brown's driver insisted on moving from the rear of the column to the front because of the dust. Rising by 4:00 A.M. each day, the column marched between fourteen and seventeen miles with a break for a midday meal, making camp after twelve difficult hours of travel. Brown was nearly "disjointed" from the wagon jolting over crude roads. Every fifth day the column stopped to rest the animals and let the nurses bake bread.

On June 12, 1755, Brown reached Fort Cumberland, "the most desolate Place I ever saw." The fort had no internal water supply and was crowded with both the wives and children of enlisted men and local families who had sought protection from Indian raids. Brown arrived ill; fever (probably malaria or dysentery) moved through the camp, striking both Brown's brother and maid in early July. Although not fully recovered, Brown nursed both of them while supervising the care of others. On July 11, 1755, the camp got first word of the Braddock defeat. Wounded began arriving on July 15, and two days later Brown's brother died. Brown herself suffered a relapse on July 20 and a month later was barely able to stand when she followed a group of troops evacuating to Frederick's Town, Maryland.

Riding on horseback, with a nurse walking beside her as companion, the still ailing Brown traveled 150 miles in ten days, sleeping on the ground all but the final night. In mid-September she made preparations to receive the sick who were being sent from Fort Cumberland on their way to Philadelphia. Choosing to travel with Mr. Cherrington, an officer she had met on shipboard, rather than with the troops, Brown's trip to Philadelphia in October 1755 was hazardous. Cherrington and she quarreled; he overturned the chaise in which they were both riding, and she was thrown from her horse. In Philadelphia she reported to the hospital, was assigned quarters, and began buying fresh provisions each day for the hospital. The hospital moved to New York City in February 1756. Taking first a ship, then a stage, and then another ship, Brown arrived in New York on February 18. After a month and a half, they moved again to Albany.

In each locale, Brown had to find quarters and scrounge for basic furnishings. As matron, she had the social status of a senior officer's wife, and she exchanged social visits with officers' wives and the elite women of the area. Deborah Franklin, for example, entertained her several times in Philadelphia. As an unattached woman traveling alone after her brother died, Brown faced questions about her reputation. In Albany, for example, some women assumed she was the mistress of Braddock or some other officer until the daughter of an officer who had known Brown in the mid-1740s vouched for her. She was then accepted into local society. Brown received another personal blow on August 10, 1756, when she received word from England of the death of her daughter and namesake.

The British king officially declared war with France on July 26, 1756, and New York saw action immediately. As sick and wounded taxed the capabilities of the hospital staff in Albany, and French and Indian attacks came uncomfortably close, Charlotte Brown found little time to write in her journal. She ended it August 4, 1757, too overwhelmed with work to write any further. What happened to Brown is unknown, but her diary has survived to provide glimpses of the life of a woman traveling with an eighteenth-century army in America.

BIBLIOGRAPHY

Deakin, Carol C. "Support Personnel: Women with General Braddock's Forces." In *Proceedings of Northern Virginia Studies Conference 1983*. Alexandria: Northern Virginia Community College, 1984.

Calder, Isabel M. *Colonial Captivities, Marches, and Journeys*. New York: Macmillan, 1935; Port Washington, NY: Kennikat Press, 1967.

Joan R. Gundersen

See also: **Camp Followers: War and Women; Families at War; Galloway, Grace: Diary of a Loyalist;**.

BUNKER HILL MONUMENT

The Bunker Hill Monument in Charlestown, Massachusetts, stands as one of the best examples of a Revolutionary War monument, preserving the memory of that war over centuries and contributing to American patriotism and identity. The monument, a 221-foot-high obelisk, was intended to stand as an eternal marker of American bravery at the Battle of Bunker Hill, and although it has largely served that purpose its meaning has also changed subtly over the years, reflecting the changing nature of the public memory of the Revolutionary War.

The Battle of Bunker Hill was the first full-scale military engagement of the Revolutionary War, and although the British won the battle the Americans proved that they were capable of fighting head-on against better trained and prepared professional soldiers who were among the most impressive military forces of that time. The battle took place on June 17, 1775, on Breed's Hill (often confused with the nearby Bunker Hill, from which the battle took its name).

The first monument erected on Bunker Hill (as Breed's Hill is popularly known) was a wooden pillar dedicated in 1794 to the memory of the most famous hero of the battle, Joseph Warren, by the King Solomon's Lodge of Freemasons. Although the wooden monument did arouse some interest as a tourist site, the larger battlefield was left largely undeveloped and unmarked until 1823, when a new generation of elite New Englanders, including Daniel Webster and Edward Everett, incorporated themselves as the Bunker Hill Monument Associ-

The Bunker Hill Monument in Charlestown, Massachusetts. © ROYALTY-FREE/CORBIS

ation. They purchased portions of the battlefield, raised money, and set about planning a large memorial.

Although they fell short of their $75,000 goal, the association raised enough money to lay the cornerstone of their monument and go ahead with a massive ceremony that coincided with the visit of the Revolutionary War hero Marquis de Lafayette in June 1825. The celebration took place on the fiftieth anniversary of the battle itself and was one of the largest American patriotic civic occasions up to that time. Participants estimated that 100,000 people turned out to witness the mile-long procession from Boston to Charlestown, which included government dignitaries, Lafayette, and veterans of the battle. Thousands gathered on Bunker Hill to watch Lafayette lay the cornerstone, to partake of refreshments, and to listen to a speech by Daniel Webster.

The plans for the monument were ambitious by the standards of the day. Horatio Greenough, then a student at Harvard College, had been awarded first prize in a de-

sign competition for the monument, although Robert Mills, later the architect of the Washington Monument in Washington, D.C., maintained that the ideas he submitted for Bunker Hill had actually been used in its construction. Boston engineer Laommi Baldwin also worked on the design, and construction plans were prepared by architect Solomon Willard. The Monument Association bought its own granite quarry in Quincy, Massachusetts, in 1825, and from 1827 to 1828 the granite was transported to Charlestown using the country's first railway system.

The Bunker Hill Monument was conceived as a way to express the gratitude of the American people for the sacrifices of the American soldiers who fought at the battle, but fund-raising went slowly, and construction lagged. By 1828, most of the granite had been quarried but funds to continue raising the monument were lacking. In 1830, believing that the lack of attention to the monument indicated a weakening of American patriotism, Sarah Josepha Hale began a campaign in her *Ladies Magazine* to raise funds from American women to complete the monument. The Massachusetts Charitable Mechanics Association, Amos Lawrence, and merchant Judah Touro, pledged significant funds. In 1840, Sarah Hale organized a Ladies' Fair in Boston, where a number of women's organizations raised the final $30,000 to complete the work. The monument was dedicated on June 17, 1843.

Visible for miles around, the Bunker Hill Monument served as a symbol of patriotism and New England pride throughout the remainder of the nineteenth century and into the following centuries. During the Civil War, a large American flag flew from the monument's top. By the time of the Bunker Hill centennial in 1875, the monument had also become a symbol of local pride in Charlestown, which was increasingly populated by Irish immigrants. The monument was deeded to the state of Massachusetts in 1919 and later became part of the Boston National Historic Park. It now occupies a place on Boston's historic Freedom Trail. The Bunker Hill Monument Association conducts annual commemorative exercises at the monument, which is one of the most popular Revolutionary War markers in the United States, symbolic of both American nationalism and local pride.

BIBLIOGRAPHY

Musuraca, Michael. "The 'Celebration Begins at Midnight': Irish Immigrants and the Celebration of Bunker Hill Day," *Labor's Heritage* 2 (1990): 54–57.

Purcell, Sarah J. *Sealed with Blood: War, Sacrifice, and Memory in Revolutionary America.* Philadelphia: University of Pennsylvania Press, 2002.

Warren, George Washington. *The History of the Bunker Hill Monument Association during the First Century of the United States of America.* Boston: J.R. Osgood, 1877.

Sarah J. Purcell

See also: **Flags; Jackson, Andrew; Lafayette's Tour; Monroe's Tour of New England; Valley Forge.**

CAMP FOLLOWERS: WAR AND WOMEN

In the eighteenth century civilians, both men and women, who traveled with the military were called camp followers. Camp followers included civilians in official, paid support roles for the military, soldiers' families, and civilians who independently sold goods and services to individual soldiers. There are no statistics on camp followers for the colonial wars, but about 20,000 women had paid positions with the American troops at some point during the American Revolution. British, Hessian, and Loyalist troops add from 3,000 to 5,000 more women to the total. Around 2,000 women traveled with Burgoyne's 7,200 troops on the 1777 invasion of New York. Two years later, 1,200 civilians, mostly wives and children, marched with John Sullivan's army from Pennsylvania into New York. In addition, an undetermined number of Indian women traveled with Indian allies to the American and British armies.

WOMEN AT WAR

During the course of a war, women slipped in and out of the different forms of camp following. A wife might take a paid position and then, if she was widowed, stay with the army. The army subjected all who traveled with them to special regulations, military discipline, and military courts. At times the army subjected women to embarrassing medical examinations for venereal disease.

Whereas the British simply accepted that an army would have camp followers and regulated the numbers who accompanied troops to America, American leaders were ambivalent about women camp followers. Washington thought they made the army look disorderly on march and slowed marches, but he also knew their presence kept men from deserting. As the war progressed, American commanders began enrolling women and children and issuing them partial rations. Officials who were struggling to keep troops from going hungry resented the extra mouths they now had to feed.

"Women of the regiment" were paid for work now done by troops with rank (engineers, cooks, supply, commissaries, laundry workers, nurses). They marched with the army on campaigns when other camp followers were ordered to stay at the base camps. The British army used a ratio of one paid woman's position for every ten enlisted men. Americans had about one woman for every fifteen men. Women cooked, did laundry, and hauled water to cool artillery.

Women of the regiment could find themselves under fire in battle. In one case, Loyalist John Simcoe scattered

MOLLY PITCHER

Historians do not agree on the true identity of Molly Pitcher, or even if she was an individual or a name given generally to women camp followers. One true-life Molly is legendary for her participation in the Battle of Monmouth during the American Revolutionary War. Although many people long believed her to be Mary Ludwig, born in Trenton, New Jersey, her true identity seems to be that of another Mary whose maiden name remains unknown. The latter Mary wed William Hays, who was a barber in Valley Forge, Pennsylvania. In 1777 he joined the Continental Army, and his Mary Hays, nicknamed Molly, came with him to the winter encampment, like other wives who prepared meals, washed clothes, and tended the ill.

Yet when spring came and other wives left, Molly marched with the Continental Army toward the colony of New Jersey. There, on a hot and humid June 28, 1778 the army engaged British forces at the Battle of Monmouth, in the town of Freehold, Monmouth County. Although the American soldiers shed unneeded clothing to cool themselves, they suffered greatly from the heat. Molly, who carried a pitcher among her supplies, realized that she could help by bringing water from a nearby spring. During this decisive battle, Molly, dodging bullets, brought pitcher after pitcher of water to the men who had collapsed from the heat. Over the noise of battle rang cries of "Molly—Pitcher!"

William Hays was firing a canon when Molly saw him collapse. After quickly determining that William's wound was not fatal, she took over loading the canon, ramming the metal balls into the barrel with a ramrod. Molly was in the thick of battle when General George Washington spied her, with her skirt and petticoat ripped by a musket ball. That evening after the battle was over, General Washington asked to speak with Molly. He granted her a field commission as a sergeant in the Continental Army.

By war's end William and Mary Hays had returned to Carlisle and Mary had resumed her former life as a servant. After William Hays died, Mary later remarried, becoming Mary Hays McCauly, and it is known from state records that in 1822 the Pennsylvania Legislature granted her a pension for her military activities. Mary Hays McCauly was buried in Carlisle in 1832, where her grave is noted by a monument on which the following poem by Sarah Woods Parkinson was engraved:

> O'er Monmouth's field of carnage drear,
> With cooling drink and words of cheer
> A woman passed who knew no fear,
> The wife of Hays, the gunner.
> With ramrod from her husband's hand,
> Beside his gun she took her stand
> And helped to wrest our well-loved land,
> From England's tyrant King.
> From the ranks this woman came,
> By the cannon won her fame
> 'Tis true she could not write her name,
> But freedom's hand hath carved it.
> Shall we then criticize her ways,
> Nay, rather give her well earned praise
> Then doff our caps and voices raise,
> In cheers for Molly Pitcher.

Whether an individual or a collective persona, Molly Pitcher's courage is commemorated today by the U.S. Field Artillery Association at Fort Sill, Oklahoma, which awards the medal Artillery Order of Molly Pitcher to a field artillery commander who has "voluntarily contributed in a significant way to the improvement of the field artillery community."

women and baggage among his encamped troops so Virginians would overestimate the size of his forces. Women bringing water sometimes were pressed into service on the guns, as happened to Mary Hays (the probable model for the Molly Pitcher story). It was reported that only four of the fifty-four women who were marching with General Braddock in 1755 survived the surprise attack by French and Indians.

The Americans had trouble recruiting the required one matron and ten nurses for every hundred wounded Revolutionary soldiers, despite offering higher pay than for other jobs because disease killed many nurses. Americans sometimes forced women to serve as nurses by threatening to cut off their rations as wives. The best account we have of the trials of an eighteenth-century army nurse is a journal kept by Charlotte Brown from 1754–1757 while serving as matron of the British hospitals during the French and Indian War.

Although women of all social classes might travel with the military, elite women lived in relative comfort. Baroness Fredericka von Riedesel and her daughters rode in a coach while following her husband, the top Hessian

Molly Pitcher at the Battle of Monmouth. Molly Pitcher is believed to have actually been Mary "Molly" Hays. During the Revolutionary War, she gained her nickname by supplying the men on the battleground with water. The cry "Molly–Pitcher!" could be heard over the noise of the battle. LANDOV

officer with General Burgoyne in 1777. As prisoners of war, the Riedesels rented a comfortable Virginia plantation. Martha and George Washington spent the winter at Valley Forge in a comfortable farmhouse entertaining staff officers generously. The 400 women on the ration rolls at Valley Forge in December 1777 drew from the same meager supplies as the ordinary soldiers and struggled to find shelter. These women were expected to walk when the army moved, although many rode on supply wagons, contrary to orders.

Many women were among the multiracial swarm of peddlers, refugees, settlers, and laborers who followed an army. The civilian camp followers provided goods and services that the army was unable to supply. Contrary to the popular image, few were prostitutes, but some were in unrecognized marriages. The British army required soldiers to get permission to marry and limited the number of married men in each regiment. Slaves seeking freedom escaped to British lines, and refugees sought protection with the armies of both sides.

The constant comings and goings of camp followers disrupted military order and provided cover to enterprising spies. One woman set up her shop in front of Washington's headquarters tent in August and September 1778 and then reported the command conversations to the British.

AFTER THE REVOLUTION

After the war, impoverished veterans and their wives petitioned for pensions. Sarah Osborne documented her camp following experience while trying to prove her husband's service. Several wives applied for pensions in their own right, including Anna Maria Lane and Margaret Corbin, both wounded in battle. As Americans embraced the idea that women's true nature was domestic, however, they forgot women's active roles in war.

The army eliminated most paid positions for women after 1804. Increasingly the army used enlisted men and officers to staff support units. In the Civil War women had to create voluntary organization such as the Sanitary Commission to offer nursing services. By World War I women could enlist as nurses and worked in support roles through organizations such as the Red Cross.

Because the army had incorporated support roles into the ranks, in World War II each branch of the service created women's auxiliaries to free men for battle. These became women's service branches after the war, then eventually integrated women into all service branches. Only reluctantly have any combat positions been opened to women. Families continue to follow soldiers, living on or near all major military bases, but unlike eighteenth-century camp followers, they do not go on active maneuvers. Throughout the centuries wars have brought new and expanded roles for women, in the process transforming American society and culture.

BIBLIOGRAPHY

Anderson, Fred. *The Crucible of War: The Seven Years' War and the Fate of Empire in British North America, 1754–1766.* New York: Knopf, 2000.

Dann, John C. *The Revolution Remembered: Eyewitness Accounts of the War for Independence.* Chicago: University of Chicago Press, 1980.

Deakin, Carol. "Support Personnel: Women with General Braddock's Forces." *Proceedings of Northern Virginia Studies Conference* (1984): 85–94.

DePauw, Linda Grant. "Women in Combat: The Revolutionary War Experience." *Armed Forces and Society* 7 (1981): 209–226.

Kerber, Linda Grant. " 'History Can Do It No Justice': Women and the Reinterpretation of the American Revolution." In *Women in the Age of the American Revolution*, edited by Ronald Hoffman and Peter J. Albert. Charlottesville: University of Virginia Press, 1989.

Gundersen, Joan R. *"To Be Useful to the World": Women in Revolutionary America, 1740–1790.* New York: Twayne Publishers, 1996.

Mayer, Holly A. *Belonging to the Army: Camp Followers and Community during the American Revolution.* Columbia: University of South Carolina Press, 1996.

Norton, Mary Beth. "Eighteenth-Century American Women in Peace and War: The Case of the Loyalists." *William and Mary Quarterly* 3d series, 33 (1976): 386–409.

Tharp, Louise Hall. *The Baroness and the General.* Boston: Little, Brown, 1962.

Joan R. Gundersen

See also: **Brown, Charlotte: Diary of a Nurse; Families at War; Sampson, Deborah.**

CIVIL LIBERTIES: KENTUCKY AND VIRGINIA RESOLUTIONS

When Americans have gone to war, measures to protect national security have often conflicted with civil liberties guaranteed in the Constitution. This conflict, inherent in American political culture, first appeared in 1798 during America's quasi-war with France. The Kentucky and Virginia Resolutions were part of the Democratic Republican response to the Adams administration's attempts to curb civil liberties during that war. Drafted secretly by Thomas Jefferson (the Kentucky Resolutions of 1798 and 1799) and James Madison (the Virginia Resolutions of 1798), the Resolutions were a formal protest by the legislatures of Kentucky and Virginia against the Alien and Sedition Acts that the Federalist-dominated Congress had passed in 1798 in the name of protecting national security.

Among other things, the Alien and Sedition Acts created a registration and surveillance system for aliens residing in the United States, provided the executive branch with the authority to deport aliens seen as a threat, and potentially made any criticism of government a crime. These acts deeply divided the nation between those who saw them as a reasonable response to a crisis situation and those who viewed the restrictions as dangerous, politically motivated, and unconstitutional. The Kentucky and Virginia Resolutions held that the Alien and Sedition Acts should be null and void because they violated numerous provisions of the Federal Constitution.

The resolutions reflected the fears of many Democratic Republicans that these acts' suppression of civil rights represented the final stages of an effort by Federalists to, as Madison put it in the Virginia Resolutions, transform the "republican system of the United States into an absolute, or at best a mixed monarchy." Those fears were built on eight years of Federalist rule that included the passage of Alexander Hamilton's financial program, the Jay Treaty with Britain, and an expansion of the federal judiciary. The crisis with France added a military buildup that triggered deep-seated worries among many Democratic Republicans that the Federalists might use the standing army to maintain power by force. Democratic Republicans viewed the Alien and Sedition Acts not as national security measures, but instead as bald attempts to silence political opposition and maintain Federalist rule.

The Kentucky and Virginia Resolutions held that the Alien and Sedition Acts were unconstitutional on a variety of grounds. Madison and Jefferson asserted that the Sedition Acts violated First Amendment protections of free speech and freedom of the press. Both resolutions claimed that the Alien and Sedition Acts breached the separation of powers laid out in the Constitution by giving the executive branch both legislative and judicial authority. In the Kentucky Resolutions, Jefferson argued that the Alien Acts also abridged the due process and jury trial provisions of the Fifth Amendment (rights he said extended to friendly aliens living on American soil).

Jefferson even argued that the provision in the Constitution preventing Congress from banning the slave trade until 1808 prevented Congress from enacting legislation limiting the migration of aliens as well. Nowhere in the resolutions did Jefferson or Madison address the question of civil rights during wartime. Indeed, the resolutions did not mention the crisis with France at all and framed constitutional rights in absolute terms.

The heart of the unconstitutionality argument in the Kentucky and Virginia Resolutions rested on a strict states' rights interpretation of the Constitution. The resolutions held that the Alien and Sedition Acts violated the Tenth Amendment which reserved to the states any powers not specifically delegated to Congress by the Constitution. Both sets of resolutions asserted that the Constitution was a compact among the states and that when Congress assumed rights not directly specified in the Constitution it violated this compact. Jefferson made the argument most forcefully in the more detailed Kentucky Resolutions: the Constitution did not give Congress either the right to punish the array of crimes laid out in the Sedition Acts or the right to limit the free speech provisions of the states. Furthermore, Jefferson argued that the Constitution did not give Congress power over aliens friendly to the United States and that foreigners therefore retained the protection of the states in which they resided.

The Kentucky and Virginia Resolutions also called on other states to take action. In the Virginia Resolutions, Madison implored other states to "interpose" to protect their Tenth Amendment rights. In the original version of the Kentucky Resolutions, Jefferson urged other states to nullify unconstitutional laws. John Breckenridge, who sponsored the resolutions on behalf of Jefferson, removed references to nullification and replaced them with a request that other states push Congress to repeal the Alien and Sedition Acts. Jefferson's nullification argument, however, was included in a separate resolution that the Kentucky legislature passed in 1799. Some historians have argued that Virginia's call to action included plans for military preparation in the event of further Federalist provocations.

Other states responded to the Kentucky and Virginia Resolutions with either silence or hostility. The southern states, although dominated by Democratic Republicans, made no comment. The states north of the Potomac River condemned the resolutions largely for the states' rights interpretation of the Constitution. Most northern state legislatures passed resolutions asserting that individual states did not have the right to declare federal laws unconstitutional.

In 1801, President Jefferson allowed the Alien and Sedition laws to expire without resolution of the fundamental issues they raised. Americans later faced the same dilemma of protecting national security while upholding civil liberties in other conflicts, including the war against international terrorism.

BIBLIOGRAPHY

Gutzman, K. R. Constantine. "The Virginia and Kentucky Resolutions Reconsidered: 'An Appeal to the *Real Laws* of Our Country.'" *Journal of Southern History* 66, no. 3 (2000): 473–496.

Koch, Adrienne and Ammon, Harry. "The Virginia and Kentucky Resolutions: An Episode in the Jefferson's and Madison's Defense of Civil Liberties." *William and Mary Quarterly* 5, no. 2 (1948): 145–176.

Sharp, James Roger. *American Politics in the Early Republic: The New Nation in Crisis.* New Haven: Yale University Press, 1993.

Smith, James Morton. "The Grass Roots of the Kentucky Resolutions." *William and Mary Quarterly* 27, no. 2 (1970): 221–245.

Terry Bouton

See also: **Alien and Sedition Acts; Quasi-War and the Rise of Political Parties.**

COMMON SENSE

More than any other speech, pamphlet or newspaper article, Thomas Paine's *Common Sense* transformed pre-Revolutionary opinion among the bickering thirteen colonies from confusion and complacency to a near-universal acceptance of full political and economic independence from England. Written in January, 1776 when America appeared to be on the verge of losing its war against Britain, *Common Sense* was both a plea to persevere and an appeal to fight for new ideals that would later be expressed in the Declaration of Independence and the Constitution. Winning the War for Independence made possible the creation of new republic that adopted those guiding principles.

Prior to the publication of *Common Sense,* citizens and leaders of the colonies were deeply divided as to the action to take as they struggled with issues such as taxation without representation. And while there was no doubt about the anger felt by most regarding the repressive policies of the British government, few were willing in 1775 to even toy with the idea of full independence. Even the more radical colonial leaders, such as John Adams and Thomas Jefferson, still believed that the crisis with England could be resolved through the political system—that the British Parliament and powerful colonial ministers could be persuaded to give New World colonists the full rights accorded British citizens in the

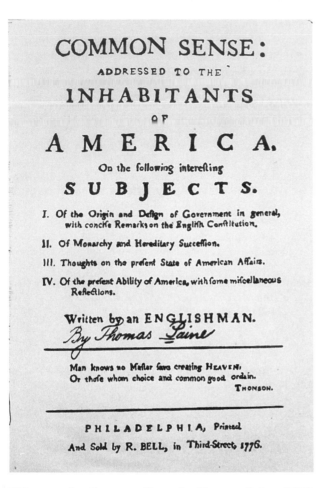

COMMON SENSE:
ADDRESSED TO THE
INHABITANTS
OF
A M E R I C A.
On the following interesting
S U B J E C T S.

I. Of the Origin and Design of Government in general,
with concise Remarks on the English Constitution.

II. Of Monarchy and Hereditary Succession.

III. Thoughts on the present State of American Affairs.

IV. Of the present Ability of America, with some miscellaneous
Reflections.

Written by an ENGLISHMAN.
By Thomas Paine

Man knows no Master save creating HEAVEN,
Or those whom choice and common good ordain.
THOMSON.

PHILADELPHIA, Printed
And Sold by R. BELL, in Third-Street, 1776.

Title page for *Common Sense* by Thomas Paine, 1776.
© BETTMANN/CORBIS

homeland. Even after violence broke out at Lexington and Concord in April, 1775, Continental Commander in Chief George Washington offered a toast to King George III at dinner while fighting the Crown's troops during the day.

A CALL TO ARMS

Ironically, the author whose document literally changed the political landscape was himself an Englishman. Born in 1737 of tradesman stock, Thomas Paine had held a variety of jobs but never quite found his niche. As an excise officer he had begun to show his skill as an author, writing a petition to the government in London to raise the salaries of his fellow tax collectors. And whereas Paine's petition fell on deaf ears, his time in London resulted in a meeting with Benjamin Franklin, who was working on behalf of the Pennsylvania colony. Self-educated and with an interest in science, Paine was able to secure from Franklin letters of recommendation; and in 1774 he decided to immigrate to the New World with the hope of changing his fortunes.

He settled in Philadelphia, at the time the largest city in the colonies, behind only London in the whole of the British Empire. In short order Paine became a successful writer and co-founder of the new *Pennsylvania Magazine.* Emboldened by the success of his articles and encouraged by Franklin, Paine decided to put pen to paper for a larger cause.

ENLIGHTENMENT UNDERPINNINGS

Given their immersion in French intellectual society, both Thomas Jefferson and Franklin were schooled in the principles of the Enlightenment movement—belief in human reason and individual liberty, skepticism of the divine right of kings. But it was Paine, fully aware of British Enlightenment theorist John Locke, who most dramatically spread the ideas of liberty, equality and individual self-governance in the practical context of the struggle with England. He declared, ". . . [T]here is something very absurd, in supposing a continent to be perpetually governed by an island."

Published on January 10, 1776, *Common Sense* put democratic theory in simple language that drew upon analogies that common citizens could understand. It went first to the crux of the issue, that people were given by God the fundamental right to form a government based on reason. Paine began with an argument that fundamentally changed the political discourse of the colonies. He protested that the monarchy claimed to be a "race of men [who] came into the world . . . exalted above the rest, and distinguished like some new species" before going on to chastise the "crowned ruffian" George III as the root of the current crisis. An example of Paine's biting analysis of monarchy: "One of the strongest *natural* proofs of the folly of hereditary right in kings, is, that nature disapproves it, otherwise, she would not so frequently turn it into ridicule by giving mankind *an ass for a lion.*"

After he hacked away at the root, Paine went on bring the entire tree down, laying out the current situation and arguing that independence was virtually the only means of improving it: "I have hear it asserted by some, that as America hath flourished under her former connexion with Great Britain, that the same connexion is necessary towards her future happiness, and will always have the same effect. Nothing can be more fallacious than this kind of argument. We may well assert, that because a child has thrived upon milk, that it is never to have meat; or that the first twenty years of our lives is to become a precedent for the next twenty."

To say that *Common Sense* spread like wildfire would be an understatement. In an era when news traveled at a snail's pace and pamphlets rarely spread beyond a local audience, the arguments in Paine's changed the entire

EXCERPT FROM *COMMON SENSE* BY THOMAS PAINE

A government of our own is our natural right: And when a man seriously reflects on the precariousness of human affairs, he will become convinced, that it is infinitely wiser and safer, to form a constitution of our own in a cool deliberate manner, while we have it in our power, than to trust such an interesting event to time and chance. If we omit it now, some, Massenello may hereafter arise, who laying hold of popular disquietudes, may collect together the desperate and the discontented, and by assuming to themselves the powers of government, may sweep away the liberties of the continent like a deluge. Should the government of America return again into the hands of Britain, the tottering situation of things, will be a temptation for some desperate adventurer to try his fortune; and in such a case, what relief can Britain give? Ere she could hear the news the fatal business might be done, and ourselves suffering like the wretched Britons under the oppression of the Conqueror. . . .

Ye that tell us of harmony and reconciliation, can ye restore to us the time that is past? Can ye give to prostitution its former innocence? Neither can ye reconcile Britain and America. The last cord now is broken, the people of England are presenting addresses against us. There are injuries which nature cannot forgive; she would cease to be nature if she did. As well can the lover forgive the ravisher of his mistress, as the continent forgive the murders of Britain. The Almighty hath implanted in us these inextinguishable feelings for good and wise purposes. They are the guardians of his image in our hearts. They distinguish us from the herd of common animals. The social compact would dissolve, and justice be extirpated the earth, of have only a casual existence were we callous to the touches of affection. The robber and the murderer, would often escape unpunished, did not the injuries which our tempers sustain, provoke us into justice. O ye that love mankind! Ye that dare oppose, not only the tyranny, but the tyrant, stand forth! Every spot of the old world is overrun with oppression. Freedom hath been hunted round the globe. Asia, and Africa, have long expelled her. Europe regards her like a stranger, and England hath given her warning to depart. O! receive the fugitive, and prepare in time an asylum for mind.

I have never met with a man, either in England or America, who hath not confessed his opinion, that a separation between the countries, would take place one time or other. And there is no instance in which we have shown less judgment, than in endeavoring to describe, what we call, the ripeness or fitness of the Continent for independence.

political debate throughout the colonies with near-miraculous speed. So popular was the pamphlet that within a year at least 500,000 copies were in circulation, roughly one copy per colonial household. As John Adams (who had written his share of pamphlets) wrote to his wife Abigail, Paine had "a better hand at pulling down the building."

And as it spread, not only did the argument of peace with England wither but George III went from a benevolent father-figure to the personification of a tyrannical oppressor. Those few who favored some new form of American monarchy virtually disappeared from public discourse as the cause of a republic became the clarion call. General Washington went from toasting the King to using *Common Sense* to inspire his beleaguered troops in the field. Soon, leaders such as Adams, Franklin and Jefferson spoke freely of total separation from England.

Paine himself joined the revolutionary army, later traveled to France in support of its own 1791 revolution, and wrote many other influential pamphlets such as *The Rights of Man*. But in a strange twist of fate Paine died in the new America in 1809, not as a founding father, but as an almost forgotten figure. Most people failed to value his contribution. Others knew better. As John Adams said at the time: "I know not whether any man in the world has had more influence on its inhabitants or affairs for the last thirty years than Thomas Paine."

In addition to his direct influence on his contemporaries, Paine captured the idea that America had a larger role to play in history. "The cause of America is in a great measure the cause of all mankind. Many circumstances have, and will arise, which are not local, but universal, and through which the principles of all Lovers of Mankind are affected. . ." This sense of a mission to be a beacon of freedom and spread democracy has been deeply imprinted upon American society, culture, and identity.

BIBLIOGRAPHY

Isaacson, Walter. *Benjamin Franklin: An American Life.* New York: Simon & Schuster, 2003.

Liell, Scott. *46 Pages: Thomas Paine, Common Sense, and the Turning Point to Independence.* Philadelphia, PA: Running Press, 2003.

Mccullough, David. *John Adams.* New York: Simon & Schuster, 2001.

Internet Resources

Brians, Paul. "The Enlightenment." Washington State University, 1993. Available from <http://www.wsu.edu/~brians/hum_303/enlightenment.html>.

Michael Davis

See also: **Boston Massacre: Pamphlets and Propaganda; Paine, Thomas; Sons of Liberty.**

COMMONWEALTH MEN

"Commonwealth Men" were those who held a well-defined set of political beliefs about the importance of liberty and the need for people to defend their rights against excessive government power. Their ideas, which had taken shape in England, became dominant in the colonies by the mid-eighteenth century, and inspired Americans to resist the Stamp Act and other forms of British taxation. The beliefs of the Commonwealth Men eventually led the colonists into revolution; they also influenced the framers of the Constitution and the political culture of the new nation. Commonwealth Men were often referred to as "Real Whigs," and their political ideas came to be known as "republicanism."

ORIGINS AND PRINCIPLES OF COMMONWEALTH THOUGHT

Commonwealth political ideas originated in England. Twice in the seventeenth century the English had deposed kings who were threatening to take absolute power at the expense of the people's rights. During these times of turmoil, political philosophers such as James Harrington and John Locke asserted that the proper role of government was to protect the liberty and property of its subjects. This idea lay at the heart of Commonwealth thought.

Calm returned to Great Britain in the eighteenth century, and Britons took pride in being the freest, best-governed nation on earth. They attributed this achievement to their constitution. In most countries, the monarch was absolutely supreme, but the British constitution had created a "mixed" government in which the king or queen, the aristocracy (through the House of Lords), and the people (through the House of Commons) all had clearly defined rights. In theory, if one of the branches of government became too powerful, or if two of them cooperated to try to dominate the nation, one or both of the others had the ability to check them and preserve the rights of all.

If most Britons were satisfied that the constitutional system was working well, events in the 1720s aroused the suspicions of the Commonwealth Men, who were only a small group on the fringes of British politics. The administration of Robert Walpole, the king's chief minister, was run by a system in which Walpole used control of parliamentary elections, the awarding of government contracts, and other means of influence to manipulate Parliament. Few Britons were worried by Walpole's practices, since the government ran smoothly. But the Commonwealth Men saw Walpole as a corrupt minister whose actions violated the constitution and endangered people's rights.

Commonwealth Men believed that liberty and power were in constant conflict, and that those holding power would always seek to expand it at the expense of liberty. Commonwealth writers outlined a series of steps that corrupt political leaders would employ to enlarge their power. These leaders, who were likely to be among the king's ministers, would first lead the nation into costly wars. The need to pay the cost of these wars would justify higher taxes, which would give the ministers more control over people's property. Through bribery and favoritism, the legislature would be neutralized or drawn into the conspirators' service. The people would be allowed to indulge in idleness and luxury, until their virtue was lost and they would either be blinded to the threat or no longer willing to defend their liberty. Then the conspirators would seize absolute power with the help of a professional army. The people would lose their political rights as well as control over their property, so that they would be no better off than the serfs and peasants in continental Europe. Commonwealth writers described this condition as a state of slavery.

According to Commonwealth principles, there were only two ways to prevent such a conspiracy from succeeding. Both depended on the people maintaining their virtue and keeping careful watch over their leaders to detect any threat to liberty. When the threat was detected, people could warn the king, who was believed to be incorruptible, so that he could remove the treacherous ministers and restore the constitutional balance. But if the king proved unwilling or unable to act, it was up to the people themselves to resist, by peaceful means if possible, but by force if necessary.

In an effort to warn the public about Walpole's dangerous practices, Commonwealth spokespeople such as John Trenchard, Thomas Gordon, and Bishop Benjamin Hoadly produced numerous books, pamphlets, and sermons in which they explained their political views. But Britons paid little attention to these writings; most of the literature produced by the Commonwealth Men was sent to America, where the colonists generally accepted and adopted their ideas.

COMMONWEALTH IDEAS AND THE AMERICAN REVOLUTION

When the British government broke with tradition and imposed direct taxation on the colonists in 1765 in the form of the Stamp Act, Americans familiar with Commonwealth ideas saw the new policy as the first step in a conspiracy to deprive them of their liberty. Believing it their duty to oppose this threat, the colonists resisted the Stamp Act, justifying their actions in pamphlets and sermons that explained both the act and their opposition to it in terms of Commonwealth thought. When repeal of the Stamp Act was followed by new taxes such as the Townshend Acts, Americans continued to justify their opposition with appeals to Commonwealth principles. By 1775 the colonists were convinced that only force could protect their liberties, and in accordance with the Commonwealth prescription, took up arms against the British government.

LEGACY

Commonwealth ideas continued to influence Americans during and after the Revolution. The Articles of Confederation, adopted as the form of government during the war, were framed according to Commonwealth principles. Power was vested in the Congress, the president had little authority, and careful watch was kept over the army. Most of the state constitutions adopted at the start of the Revolution followed a similar pattern.

The U.S. Constitution also incorporated many Commonwealth principles, though some were modified by the lessons learned during the Revolution. The framers, recalling how difficult it had been for the Confederation Congress to agree on and carry out policy, created a stronger executive. But they carefully crafted a system of checks and balances between the presidency, Congress, and the judiciary to prevent any branch of government from becoming too powerful, or falling under the control of a corrupt faction. In addition, the framers provided for a distribution of power between the federal and state governments, and placed the military under civilian control. Later, the Bill of Rights was added to guarantee specific liberties to the people. In these and other aspects, the new nation and its Constitution reflected the important influence of the Commonwealth Men.

BIBLIOGRAPHY

Bailyn, Bernard. *The Ideological Origins of the American Revolution.* Cambridge, MA: Belknap Press of Harvard University Press, 1992.

Robbins, Caroline. *The Eighteenth-Century Commonwealthman: Studies in the Transmission, Development and Circumstance of English Liberal Thought from the Restoration of Charles II until the War with the Thirteen Colonies.* Cambridge, MA: Harvard University Press, 1961.

Jim Piecuch

See also: **Constitution: Creating a Republic; Federalist Papers; Republicanism and War; Stamp Act Congress.**

CONSTITUTION: BILL OF RIGHTS

The first ten amendments to the U.S. Constitution, known at the Bill of Rights, list more than twenty-five rights. Initially significant as a symbol of the nation's aspirations than for their substance, these provisions have become increasingly important as the modern Supreme Court has applied them not only to the national government but also to the states to define the meaning of individual liberty, legal and civil rights, and the extent of government authority.

ORIGINS IN STATE CONSTITUTIONS

When the Second Continental Congress declared independence in July 1776, it encouraged states to adopt constitutions and most of them did so. Almost all incorporated declarations, or bills, of rights, like Virginia's Declaration of Rights, written by George Mason in 1776. The idea that governments should recognize such rights goes at least as far back in English history as the Magna Charta (1215), through which English noblemen had embodied written concessions from the English king at Runneymede, through the English Bill of Rights (1689), and the Act of Settlement (1701).

The first government to succeed that of Britain in the colonies was formed under the Articles of Confederation (1781–1788). It was premised on the idea of continuing individual state sovereignty and therefore invested little power in the Congress. Since few powers had been delegated to the national government, few rights needed to be reserved. On the state level, declarations of rights did not always succeed in keeping state assemblies from trampling on individual liberties in the absence of checks and balances.

THE UNITED STATES CONSTITUTION

When the delegates met in Philadelphia in the summer of 1787 to write a new Constitution, they were primarily concerned with strengthening the national government, but they were aware that with strength would come danger. Thus, although they invested such significant new powers in Congress as the power to regulate interstate and foreign commerce and the power to act directly on individual citizens, the framers of the constitution were also concerned to corral these new powers. Accordingly they divided Congress into two houses, and created an independent executive and judiciary. James Madison, a key architect of the new document, argued that the new government would be less likely to result in individual injustice than would state governments.

In a sense, the entire Constitution was intended to be a bill of rights. The founders chiefly relied on institution protections for such rights, but they also built specific limitations into the Constitution. Thus, Article I, Section 9, prohibits Congress from interfering with the states' rights to import slaves for twenty years, from laying direct taxes other than according to the census, from taxing exports, and from granting titles of nobility. This article also protects individual rights by prohibiting Congress from suspending the writ of habeas corpus (requiring the government to specify charges against individuals who were imprisoned) except in limited circumstance or from adopting bills of attainder (legislative punishments without benefit of a trial) or ex post facto (retroactive criminal) laws. Similarly, Article I, Section 10 also prohibited states from enacting bills of attainder, ex post facto laws, or impairing the obligation of contracts. In like manner, Article VI prohibited any "religious Test" as a condition for federal office.

Perhaps because they still envisioned a relatively limited government, the framers of the Constitution did not give much consideration to a bill of rights. George Mason waited until near the end of the Convention to propose the addition of a bill of rights, and the states present unanimously defeated his motion.

RATIFICATION DEBATES

The delegates bypassed the amending mechanism under the Articles of Confederation and provided that the new Constitution would go into effect when conventions in nine or more states ratified it. Although some states ratified relatively quickly, it was soon clear that ratification would not be easy. Those who supported the Constitution, the Federalists, quickly faced strong Anti-federalist opposition, especially in key states like Virginia, New York, and Massachusetts. Anti-federalists expressed a variety of fears, many centering on the unknown consequences of adopting such a radically new form of government. Charging that the new government would

become overly aristocratic, or monarchical, and that it would swallow the states, Anti-federalists raised fears that the new government would destroy the individual liberties for which the Revolutionary War had been fought. The French philosopher the Baron de Montesquieu, had argued that republican government was impossible over a large land area, and Madison's arguments that an extended republic would in fact make injustice more unlikely did not offer the same security as specifically delineated rights.

Initially, Federalists argued that a bill of rights was unnecessary and could even prove dangerous-giving the government the authority to say that any right not specifically identified could be taken away. Some Federalist friends, however, argued that a bill of rights might help and could do no harm. Thomas Jefferson was among those who wrote to James Madison arguing that rights specifically incorporated into a bill of rights might serve not only to enlighten the public as to their rights but also as a mechanism through which wise judges might strike down unconstitutional provisions.

Although they rejected the idea that states could conditionally ratify the Constitution, key Federalists expressed a willingness to consider a bill of rights once the Constitution was ratified. Fortunately, Madison served in the first House of Representatives, where he combined and condensed various rights that states had proposed when debating the Constitution with provisions in existing state declarations of rights. Two-thirds majorities of both houses of Congress eventually proposed twelve amendments, ten of which the requisite three-fourths of the states adopted in December 1791 as the bill of rights.

THE CONTENT OF THE BILL OF RIGHTS

The First Amendment prohibits Congress from making laws respecting the establishment of religion or prohibiting its free exercise and guarantees rights of freedom of speech, press, peaceable assembly, and petition. The Second Amendment allows for a right to bear arms, and the Third Amendment prohibits an abuse that the colonies observed during the Revolutionary War by prohibiting the quartering of troops in private homes without the owners' consent. The Fourth prohibited unreasonable searches and seizures (another colonial grievance that led to the Revolutionary War). The Fifth, Sixth, and Seventh Amendments primarily protect the rights of individuals accused of crimes, or on trial. The Eighth Amendment includes protection against cruel and unusual punishments, and the Ninth and Tenth Amendments recognize the existence of unnamed rights reserved to the states and to the people.

ENFORCEMENT OF THE BILL OF RIGHTS

The Bill of Rights would signal little more than national aspirations if U.S. courts did not exercise the power, known as judicial review (established by Chief Justice John Marshall in *Marbury v. Madison*, 1803), to void legislation that is unconstitutional. Even then, courts are not always sympathetic to the protection of rights. No court invalidated the notorious Sedition Act of 1798 (prohibiting criticism of the president at a time of rising tension with France) during its short existence, and courts have been better at proclaiming the existence of rights after wars were over than enforcing them while wars were being waged. It was not until *Ex Parte Milligan* (1866) that the Court invalidated military trials of civilians during the Civil War. Similarly, while sidestepping the issue of their incarceration in detention camps, in *Korematu v. United States* (1944) the Court upheld the exclusion by executive order of Japanese Americans from their homes and businesses on the West Coast.

THE EXPANDED APPLICATION OF THE BILL OF RIGHTS

The most important development in the history of the Bill of Rights has been its application to the states, rather than just to the federal government. In *Barron v. Baltimore* (1833), Chief Justice John Marshall decided that the bill of rights had been designed as a limitation on the national government rather than on the states. His argument was supported by the fact that the First Amendment began with the words "*Congress* [an instrumentality of the national government] shall make no law." After the turn of the twentieth century, the Bill of Rights was applied to the states.

The scope of the Bill of Rights was broadened when the Fourteenth Amendment guaranteed key rights for all Americans. Historians still debate whether those who authored and ratified this amendment intended to apply the bill of rights directly to the states, but it seemed clear that, as the embodiment of key values, violations of constitutional rights would constitute a denial of due process of law or of the privileges and immunities of U.S. citizenship. Chiefly beginning with the case of *Gitlow v. New York* (1925), the Supreme Court has proceeded, through the doctrine of "selective incorporation," to apply the most essential provisions in the bill of rights to the states. Over time, the court has decided that almost all of these provisions can be considered essential to liberty. Indeed, many justices have ruled that there are penumbral rights (such as the right to privacy) that apply to both state and national governments, even though they are not directly stated within the Constitution.

SUMMARY

The Bill of Rights was in part a product of English tradition, colonial resistance to English rule, and the experience of making constitutions and government during the Revolutionary War. Fear of tyrannical government and the desire to define and protect rights guided the creation of the Constitution and later the Bill of Rights. The idea of state declarations of rights grew into the national bill of rights. This bill of rights was, in turn, expanded and nationalized through judicial interpretations of the Fourteenth Amendment. Courts have increasingly enforced rights once largely considered to be constitutional aspirations. Thus the struggle to end segregation and debate over the kind and extent of individual rights, such as the right of privacy or choice, and the controversy over the limits of government power in time of war, trace their origins to the American Revolution.

BIBLIOGRAPHY

Abraham, Henry J., and Perry, Barbara A. *Freedom & the Court: Civil Rights & Liberties in the United States*, 8th ed. Lawrence: University Press of Kansas, 2003.

Cogan, Neil. ed. *The Complete Bill of Rights: The Drafts, Debates, Sources and Origins*. New York: Oxford University Press, 1997.

Conley, Patrick T., and Kaminski, John P., eds. *The Bill of Rights and the States: The Colonial and Revolutionary Origins of American Liberties*. Madison, WI: Madison House, 1992.

Kurland, Philip B., and Lerner, Ralph. *Amendments I-XII*. In *The Founders' Constitution*, Vol. 5. Chicago: The University of Chicago Press, 1987.

Veit, Helen E.; Bowling, Kenneth R.; and Bickford, Charlene Bangs, eds. *Creating the Bill of Rights: The Documentary Record from the First Federal Congress*. Baltimore, MD: The Johns Hopkins University Press, 1991.

Vile, John R. *Encyclopedia of Constitutional Amendments, Proposed Amendments, and Amending Issues, 1789–2002*. Santa Barbara, CA: ABC-CLIO, 2003.

John R. Vile

See also: **Anti-Federalists; Articles of Confederation; Commonwealth Men; Declaration of Independence; Federalist Papers.**

CONSTITUTION: CREATING A REPUBLIC

In early 1788, in defense of the proposed constitution, James Madison wrote in Federalist Paper 51: "If men were angels, no government would be necessary. If angels were to govern men, neither external nor internal controls on government would be necessary. In framing a government which is to be administered by men over men, the great difficulty lies in this: you must first enable the government to control the governed; and in the next place oblige it to control itself." Here, Madison described the dilemma of government in a democratic republic: The role of government is to prevent the excesses of personal license and political tyranny while ensuring the broadest range of individual liberty.

PRESERVING THE REVOLUTION AND UNION

Madison's support of the Constitution sought to preserve the ideals and values of the Revolution by sustaining the unity of the new nation. In the spring of 1787 the United States had been on the verge of breaking into independent states and regional confederations. Its economy was crippled by a variety of currencies, state tariffs, threats of secession in the west, a huge national debt, and the inability to defend American merchants from pirates. Popular uprisings, the most famous being Shays' Rebellion in western Massachusetts, destabilized states. Madison believed that the near-collapse of the nation had resulted from the desire of each state to promote its own interest and from the weakness of the national government.

The national government had been created during the Revolutionary War by the Articles of Confederation. Under the Articles, sovereign states agreed to join a loose national federation that had a weak central government composed of representatives from each state. Each state had one vote in the federal congress. There was no executive and no system of federal courts. This form of government reflected the views and experiences of the people who led Americans to war against Britain. Americans fought for independence from England partly because they believed that Parliament had too much authority, had weakened the powers of the provincial legislatures, and had "enslaved" citizens by depriving them of their rights. Revolutionary leaders responded by giving most power to the states and making the national government the servant of the states.

THE CONSTITUTIONAL CONVENTION

Disunion, with states becoming independent countries, could result in divisions similar to those in Europe that had been the source of centuries of warfare. Facing this prospect, leaders had to rethink the political principles and government structures that had dominated during the Revolution. The Continental Congress authorized a convention to propose amendments to the Articles of Confederation that would strengthen the national government. Meeting in Philadelphia through the summer of 1787, delegates chosen by the states followed a path laid out by Madison. Rather than reform the existing system, they would create a new form of government. Their goal was revolution, not revision.

The fate of the nation was in the hands of a few men. Of the seventy-four delegates only fifty-five attended the Philadelphia convention. Nearly all had served in their state legislatures and the Continental Congress; thirty had served in the army. The selection of George Washington as presiding officer put the convention above politics in the public's mind. For three months delegates met in secret to permit open and candid discussion of ideas and conflicting views. The result was a novel form of government that would preserve the principles of the Revolution and American society for "generations yet unborn."

FEATURES OF THE CONSTITUTION

James Madison, often referred to as "The Father of the Constitution," presented a proposal that would vastly increase the power of the national government and give most power to the most populous states. His Virginia Plan provided for proportional representation in the House and Senate based on a state's population. Following the lead of many state constitutions, Madison introduced the idea of separation of powers on the national level, proposing a separate judiciary and executive. He also proposed that the national government have the power to tax citizens directly and to declare state laws null and void.

Delegates from states that were poor and had small populations vigorously opposed Madison's plan. The conflict between small states and large states over their powers in the national government nearly broke up the convention. Madison's opponents insisted they had not fought a war for independence against the tyranny of a King and Parliament just to exchange one master for another. The compromise offered by Roger Sherman of Connecticut resolved the controversy. It initiated a succession of compromises that led to near unanimous approval of the draft constitution.

The delegates agreed that the House would be composed of popularly elected delegates in proportion to the population of each state, but that each state would be equally represented in the Senate by two delegates chosen by their state legislatures. The compromise also revealed a paradox of the Constitution. It was to be not an elegantly consistent blueprint based on one theory, but a mixture of principles, pragmatically arranged, that reflected a variety of values engrained in American society. It also reflected the delegates' view of human nature, based on their experiences in war and peace.

The Three-fifths Clause was another compromise. Under the Articles of Confederation each slave counted as three-fifths of a person, a figure that had determined a state's assessment to pay for the war against England. This clause was incorporated into the Constitution, despite some opposition to slavery, to ensure southern acceptance of the new form of government. The external slave trade would continue until 1808. When delegates were forced to choose between the Union or abolishing slavery, they chose the Union.

The final draft was submitted to the Continental Congress, which had been created under the Articles and

The Liberty Bell in Philadelphia, Pennsylvania. Philadelphia served as the capital of the United States from 1777 to 1800. It was during the summer of 1787 that the members of the Continental Congress debated and redrafted the Articles of Confederation into the Constitution.

which had authorized the convention. That congress agreed to submit the draft to individual states for approval. In doing so the congress authorized its own demise and the replacement of the Articles by the Constitution as soon as nine of the thirteen states approved the draft. In short, the Continental Congress authorized its own overthrow by ballots, not bullets. The draft produced widespread debate on the principles and functions of government, provoking an extraordinarily intense and creative period in American political history during which the nation debated the meaning of the Revolution and the future of the United States.

The provisions of the Constitution were seen as novel, but not new. Some of its features resembled those already found in some state constitutions. The Constitution incorporated the principle of separation of powers by dividing the legislative, judicial and executive functions of government between three distinct branches rather than blending them as had been done in Great Britain. The Constitution enumerated the powers of the

national government, yet provided for elasticity in exercising those powers. It also distributed powers between the national government and the state governments. In doing so, the Constitution made individuals citizens both of their states and of the nation. This dual citizenship, a basis for later claims of states' rights, fostered conflict over a variety of issues, such as the right of citizens to own slaves. While it did not contain a bill of rights (which was added in 1791), the Constitution did protect individual liberties. For example, it provided for habeas corpus, which permits an imprisoned person to demand that he or she be brought before a court to hear the charges. No existing state constitution incorporated all of the Constitution's provisions. Even more important, the Constitution proposed a federal republic of a type and scope never before seen in history.

APPROVING THE CONSTITUTION

Voters in each state had to decide whether to accept or reject the Constitution as presented. Following the model created by Massachusetts, candidates sought election to their state's convention on whether they supported or opposed the constitution. The conventions met, cast one vote, and then dissolved. Thus, approval of the Constitution reflected the will of the majority of voters through elected delegates. Furthermore, the Constitution was to be the written framework to organize and restrict the powers of government, and as such was conceived as "higher law." It not only was the supreme law of the land, but represented the principle that no person was above the law.

In June, 1788 New Hampshire became the ninth state to approve the Constitution and with that, the Articles of Confederation became null and void. Implementing the new form of government began with elections to the House of Representatives, the selection of senators by state legislatures, and the choice of president of the United States by the Electoral College. George Washington's inauguration in April 1789 formally ended that phase of the political revolution. Under this novel Constitution, the United States initiated an experiment in self-government in a federal republic guided by the ideals of the Declaration of Independence.

LEGACY

The Constitution, a product of a period of political dissent, war, and post-war turmoil, has had a major influence in shaping American culture, society, and identity. The debate over ratification expressed in the Federalist Papers and the Anti-Federalist replies created the most important source of American political thinking, one that continues to influence modern politics. The Constitution became an object of veneration that celebrated "American Exceptionalism," the idea that the United States is unique and had a special role to play in history. It has also come to symbolize American belief that the United States is a society governed by law and that no person is above the law. Constitutional law has proved to be organic, capable of applying and extending the Constitution's principles to unforeseen circumstances through amendments and interpretations made by the Supreme Court. Finally, the Constitution has been a means through which to express popular opinion and America's deepest cultural ideals, as seen in decisions such as *Plessy v Ferguson* (1896) that upheld segregation and *Brown v Board of Education* (1954) that declared segregation unconstitutional.

BIBLIOGRAPHY

Collier, Christopher and Collier, James. *Decision in Philadelphia.* New York: Random House, 1986.

Cornell, Saul. *The Other Founders: Anti-Federalism and the Dissenting Tradition in America.* Chapel Hill: University of North Carolina Press, 1999.

Kammen, Michael. *A Machine That Would Go Of Itself: The Constitution in American Culture.* New York: Knopf, 1986.

Rakove, Jack N. *Original Meanings: Politics and Ideas in the Making of the Constitution.* New York: Vintage Books, 1997.

John P. Resch

See also: Articles of Confederation; Constitution: Creating a Republic; Continental Congresses; Declaration of Independence; Madison, James; Shay's and Whiskey Rebellions; Washington, George.

CONTINENTAL CONGRESSES

In September 1774, the First Continental Congress convened in Philadelphia, the first intercolonial meeting since the Stamp Act Congress of 1765. Fifty-five elected delegates from twelve colonies (excepting Georgia, Florida, Quebec, and Nova Scotia) met to discuss the Coercive Acts passed by the North ministry in England early in the year. The delegates agreed to formulate a common response despite acknowledged differences of religious persuasion, territorial claims, professional training, sectional economic interests, and political beliefs, and alongside the proliferation of local and provincial committees springing up throughout the colonies. They established that each colony would have one vote, ensuring a basic equality among all the provinces and establishing a principle that would last until the Constitutional Convention in 1787.

FIRST CONTINENTAL CONGRESS

A bold resolution brought by the Massachusetts delegates, the Suffolk Resolves, demanded colonial resistance to the Coercive Acts and preparations for military defense. But delegates from New York, Pennsylvania, and Delaware did not yet wish for such far-reaching rejection of Parliament's authority over them, insisting that the First Continental Congress distinguish between colonial internal taxes and local courts, which Parliament had no right to forbid, and external trade, which many delegates agreed Parliament might still regulate. In an effort to stall any decisions that might lead to outright war in the empire, Pennsylvania's moderate Joseph Galloway proposed a Plan of Union, at the center of which would be a Grand Council that combined colonial and imperial authority for governing and taxing throughout the empire. Despite the heated disagreements that ensued, including Patrick Henry's expression of a new identity, "I am not a Virginian, but an American," a compromise document emerged. The Declaration of Rights condemned the legislation of Parliament since 1763 while still recognizing the king's sovereignty over them. In the declaration, the Continental Congress underscored that all colonists enjoyed certain rights, which were secured by "the immutable laws of nature, the principles of the English constitution, and the several charters" originally granted to the colonies, wording that previewed the Declaration of Independence. While Parliament had the right to regulate imperial commerce, efforts to destroy colonial systems of justice with new admiralty courts, to decree internal taxes, to close their assemblies, or to revoke crown charters were unmistakable signs of Parliament's utter corruption. Colonists had rehearsed these ideas many times in the preceding years, but in 1774 their unified voice in a delegated Congress added significant weight to the charges.

Without waiting for the king's reply, Congress initiated a non-importation agreement (the third major boycott of British goods since 1765) to begin on December 1, 1774. They further resolved that if repeal were not forthcoming in early 1775, a non-exportation movement would begin in September 1, 1775. A broad intercolonial Association Agreement also urged colonists to pledge themselves to nonconsumption of English goods, to practice frugality, economy, and industry (all familiar terms to eighteenth-century ears) and to avoid unnecessary spending and entertainments until Parliament repealed post-1763 legislation. Committees of Inspection would enforce the boycott and keep order in local communities.

RESISTANCE AND COLONIAL IDENTITY

The Continental Congress's actions made important new steps toward shaping a unified political community and were widely popular to both colonists who hoped for reconciliation with the mother country, and to those (Richard Henry Lee and Sam Adams among them) who wished to press onward toward independence. A broad public discussion developed in pamphlets and newspapers that circulated across colonial boundaries. Daughters of Liberty and local "spinning schools" made homespun wool and produced substitutes for imported tea in myriad communities. Even after official non-importation ended, women from dozens of small towns pledged to continue wearing modest forms of dress, scale down funerals, and celebrate holidays less ornately. Moreover, during 1775 thousands of colonists helped forge a new intercolonial identity by supporting the Committees of Inspection and the Committees of Safety sanctioned by the Continental Congress. Alongside the provincial congresses forming as a dual authority to the crown's, the Continental Congress pressed colonists to declare their beliefs openly, punish those who wavered or disagreed, forge new links across the colonies, and use new terms such as nation, America, and states.

SECOND CONTINENTAL CONGRESS: MAKING WAR

Delegates to the Second Continental Congress began deliberations in May 1775, less than a month after the bloody events at Lexington and Concord. Delegates urged the Committees of Inspection and Committees of Correspondence to become more active and aroused the militia to begin taking over "loyalist nests." This time, Georgia sent delegates, but Canadians rebuffed Congress's overtures, and the multiethnic, multiracial population in East and West Florida remained under tight British control. Assemblies of Grenada, Jamaica, and Barbados opted to join the American independence movement, but crown forces on the islands overwhelmed the rebels. In the future, these islands would attract many fleeing loyalists.

Military preparedness began from April 1775 to June 1775, a full year before delegates seriously considered the Declaration of Independence. Yet although Congress resolved that "we must put ourselves in an armed condition" by creating a Continental Army, Thomas Jefferson noted the general public's distrust of standing armies, especially since the French and Indian War, and asserted that Congress had no authority to create a pan-colonial military force. But other delegates insisted that since the resistance movement "engaged a continent," it required a trained and centrally commanded force. Militiamen served short terms of enlistment; their loyalty often stemmed from serving under officers of their choosing and from their locales; and they had little comprehension of sustained warfare and their propensity to return home between battles would seriously harm the rebel cause. In June 1775, the Continental Congress voted unanimously to raise a Continental Army and place the forty-three-year-old George Washington in charge. A few days later, Congress gave Washington a staff of major generals and voted to issue $2 million in congressional paper currency to fund the troops.

RECONCILIATION OR WAR

Despite such mobilization, on July 5, 1775 John Dickinson of Pennsylvania had presented the Olive Branch Petition to Congress, a document delegates voted to send to George III affirming colonial loyalty to the monarch, asking that British army hostilities cease, and proposing a joint discussion of differences. But Dickinson himself helped Thomas Jefferson draft a Declaration of the Causes and Necessities of Taking Up Arms the day after Congress sent the Olive Branch Petition to the king. In early August, a few congressional delegates began negotiations with Indians in the mid-Atlantic region, especially the Iroquois, to win either their support or promise of neutrality. Congress also appointed Benjamin Franklin as postmaster general in charge of coordinating intercolonial communication.

George III refused to read the Olive Branch Petition, giving Congress little choice but to entrench itself deeper in war. In the fall of 1775, the small Continental Army marched into Canada to grab territory and win over the citizenry where the British were weak, only to lose hundreds of soldiers in desperate maneuvers and waves of smallpox. Southern patriots engaged with loyalists, and in Virginia the former Governor Dunmore organized slave regiments to defend crown interests. Southern patriot merchants began honoring the conditions of Congress's Association Agreement, which stipulated a halt to all trade with Britain. But the Second Continental Congress hesitated, still, to declare independence. They continued, in their majority, to support British control of their trade and refused to countenance open foreign trade at American ports or seek foreign financial support, hoping their petitions and commercial boycott would bring reconciliation. Congress had created an army, a commander, a military staff, and an intercolonial currency; but it had no authority to coerce colonies or citizens to support their measures, nor had it yet defined long-range political goals of all "confederated colonies in congress."

But by late Fall 1775, the king's closest advisors declared the colonies to be in open rebellion, the British navy blockaded major colonial ports, Parliament had passed restraining acts against trade from most of the colonies during the year, and recruitment officers sent out a general call for foreign (mainly German) mercenaries. On December 22, 1775 Parliament assented to a Prohibitory Act that declared all American vessels and goods would be forfeit to English admiralty officials, a measure that legalized blanket seizures.

INDEPENDENCE

In February 1776 the Second Continental Congress began to openly debate independence, although even then, the important mid-Atlantic provinces opposed it. On April 6, 1776, Congress threw open American ports to all nations except Britain and its loyal colonies. Economic independence was, in effect, declared. Through May and June, individual colonial assemblies instructed delegates sitting in Philadelphia to support a call for political independence. On June 7, Richard Henry Lee presented a resolution that "these United Colonies are, and of right ought to be, free and independent states." One after another the colonies (many of them already in the process of becoming new states) assented to the Declaration of Independence in July 1776.

CONGRESS AND THE REVOLUTIONARY WAR

Congress faced numerous difficulties during the war. The Army was never as large as Congress (and Washington) wished it to be, and always dependent on the sacrifice of citizens in the several states as well as a contracting system that was deeply flawed. Foreign aid came with a high price tag. Congress drafted the Articles of Confederation in 1776, and submitted them to the states in November 1777, in order to clarify the relationship of Congress to the emerging state governments and citizens as a whole. However, only the principle of dispersing power and retaining one-state-one-vote were established in the heated debates for months to come. How the war would be funded and how new western lands would become a part of Congressional powers remained thorny points of debate from early 1777 to 1781. The Articles carried no provisions to tax citizens or states, or to coerce compliance with its needs for central rule and national defense, and repeated efforts to establish an import duty on foreign goods met constant disapproval in the revolutionary states. Only at the end of the war did the new states approve the Articles. In the next years, Congress would be saddled with a tremendous debt to citizens, states, and foreign governments. However, before its business was superceded by the national government, Congress bequeathed the Northwest Ordinance, adopted on July 13, 1787, which stipulated principles and practical means to organize a national domain which would contain new states.

LEGACY

From 1774 through 1787, the Continental Congresses were the central delegated authority of first the colonies and then the new states. The first congress was a forum for protesting British policies and for intercolonial cooperation. The second congress conducted the war for Independence and wrote the Articles of Confederation, which was approved by delegates of the infant states at the close of the war and stipulated the extent and limitations of central government authority. Until the Constitutional Convention convened in May 1787, the second Continental Congress continued to exercise limited central authority over citizens and to negotiate certain international and Indian relations.

BIBLIOGRAPHY

Ammerman, David. *In the Common Cause: American Response to the Coercive Acts of 1774.* New York: Norton, 1974.

Burnett, Edmund C. *The Continental Congress.* New York: Macmillan, 1941.

Countryman, Edward. *The American Revolution.* New York: Hill and Wang, 1985.

Ferguson, E. J. *The Power of the Purse: A History of American Public Finance, 1776–1790.* Chapel Hill: University of North Carolina Press, 1961.

Greene, Jack, ed. *The American Revolution: Its Character and Limits.* New York: New York University Press, 1978; reprinted 1987.

Jensen, Merrill. *The Articles of Confederation: An Interpretation of the Social-Constitutional History of the American Revolution, 1774–1781.* Madison: University of Wisconsin Press, 1940; reprinted 1959.

Rakove, Jack N. *The Beginnings of National Politics: An Interpretive History of the Continental Congress.* New York: Alfred A. Knopf, 1979.

Cathy Matson

See also: Articles of Confederation; Commonwealth Men; Declaration of Independence; Constitution: Creating a Republic; Stamp Act Congress; States and Nation Building, 1775–1783.

COOPER, JAMES FENIMORE

(b. September 15, 1789; d. September 14, 1851)
American writer known for early U.S. war novels.

James Fenimore Cooper was part of the generation of writers who created the first distinctively American literature following the Revolutionary War. Critics debate whether or not he was a great writer, but it does seem safe to say that Cooper was the father of the American novel, and more specifically of the American war novel. This is probably all that can be said about him without argument. Mark Twain famously and wittily despised him, more for his squirishness, perhaps, than for his writing. He was often criticized in his own century for too greatly admiring (and imitating) British writers, and more recently he has been criticized for his patronizing attitude toward Native Americans, as well as for his turgid and overwritten prose.

EARLY WORKS

The scion of a landed upstate New York family (which lent its name to Cooperstown, New York), James Fenimore Cooper was raised to be a gentleman farmer, but his family's fortunes were already on the wane when in 1818, at the age of twenty-nine, he moved with his new bride Susan (née DeLancey) to her native Westchester county. There he was the owner of a substantial property called Angevine, in Scarsdale, which he managed as a gentleman farmer; but he was beset by increasing financial uncertainty, in part due to his family's financial difficulties. His decision to become a writer may well have been prompted by his need to earn money.

In 1821, Cooper published the first U.S. war novel, *The Spy,* which combined national pride with unabashed adulation of America's natural beauty, themes both well matched to the spirit of U.S. nationalism in the years following the War of 1812.

WAR NOVELS

Within a year after the appearance of *The Spy,* one contemporary critic had already dubbed Cooper the first distinguished American novelist, and he was already at work on *The Pioneers* (1823), which he called a "Descriptive Tale" set in the frontier wilderness near the area where he grew up in upstate New York. The novel is most significant for its introduction of the character of Natty Bumppo, who went on to be the central character in the Leatherstocking series, which included Cooper's novel of the French and Indian War and arguably his best known work, *The Last of the Mohicans* (1826). In 1824, he published *The Pilot,* which takes place during the Revolution, using the activities of the real-life war hero John Paul Jones off the coast of England as a backdrop for its plot. Cooper had been a sailor in his youth and *The Pilot* drew heavily on his knowledge of the sea.

In addition to *The Pilot,* the final volumes of the Leatherstocking series—*The Pathfinder* (1840) and *The Deer Slayer* (1841)—and *Oak Openings* (1848), Cooper wrote several novels portraying Americans at war or engaged in conflict with hostile native populations, including his 1829 novel, *The Wept of Wish-ton-wish,* which portrayed the Puritan conflict with the American Indians in King Philip's War. He also wrote a number of works of nonfiction, including *The History of the Navy of the United States of America* (1839), which contains a useful, although disputed, description of the Battle of Lake Erie, and a series of biographies published as *Lives of Distinguished American Naval Officers.*

In the final decade of his life, Cooper wrote a trilogy known as the Littlepage novels (after the name of a family whose experiences are central to the story), portraying Americans involved in the Rent War of the 1840s in New York's Ulster and Delaware counties. As a member of one of the state's oldest property-owning families, he portrayed this anti-rent struggle as representative of moral decay and social decline.

Charles B. Potter

See also: Fort William Henry Massacre, Cultural Legacy; King Philip's War, Legacy of; Memory and Early Histories of the Revolution; *The Spy;* First American War Novel.

DECLARATION OF INDEPENDENCE

The American Revolution was both a war for independence and a conflict that gave rise to a new society and political culture. The Declaration of Independence was the document in which the people of the thirteen British North American colonies declared their separation from Great Britain and set forth the broad principles on which America built, and continued to build, the nation. Unhappy with the way in which the British government was ruling the colonies, the colonists began the Revolutionary War in April 1775 to establish their rights within the British Empire. Later, many of them began to call for outright independence, resulting in the formal adoption of the Declaration of Independence on July 4, 1776, by the Second Continental Congress convened in Philadelphia.

THE DECLARATION ON TAKING UP ARMS

When the colonists began their revolt against Great Britain, they did not initially seek independence. However, they had to justify their armed resistance against the British. To this end, the Second Continental Congress issued the Declaration on Taking up Arms, which it approved on July 6, 1775. Thomas Jefferson originally composed this document, although John Dickinson extensively revised it. The Declaration on Taking up Arms listed the colonists' grievances, most of which later appeared in the Declaration of Independence. According to the document, the British actions had led colonists to choose between "an unconditional submission to the Tyranny of irritated Ministers, or Resistance by Force." The colonists chose resistance. However, they indicated that they were willing to lay down their arms if the British addressed the grievances.

CREATION OF THE DECLARATION
OF INDEPENDENCE

As the war progressed, more and more colonists began to call for outright independence. In December 1775, the Second Continental Congress denied the sovereignty of the British parliament over the colonies. In January 1776, Thomas Paine's *Common Sense* whipped up public support for the cause of independence. In April, the colonists opened their ports to trade with other nations, clearly violating the restrictive mercantilist policies of the mother country. In May 1776, the congress declared that the authority of the king was to be suppressed and that it would establish its own government to administer the colonies,

In CONGRESS, July 4, 1776.

A DECLARATION

By the REPRESENTATIVES of the

UNITED STATES OF AMERICA,

In GENERAL CONGRESS ASSEMBLED.

WHEN in the Course of human Events, it becomes necessary for one People to dissolve the Political Bands which have connected them with another and to assume among the Powers of the Earth, the separate and equal Station to which the Laws of Nature and of Nature's God entitle them, a decent Respect to the Opinions of Mankind requires that they should declare the causes which impel them to the Separation.

We hold these Truths to be self-evident, that all Men are created equal, that they are endowed by their Creator with certain unalienable Rights, that among these are Life, Liberty, and the Pursuit of Happiness---That to secure these Rights, Governments are instituted among Men, deriving their just Powers from the Consent of the Governed, that whenever any Form of Government becomes destructive of these Ends, it is the Right of the People to alter or to abolish it, and to institute new Government, laying its Foundation on such Principles, and organizing its Powers in such Form, as to them shall seem most likely to effect their Safety and Happiness. Prudence, indeed, will dictate that Governments long established should not be changed for light and transient Causes; and accordingly all Experience hath shewn, that Mankind are more disposed to suffer, while Evils are sufferable, than to right themselves by abolishing the Forms to which they are accustomed. But when a long Train of Abuses and Usurpations, pursuing invariably the same Object, evinces a Design to reduce them under absolute Despotism, it is their Right, it is their Duty, to throw off such Government, and to provide new Guards for their future Security. Such has been the patient Sufferance of these Colonies; and such is now the Necessity which constrains them to alter their former Systems of Government. The History of the present King of Great-Britain is a History of repeated Injuries and Usurpations, all having in direct Object the Establishment of an absolute Tyranny over these States. To prove this, let Facts be submitted to a candid World.

He has refused his Assent to Laws, the most wholesome and necessary for the public Good.

He has forbidden his Governors to pass Laws of immediate and pressing Importance, unless suspended in their Operation till his Assent should be obtained; and when so suspended, he has utterly neglected to attend to them.

He has refused to pass other Laws for the Accommodation of large Districts of People, unless those People would relinquish the Right of Representation in the Legislature, a Right inestimable to them, and formidable to Tyrants only.

He has called together Legislative Bodies at Places unusual, uncomfortable, and distant from the Depository of their public Records, for the sole Purpose of fatiguing them into Compliance with his Measures.

He has dissolved Representative Houses repeatedly, for opposing with manly Firmness his Invasions on the Rights of the People.

He has refused for a long Time, after such Dissolutions, to cause others to be elected; whereby the Legislative Powers, incapable of Annihilation, have returned to the People at large for their exercise; the State remaining in the mean time exposed to all the Dangers of Invasion from without, and Convulsions within.

He has endeavoured to prevent the Population of these States; for that Purpose obstructing the Laws for Naturalization of Foreigners; refusing to pass others to encourage their Migrations hither, and raising the Conditions of new Appropriations of Lands.

He has obstructed the Administration of Justice, by refusing his Assent to Laws for establishing Judiciary Powers.

He has made Judges dependent on his Will alone, for the Tenure of their Offices, and the Amount and Payment of their Salaries.

He has erected a Multitude of new Offices, and sent hither Swarms of Officers to harrass our People, and eat out their Substance.

He has kept among us, in Times of Peace, Standing Armies, without the consent of our Legislatures.

He has affected to render the Military independent of and superior to the Civil Power.

He has combined with others to subject us to a Jurisdiction foreign to our Constitution, and unacknowledged by our Laws; giving his Assent to their Acts of pretended Legislation:

For quartering large Bodies of Armed Troops among us:

For protecting them, by a mock Trial, from Punishment for any Murders which they should commit on the Inhabitants of these States:

For cutting off our Trade with all Parts of the World:

For imposing Taxes on us without our Consent:

For depriving us, in many Cases, of the Benefits of Trial by Jury:

For transporting us beyond Seas to be tried for pretended Offences:

For abolishing the free System of English Laws in a neighbouring Province, establishing therein an arbitrary Government, and enlarging its Boundaries, so as to render it at once an Example and fit Instrument for introducing the same absolute Rule into these Colonies:

For taking away our Charters, abolishing our most valuable Laws, and altering fundamentally the Forms of our Governments:

For suspending our own Legislatures, and declaring themselves invested with Power to legislate for us in all Cases whatsoever.

He has abdicated Government here, by declaring us out of his Protection and waging War against us.

He has plundered our Seas, ravaged our Coasts, burnt our Towns, and destroyed the Lives of our People.

He is, at this Time, transporting large Armies of foreign Mercenaries to compleat the Works of Death, Desolation, and Tyranny, already begun with circumstances of Cruelty and Perfidy, scarcely paralleled in the most barbarous Ages, and totally unworthy the Head of a civilized Nation.

He has constrained our fellow Citizens taken Captive on the high Seas to bear Arms against their Country, to become the Executioners of their Friends and Brethren, or to fall themselves by their Hands.

He has excited domestic Insurrections amongst us, and has endeavoured to bring on the Inhabitants of our Frontiers, the merciless Indian Savages, whose known Rule of Warfare, is an undistinguished Destruction, of all Ages, Sexes and Conditions.

In every stage of these Oppressions we have Petitioned for Redress in the most humble Terms: Our repeated Petitions have been answered only by repeated Injury. A Prince, whose Character is thus marked by every act which may define a Tyrant, is unfit to be the Ruler of a free People.

Nor have we been wanting in Attentions to our British Brethren. We have warned them from Time to Time of Attempts by their Legislature to extend an unwarrantable Jurisdiction over us. We have reminded them of the Circumstances of our Emigration and Settlement here. We have appealed to their native Justice and Magnanimity, and we have conjured them by the Ties of our common Kindred to disavow these Usurpations, which, would inevitably interrupt our Connections and Correspondence. They too have been deaf to the Voice of Justice and of Consanguinity. We must, therefore, acquiesce in the Necessity, which denounces our Separation, and hold them, as we hold the rest of Mankind, Enemies in War, in Peace, Friends.

We, therefore, the Representatives of the UNITED STATES OF AMERICA, in GENERAL CONGRESS, Assembled, appealing to the Supreme Judge of the World for the Rectitude of our Intentions, do, in the Name, and by Authority of the good People of these Colonies, solemnly Publish and Declare, that these United Colonies are, and of Right ought to be, FREE AND INDEPENDENT STATES; that they are absolved from all Allegiance to the British Crown, and that all political Connection between them and the State of Great-Britain, is and ought to be totally dissolved; and that as FREE AND INDEPENDENT STATES, they have full Power to levy War, conclude Peace, contract Alliances, establish Commerce, and to do all other Acts and Things which INDEPENDENT STATES may of right do. And for the support of this Declaration, with a firm Reliance on the Protection of divine Providence, we mutually pledge to each other our Lives, our Fortunes, and our sacred Honor.

Signed by ORDER and in BEHALF of the CONGRESS,

JOHN HANCOCK, PRESIDENT.

ATTEST.
CHARLES THOMSON, SECRETARY.

PHILADELPHIA: PRINTED BY JOHN DUNLAP.

Declaration of Independence AP/WIDE WORLD PHOTOS

which it soon did. It formed the Continental Army, issued a currency, and established a post office. King George declared the colonies in rebellion and began to hire German mercenaries to fight in North America. To the colonists, such actions only proved that the king was treating them as foreigners and not as British citizens.

By mid-May 1776, eight of the thirteen colonies supported the idea of complete independence from England. The Virginia Convention resolved that their delegates should propose to the Second Continental Congress that independence be declared. On June 7, 1776, Richard Henry Lee of Virginia read a resolution to the Continental Congress that called for ending the formal connection between the colonies and Great Britain, thus making the colonies independent of British rule. This resolution was a reflection of what had already been happening in the colonies since the previous year.

After Lee's resolution, the Congress appointed a five-man committee to draft a document proclaiming independence. The committee members were John Adams of Massachusetts, Roger Sherman of Connecticut, Benjamin Franklin of Pennsylvania, Robert Livingston of New York, and Thomas Jefferson of Virginia. The Declaration of Independence went through several versions. Jefferson drafted the original version. Then, other committee members commented on Jefferson's draft. On July 2, twelve colonies voted in favor of the Lee resolution, with New York abstaining. On July 3–4, the Congress discussed the Declaration, altering and deleting portions of the committee draft. Finally, on July 4, 1776, Congress adopted the Declaration of Independence.

Once adopted, the Declaration had to be printed. John Dunlop, the official printer to Congress, made copies. Starting on July 5, delegates distributed them to assemblies and conventions throughout the colonies, as well as to colonial military commanders.

CONTENT OF THE DECLARATION OF INDEPENDENCE

The Declaration contained five parts. The first part was the Introduction, consisting of a single long paragraph. One key aspect of the Introduction was that it elevated the dispute between the colonists and the British from a relatively petty political dispute to a major event in modern history by placing the colonial rebellion in the "course of human events." The Introduction also helped to dignify the colonists' fight and gave them a certain moral legitimacy by evoking the laws of nature. This section was objective in tone, presented as simple observation rather than as an interpretation open to questioning.

The second section of the Declaration was the Preamble. This general section outlined the philosophy of government that made revolution possible. The Preamble contained several propositions. It stated first, that all men are created equal. Second, that all men are endowed with certain unalienable rights. Third, that these rights include "life, liberty, and the pursuit of happiness." Fourth, that governments are instituted to secure these rights. And fifth, that it is the right of the people to abolish any government that does not secure these rights.

The third section of the Declaration was an indictment of King George III of Great Britain. This section was the first to refer explicitly to the conflict between the colonists and Great Britain. Here, the colonists sought to prove that King George was a tyrant and bad ruler. The Declaration listed twenty-eight grievances ranging from taxation without representation to the suspension of colonial laws. Five of the grievances were related to war: (1) by waging war against the colonists, King George had abdicated his right to govern the colonies; (2) the king had "plundered our seas, ravaged our Coasts, burnt our towns, and destroyed the Lives of our people"; (3) he had used foreign mercenaries; (4) the British had taken captives on the high seas and forced them to bear arms; and (5) they had attempted to incite the Indians to fight against the colonists.

The fourth section was a denunciation of the British people. The Declaration stated that the colonists had appealed in vain to the people of Great Britain. The fact that such appeals had fallen on deaf ears further showed the conditions that justified revolution.

Finally, the fifth section of the Declaration actually declared separation from Great Britain. Here the colonists claimed the power to wage war, conclude peace, make alliances, and do everything else that independent countries have the right to do.

ABRAHAM LINCOLN, THE CIVIL WAR, AND THE DECLARATION OF INDEPENDENCE

Americans have evoked the Declaration of Independence in subsequent wars. During the 1850s, Abraham Lincoln went so far as to say that the sentiments of the Declaration influenced all of his political ideas. Soon, Lincoln's understanding and interpretation of the document became that of the country as a whole. The future president's concern with the Declaration emerged during his debates with Stephen Douglas in the 1858 campaign for Senate. One of the key issues of the campaign was the future of slavery. Both men utilized the Declaration to defend their position.

Douglas defended the Kansas-Nebraska Act, pointing out that each colony retained its rights and privileges even when it voted in favor of independence from Great Britain. Furthermore, he argued that the Declaration applied only to people of European descent and that the document's only true purpose was to justify American political independence.

Lincoln offered a different interpretation. He believed that the Declaration applied to all men and that no person or government could rule over another without consent. Furthermore, Lincoln claimed that the Declaration not only justified the American Revolution, but set standards of equality that would lead to the eventual extinction of slavery. Later, as president, he felt that the Civil War was not merely to end slavery, but to save a form of government "whose leading object is to elevate the condition of men" as outlined in the Declaration. He argued that the southern states were attempting to overthrow the principle that all men are created equal.

THE DECLARATION OF INDEPENDENCE AND WORLD WAR II
In 1943, the United States government dedicated the Jefferson Memorial in Washington, D.C., to mark the two-hundredth anniversary of Thomas Jefferson's birth. As part of tribute to the Declaration's author, Julian Boyd published *The Declaration of Independence: The Evolution of the Text*. Archibald MacLeish, the Librarian of Congress, was charged with writing the foreword to the book. MacLeish's job was not an easy one. The country was fighting World War II and the United States and Great Britain were allies, yet MacLeish had to write about a document that celebrated the break between the two countries nearly two hundred years earlier.

In his foreword, MacLeish did not focus on the split between the United States and Great Britain. Rather, he interpreted the Declaration of Independence as a document that could unify the countries of the world. He described it as a declaration of the basic principles of human liberty that would flourish in the future, once fascism was defeated. Furthermore, he emphasized that the Declaration was part of a larger tradition of liberty in the English-speaking world. He likened it to the Magna Carta, arguing that the positive principles contained in such documents had never been more important than during World War II, as the allies fought against fascist dictatorships.

BIBLIOGRAPHY
Armitage, David. "The Declaration of Indpendence and International Law." *The William and Mary Quarterly* 59, no. 1 (2002): 39–64.

Bush, Harold K. *American Declarations: Rebellion and Repentance in American Cultural History*. Urbana: University of Illinois Press, 1999.

Lucas, Stephen. "Justifying America: The Declaration of Independence as A Rhetorical Document." In Thomas W. Benson, ed. *American Rhetoric: Context and Criticism*. Carbondale: Southern Illinois University Press, 1989.

Maier, Pauline. *American Scripture: Making the Declaration of Independence*. New York: Knopf, 1997.

Internet Resources
"Declaration of Independence." U.S. National Archives. Available from <http://www.archives.gov/national_archives_experience/charters/declaration_transcript.html>.

Ronald Young

See also: **Articles of Confederation;** *Common Sense;* **Constitution: Creating a Republic; Continental Congresses; Jefferson, Thomas; Paine, Thomas.**

DRINKER, ELIZABETH
(b. February 27, 1735; d. November 24, 1807) Quaker diarist who described hardships of the Revolutionary War for neutrals.

Elizabeth Drinker's diary chronicles the impact of the Revolutionary war on neutral Quakers in Philadelphia. A native Philadelphian, Drinker was born to prosperous Quakers, William Sandwith and Sarah Jervis, who gave their daughters a better-than-usual education. After her parents' death in 1756, the twenty-one-year-old Elizabeth and her older sister Mary lived with friends until Elizabeth married the widower Henry Drinker on January 13, 1761.

Henry Drinker was a partner in one of the city's leading import-export firms. The couple had nine children between 1761 and 1781, of whom five survived to adulthood. The household also included Elizabeth's sister Mary and several servants. In 1771, the family demonstrated their elite status by moving to a large, three-story brick house on Front Street, overlooking the Delaware River. A large yard in the back housed a garden, stables, well, and wash house.

In 1773, the British government appointed the firm of James and Drinker to receive and sell East India tea imported under the Tea Act. Drinker and his partner resigned their appointments amidst heavy public pressure. Even though Elizabeth Drinker, her sister, and her daughter Sally provided medical help to Americans held as prisoners of war in occupied Philadelphia, they could not erase the public suspicion that they were British supporters.

In order to maintain their neutrality, Quakers refused to sign non-importation agreements, illuminate their houses to celebrate American victories and independence, supply belligerents, or take paper money issued by the new governments. They also refused to swear (or affirm) loyalty oaths. In September 1777, Pennsylvania arrested twenty leading Quakers men, including Henry Drinker, and sent them into captivity in Virginia, supposedly to prevent them from aiding the approaching British. Thus Elizabeth Drinker faced the British occupation of Philadelphia in 1777 and 1778 as a single head of a household that included five children aged three to sixteen, her sister, and a series of constantly changing servants.

Elizabeth Drinker was unable to prevent one of her female servants from running off with a soldier, or to protect her household from break-ins by soldiers. One soldier simply walked in and took blankets from the house. She reluctantly agreed to provide quarters for a British officer who took over the front of the house, the stables, and the kitchen. Although his presence crowded the Drinkers, the officer and the family had a generally good relationship, and after the British withdrew they maintained a correspondence until his death late in the war. The officer's presence afforded the family some protection from other incursions.

Despite Drinker's belief that women should not take public roles, she joined with the wives of the other detainees to draw up a petition to Congress. She had already defied regulations by sewing money inside the clothes she sent to her husband. Drinker was one of four women sent by the detainees' families in April 1778 to present their case to General George Washington and Congress, then sitting in Lancaster. At Valley Forge, Washington and his wife entertained the women but could not do more than give them passes through American lines. On April 24, 1778, after a month of negotiation, the surviving men, including Henry Drinker, were released and allowed to return to Philadelphia. Two had died in captivity.

The return of the American forces to Philadelphia brought the Drinkers no relief from harassment. Americans searched their home several times for British trade goods, confiscated blankets and horses to supply the army, and seized numerous pieces of fine furniture to satisfy fines levied against Quaker noncombatants. The Drinkers, however, did not suffer the fate of some of their friends who openly worked with the British. Two were hung, and others had their land and all their property confiscated. Elizabeth Drinker maintained her friendships with these families. In October 1781, a mob targeted Quakers who had not put candles in their windows to celebrate the victory at Yorktown. They broke over seventy panes of glass and smashed the front door in the Drinker home.

Once peace was restored, the Drinkers resumed their normal life and work. As their children came of age and married, the family shrank and Drinker had more time to write and read, including such contemporary authors as Mary Wollstonecraft. She continued to provide medical advice for her family and enjoyed long visits with her grandchildren. A near invalid and in great pain, Drinker lost heart after the death of her daughter, Sally, from cancer and died two months later on November 24, 1807. Her beloved companion, Henry, died in 1809. Her life illustrates the dangers suffered—at the hands of both loyalists and patriots—by those whose religious convictions required them to remain neutral during war.

BIBLIOGRAPHY

Crane, Elaine Forman, ed. *The Diary of Elizabeth Drinker*, 3 volumes. Boston: Northeastern University Press, 1991.

Crane, Elaine Forman, ed. *The Diary of Elizabeth Drinker: The Life Cycle of an Eighteenth-Century Woman*. Boston: Northeastern University Press, 1994.

Evans, Elizabeth. "Elizabeth Sandwith Drinker." In *Weathering the Storm: Women of the American Revolution*. New York: Scribner, 1975.

Joan R. Gundersen

See also: **Adams, Abigail; Generals' Wives: Martha Washington, Catherine Greene, Lucy Knox; Madison, Dolley; Republican Womanhood; Sampson, Deborah.**

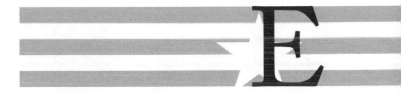

EMBARGO

The most comprehensive and controversial economic sanction ever adopted by the United States was the Embargo. Also known as the Long Embargo, this measure was in force from December 22, 1807, to March 1, 1809. Essentially a non-exportation law, the Embargo prohibited American ships and goods from leaving port. It was designed to force Great Britain and France to show greater respect for American rights during the Napoleonic Wars (1803–1815) by depriving them of American trade. Its purpose was also to protect American ships and seamen by keeping them in port. The Embargo failed as a coercive measure, and whatever protection American ships and seamen derived from their forced inactivity was more than offset by the adverse impact that the measure had on American trade and prosperity.

The Embargo was the most ambitious of a series of economic sanctions, collectively known as the restrictive system, adopted prior to the War of 1812. The American colonies had employed non-importation, non-exportation, and non-consumption in the 1760s and 1770s to force the British to modify their tax and trade policies. Although these measures probably did not play a decisive role in securing a change in policy, American leaders like Thomas Jefferson and James Madison interpreted history otherwise. Convinced that the U.S. held the key to the prosperity of Great Britain and France as well as their West Indian colonies, Republican leaders were determined to protect American rights in the Napoleonic Wars by using the nation's trade as an instrument of foreign policy.

The Embargo was preceded by a partial non-importation law against Great Britain that was enacted in 1806 but was suspended repeatedly until early December 1807. Shortly thereafter, President Jefferson recommended an embargo, and the Republican-controlled Congress complied. This law was followed by four increasingly draconian enforcement acts designed to close loopholes and suppress smuggling.

The Embargo had a disastrous effect on the U.S. economy. Ships were idled in port, and neither merchants nor farmers could get their produce or goods to foreign markets. Domestic exports, which had soared from less than $20 million in 1790 to almost $49 million in 1807, plummeted to $9 million in 1808. Because the nation's economy was so closely tied to the sea, virtually everyone in the U.S. felt the chilling effects of the Embargo. Government revenue, which was derived almost entirely from

John Paul Jones capturing the British ship HMS *Serapis*. Jones set sail in 1779 to raid English shipping. In 1807, the Embargo closed American ports to English and French ships.

taxes on shipping and trade, suffered as well. After increasing from $2 million in 1790 to $17 million in 1808, government income fell to less than $8 million in 1809.

CONSTITUTIONAL ISSUES AND POLITICAL DISSENT

The Embargo also raised serious constitutional issues. There was extensive smuggling, not only on the Atlantic seaboard but also across the Canadian border, where smugglers often clashed with government officials. Although it is unlikely that the suppression of this trade would have rendered the Embargo any more successful, Republicans leaders were willing to push the limits of the Constitution to give the measure every chance.

The administration asked Congress for increasingly broad powers. When Secretary of the Treasury Albert Gallatin told Jefferson that the Embargo could be enforced only if government officials were given powers that were "arbitrary" and "equally dangerous and odious" (Gallatin, July 29, 1808) the president was undeterred. "Congress," Jefferson replied, "must legalize all *means* which

may be necessary to obtain its *end*" (Jefferson, August 11, 1808). The climax came in 1809 with the fourth and final enforcement act, which gave customs officials sweeping powers and authorized the use of the army and navy to suppress smuggling.

The last enforcement act probably violated the Fourth Amendment guarantee governing search and seizure. In addition, President Jefferson repeatedly exceeded his constitutional authority. He routinely used the army and navy to enforce the law; he claimed that areas where defiance was widespread were in a state of insurrection; he insisted that some smugglers be tried for treason to set an example; and he ordered government officials to ignore a court order that he disagreed with. Enforcing the Embargo showed Jefferson at his worst, determined to go to almost any lengths to bend reality to uphold a flawed ideal that was probably unattainable.

The Embargo also fueled a revival of the Federalist party, which had been in decline ever since the election of 1800 and seemed headed for extinction. Buoyed by rising discontent over the Embargo, the Federalists made significant election gains, especially in New England, where the destruction of shipping and trade caused widespread suffering and extensive economic losses.

LEGACY

In spite of the huge price paid by Americans, the Embargo did not have a significant impact on England or France. Although American commodities became more dear abroad, the effects everywhere were less devastating than U.S. leaders had anticipated. The European belligerents found alternative sources for food and raw materials as well as new markets for their exports. Instead of making concessions to secure an end to the Embargo, Britain welcomed the withdrawal of a commercial rival from the high seas and France used the measure as a pretext for confiscating additional American maritime property.

In March of 1809, after fifteen months of national suffering and on the eve of Jefferson's retirement from office, the Embargo was repealed. Although the Embargo was an obvious failure, most Republicans retained their faith in the restrictive system. The Embargo was succeeded by a non-intercourse act in 1809 and a non-importation act in 1811, but these measures proved no more effective.

Even though the Embargo and its successors were defended as a peaceful alternative to war, Republicans steadily expanded the restrictive system during the War of 1812. The climax came in late 1813, when a second embargo was adopted, one that included all the enforcement machinery of the Long Embargo. This measure was repealed in 1814, when news arrived that Napoleon's defeat at Leipzig had opened all of northern Europe to

British trade. At last thoroughly discredited, economic sanctions were not revived as an instrument of foreign policy until the twentieth century, and never again would the nation adopt any restriction that was as comprehensive as the Embargo.

BIBLIOGRAPHY

Adams, Henry. *History of the United States of America during the Administrations of Jefferson and Madison,* (1889–1891), abridged and edited (one volume) by Ernest Samuels. Chicago: University of Chicago Press, 1967.

Gallatin, Albert. "Letter to Thomas Jefferson, July 29, 1808." *Jefferson Papers.* Washington, DC: Library of Congress. Microfilm.

Heaton, Herbert. "Non-Importation, 1806–1812." *Journal of Economic History* 1 (1941): 178-98.

Jefferson, Thomas. "Letter to Albert Gallatin, August 11, 1808." *Jefferson Papers.* Washington, DC: Library of Congress. Microfilm.

Jennings, Walter W. *The American Embargo, 1807–1809.* Iowa City: University of Iowa, 1921.

Levy, Leonard W. *Jefferson and Civil Liberties: The Darker Side.* 2d edition. New York: Quadrangle/New York Times Book Co., 1973.

Sears, Louis Martin. *Jefferson and the Embargo.* Durham, NC: Duke University Press, 1927.

Spivak, Burton. *Jefferson's English Crisis: Commerce, Embargo, and the Republican Revolution.* Charlottesville: University Press of Virginia, 1979.

Donald R. Hickey

See also: **Hartford Convention; Jefferson, Thomas; Madison, James; Monroe, James; Pirates and the Barbary War; Quasi-War and the Rise of Party Politics.**

EUROPEAN INVASION OF INDIAN NORTH AMERICA, 1513–1765

Indian North America was peopled in 1500 by some five hundred societies who fully used the continent—which their ancestors had inhabited for about 25,000 years—to sustain themselves by hunting and gathering, slash and burn migratory farming, or, especially in the south, by settled agriculture. There is much debate about the total population of that continent, with serious estimates ranging from one to eighteen million people, but there is some consensus that individual societies or confederacies very seldom contained more than 30,000 people.

EUROPEAN INVASION

By far the worst war for all American Indian people after 1500 was the war against alien diseases that invaded more stealthily, quickly, and pervasively than the accompanying Europeans. The human intruders did not arrive or multiply fast enough to match the devastation of Indian North America, and the total population of the continent continued to decline until at least 1700. Natural immunities to new diseases take generations to develop and interaction between migrating peoples from three continents initially proved deadly, and particularly so for American Indians. Endemic malaria plagued European immigrants to the southeast, but "virgin land" infections of smallpox, measles, influenza, cholera, and yellow fever could kill the majority in an American Indian society. Indigenous medicine proved helpless—and lost credibility—against these infectious killers that often hit hardest at more densely-peopled farming societies like the Massachusetts, Huron, and Iroquois, and gave a relative advantage to the more remote and to scattered hunter-gatherers. Spasmodically repeating the devastation, migrants, traders, and armies brought recurring epidemics. These sudden losses created a frightening new world for American Indian survivors even before invading people, animals, and plants brought other revolutions and wars. Depopulation and war prompted the creation of new communities, like the Choctaw, Creek, and Powhatan confederacies. Some decimated societies made room for European strangers in places such as Québec (1608), Plymouth (1620), and Massachusetts (1630); the Iroquois Confederacy reacted to epidemics with a series of successful wars to replace their dead with captives.

FLORIDA INDIANS CONFRONT THE SPANISH, 1513–1565

American Indians defeated all the early Spanish "explorers" of Florida. The Calusa and Timucua of south Florida were likely the first North Americans to meet Europeans when Spanish slavers raided to replace rapidly-dying Arawak workers at their new Caribbean gold mines, farms, and ranches. Timucua and Calusa archers repelled all three attempts of Juan Ponce de León's well-equipped fleet attempting to land in Florida in 1513, and drove off other Spanish fleets in 1517 and 1521. The Guale, in what eventually became Georgia, initially welcomed 1,100 Spanish colonists who arrived in 1528; most of these died of malaria, leaving a remnant whose dependence on the Guale for food led to conflict and the evacuation of the surviving Spanish.

Fabulous Spanish success against the Aztecs and the Incas were unrepeatable examples of imperial success in the Americas, but numerous Spanish expeditions sought comparable wealth in the North American southeast. An army of six hundred landed in Timucuan territory in 1527 and trudged through north-central Florida in heavy metal armour, only to be killed by Apalachee and Aute bowmen, malaria, or shipwreck during escape; only four returned to Spanish territory. Eleven years later a comparable force organized by a leading Spanish conqueror of the Inca, Hernando De Soto, began four years of rambling destruction: taking leaders hostage, extorting food and labor, and leaving disease and starvation in their wake from Georgia to Texas. This army fought only one pitched battle, destroying Mabila (near present day Selma, Alabama) where some 2,500 Choctaw died, either in their burning town or facing mounted Spanish lancers wearing light and effective Aztec body armor. Subsequent casualties from disease remain unnumbered, but the extensive Creek chiefdom of Coosa, on the Alabama River, is known to have been destroyed. De Soto and half his army had also died before the survivors built a brigantine and escaped down the Mississippi in 1542, with war canoes in pursuit. A smaller Spanish expedition hunted in vain for the Seven Cities of Gold in the southwest between 1540 and 1542, and four more expeditions failed in Florida between 1559 and 1562. The American Indians of the southeast had, at a price, completely defeated the Spanish intruders in the first half-century of contact.

Spain was anxious to keep other Europeans well away from the Florida coasts, past which treasure fleets from the Caribbean sailed homeward to Spain. However, the Timucua allowed one French expedition to stay, in return for support in a local war. The Spanish destroyed this French privateering base and replaced it with the first permanent European community in North America, the expensive fort of San Agustín (1564–1565). Missionaries proved more tolerable than soldiers in spreading the Spanish presence, particularly among the Apalachee and the Guale, as well as the Pueblo of New Mexico. Occasionally missionaries were martyred and missions destroyed in wars of resistance like those of the Pueblo in 1580, the Guale in 1597, and the Apalachee in 1647. Although the Spanish military retaliated, missions remained the comparatively inexpensive Spanish method of empire in the American borderlands. The system would collapse in the southeast between 1670 and 1704, when Creek and English slavers captured an estimated 51,000 for Carolina or English West Indian plantations.

IROQUOIS, HURON, AND ALGONQUIN MEET THE FRENCH, 1534–1649

The Laurentian Iroquois dominated the St. Lawrence Valley in 1534, when the first French expedition visited Stadacona (later Québec). The French were more aggressive when returning the next year, insisting on exploring upriver over local objections, fortifying their scurvy-ridden camp, and meddling in local politics. The next time the French returned, in 1541, they numbered 1,500 and intended to settle. Initial Iroquois curiosity turned to suspicion and then hostility; in 1543 the harrassed French evacuated, becoming the second nation of

Europeans to be driven from North American beach-heads. When the French returned to found Québec in 1608 they settled without facing any resistance, for the Laurentian Iroquois had mysteriously disappeared and the Montagnais, Algonquin, and Huron readily enlisted the unwitting newcomers in fighting the Five Nations of the Iroquois.

Fur trading would reshape American Indian diplomacy and war, while inviting and funding French, Dutch, and English outposts that became permanent. Furs became fashionable in Europe after 1600, amid climatic cooling, and American Indian hunters readily joined a trade that built mutual dependence and more-enduring alliances than those possible with land-hungry European farming societies. A minor Micmac victory over the Abenaki in Maine in 1607 demonstrated the advantage of trading for French-supplied metal spear and arrow heads, daggers, cutlasses, plus a few matchlock muskets; the defeated Abenaki became very interested in an English trading station established at Sagadohoc that year. Although the French and English depended on matchlock muskets, American Indians were reluctant to trade the bow and arrow for a heavy weapon that was inaccurate, unreliable in rain, and needed a burning matchcord that emitted a smell, sound, and light that precluded surprise. However, the matchlock could be a terrifying novelty; within weeks of a Mohawk defeat by the Huron at Lake Champlain (1609), the Mohawk were trading with newly-arrived Dutch, led by Henry Hudson. Trade was a factor in the Mohawk-Canadian wars of 1609 to 1624, 1650 to 1667, and 1684 to 1701, which brought each side near destruction, but ended in a draw. The Huron were the premiere fur trade partners, trading, raiding, and praying with the French. However, they were devastated by disease in the 1630s, were divided into competing Christian and traditionalist factions by the 1640s, and were conquered and scattered by the Five Nations in a massive winter assault in 1649.

IROQUOIS MEET THE DUTCH AND ENGLISH, 1608–1701

The Five Nations of the Iroquois was one American Indian culture that grew in military and economic power after European contact. The Iroquois Confederacy developed from an earlier nonaggression pact among the Mohawk, Oneida, Onondaga, Cayuga, and Seneca who inhabited the lands between the Hudson River and Lake Erie. The Mohawk met Dutch maritime traders on the Hudson annually between 1609 and 1624, when the Dutch West India Company established Fort Orange (Albany). The Mohawk ended their war against Canada in order to defeat the Mahicans and monopolize American Indian access to the Dutch post. The Dutch trod carefully after sending six Dutch musketeers with a Mahican war party in 1628 that was ambushed by Mohawks, killing four of the Dutch. As the Mohawk depleted the beaver of their own territory, they intensified attacks on rival Huron and Algonquin fur convoys bound for Québec.

In a smallpox epidemic that ravaged American Indian communities from New England to Huronia in 1633 to 1634, the population of the Iroquois Confederacy was suddenly halved and the Mohawk were reduced from 8,100 to 2,000 people. The Mohawk-Dutch alliance was vital to both parties and was bolstered between 1643 and 1645 when the Dutch supplied some four hundred muskets to the Mohawk. This armament coincided with a new Mohawk role, assisting the Dutch in controlling smaller tribes down the Hudson Valley who resisted taxation and the expansion of Dutch farming. In Kieft's War (1643–1645), Mohawk musketeers attacked several resisting bands, taking prisoners for adoption. The Mohawk did not join Dutch colonists and soldiers in encircling and setting fire to a fortified Weequaesgeek village (1644) and slaughtering an estimated five hundred fleeing people while suffering only one fatality. The Mohawk and Dutch were victorious against the Susquehannock and a Swedish trading colony on the Delaware River in the early 1650s, and Mohawk helped the Dutch in three wars against the Delaware tribe (1655–1657, 1659–1660, 1663–1664). The Iroquois rebuilt their population through a series of "mourning wars" to replace their dead with adopted captives, destroying and dispersing Iroquois-speaking Huron (1649), Petun (1650), Erie (1657), and Susquehannock (1680).

The Five Nations, led by the Mohawk, had no trouble making trade and diplomatic adjustments when the English captured New Netherlands from the Dutch in 1664 and 1672. The English had a considerable West Indian and North American empire by then, and had destroyed both the Powhatan confederacy in Virginia and the Pequot of New England (1637). The Mohawk played a significant role in the eventual English victory over Wampanoag King Philip, and the English and Five Nations formalized a "Covenant Chain" of trade and diplomacy in 1677. Although this covenant chain eventually benefited both parties, the Iroquois received little help from the English as they suffered renewed French attacks after 1684. In the face of severe losses, and continuing attacks by Ojibwa allies of the French, the Iroquois made peace in 1701 and lived in profitable neutrality during the next half-century of Anglo-French rivalry and war.

AMERICAN INDIANS AND THE ANGLO-FRENCH COLONIAL WARS 1689–1748

American Indians generally benefited from the Anglo-French wars (1689–1697; 1702–1714; 1744–1748; 1754–1763), for these rivals vied for American Indian alliances, providing diplomatic gifts as well as trade goods and weapons. This situation entirely masked the growing American Indian dependency on European flintlock muskets, gunpowder, and shot. The Anglo-French wars also funded American Indian forces conducting wars of their own, rolling back the encroaching white settlements. Warriors from game-depleted regions of the northeast could profitably hunt for captives to sell in labor-short New France. It is also noteworthy that American Indians allied to either power became increasingly reluctant to attack American Indian allies of the other Europeans; the European colonists and armies were the American Indians' targets.

A most dangerous time for American Indians occurred late in each Anglo-French war, when colonials were prone to attack American Indians rather than colonial enemies. The Anglo-French Peace of Ryswick (1697) only intensified French-backed attacks on the Iroquois. As the second Anglo-French war drew to a close, the French and their allies opened a generation of intermittent warfare against the Fox (1712–1738), destroyed the Natchez (1729–1730), and attacked the Chickasaw (1736–1739). The English of Massachusetts had used the peace of 1697 to concentrate on their war with the Abenaki (1688–1699), which resumed again (1723–1727) during the next intercolonial peace. Although English and Creek slavers had opened Queen Anne's War in the south by completely destroying the Spanish missions, it was near the end of this war that Creek, Cherokee, Catawba, and Yamasee joined the English to attack and disperse the Iroquoian-speaking Tuscarora (1711–1713), sending enough refugees north to turn the Five Nations into the Six Nations. Within two years, offended Yamasee built a broad American Indian coalition that nearly destroyed the vulnerable South Carolina colony (1715–1717), where African slaves outnumbered their enslavers. Although this pan-American Indian alliance disintegrated after the Catawba withdrew and the Cherokee joined the English, the Yamasee War would trail on for another eleven years, as some Yamasee and Guale continued to raid Carolina from new villages in Spanish Florida. In switching sides, the Cherokee provoked a bitter Creek-Cherokee war (1716–1727) in which the Creeks used their geographical position to make allies of the English, Spanish, and French, in turn.

FRENCH AND INDIAN "SEVEN YEARS WAR," 1754–1763

Shawnee, Delaware, and Mingo (Six Nations Iroquois migrants) farmers and hunters had lived in the Upper Ohio Valley for a generation when they welcomed English traders, thereby prompting French military intrusion. Ohio American Indian objections were ignored by the French, appeals to Six Nations kin were met with

European confrontation with Indians. Although initially disease brought by European intruders proved the most deadly, ultimately it was the colonists ability to marshall people, taxes, and resources for war that conquered the Native Americans. THE LIBRARY OF CONGRESS

insistence on neutrality, and the Pennsylvanians offered trade goods, alliances, and sympathy but their Quaker-led assembly would not fight the French. It was Virginian land speculators who answered the call for help and initiated a confrontation with the French that would herald a global imperial war.

Like most American Indians in eastern North America, those of the Ohio country soon saw the French as the lesser evil and used French assistance to pursue a devastating war that pushed some English colonial frontiers back two hundred miles. Meanwhile the French and a broad coalition of allied American Indians defeated the English on the New York frontier by capturing Fort Oswego (1756) and Fort William Henry (1757). However, as the British began to win the maritime war and the American war became increasingly European, the Ohio American Indians negotiated a calculated withdrawal that ensured that Fort Duquesne would fall (1758). The Iroquois joined the British to take Fort Niagara (1759), and American Indian allies of a collapsing New France withdrew and thereby generally escaped the vengeance dis-

played in Robert Rogers's destruction of the Abenaki village of St. Francis (1759).

American Indians were well aware that the fall of New France (1760) exposed them to triumphant English power that was harder to avoid without diplomatic, military, or trading alternatives. The Cherokee, who had been allied with the British, launched a badly-timed war against them (1759–1761), without being able to acquire any American Indian allies. Despite some Cherokee successes, the British sent readily-available regular troops who invaded annually to burn ripening crops and a total of nineteen towns. Privation and the increasing shortage of gunpowder brought the Cherokee to negotiate a peace that included a specified frontier line between the two cultures.

"PONTIAC'S WAR," 1763–1765

American Indians of the Great Lakes region launched a war, misnamed "Pontiac's War," in 1763 when they learned that the French had presumed to forfeit American Indian lands to the British, that English settlers were moving onto those lands, and that the victorious British were reducing diplomatic gifts and restricting trade goods.

The conflict erupted when warriors of fifteen tribes captured nine widely dispersed up-country British posts in May and June of 1763. The stronger and well provisioned posts of Fort Pitt, Fort Detroit, and Fort Niagara were besieged in vain, but reinforcements for the last two of these posts were destroyed. In raids against Maryland, Virginia, and Pennsylvania frontiers, American Indians killed and captured about two thousand settlers. The Royal Proclamation of 1763, with its provision of a clear line dividing the European colonies from American Indian-controlled land, came too late to avert the conflict, but became part of the negotiated peace in a stalemated war.

American Indians certainly lost more than either the French or the Spanish in the outcome of the long imperial battle to control and inhabit eastern North America. The European immigrant invasion of American Indian country now accelerated, while a heavily-indebted British government was unable to police the new frontiers, and colonists wanted neither the policing nor the additional imperial taxes to pay for it. The conquest of Canada, and the Spanish surrender of Florida, suspended the American Indian strategy of playing one European power against another, but the "white men" were about to subdivide again with the rebellion of the British American colonies.

LEGACY

By 1765, Indian North America was in retreat. Nearly two million Europeans and Africans occupied the lands east of the Appalachians. Disease and intertribal war had distorted the contest between the people of the bow and arrow and those with steel weapons and matchlock muskets. By 1675, the flintlock musket had invaded both American Indian and European America, but this equality was illusory because guns and gunpowder were available only from Europe, and gunpowder deteriorated easily. The Anglo-French wars encouraged the spread of flintlocks to American Indian allies, while masking the dependence on European suppliers during the lifetime between King Philip's War and those of the Cherokee and Pontiac. The Six Nations Iroquois were particularly successful, based upon martial reputation, rebuilt populations, location between European rivals, diplomatic shrewdness, and imperial ambitions that worked well with those of the British.

In many respects, the colonial wars established the territorial and cultural roots of the United States. Long before they established the right to bear arms, American colonists were familiar with guns. Although the performance of colonial militias and short-term contract soldiers was often unimpressive, by 1765 militia duty was presumed in all colonies except Pennsylvania. Colonial and imperial governments more readily marshalled people, taxes, and resources for war than for any other purpose. With minor exceptions, European intruders and their descendants had conquered the region from the eastern seaboard to the Appalachians from American Indians and from each other; this pattern would continue in U.S. expansion to the Pacific Ocean.

Although confiscation of the continent was routinely justified by "rights of conquest," such rights have always been seen as morally inadequate. Another supposed justification came from the myth that the land had been quite empty and underused. To claim a civilizing and redeeming role, the invaders also projected savagery exclusively on the American Indians, through fireside tales, vivid and popular "captivity narratives," and more recently, novels and films. However, it remains striking that the traditional rivalries, either among American Indian societies or among European immigrant societies, almost always took precedence over any racial alliances. Slavery was part of colonial warfare from the beginning, and a sense of race eventually emerged. By 1763, American Indians were uniting to resist what had just become the lone victorious European power, and the idea of a clear line between American Indian and white cultures and between American Indian and white lands was appealing to American Indian negotiators as well as to the British government. Colonials had come to accept the line between cultures, but regarded permanent American Indian land ownership as intolerable, whether imposed by the Royal Proclamation of 1763 or the Quebec Act of 1774.

BIBLIOGRAPHY

Axtell, James. *The Invasion Within: The Contest of Cultures in Colonial North America.* New York: Oxford University Press, 1985.

Calloway, Colin G., ed. *The World Turned Upside Down: Indian Voices from Early America.* Boston: St. Martin's Press, 1994.

Chet, Guy. *Conquering the American Wilderness: The Triumph of European Warfare in the Colonial Northeast.* Amherst: University of Massachusetts Press, 2003.

Dowd, Gregory Evans. *A Spirited Resistance: The North American Indian Struggle for Unity, 1745–1815.* Baltimore, MD: Johns Hopkins University Press, 1992.

Ferling, John. *Struggle for a Continent: The Wars of Early America.* Arlington Heights, IL: Harlan Davidson, 1993.

Gallay, Alan, ed. *Colonial Wars of North America, 1512–1763: An Encyclopedia.* New York: Garland, 1996.

Jennings, Francis. *The Invasion of America: Indians, Colonialism, and the Cant of Conquest.* New York: Norton, 1976.

Merrell, James H. *The Indians' New World: Catawbas and their Neighbors from European Contact to the Era of Removal.* Chapel Hill: University of North Carolina Press, 1989.

Richter, Daniel K. *Facing East from Indian Country: A Native History of Early America.* Cambridge, MA: Harvard University Press, 2001.

Starkey, Armstrong. *European and Native American Warfare, 1675–1815.* Norman: University of Oklahoma Press, 1998.

Steele, Ian K. *Warpaths: Invasions of North America.* New York: Oxford University Press, 1994.

Ian K. Steele

See also: Jamestown; Legacy of the Massacre of 1622; King Philip's War, Legacy of; Legacies of Indian Warfare; Native Americans: Images in Popular Culture.

FAMILIES AT WAR

If asked about the impact of the American Revolution on family life, those who experienced the conflict would most likely have pointed to practical difficulties: the absence of men in military service, the economic disruptions of war, and, for some, the loss of homes and livelihood. Over the long term, however, pressures that the Revolution placed on the form and function of the traditional household have proven far more significant than its immediate effects on community life. One of the great paradoxes of the Revolution was that it created a new political order without replacing old patterns of household government.

The wartime correspondence between Abigail and John Adams illustrates the various tensions the Revolution placed on family and household. The letters frequently refer to the difficulties of maintaining a household in wartime and to the emotional strains of separation, concerns that were important but not unique to the Revolution. It is the letters' political content that sets them apart. In particular, they have become famous for a brief exchange acknowledging—and dismissing—the potential of Revolutionary ideology to reshape the government of households. In the spring of 1776, Abigail asked John to "remember the Ladies" in the "new Code of Laws" to be enacted by the Continental Congress. "All Men would be tyrants if they could," she noted, and existing laws invited abuse by putting virtually "unlimited power in the hands of the Husbands." Half jokingly, she threatened that neglect of this issue would lead women to "foment a Rebelion" of their own. We "will not hold ourselves bound by any Laws in which we have no voice, or Representation," she declared.

Abigail Adams's observation about the formidable powers colonial laws gave to husbands also applied to other relations of legal dependence: master and servant (or slave), parent and child, guardian and ward. (All of these ties were also deemed "family" relationships; in eighteenth-century usage, the term was not yet reserved primarily for connections of blood and affection.) Within this early modern legal framework, male heads of households represented the political interests of most of the population. Wives, servants and slaves, children, and others categorized as dependent had no direct claim on the state. Abigail Adams implied that the Revolution would be incomplete if its legal reforms failed to come to terms with the immense authority this arrangement gave individual men over their dependents.

"REMEMBER THE LADIES"

This March 31, 1770 letter from Abigail Adams to her husband, John Adams is known as the "Remember the Ladies" letter. In it Abigail expresses her feelings about the rights of women to John, who was in Philadelphia as a Massachusetts delegate to the Continental Congress. Knowing that he is on the committee to draft The Declaration of Independence, she asks her husband to promote laws that would improve the legal status of women, who in that era had few rights.

I have sometimes been ready to think that the passion for Liberty cannot be Eaquelly Strong in the Breasts of those who have been accustomed to deprive their fellow Creatures of theirs. Of this I am certain that it is not founded upon that generous and christian principal of doing to others as we would that others should do unto us. . . .

Tho we felicitate ourselves, we sympathize with those who are trembling least the Lot of Boston should be theirs [Many homes were ruined by looters.] But they cannot be in similar circumstances unless pusilanimity and cowardise should take possession of them. They have time and warning given them to see the Evil and shun it.—I long to hear that you have declared an independency—and by the way in the new Code of Laws which I suppose it will be necessary for you to make I desire you would Remember the Ladies, and be more generous and favourable to them than your ancestors. Do not put such unlimited power into the hands of the Husbands. Remember all Men would be tyrants if they could. If perticuliar care and attention is not paid to the Laidies we are determined to foment a Rebelion, and will not hold ourselves bound by any Laws in which we have no voice, or Representation.

That your Sex are Naturally Tyrannical is a Truth so thoroughly established as to admit of no dispute, but such of you as wish to be happy willingly give up the harsh title of Master for the more tender and endearing one of Friend. Why then, not put it out of the power of the vicious and the Lawless to use us with cruelty and indignity with impunity. Men of Sense in all Ages abhor those customs which treat us only as the vassals of your Sex. Regard us then as Beings placed by providence under your protection and in immitation of the Supreem Being make use of that power only for our happiness.

[SOURCE: *The Book of Abigail and John: Selected Letters of the Adams Family, 1762–1784*, edited and with an introduction by L. H. Butterfield, Marc Friedlaender, and Mary-Jo Kline, Harvard University Press, 1975.]

For John Adams and most of his contemporaries, in contrast, the thought of applying revolutionary ideology to household government was a recipe for anarchy. John informed Abigail that he could only laugh at her "extraordinary" proposal. "We have been told that our Struggle has loosened the bands of Government every where. That Children and Apprentices were disobedient . . . that Indians slighted their Guardians and Negroes grew insolent to their Masters." The social order, as John Adams depicted it, rested on the foundation of female dependence. Challenges to any one set of household relationships were bound to disrupt others.

John Adams used this reasoning to support his belief that political power should be restricted to the propertied elite. But male dominance over the household could also provide justification for extending political rights to white men of all classes. In the *Pennsylvania Gazette* of January 26, 1785, a writer who called himself Cato explained that "every man . . . has what is supposed by the constitution to be property: his life, personal liberty, perhaps wife and children, in whom they have a right, the earnings of his own or their industry." By emphasizing the rights of possession accorded to male household heads, the writer recast poor men as independent property holders and defended their claim to the vote. Their political gains helped cement the political exclusion of women and other dependents.

Abigail Adams was not the only American sensitive to this contradiction. Thousands of slaves and servants attempted to claim their own personal liberty during the Revolution by running away from their masters' "families." John Adams might have been thinking of these runaways when he referred to unruly Indians and Negroes. He might also have had in mind the formal legislative petitions by which African New Englanders sought to end slavery and claim the right to form autonomous families of their own. Although the Revolution did contribute to the gradual end of legal slavery in several Northern states, it did not end the legal patterns of discrimination that forced most free people of color to labor as dependents in white households.

The distinction we now make between family and household—between ties of "natural" affection and bonds of formal obligation—is in part a product of Revolutionary-era efforts to justify the persistence of traditional household government. The celebration of the affectionate, nurturing family as the source of civic virtue gave women new claims to social authority. John Adams employed this rhetoric in his light-hearted dismissal of Abigail's concerns. He assured her that husbands had "only the Name of Masters"; emotional ties gave women the real power in families. Surrendering formal legal power, he suggested, would place men wholly under the emotional sway of their wives and "completely subject Us to the Despotism of the Petticoat."

For most Americans after the Revolution, the "new Code of Laws" contained very little that was new with regard to family life. Household government remained the form of government most immediate to the inhabitants of the new country. Divisions over slavery helped keep all domestic relations under the final jurisdiction of state and local authorities, and actually served to reinforce patriarchal authority, especially in the South. But the Revolution's celebration of egalitarian ideals and the right of individuals to a voice in government provided a potent justification for protests against this order, giving impetus to the powerful movements for dependents' rights that flowered in the nineteenth century and continue today.

BIBLIOGRAPHY

Aptheker, Herbert. *A Documentary History of the Negro People in the United States*, vol. 1. New York: Citadel Press, 1967.

Crane, Elaine Forman. "Political Dialogue and the Spring of Abigail's Discontent." *William and Mary Quarterly* 56, no. 4 (1999): 745–774.

Frey, Sylvia R. *Water from the Rock: Black Resistance in a Revolutionary Age*. Princeton, NJ: Princeton University Press, 1991.

Nash, Gary B., and Soderlund, Jean R. *Freedom by Degrees: Emancipation in Pennsylvania and Its Aftermath*. New York: Oxford University Press, 1991.

Shammas, Carole. *A History of Household Government in America*. Charlottesville: University Press of Virginia, 2002.

Smith, Billy G. "Runaway Slaves in the Mid-Atlantic Region during the Revolutionary Era." In *The Transforming Hand of Revolution: Reconsidering the American Revolution as a Social Movement*, edited by Ronald Hoffman and Peter J. Albert. Charlottesville: University Press of Virginia, 1995.

Tadmor, Naomi. "The Concept of Household Family in Eighteenth-Century England." *Past and Present* 151 (1996): 110–140.

Internet Resource

Correspondence of Abigail and John Adams. Available from <http://www.masshist.org/digitaladams>.

Kirsten D. Sword

See also: Adams, Abigail; Drinker, Elizabeth; Generals' Wives: Martha Washington, Catharine Greene, Lucy Knox; Republican Womanhood.

FEDERALIST PAPERS

The Federalist Papers, a series of eighty-five essays written by Alexander Hamilton, James Madison, and John Jay, were intended to win public support for the Constitution by explaining in detail how the proposed system of government would work. The essays, signed with the pseudonym "Publius," appeared in several New York newspapers from October 1787 to April 1788, and were also reprinted in other states. Their carefully crafted arguments in favor of the Constitution convinced many Americans to support its ratification and influenced later interpretations of constitutional principles.

ORIGINS AND AUTHORSHIP

Supporters of the Constitution realized that winning ratification in New York would be a difficult task. Governor George Clinton, who led the opposition, attacked the Constitution in several published letters signed "Cato," charging that the framers had no authority to devise a new system of government, and that the Constitution threatened the rights of the citizens as well as the states.

Hamilton realized that an effective response was necessary. Believing that a well-reasoned defense of the Constitution would win over many voters, he decided to publish a series of papers explaining the principles of the Constitution and why it was an improvement over the current Confederation government. Hamilton wrote the first "Publius" letter and enlisted John Jay and, later, James Madison to assist in the undertaking. Madison composed about one-third of the essays, Jay five, and Hamilton the remainder (the authorship of several is uncertain). The essays describe how the Constitution would operate as well as how the new system of government would mesh with both the principles that had inspired the Revolution and the lessons learned from the experience of the Revolution itself.

KEY POLITICAL PRINCIPLES

More than half of the essays emphasized the need for a stronger central government. The Federalist arguments for this were based on the need to preserve liberty while maintaining domestic order, and the essays sought to modify the political ideas of republicanism in light of the lessons of the Revolution. Republican ideology held that the virtue of the people would insure their commitment to the common good, but wartime experience

**MADISON'S DEFINITION OF A FACTION
FROM FEDERALIST PAPER NO. 10**

"By a faction, I understand a number of citizens,
whether amounting to a majority or minority of the
whole, who are united and actuated by some common impulse of passion, or of interest, adverse to
the rights of other citizens, or to the permanent and
aggregate interests of the community."

had convinced the Federalists that people were more
likely to ignore political ideals to pursue selfish ends at
the expense of the public interest.

During the Revolution power had remained in the
hands of Congress and the states. Because state and sectional interests were often in conflict, the United States
had found it difficult to formulate and carry out policy
even in times of crisis. States had refused to contribute
the taxes and troops demanded by Congress, jeopardiz-
ing the war effort. Sectional disputes over the goals
sought in peace negotiations had caused difficulty in settling the treaty with Great Britain. American farmers had
refused to sell grain to their own troops for Continental
paper money, yet sold food to their British enemies for
gold. Without an executive strong enough to carry out
the mandates of Congress, or a mechanism to compel either states or individuals to comply with congressional
decisions, it proved nearly impossible to execute any coherent policy. This was demonstrated again after the war,
when the Confederation government was unable to respond effectively to Spain's closure of the Mississippi
River to American commerce, or to Britain's refusal to
evacuate forts as required by the peace treaty.

The authors of the Federalist Papers explained at
length how the Constitution would remedy these defi-
ciencies. In Federalist No. 26, Hamilton declared that an
energetic government was not the enemy of liberty, but
rather the best means of securing people's rights. For
Hamilton, the energy of this government was centered
in the executive. A strong president, he asserted in Federalist No. 70, is necessary for government to be effective. "A feeble executive implies a feeble execution of the
government," he wrote, and this was equivalent to "a bad
execution; and a government ill executed . . . must be in
practice, a bad government."

Hamilton also refuted claims that because the Constitution granted the federal government direct power over
citizens, it threatened liberty. He noted in Federalist No.
21 that the Confederation's inability to enforce its own
laws was a "striking absurdity." This weakness was a
greater threat to liberty than the power granted to the national government, for the current Confederation government was powerless to intervene if a tyrant should gain
control of a state and oppress the citizens. Furthermore,
Hamilton explained in Federalist No. 31, without the
power to collect taxes, the national government would be
unable to meet even its ordinary financial needs. The Revolution had shown that the states could not be relied upon
to supply requested funds—only the authority to collect
taxes directly from the people could provide the revenues
that were the "essential engine" of effective government.

In a glaring break with republican beliefs, Hamilton
argued in favor of the Constitution's provision for a standing army. The idea that a professional army could be employed to oppress the people was a key element of
republican thought, and the Constitution's creation of a
powerful federal government combined with the possibility of a standing army at its disposal frightened many
Americans; opponents of the Constitution found this to
be a powerful argument against ratification. Hamilton
maintained that a standing army would not be an instrument of tyranny, but instead leave citizens free to pursue
their livelihoods to their benefit and that of the United
States. In Federalist No. 24 he stated that taking people
from their farms and businesses for extended militia service "would be as burdensome and injurious to the public
as ruinous to private citizens." Hamilton dismissed the idea
of the army being used to oppress the people in Federalist No. 26, noting that such a scheme would require the
unlikely collusion of the executive and legislative branches,
while in Federalist No. 27 he stated that there would be
no need to use the army to enforce the laws, as the Constitution granted that power to the federal judiciary.

Another key principle of republican thought invoked
by opponents of the Constitution was the belief, based
on historical examples, that a large republic could not survive for long without falling under the grip of tyranny.
Madison addressed this issue in Federalist No. 10. He
did so by focusing on a fear shared by supporters and opponents of the Constitution, that of faction, which he
defined as "a majority or minority . . . united and actuated by some common impulse of passion, or of interest,
adverse to the rights of other citizens, or to the permanent and aggregate interests of the community." Should
any faction gain power, Americans believed their liberty
would be endangered. Madison conceded that faction
could not be eliminated, only controlled, but that it was
more easily controlled in a large republic than a small
one. A large republic would benefit from a larger electorate as well as from a larger pool of qualified leaders,

both of whom were less likely to fall under the influence of factions. Also, competing regional interests would be better balanced in a geographically large country.

Other key points discussed in the Federalist Papers included the separation of powers, the role of the judiciary, and the limits of federal power. Madison dealt with the first as it related to the division of state and national power in Federalist No. 14, writing that the two-tiered system allowed the federal government to focus on issues of national concern while the states focused on domestic responsibilities, so that the people would be well served in both spheres. In Federalist No. 51 he added that the state and national governments would help preserve liberty by serving as a check upon one another; Madison also noted that the structure of the federal government would protect liberty by distributing power between the executive, legislative, and judicial branches, a point also made in Federalist No. 47. Hamilton addressed the function of the federal judiciary in Federalist No. 78, in which he stated that the primary role of federal judges was to review laws to insure their compatibility with the Constitution. By invalidating laws that conflicted with constitutional principles, judges would uphold the will of the people as expressed by their ratification of the Constitution. Hamilton defended the Constitution's controversial "necessary and proper" clause in Federalist No. 33, declaring that it merely gave the federal government the means to carry out the responsibilities granted to it by the Constitution. The national government itself and the people were, Hamilton, wrote, the final judges of what policies were necessary and proper.

THE FEDERALIST LEGACY

The Federalist Papers had a lasting influence on how Americans have understood the Constitution, and thus on American society and culture. Acting on principles contained in the Federalist Papers regarding the need to control factional domestic unrest, George Washington suppressed the Whiskey Rebellion in 1794, Andrew Jackson demanded South Carolina's compliance with federal tariff laws in 1832, and Abraham Lincoln resisted secession in 1861. The elasticity of federal powers contained in the "necessary and proper" clause has justified a variety of actions, including Thomas Jefferson's 1803 Louisiana Purchase and Franklin Roosevelt's internment of Japanese Americans in World War II. The principle of judicial review proved crucial to the success of the Civil Rights Movement by enforcing the terms of the Fourteenth Amendment. In explaining how the framers intended the Constitution to work, the Federalist Papers have enabled subsequent generations of Americans to better comprehend and apply constitutional principles, and the Federalist Papers remain among those documents that best define American political ideas.

BIBLIOGRAPHY

Carey, George W. *The Federalist: Design for a Constitutional Republic.* Urbana: University of Illinois Press, 1989.

Kramnick, Isaac. "The 'Great National Discussion': The Discourse of Politics in 1787." *William & Mary Quarterly* 45, no. 1 (January 1988): 3–32.

Wright, Benjamin Fletcher, ed. *The Federalist, by Alexander Hamilton, James Madison, and John Jay.* Cambridge, MA: Belknap Press of Harvard University Press, 1961.

Jim Piecuch

See also: **Articles of Confederation; Commonwealth Men; Constitution: Creating a Republic; Declaration of Independence; Shays's and Whiskey Rebellions.**

FEDERALIST PARTY

The Federalist Party, along with the Democratic-Republican Party, was one of the first two political parties in the United States, and hence in the world. It arose in the executive and congressional branches of government during George Washington's first administration (1789–1793) and dominated the government until John Adams's failed bid for reelection to the presidency in 1800. After that, the party never again held the White House, although it continued as a force in Congress until after the War of 1812, and in some states until the 1820s. Its remaining members then joined both the Democratic and Whig parties.

Among leading Federalist figures such as John Adams, Alexander Hamilton, John Jay, and John Marshall, George Washington was the greatest. Although he disdained political parties and disclaimed party loyalty, his policies and inclinations were those of a Federalist. The party's leading men had headed the movement in 1787 for a new, more effective constitution. Yet because their eventual opponents, led by Thomas Jefferson and James Madison, had also backed the constitution and joined the government formed under it, Federalists cannot be considered direct descendants of the pro-constitution group, who were also called "federalists," of the 1780s. The Federalist Party, like its opposition, arose under fresh conditions around fresh issues in the 1790s.

The Federalist Party attracted those who wanted to strengthen national power by establishing a national banking system, protecting American commerce, exercising authority over the states, and employing military might against both domestic and foreign threats. The party's style was generally elitist, and its leaders opposed the spread of political and social democracy. Its centers of power were the commercial northeast, Delaware, parts of Virginia and North Carolina, and South Carolina. But it never appealed to slave-owning plantation owners or small farmers in the South and West. Its policies, ideology, and geographic limitations led to its defeats and demise.

FEDERALIST POLICIES

The party formed around the successful 1790 proposals of Hamilton, the nation's first treasury secretary, that the federal government assume the states' revolutionary war debts, pay those debts at par rather than at their depressed market value, and charter a national bank. Secretary of State Jefferson and Congressman Madison led opposition to the plan. But it was only when the administration ordered troops to quell the Whiskey Rebellion in western Pennsylvania in 1794 and later when Congress debated the ratification and implementation of Jay's treaty with Great Britain in 1795 and 1796 that two political parties took public shape. With Hamilton's leadership, the Federalist Party became champion of a strong national government under executive leadership and judicial oversight, firm links with Britain, opposition to the French Revolution (or at least to a foreign policy that might favor France), and internal order imposed if necessary by military force. The classic statement of the party's philosophy, prepared with Hamilton's help, was Washington's celebrated Farewell Address of 1796 that deplored partisan division and urged avoidance of all permanent alliances with foreign powers (a veiled attack on the 1778 wartime alliance, still in force, with France). Washington's views now became firm party doctrine.

Succeeding Washington as an avowed Federalist in 1797, vice president John Adams became the first person to gain the presidency as a partisan. Adams at first maintained Washington's cabinet and policies. Adams engaged the United States in an undeclared naval war with France, the nation's first external military action since the revolution. Adams also supported the infamous Alien and Sedition acts after congressional Federalists, gaining control of both the House and Senate in the 1798 elections, introduced them. This marked the apogee of Federalist power.

A public storm greeted the Alien and Sedition Acts, which curbed free speech and made immigrants suspect. Also weakening the party, Hamilton's wing attacked Adams's priorities when in 1799 Adams opened negotiations with France to end the quasi war. The Hamiltonians finally broke with Adams when he reorganized his cabinet with men under his own control. Despite these actions, which Adams took in part to shore up his own political position, they were not enough to gain Adams's reelection. Before leaving office, however, he concluded peace with France and secured confirmation in the Senate of John Marshall, his choice for chief justice. While the party never regained the presidency, Marshall's court embedded its principals in constitutional law.

OPPOSITION PARTY

Now in the minority, Federalists at last accepted the need to create a system of state party organizations and democratic electoral tactics to parallel those of the Democratic-Republicans. Even so, they became in effect a sectional minority party whose greatest strength was now found in Massachusetts, Connecticut, and Delaware. By opposing Jefferson's popular 1803 purchase of Louisiana as too costly in funds and dangerous to northern influence in government, the party again lost to Jefferson in 1804.

WAR OF 1812: DEATH OF THE FEDERALIST PARTY

The presidential defeat and Hamilton's death the same year threatened to derail the party permanently. But Jefferson's 1807 embargo on all foreign trade revived it, although the party's candidate, Charles Cotesworth Pinckney, could not defeat Madison for the presidency the next year. Not even Madison's declaration of war against Great Britain in 1812, when Federalists carried New York, New Jersey, and much of Maryland as well as its normal New England strongholds, could help the Federalist Party regain the presidency.

When Federalists followed up their opposition to declaring war with outright obstruction of the war effort, their newfound popularity quickly waned. The Hartford Convention of 1814, unjustly accused of secessionist and treasonous intentions, was a setback from which the party never recovered. Rufus King carried only Massachusetts, Connecticut, and Delaware against James Monroe in 1816.

After that, the party never regained a national following. By 1828 it became the first American political party to die out because it could not adjust to an increasingly democratic national spirit, especially in the nation's towns and cities. And among most Americans, mainly farmers suspicious of government, its policies of strong federal involvement in the economy kept it unpopular. Inconsistency in its stance toward military action (first undertaking a naval war with France, then treating for peace with that same nation, then actively opposing war with Britain) made the Federalist Party's true intentions suspect and laid it open to charges that it was nothing but an opposition party without consistent foreign or military policies of its own and was unwilling to defend the national interest.

Yet the party's contributions to the nation were extraordinary. Its principles were the foundations of the new government. Its leaders defined a national economy, created the judicial system, and gave voice to enduring principles of American foreign policy, chief among them a wariness of involvement in troubles overseas.

BIBLIOGRAPHY

Banner, James M., Jr. *To the Hartford Convention: The Federalists and the Origins of Party Politics in Massachusetts, 1789–1815.* New York: Alfred A. Knopf, 1970.

Ben-Atar, Doron and Oberg, Barbara B., eds. *Federalists Reconsidered.* Charlottesville: University Press of Virginia, 1998.

Elkins, Stanley and McKitrick, Eric. *The Age of Federalism: The Early American Republic, 1788–1800.* New York: Oxford University Press, 1993.

James M. Banner, Jr

See also: **Embargo; Hamilton's Reports; Hartford Convention; Quasi-War and the Rise of Political Parties.**

FLAGS

For hundreds of years, flags have been symbols of national identity all over the world. As a symbol of freedom and democracy, the American flag has been an especially powerful beacon of hope for some people and an unpleasant reminder of American imperialism for others. Besides being flown atop public buildings and in public squares, flags have been wielded by the military, by explorers, and displayed prominently in parades on Memorial Day, Veterans Day, and Independence Day.

The first flag that flew in America was the British Union Jack, a combination of the white St. Andrew's cross and the Red St. George's cross. Another flag in use before the Revolution was the British Red Ensign, which featured a field of red with the Union Jack in the canton (the upper right corner).

The war that broke out in 1775 brought a disdain for what was now the enemy flag. A new Union flag was raised by General George Washington in 1776 and served as the American flag for about a year and a half. It featured red and white stripes and a Union Jack in the canton. Other flag variations were created during the Revolution. In 1776 Colonel Christopher Gadsden presented to the provincial Congress a flag that featured a coiled rattlesnake with the words, "Don't tread on me." The Pine Tree flag featured a pine tree in one quadrant of a red cross on a white field in the canton of a flag with a field of blue. The Moultrie flag, with a white crescent on a field of blue, was flown in Carolina in 1776 (one variety of the Moultrie flag added the word "liberty.")

The Stars and Stripes design was officially approved by Congress in 1777. This successor to the Union flag retained the red and white stripes but replaced the Union Jack with thirteen stars (one for each American colony) in a field of blue. For many years schoolchildren have heard the story of a young seamstress named Betsy Ross who created the Stars and Stripes, but no definitive proof that she did so exists.

In 1794 a new flag was created that replaced the circle of stars with five rows of three stars each and that had fifteen stripes. This flag flew for twenty-three years, until 1818, when the flag was returned to thirteen stripes, and a number of stars that varied according to the number of states in the Union. Since the addition of a star for Hawaii on July 4, 1960, the flag has had fifty stars.

Throughout American history, the flag has taken on extra meaning during wartime, both on the battlefield and on the homefront. After the Revolution, the next time the flag would stir the population was during the War of 1812. In September 1814 an attorney and amateur poet named Francis Scott Key stood on the deck of a ship in the harbor of Baltimore as he watched the bombardment of the American Fort McHenry by the British fleet. After the night of attack, Key observed that the 30-by 42-foot flag that flew over the fort had survived. He wrote a poem called "The Star-Spangled Banner," which was soon published in a local newspaper. In 1931 that poem became the words of our national anthem, set to the tune of an old song. The remains of the inspiring flag are housed in the Smithsonian Institution in Washington, D.C.

During the Civil War (1861–1865), the American flag was again the centerpiece of strong feelings of patriotism. With the secession of the South, the American Stars and Stripes flag was now opposed by an enemy flag, the Stars and Bars of the Confederacy.

Writers took up the flag as an emblem of patriotism. An 1861 poem by Elmer R. Coates called "Awake! Awake!" declared that "the Star-Spangled Banner this moment implores you" to wake up and fight. In an 1861 letter to Kentuckians, Joseph Holt began: "Let us twine each thread of the glorious tissue of our country's flag about our heart strings." The poet Henry Wadsworth Longfellow commemorated a scene in 1862 when "the flag still floated over the main mast-head" of the Union ship *Cumberland* after it was sunk by the *Merrimac*, an ironclad Confederate ship. The poet Oliver Wendell Holmes wrote a Civil War poem called "Union and Liberty" that began, "Flag of the heroes who left us their glory, / Borne through their battle-fields' thunder and flame, / Blazoned in song and illumined in story, / Wave o'er us all who inherit their fame!"

When the United States entered World War I in 1917, the American people once again embraced the symbolism of the flag. A 1917 government advertisement titled "I Wish I Was Old Enough to Fight" featured a

THE STAR SPANGLED BANNER

From 1793 until 1814 the emperor of France, Napoleon Bonaparte, had been waging war against many European countries, including England. Needing more sailors, the British Navy began boarding American ships and taking both British deserters and American sailors to fight for Britain. In June of 1812 the United States declared war on England, beginning what became known as the War of 1812, which lasted for two years. During this time, British forces came ashore in Maryland and burned Washington, including the White House.

On the evening of September 13, 1814, the young lawyer Francis Scott Key was sent as an envoy under the white flag of truce to the British fleet that was anchored in Chesapeake Bay. His job was to negotiate the release of a doctor whom the British had captured. While Key was on board the British man-'o-war, its commander ordered that it fire upon Fort McHenry, in Baltimore, Maryland.

Throughout the night as the bombardment took place, Key watched and wondered about the outcome. By morning it was evident to all from the sight of the tattered American flag flying above Fort McHenry that the Americans had held the fort. Encouraged by the sight and with the tune from a popular British drinking song in mind, Key scribbled down the poem "Defence of Fort M'Henry" while still on the British ship. Later he made a few changes and the poem was first published on September 20, 1814 in the *Baltimore Patriot*.

During the 1890s the ever-more popular tune became the official song of the U.S. Army and Navy, and in 1916 President Woodrow Wilson asked that it be played at official government events. Finally, on March 3, 1931, Congress designated "The Star Spangled Banner" the official anthem of America.

Oh, say, can you see,
By the dawn's early light,
What so proudly we hailed
At the twilight's last gleaming?
Whose broad stripes and bright stars,

Thro' the perilous night,
O'er the ramparts we watch'd
Were so gallantly streaming?
And the rockets' red glare,
The bombs bursting in air,
Gave proof thro'
the night that our flag was still there.
Oh, say, does that star-spangled banner yet wave,
O'er the land of the free and the home of the
brave?

On the shore dimly seen through the mists of the
deep,
Where the foe's haughty host in dread silence re-
poses,
What is that which the breeze, o'er the towering
steep,
As it fitfully blows, half conceals, half discloses?
Now it catches the gleam of the morning's first
beam,
In full glory reflected now shines on the stream.
'Tis the star-spangled banner, oh, long may it wave
O'er the land of the free and the home of the
brave.

And where is the band that so vauntingly swore
That the havoc of war and the battle's confusion,
A home and a country shall leave us no more?
Their blood was washed out their foul footsteps's
pollution.
No refuge could save the hireling and slave,
From the terror of death and the gloom of the
grave.
And the star-spangled banner in triumph doth wave
O'er the land of the free and the home of the
brave.

Oh, thus be it ever when freemen shall stand
Between their loved homes and the war's desola-
tion;
Blessed with vic'try and peace, may the heaven-
rescued land
Praise the power that hath made and preserved us
a nation.
Then conquer we must, for our cause it is just,
And this be our motto: "In God do we trust."
And the star-spangled banner in triumph shall wave
O'er the land of the free and the home of the
brave.

young boy, who was visiting his older brother at an army camp, saying: "The band began to play 'The Star-Spangled Banner' and the Color Sergeant and the Color Guard hauled down the Big Beautiful Flag, and there was a lump in my throat, but I didn't want to cry."

During World War II, a bloody battle took place between the Americans and the Japanese for control of Iwo Jima, a barren South Pacific island. When Americans finally reached the summit of the chief mountain on the island in February 1945, they raised the flag, and the

The "Star-Spangled Banner" that inspired Francis Scott Key's poem, in 1874. It was moved to the Smithsonian Institute in 1907. © BETTMANN/CORBIS

moment was captured in a famous photograph showing six Marines holding the flag at an angle as they positioned it into the ground. The bronze sculpture based on that photograph stands in Arlington National Cemetery and features a cloth flag—one of the nation's most powerful uses of the flag as an emblem of patriotism.

Perhaps the most auspicious moment for the American flag was when astronauts Neil Armstrong and Buzz Aldrin landed on the moon in July 1969. After stepping out of the lunar module, they planted the flag into the dusty soil, in effect claiming the moon for the United States. A photo of Aldrin, standing next to the crisp and bright flag, captures the ideals of a generation and marks the end of one aspect of the Cold War—the space race between the Soviet Union and the United States.

After September 11, 2001, the American flag again took on a deep meaning. A much-publicized American flag flew at Ground Zero, the site of the destroyed World Trade Center. As the United States went to war on terrorism, flag sales soared. The flag is a symbol of unity and patriotism as well as American cultural identity. Wars have helped to shape that identity, and the flag has come to represent the sacrifice of men and women in defending the nation and upholding its most cherished values.

BIBLIOGRAPHY

Adams, John Winthrop, ed. *Stars and Stripes Forever: The History of Our Flag*. New York: Smithmark Publishers, 1992.

Quaife, Milo M.; Weig, Melvin J.; and Appleman, Roy E. *The History of the United States Flag: From the Revolution to the Present, Including a Guide to Its Use and Display*. New York: Harper and Row, 1961.

Sedeen, Margaret. *Star-Spangled Banner: Our Nation and Its Flag*. Washington, DC: National Geographic Society, 2002.

Thornhill, Thomas E. *Flags Over Carolina*. Charleston, SC: Provost Press, 1975.

Williams, Earl P., Jr. *What You Should Know About the American Flag*. Lanham, MD: Maryland Historical Press, 1987.

Richard Panchyk

See also: Bunker Hill Monument; Lafayette's Tour; Memorials and Monuments; Montgomery, Richard; Valley Forge.

FORT WILLIAM HENRY MASSACRE, CULTURAL LEGACY

Writers, artists, and filmmakers have made the 1757 siege of Fort William Henry into a cultural icon, imprinting their visions of that event on American society, culture, and identity. The portrayals of the siege and subsequent massacre illustrate how the events in a war can take on a larger meaning in the nation's history and consciousness.

During the French and Indian War, two English forts were of particular interest to the French. Fort Edward, along New York's Hudson River, and Fort William Henry, on Lake George in the Adirondack Mountains, were about twenty miles from each other. In early 1757 the French, under the command of General Louis-Joseph de Montcalm, were preparing to attack Fort William Henry. Lieutenant Colonel George Monro, commander of the fort, had only 2,000 men under his command within it. On the French side, there were 8,000 soldiers and hundreds of Indians, among them Huron, Algonkin, Seneca, Cayuga, Ottowa, Chippewa, Delaware, and Shawnee. Monro sent word to Major General Daniel Webb at Fort Edward that reinforcements were needed. Webb decided against sending any men, but his messenger was intercepted by General Montcalm's soldiers.

The attack began with cannon and mortar on August 7. Inside the fort, where many were sick with smallpox, women and children were hidden in the safest part. The French sent a truce flag and an officer asking Monro to surrender the fort. Learning that no reinforcements were on the way, Monro agreed to surrender. Terms of the surrender included safe passage to Fort Edward, but the Indians defied Montcalm's orders and killed hundreds. When Montcalm finally put a stop to the slaughter, the Indians were upset that they could not take further revenge on their British enemies.

In the nineteenth century, the attack and massacre became part of American myth. Perhaps the most famous story of the attack is James Fenimore Cooper's historical novel, *The Last of the Mohicans* (1826). The hero of the novel is a woodsman named Hawkeye, who was raised as a Mohawk and shares many adventures with his friends, the Mohican chief Chingachgook and his son Uncas. The battle and surrender of the fort serve as the backdrop to an adventure story of both historical and fictional characters.

In the novel, a group of British, including General Monro's daughters, Alice and Cora, are being escorted from Fort Edward to Fort William Henry by a British major and an Indian scout, Le Renard Subtil. In the woods they meet Hawkeye, Chingachgook, and Uncas. Hawkeye and the Mohicans help the party escape an ambush planned by the scheming Le Renard. After another attack by Le Renard and his men, the British party is captured. Le Renard wants Cora to become his bride as revenge against Monro; then, he says, he will free the others. She refuses. Hawkeye and the Mohicans rescue Cora and the rest of the party and lead them to Fort William Henry just as the attack on the fort is beginning. After the surrender of the fort, Le Renard captures

Montcalm trying to stop the Fort William Henry Massacre. THE LIBRARY OF CONGRESS

Alice and Cora. With Heyward and Monro, Hawkeye and the Mohicans plan a daring rescue. Le Renard takes Cora as his wife, but she is killed by another Indian before the rescue takes place.

Cooper's story was the basis for several movies. The 1992 film directed by Michael Mann dramatically captures the events leading up to Fort William Henry's capture. It also creates a love affair between Hawkeye, played by Daniel Day-Lewis, and Alice. In this telling of the story, Cora kills herself rather than live as an Indian bride.

The Fort William Henry massacre has also given inspiration to painters. Thomas Cole (1801–1848), the founder of the Hudson River School style of painting, depicted several scenes from Cooper's book, using the Hudson River Valley as his backdrop. The human figures in the paintings are more like bit players on the grand stage of nature. One 1827 canvas depicts a tense scene of Indians standing in a circle on a mountain ledge. The events have been subsumed by the grandeur of the landscape. In Cole's vision, our cultural impression of the French and Indian War and of Indians in general is intricately connected with nature. The woods are a myste-

rious place where the white man is a novice and the Indian is at home.

The Fort William Henry massacre, and the events leading up to it, has shaped cultural attitudes toward Indians in conflicting ways. Cooper's novel refers to the dangerous "savages" and shows their willingness to kill. The book creates a lasting impression of the untrustworthiness and dangerousness of Indians in general. Time and again since the early nineteenth century, Indians have been portrayed as revenge-seeking troublemakers looking to scalp their enemies.

Yet *The Last of the Mohicans* also highlights the friendship between Hawkeye and Chingachgook. At the close of the novel, the two woodsmen grasp hands as Hawkeye proclaims that the Indian is not alone. Despite their different skin colors, Hawkeye says, God put white men and Indians on the same path. This sense of common ground has also found expression in American culture.

The Fort William Henry massacre, and artists' interpretations of it, helped shape Americans' view of themselves as a heroic and honorable people. On the other side of that pride are conflicting feelings toward

Indians, who both helped and hindered the newcomers to the land.

BIBLIOGRAPHY

Eckert, Allan W. *Wilderness Empire: A Narrative.* Boston: Little, Brown, 1969.

Hamilton, Edward P. *The French and Indian Wars: The Story of Battles and Forts in the Wilderness.* New York: Doubleday, 1962.

Yaeger, Bert D. *The Hudson River School: American Landscape Artists.* New York: Smithmark Publishers, 1996.

Richard Panchyk and Caren Prommersberger

See also: **Cooper, James Fenimore; Memory and Early Histories of the Revolution; Spy, The: First American War Novel.**

FOURTH OF JULY

"The Second Day of July 1776," John Adams wrote to his wife Abigail, "will be the most memorable Epocha [fixed moment] in the History of America . . . it will be celebrated . . . as the great anniversary Festival." Perhaps only John Adams realized that delegates to the Continental Congress had given birth to the modern national holiday, which came to be celebrated on the fourth, when the Declaration of Independence was approved. The day, he told Abigail, "ought to be commemorated, as the Day of Deliverance. . . It ought to be solemnized with Pomp and Parade."

The Fourth of July provided a rallying point for revolutionary fervor throughout the war. The Continental Army celebrated by firing salutes, distributing extra rum, and pardoning prisoners. Holiday rituals included bell ringing, thirteen-gun salutes, fireworks, military parades, oratory, sermons, dinners, and toasting. A consensus emerged on these rituals and the national symbols of the Declaration of Independence, George Washington, and the flag. Despite this symbolic consensus, conflicts marked celebrations of the Fourth from the start. During the war revolutionary leaders downplayed the fact that a significant number of Americans were Loyalists, while rank-and-file patriots marked and publicly punished Loyalists by breaking their windows on the Fourth.

Conflicts over the meaning of the Fourth and the nation continued after the war. Federalists and anti-Federalists used the Fourth to legitimize their causes during the contest over ratification of the Constitution. Federalists suggested that the Constitution was the fulfillment of the Revolution by holding ratification processions on July 4, 1788. Anti-Federalists countered with

Fourth of July fireworks at the Washington Monument in Washington, D.C. AP/WIDE WORLD PHOTOS

rituals and oratory opposing ratification, going so far as to burn a copy of the Constitution in Albany, New York.

CREATING NATIONAL IDENTITY: CONSENSUS AND CONFLICT

By the late eighteenth century, Fourth of July celebrations contained four standard features: (1) the oration and the reading of the Declaration of Independence; (2) a military parade and drill; (3) dinners and toasting; and (4) fireworks and illuminations. The oration was the centerpiece of the celebration and taught the lessons of the Revolution. Speakers proclaimed that Americans were by nature a liberty-loving people, which was why they had risen up against England's tyranny. Because power resided with the people, orators continued, Americans must be both virtuous and vigilant to preserve their liberties. Finally, they asserted that unity was essential to the nation's continued independence and lauded the Declaration of Independence and the Constitution as symbols and guarantors of that union.

Despite calls for unity, underlying divisions over the nature of the republic continued to flare up on Independence Day. By the mid-1790s Federalists and Republicans were holding separate celebrations in Boston, New

York, and other cities, with each party proclaiming itself the true heir of the Revolution. Republicans rallied for the French Revolution, comparing it to America's own, whereas Federalists condemned its anarchy. Both parties lauded the Constitution as the guarantor of independence, but Republicans read the Declaration of Independence at their exercises, whereas Federalists preferred to keep it and its potentially radical implications well in the past. Each party annually berated the other as an illegitimate faction seeking to undermine the republic. Although both paid tribute to George Washington, Republicans in the 1790s attacked his and Adams's administrations; once the Republicans took over the presidency in 1801, Federalists used the Fourth to assail Thomas Jefferson's administration.

Rather than leading to renewed unity, the War of 1812 intensified these partisan divisions. Republicans used the Fourth to rally support for the war, proclaiming that its causes were the same as those of the Revolution, whereas Federalists condemned the war and James Madison's administration. After the War of 1812, partisan ferocity declined along with the Federalist party, but politically divisive Fourths reemerged in the antebellum era with rising tensions over slavery.

SLAVERY AND ABOLITION

African Americans faced harassment from whites on the Fourth. Some refused to observe the day in protest of its hypocrisy, while others organized separate exercises to agitate for emancipation and point out the incongruity of slavery in the land of liberty. Abolitionists turned the Fourth into a pointed attack on America's fall from the promise of 1776. In an 1852 address, the abolitionist and writer Frederick Douglass denounced the holiday as a cruel joke to African Americans and asserted that they could not celebrate it until they were free. On another Fourth, the more radical abolitionist William Lloyd Garrison burned a copy of the Constitution to protest its acceptance of slavery.

Although abolitionists attacked the Constitution on the Fourth, white Southerners embraced its protection of slavery. During the Civil War, however, Southerners returned to the Declaration of Independence to support secession, which they heralded as the completion of the Revolution. Northerners, in contrast, used wartime Fourth of July celebrations to proclaim unity and loyalty to the republic and its Constitution. During Reconstruction white Southerners refused to commemorate the Fourth, whereas African Americans celebrated it and their newly won independence vigorously.

PATRIOTISM

Since the Civil War, the Fourth of July has continued to serve as a periodic rallying cry for Americans at war. During the war against Filipino insurgents at the turn of the century, pro- and anti-imperialists promoted their respective causes in holiday oratory. In 1915 more than a hundred towns celebrated the Fourth as National Americanization Day. In response to pressure to demonstrate their patriotism during World War I, immigrant leaders worked with the Committee on Public Information to make the 1918 Fourth of July a showcase of loyalty. In World War II as well, the Fourth was an occasion to demonstrate patriotism. Congress even created a new citizenship holiday, dubbed "I Am an American Day." During the Cold War (1946–1991), Fourth of July orators often propounded on American freedom and denounced communism. During the Vietnam War (1965–1973), pro- and antiwar forces agitated.

Today naturalization ceremonies remain a feature of the Fourth, with the most symbolic at Monticello, Thomas Jefferson's home in Virginia. In the aftermath of the terrorist attacks on September 11, 2001, the Fourth again became a rallying point, this time for the war on terrorism. Although picnics, family reunions, fireworks displays, and sporting events are popular ways to celebrate the contemporary Fourth, the holiday clearly retains the potential to revive revolutionary passions and renew patriotic values.

BIBLIOGRAPHY

Appelbaum, Diana Karter. *The Glorious Fourth: An American Holiday, an American History.* New York: Facts on File, 1989.

Dennis, Matthew. *Red, White, and Blue Letter Days: An American Calendar.* Ithaca, NY: Cornell University Press, 2002.

Litwicki, Ellen M. *America's Public Holidays, 1865–1920.* Washington, DC: Smithsonian Institution Press, 2000.

Newman, Simon P. *Parades and the Politics of the Street: Festive Culture in the Early American Republic.* Philadelphia: University of Pennsylvania Press, 1997.

O'Leary, Cecilia Elizabeth. *To Die For: The Paradox of American Patriotism.* Princeton, NJ: Princeton University Press, 1999.

Sweet, Leonard I. "The Fourth of July and Black Americans in the Nineteenth Century: Northern Leadership Opinion within the Context of Black Experience." *Journal of Negro History* 61 (July 1976): 256–275.

Travers, Len. *Celebrating the Fourth: Independence Day and the Rites of Nationalism in the Early Republic.* Amherst: University of Massachusetts Press, 1997.

Waldstreicher, David. *In the Midst of Perpetual Fetes: The Making of American Nationalism, 1776–1820.* Chapel Hill: University of North Carolina Press for the Omohundro Institute of Early American History and Culture, 1997.

Ellen M. Litwicki

See also: Bunker Hill Monument; Lafayette's Tour; Valley Forge.

FRANKLIN, BENJAMIN

(b. January 17, 1706; d. April 17, 1790) Printer and publisher, scientist and inventor, ambassador and statesman, politician.

Benjamin Franklin's impact on America's independence movement and its aftermath cannot be overstated. Franklin fled Boston, the city of his birth, at age seventeen. In Philadelphia, after many false starts, he set up a flourishing printer's shop on Market Street and married Deborah Read, retiring at age forty-two. With his son William, he conducted his famous kite experiment demonstrating the connection between lightning and electricity, which immediately garnered him international fame as a scientist. He also began his political career by winning a seat as Philadelphia's representative to the Pennsylvania legislature. He organized the colony's militia at the beginning of King George's War, presented his abortive "Plan of Union" to the Albany Conference in 1754, and spearheaded the drive for Pennsylvania to become a royal colony. The effort to throw off the proprietary yoke of the Penn family brought Franklin to England in 1757 and again in 1764. He remained there until 1775, when it became clear to him that the destiny of the colonies lay in independence.

At the age of seventy, Benjamin Franklin was one of America's most vociferous supporters of independence even though he had once been a staunch defender of the monarchy. A true "empire man," Franklin was proud of his heritage and had been eager to serve the Crown. He helped his son obtain an appointment as New Jersey's royal governor, and sought a Crown appointment for himself. While he was convinced that England would one day need the vast and wealthy colonies more than the colonies would need England, he did not imagine that America would be impelled to sever its connection to the mother country. During the Stamp Act crisis of 1765, Franklin was temporarily caught off guard by the violent reaction in the colonies to parliamentary taxation. If he was slow to recognize the implications of the Stamp Act, he quickly landed on his feet, and worked to persuade the new Rockingham ministry to repeal the legislation in 1766.

He still continued to occupy the middle ground. He became the colonial agent for New Jersey, Georgia, and Massachusetts, representing American interests in London, and explaining England's unpopular decisions to the colonies. But each parliamentary effort to tax the colonies and to place Americans in a subordinate position alienated him a little more. With the crisis engendered by the Boston Tea Party in 1773, Franklin determined that the chances for the imperial unity for which he had fought no longer existed.

In 1775, Franklin returned home a widower, determined to represent Pennsylvania in the second Continental Congress, and to persuade his reluctant compatriots to sever their ties to England. His son, William, opposed independence. No patriot would have blamed Franklin had he decided merely to retire from public affairs. Instead, he became an indefatigable member of the "radical" contingent of rebellious Americans. Franklin was one of five men appointed by the Continental Congress to write what became known as the Declaration of Independence. If Thomas Jefferson was the scribe, Franklin was the diplomat, soothing the ruffled egos of the contentious committee members.

With independence declared and the war against England begun in earnest, Franklin once more embarked for Europe, serving as the Continental Congress's ambassador to the court of Louis XVI. If it is true that America could not have defeated England without French aid, it is possible that such assistance would not have materialized without Franklin's efforts. He was not America's only representative in France, of course. Silas Deane, John Adams, and Arthur Lee did their part, but none of these men were as successful as Franklin. He

Benjamin Franklin in a painting by Joseph Duplesses.
THE LIBRARY OF CONGRESS

used his fame as the man who brought the lightning from the skies to become a court favorite. He catered to the French, appealing to their hardheaded desire to humiliate the English and to their romantic fascination with "republican America." While he was often exasperated by his fellow ambassadors (and they by him), he controlled his anger. After the news of America's victory at Saratoga, he persuaded the French to enter the war on the side of the former colonies.

Franklin remained in France until the war's end. After Yorktown, he, John Jay, and John Adams sat down with the British to discuss the terms for peace. With the Peace of Paris ratified in 1783, Franklin finally returned home.

Even then, he continued to serve his country. At the age of eighty-one, he was America's oldest delegate to the Constitutional Convention, which met in Philadelphia in 1787. While his substantive contributions to the body were few, he constantly drew the delegates' attention to the "republican" principles of 1776. His colleagues usually rejected his suggestions, but few could simply ignore the words of a man who had helped launch America's existence as an independent nation. After his death, Franklin, the Legendary Revolutionary, soon became an icon that symbolized the genius of the new American society.

BIBLIOGRAPHY

Lopez, Claude Anne, and Herbert, Eugenia W. *The Private Franklin: The Man and His Family.* New York: Norton, 1975.

Middlekauff, Robert. *Benjamin Franklin and His Enemies.* Berkeley: University of California Press, 1996.

Morgan, Edmund Sears. *Benjamin Franklin.* New Haven, CT: Yale University Press, 2002.

Newcomb, Benjamin H. *Franklin and Galloway: A Political Partnership.* New Haven, CT: Yale University Press, 1972.

Van Doren, Carl. *Benjamin Franklin.* New York: Viking Press, 1938.

Wright, Esmond. *Franklin of Philadelphia.* Cambridge, MA: Harvard University Press, 1986.

Sheila L. Skemp

See also: Adams, John; Jefferson, Thomas; Madison, James; Monroe, James; Peace of Paris 1763; Sons of Liberty; Washington, George.

FRENCH AND INDIAN WAR, LEGACY OF

The French and Indian War, or Seven Years' War as it is termed in Europe, began in North America in 1754 when George Washington's forces clashed with the French in western Pennsylvania (war was not formally declared between Britain and France until May 1756), and ended in 1763 with the Treaty of Paris, although major hostilities in North America ceased with the British capture of Canada in 1760.

CAUSES AND COURSE OF THE WAR

The causes of the war lay in both global and regional issues. Britain and France had conflicting colonial claims, particularly in North America, and especially in the upper Ohio Valley. When Pennsylvania traders and Virginia land-speculators began to take an interest in the region in the late 1740s, the French began construction of a series of forts from which they could exclude British influence. Virginia responded by dispatching an expedition commanded by the inexperienced George Washington. However, the French surrounded and captured Washington's expedition at Fort Necessity. London now dispatched an entire army commanded by Major General Edward Braddock. When this force was routed at the Battle of the Monongahela in July 1755, a full-scale war began.

The early years of the war saw the British colonies suffering a series of defeats. The important forts of Oswego and Fort William Henry surrendered to the French in August 1756 and August 1757 respectively, while Indian raiders devastated the frontier from New England to the Carolinas, killing or capturing several thousand colonists. However, in 1758 the fortunes of war began to change. In London, a new administration headed by William Pitt determined to use Britain's financial power to destroy the French Empire. Pitt was prepared to fund a massive war effort and to reimburse the colonies for any expenses incurred. He committed over 20,000 regular troops to North America while over 14,000 seamen were engaged in American waters. Britain's power soon began to tell. In 1758 British troops, assisted by colonial forces, captured Fort Duquesne on the Ohio and the strategic French fortress of Louisbourg in Acadia. Then in 1759 the British seized Quebec, the capital of French Canada. In 1760 the remaining French forces in Canada surrendered and the war in North America was essentially concluded.

ECONOMIC IMPACT OF THE WAR

In the early stages of the war, the effects of frontier raids and the thousands of refugees disrupted the colonial economies. Fierce fighting also left a legacy of widows and orphans, particularly in New England, who were forced to seek poor relief. Trade was badly depressed as the British imposed a series of embargoes on traffic to enemy and neutral ports. Once out of port, merchant vessels fell prey to French warships and privateers. Insurance rates increased while trade slumped. By 1757 the legacy of refugees, widows and disrupted trade fuelled widespread discontent with the progress of the war.

However, from 1757 onwards, the increased demands of the British and provincial armies for provisions, demands from the Royal Navy for supplies, and the increased flow of funds from Britain to pay American soldiers more than compensated the negative economic effects. The provincial economies went into a boom. In addition, as the Royal Navy swept French ships from the seas, trade resumed and soon many colonial merchants were able to make illegal, but lucrative, profits by shipping grain and other foodstuffs to the all but starving French colonies in the West Indies. New economic opportunities also opened up for provincial merchants, particularly in New York, to build and fund their own privateers to plunder French commerce and over 200 privateers took to the seas during the war.

TERRITORIAL AND STRATEGIC LEGACY OF THE WAR

At the conclusion of the war at the Treaty of Paris in 1763, the most obvious legacy was the removal of the French presence in North America. For 150 years the French had threatened the security, indeed the very existence, of the British North American colonies. Now the French were gone and the colonies had a degree of security that had been unthinkable previously. Indeed, it is highly unlikely that the colonists would have felt secure enough to challenge the British Empire in the 1770s had the French threat remained. In addition, the British gained a vast swathe of territory from the Appalachians to the Mississippi River. The future of this territory was to pose a major problem for British policy makers.

The frontier raids had also demonstrated the ability of the Indians to devastate the colonial frontier at will. For British policy-makers prevention of any future war, and its associated costs, was a central theme of western policy after the war. Consequently, the British sought to separate colonists and Indians by defining a clear boundary to the colonies. This policy was formally recognized in the Royal Proclamation of 1763, which forbade all settlement across the Appalachians. However, colonists felt that much of their blood had been shed in an attempt to protect their homes from Indian raiders and that western lands were their deserved reward. From 1763 onwards, colonists viewed both British and Indians with increasing anger which sometimes boiled over into violence, as in December 1763 in Lancaster County, Pennsylvania, when a band of frontiersmen calling themselves the Paxton Boys massacred a band of Conestoga Indians.

RELATIONS WITH GREAT BRITAIN

For the British, another legacy of the war was a debt of 137 million pounds. Following the peace, the British sought every means possible to reduce the debt by reducing government expenditures and increasing income. Since a principal item of expenditure was the cost of garrisoning the newly conquered territories in North America, London did not see why the American colonists should object to paying a share of these costs. Such a policy led directly to the revenue acts of the 1760s, most infamously the Stamp Act of 1765, and the resulting political crisis.

The political legacy of the war extended far beyond the simple issue of taxation. The failure of the provincial governments during the war to halt smuggling, to raise troops, to provide quarters for British troops or to provide adequate funds or supplies, all suggested that government of the colonies, which had previously been all but neglected by London, needed much closer supervision. Colonial affairs now received more attention in London and the British began to strengthen colonial administration, such as giving governors greater powers and removing some trials from civil courts. All these reforms generated substantial resentment in the colonies. The presence of British troops also became a major political issue, particularly as the British began to abandon western posts, because of their high costs, and instead garrison troops in port towns such as Boston. Finally, the war also strengthened the powers of the colonial assemblies who found themselves responsible for raising armies and supplying provisions to British and provincial armies. These wartime responsibilities greatly expanded the scope and activity of the colonial assemblies.

IMPACT ON COLONIAL IDENTITY

The war had seemingly conflicting effects on colonists' perception of their identity. Colonists took great pride in the British victory, and as the war closed, viewed themselves more than ever as Britons. As such they demanded the full political rights of Englishmen, and these demands would provide the fuel for the coming Revolutionary conflict. But the war had also highlighted differences between the colonies and Britain. The presence of British troops in the colonies, and the service of many thousands of colonists alongside them, had highlighted the differences between the profanity and debauchery of the British rank and file and the morality and sobriety of the American troops. British officers had demonstrated their disdain not only for the rank and file, but also for members of the American elite and for the colonial assemblies. The experience of war thus created a clear sense of the differences between colonists and Britons.

The war also helped colonists to define American identity in other ways. The struggle with the Catholic French and "heathen" Indians was often viewed with strong religious overtones. The colonies had suffered terrible defeats and hardship; they had been brought to the

Death of General Wolfe, **by Benjamin West, depicting the death of the British general during the French and Indian War.** GETTY IMAGES

edge of defeat, but they had emerged victorious. Many colonists, particularly in New England, perceived in this rescue from disaster the hand of God. This led to the rise of "civil millennialism" that increasingly stressed America's unique position in the world. The war also led to a new perception of America's role in the world and a confidence in America's future as colonists noted the implications of America's expansion into the west. Benjamin Franklin, in particular, noted how the acquisition of western territory would ensure that America would soon become greater in power and population than Britain.

The French and Indian War succeeded in providing security for the American colonies. More importantly, it contributed to the identity of the American colonists, especially the view that they had a unique and divine role to play in the world. Between 1763 and 1776, the difference between the American and British cultures contributed to the conflict between colonists and British authorities over the imperial policies, and to the decision in 1776 to seek independence rather than reconciliation with England.

BIBLIOGRAPHY

Anderson, Fred. *Crucible of War: The Seven Years' War and the Fate of Empire in British North America, 1754–1766.* New York: Knopf, 2000.

Leach, Douglas Edward. *Arms for Empire: A Military History of the British Colonies in North America, 1607–1763.* New York: MacMillan, 1973.

Lenman, Bruce. *Britain's Colonial Wars, 1688–1783.* Harlow, UK: Longman, 2001.

Middleton, Richard. *The Bells of Victory: The Pitt-Newcastle Ministry and the Conduct of the Seven Years' War, 1757–1762.* Cambridge, UK: Cambridge University Press, 1985.

Nash, Gary B. *The Urban Crucible: The Northern Seaports and the Origins of the American Revolution.* Cambridge, MA: Harvard University Press, 1986.

Rogers, Alan. *Empire and Liberty: American Resistance to British Authority, 1755–1763.* Berkeley: University of California Press, 1974.

Steele, Ian K. *Warpaths: Invasions of North America.* Oxford: Oxford University Press, 1994.

Trask, Kerry. *In the Pursuit of Shadows: Massachusetts Millennialism and the Seven Years War.* New York: Garland, 1989.

Ward, Matthew C. *Breaking the Backcountry: The Seven Years' War in Virginia and Pennsylvania, 1754–1765*. Pittsburgh, PA: University of Pittsburgh Press, 2003.

Matthew C. Ward

See also: Fort William Henry Massacre, Cultural Legacy; Mobilization: French and Indian War; Peace of Paris, 1763; Stamp Act Congress; Washington, George.

GALLOWAY, GRACE: DIARY OF A LOYALIST

The experiences of Grace Growden Galloway (1727–1782) illustrate the challenges Loyalists faced when they remained in the colonies during the American Revolution. Her wartime diary, kept in Philadelphia from 1778 until 1781, reveals how the absence of male family members and the hardships of military conflict transformed women's daily lives. For Galloway, American independence meant poverty, abandonment, loss of social precedence, and the devastating disappearance of the prewar world she had known.

Galloway's father, Lawrence Growden, was a prominent businessman, landowner, and politician with considerable influence in Pennsylvania. In 1753 she married Joseph Galloway, a successful lawyer, who converted to Anglicanism from Quakerism in order to marry her. Galloway's earliest writings convey the turbulence of her marriage, as in these lines from a poem: "never get Tyed to a Man / for when once you are yoked / Tis all a Mere Joke / of seeing your freedom again." On another occasion she wrote that she had been "turn'd to that heavy lifeless lump of a wife" (as quoted in Norton, p. 45).

The Galloways adopted Loyalist opinions in the early 1770s. In 1777 Lord Howe appointed Joseph Galloway civil commissioner of Philadelphia while the British occupied the city. After the British retreated to New York, Joseph Galloway and the couple's only surviving child, Betsey, sailed for London in October 1778. Galloway stayed behind, like many Loyalist wives, because she and her husband assumed that the British would prevail. All she needed to do in her family's absence was retain control of their property and business interests. Her initial diary entries after his departure show her frustration in this endeavor: "It seems," she wrote on August 13, 1779, "as if ye world was in league against us."

Although Galloway relied initially on her husband's friends and business partners for advice, after Revolutionaries confiscated her house in September 1778 she pursued a campaign to protect her dower properties for her daughter on her own. This property, which she had inherited from her father, included five estates in Pennsylvania and Delaware totaling over 1,800 acres and a 30 percent share in the Durham Iron Works. Pennsylvania authorities eventually ruled that she could not control land she inherited from her father until after her husband's death. Only after Joseph's death in 1803 was Betsey able to inherit.

EXCERPT FROM THE DIARY OF GRACE GROWDEN GALLOWAY, PHILADELPHIA, JULY 1778

Thursday y⁰ 9. Thomas Stackhouse he paid Me thirty pounds Israel Pemberton he advised Me to see Lawers [lawyers?] as the men were nominated to seize our estate; sent for Lewise gave him ten guineas . . . he promised to Consult Abel James & Mr. Chew [Benjamin Chew, the last chief-justice under the proprietors] to see if I cou'd have dower.

Friday y⁰ 10th. Jones girls here in ye afternoon & told me 12 french ships of ye line was gone for New York & I was quite Mad with How[e] for betraying us to the provincials as it was in his power to have settled ye affair . . . Mr Chew here at Night . . . he do[es] not seem so kind as at first; & told me he cou&d not come often as he was afraid . . .

Saturday y⁰ 11th. Nurse at y⁰ generals [likely General Cadwalader] all day . . . they had a Turtle . . . sent me some soop. Chew girls here at Night told me the Roebuck was taken [British ship H.M.S. *Roebuck* was driven ashore on July 14, 1778 and deserted by the crew]; they boast of the kindness of english officers & I was very low & mad to think we that are ruin'd by them was the least noticed . . . everything wears a gloomy appearance . . . am quite low.

Sunday y⁰ 12th. was very unwell in ye morn & the french Ambassadore came this day . . . I look'd out & saw the Cannon & soldiers & I thought it was like the execution of my husband & turn'd away determine'd to see no more of it but Nancy Clifton came & I went down to her & she told me the Roebuck was not taken which raised my spirits & I look out & saw ye Contemptable [sic] sight . . . there was eighty two Men drawn Up before the generals & our house on ye opposeite side of the street, Under arms & general Cadwallader & Mr Morrise with some of ye Aid de Camps came with them . . .

Tusday y⁰ 21st. was in very good spirits . . . Sucky Jones came in ye morn to tell me the Men [agents entrusted with the disposal of confiscated estates] was at Shoemakers yesterday [Samuel Shoemaker had supported the British cause and he was attainted, like Galloway, and his estates confiscated]: Mrs Jones here & about 2o'clock they came—one smith[,] a hatter & Col Will & one Shriner & a Dutch Man I know not his Name . . . they took an inventory of everything even to broken China & empty bottles. . . . I had such spirits that I appear'd Not Uneasy . . . they told Me they must advertise the house. I told them they may do as they pleased but till it was decided by a Court I wou'd not go out Unless by ye force of a bayonet but when I knew who had a right to it I should know how to Act; . . .

[SOURCE: *Diary of Grace Growden Galloway*, New York: Arno Press, 1971, pp. 38–41.]

Galloway worried over the fate of her daughter and husband, from whom she received letters infrequently. Correspondence she received from them on May 4, 1779, left her feeling "more easey as I hope from what they write we shall not sink & they are well & happy." Galloway also feared the potential for violence against Loyalists. One night she "awoke early in a fright Dreamed I was going to be hang'd." The earlier hanging of Loyalist George Spangler must have made an impression on her.

Although Galloway socialized daily with an extensive network of female friends, she confided her fear and isolation to her diary. After she was evicted from her house, she boarded with Quaker Deborah Morris. While she lived with "dear Debby," a steady stream of visitors came to take tea with the two women, although these visits were not always to Galloway's liking. During one visit Galloway and an acquaintance "had a Dispute" over whether Britain or America was better. "We got at last very ernest & hated each other freely." Politics and war invaded women's social gatherings and tested Galloway's Loyalist sympathies.

Galloway found her material circumstances altered by the war. She had to make arrangements for basic daily needs with devalued Continental currency. She described the arduous process of purchasing firewood, salt, cider, and other necessities. Galloway resented other changes too, writing late in 1778 that "My dear child came into My Mind & what she wou'd say to see her Momma walking 5 squares in the rain at Night like a common Woman & go to rooms in an Alley for her home."

Galloway was not alone in her struggles. Many Loyalist wives stayed in the colonies to protect property;

sometimes their husbands abandoned them when they resettled in Canada or Great Britain, as Joseph Galloway seemed to have done, as Linda Kerber noted in *Women of the Republic*. As it became clear there was little hope of acquiring title to their American properties, Galloway wrote: "I am Determin'd to go from this wicked place as soon as I hear from JG [Joseph Galloway] & Not by My own impatience put it out of my power to leave this Sodom...." But she received no instructions from her husband. Her poor health and precarious financial situation frustrated her in the final months of her diary: "all is Cloudy & I am wrap[p]ed in impenetrable Darkness will it Can it ever be removed & shall I once More belong to somebody for Now I am like a pelican in y⁰ Desert."

Galloway died in Philadelphia in February 1782. Although histories of the American Revolution commonly celebrate the victors and sacrifices of patriots, Grace Galloway's diary reminds us that a large number of Americans paid a terrible price, especially wives of Tories, for opposing America's War for Independence.

BIBLIOGRAPHY

Evans, Elizabeth. *Weathering the Storm: Women of the American Revolution.* New York: Scribners, 1975.

Kerber, Linda K. *Women of the Republic: Intellect and Ideology in Revolutionary America.* Chapel Hill: University of North Carolina Press, 1980.

Norton, Mary Beth. *Liberty's Daughters: The Revolutionary Experience of American Women, 1750–1800.* Boston: Little, Brown, 1980.

Werner, Raymond C., ed. *The Diary of Grace Growden Galloway.* New York: Arno Press, 1971.

Rebecca Goetz

See also: Brown, Charlotte: Diary of a Nurse; Camp Followers: War and Women; Families at War; Sampson, Deborah; Women and the Homefront: Diaries.

GENERALS' WIVES: MARTHA WASHINGTON, CATHARINE GREENE, LUCY KNOX

During the War for Independence, many women moved between their homes and military encampments as they joined their husbands in the Continental Army for varying lengths of time. Although they may all be called camp followers, at that time people distinguished between the women who followed the soldiers and those who were the consorts of officers. The consorts, in turn, were further divided by social and military rank. Martha Washington, Catharine Greene, and Lucy Knox, as generals' wives, represent the elite women within early America's

civil and military societies. That shared status, however, should not obscure the differences in their cultural origins, economic situations, and postwar circumstances.

Over the course of the Revolution, Martha Dandridge Custis Washington (1731–1802) became the new nation's First Lady. Such a position was not even to be imagined in 1759, when the wealthy young widow and mother accepted George Washington (1732–1799) as her second husband. Like many other southern gentlewomen faced with administering an estate, Martha Custis had simply thought of finding an amiable spouse who could ably handle their public interests while she managed the domestic ones. The Washingtons created an affectionate, productive partnership that strengthened in the face of the Revolution's challenges.

When George Washington left Virginia to assume command of the Continental Army in 1775, Martha Washington initially remained at their home, Mount Vernon. That winter, however, she traveled up to the encampment around Boston. Catharine Greene and other officers' wives did the same, starting what would be a pattern throughout the war. Although there were exceptions, these women generally—unless home, health, or other issues intervened—joined their husbands after the active campaigning had ended in one year and left when the army readied for action in the next. The necessity of leaving the encampments was made clear early in the war. Martha Washington, Catharine Greene, and Lucy Knox had followed their husbands into New York City in the spring of 1776 only to have their spouses hurry them out in July when news came that the British might be coming. When the British did not immediately show up, Catharine Greene returned and Lucy Knox clamored to do the same. Greene's husband, however, regretted allowing his wife to return, and Knox's simply refused. General Washington did not have that worry, for Martha Washington understood the difference between providing comfort when the army was in garrison and creating a distraction when it was readying for a fight.

That understanding reflected the differences between these generals' wives in temperament, experience, and domestic arrangements. Martha Washington was longer married and a generation older than Catharine Littlefield Greene (1753–1814), who married Nathanael Greene (1742–1786) in July 1774, and Lucy Flucker Knox (1756–1824), who had married Henry Knox (1750–1806) just a month earlier in June 1774. Lady Washington (as she was often called) also had an established, extensive household to run. Her young compatriots were just starting their families and had not yet laid the foundations for their permanent homes.

Catharine Greene married into a Rhode Island Quaker family with farming, mercantile, and manufacturing interests. Because of the war, the young wife often found herself more with the family than the man—and that was not something she liked. Neither a Quaker (nor was Nathanael any longer because of his military activities), nor of strong domestic interests and skills, Catharine Greene often felt at odds with her brothers and sisters in law. She was always eager to join her husband (often leaving her children with the family) and engage in the social activities that were part of life at headquarters.

Lucy Flucker Knox's loyalist family (her father was the Royal Secretary of the Province of Massachusetts Bay, and her brother served in the British army) rejected her when she chose Knox, a bookseller and Whig. They disapproved of the match as socially, economically, and politically imprudent. When the British forces abandoned Boston in March 1776, the Fluckers fled, turning estrangement from Lucy into permanent separation. This may explain why Lucy cleaved all the more strongly to Henry: she had no other close family besides him and his brother. Lucy Knox attempted to help her brother-in-law run the bookseller business for a while during the war, but the business failed. She also stayed with friends or in rented lodgings at times during the war, but she always preferred to be with her husband. As a result of both need and determination, she managed numerous, lengthy visits to camp, where she started to raise her family and served as a prominent social hostess.

AFTER THE REVOLUTION

All three generals' wives faced various private and public pressures after the war. Martha Washington's duties as mistress of Mount Vernon increased as visitors consulting with her husband multiplied. Her social graces and experience at handling a large household stood her in good stead then and when her husband became president.

Although the Washingtons did have financial concerns, they were nothing like the problems facing the Greenes and Knoxes. Economic necessity drove the Greenes south. Unable to pick up where he left off in Rhode Island, and with debts from the war, Nathanael Greene gratefully accepted lands offered by South Carolina and Georgia. Still, when he died in 1785 he left his wife and children in a financial bind. Catharine Greene had to go to friends for help and practice the stringent housewifery she so despised. She learned to manage her affairs with the help of Phineas Miller, whom she married in 1796. She and Miller also served as patrons for Eli Whitney, who invented the cotton gin. Lucy Knox

continued as a society hostess after the war, when her husband served as Secretary at War in the Confederation government and then as Secretary of War under Washington. He accepted those positions both out of a sense of public service and out of the need to support his family. The Knoxes continued to live beyond their means and without a permanent home through those years. Knox resigned in December 1794 and the following spring settled his family in Maine. After Henry died in 1806, Lucy became reclusive and sold much of her property to pay off debts and support herself.

These generals' wives served the Revolution through their domestic endeavors, but their private efforts contributed to public results by sustaining the Continental Army's leaders. In doing so, their lives reflected the dynamics of American society during the Revolutionary and federal periods. Like many others, these members of the provincial elite became part of the new American elite. Yet that was not an easy process or guaranteed result, for they had to cope with social and economic instability and the mobility of the time.

BIBLIOGRAPHY

Callahan, North. *Henry Knox: General Washington's General.* New York and Toronto: Rinehart, 1958.

Freeman, Douglas Southall. *Washington.* Abridgment in one volume by Richard Harwell of the seven-volume *Washington* (1968). New York: Collier Books; Maxwell Macmillan International, 1992.

Greene, Nathanael. *The Papers of General Nathanael Greene,* edited by Robert E. McCarthy. Microform edition. Wilmington, DE: Scholarly Resources, 1989.

Stegeman, John F., and Stegeman, Janet A. *Caty: A Biography of Catharine Littlefield Greene.* Athens: University of Georgia Press, 1985.

Washington, George. *The Papers of George Washington.* Revolutionary War Series, edited by Philander D. Chase. Charlottesville: University Press of Virginia, 1985–2002.

Internet Resource

"Martha Washington Collection." Mount Vernon Library and Special Collections. Available from <http://www.mountvernon.org/learn/collections>.

Holly A. Mayer

See also: **Adams, Abigail; Brown, Charlotte: Diary of a Nurse; Camp Followers: War and Women; Families at War; Madison, Dolley; Sampson, Deborah; Warren, Mercy Otis.**

HAMILTON, ALEXANDER

(b. January 11, ca. 1755; d. July 11, 1804) Key aide to General Washington during Revolutionary War; first U.S. Secretary of the Treasury.

As a penniless boy in the British West Indies, Alexander Hamilton dreamed of war and winning fame as a general. Older men saw promise in Hamilton, who had a genius for business facts and figures, and sent him to Britain's North American colonies for an education. He became one of General George Washington's key aides in the American Revolution and played an even more prominent role in the new nation.

Arriving in 1772, Hamilton enrolled in King's College (now Columbia University) in New York. By 1774 his wished-for war loomed on the horizon. The thirteen colonies on the Atlantic seaboard were quarreling with the British parliament about taxation and the right to self-government by their local legislatures. Hamilton sided with the Americans, writing rebellious essays and giving defiant speeches. When war broke out, he became captain of the New York Provincial Artillery. They were among the few units who kept their esprit de corps during the near-ruinous defeats the American army suffered in the latter half of 1776.

In 1777 General Washington invited Hamilton to become a member of his staff with the rank of lieutenant colonel. War had catapulted Hamilton to the summit of the new nation's power structure. He drafted letters for Washington's signature, dealt with generals and visiting congressmen, and soon acquired strong opinions about what was wrong with the revolutionary American government. The Continental Congress lacked power—above all the power to tax. That was why soldiers starved at Valley Forge and other winter camps and went for months without pay.

In 1780 Hamilton married Elizabeth Schuyler, the daughter of General Philip Schuyler, owner of thousands of acres in the Hudson River Valley. The marriage made him a member of upper-class American society. When the Revolutionary War ended in American independence in 1783, Hamilton became a leading spokesman for the reform of the American constitution. At the Constitutional Convention of 1787, he revealed an elitist view of politics, recommending, among other things, a presidency for life.

In 1789 President Washington invited Hamilton to become his secretary of the treasury. The United States was sinking under an $80 million war debt. Its currency was worthless, and there was an alarming shortage of

Alexander Hamilton.

Hamilton as his second in command, with the rank of major general. The army fought no battles, but Hamilton henceforth styled himself as "General Hamilton."

When Jefferson defeated Adams in the 1800 race for the presidency, Federalist party leaders blamed Hamilton. By 1804 he was virtually out of politics and could do little but snipe from the sidelines when Aaron Burr, a colonel in the Revolution, ran for governor of New York with the backing of most of the state's Federalists. Burr had been elected vice president in 1800, but had fallen out with Jefferson. New England Federalists, fearing Jefferson's 1803 purchase of the Louisiana Territory would make them an impotent minority, were considering secession. Burr promised to take New York into this new confederacy.

When Burr lost the election, he decided that only a triumph over General Hamilton would enable him to become the military leader of the secessionists if New England left the union and a civil war broke out. Burr challenged Hamilton to a duel, claiming to be insulted by Hamilton's relatively trivial attack on him when he launched his race for governor.

General Hamilton accepted the challenge in order to stay in the running for the same military role. He too thought a civil war was likely. On July 11, 1804, Burr mortally wounded Hamilton with his first shot, ending a career that had been made—and finally unmade—by war.

BIBLIOGRAPHY

Fleming, Thomas. *Duel: Alexander Hamilton, Aaron Burr and the Future of America.* New York: Basic Books, 1999.

Flexner, James Thomas. *The Young Hamilton.* Boston: Little, Brown, 1978.

Gordon, John Steele. *Hamilton's Blessing.* New York: Walker, 1997.

Hamilton, Alan McClane. *The Intimate Life of Alexander Hamilton.* New York: Scribners, 1910.

Hendrickson, Robert. *Hamilton.* 2 vols. New York: Mason/Charter, 1976.

Kline, Mary-Jo, ed. *Alexander Hamilton: A Life in His Own Words.* New York: Newsweek Books, 1973; distributed by Harper and Row.

McDonald, Forrest. *Alexander Hamilton.* New York: Norton, 1979.

Thomas Fleming

See also: **Hamilton's Reports; Jefferson, Thomas; Valley Forge; Washington, George.**

circulating money. In a series of brilliant state papers, Hamilton persuaded Congress to turn the debt into bonds backed by the full credit of the federal government, which now had the power to raise money by taxes and tariffs. When Hamilton left office in 1795 to practice law in New York, the new republic's credit rating was the highest in the world, and a reliable money supply was fueling prosperity from Boston to Savannah.

In 1794 farmers in western Pennsylvania threatened to revolt over a tax on whiskey. Hamilton persuaded President Washington to raise an army of 15,000 men and crush the Whiskey Rebellion. Hamilton also persuaded Washington to declare America neutral in the war that had broken out between Great Britain and revolutionary France. The neutrality had a distinct tilt toward the English, whose trade was supplying most of the money for Hamilton's financial system. A great many Americans, led by Thomas Jefferson, disagreed with these policies. They already disliked Hamilton's monetary reforms, which seemed to favor the rich. The dissidents formed the Democratic-Republican Party, which contested the Hamilton-led Federalists after Washington left office in 1796.

In 1798 relations with revolutionary France deteriorated into undeclared war. President John Adams expanded the Navy and appointed George Washington head of a 10,000-man army. Washington selected

HAMILTON'S REPORTS

The War for Independence (1775–1783) created a new nation and an opportunity to chart a future very different from the one inherited from Great Britain. With the implementation of the Constitution in 1788, the American people formally rejected monarchy and aristocracy in favor of a democratic republic. Yet the economic, cultural, and social shape of the new nation was unformed. Beginning in 1790 with Alexander Hamilton's reports to Congress, the national government began to shape the country's future direction and identity. Hamilton submitted three reports to Congress from 1790 to 1791 that charted a vision of the early American republic. As secretary of the treasury in George Washington's administration, Hamilton wrote his reports to secure the legacy of the war for American independence and chart the nation's path toward greater power and prestige. The reports evoked protest that produced the first American political party system.

REPORT ON THE PUBLIC CREDIT

On January 14, 1790, Congress read Alexander Hamilton's first report on public finance and debt. Hamilton declared that the debt of the United States was the cost of liberty and that its payment would generate respect among nations, a widely held view. A nation's reputation, like an individual's, depended on honoring the commitments and obligations made toward others. More daringly, Hamilton argued for transforming the debt into an asset of the national government to be used as money. Hamilton proposed dividing the debt into two categories, domestic and foreign. Foreign debt would be paid in full, while domestic debt would be paid at market value, or par, with the money going to the current owner. It did not matter if either the original owner held the debt or the original value differed from the current market rate. Hamilton asserted that the domestic debt encompassed that of the national government and respective states. To pay the total debt of $85 million, Hamilton outlined the floating of a new loan with varying interest rates and annuities; he also proposed taxes on coffee, tea, wine, and alcohol, and postal revenues.

Hamilton's vision in the *Report on Public Credit* was twofold. First, a debt-based currency would smooth economic transactions and reduce reliance on barter or undisciplined schemes of paper money. Second, stronger ties between the national government, the financial classes, and the states would stabilize American independence.

Critics assailed the report. Led by Representative James Madison of Virginia, Hamilton's critics accused him of favoring financial speculators over workers and farmers. Madison believed that many original debtholders were poor and had sold their obligations to people that dealt with money for a living. Madison charged that the plan gave the national government too much power and invested a small group of people with selfish motivations, particularly in the North, to protect the national government at the expense of the states.

Congress grappled until mid-1790 with the proposals embedded in the *Report on Public Credit*. Then, in a secret deal between Hamilton and the Virginia delegation and with Jefferson's approval, a small section of Virginia became the site of the nation's proposed capital in exchange for Congress's passage of Hamilton's plan.

REPORT ON A NATIONAL BANK

The report on public credit lacked a key ingredient. Hamilton had articulated the "what" but not the "how." On December 14, 1790, almost a year after his first report, he sent to the House of Representatives a *Report on a National Bank*. The "how" had arrived, and with it the sparks of opposition exploded.

Hamilton described a Bank of the United States. It would be capitalized at $10 million and comprised of 25,000 shares. The national government would own one-fourth of the shares, and the public could purchase the rest. One-fourth of the shares could be bought in coin or hard money, while three-fourths could be secured with the debt-based paper mentioned in the first report. Twenty-five directors would govern the bank, most of whom would be private shareholders and not government officials. The bank could issue paper notes as legal tender for all debts owed to the United States and could open branch offices. For twenty years the bank would function under a charter and at the end of that time seek a renewal for continued operations.

The bitter debate of 1790 returned. In early 1791 the House of Representatives examined the report and a bill for establishing the bank. A representative from Georgia repeated arguments heard in opposition to the debt plan, including favoritism to speculators. Opposition took on new tones when James Madison rose to speak. Known as an active and forceful participant in the Constitutional Convention of 1787, Madison declared that the Constitution gave the national government limited powers that did not include establishing a bank. The bill was therefore "unconstitutional." Hamilton's backers retorted that several laws had been adopted through powers "implied" in the Constitution. Against furious opposition, both houses of Congress passed the bank bill.

The debate illuminated two visions of the American nation. Hamilton envisioned a national government that used its power creatively and aggressively, and an economy that thrived on trade. An interlocking relationship would connect the national government to financial and economic institutions. For Hamilton, the American identity was best expressed in the vitality of its national government. By mid-1791 Hamilton's vision became the central ideology of the Federalist Party.

James Madison and Thomas Jefferson developed alternative ideas. They desired a smaller, restrained national government with greater emphasis on state and local autonomy. They interpreted the Constitution as the final barricade of national governmental power, not the first tool it could use to find and wield new powers. The American identity resided in the connections that people had with farming and the land, and those layers of government closest to them, the states and localities. These became the tenets of the new Jeffersonian Republican Party.

The debate revealed a divide beyond political parties. An observer perceived a geographic split on significant constitutional questions. Another commentator went further and said North and South had radically different opinions on the Constitution and government, and that these differences threatened the viability of the national union. The twin reports of Alexander Hamilton had crystallized divergent views among two political parties, regions, and ways of life.

THE REPORT ON MANUFACTURES

Hamilton owed Congress a third report from early 1790, on how to encourage manufactures in the United States. Congress believed the nation would be more secure, particularly in military material, if a stable manufacturing base existed in the United States. Hamilton had made his public credit and banking reports higher priorities, but now that both were law, he submitted the *Report on Manufactures* on December 5, 1791.

Hamilton's third report demonstrated his ability to research, analyze, and write with breadth and creativity. He had gathered data for this report since spring 1790, seeking input from manufacturers in the United States, Europe, and Asia. He encouraged manufacturers to write their views in letters and to convene discussion groups among their peers. He ordered government officials charged with collecting public revenues to amass information on manufacturing in their respective regions. This great flood of data swept into Hamilton's office, where he sorted and sifted until he produced a startling set of conclusions.

In the third report Hamilton recognized the centrality of agriculture in American life. He noted that many regarded agriculture as the best form of human economy and an enhancer of the nation's wealth, stability, and population. Hamilton wrote that agriculturists preferred that government not act to support manufacturing because it might transfer wealth to a less desirable form of economic endeavor.

Hamilton stated that the American economy needed manufacturing. He made three points. First, manufacturing complemented agriculture. As more people worked in manufacturing, the demand for agricultural products would increase, benefiting farmers. Second, manufacturing enabled the nation to make better use of diverse resources and population, especially in using women and children in a labor force stretched thin. Third, unless officials nurtured domestic manufacturing, other nations with robust manufacturing would continue to trade with the United States from a position of superiority. Strong American manufacturing would permit the United States to trade abroad on an equal footing.

Hamilton made several recommendations. He urged tariffs on foreign goods; prohibition of manufacturing imports; bounties for specific American industries; stimulation of inventions; governmental inspection of manufacturing goods; and a transportation system to haul raw materials and finished goods. Through these measures, the third piece of Hamilton's economic triad would fall into place—sound public finances, a thriving national bank, and a growing manufacturing sector.

Jefferson and the agriculturists seethed at the report. Jefferson predicted that women and children would be dragged from farms to work with machines in filthy settings. He warned that manufacturing workers would lose their independence in factories and would form mobs. Jefferson's criticisms, combined with the Republicans' hatred of Hamilton's entire economic vision, led to vigorous opposition to the report, which nevertheless passed both houses of Congress.

CONCLUSION

The memory of war was a thread that ran through Hamilton's reports. As an officer and aide to General Washington, Hamilton witnessed the effects of disintegrating currency, incoherent public finances, and weak manufacturing. These weaknesses had nearly destroyed the Continental Army and the cause of American independence. The vision outlined in the reports reflected Hamilton's desire to strengthen the new American government that had emerged with the Constitution of 1787. But although many agreed with the memory, they did not agree with the vision, and from the controversy over Hamilton's works sprang the American political party system.

BIBLIOGRAPHY

Chernow, Ron. *Alexander Hamilton*. New York: Penguin Press, 2004.

Cunningham, Noble E. *Jefferson vs. Hamilton: Confrontations that Shaped a Nation*. Boston: Bedford/St. Martin's, 2000.

Randall, Willard Sterne. *Alexander Hamilton: A Life*. New York: HarperCollins, 2003.

Daniel T. Miller

See also: **Hamilton, Alexander; Memory and Early Histories of the Revolution; Revolution and Radical Reform.**

HARTFORD CONVENTION

The Hartford Convention was a gathering of Federalist Party delegates from five New England states that met in Hartford, Connecticut, between December 15, 1814, and January 5, 1815. Its members convened to discuss their long-held grievances against the policies of the successive Democratic-Republican administrations of Thomas Jefferson and James Madison. But its immediate cause was Madison's conduct of the War of 1812 with Great Britain. Delegates also met to propose changes in government policies and structures that would deal with their concerns.

CAUSE OF PROTEST

By the summer of 1814, the prosecution of the war with Britain, which had never gone well to begin with, reached its low point. In August as British troops burned the city of Washington, President Madison was forced to flee. Then, having defeated Napoleon in Europe, Britain began to move troops to North America for a major offensive and blockaded the east coast of the United States. In September, the British invaded New York State from the north and occupied much of Maine.

To make matters worse, the federal government was on the edge of bankruptcy. Seeking to prevent smuggling, Congress had enacted a coastal trade embargo, which not only depressed the economy but reduced federal revenues. The administration was also considering nationalizing the state militias, including those of the New England states. New England Federalists believed they had ample grounds to protest policies that put their region's security and interests at stake.

As usual, Massachusetts Federalists took the lead in seeking a political solution to their region's distress. Massachusetts governor Caleb Strong called the General Court (the state's legislature) into special session in early September to consider measures that "the present dangerous state of public affairs may render expedient." Party moderates turned back proposals for extreme actions, such as prohibiting the collection in Massachusetts of federal customs duties. This illegal act would have qualified as nullification—a refusal to implement federal law. Instead, the legislature adopted a call for a meeting of delegates from New England to prepare the region's defense, promote a "radical reform" in the federal Constitution, and take other measures "not repugnant to their obligations as members of the union."

GRIEVANCES AND RESOLUTIONS

The Hartford Convention, like the earlier Continental Congress, was an extralegal (that is, not regulated by law), not illegal, gathering. It opened with twenty-six delegates, only three of whom, elected by Federalist meetings in Vermont and New Hampshire counties, were popularly elected. The rest were experienced political figures appointed by their state legislatures and disinclined to take radical measures.

Like the meetings of the Constitutional Convention of 1787, the Hartford Convention's meetings were held in secret, a circumstance that has since kept alive speculation that its members contemplated breaking away from the union. But all evidence points to measured proceedings under the leadership of Massachusetts elder statesman George Cabot. No expressions of disloyalty or treasonous intent mar the convention's official record. The convention's final report, written by Harrison Gray Otis, also of Massachusetts, was moderate. The report assailed conditions that had reduced New England's national influence and rendered the region without security. To substantiate its charges, the report cited the following grievances: the admission of new states in the trans-Appalachian West; the Constitution's three-fifths clause, which gave the South extra representation in Congress; the easy naturalization of immigrants; the administration's patronage policies favoring the South and West; and the conscription of state militias for prosecution of a failing war. The report went on to urge Congress to authorize each state to defend itself and to rebate federal tax revenues to the states for that purpose. Significantly, it did not endorse the nullification of federal laws. Instead, the report argued that such an extreme measure was justifiable, "especially in time of war," only by "absolute necessity." But it is worth noting that the idea was thus not entirely dismissed.

To give teeth to its views, the Convention proposed seven constitutional amendments to address New England's situation. The first, to reduce the South's advantage in Congress, would have counted only the free white population but none of the slaves in apportioning congressional representation and federal direct taxes. Others would have required a two-thirds vote in Congress for the admission of new states, the passage of embargoes, and declarations of war. One would have limited embargoes to sixty days. Another would have barred from Congress and other national offices all nonnative-born citizens (who were thought to favor the opposition party overwhelmingly). And a seventh, aimed at the presidency's "Virginia Dynasty," would have prohibited successive elections of presidents from the same state. Well received by Federalists throughout the nation, the report was officially adopted by the governments of Massachusetts, Connecticut, and Rhode Island and conveyed to Washington, D.C.

Yet even as the Convention met, American diplomats were concluding peace with Great Britain at Ghent, Belgium. Then in early January 1815, shortly after the

Convention had adjourned, Andrew Jackson's forces decisively defeated British regulars at New Orleans. When Americans learned in mid-February of both events, they ridiculed the Convention's actions. The Federalist Party never recovered.

SIGNIFICANCE

The Hartford Convention, an institutionalized partisan expression of people's grievances, had, and retains, wide significance. As the first concerted expression of opposition to war under the Constitution (and during the first full-scale war fought under that Constitution), it originated and gave legitimacy to a long American tradition of antiwar sentiment and pressure. It revealed how responsible leaders, during war as well as peace, can steer rebellious inclinations into constitutional channels. It raised serious questions about the responsibility of government to all people, regions, and interests, especially with regard to their military security. Its proposal to end the counting of three-fifths of the South's slaves in apportioning the House of Representatives bore fruit finally with Union victory in the Civil War. On the other hand, and most ominously, the Hartford Convention, even while shying away from any talk or threat of disunion, gave added force to notions of interposition (putting the sovereignty of states ahead of that of the federal government) and nullification. These ideas gained enough currency in the South by 1861 to help justify secession.

BIBLIOGRAPHY

Banner, James M., Jr. *To the Hartford Convention: The Federalists and the Origins of Party Politics in Massachusetts, 1789–1815.* New York: Alfred A. Knopf, 1970.

Stagg, J. C. A. *Madison's War: Politics, Diplomacy, and Warfare in the Early American Republic, 1783–1830.* Princeton, NJ: Princeton University Press, 1983.

James M. Banner, Jr.

See also: **Embargo; Federalist Party; Fourth of July; War of 1812.**

HEWES, GEORGE ROBERT TWELVES

(b. 1742; d. November 5, 1840) Source for two workingman's accounts of events during the American Revolution.

George Hewes was a poor shoemaker in Boston before the American Revolution, a sailor and militiaman during the war, and a poor farmer afterward. He was not a political leader, though he once set off a small riot. Instead, Hewes was a face in the crowd at the Boston Massacre and Boston Tea Party. In two books he left a man-on-the-street's view of America's break with Britain. Hewes's participation in the protest leading to the Revolutionary War and in the war itself changed his self-image from a subject restricted by class and custom to a citizen judged on his merits. In many ways, Hewes's personal transformation from subject to citizen reflected the larger change in American culture, society, and identity that were part of the American War for Independence.

Hewes was born into a family of tanners striving for gentility; his father held minor town offices, and he remembered his mother buying a slave. But the family fortunes declined after Hewes's father died in 1749. His own prospects were limited: he was a mediocre scholar and, at five feet one inch, too small for heavy labor. The young man was sent to a relative's farm in Wrentham, twenty miles away, then returned to Boston as apprentice to a shoemaker—a profession that promised work but no wealth.

Hewes's apprenticeship coincided with the French and Indian War. When his first master's business failed, he tried to enlist in the British army. But he was rejected as too short, even after he built up his shoes.

At age twenty-one Hewes opened a small shop on Griffin's Wharf, and in 1768 he wed Sally Sumner, a teenage laundress. Their marriage lasted sixty years, but they never escaped poverty. A lone shoemaker could not compete with early manufacturing centers like Lynn, Massachusetts, whose artisans in 1767 produced 40,000 pairs of shoes. Hewes therefore occasionally worked on fishing boats off Newfoundland, and in 1770 was jailed for a £7 debt.

Hewes started to turn against the royal government after it sent troops into Boston in 1768. He learned to carry rum to placate sentries. Once, he complained to a captain about a sergeant's not paying for shoes, then was horrified by how harshly the army punished the man: 300 lashes. Later, he saw a grenadier steal a bundle of clothing; he chose to confront this man privately.

On March 5, 1770, Hewes saw the captain and the grenadier again, part of a squad facing a violent crowd on King Street. The soldiers shot into the townspeople. A mariner fell, mortally wounded, into Hewes's arms. The angry shoemaker testified twice to magistrates about what Bostonians considered a massacre.

Three years later, the town was caught up in a fervor over three shiploads of taxable tea. On the night of December 16, Hewes spotted a crowd of men in disguise heading toward Griffin's Wharf, near his shop. He grabbed a blanket, rubbed his face with soot, and joined them in dumping the tea into the harbor.

Pre-Revolutionary newspapers mentioned Hewes only once, after a violent incident on January 25, 1774.

He told a customs official, John Malcolm, to stop threatening a boy. Malcolm replied that Hewes "should not speak to a gentleman." Hewes noted how Malcolm had recently been tarred and feathered over his clothing in New Hampshire. Irked, Malcolm clubbed Hewes with his cane. While some people carried the unconscious shoemaker to a doctor, others pursued his attacker, telling gentlemen who tried to intervene that they no longer trusted royal justice. That evening, a mob stripped Malcolm, covered him with tar and feathers, and carted him around town, whipping him viciously. When the two injured men met again on the street weeks later, Hewes was pleased to hear the customs man speak more politely.

After the Revolutionary War began in April 1775, Hewes sent his wife and children to his Wrentham relatives, then smuggled himself out of the besieged town on a fishing boat. That winter, his deserted shop was torn down for firewood.

Hewes never again lived in Boston. During the war, he served in the militia and on two privateering ships, working for a share of whatever British cargoes his vessels might capture. But he refused to sail with a ship's officer who insisted "he take off his hat to him," a sign of new republican pride. For decades after independence Hewes farmed in Wrentham. Although in his seventies during the War of 1812, he nonetheless tried to enlist in the U.S. Navy before moving in with sons in upstate New York.

Hewes would have remained obscure had he not been discovered in the 1830s by young writers eager for Revolutionary lore. His memories, once common but by then rare, became the core of two books that preserved both his name and a workingman's perspective on the American transition from monarchy to republic.

BIBLIOGRAPHY

Hewes, George R. T. [as told to James Hawkes]. *A Retrospect of the Boston Tea-Party*. New York: S. S. Bliss, 1834.

Hewes, George R. T., as told to "A Bostonian" [Benjamin Bussey Thatcher]. *Traits of the Tea Party*. New York: Harper and Brothers, 1835.

Young, Alfred F. *The Shoemaker and the Tea Party: Memory and the American Revolution*. Boston: Beacon Press, 1999.

J. L. Bell

See also: **Boston Tea Party: Politicizing Ordinary People; Bunker Hill Monument; Constitution: Creating a Republic; Madison, James; Memory and Early Histories of the Revolution; Sampson, Deborah.**

JACKSON, ANDREW

(b. March 15, 1767; d. June 8, 1845) Victor of the Battle of New Orleans; general of the War of 1812; Seventh U.S. president (1829–1837).

Andrew Jackson was born to Scottish-Irish immigrant parents and grew up on the Carolina frontier. As a boy, he fought in the Revolution with patriot irregulars and was captured. By his own later account, a British officer slashed him with a sword for refusing to clean his boots, leaving a permanent scar.

After the war, Jackson read law in North Carolina and in 1788 moved west to Nashville. In the new state of Tennessee, he won quick political promotion, and in 1802 was elected major general of the state militia. Jackson thirsted for the field, offering his men for service against every possible foe, including the Burr conspirators, the Spanish, the British, and the border American Indian tribes.

Congress declared war against Britain in June 1812, and in November Jackson's Tennessee troops were ordered to New Orleans. Jackson led two thousand men as far as Natchez, where he received an abrupt order dismissing them without pay or provisions. On his own responsibility, Jackson held the command together for the return home. His willingness to share his men's privations on this march earned him the name "Old Hickory."

In 1813 Jackson was ordered to suppress a group of hostile Creek in Mississippi Territory (later the state of Alabama). Commanding Tennessee troops and allied Indians, Jackson penetrated into the heart of Creek territory and fought a series of engagements. At Horseshoe Bend in March 1814, he destroyed the main Creek force. His victories paved the way for later treaties—some negotiated by Jackson himself—in which the Creek and other southern tribes (including those who had fought alongside Jackson) relinquished millions of acres to the United States.

Jackson's success against the Creek won him a commission as U.S. Major General in charge of defending the Gulf Coast. Jackson beat off a British strike at Mobile and drove the British from their post in Spanish (and ostensibly neutral) Pensacola, Florida. The main encounter came in January 1815 at New Orleans, where Jackson's motley force of regulars, militia, free blacks, and pirates repulsed an invading army of British veterans. In the main action, a frontal assault on Jackson's lines astride the Mississippi on January 8, the British lost two thousand men; the Americans, only a few dozen.

Andrew Jackson at the Battle of New Orleans, in a painting by Charles Severin.

With its astounding casualty ratio and stirring (though apocryphal) image of American backwoods riflemen picking off British regulars, the Battle of New Orleans passed instantly into patriotic myth. Unbeknownst to both sides, the battle was fought two weeks after the Treaty of Ghent and did not affect the war's outcome. Still, for Americans it put a crown of glory on what had been a frustrating and humiliating military effort. Jackson himself became a hallowed hero, a living symbol of republican martial prowess.

Jackson remained in the postwar army as one of its two major generals. In 1818, in pursuit of a raiding band of Seminole, he led a force into Spanish Florida, captured Spanish bastions at St. Marks and Pensacola, and arrested and executed two British nationals. Jackson's unauthorized invasion sparked a diplomatic furor and a congressional investigation. But it served American ends by nudging Spain to cede Florida in an 1819 treaty.

In 1821 Jackson resigned his commission. He served briefly as Florida governor and in 1824 stood for the presidency. Jackson's military background furnished both his prime qualification for the presidency and his main handicap, for virulent controversy had accompanied battlefield

successes throughout his army career. Jackson's stern sense of discipline, his obsession with personal honor, and his explosive temper had embroiled him in endless quarrels with both superiors and subordinates. As a commander he had sometimes defied civil authority. Outside the army he had fought duels and street brawls. To some Americans, he seemed a paragon of martial purity and forthrightness, a simple soldier called from retirement to rescue his country from devious and corrupt politicians. But to others he was a mere warrior chieftain, bloodthirsty and capricious, a tyrant and bully in the mold of Caesar or Napoleon.

Jackson led the vote in the multicandidate election of 1824, but lost to John Quincy Adams in the House of Representatives. In 1828 Jackson defeated Adams. Jackson's two-term presidency, like his generalship, was bold and steeped in controversy. His conduct in office was hailed as decisive and denounced as high-handed, furnishing evidence for both sides in the enduring argument over the fitness of military characters for the presidency.

BIBLIOGRAPHY

Heidler, David S., and Heidler, Jeanne T. *Old Hickory's War: Andrew Jackson and the Quest for Empire.* Mechanicsburg, PA: Stackpole Books, 1996.

Owsley, Frank Lawrence, Jr. *Struggle for the Gulf Borderlands: The Creek War and the Battle of New Orleans.* Gainesville, FL: University Presses of Florida, 1981.

Remini, Robert V. *Andrew Jackson and the Course of American Empire, 1767–1821.* New York: Harper and Row, 1977.

Remini, Robert V. *The Battle of New Orleans.* New York: Viking, 1999.

Remini, Robert V. *Andrew Jackson and His Indian Wars.* New York: Viking, 2001.

Daniel Feller

See also: **Battle of New Orleans; Lafayette's Tour; Monroe, James; Republicanism and War; War of 1812.**

JAMESTOWN: LEGACY OF THE MASSACRE OF 1622

On March 22, 1622, Indians of the Powhatan Confederacy in eastern Virginia killed around 347 English colonists, nearly a quarter of the entire English population in Virginia. This well-planned, coordinated attack, which the English called a "great massacre," resulted from numerous causes and had a lasting impact on the direction of English-Indian relations in colonial America.

Ever since the Virginia Company established the Jamestown colony in 1607, the settlers had sought a

Engraving of the Jamestown Massacre, 1634. © BETTMANN/CORBIS.

moneymaking product that could be extracted from the Virginia environment. By 1613 John Rolfe (who married Pocahontas in 1614) had developed a new strain of tobacco that gave the colony its first real source of revenue and committed Virginia to a farming and plantation economy. Jamestown colonists quickly expanded their settlements to grow tobacco, but tobacco leached nutrients out of unfertilized soil in just a few years, requiring the farmers to constantly acquire and till new lands. The Virginia colonists suddenly became land hungry, putting increasing pressure on the Powhatans to sell or give up their land. In the opinion of the English, so-called empty or unfarmed land should be converted to agricultural uses, whereas the Powhatans viewed wooded and unoccupied areas around their villages as crucial hunting areas and buffer zones between villages.

Around 1616, the aging Chief Powhatan was replaced by two of his maternal brothers, Itoyatan and Opechancanough. Powhatan had committed to living at peace with the English, particularly after the capture of his daughter Pocahontas and her marriage to Rolfe in 1614, but his successors viewed the English warily and it was Opechancanough who planned and led the 1622 at-

tack (he was also the war leader who captured Captain John Smith in December 1607, resulting in Smith's metaphorical adoption by the Powhatans via his rescue by Pocahontas).

In 1620, Virginia Company officials, especially George Thorpe, began pressuring the Powhatans to send some of their children to be educated among the colonists, a request the Powhatans found intolerable. Moreover, imported diseases such as smallpox had killed Powhatans by the dozens in the 1610s and placed stress on their traditional culture when the deaths could not be prevented by conventional healing methods. Finally, just two weeks before the 1622 attack, English settlers killed a leading Powhatan warrior and shaman named Nemattanew, providing the spark needed to inflame an increasingly edgy situation.

Scholars debate what Opechancanough and the Powhatans intended with their one-day attack. Some argue the Powhatans hoped to remove the English presence from Virginia but failed to follow up on their initial military success and eventually lost the fight to keep Virginia. It is more likely, however, that the Powhatans never planned to exterminate every English person and instead meant to send a powerful warning that the English needed to recognize Powhatan superiority, behave appropriately, and restrict their settlements to the original Jamestown area. This interpretation is supported by the actions of Opechancanough who sent a messenger to warn Jamestown of the attack and concentrated hostilities on the outlying English settlements. The English failed to heed the warning, however, and instead redoubled their efforts to secure a foothold in Virginia and gain permanent occupation of Powhatan lands.

Many of the surviving English settlers welcomed the attack as a justification for assaulting the Powhatans and driving them from their lands. Edward Waterhouse wrote after the attack, "Our hands, which before were tied with gentleness and fair usage, are now set at liberty by the treacherous violence of the savages . . . So that we . . . may now by right of war, and law of nations, invade the country, and destroy them who sought to destroy us . . . Their cleared grounds in all their villages . . . shall be inhabited by us" (Gleach, p.159). Acquiring land by right of conquest had guided European relations with Indians since Columbus first encountered the Americas, but the aftermath of the 1622 attack was the first time the English employed the notion in North America. Open warfare lasted ten years in Virginia before an uneasy truce kept the peace for over a decade.

The most important immediate impact of the 1622 attack was that in 1624 the Virginia Company lost title over the colony to the crown of England, making Virginia a royal colony. From that time onward, imperial concerns intruded into Virginia relations with Native Americans and affected the policies the Virginia government pursued. Warfare and diseases caused the Powhatan population to continue to drop from a high of around 25,000 in 1607 to a few thousand by the 1630s, and many of their villages were abandoned. On April 18, 1644, the Powhatans, still under the leadership of the elderly Opechancanough, attacked again, killing over 400 English colonists. That war ended within two years, Opechancanough died in a Jamestown jail cell, and Powhatan dominance in Virginia ended.

For the English to term the 1622 attack a "massacre" meant that their subsequent decade-long war against the Powhatan "savages" was an act of justifiable retribution, as Edward Waterhouse suggested. One group's "massacre" is often another group's justifiable retribution or "freedom fight," however; and the subjective meaning of "massacre" to make one party seem innocent in an act of violence should be examined critically. The use of the term "massacre" by Euro-Americans to describe attacks by Native Americans throughout American history automatically places the blame for such violence on Native Americans, while relinquishing Europeans or Americans of their own culpability. According to the standard narrative of American history that impacted decision making from 1622 onward, only one side in this great cultural encounter committed "massacres" whereas the other merely responded with violence out of self-defense. So-called justifiable vengeance contributed to a still-prevalent view by Americans that they only attacked other peoples when provoked and were always reasonable with their response.

BIBLIOGRAPHY

Fausz, J. Frederick. "The 'Barbarous Massacre' Reconsidered: The Powhatan Uprising of 1622 and the Historians." In *Explorations in Ethnic Studies* 1 (1978): 16–36.

Fausz, J. Frederick. "George Thorpe, Nemattanew, and Powhatan Uprising of 1622." In *Virginia Cavalcade* 28 (1979): 110-117.

Gleach, Frederic W. *Powhatan's World and Colonial Virginia: A Conflict of Cultures.* Lincoln: University of Nebraska Press, 1997.

Rountree, Helen. *The Powhatan Indians of Virginia: Their Traditional Culture.* Norman: University of Oklahoma Press, 1989.

Rountree, Helen. *Pocahontas' People: The Powhatan Indians of Virginia Through Four Centuries.* Norman: University of Oklahoma Press, 1990.

Rountree, Helen, ed., *Powhatan Foreign Relations, 1500–1722.* Charlottesville: University Press of Virginia, 1993.

Greg O'Brien

See also: **Bacon's Rebellion; European Invasion of Indian North America, 1513–1765; King Philip's War, Legacy of; Legacies of Indian Warfare; Native Americans: Images in Popular Culture.**

JEFFERSON, THOMAS

(b. April 13, 1743; d. July 4, 1826) Third president of the United States (1801–1809).

Thomas Jefferson was among the preeminent founders of the United States, advocating strong states' rights and separation of church and state. He drafted the Declaration of Independence, founded the University of Virginia, served as governor of Virginia, minister to France, secretary of state, vice president (1796–1800), and finally president (1801–1809). Although he was never in the military, war nevertheless tested Jefferson's philosophy and political will.

Jefferson was a highly idealistic and complex individual; he believed and argued for a small and weak federal government, strong states' rights, a conservative reading of the Constitution, and peaceful means to end conflict. He drafted the inspiring "all men are created equal" words of the Declaration of Independence. However, he constantly agonized over the details of these ideals and, in practice, contradicted himself for the benefit of the new nation and his own personal desires—for example, by upholding slavery even though he had a long term relationship and fathered children with his slave, Sally Hemings.

Thomas Jefferson was born in Albemarle County, Virginia. His mother, Jane Randolph, was from one of the most famous Virginia families, giving Jefferson contact with prominent citizens. He received a huge inheritance of land, of which his estate Monticello was a part, and his marriage to Martha Wayles Skelton doubled his holdings. He studied at the College of William and Mary, then read law under George Wythe, the leading law teacher of his generation.

Jefferson practiced law until the revolution suspended the courts in 1774, and he went on to represent Virginia in the Continental Congress, drafting *A Summary View of the Rights of British America*, which foreshadowed the Declaration of Independence. During the Revolution, he served as governor of Virginia. There was an inquiry into his conduct as governor due to the loss of Richmond to the British, but he was exonerated; the incident haunted him politically for decades.

While vice president, Jefferson argued against the Alien and Sedition Acts, which allowed the government to deport people who were deemed dangerous and punished writings against the government with fines and imprisonment. He argued that these acts were unconstitutional because the Tenth Amendment gave states the powers not delegated to the federal government by the constitution and that therefore, states could nullify federal legislation in order to protect their citizens' rights.

During his first term as president, when Napoleon offered the Louisiana Territory to the United States, Jefferson disregarded his unease about the federal government acting on its own to add territory without a constitutional amendment and sent negotiators to France. The Louisiana Purchase helped the United States double in size and guaranteed access to the Mississippi river and interior territories, but also set the stage for troublesome wars to come. The question of slavery in the new territories and the balance of power between slave and free states, key issues leading to secession and the Civil War, was debated at this time. Displacement of American Indian tribes by the U.S. government would also accelerate, resulting in increasing armed conflict over the next century.

Jefferson expanded the executive powers of the presidency by fighting undeclared wars such as the Barbary Coast Wars (1802–1805), when Jefferson sent the Navy and Marines during a congressional recess. During his second term, the conflict between Britain and France was intensifying, putting the neutrality of the United States

in danger because of those two nations' shipping blockades. Furthermore, Britain actually removed sailors from American ships to impress them into its navy. The attack on the American frigate *Chesapeake* in 1807 led Jefferson to the verge of war with England. He tried to bring pressure on both sides by suspending commerce through the Embargo Act, and to enforce the embargo, he infringed on individual and states' rights by ordering the U.S. army and navy to act against its own citizens in a time of peace (one of the main complaints against King George III listed in the Declaration of Independence). The Embargo did not have the desired economic effect on Britain and France, and commerce states (mainly New England) suffered so much that there was talk of "disunion." The Embargo Act, along with the Non-Importation Act, was repealed in 1809 with Jefferson's consent in order to save the Union. Weaker measures enacted did nothing to avoid the War of 1812.

After his presidency, Jefferson retired to Monticello but maintained an active correspondence with Democratic Republican party members and elected officials. After the British burned the capitol in the War of 1812, he sold his library of 6,487 books as a replacement for the Library of Congress lost in the fire. In 1823 he advised Monroe on what became the Monroe Doctrine—essentially non-intervention and an end to colonization by European powers in the Western Hemisphere. Always wary of European influence, Jefferson wanted to keep the Western Hemisphere free so republics could flourish; he supported a joint declaration desired by the formerly distrusted England in order to secure this ideal.

Thomas Jefferson helped to forge the nation. The Declaration of Independence and the Virginia Statute on Religious Freedom that he drafted were products of the American Revolution and Enlightenment ideals, fused and powerfully expressed by him. Jefferson was a slaveholder who wrote eloquently about liberty; he favored a federal union but feared the power of central government; he wanted limited government, but expanded executive powers and stretched the limits of the Constitution to serve his policies; he was suspicious of a strong military, but conducted undeclared wars. In many ways his ideals and contradictions, forged in war and the making of a new nation, represent enduring features of American society and culture.

BIBLIOGRAPHY

Beran, Michael Knox. *Jefferson's Demons: Portrait of a Restless Mind*. New York: Free Press, 2003.

Bernstein, Richard B. *Thomas Jefferson*. New York: Oxford University Press, 2003.

Bishop, Arthur, ed. *Thomas Jefferson, 1743–1826: Chronology, Documents, Bibliographic Aids*. Dobbs Ferry, NY: Oceana Publications, 1971.

Bowers, Claude G. *Jefferson in Power: The Death Struggle of the Federalists.* Boston: Houghton Mifflin, 1936.

Brodie, Fawn M. *Thomas Jefferson: An Intimate History.* New York: Norton, 1974.

Kaplan, Lawrence S. *Jefferson and France: An Essay on Politics and Political Ideas.* New Haven, CT: Yale University Press, 1967.

Malone, Dumas. *Jefferson and His Time: The Sage of Monticello.* Boston: Little, Brown, 1981.

Mayo, Bernard, ed. *Jefferson Himself: The Personal Narrative of a Many-Sided American.* Charlottesville: University Press of Virginia, 1970.

McDonald, Forrest. *The Presidency of Thomas Jefferson.* Lawrence: University Press of Kansas, 1976.

Onuf, Peter S. *Jefferson's Empire: The Language of American Nationhood.* Charlottesville: University Press of Virginia, 2000.

Vidal, Gore. *Inventing a Nation: Washington, Adams, Jefferson.* New Haven, CT: Yale University Press, 2003.

Wills, Garry. *Negro President: Jefferson and the Slave Power.* Boston: Houghton Mifflin, 2003.

Robert A. Arlt

See also: **Declaration of Independence; Embargo; Jeffersonian Republican Party; Madison, James; Monroe, James; Revolution and Radical Reform; Slavery and the Home Front, 1775–1783.**

JEFFERSONIAN REPUBLICAN PARTY

Jeffersonian (or Madisonian) Republicans appeared within three years of the inauguration of the federal Constitution, as Thomas Jefferson, James Madison, and lesser figures in the infant federal government united with, encouraged, and assumed the leadership of popular opposition to Alexander Hamilton's financial programs. This resistance, though, assumed the shape of the first political party only as a conflict over foreign policy politicized and mobilized a mass electorate for national competition. In this sense, the Jeffersonian Republicans originated in conflicting sympathies about the French Revolution and were preoccupied, throughout their history, with the revolutionary and Napoleonic wars.

Alexander Hamilton's proposals for the funding of the national debt, federal assumption of the revolutionary obligations of the states, creation of a national bank, and federal encouragement of native manufacturers were intended to equip the new United States with economic and financial institutions similar to those that had permitted Britain to compete successfully in four great eighteenth-century wars. But imitation of the British, the

constitutional interpretations necessary to defend such institutions, and the obvious contempt by some supporters of these measures for political involvement by the rabble, all generated potent fears that the republic was in danger. Some believed the pro-administration forces were conspiring to reintroduce hereditary power, which is why the opposition referred to itself as the "Republican interest." Such policies were clearly incompatible with the primarily agrarian economy and relatively modest differences between the rich and poor that Jefferson and Madison considered more appropriate for sound republics. By the end of 1791, the two Virginians and their allies in the Congress were reaching out for links with local politicians, had taken measures to secure initiation of a national newspaper to support their views, and were attacking their opponents' rising criticisms of developments in France.

WAR IN EUROPE AND AMERICAN POLITICS

Foreign policy had influenced the dispute between the governmental factions even as it first took shape. In 1789, on the first day of business for the first federal Congress in the House of Representatives, Madison moved for commercial regulations that would discriminate against Great Britain, insisting that the Constitution had been framed and ratified in order to permit a stronger central government to retaliate against European restrictions on American commerce and ease the economic suffering that had marked the postwar years. Freer oceanic trade seemed indispensable if the United States was to avoid a premature transition to an urbanized and manufacturing economy. Madison and Jefferson believed the United States was capable of forcing freer trade by favoring nations, such as France, which had commercial treaties with the union, or by withholding exports of the food and other raw materials which they defined as absolute necessities of life. Hamilton opposed and helped defeat their yearly efforts to enact such measures, believing America would lose in any confrontation with a more developed power and that his financial system would be shattered in the process.

Then, in February 1793, the revolutionary French Republic, already heavily engaged with Austria and Prussia, declared war on Great Britain as well, initiating twenty years of worldwide conflict. Contrasting sympathies toward revolutionary France and Britain, both of which attempted to deny their enemy the benefits of neutral commerce, drew thousands of Americans into the party contest. Though neither party wanted the United States to get involved in European conflict, strict neutrality between Great Britain and republican France, to which America was linked by the treaty of 1778, was widely unpopular at first. During Washington's second administration, British seizures of several hundred American ships deepened opposition anger over what Republicans perceived as subservience to that country. When the crisis in Anglo-American relations was resolved, not by commercial confrontation, but by John Jay's Treaty of 1795, which Republicans considered damaging, demeaning, and likely to provoke a confrontation with France, Madison attempted to defeat it in the House of Representatives by refusing the appropriations necessary to carry it into effect. During the administration of John Adams, who defeated Jefferson in the election of 1796, the British treaty did provoke resentment, retaliation, and a limited naval war with revolutionary France. Concurrent Federalist attempts to suppress the Jeffersonian opposition culminated in the Alien and Sedition Acts of 1798 and Jefferson's and Madison's Kentucky and Virginia Resolutions. Wartime taxes and the crisis laws contributed importantly to the Republican victory in 1800.

JEFFERSONIAN POLICIES

The Jeffersonian Ascendancy, stretching through the administrations of Jefferson and Madison and into that of James Monroe, was characterized by the consistent pursuit of the policies outlined during the 1790s. In foreign policy, the critical objectives were expansion to the west (especially by way of the Louisiana Purchase of 1803), freer oceanic trade, and commercial confrontation with nations that denied it. Economic warfare, mostly with Great Britain, climaxed in the Great Embargo of 1807, four years of fruitless search for other ways to use the weapon of withholding U.S. trade to force the British to relax their damaging, demeaning violations of the "rights" of neutrals, and eventual abandonment of these in favor of the War of 1812. Only after the conclusion of the war, as the Federalists collapsed and the country entered on a period of single-party rule, did the Jeffersonians approve creation of a second national bank, a moderately protective tariff, larger peacetime forces, and other policies they had initially opposed. By the mid-1820s, both the National Republicans (later Whigs) and their Jacksonian opponents claimed to be the rightful heirs of the Jeffersonian tradition.

BIBLIOGRAPHY

Banning, Lance. *The Jeffersonian Persuasion: Evolution of a Party Ideology.* Ithaca, NY: Cornell University Press, 1978.

Elkins, Stanley, and McKitrick, Eric. *The Age of Federalism: The Early American Republic, 1788–1800.* New York: Oxford University Press, 1993.

McCoy, Drew R. *The Elusive Republic: Political Economy in Jeffersonian America.* Chapel Hill: University of North Carolina Press, 1980.

Tucker, Robert W., and Hendrickson, David. *Empire of Liberty: The Statecraft of Thomas Jefferson.* New York: Oxford University Press, 1990.

Lance Banning

See also: Federalist Party; Hartford Convention; Quasi War and the Rise of Political Parties; War of 1812.

KING PHILIP'S WAR, LEGACY OF

King Philip's War cataclysmically ended a generation of peaceful interdependence among New England's various groups of English colonists and American Indians. After the Pequot War, the New England colonies and American Indian tribes had coexisted in a delicate balance of power with their communities linked economically and politically. The English population grew rapidly, however, to the point that colonists outnumbered Indians three to one. The resulting pressures on American Indian land, combined with divisions among the Indians over the spread of Christianity, created fissures in the biracial society.

What began with a minor skirmish in June 1675 escalated into a war that involved all of New England and was far more harsh than any American Indian-English conflict preceding it. Indians fought on both sides of the conflict, and though the English colonies did not fight against one another, their unity was fragile. The English had at least several hundred casualties and had to abandon many of their western settlements. American Indians fared far worse, with their populations shrinking by roughly 60 percent. Many of those Indians who did not die of battle wounds or disease either fled New England or found themselves transported to the Caribbean as slaves by the English. The war devastated the Indian population to the point that New England had only one American Indian for every ten colonists at conflict's end.

Though American Indians did not vanish entirely from the region, their demographic collapse resulted in its political, cultural, and social reorganization. Tribes lost most of their power, creating a political vacuum that spurred bickering among factions of English in Connecticut, Massachusetts, Plymouth, and Rhode Island. The colonists argued over topics ranging from colonial boundaries to blame for the bloody conflict from which they had just emerged. This factionalism eventually drew the attention of England's imperial authorities who, until this point, had largely ignored the activities of New Englanders. In 1686, Royal officials finally created the Dominion of New England, which put the New England colonies under the rule of New York's Governor Edmund Andros. Ironically, even though New England's colonies had prevailed on the battlefield, King Philip's War led to the loss of much of their political autonomy.

The conflict between colonists and Native Americans known as King Philip's War, was one of the bloodiest (per capita) battles in American history. © BETTMANN/CORBIS

WITCHES AND SATAN

The New England colonists also faced spiritual challenges that can be traced directly to King Philip's War and subsequent frontier violence in Maine. The New England colonists were devout Puritans who saw themselves as God's chosen people. In turn, they usually interpreted their wars with Indians as a sign of God's displeasure. Many English refugees from these Indian wars sought safety in towns like Salem and Boston. Their fear of both American Indians and the Devil turned into hysteria during the infamous Salem witchcraft trials of 1692.

Pivotal individuals in the trials such as George Burroughs and Abigail Hobbs had been terrorized by wars with the Indians. Though they did not equate American Indians with witches, they and their neighbors did come to associate the visible assaults of Indians with the invisible attacks of the Devil. In their confessions, accused witches would describe the devil as resembling an American Indian. Their fear of Indians, having grown exponentially since the outbreak of King Philip's War, had heightened their fear of witches, which eventually led to the execution of twenty individuals.

That American Indians and the Devil had become intimately entwined in the minds of many colonists indicates just how much King Philip's War had reinforced racial identity and the divide between English colonists and native peoples. This new mentality had a lasting impact on future colonists and even the United States. The New Eng-

land colonists wrote far more about King Philip's War than did other English colonists about their conflicts with Indians. They waged a war with their pens that justified their actions and cast all American Indians as the enemy. All of the ink these colonists spilled created a lasting, however skewed, memory of the war that shaped American culture and subsequent American Indian-white relations.

LITERATURE AND CULTURE

Shortly after the war, for example, Mary Rowlandson wrote about her life as an Indian captive in *The Sovereignty and Goodness of God* (1682). It became America's first best seller and the most widely read captivity narrative ever published, helping to establish many of the genre's key elements. It offered a gripping tale of Rowlandson's capture during an American Indian attack on the town of Lancaster and how she endured months of captivity, never losing faith in God and resolutely clinging to the superiority of English ways. The most enduring legacies of the work were the reinforcement of the Anglo-American belief of American Indians as savages and masking the lack of attention paid to American Indian captivity experiences.

Rowlandson's work was only the first of many highly popular depictions of King Philip's War. In the 1830s writers such as James Fenimore Cooper, Edwin Forrest, and William Apess, a Pequot American Indian, drew on the memory of King Philip's War in ways that made readers and theater viewers think about contemporary American Indian policy. They presented fictional and romanticized accounts of Indian resistance to English expansion. They presented conflict between English and American Indians as inevitable, and, in many cases, provided a rationale for the Indian removals under President Andrew Jackson.

BIBLIOGRAPHY

Drake, James D. *King Philip's War: Civil War in New England, 1675–1676*. Amherst: University of Massachusetts Press, 1999.

Lepore, Jill. *The Name of War: King Philip's War and the Origins of American Identity*. New York: Knopf, 1998.

Norton, Mary Beth. *In the Devil's Snare: The Salem Witchcraft Crisis of 1692*. New York: Knopf, 2002.

Salisbury, Neal, ed. *The Sovereignty and Goodness of God by Mary Rowlandson*. Boston, MA: Bedford Books, 1997.

James D. Drake

See also: **Bacon's Rebellion; Cooper, James Fenimore; Native Americans: Images in Popular Culture; Rowlandson, Mary.**

LAFAYETTE'S TOUR

The visit of Marie Joseph Paul Yves Roch Gilbert Motier, the Marquis de Lafayette, to the United States in 1824 and 1825 marked a high point of early American nationalism. Lafayette's triumphal tour of the United States signaled that memories of the Revolutionary War would continue to play a significant role in American culture. It also served as a high-water mark in the on-again, off-again love affair between the United States and France.

The Marquis de Lafayette was just a nineteen-year-old wealthy nobleman when he came to the United States in 1777 to lend his support to the cause of American independence, but he soon was commissioned a major-general in the Continental Army and became an important member of George Washington's staff. Lafayette helped persuade the French government to recognize the United States and to send military aid, although he was not close to the commander of French forces in the United States, the Comte de Rochambeau. Lafayette's greatest military contribution came at the end of the war in Virginia, where he was instrumental in securing the American victory at Yorktown. During the Revolutionary War, Lafayette became close friends with George Washington, whom he referred to as his "adopted father," and he garnered great affection from the troops he commanded, whose pay he sometimes supplemented with his own fortune.

Lafayette returned to France in 1781, and he was soon caught up in the politics of the French Revolution. Lafayette supported the idea of a constitutional monarchy, and although he initially supported the revolution, when the Jacobins turned increasingly violent in 1792, Lafayette disapproved. Lafayette was imprisoned by his enemies in Austria for five years. Napoleon Bonaparte freed Lafayette, but the general mainly stayed out of politics until after Napoleon was deposed in 1815. Lafayette spent the following decade mostly in retirement at his estate, La Grange, where he experienced increasing financial problems, since most of his wealth had been confiscated during the French Revolution.

What Americans saw as Lafayette's support for moderate democracy during the French Revolution had only increased his popularity in the United States, and news of his every move during the French Revolution had filled U.S. newspapers. Early in 1824, President James Monroe invited the general to return to the United States for a visit to accept money and land-grants from Congress and praise from the American people. Lafayette saw the trip as not

Marquis de Lafayette, wounded and laying on the ground, at the Battle of the Brandywine, 1777. Lafayette's tour of the United States in 1824 and 1825 marked a high point of early American nationalism. GETTY IMAGES

only financially a good move, but also a way to promote French ties with the American republic, and he gladly accepted the invitation. Lafayette took with him on the tour his son, George Washington Lafayette, a secretary named Auguste Levasseur, who wrote a French account of their journey, and, at various stages of the journey, a collection of other European friends including the Scottish writer and reformer Frances Wright. Congress instructed the American people that Lafayette, as the "nation's guest," should not be allowed to expend one cent of his own money during his trip, and people all over the United States prepared to greet one of their favorite Revolutionary heroes.

LAFAYETTE AND NATIONAL IDENTITY

Lafayette's visit to the United States in 1824 came at an important time for the nation to reconfirm its allegiance to the ideas of the American Revolution and the memory of the Revolutionary War. The Revolutionary generation was dying off, and the country was moving in a more modern direction in the nineteenth century. Amidst all the changes, however, most Americans felt it was necessary and positive to remind themselves of the country's glorious military past and to express a continued belief in republican and democratic ideals. When Lafayette arrived

in New York City August 15, 1824, he provided the greatest possible living reminder of America's Revolutionary past. Lafayette seemed to be the perfect inspiration for Americans to celebrate their past, their "pure" politics of liberty, and their ideals of progress.

During his visit to the United States, Lafayette visited all twenty-four states, and at every stop along the way, he faced an outpouring of thankfulness from the American people that took the form of ceremonies, balls, parades, fireworks, and any other form of celebration they could think of. The general attended a huge two-day commemoration of the Battle of Yorktown, during which he received visitors directly on the battlefield. He was present in Washington D.C. as the contested presidential election of 1824 was decided by Congress, and some observers credited his presence for helping to divert public attention from the crisis and for calming the situation. Lafayette visited former presidents James Madison and Thomas Jefferson, and he made a gut-wrenching pilgrimage to George Washington's grave. In June 1825, Lafayette laid the cornerstone of the Bunker Hill Monument in Charlestown, Massachusetts, the most important of the countless libraries, memorials, and other public buildings he dedicated on his journey. At every turn, Lafayette stopped to speak with visitors (including slaves, which embarrassed his Southern hosts), and the public took particular notice of his affection for Revolutionary veterans everywhere.

Lafayette's visit built up a sense of American nationalism, not only by reminding the people who turned out to greet him around the country of the Revolutionary past, but also because the American press followed his every move. Newspapers reported every day on Lafayette's movements, his speeches, his clothing, and how many grateful viewers turned out to laud him. The publicity helped to link disparate parts of the nation together in the mutual admiration for Lafayette. In addition, a huge number of souvenirs (sheet music, cleaning brushes, china, and glass bottles), many bearing images of Lafayette, allowed Americans to express their patriotism through commercial activity. When Lafayette departed for France in September 1825, the American people would long remember not only him, but also the excitement of his visit.

Americans have not lost their affection for Lafayette over the years, witnessed by the number of "Lafayette" place names, the several societies dedicated to his memory, and the hot collector's market for souvenirs of his visit. When U.S. general John Pershing landed the American Expeditionary Force in France during World War I, his first words were "Lafayette, we are here!" Lafayette's memory signals that the relationship between the United States and France, although it may wax and wane, will probably always have a solid basis in a past of Revolutionary friendship.

BIBLIOGRAPHY

Klamkin, Marian. *The Return of Lafayette: 1824–1825*. New York: Scribners, 1974.

Kramer, Lloyd. *Lafayette in Two Worlds*. Chapel Hill: University of North Carolina Press, 1996.

Loveland, Anne C. *Emblem of Liberty: The Image of Lafayette in the American Mind*. Baton Rouge: Louisiana State University Press, 1971.

Purcell, Sarah J. *Sealed with Blood: War, Sacrifice, and Memory in Revolutionary America*. Philadelphia: University of Pennsylvania Press, 2002.

Sarah J. Purcell

See also: **Bunker Hill Monument; Flags; Montgomery, Richard; Valley Forge.**

LEGACIES OF INDIAN WARFARE

Early America was often a violent time and place. Conflicts between American Indian groups and between American Indians and Europeans characterized the colonial and early national periods, impacting both American Indians and Europeans in significant ways. Causes of conflict remained as varied as the many different nations and peoples that encountered one another in early America. Like Europeans, American Indian peoples fought against each other before Europeans arrived in the Americas, and war formed a crucial component of their cultures, especially among men. The frequency and deadliness of warfare increased dramatically after contact with Europeans, however, and American Indian cultures adapted by making war and preparation for war a more vital element of their societies than ever before. The introduction of new technologies increased the mortality of war, forcing Europeans and American Indians to adapt new tactics and styles of warfare. This new world of nearly constant warfare in early America presented all peoples with new challenges, permanently altered the course of history, and thereby helped to shape American society and culture.

CAUSES OF WARFARE

American Indians and Europeans fought among themselves and against each other for a variety of reasons. Revenge for the murder of a kinsman provided the most likely reason for American Indian groups to fight against each other. The family and clan members of a murdered American Indian killed the murderer or a member of the murderer's family to avenge their deceased relative, which often sparked further revenge killings in response, sometimes spiraling into full-fledged war between different American Indian groups. Repeatedly, the need to avenge the deaths of murdered kinsmen also brought American Indians and Europeans into open conflict as European settlers fought with and killed American Indian warriors who were then avenged. Occasionally, American Indians fought against each other to protect or acquire resources, such as horses (valuable new animals introduced by Europeans) or game-rich hunting lands. After European diseases introduced into North America killed American Indians by the tens of thousands, American Indian groups like the Iroquois warred against other native peoples to acquire captives to adopt into their tribes and replenish their depleted populations. As American Indians fled these attacks or moved away from European settlements, they displaced other groups that frequently reacted by attacking the newcomers to their region.

All American Indian groups had traditional enemies by the time Europeans arrived on the scene, and they often attempted to recruit their new technologically advanced neighbors as allies in their preexisting disputes. Trade with Europeans became a source of tension between American Indian groups as tribes competed over access to manufactured goods. American Indian groups with access to guns through trade found they had a

INDIAN WARS, 1609–1824

1609 Samuel de Champlain and Algonquians attack Mohawks

1609–1614 First Anglo-Powhatan War

1622–1632 Second Anglo-Powhatan War

1636–1637 Anglo-Pequot War in New England

1640–1685 Iroquois wage "Mourning Wars"

1644–1646 Third Anglo-Powhatan War

1675–1676 King Philip's War in New England

1676 Bacon's Rebellion in Virginia

1680 Pueblo Rebellion against the Spanish in the southwest

1689–1697 King William's War between England and France and their respective Indian allies

1702–1713 Queen Anne's War: England and her Indian allies against France and Spain and their respective Indian allies

1703–1704 South Carolina War against the Apalachees and their Spanish missions in north Florida

1711–1713 Tuscarora War in North Carolina

1715–1728 Yamasee War in South Carolina

1720–1752 French and Choctaw wars against the Chickasaws

1729–1731 Natchez War in lower Mississippi Valley

1744–1748 King George's War between England and France and their respective Indian allies

1754–1763 North American component of the Seven Years War between England and France and their respective Indian allies

1760–1761 Cherokee War in South Carolina

1763–1765 Pontiac's Rebellion in Ohio Valley and Great Lakes area

1774 Lord Dunmore's War in Virginia against the Shawnees

1775–1783 American Revolution between United States and England and their respective Indian allies

1790–1794 Little Turtle's War between Ohio Valley Indians and the United States

1809–1815 Ohio Valley Indian Confederacy war against the United States

1812–1815 War of 1812 between United States and England and their respective Indian allies

1813–1814 Red Stick War among the Creek Indians and against the United States

1817–1818 First Seminole War in north Florida

1819–1824 Kickapoo War against the United States

major advantage over their native neighbors who had not yet acquired the new weapons. Finally, the various European powers in colonial North America sought allies and trade partners among American Indian groups. When Europeans went to war against one another, they pulled American Indians into the conflicts by offering them incentives to fight or by attacking them for being allies of their opponent. Europeans also paid American Indians to attack each other for economic gain, as the English did in South Carolina in the late 1600s and early 1700s by arming and paying their native allies to seize captives from other American Indian groups to be sold as slaves in the Caribbean.

COLONIAL WARS OF AMERICAN INDIAN RESISTANCE: SEVENTEENTH CENTURY

Throughout North America and from the times of earliest contact with Europeans, many American Indian peoples violently resisted European encroachments on their land, culture, and independence. Although many American Indian groups welcomed Europeans initially as trading partners and allies, those friendly relations often degenerated into animosity, distrust, and violence. European arrival in the Americas brought Europeans, American Indians, and Africans into contact for the first time. Their respective cultures, values, and languages differed markedly, and those differences encouraged misunderstandings that frequently led to conflict. American Indians who lived near a European settlement watched new diseases kill their relatives, European hunters dispatch their game animals, European livestock eat their crops, European men assault their women, Christian missionaries condemn their religion, and European farms consume their land. Some native peoples adapted to these new pressures without resorting to violence, but many others felt pushed to the limit of toleration and lashed out at the injustices they perceived were being perpetrated upon them.

In the area that later became the United States, American Indian resistance occurred most often against English colonists. In 1609, within two years after establishing Jamestown, Virginia Company officials found themselves involved in a low intensity conflict, known as the First Anglo-Powhatan War, that lasted five years. Overbearing English demands for food and land convinced the Powhatan to launch a devastating attack in March 1622 that killed hundreds of English people and ignited a decade-long war that ended largely in a stalemate. The last major attempt by the Powhatan to violently preserve their autonomy occurred in another one day attack in April 1644 that killed over 400 English colonists but resulted in Powhatan defeat after two years of conflict.

In New England, the Pequot fought against land encroachment and an attempt to monopolize the wampum trade by English Puritan colonists in 1636 to 1637. The war ended in a overwhelming defeat for the Pequot as the English surrounded their main village, set it on fire, and killed over 600 of the fleeing American Indians as they emerged from the flames. Some surviving Pequot, including their principal chief Sassacus, fled west to Mohawk territory where the Mohawk killed them to prove they were not involved in the attacks on the English. The English captured still other survivors and sold them into slavery in the Caribbean or gave them to their American Indian allies such as the Mohegan, Narraganset, and Niantic. King Philip's War is the name given to the next major uprising of New England Indians in 1675 to 1676. English land encroachment and attempts to force American Indians in New England to live under English law provided the central causes of this conflict with the Wampanoag and other American Indian groups. English superiority in numbers of soldiers and firepower, and the aid of their American Indian allies, wore the Indian alliance down and virtually eliminated the Wampanoag, Nippmuc, and Narragansett tribes, resulting in the end of large scale American Indian resistance in New England.

COLONIAL WARS OF AMERICAN INDIAN RESISTANCE: EIGHTEENTH CENTURY

In the Carolinas, the Tuscarora and Yamasee tribes rebelled against the English presence in 1711 to 1713 and 1715 to 1728 respectively. In both wars, trade abuses by the English, such as seizing American Indian women and children in payment for American Indian trade debts, provoked the American Indians into attacking. Eventually, both groups were militarily defeated, with Tuscarora survivors fleeing north to New York to join their Iroquois relatives and Yamasee refugees joining the Creek confederacy in the deep South. Similarly, the Natchez re-

belled against French arrogance and land encroachments in 1729 to 1731 by killing hundreds of French people settled in Natchez on the Mississippi River. France and her Choctaw allies eventually routed the Natchez, killing hundreds, seizing dozens for sale into slavery in the Caribbean, and forcing dozens more to flee and join other American Indian groups such as the Chickasaw, Creek, and Cherokee.

In 1760 to 1761, the Cherokee struck the British in South Carolina during the turmoil of the Seven Years' War (known in America as the French and Indian War) because some of their warriors were attacked and killed while traveling back and forth to Virginia to assist George Washington's forces against the French. The Cherokee seized the advantage of fighting in their mountainous homeland and defeated Carolina forces, before a regular British army force turned the tables and forced the Cherokee to sign a peace treaty ceding large portions of their territory. After the Seven Years' War ended in 1763, American Indians in the Ohio Valley and Great Lakes area who had formerly been allied to France united to assail the British takeover of French forts in those areas. After initial success in this war, called Pontiac's Rebellion after one of the principal war leaders, the American Indians and the British eventually settled on a nervous truce in 1765.

WARS OF AMERICAN INDIAN RESISTANCE AGAINST THE UNITED STATES, 1790s TO 1820s

During George Washington's term as president of the United States, Shawnee, Ojibway, Miami, Delaware, Potawatami, and Ottawa in the Ohio Valley, under the nominal leadership of Miami war chief Little Turtle, revolted against American intrusion on their lands. They defeated two American armies before eventually suffering defeat at the hands of a third army under General Anthony Wayne in 1795. A little more than a decade later, American Indians from the Great Lakes to the Gulf Coast joined a war of resistance against American land grabbing and cultural interference. The Shawnee brothers Tecumseh and the Shawnee Prophet organized much of this insurgency and folded their fight into the War of 1812 between Britain and the United States on the side of the British. American forces eventually defeated them and their British supporters in Canada. Similarly, the Red Stick faction of the Creek fought against other Creek and Americans at the same time until suffering defeat at the hands of Andrew Jackson and American Indian groups such as the Choctaw and Cherokee who allied with the United States. Some of the Red Stick Creek survivors fled south into north Florida to join their Seminole brethren and continued the fight against the United States in what became known as the First Seminole War, from 1817 to 1818. Around the same time, the Kickapoo fought briefly against American veterans of the War of 1812 who had been promised land in Illinois in compensation for their service.

IMPERIAL WARS

Besides the wars of resistance, native peoples also fought in every war between their European neighbors. In all of the imperial wars during the colonial and early national periods, American Indians fought on both sides, providing crucial intelligence and fighting strength to the European forces and enduring death, deprivation, and sometimes victory for their efforts. The major imperial wars that also engaged American Indian warriors include: King William's War between England and France and their respective American Indian allies from 1689 to 1697; Queen Anne's War with England and her American Indian allies against France and Spain and their respective American Indian allies from 1702 to 1713; King George's War between England and France and their respective American Indian allies from 1744 to 1748; the North American component of the Seven Years' War between England and France and their respective American Indian allies from 1754 to 1763; the American Revolution between the United States and England and their respective American Indian allies from 1775 to 1783; and the War of 1812 between the United States and England and their respective American Indian allies from 1812 to 1815.

IMPACTS OF WARFARE ON AMERICAN INDIAN CULTURE

Because of the nearly constant state of warfare in North America after 1607 and the need for American Indians to participate in these conflicts, Europeans and Americans tended to view American Indians as inherently warlike people whose "savage" nature led them to launch sneak attacks on unsuspecting men, women, and children. There is evidence that the so-called American Indian style of warfare consisting of small-scale attacks under concealment of darkness and forests arose as a response to European firearms technology. In 1609, Frenchman Samuel de Champlain led a party of French soldiers accompanied by Algonkin and Montagnais in canoes down Lake Champlain where they encountered a Mohawk war party of about 200 men. The two opposing American Indian groups beached their canoes and made preparations for a ritual battle whereby the two forces dressed in wooden armor and massed a few hundred yards apart. War leaders from each side leapt into the clear space between the forces, taunting and daring individuals from the other side to fight. Champlain grew tired of the lack of real fighting and ordered his soldiers to fire at the Mohawk with their guns. The French sol-

diers immediately killed three Mohawk chiefs, distinguishable by their ornate apparel, shocking the Mohawk and forcing them to flee. Because guns and bullets made such tactics obsolete, never again would American Indians in the northeast fight large scale ritualized battles with wooden armor, and, ironically, the new fighting techniques they devised came to be known by Europeans as a particularly American Indian way of fighting.

CULTURAL IMPACTS

American Indian cultures adapted in a variety of significant ways to the new world of warfare that confronted them after European arrival. War chiefs, who normally only exercised authority while leading a war party, assumed greater leadership roles over time than their peace or civil chiefs, who normally directed day-to-day functions, since a state of war became perpetual. Europeans also preferred to negotiate with war leaders in order to recruit native allies in their wars against other Europeans, thus elevating the status of war chiefs and warriors in diplomacy.

Economically, American Indian groups became increasingly dependent on trade with Europeans to acquire the guns, gun powder, and ammunition necessary to survive against native and European enemies. Dependence on European trade made American Indians vulnerable to manipulation by Europeans and Americans who often insisted on land cessions in order to pay trade debts. Continual warfare resulted in the deaths of large portions of many generations, especially among young men. Survivors of war often became refugees who joined other American Indian tribes in order to find mates and subsist. Coupled with the killer diseases introduced to the Americas by Europeans, the new world of unrelenting war wiped out many American Indian communities, forced others to migrate, and made the threat of violence a basic reality of American Indian life.

BIBLIOGRAPHY

Calloway, Colin G. *New Worlds for All: Indians, Europeans, and the Remaking of Early America.* Baltimore, MD: Johns Hopkins University Press, 1997.

Holm, Tom. "American Indian Warfare: The Cycles of Conflict and the Militarization of Native North America." In *A Companion to American Indian History,* edited by Philip J. Deloria and Neal Salisbury. Malden, MA: Blackwell Publishers, Inc., 2002.

Nardo, Don. *North American Indian Wars.* San Diego, CA: Greenhaven Press, Inc., 1999.

Starkey, Armstrong. *European and Native American Warfare, 1675–1815.* Norman: University of Oklahoma Press, 1998.

Waldman, Carl. *Atlas of the North American Indian.* New York: Facts on File, 1985.

Washburn, Wilcomb, ed. *History of Indian-White Relations.* Washington, DC: Smithsonian Institution, 1988.

Greg O'Brien

See also: Armed Conflicts in America, 1587–1815; Jamestown: Legacy of the Massacre of 1622; King Philip's War, Legacy of; Native Americans: Images in Popular Culture; Slavery in America; War of 1812.

LOYALISTS

An examination of loyalists of the American Revolution opens up an elusive world of changing terms and historical interpretations. Technically all American colonists were "loyal" until the Declaration of Independence in 1776 forced them to take sides publicly. But in the preceding decade, as resistance to Parliament and its policies escalated, the question facing Americans was whether their acknowledged grievances justified riots, boycotts, armed protests, and, ultimately, revolution. Those who maintained the faith that the British government would rectify colonial complaints through the legal legislative system were contemptuously dubbed "Tories" by their more aggressive "Whig" opponents—terms drawn from seventeenth-century English politics. After 1776, "Tory" and the somewhat more dignified label, "Loyalist," became synonymous.

LOYALISTS AND HISTORIANS

As the "losers" in the Revolution, loyalists did not fare well in revolutionary-era histories. Although comprising half a million of British America's white population of 2.5 million, they became a topic of objective historical examination only by the mid-nineteenth century chiefly as biography (Smith 1968, p. 269). Historians of the early twentieth century tended to interpret loyalism in socio-economic terms, and later as an intellectual phenomenon. The Vietnam War, the Bicentennial, and the Civil Rights movement, however, sparked a new interest in dissent and in issues of race, class, and gender which help to explain the appearance of a vast number of loyalist studies since the 1960s. The result has been to depict loyalism as a vertical cross section, rather than a horizontal segment, of American society, with the addition that loyalism generally predominated among recent immigrants and cultural minorities who valued royal government as protection against discrimination by local majorities.

ARTICULATE LOYALISTS

Revolutionary governments found it as difficult as modern historians to distinguish between loyalists and Whig "patriots." High profile, outspoken loyalists, such as royal governors, imperial officials, and clergy of the Church of England who clung to their oaths to God and king and who profited from their appointments were not hard to spot and to neutralize. Equally vulnerable were provincial elites, politicians, lawyers, overseas merchants, who openly expressed their convictions that rebellion against the powerful British government could never succeed, and if by chance it did, Americans would fall victim to republican anarchy which would, in turn, open the way to a French-imposed despotism far worse than anything suffered under Great Britain. Collectively, government officials and outspoken opponents of revolution constituted the most prominent of the 80,000 to 100,000 loyalists who eventually fled from the Revolution to other parts of the empire (Brown, 192).

PRAGMATIC LOYALISTS

Other less articulate Americans expressed their loyalty by bearing arms in the king's cause. At one time or another during the war, an estimated 20,000 American loyalists fought for the crown as provincial regulars (Smith 1968, p. 266). In addition, wherever the British were a military presence, as in Savannah, Charleston, New York, and even the town of Castine in Maine, local loyalists flocked to the royal standard as irregular militia, turning revolution into bloody civil war. In the Carolina backcountry, around Long Island Sound, and along Maine's coast, revolution offered both sides the opportunity for pursuing long smoldering feuds and personal vengeance under the cover of political ideology.

Another group that defined their loyalism by deeds rather than words were an estimated 100,000 African slaves, one-fifth of the total black American population (Walker, 3). The process began as early as 1775 when Virginia's royal governor, Lord Dunmore, issued a call for recruits and promised freedom to slaves owned by rebels. In short order, Dunmore had three hundred former slaves enlisted in his "Ethiopian Regiment," and in the course of the war, Virginia alone lost some 30,000 slaves, though not all by flight because some were captured in raids on rebel estates (Walker, 3). Thus from the start the British were committed to emancipation, but only as a wartime expedient and with varied and contradictory results. While the war continued, many escaped slaves were pressed into the royal navy or into the British army as "auxiliaries," such as teamsters, laborers, cooks, and as officers's personal servants. Slave owning loyalists who escaped to British protection were not only allowed to retain their own slaves, but sometimes received as compensation for lost labor the slaves seized as booty of war from rebel estates.

THE SILENT LOYALISTS

The loyalists that Whigs feared the most were the ones they could not see. The silent subversives (Tories of the heart), whose allegiances were suspect, stayed quiet waiting for the time when the King's forces would eventually prevail. Long before the Declaration of Independence,

Tarring and feathering of an English loyalist by American colonists. © BETTMANN/CORBIS

the Continental Congress warned the states to disarm citizens who refused to join the Association enforcing the embargo against Britain. The Declaration of Independence stimulated a torrent of anti-loyalist legislation. All thirteen states formulated test oaths administered by local committees to adult males. Often public exposure, hu-

miliation, the threat of mob action and of social ostracism were sufficient to win converts. If not, loss of public office, bonds for good behavior, fines, prison, and even banishment with confiscation of property awaited those who refused to renounce their loyalty to the king, with severity depending on the suspect himself and local circumstances. In Massachusetts, at least, the plight of loyalist refugees worsened when the state government in 1778 passed a banishment law that not only proscribed over 300 prominent refugees by name, but threatened with death those who persisted in their efforts to return.

Penalties applied only to male family members, and so loyalists facing flight or banishment often consigned their property to wives, relatives or friends who stayed behind in the expectation that family and property could be reunited after the British won the war. In such circumstances Tory wives were suddenly yanked from domestic obscurity to manage and defend all alone the family possessions from rapacious neighbors and an unsympathetic legal system.

THE LOYALIST REFUGEES

American independence in 1783 posed a huge dilemma to the British government as well as to the thousands of loyalists who left their homes to seek sanctuary under British protection. As early as 1776, over a thousand civilian loyalists had joined the British troops evacuating Boston for Halifax. As far as refugees go, they were the lucky ones, for they had comparatively ready access to local sympathy, occupations, and land. But when the war ended, a veritable deluge of impoverished refugees abandoned the fortified enclaves along the American coast where they had been sheltered and flooded into nearby British possessions, completely outstripping the ability of those regions to absorb such numbers. Thirty thousand refugees landed in Nova Scotia alone, destitute of resources and of hope (Brown, 192).

Refugees with sufficient means, economic and political, might travel to England where they tried to capitalize on their connections to re-create a respectable life. Persistent applications to the British government for compensation finally led to the creation of a Court of High Commission to investigate claims against the government. Eventually the Court authorized payment of over three million pounds to more than four thousand claimants as at least token compensation for their loyalty and losses (Brown, 188). Additionally, the British government awarded pensions and offices, both political and religious, to leading loyalists as well as thousands of land grants to refugees in Canada. But all this was small satisfaction to the vast majority of loyalist refugees whose losses, though personally devastating, were insufficient to attract the Commission's attention. Regardless of their condition or location, all refugees shared a common sense of bewilderment over Britain's loss and their own lonely plight as aliens in a strange land.

None could have felt it more than the "emancipated" slaves that accompanied the civilians and troops that evacuated America. From Savannah and Charleston, several thousand black refugees ended up in Spanish-held Florida and the British West Indies. At least 3000 former slaves from New York were deposited in Birchtown, near Shelburne, on Nova Scotia's southern tip (Walker, 12). Without sufficient government aid or means of self-support, the black refugees of Nova Scotia subsisted through a form of indentured servitude and petty crime until their plight came to the attention of a group of London philanthropists. Operating through the Sierra Leone Company, the London group acquired land on the west coast of Africa. In January 1792, 2,000 black loyalists in a convoy of fifteen vessels set sail from Nova Scotia to start a new life in a new British colony, Sierra Leone, the capitol of which would be named "Freetown."

THE RETURNEES

The conclusion to the fighting convinced some loyalists to attempt a return to their homes in America. Two provisions in the peace treaty gave them some ray of hope. One stipulated that the Continental Congress would urge the states to place no obstacles in the way of loyalists returning to recover property and debts, and in the other, Congress agreed to recommend that the states cease all prosecutions and confiscations of loyalist property. In areas where fighting had been recent and intense, local authorities simply ignored Congress. In Maine, New York and Connecticut, returning loyalists were arrested, physically abused, and summarily expelled; in South Carolina, one loyalist was lynched. But elsewhere, depending on local circumstances and the returnees themselves, the response could be considerably more friendly. In commercial centers such as Boston, New York City, and Charleston, prominent Tory merchants, valued for their skills and wealth, were welcomed back and some even recovered a portion of their confiscated estates. Gradually, as the United States came to grips with a postwar depression, Americans everywhere accepted, if not welcomed, returning loyalists as a means of economic revival. As the loyalists gradually returned to respectable obscurity in the new republic they had once opposed, the term, "Tory," retained its usefulness long into the nineteenth century as a means of denouncing one's political opponents.

BIBLIOGRAPHY

Bailyn, Bernard. "The Losers: Notes on the Historiography of Loyalism" (appendix). In *The Ordeal of Thomas Hutchinson*. Cambridge, MA: Harvard University Press, 1974.

Brown, Wallace. *The Good Americans: The Loyalists in the American Revolution*. New York: Morrow, 1969.

Calhoon, Robert M.; Barnes, Timothy M.; and Rawlyk, George A., eds. *Loyalists and Community in North America*. Westport, CT: Greenwood Press, 1994.

Nelson, William H. *The American Tory*. London: Oxford University Press, 1961.

Quarles, Benjamin. *The Negro in the American Revolution.* Chapel Hill: University of North Carolina Press, 1961.

Smith, Paul H. *Loyalists and Redcoats: A Study in British Revolutionary Policy.* Chapel Hill: University of North Carolina Press, 1964.

Smith, Paul H. "The American Loyalists: Notes on Their Organization and Numerical Strength." *William and Mary Quarterly*, 25 no. 2 (1968): 259–277.

Walker, James W. St. G. *The Black Loyalists: The Search for a Promised Land in Nova Scotia and Sierra Leone, 1783–1870.* London: Dalhousie University Press, 1976.

James S. Leamon

See also: **Association Test; Galloway, Grace: Diary of a Loyalist; Mobilization: War for Independence.**

MADISON, DOLLEY

(b. May 20, 1768, d. July 12, 1849) As First Lady, saved many documents and White House treasures prior to burning of Washington, D.C. by the British during the War of 1812.

Throughout the history of the United States, only three First Ladies have come close to matching the fame of their husbands. Jacqueline Kennedy was much admired for her beauty, grace, and elegance. Eleanor Roosevelt was respected worldwide for her dignity, generosity, and greatness of spirit. Dolley Madison was known at first for her skills as a social hostess in the White House; but during war with the British, she proved herself both courageous and quick-thinking.

Dolley Payne, born in Piedmont, North Carolina, on May 20, 1768, was raised in rural eastern Virginia, the land of her parents, John and Mary Coles Payne. Her mother was a Quaker, and Dolley, one of eight children, was raised in that faith. John Payne freed his slaves in 1783 and moved the family to Philadelphia. After his death in 1793, Dolley's mother returned to Virginia with her two youngest children. By that time, Dolley had married John Todd, a young Quaker lawyer.

Yellow fever hit Philadelphia in 1793, and Dolley took her two sons, John Payne and William Temple, to escape the city. Nonetheless, William died of the fever that year, as did Dolley's husband. The following year, Aaron Burr, then a U.S. Senator, introduced the young widow to a mild-mannered, frail-looking bachelor seventeen years her senior. At the time, James Madison, who had served in the Continental Congress and had sponsored the first ten amendments to the Constitution, was a member of the House of Representatives. The vivacious Dolley and the shy James were married in 1794.

When Madison became the nation's fourth president in 1809, Dolley became the first First Lady to serve a full term in the White House. The president's home had not been built during Washington's years in office; John and Abigail Adams spent only four months there; and Thomas Jefferson was a widower. In fact, Dolley had often taken on the role of official hostess during Jefferson's administration.

Once in the White House, Dolley transformed the rather austere and neglected mansion into a visitor's paradise. She called upon architect Benjamin Henry Latrobe and his wife Mary for assistance. New paint and tasteful decorations brightened every room. They were neither too fancy nor too foreign. The front entrance was fixed

Dolley Madison saving the Declaration of Independence before fleeing the White House prior to the British invasion of Washington, D.C., during the War of 1812. © BETTMANN/CORBIS

so that visitors no longer had to fear falling into a pit upon entering. Before long, White House functions were the most coveted invitation in town. And Dolley Madison, with her gowns of silk and satin and an ostrich feather stuck in her hair, established a ritual for every other First Lady to follow—that of showing off the nation's presidential home with pride. Since that time all First Ladies have followed her lead to a lesser or greater degree, although few have matched the elegance of Dolley Madison.

At the beginning of Madison's second term, war broke out between the United States and Great Britain over grievances arising from oppressive shipping practices during the Napoleonic Wars. Ironically, Madison asked Congress to declare war on Great Britain the day after the British had lifted the trade restrictions. Without telephone or other communication, it was some time before either side knew what the other had done. By then, the so-called War of 1812 was in full force.

The United States was ill-prepared for war against Great Britain. Despite some early and surprising U.S. Navy successes, by 1814 the British had landed in Maryland. On a late August morning, Madison rode out on his horse to investigate cannon fire. Dolley was left at the White House with 100 soldiers as guard and one spyglass. Before long, most of the guard left to join the fight.

Dolley spent the day peering through windows with her spyglass and trying to decide what she must save if the British came. After a soldier returned with the President's message to leave and meet him in Virginia, Dolley loaded as many Cabinet papers as possible into a wagon as well as any silver that could be carried. She was also determined to save the portrait of George Washington by famed painter Gilbert Stuart. When it proved too time-consuming to unscrew the frame from the wall, she ordered the frame to be broken and the canvas taken out and rolled up. Now restored, the portrait is the only object that has been in the White House since 1800.

Before she left, Dolley spent a few moments writing a short letter to her sister Anna. She ended it by saying, "I must leave this house, or the retreating army will make me a prisoner in it by filling up the road I am directed to take."

The British did arrive shortly thereafter and burned the city and the White House. It was a harsh blow to American pride. The Madisons returned to find their home in ruins. They never lived again in the White House, but it was rebuilt in three years, grander than before.

Dolley and James retired to Montpelier, Virginia, where she continued to entertain in her lavish style. After Madison died in 1836, Dolley went back to the Washington society she loved. She died at the age of 81 in 1849, shortly after attending a ball for President James K. Polk. Her funeral attracted thousands of mourners. Dolley Madison had become a folk hero and an icon in American culture for the courage she had shown in 1814 when Washington came under attack.

BIBLIOGRAPHY

Editors of American Heritage. *The American Heritage Book of the Presidents and Famous Americans*, Vol. 2. New York: Dell, 1967.

Whitney, Robin Vaugh. *The American Presidents*, 8th edition. Pleasantville, NY: Reader's Digest Books, 1996.

Internet Resources

"The Dolley Madison Project." Virginia Center for Digital History. Available from <http://moderntimes.vcdh.virginia.edu/madison>

Madison, Dolley. "The Burning of Washington, August 23, 1814." National Center for Public Policy Research. Available from <http://www.nationalcenter.org/WashingtonBurning1814.html>

The White House: First Ladies' Gallery. Available from <www.whitehouse.gov/history/firstladies>

Corinne J. Naden and Rose Blue

See also: **Adams, Abigail; Drinker, Elizabeth; Generals' Wives: Martha Washington, Katherine Greene, Lucy Knox; Republican Womanhood; Women and the Homefront: Diaries.**

MADISON, JAMES

(b. March 16, 1751; d. June 28, 1836) Father of the U.S. Constitution, coauthor of *The Federalist*, draftsman of the Bill of Rights, and fourth President of the United States (1809–1817).

James Madison was centrally concerned, throughout his public life, with war or the prospect of war. He became a member of the Continental Congress in December 1779, perhaps the darkest moment of the Revolutionary War, and rose to be regarded as the most effective member of that body. He helped secure approval of the Articles of Confederation, struggled constantly with the financial problems facing the union, and supported proposals for a set of independent federal taxes. After 1783, he returned to the Virginia legislature's lower house and came to be committed to elemental changes in the structure of the new republic. This commitment to reform led to the drafting of the Constitution.

Madison believed that the continental union was not just ineffective, but increasingly in danger of a speedy dissolution. Moreover, he was convinced that the Revolution could not survive disintegration of the union. It was the union that protected the Revolution's experiments in republican governance from foreign intervention and secured the states against the rivalries and fragmentation that had splintered Europe and condemned its peoples to oppressive taxes, swollen military forces, tyranny, and wars. As it was, he reasoned, federal inability to act against the postwar economic slump, which he attributed to European regulations limiting the country's trade, was probably the leading cause of popular commotions in the several states and local legislation violating basic rights or sacrificing long-term public needs to more immediate considerations. "Most of our political evils," he wrote, "may be traced up to our commercial ones, as most of our moral may to our political."

At the Constitutional Convention in 1787, Madison assumed the lead of delegates who urged a thorough federal reform. Although the full convention greatly altered his original proposals, he soon concluded that the finished Constitution was the best solution to the classic riddles of a liberal democracy that humankind had yet devised. He collaborated with Alexander Hamilton in writing the *Federalist Papers*, the most impressive public defense of the reform. He then ensured the Constitution's success by taking on himself, as leader of the new House of Representatives, the preparation of a Bill of Rights.

In 1793, however, revolutionary France initiated twenty years of war with Britain and much of Europe. Madison and Thomas Jefferson were already at the forefront of opposition to Hamilton's financial policies. They now took the lead, as well, of swelling numbers who supported the French Revolution and condemned a foreign policy that seemed to favor Britain, although the British posed the greater threat to neutral trade. During Washington's administration, Hamilton and others favored diplomatic efforts to resolve the crisis with Great Britain, backed by stronger military preparations. Madison and Jefferson, at the head of what was rapidly becoming the first political party, the Democratic-Republican Party, preferred commercial warfare with the British. Both regarded John Jay's Treaty of 1795 as an abject surrender to the British and the leading cause of rising trouble with the French.

During the later 1790s, several factors—a quasi war with France, enlargement of the army, and legislative efforts to suppress domestic opposition—persuaded the Republicans that a conspiracy to undermine the constitutional republic had burst into the open. Federalist conspirators, they feared, were moving toward a permanent alliance, maybe even a reunion, with Great Britain. With all three branches of the federal government in their opponents' hands, Madison and Jefferson used the legislatures of Virginia and Kentucky to challenge the federal Alien and Sedition Laws, developing a compact theory of the nature of the Constitution and initiating the campaign that led to Jefferson's victory in the election of 1800.

From 1801 to 1809, Madison served not only as Jefferson's secretary of state, but also as a principal advisor on domestic policy, which they were mutually determined to revise. They also decided to employ commercial confrontation as a viable alternative to war. By the time that Madison succeeded Jefferson as president, however, the Great Embargo had failed to achieve that goal. Madison was preoccupied throughout his presidency with a search for ways to use the economic weapon that would damage France and Britain more than the United States. By the winter of 1811–1812, commercial warfare had been pressed, in one form or another, for a full four years without securing a repeal of the damaging and nationally demeaning British policies to which the Jeffersonian Republicans objected. Before the new, Twelfth Congress met, the president reluctantly decided that his only choices were submission to these British policies or war. On June 18, 1812, in what was basically a party vote, a declaration of war passed the Congress.

BIBLIOGRAPHY

Banning, Lance. *The Sacred Fire of Liberty: James Madison and the Founding of the Federal Republic.* Ithaca, NY: Cornell University Press, 1995.

Ketcham, Ralph. *James Madison: A Biography.* New York: Macmillan, 1971.

McCoy, Drew R. *The Last of the Fathers: James Madison and the Republican Legacy.* Cambridge, U.K., and New York: Cambridge University Press, 1989.

Rakove, Jack N. *James Madison and the Creation of the American Republic.* New York: Longman, 2002.

Lance Banning

See also: **Alien and Sedition Laws; Constitution: Bill of Rights; Constitution: Creating a Republic; Federalist Papers; Hamilton, Alexander; Jefferson, Thomas; Madison, Dolley; Monroe, James; Washington, George.**

MEMORY AND EARLY HISTORIES OF THE REVOLUTION

Memories of the American Revolution have been a powerful element in American nationalism from the beginning of the country. Even while the Revolution was taking place, Americans hoped they were participating in a series of events that would long be remembered and commemorated by their fellow countrymen and -women, and this helped them cast the Revolution and the Revolutionary War in glorious terms. Afterwards, Americans remembered the Revolution by reading books, buying artwork, marching in parades, and passing on oral traditions. Many of the important themes and patterns in this remembrance were set from the start, and although some of the meanings assigned to the Revolutionary past have shifted over the decades, some remain almost unchanged into the twenty-first century.

REVOLUTIONARY MEMORY IN THE EARLY REPUBLIC

Almost as soon as Revolutionary events occurred, Americans concerned themselves with how they would be remembered and commemorated, and Revolutionary memory was one of the most important components of public culture in the United States during the entire early national period. At the heart of that public memory lay images of Revolutionary War heroism and sacrifice. Decisive battles and the contributions of well-born gentlemen, especially of those who died for the cause, were the most common subjects of the early commemorations.

Although many commemorations took place on a local level (and often praised the actions of local men), the burgeoning print culture helped to spread important Revolutionary War memories to the entire nation. For example, beginning in the first year after the Battle of Lexington, which began the Revolutionary War, local residents held commemorative exercises on the Massachusetts battlefield. They gathered to hear commemorative sermons, to praise the men who gave up their lives, and to ensure that the events of April 19, 1775, would be remembered. Their local actions took on a wider importance when the annual sermons were subsequently published as pamphlets and newspapers around the country began reporting on the activities. The local ceremonies took on even greater formality once the war ended, and by the end of the 1790s Lexington residents had raised funds to erect a monument on the battlefield. The monument drew visitors to the town and helped perpetuate the memory of the battle.

Even more important were commemorations of Revolutionary War heroes, which came to be linked to the same kind of ceremonies, print culture, and monuments—albeit on a much larger scale. Richard Montgomery, who was killed in the early American invasion of Canada, and Joseph Warren, who lost his life at the Battle of Bunker Hill, became the two most prominent martyrs of the war. For decades after 1775, when they were killed, each was commemorated in countless pamphlets, stage plays, poems, songs, toasts, ceremonies, paintings, and engravings, and each was commemorated with a monument. Important military officers who survived the war—most especially George Washington, the Marquis de Lafayette, and Nathanael Greene—also became the subjects of a great deal of heroic writing, singing, and other forms of public culture.

Public memorials to these war heroes invited Americans to ponder their national allegiance as they gathered together (either literally or figuratively) to praise the symbols of their Revolution. Local commemorative occasions—like the battle anniversaries celebrated each year in Bennington, Vermont, or Charleston, South Carolina—sometimes took on a regional character. Occasions like the Fourth of July, which was popularly celebrated all over the United States from 1776 onward, formed the basis of the national civic calendar, even though localities might shape the festivities to suit their own regional tastes. By the time of the Civil War, both Southerners and Northerners believed themselves heirs to the memory of the Revolutionary War, but they disagreed violently over what that legacy meant.

EARLY REVOLUTIONARY HISTORIES

Some writers began to craft formal histories of the period, most of them driven by the same nationalistic impulses that shaped the early public commemorations. The conventions of historical writing in the late eighteenth and early nineteenth centuries shaped their writing, and most of the early histories of the American Revolution were highly partisan in tone; many of them also contained material that was not entirely original to their authors.

But at the same time that these authors helped bolster American nationalism, they simultaneously moved toward a more modern and objective form of historical writing.

Several modern scholars have argued that the early Revolutionary historians began to separate themselves from an earlier tradition of historical writing, which attributed most events to the workings of Providence, but that they nonetheless communicated a strong message that America was destined to become a great nation. None of the early writers were full-time professional historians. David Ramsay, who published his *History of the Revolution of South Carolina* in 1785 and expanded his analysis four years later with his *History of the American Revolution*, took a strongly nationalist tone. Ramsay was a successful South Carolina physician, but most other early historians were New Englanders. Jeremy Belknap, William Gordon, and Jedidiah Morse, all New England ministers, presented heroic narratives of the nation's founding and of the war. The other major Southern historian of the war was the future Chief Justice John Marshall, who published a highly popular heroic biography of George Washington at the turn of the nineteenth century.

These early histories advanced a laudatory view of the Revolution, but they were also caught up in the domestic political battles that began in the 1790s. The authors supported the Federalist Party, which developed under the leadership of Alexander Hamilton and whose aristocratic leanings fitted well with their great man approach to historical writing. The main exception also stands out because she was female. The most prominent history of the Revolution written by a supporter of the rival Democratic-Republican Party was penned by Mercy Otis Warren, a Massachusetts patriot and writer whose husband was a prominent Revolutionary politician. Warren's 1804 *History of the Revolution* openly criticized many postwar Federalist policies. Warren's version of events caused a rift with her friend the Federalist former president John Adams, who was openly critical of the idea of a woman historian.

Although Warren's Democratic-Republican version of events was controversial, it was nowhere near as unpopular as histories that questioned the Revolution. For example, Andrew Oliver, a famous Loyalist, could find no publisher for his highly critical history, and it remained unpublished until the twentieth century. No book that questioned the Revolution appeared until well after the war ended.

REVOLUTIONARY MEMORY IN THE NINETEENTH AND TWENTIETH CENTURIES

The mixture of patriotic memory and histories praising the American Revolution continued well into the nine-

teenth century, and only in the twentieth century did many historians adopt a less openly patriotic tone. Popular memory of the Revolutionary War continued its patriotic tone, although it did become a bit more democratic in the years following the War of 1812, when a number of common soldiers' memoirs became popular and some historians broadened their focus to take in more than just the greatest war heroes. By midcentury, historians like Benson Lossing and Elizabeth Ellet had published books focusing to a degree on the common experience in the Revolutionary War, although they still retained a strong patriotic tone.

Popular symbols of the Revolutionary War, including some of the original war heroes such as George Washington, retained their status, but they were joined in the late nineteenth and early twentieth centuries by other symbols and myths that stressed the bravery of average men and women. Stories of the suffering of average soldiers at Valley Forge, Pennsylvania, and of heroic actions by people like Molly Pitcher began to give a more egalitarian sense of American nationalism.

Whatever their political tone, memories of the American Revolution retain great cultural power in the United States, and they continue to inspire a sense of American nationalism. In the celebration of Independence Day and in the near-religious reverence for the founding fathers, memories of the country's founding period, and especially of the war, stand at the heart of American national myth-making.

BIBLIOGRAPHY

Cohen, Lester H. *The Revolutionary Histories: Contemporary Narratives of the American Revolution.* Ithaca, NY: Cornell University Press, 1980.

Kammen, Michael. *A Season of Youth: The American Revolution and the Historical Imagination.* New York: Knopf, 1978.

Purcell, Sarah J. *Sealed with Blood: War, Sacrifice, and Memory in Revolutionary America.* Philadelphia: University of Pennsylvania Press, 2002.

Sarah J. Purcell

See also: Bunker Hill Monument; Flags; Fourth of July; Spy, The: First American War Novel; Valley Forge.

MOBILIZATION, FRENCH AND INDIAN WAR

The origins of the French and Indian War lay in conflicting British and French claims, particularly in the Ohio Valley and Nova Scotia. The war began in the Ohio Valley in 1754 but soon spread to the rest of North

Engraving of British ships surrounding the walled city of Louisbourg, Cape Breton Island, Canada, during the siege of 1758. GETTY IMAGES

America and eventually became a global war, known in Europe as the Seven Years' War.

CAUSES AND COURSE OF THE WAR

The early years of the war went badly for the British. In 1755, a British army was routed at the Battle of the Monongahela and in the following year the British surrendered the important fort of Oswego on Lake Ontario. Meanwhile, Indian raiders devastated the colonial frontier. In 1757, the French captured Fort William Henry and there were fears of a French invasion of New York. By 1758, the British had committed over 20,000 troops to North America. This turned the tide of war. An amphibious force captured the strategic French fortress of Louisbourg on Cape Breton Island, and in the Ohio Valley another army seized Fort Duquesne. In 1759, the British won their greatest victory when an army under Major General James Wolfe captured Quebec, and in the following year the remaining French forces in Canada surrendered.

MOBILIZING COLONIAL RESOURCES

The war mobilized colonial resources in various ways, the most basic of which was the recruitment of colonists into the armed forces. Most British regiments were under

strength when they were shipped to North America and once in America recruited thousands of colonists. To make recruitment easier, the British created the Royal American regiment, where foreigners, forbidden from holding high rank in other units, could hold command. Even more men served in the provincial forces. During the French and Indian War, nearly all colonies created their own military forces, which undertook operations independent of the British army or served alongside regular units or under the ultimate command of regular officers. Unlike soldiers in the regular army, who enlisted essentially for life, men enlisted in the provincial forces for short terms, often only for that year's campaign. At the height of the war, about 20,000 troops were serving in provincial regiments: over 10,000 from New England; nearly 3,000 each from Virginia and Pennsylvania; about 2,000 from New York; and smaller numbers from North and South Carolina.

In addition to the regular army and provincial forces, nearly all men would have served at some time in the militia. Most colonies had their own militias, and they formed the backbone of local defense and in times of emergency defended provincial forts or served alongside regular and provincial units. Hundreds of women also served, working as cooks or washerwomen alongside the regular and provincial forces, as well as unofficially accompanying their husbands on campaign. Other civilians were also contracted to work for the army as laborers or craftsmen. These camp followers played a vital role in allowing the armies to function.

The mobilization of such substantial forces boosted the provincial economies during the war. Money flooded into the provinces as Britain provided funds to raise these forces, much of which was spent on wages and bounties to lure men into service. These varied from colony to colony and from year to year, but in some cases the bounty amounted to over one and a half years' pay for a typical laborer. The lure of bounties and wages attracted specific types of men into the provincial forces. In New England, the provincial forces were composed principally of the sons of farmers who were waiting for their inheritance and these forces were representative of the communities from which they were recruited. Further south, in New York, Virginia, and Pennsylvania, the provincial forces attracted more immigrants, landless poor, and indentured servants, and recruits tended to represent the lower levels of society.

LEGACY: COLONIAL SOCIETY AND REVOLUTION

The creation and supplying of these provincial forces provided an important precedent for the Revolutionary War. Whereas New England had previously raised provincial forces, most other colonies had not. In 1775, this experience would prove central in assuring the colonies that they could raise their own forces with which to oppose Great Britain. The French and Indian War also provided many colonists with important military experience. It was little wonder that at the start of the Revolutionary War the Continental Congress turned to the officer who had gained the greatest experience of command during the French and Indian War, George Washington, who had commanded the Virginia Regiment.

Mobilization also provided conflicting lessons for the British and their colonists. The British noted the successes of the regular army in the campaigns at Louisbourg and Quebec. To British officers, provincial troops seemed undisciplined and unruly, little more than a rabble, unable to fight or even defend themselves. In contrast, American colonists noted the ineptitude of British commanders such as Major General Edward Braddock and Major General James Abercromby, whose armies were routed by French and Canadian forces. British troops seemed reliant on large supply convoys and unable to march without a substantial baggage train. Both sides viewed the other as militarily weak, and these perceptions fed their willingness to resort to war in 1775. British officers also noted the failures of the colonial militia to fight effectively and concluded that the militia had limited military use. George Washington drew similar conclusions and developed a clear preference for regular troops over militia. These perceptions would shape the attitudes of British commanders and Washington during the Revolutionary War and largely account for the failure of the British to perceive the value of the American militia and Washington's belief that the preservation of the Continental army was central to the revolutionary cause.

Mobilization during the war also affected perceptions of colonial identity. The many colonists who had served alongside the British were shocked at what they saw as the immorality of British troops, their failure to observe the Sabbath, profanity, and frequent gambling, and the arrogance of their officers. To these Americans, the only reason for British military discipline was fear. This contrasted to the provincial forces, where officers were often elected and commanded their men as much through influence and cajoling as through coercion and fear. This seemed to underline the different natures of the British and colonial societies and was central in defining a sense of colonial identity in the years before the Revolution.

Mobilization during the French and Indian War affected colonial societies in many different ways. However, perhaps its most lasting legacy was the manner in which it prepared the colonies, both militarily and psychologically, for the coming Revolutionary War.

BIBLIOGRAPHY

Anderson, Fred. *A People's Army: Massachusetts Soldiers and Society in the Seven Years' War.* Chapel Hill: University of North Carolina Press, 1984.

Higginbotham, Don. *George Washington and the American Military Tradition.* Athens: University of Georgia Press, 1985.

Nash, Gary B. *The Urban Crucible: The Northern Seaports and the Origins of the American Revolution.* Cambridge, MA: Harvard University Press, 1986.

Selesky, Harold E. *War and Society in Colonial Connecticut.* New Haven, CT: Yale University Press, 1990.

Shy, John. *Toward Lexington: The Role of the British Army in the Coming of the American Revolution.* Princeton, NJ: Princeton University Press, 1965.

Titus, James. *The Old Dominion at War: Society, Politics, and Warfare in Late Colonial Virginia.* Columbia: University of South Carolina Press, 1991.

Ward, Matthew C. *Breaking the Backcountry: The Seven Years' War in Virginia and Pennsylvania, 1754–1765.* Pittsburgh: University of Pittsburgh Press, 2003.

Matthew C. Ward

See also: **Fort William Henry Massacre, Cultural Legacy; French and Indian War, Legacy of; Stamp Act Congress; Washington, George.**

MOBILIZATION, WAR FOR INDEPENDENCE

Mobilization in the War for Independence is the process by which America raised and organized the military forces to wage war against the British Empire. After the conclusion of the French and Indian War (1756–1763), a decade of political controversy between Americans and Great Britain prompted Americans to reinvigorate their local militias in preparation to defend their property rights and civil liberties. Americans ousted royalist officers from their militia companies, stepped up training exercises, and collected military stores. Volunteers from the militia formed minuteman companies that were to be ready to march at a minute's notice in the event that British troops threatened to use force against Americans. When political disagreements transformed into actual hostilities in 1775, the American people mobilized as citizen-soldiers in the colonial militia tradition of universal male citizen service.

THE FIRST MOBILIZATION AND THE NEW ENGLAND ARMY

On April 19, 1775, alarm riders alerted American minutemen of a British expedition from Boston sent to destroy American military supplies in Concord. When American minutemen confronted the British troops in Lexington and Concord, gunshots shattered the uneasy peace. As the British withdrew toward Boston, the minutemen used traditional militia tactics, taking concealed positions behind stonewalls and trees to pour devastating fire upon the retreating British. The rapid mobilization at the Concord alarm was an inspiring success for the Americans, and it highlighted the strength of the militia for irregular fighting.

Within days, thousands of American militiamen, who were mostly farmers and artisans, surrounded the British garrison at Boston. The Massachusetts Provincial Congress took charge of the impromptu army and voted to enlist 30,000 militiamen for the remaining eight months of the year. New England governments granted prominent men authority to "raise for rank," by which the award of an officer's ranking was proportionate to the number of men he enlisted. It was an expedient method of mobilizing troops, but it made officers dependent on their popularity and compromised professional military standards.

The New England militia army showed itself formidable at the Battle of Bunker Hill on June 17, 1775, when the American citizen-soldiers fought fiercely against the best of the British army. After that bloody battle, British General Gage wrote that the Americans were "not the despicable rabble too many supposed them to be . . . the conquest of this country is not easy" (Ward, 1:97). But the strong showing of the militia at Bunker Hill hid the militia's limitations when forced to match up against British regulars in the open field.

THE CONTINENTAL ARMY

On June 15, 1775, the Second Continental Congress adopted the New England militia army and transformed it into a Continental Army to represent all thirteen colonies. First, they appointed an experienced Virginia officer, George Washington, as commander in chief. Second, the Continental Congress ordered regiments of volunteer riflemen from Virginia, Maryland, and Pennsylvania to reinforce the New England soldiers at Boston, making it a genuinely "continental" effort. Washington determined to create a "respectable army" by instituting military regulations. But, even as he undertook that task in the fall of 1775, an alarmed Washington watched his volunteer army disperse as his soldiers' enlistments expired. By January 1776, Washington's manpower dropped to less than 12,000 soldiers.

General Washington complained to Congress that by the time soldiers learned their duties, a little discipline, and a few maneuvers, they were ready to go home, only to be replaced by other untrained recruits. According to Washington, longer enlistments were the solution. Although many members of Congress were concerned that a professional, or "standing," army posed a potential threat to civil liberty, Congress conceded to one-year enlistments for soldiers to fill the ranks of twenty-seven Continental regiments. By February 1776, Washington's troop strength was back up to 20,000.

The first test of the new Continental Army in a large-scale battle was at New York City in August 1776. The American citizen-soldiers were overwhelmed by the well-trained British and Hessian regulars in the open field, and only a heroic retreat saved the American army from capitulation. The failure of the American army at New York persuaded Congress that a regular army of long-term recruits was a necessity.

In September 1776, Congress agreed to establish a regular army to consist of eighty-eight regiments (60,000 troops) enlisted for the duration of the war. Virginia and Massachusetts were obligated to provide the largest contingents, and other states contributed regiments in proportion to their populations. In later years, Congress reduced the number of authorized regiments, mainly because there was never enough manpower or resources to complete all the regiments envisioned in 1776. The Continental Army never fielded more than 30,000 soldiers at one time and often relied on the turnout of the militia when major battles loomed, as at Saratoga in 1777.

Revolutionary minutemen leaving for battle.

Nonetheless, the Continental Army was of critical importance not only because of its military role, but as the focal point of the American cause around which the militia could rally when called.

RECRUITING: SOCIETY AND SOLDIERS

The public did not respond enthusiastically to open-ended enlistments for the duration of the war, and the Continental Congress quickly offered an option for a limited term of three years. Besides the shorter term, the Continental Congress and the states offered bounties to attract volunteers. Bounties were incentives for recruits, usually consisting of cash, extra pay, and sometimes land grants. For example, the Continental Congress's bounty for a Continental enlistment was twenty dollars plus a grant of one hundred acres of land. Despite a variety of bounties, large numbers of men preferred the shorter terms of service in the militia.

To meet the manpower needs of the Continental Army, Congress requested the states to fill enlistment quotas. In turn, the state legislatures designated quotas for each town in proportion to their population. When bounties failed to produce enough volunteers, legislatures ordered towns to set up committees to divide the town's male population into as many groups as the number of recruits required of them. Each group, or "class," had responsibility to produce a recruit or pay a stiff fine. Hiring substitutes was acceptable, and some young men were drawn to the chance to advance themselves financially.

African Americans and Native Americans also filled the ranks. Free Blacks and American Indians participated in the initial mobilization of 1775, but American commanders were concerned about having Black soldiers fighting for liberty while the majority of African Americans were enslaved. At first Washington lobbied to disallow Blacks and American Indians from military service. However, after the royal governor of Virginia, Lord Dunmore, offered freedom to slaves who deserted their masters to serve with British forces in late 1775, Americans reconsidered their ban, fearful that it might drive more Blacks to the British lines. Americans agreed to enlist free Blacks, but declined to enroll slaves primarily because slave owners were generally unwilling to relinquish their property and were fearful of arming their slaves. Nonetheless, thousands of Blacks did join both sides, fighting for their own civil liberty.

American Indians likewise aligned with whichever side seemed to offer them the best chance of maintaining their own lands and independence. Some, like the Abnaki, worked for both sides at different times. Generally, Native Americans within areas of white settlement, including the Wampanoag and Natick of New England, sent soldiers to fight with American forces. However, most frontier American Indians like the Iroquois in the north and Cherokee in the South saw their advantage with the British, who were important trade partners and who promised to prevent Americans from pushing them off their lands.

SOCIETY IN WAR

More than 200,000 Americans served in the militia and Continental armies, and about 25,000 of them died in the War for Independence. As a percentage of population, the death rate was second only to the American Civil War. Not only did the war exact a toll on America's human resources, but it also disrupted the American economy, especially exports of wheat, rice, and tobacco to Europe, and trade with the West Indies. Likewise, imports were choked off and hard currency became scarce. Within the country, exchange networks between farmers and their markets were interrupted by the passing armies, and the British Navy effectively closed the ports and grounded the fishing fleets. To make matters worse, the cost of mobilization precipitated rampant inflation that devalued the currency so fast that families could barely keep up.

It was an especially difficult economy for the families whose men were off in the service. Some women and their families worked for and traveled with both British and American armies, but most women assumed, in addition to their own work, their husbands' roles in order to keep farms and shops operating. Often, towns contributed to the support of the families of the men who were off in the service. In Plymouth, for example, direct expenses for soldiers' families consumed fully one-half of the town budget presented in September 1779. Everyone contributed to the mobilization.

The War for Independence began with mobilization in the militia tradition. However, as the war grew continental in scope and extended into years of struggle, Americans reluctantly accepted the necessity of creating a regular national army, known as the Continental Army. The Continental Army provided the symbolic center of the American cause, but it remained small and dependent on the support of the citizen-soldier militia. Together, the militia and the Continental Army ensured that the American Revolution would be a "people's war." The country mobilized hundreds of thousands of young men and the resources of their families and communities in the eight-year war for independence.

BIBLIOGRAPHY

Calloway, Colin G. *The American Revolution in Indian Country: Crisis and Diversity in Native American Communities.* Cambridge, UK: Cambridge University Press, 1995.

Higginbotham, Don. *The War of American Independence: Military Attitudes, Policies, and Practice, 1763–1789.* New York: Macmillan, 1971.

Lesser, Charles H, ed. *Sinews of Independence: Monthly Strength Returns of the Continental Army.* Chicago: University of Chicago Press, 1974.

Quarles, Benjamin. *The Negro in the American Revolution.* New York: Norton, 1961.

Royster, Charles. *A Revolutionary People at War: The Continental Army and American Character, 1775–1783.* Chapel Hill: University of North Carolina Press, 1979.

Ward, Christopher. *The War of the Revolution.* Edited by John R. Alden. 2 vols. New York: Macmillan, 1952.

Walter L. Sargent

See also: **Mobilization: French and Indian War; Camp Followers: War and Women; Association Test.**

MONROE, JAMES

(b. April 28, 1758; d. July 4, 1831) Fifth U.S. president (1817–1825).

James Monroe led a life shaped by war. As a young man he served with distinction in the Continental Army during the War of Independence, and as a two-term president (1817–1825) he avoided potential war with Spain. His most important accomplishment, however, was creating the "era of good feelings," a period of unprecedented unity and nationalism, out of the partisan bitterness left from the War of 1812.

As president, Monroe held two particular distinctions. He was the last of the so-called Virginia Dynasty of presidents, which included such luminaries as the Father of the Nation, George Washington; the author of the Declaration of Independence, Thomas Jefferson; and the framer of the Constitution, James Madison. Monroe was also the "last of the cocked hats," or the last chief executive who was a veteran of the War of Independence. He was a senator, an ambassador, and President Madison's secretary of state as well as acting secretary of war during key moments of the War of 1812.

The War of 1812 ended in peace with the Treaty of Ghent in 1814, yet in 1817, when Monroe became president, the nation still felt its effects. Monroe faced a divided nation torn across political and regional lines, and met it with an elaborate personal tour. Most significant, he visited New England, the seedbed of much partisan opposition, where he met with political rivals. A combination of his humility—paying for his expenses, traveling as a private citizen, wearing simple, Revolutionary-era clothing—and his symbolic acts—visiting key locations from the War of Independence and the War of 1812, honoring veterans, and invoking the memory of George Washington and other past war heroes—made his tour a great success. The unity and nationalism fostered by Monroe's goodwill campaign energized the country's spirit, economy, and expansion.

Monroe also faced other challenges during his tenure in executive office, many of which he inherited from his predecessors. One involved the U.S. military chain of command. General Andrew Jackson, the hero of the Battle of New Orleans during (though technically after) the War of 1812, protested the fact that one of President Madison's cabinet members had issued an order to one of Jackson's inferiors, thus bypassing Jackson. Monroe ably handled the problem with a compromise that spared Jackson's pride but also removed any block to direct orders from Washington, D.C. The situation grew more complicated when Jackson captured Spanish holdings in Pensacola without authorization. Monroe not only managed to avoid hostilities with Spain over Jackson's reckless actions, but also convinced Spain to sell its Florida lands and define boundaries for its remaining territories. The problem could have led to war, but Monroe's solution proved both peaceful and popular.

Monroe also inherited the problem of slavery from earlier presidents. Slaveholding and non-slaveholding representatives were perfectly balanced in the Senate when Missouri, a territory allowing slavery, applied for statehood, threatening to tip that balance. Maine, a northern and non-slaveholding part of Massachusetts, soon applied for statehood as well. Eventually, through the Missouri Compromise, the two territories became states, thus canceling out each other's Senate votes and preserving a fragile balance between the two opposing interests. New law prohibited slavery in territories above Missouri's northern border. The resolution avoided civil war but was only a temporary solution at best, despite Monroe's plea for an end to regional self-interest in politics.

As president, Monroe repositioned the United States on the world stage by creating a policy known as the Monroe Doctrine. Because of the increase of Latin American revolutions against colonial powers and hostil-

James Monroe.

ities in Europe that threatened to spill over into other parts of the Western hemisphere, Monroe felt it was time to articulate a clear role for the United States in international affairs. Monroe pledged U.S. neutrality in Europe but explained that European powers could no longer colonize in the Americas. The Monroe Doctrine proclaimed the Western hemisphere a "hands-off zone" that would be protected by the United States.

Other challenges, such as funding internal improvements and building coherent policy toward American Indians, also arose during Monroe's administration. In the final analysis, Monroe avoided war, rethought U.S. foreign policy, erred on the side of compromise when he could, and postponed crises that had no simple solution. With his New England tour, his measured rhetoric, and his command of symbolism, Monroe built unity from a bitter postwar nation, reviving Revolutionary spirit in the unstable aftermath of the War of 1812 and ushering in the "era of good feelings."

BIBLIOGRAPHY

Ammon, Harry. *James Monroe: The Quest for National Identity.* Reprint, Charlottesville: University of Virginia Press, 1990.

Cunningham, Noble E., Jr. *The Presidency of James Monroe.* Lawrence: University Press of Kansas, 1996.

Dangerfield, George. *The Era of Good Feelings*. Chicago: Ivan R. Dee, 1989.

Ketchum, Ralph. *Presidents above Party: The First American Presidency, 1789–1829*. Chapel Hill: University of North Carolina Press, 1984.

Monroe, James. *The Papers of James Monroe*. Edited by Daniel Preston. Westport, CT: Greenwood Press, 2003.

Sturgis, Amy. *Presidents from Washington through Monroe, 1789–1825: Debating the Issues in Pro and Con Primary Documents*. Westport, CT: Greenwood Press, 2002.

Internet Resources

"The James Monroe Museum and Memorial Library." Mary Washington College. Available from <http://www.mwc.edu/jmmu>.

Monroe, James. "The Papers of James Monroe." The Avalon Project at Yale Law School. Available from <http://www.yale.edu/lawweb>.

Amy H. Sturgis

See also: **Bunker Hill Monument; Jefferson, Thomas; Lafayette's Tour; Madison, James; Monroe's Tour of New England; Supreme Court and War Powers; War of 1812.**

MONROE'S TOUR OF NEW ENGLAND

During his two terms in office (1817–1825), President James Monroe transformed a bitter, divided, partisan nation in the wake of the War of 1812 into a unified country with an unprecedented sense of national identity and patriotism. Monroe's tour of New England ushered in the "era of good feelings" by invoking the symbols of the War of Independence and focusing on citizens' common background and victories.

As the last so-called "Virginia Dynasty" president, Monroe inherited a number of national issues from his predecessors—Washington, Adams, Jefferson, and Madison. Among them were the slavery question, American Indian policy, westward expansion, and state-federal government relations. Perhaps the most pressing challenge he faced in his two terms was rebuilding the nation's postwar economy, unity, and sense of nationalism.

The war was the chief preoccupation and major event of James Madison's presidency (1809–1817). Although quasi wars with Great Britain had erupted since the U.S. founding, previous chief executives had managed to avoid official hostilities with the parent nation. By Madison's time, war seemed inevitable in order to protect domestic and foreign trade. Although critics argued that a war to protect commerce actually would result in a loss of international consumers of U.S. goods and a wounded national economy, Congress nevertheless answered Madison's request by declaring war against Great Britain

in June 1812. The war went badly: In America's worst moment, British troops sacked Washington, D.C., and burned the Capitol building. An attempt to conquer Canada failed. Perhaps the worst consequence of the war was the bitter divisions it created within the nation. In December 1814, while peace was being negotiated in Europe, leaders in New England, where opposition to the war was most intense, met at Hartford, Connecticut, to demand changes in the Constitution to curb the war-making powers of the federal government. They threatened to lead New England out of the union if their demands were not met. When peace came with the Treaty of Ghent in December 1814, the nation found itself economically weakened and bitterly divided along political and regional lines.

Monroe, who had served as Madison's secretary of state and at times acting secretary of war during the War of 1812, became president of a nation still coming to terms with what a postwar United States should be. Monroe embraced the opportunity this unique moment afforded him and chose to rally and unify the country through an elaborate schedule of personal tours, from the oldest birthplaces of the former colonies to the newly opened West. The most significant of his tours took place in 1817 in New England, where the hottest opposition to the War of 1812 had seethed. The region was also the home of the Federalist Party, the direct competitor to Monroe's Democratic-Republicans.

The president pursued his goal—healing the bitter rift of party factionalism so recently intensified by war—by invoking the symbol of the nation's first war hero and chief executive, George Washington. This worked on two levels: Monroe was not only the final Virginia Dynasty president, but also "the last of the cocked hats," or the last president to have served in the War of Independence. As a veteran of the Revolution and the inheritor of Washington's tradition of leadership, Monroe orchestrated every detail of his trip to New England to recall the enthusiasm and patriotism of the War of Independence. He journeyed as an independent citizen without official escort or ceremony and paid for his travel expenses out of his own pocket. Instead of the day's current fashions, he wore simple knee-buckled breeches and, significantly, three-pointed, Revolution-era hats.

Where Monroe traveled was just as noteworthy as how he traveled. The president visited Baltimore, Philadelphia, and New York, careful to make appearances at sites important to either the War of Independence or the War of 1812 and honor veterans in the process. He went to Boston, the birthplace of the Revolution, on the Fourth of July for the anniversary of the nation's independence. While there he visited important symbols of Revolutionary action such as Bunker Hill, "Old Ironsides," and the Boston Athenaeum. Touring more as an old patriot than a new president, meeting with leading political adversaries such as the Federalists John Adams and Timothy Pickering, and choosing memorable places and dates for his visits marked Monroe's New England journey as a tour of goodwill.

Monroe's success was immediate and undeniable. In contrast to his own understated and personable appearance and manner, enthusiastic locals at each stop along his tour met him with regal pomp and ceremony, flags and songs, as if Monroe had won both the War of Independence and the War of 1812 single-handedly. Celebrations at his many stops and along the routes that connected them turned his modest tour into a triumphant procession. Newspapers wrote about how Monroe's non-partisan, patriotic appearances seemed focused on unity and healing, proving that his tenure as president would make one people out of a nation that had been deeply divided. One Boston newspaper coined a phrase that would come to describe Monroe's two administrations: Monroe, it was said, had ushered in an "era of good feelings." The positive spirit fed by Monroe's travel revived not only the nation's self-image but also its economy and expansion. The tour was so successful, in fact, that Monroe and Congress invited Revolutionary hero Marquis de Lafayette to the United States for a similar goodwill tour during Monroe's second term.

Turning postwar dissent and factionalism into an opportunity to foster unity and active nationalism was perhaps Monroe's most important achievement in office. As he prepared to leave the executive branch, Monroe understood that bringing the Virginia Dynasty to an end was exactly what the nation needed. Concerned that too many like-minded Southern presidents would undo the inclusive nonpartisanship he had fostered, Monroe prepared his New Englander secretary of state, John Quincy Adams, to succeed him as president. And indeed, Adams's presidency maintained Monroe's legacy of optimism and unity. Appropriately for one who had linked himself so closely with the Revolutionary experience, Monroe died on July 4, 1831, becoming the third of five presidents to die on the nation's birthday.

Monroe's tour of New England was a symbolic act that not only bound a divided nation but also demonstrated how the memory of the Revolution and American military triumphs could energize and define the nation's self-image. The tour proved that war and the way in which Americans are led to remember their wars could be used as a powerful political force to forge national identity and shape the country's culture.

BIBLIOGRAPHY

Ammon, Harry. *James Monroe: The Quest for National Identity*. Reprint, Charlottesville: University of Virginia Press, 1990.

Cunningham, Noble E., Jr. *The Presidency of James Monroe*. Lawrence: University Press of Kansas, 1996.

Dangerfield, George. *The Era of Good Feelings*. Chicago: Ivan R. Dee, 1989.

Ketchum, Ralph. *Presidents above Party: The First American Presidency, 1789–1829*. Chapel Hill: University of North Carolina Press, 1984.

Monroe, James. *The Papers of James Monroe*. Edited by Daniel Preston. Westport, CT: Greenwood Press, 2003.

Sturgis, Amy. *Presidents from Washington through Monroe, 1789–1825: Debating the Issues in Pro and Con Primary Documents*. Westport, CT: Greenwood Press, 2002.

Internet Resources

"The James Monroe Museum and Memorial Library." Mary Washington College. Available from <http://www.mwc.edu/jmmu>.

Monroe, James. "The Papers of James Monroe." The Avalon Project at Yale Law School. Available from <http://www.yale.edu/lawweb>.

Amy H. Sturgis

See also: **Bunker Hill Monument; Federalist Party; Flags; Hartford Convention; Lafayette's Tour; Valley Forge.**

MONTGOMERY, RICHARD

(b. December 2, 1738; d. December 31, 1775) Revolutionary War hero.

Richard Montgomery was born in County Dublin, Ireland, in 1738 to a wealthy gentry family. Richard's father, a member of the Irish parliament, and his older brother, an army captain, encouraged him to seek a position in the British Army, and in 1756 he enlisted. He rose fairly quickly through the ranks to become a captain by 1762, due in part to his good service in North America during the Seven Year's War and in part to the army's typical promotion of sons of privilege.

During his stay in North America, Richard Montgomery formed a favorable impression of the British colonists there, unlike most of his fellow British officers. Upon his return to England in 1765, he was outspoken on behalf of the colonists as conflicts over taxes and other imperial matters worsened. Montgomery resigned his army commission in 1772 and migrated to New York State, where he hoped to become a prosperous farmer.

Montgomery became a successful landowner, and he greatly enhanced his status the following year, when he married Janet Livingston, the wealthy daughter of New York scion Robert Livingston. Janet's wealth and family connections would influence not only the course of Montgomery's life, but also his fame after death.

The Death of General Montgomery at Quebec, copy of an engraving by W. Ketterlinus after John Trumbull. LANDOV

As the imperial crisis between the American colonies and Great Britain heated up, Montgomery found a new chance to become an important public man in his adopted country. In 1775 he was elected to the Provincial Congress of New York, and when the Revolutionary War broke out that same year, the Continental Congress appointed Montgomery a brigadier-general of the Continental Army. Montgomery was appointed second-in-command of a planned invasion of Canada, but when his commander, Major General Philip Schuyler, became ill, most of the planning and everyday command of the operation fell to Montgomery.

Montgomery's Canadian expedition set out in September 1775, and, although his underprepared band of mostly New England troops faced a hard winter march through rough terrain, Montgomery's force was quite successful at first, capturing several forts and then the city of Montreal on December 13. Montgomery connected with another group of American troops commanded by Benedict Arnold outside of Quebec, and together the two forces laid siege to that city, hoping to capture it before the end of the year, when the first Continental Army enlistments formally expired. The American forces were

weak and undersupplied, and with their siege failing, they attempted an attack on the city on the last day of the year. Montgomery was killed during the attack on Quebec, which ultimately also failed.

Immediately after his death, Montgomery's even more important career as an American martyr began. Montgomery, the well-born British army officer, who had chosen to cast his lot with the Americans during their revolution, became a symbol of the elite brand of heroism that expressed the sacrifice of the Revolutionary War to the American public and helped to inspire allegiance to the new American nation. Even the British instantly recognized Montgomery as a heroic figure. After the battle at Quebec, the British forces buried his body with honors outside the city's gates.

The Continental Congress learned of Montgomery's death on January 17, 1776, and the representatives, hoping to boost public support for the war and for the cause of American freedom, took immediate steps to commemorate him. A congressional committee commissioned a marble monument to Montgomery's memory, and the entire Congress convened in Philadelphia for a public funeral for Montgomery on February 19, 1776.

Montgomery, along with Joseph Warren, a martyred hero of the Battle of Bunker Hill, became the subject of laudatory poems, pamphlets, and other popular printed materials. Praise for his bravery and sacrifice helped to cement support for American independence in July 1776, and he remained a potent figure of patriotic inspiration throughout the Revolutionary War.

Montgomery's memory lived on in the postwar years. In 1787 the monument to Montgomery commissioned by Congress was erected in Trinity Church in New York City. It became a popular tourist destination and the inspiration for further writings lauding Montgomery. Janet Livingston Montgomery did much to preserve the memory of her husband in the public mind. In 1818 she spearheaded a drive to have his remains reinterred in New York City at the site of his monument. This second burial was again accompanied by great public ceremony and praise, and the occasion provided an opportunity for Americans to rededicate their allegiance to the memory of the American Revolution, a primary basis of early American nationalism.

Although Richard Montgomery's symbolic importance receded somewhat by the end of the nineteenth century, he retained his reputation as a semi-aristocratic hero who served to inspire allegiance to the American revolutionary cause during the early republican period. Montgomery, as a heroic figure much praised by the public, embodied the values of the Revolutionary War and the American nationalism that grew out of it.

BIBLIOGRAPHY

Gabriel, Michael P. *Major-general Richard Montgomery: The Making of an American Hero.* Madison, NJ: Fairleigh Dickinson University Press, 2002.

Purcell, Sarah J. *Sealed with Blood: War, Sacrifice, and Memory in Revolutionary America.* Philadelphia: University of Pennsylvania Press, 2002.

Shelton, Hal T. *General Richard Montgomery and the American Revolution: From Redcoat to Rebel.* New York: New York University Press, 1994.

Sarah J. Purcell

See also: **Bunker Hill Monument; Flags; Lafayette's Tour.**

MUSIC AND THE REVOLUTION

During the Revolution, American patriots, loyalists, and British occupants alike heard, performed, and enjoyed a wide variety of music. While the period is often remembered mainly for its political and military events, music animated many pursuits of daily life, even during the disruption of war. At a militia muster, young fifers and drummers stirred the morning air, while trained wind bands accompanied the Continental Army on the move with a brisk march. By night, army bands played elegant minuets and country dances for the entertainment of officers, while talented slaves and freemen alike accompanied frequent civilian balls that provided important social intercourse. Newly popular choirs and singing school youths sang sacred psalm settings and anthems in church, while sailors and soldiers sang war songs and bawdy ballad tunes at the tavern table. At home, an educated elite performed art songs for private parlor audiences, while public instrumental and vocal concert programs reflected the latest from London in the world of George III. Despite lingering local laws against the sin and expense of theatrical productions, the public still found means to enjoy a lengthy evening of favorite British ballad operas and light comic operas, sometimes as "lecture" readings in place of banned performances. New American public celebrations, for the Fourth of July, Washington's birthday, and the like, came to life with festive songs set to popular music of the day, afterward widely distributed through quick newspaper and broadside publication. Indeed, fledgling government and military leaders understood the importance of music, its prevalence, and its unique power to rally the troops. Richard Peters, Secretary to the Board of War, wrote in 1779: "I wish often to see ballads dispersed among the soldiery, which, inspiring in them a thirst for glory, patience under their hardships, a love of their General, and submission to their officers, would animate them to a cheerful discharge of their duty, and prompt them to undergo their hardships with a soldierly patience and pleasure" (Anderson, p. x).

REVOLUTIONARY SONGS

Songs and ballads of the Revolution formed perhaps the most accessible, influential, and lasting type of music from the period. Their texts told a story, often inspired by current events like a recent battle and infused with a political message. While some songs indeed died a quiet death, with inferior texts wedded to events of passing interest, a few remained wildly popular over time. Amateur poets of the educated elite were usually the authors responsible for their quick creation and publication. They were not composers of the music, however. Adopting a simple technique common to colonial culture in British North America, poets set their newly composed verses to preexisting tunes known by the public. An array of familiar British songs and marching tunes, many of folk origin or derived from eighteenth-century theater and pleasure-garden entertainments, supplied an ever-ready source of these melodies. Especially popular were tunes from British nationalistic songs that in their original texts extolled the might of king, army, and especially the proud

REVOLUTIONARY TEA

In November of 1773, a group of Boston men disguised as Mohawks in Indian war paint boarded and dumped 342 chests of tea overboard to protest the Tea Act that placed a three pence per pound tax on all Dutch tea exported to America. "Revolutionary Tea" celebrates this famous anti-tax protest for which the rallying cry was "No taxation without representation."

There was an old lady lived over the sea,
And she was an Island Queen.
Her daughter lived off in a new country,
With an ocean of water between.
The old lady's pockets were filled up with gold;
But never contented she.
So she called on her daughter to pay a tax
Of three pence a pound on the tea.
Of three pence a pound on the tea.

"Now mother, dear mother," the daughter replied
"I shan't do the thing that you ax;
I'm willing to pay a fair price for the tea,
But never a three-penny tax."
"You shall," quoth the mother, and reddened with
rage,

"For you're my own daughter, you see.
And sure 'tis quite proper the daughter should pay
Her mother a tax on the tea,
Her mother a tax on the tea."

And so the old lady her servant called up,
And packed off a budget of tea.
And eager for three pence a pound, she put in
Enough for a large family.
She ordered her servant to bring home the tax,
Declaring her child should obey,
Or old as she was, and a woman most grown,
She'd half whip her life away,
She'd half whip her life away.

The tea was conveyed to the daughter's front
door,
All down by the ocean side,
But the bouncing poured out every pound
In the dark and the boiling tide.
And then she called out to the Island Queen,
"Oh mother, dear mother," quoth she,
"Your tea you may have when it is steeped
enough,
But never a tax from me,
But never a tax from me."

SOURCE: Silverman, Jerry *Of Thee I Sing: Lyrics and Music for America's Most Patriotic Songs*, Citadel Press, 2002.

royal navy that ruled the seas and defended the treasured rights and liberties of British citizens against despotic foes. Like their British counterparts, most printed versions of new American songs provided texts only without music, making it sadly impossible to recreate the full repertoire of Revolutionary song.

Some of the tunes American authors chose were so widely known and popular that they were applied repeatedly to different texts. Such was the case, for example, with our first truly American patriotic song—John Dickinson's "Liberty Song" of 1768, a pre-Revolutionary critique of the Townshend duties (a set of import taxes) imposed by Parliament. Set to the tune "Hearts of Oak," a rousing theater song by William Boyce praising British ships and sailors, the "Liberty Song" applied the patriotic sentiment of the original song to America's own new cause. It was quickly parodied by Tory critics and, in response, by another patriot author.

After the outbreak of hostilities, the first actual war song to spread like wildfire throughout the colonies was "War and Washington" (May 1775), which set words by New Hampshire lawyer Jonathan Mitchell Sewall to "British Grenadiers." The original song celebrated the earlier exploits of that same elite branch of the British army that helped provoke the first bloodshed at Lexington and Concord a month before. The deliberate irony of setting new words in praise of General Washington to this tune thus enhanced its boldly patriotic effect. This, no doubt, was the war song heard "at every Continental camp-fire," and the one that "led the gallant soldier on to battle, and returned him from the field of victory triumphant in deathless verse." Also noteworthy was an independence song composed by Sewall in 1776 (tune unspecified), which was among the earliest of any to point the finger beyond bungling ministers at King George III himself as troublesome tyrant: "George the Third, of Great Britain, no more shall he reign, / With unlimited sway o'er these free States again" (Spicer, pp. 20–22).

"Yankee Doodle" and "Chester," songs of different origins that preceded the Revolution, were the two most closely associated with the patriot cause. Eventually they became the signature songs of the marching army. First referenced in 1767, "Yankee Doodle" derives from a complex folk history that, despite much research and speculation by music historians, is still not fully understood. Before the war, the tune was used by the British in deliberate derision of country-bumpkin colonists, while changing the guard within earshot of Boston Sunday church meetings, for example. After war began, Americans usurped the tune as their own and turned its significance on end. It then became associated with an explosion of new texts, as Americans enjoyed using the jaunty tune more than any other in the creation of further patriotic song; both sides found the tune a fitting vehicle for mocking the other's misfortunes. At the 1781 Yorktown surrender, in fact, it was because Lafayette requested soldiers of the defeated British light infantry to strike up the hated "Yankee Doodle" that many broke their arms upon the ground with bitter rage. The words most commonly associated with the tune, including the rhyme of "pony" with "macaroni," did not appear until 1842.

"Chester" appeared in the first publication of sacred music all by an American composer, *The New-England Psalm-Singer* (1770) by William Billings, an eccentric Boston leather tanner. Though musically untrained, Billings became a passionate and prolific composer of original music for the singing school, a thriving social as well as musical institution especially popular with young adults. The music Billings composed took several different forms, from straightforward hymnlike settings to more complex anthems. The several verses of "Chester" are set simply in four voices, with the tune in the tenor rather than in the top voice, as is now customary. Eight years later it reappeared in a second publication by Billings (*The Singing Master's Assistant*, 1778) with new verses added to reflect recent events of the war.

MILITARY MUSIC

During the Revolution Americans also heard the strains of military band music, but not like that we hear today. The instruments, the ensembles, and the music they played were all different than those that evolved after the 1830s, and all were directly patterned after contemporary British models. In particular, two entirely separate groups of musicians accompanied the British army by the time occupying forces arrived in Boston in 1768. These included not only the all-important field musicians—the more familiar fifers and drummers who gave the critical signals telling the troops what to do from battle to bedtime—but also a few very fine bands of musicians. These were not the brass bands of the nineteenth century, nor the larger mixed ensembles of today, but rather small wind octets of paired oboes, clarinets, horns, and bassoons. The officers whom they served organized and paid for the bands for ceremonial, concert, and dance entertainment. Before the war, Bostonians objected to offensive performances by British field musicians; but they hired and took great pleasure in the musical refinements of British bands, which gave regular concerts between 1769 and 1774.

When the American Continental Army was formed, it organized both field musicians and bands exactly in the British tradition. Washington ultimately appointed John Hiwell as Inspector and Superintendent of Music to train and maintain the quality of his field musicians. Hiwell also continued to direct one of several fine bands that formed during the war, with duties ranging from morning parade to evening entertainment, even during the worst winters at Valley Forge and Morristown.

Though very few American military instruments from the Revolution survive with reliable verification, a number of manuscript music books for fife and drum do. They show that the repertory played by both British and American army bands was essentially the same—the very march, dance, and folk tunes that inspired Revolutionary song.

Perhaps the best known tradition of military music from the Revolution is false folklore—that the British under Cornwallis marched in defeat at Yorktown to the nursery tune "The World Turned Upside Down." Schrader (1998) documents exhaustive detective work showing that this "tradition" was likely a later invention of an unreliable historian of the early nineteenth century, nevertheless repeated as accepted truth through the generations thereafter.

MUSIC IN AMERICAN CULTURE AND IDENTITY

Even while Americans fought and sacrificed for political independence from Britain, their musical culture remained wholly dependent on British traditions throughout the war and beyond, as Americans forged a new national identity into the nineteenth century. A familiar repertory of largely British tunes continued to accompany new American public celebrations, for ratification of the Constitution, the Fourth of July, battle victories, town bicentennials, and the like.

Similarly, music played an important ceremonial role in nineteenth-century commemorations of the Revolution. New generations of Americans increasingly redefined and romanticized the Revolution during anniversary observations that first gained momentum at the 1825–1826 Jubilee and reached a peak during centennial events beginning in 1875.

Festive celebration accompanied the dedication of many new battle monuments; but there was sad ceremony, too, for the reburial of patriot remains and grand public funerals of otherwise unknown last surviving veterans. The funeral in 1854 for fifer Jonathan Harrington of Lexington, who died at age ninety-four, attracted some 5,000 people, for example. In all cases there was but modest use of wartime repertoire. Rather, an evolving musical culture after the 1820s dictated the use of Masonic song at the laying of cornerstones, the setting of commemorative texts to newly popular parlor song for solo voice, martial music for new all-brass bands in parade, and the addition of large choruses, often performing excerpts from favorite oratorios, like Handel's *Judas Maccabaeus* and Haydn's *The Creation*. In American public life today, music continues to provide powerful accompaniment. Though the popular tunes from our British colonial past are largely long gone, some of the music we still hear can trace its roots to the American Revolution.

BIBLIOGRAPHY

Bowman, Kent A. *Voices of Combat: A Century of Liberty and War Songs, 1765–1865*. New York: Greenwood Press, 1987.

Camus, Raoul. *Military Music of the American Revolution*. Chapel Hill: University of North Carolina Press, 1976.

Camus, Raoul. "Military Music of Colonial Boston." In *Music in Colonial Massachusetts, 1630–1820*, vol. I: *Music in Public Places*. Boston: Colonial Society of Massachusetts, 1980.

Crawford, Richard. *The Birth of Liberty: Music of the American Revolution*. Notes to New World Records LP NW 276 (1976). Rereleased on CD as New World Records 80276-2 (1996).

Hazen, Margaret Hindle Hazen. "Songs of Revolutionary America." *The New England Historical and Genealogical Register* 130 (July 1976): 179–195.

Schrader, Arthur. "'The World Turned Upside Down': A Yorktown March, or Music to Surrender By." *American Music* 16, no. 2 (summer 1998): 180–215.

Silverman, Kenneth. *A Cultural History of the American Revolution: Painting, Music, Literature and the Theatre in the Colonies and the United States from the Treaty of Paris to the Inauguration of George Washington, 1763–1789*. New York: Columbia University Press, 1987.

Spicer, Richard C. "Popular Song for Public Celebration in Federal Portsmouth, New Hampshire." *Popular Song and Society* 25, nos. 1–2 (spring/summer 2001): 1–99.

Other Resources

Anderson, Simon Vance. *American Music during the War for Independence, 1775–1783*. Ph.D. diss. University of Michigan, Ann Arbor, 1965.

Song Text and Tune Sources

Anderson, Gillian B. *Freedom's Voice in Poetry and Song*. Wilmington, DE: Scholarly Resources, 1977.

Brand, Oscar. *Songs of '76: A Folksinger's History of the Revolution*. New York: M. Evans and Company, 1972.

Corry, Mary Jane; Keller, Kate Van Winkle; and Keller, Robert M. *The Performing Arts in Colonial American Newspapers, 1690–1783: Text Database and Index* (CD-ROM). New York: University Music Editions, 1997.

Dannett, Sylvia G. L. *The Yankee Doodler*. South Brunswick, NJ and New York: A. S. Barnes and Company, 1973.

Keller, Kate Van Winkle, ed. *Giles Gibbs, Jr. His Book for the Fife*. Hartford: Connecticut Historical Society, 1974.

Keller, Kate Van Winkle, and Rabson, Carolyn. *The National Tune Index* (microfiche). New York: University Music Editions, 1980.

Lawrence, Vera Brodsky. *Music for Patriots, Politicians, and Presidents: Harmonies and Discords of the First Hundred Years*. New York: Macmillan, 1975.

Moore, Frank. *Songs and Ballads of the American Revolution* (1856). Port Washington, NY: Kennikat Press, 1964.

Rabson, Carolyn. *Songbook of the American Revolution*. Peaks Island, ME: Neo Press, 1974.

Schrader, Arthur F. "Songs to Cultivate the Sensations of Freedom." In *Music in Colonial Massachusetts, 1630–1820*, vol. I: *Music in Public Places*. Boston: Colonial Society of Massachusetts, 1980.

Silber, Irwin. *Songs of Independence*. Harrisburg, PA: Stackpole Books, 1973.

Richard C. Spicer

See also: **Memory and Early Histories of the Revolution;** *The Spy*: **First American War Novel.**

NATIVE AMERICANS: IMAGES IN POPULAR CULTURE

Starting with the earliest contact between Europeans and American Indians, Europeans viewed native people through cultural blinders that often confused them about the realities of Native American life. Images of other peoples and places can play a dominant role in affecting how two (or more) societies interact, and decisions made on the basis of ethnocentric imagery usually lead to confusion, misunderstanding, and war between peoples. European views of Indians in early America rarely reflected the nuanced reality of life for native populations. Indigenous peoples came to symbolize many things for Europeans, depending on the background and motivations of the person discussing them, although popular conceptions of Indians followed a particular historical progression as Euro-American people experienced more contact with Indians. Indians were often portrayed in a negative light, although by the time of the American Revolution, if not before, some Europeans living in North America also began borrowing elements of what they considered Indian culture. For many Euro-Americans, Indians also came to symbolize America as a land different from Europe and the Euro-American populace sometimes portrayed themselves with Indian symbols to distinguish themselves from Europeans.

INITIAL CONCEPTIONS

The English adopted the term *Indian* from the Spanish to generically describe the native inhabitants of North America, even though Indian people almost never used such a collective term, instead preferring the actual tribal or community designation of an individual. The manner in which Indians identified other Indians emphasized their uniqueness, whereas Europeans tended to lump all Indians together when portraying their cultural values. Thus, from the beginning of contact, Euro-Americans in positions of cultural influence as writers, publishers, military officials, or politicians relied on generalizations about how Indians lived, why they acted the way they did, and what concerned them. Europeans usually described Indians in ways that differentiated Indians as the Other—as something not European, not "civilized."

STEREOTYPING

General English conceptions of Indians in early America fell into two categories: ignoble savages and noble savages. Both notions portrayed Indians as primitive in comparison to Europeans, but the ignoble savage view focused on perceived negative characteristics of Indian culture and the noble savage perspective saw much to admire, if not necessarily to emulate, in Indian cultures. Whether ignoble or noble, Indians in European eyes remained primitive and exotic, worthy of either scorn or pity but not equality. The ignoble Indian was always lacking something that European civilization took for granted, such as permanent housing, proper clothing, political institutions, religion (meaning Christianity), a written language (or indeed any language at all worthy of the name), correct morals, agriculture, livestock, and appropriate gender roles. The character of such Indians was described as warlike, lewd, barbarous, cannibalistic, filthy, lazy, and so on. Descriptions of Indians as ignoble beastlike devils can be found among the earliest reports emanating from the colonies and from Europe, but they reached their most influential distribution in captivity narratives.

CAPTIVITY NARRATIVES

No literary genre in early America did more to shape the average Euro-American's perceptions of Indians than the captivity narratives. Particularly popular among the literate population of Puritan New England, captivity narratives first appeared in the late seventeenth century as a result of numerous actual captive-taking episodes arising from the wars between France and England, such as King William's War (1689–1697) and Queen Anne's War (1702–1713). The narratives told of devilish Indians preying like packs of wolves on innocent English families who lived on the edges of Euro-American settlement in western and northern New England. God and Satan, Puritan and Indian, battled for lives and souls as Indians allied with the Catholic French in Canada killed Puritan men and seized Puritan women and children. Puritan ministers used the narratives to preach about God's wrath on sinful people (in the form of Indian attacks) and to point out the power of redemption when some captives returned to English territory after months or years of captivity, usually after being ransomed.

Women captives who returned remained suspect if they did not wholeheartedly renounce their experience and their captors as heathenish. Witness the long title of one of the most famous and earliest captivity narratives: *The Sovereignty and Goodness of God, Together with the Faithfulness of His Promises Displayed: Being a Narrative of the Captivity and Restauration of Mrs. Mary Rowlandson; Commended by Her, to All that Desire to Know the Lord's Doing to, and Dealings with Her* (1682). Indian warriors, so the narratives said, wanted nothing more than to rape chaste English women, and only the most devout Puritan woman could resist their charms and co-

ercion. In reality, warriors never engaged in sex on a war party because of the ritualized strictures associated with war and because they wanted to avoid the possibility of incest since their captives might be adopted into their own family. Indians did seek to convert their captives to their way of life, and hundreds of English children and young women remained the rest of their lives among their new Indian families.

In the eighteenth century, the captivity narratives abandoned all pretense of impartiality and became the gothic novels of their day, with a hint of forbidden love thrown in for good measure. This genre of literature, and its negative stereotyping of Indians, especially of Indian men, continued in the nineteenth-century dime novel and the twentieth-century Hollywood Westerns.

THE "NOBLE" INDIAN

Some Europeans found much to admire in the perceived primitiveness of Indians and thought of them as noble savages. This characterization emphasized their assumed honesty, hospitality, generosity, handsome physical stature, stamina, dignity, pride, simplicity, and innocence; in short, it portrayed them as children of nature, much like Adam and Eve of the Old Testament. Frequently coupled with this view was a belief that Indians were a vanishing race. The ultimate example of these portrayals is James Fenimore Cooper's *Last of the Mohicans* (1826), but the notion was already popular by the mid-eighteenth century. Here Indian resistance and tenacity—their ability to hold onto a traditional lifestyle until death—was honored despite its inherent naiveté. It was this conception of Indians that motivated the Bostonians who threw British tea into the harbor during the Boston Tea Party (1773) to dress as Indians. Disguise mattered little—everyone knew who they were. Distinguishing themselves as something quintessentially American, in opposition to the European British, meant everything.

IMPACTS OF IMAGES ON INDIAN-WHITE RELATIONS

The impact of these images can be hard to assess in specific actions by European or American governments and citizens, but their overall impacts are clear. As a tool of imperial expansion, these images justified the takeover of Indian lands, with force if necessary. Since Indians supposedly did not farm and did not live in permanent homes, they did not make proper use of the land and therefore forfeited their right to continue to possess it. Euro-Americans promoting this image focused on Indian men who hunted to contribute to their family's subsistence and ignored Indian women who raised crops among most groups east of the Mississippi River, although agriculture (corn, squash, beans, sunflowers, and

The Buffalo Hunter by Seth Eastman, ca. 1808–1875. The "noble savage," the Indians' ability to hold onto traditional lifestyle, was a popular image by the eighteenth century. © GEOFFREY CLEMENTS/CORBIS

so on) supplied a major portion of Indian diets. Women's efforts mattered little to the Euro-American male image-makers, so if Indian men did not farm, then Indians did not farm. If Indian men hunted and roamed about the countryside, then Indians were nomadic, and nomadic people could not rightly claim particular patches of land. Warlike, bloodthirsty Indians could not change their ways or live in peace near Europeans, so the imagery said, and therefore they needed to be removed or exterminated. As non-Christians (although significant numbers of Indians became at least nominally Christian by the eighteenth century), Indians could not expect to enjoy the same rights as Europeans. As a vanishing race, Indians stood in the way of progress if they resisted white expansion. They might need special attention and care from their white "fathers," but only under Euro-American laws and according to Euro-American priorities. Such images played on Euro-Americans' fears and distorted reality while simultaneously justifying ill treatment of Indians.

The pervasiveness of this imagery did not allow for the possibility of Euro-Americans accepting Indians according to Indian values or from Indian perspectives.

Comparison was always made to an idealized notion of Euro-American life, and Indians always came up lacking. Intolerance of difference has characterized all periods of American history in one manner or another, Indians bore an inordinately large share of the consequences of those beliefs. American society and culture have been shaped by these images of Indians, resulting in wars of removal and extermination, well-meaning paternalism to "civilize" Native Americans, and the perpetuation of stereotypes.

BIBLIOGRAPHY

Berkhofer, Robert F., Jr. *The White Man's Indian: Images of the American Indian from Columbus to the Present.* New York: Random House, 1979.

Calloway, Colin G. *New Worlds for All: Indians, Europeans, and the Remaking of Early America.* Baltimore, MD: Johns Hopkins University Press, 1997.

Deloria, Philip J. *Playing Indian.* New Haven, CT: Yale University Press, 1998.

Drinnon, Richard. *Facing West: The Metaphysics of Indian Hating and Empire Building.* New York: Schocken, 1980.

Green, Rayna. "The Pocahontas Perplex: The Image of Indian Women in American Culture." In *Native American Voices: A Reader,* edited by Steve Talbot. Upper Saddle River, NJ: Prentice Hall, 2001.

Kupperman, Karen Ordahl. *Indians and English: Facing Off in Early America.* Ithaca, NY: Cornell University Press, 2000.

Lepore, Jill. *The Name of War: King Philip's War and the Origins of American Identity.* New York: Knopf, 1998.

Scheckel, Susan. *The Insistence of the Indian: Race and Nationalism in Nineteenth-Century American Culture.* Princeton, NJ: Princeton University Press, 1998.

Greg O'Brien

See also: **Cooper, James Fenimore; Indian Removal and Response.**

PAINE, THOMAS

(b. January 29, 1737; d. June 8, 1809) Political pamphleteer, radical advocate of American independence

Thomas Paine, who was born into a Quaker family in Thetford, England, was a soldier in the Continental Army and author of *Common Sense,* the most influential pamphlet calling for American independence. He was a radical advocate of republican principles in both the American and French Revolutions.

Paine left the local grammar school at age thirteen, became an apprentice in his father's corset factory, went to sea briefly at age sixteen, returned to apprenticeship, and later became a tax collector but was dismissed from that job. Impoverished, separated from his wife, and with few prospects, Paine immigrated to Philadelphia in 1774 at the urging of Benjamin Franklin whom he had met by chance in London.

Paine became a printer and political propagandist, advocating, among other things, the abolition of slavery. In 1774 he became involved in the protests against English "tyranny" and in December, 1776 was with Washington's beleaguered army. Facing defeat, Paine wrote an inspirational pamphlet, *The Crisis,* that boosted the morale of the troops and rallied patriots to the cause. The opening lines have become embedded in American culture: "These are the times that try men's souls. The summer soldier and the sunshine patriot will, in this crisis, shrink from the service of their country; but he that stands it now, deserves the love and thanks of man and woman. Tyranny, like hell, is not easily conquered."

In January, 1776 Paine published his most important work, *Common Sense,* which made the case for American independence. While some leaders of the resistance still thought that reconciliation with Britain was possible, Paine argued that America should not only become independent but more importantly, should create a new form of government based on radical republican principles. Paine's ridicule of monarchy and aristocratic rule reflected his Quaker egalitarianism and the influence of Enlightenment belief in human reason and social progress. His ideas struck a popular nerve, shown by the initial production of over 100,000 copies of *Common Sense.* Historian Eric Foner observed, "The success of *Common Sense* reflected the perfect conjunction of man and his time, a writer and his audience, and it announced the emergence of Paine as the outstanding political pamphleteer of the Age of Revolution" (Foner, 87).

Thomas Paine.

Something of a gadfly, more adept at tearing down than building up, Paine did not involve himself in creating the republican institutions he had idealized. Although he wrote more pamphlets, later compiled as *The American Crisis,* to boost morale during the war with England, he devoted part of his time to experiments in making smokeless candles and iron bridges. Restless, he returned to England in 1787 to pursue these two enterprises.

In 1790, with the French Revolution moving toward the establishment of a constitutional monarchy, Paine resumed his role as a pamphleteer advocating radical republicanism. In response to criticism of the revolution in France by British statesman Edmund Burke, who had been his friend, he wrote his finest work on democratic philosophy, *The Rights of Man* (1790–1791). In this pamphlet, which was banned by the British government, Paine argued against hereditary government, even suggesting the abolishment of the House of Lords. He held that all men over the age of 21 should have equal political rights. He also proposed such extreme innovations as progressive taxation, family allowances, old age pensions, and maternity grants. Outlawed for sedition, Paine went to France to escape arrest. Despite the ban, *The Rights of Man* became one of the most important political pamphlets in British history among the working and rising middle classes.

Paine became a French citizen and a member of the National Convention, but proved to be more republican than radical. In 1793 he voted against the execution of Louis XVI and was put in jail in 1794 by the Jacobins. Fearing that he might not have long to live, Paine spent his time in prison completing *The Age of Reason* (1794–1796), in which he expressed his Deist religious convictions more vehemently than had eighteenth-century Deists whose writings were addressed to scholars. Because he wrote for common people and tactlessly ridiculed Christian beliefs in addition to presenting arguments against them, this book aroused a storm of protest.

Returning to the United States from France in 1802, Paine discovered that his attack on Christianity had made him an outcast. Upon his death in 1809 a new generation of Americans ignored Paine's passing and his contributions to the Revolution. Only in the latter part of the twentieth century did Paine, the radical pamphleteer whose words helped lead America to independence, republicanism and democracy, become an important part of the nation's culture and revolutionary tradition.

BIBLIOGRAPHY

Fast, Howard. *Citizen Tom Paine.* New York: Grove Press, 1983.

Foner, Eric. *Tom Paine and Revolutionary America.* New York: Oxford University Press, 1976.

Foner, Eric, ed. *Thomas Paine: Collected Writings.* New York: Library of America, 1995.

Keane, John. *Tom Paine: A Political Life.* London: Grove Press, 1995.

Internet Resource

"Thomas Paine." (Includes complete texts of his major works.) Independence Hall Association. Available from <http://www.ushistory.org/paine/>.

John P. Resch

See also: **Adams, John; Boston Massacre: Pamphlets and Propaganda;** *Common Sense;* **Continental Congresses; Franklin, Benjamin; Mobilization; War of Independence; Sons of Liberty; Stamp Act Congress.**

PAINTERS AND PATRIOTISM, LATE EIGHTEENTH AND EARLY NINETEENTH CENTURIES

American art in the late eighteenth and early nineteenth centuries was used as a didactic tool to celebrate the republican and patriotic ideals fostered by the American Revolution. The new values of the Revolution recalled the old virtues of ancient Greece and republican Rome, thus the artistic style that illustrated them to American audiences evoked the style of the classics in its abolishment of everything that was decorative and superfluous. This focus on the essential was what united the American Puritan tradition and the neoclassic style of the late eighteenth century. As art critic Robert Hughes claims in his 1997 book *American Visions*, "there was no real conflict between the values of American neoclassicism and those of the Puritan tradition; one flowed into the other, sharing a common radicalism."

Paradoxically, the painter who influenced this new direction of American art did not paint scenes of the American Revolution and spent the best part of his life in Europe under the patronage of George III. Benjamin West was the first American artist to combine a contemporary historical event with a neoclassical composition in his controversial *The Death of General Wolfe* (1770). It addresses the death of the British commander, Major General James Wolfe, while defeating the French army at the battle for Quebec in 1759. The painting is organized according to classical principles with the dying hero at its center looking skyward, thus prefiguring the ascension of Wolfe's soul and echoing scenes of Christ's deposition from the Cross. At the time, the painting caused heated debates in artistic circles, as many thought that historical painting required antique drapery rather than a detailed portrayal of modern uniforms and weaponry.

West's reply to these objections would influence a whole generation of American artists: "The event to be commemorated took place . . . in a region of the world unknown to the Greeks and Romans, and at a period of time when no such nations, nor heroes in their costumes, any longer existed . . . The same truth that guides the pen of the historian should govern the pencil of the artist . . . I want to mark the date, the place and the parties engaged in the event."

PAINTERS OF THE AMERICAN REVOLUTION

John Singleton Copley applied West's intuition about historical painting to subjects taken from the American Revolution. Copley's portraits form a gallery of the men and women who contributed to the founding of the American republic. Hughes views Copley as the founder of that current of American empirical realism "which, disdaining frills of style and 'spiritual' grace notes, tried in all its sharpness and bluntness to engage the material world as an end in itself." Though Copley also painted many Tories of his native Boston and his own political allegiances are unknown, his paintings devoted to revolutionary personalities such as Paul Revere and Samuel Adams have become fundamental statements about the American character.

Revere, a silversmith who warned the patriot troops at Lexington of the impending arrival of the British, is defined in Copley's portrait through his profession, as he is holding a silver teapot while three etching instruments are on the table. The painting, whose subject would also be featured in a work by the twentieth-century American regionalist painter Grant Wood, rejects any embellishment of the material world of Revere's profession. Thus, Hughes sees it as "a manifesto of democratic American pride in work. The radical as craftsman."

John Trumbull's political faith in the American Revolution has never been in doubt. Writing to Thomas Jefferson in 1789, Trumbull stated that his paintings were motivated by "the wish of commemorating the great events of our country's revolution." To Trumbull, the potentially frivolous profession of painter was given dignity by the task of preserving the memory of the greatest events and heroes in human history. This celebrative intent led Trumbull to plan a series of thirteen scenes from the American Revolution, of which he managed to complete eight. *The Declaration of Independence, 4 July 1776* (1787–1820) with its from-life portraits of Jefferson, John Adams and Benjamin Franklin, is surely the best-known of the group and is based on a description of the Assembly Room in the Pennsylvania State House given by Jefferson. Trumbull also memorialized the events of the Revolution for the rotunda in the Capitol, focusing on *The Declaration of Independence*, the engraving of which established the reputation of Asher B. Durand; *The Surrender of Burgoyne; The Surrender of Cornwallis;* and *The Resignation of Washington* (1817–1824).

Other late eighteenth-century painters who used art as a patriotic tool were Charles Wilson Peale, who painted several events where Washington had been the hero; his son Rembrandt Peale, whose Porthole portrait of Washington contributed to the growth of the president's iconography; and Gilbert Stuart, whose unfinished head of Washington has attained iconic status. Washington was also the hero of William Trego's *The March to Valley Forge* (1883).

LANDSCAPE PAINTING AND AMERICAN VALUES

Though concerned mostly with landscape painting, the Hudson River School, led initially by Thomas Cole and then by Asher Durand, contributed to the fostering of patriotic values as it established, at the beginning of the nineteenth century, the myth of American wilderness. Active from the 1820s to the 1870s, the members of the school painted distinctively native landscapes, scenes not only of the Hudson River Valley but also of the American wilderness and of the West. Their paintings were part of the larger cultural trend of the nineteenth century, the exploration of nature in its mediating relationship between the human and the divine spheres. The paintings of the Hudson River School, particularly those by Thomas Cole, responded perfectly to the expectations of the rich New York Federalist families and their yearning for an idealized, purer America, unspoiled by the populism of Andrew Jackson's presidency. Cole's landscape paintings symbolize the dangers and the threats besieging Arcadian America, thus representing the anxiety over social and economic change shared by many of his patrons.

Cole's Arcadian landscapes were always beset by the storms of change (*The Oxbow*, 1836, being the clearest example) and they should therefore be set against the ambitious social reforms favored by Andrew Jackson's populist democracy. Cole's didactic and allegorical intent is apparent in *The Course of the Empire* (1834–1836), a series of five paintings commissioned by New York millionaire Luman Reed for the then enormous sum of $5,000. *The Course of the Empire* was an appeal for a return to the republican virtues of the forefathers who had been forsaken by Cole's generation. Set against the same natural backdrop (a natural harbor dominated by a rock, representing the endurance of nature and the caducity of human history), the cycle takes the viewer from *The Savage State* (1834) and *The Arcadian or Pastoral State* (1836), when humans were still honest and virtuous, to the corruption implied in *Consummation* (1836) and leading to the gloom of *Destruction* (1836) and *Desolation* (1836).

Though the subject matter changed over time, the late eighteenth and early nineteenth centuries witnessed the emergence of a distinctively American school of painting, in which historical events and natural scenery provided a constant source of patriotic inspiration for artists and their audiences.

BIBLIOGRAPHY

Cooper, Helen. *John Trumbull: The Hand and Spirit of a Painter.* New Haven, CT: Yale University Press, 1982.

Hughes, Robert. *American Visions: The Epic History of Art in America.* London: The Harvill Press, 1997.

Miles, Ellen Gross, ed. *The Portrait in Eighteenth-Century America.* Newark: University of Delaware Press, 1993.

Novak, Barbara. *Nature & Culture: American Landscape and Painting, 1825–1875.* New York: Oxford University Press, 1980.

Truettner, William H. and Wallach, Alan, eds. *Thomas Cole: Landscape into History.* New Haven, CT: Yale University Press, 1994.

Yaeger, Bert D. *The Hudson River School: American Landscape Artists.* New York: Smithmark Publishers, 1996.

Luca Prono

See also: **Bunker Hill Monument; Lafayette's Tour; Memory and Early Histories of the Revolution; Valley Forge.**

PEACE OF PARIS, 1763

The Peace of Paris, signed by Britain, France, Spain, and Portugal, was ratified on February 10, 1763. Together with the Treaty of Hubertsburg (February 15, 1763) between Prussia and Austria, it ended the series of European conflicts that were fought worldwide and known collectively as the Seven Years' War, or in America, the French and Indian War.

TERMS

As befit the global character of Britain's triumph, the settlement's terms were overwhelmingly favorable to the subjects of George III. In North America, France and Spain recognized Britain's title to all territory east of the Mississippi River except New Orleans. Britain's new possessions included the French colonies of Acadia, Cape Breton, Quebec, and the Spanish East and West Florida, which Spain ceded in exchange for the restoration of Cuba. In the West Indies, Britain acquired Grenada, Saint Vincent, Dominica, and Tobago from France while restoring Martinique, Guadeloupe, and Saint Lucia. In Europe, France returned Minorca in exchange for Belle-Île, and France and Spain promised to withdraw their forces from Germany and Portugal, respectively. In West Africa, Britain restored Gorée to France but kept Senegal, and in India France regained its possessions of 1749 but on an exclusively commercial basis. The British government returned Spanish Manila, which the East India Company had captured in 1762, without territorial compensation; however, the peace confirmed the rights of British settlers to cut logwood on the Spanish coast of Honduras Bay. Spain also renounced all claims to the Newfoundland fishery, although France kept its fishing rights off Newfoundland and in the Gulf of Saint Lawrence, as well as the islands of Saint Pierre and Miquelon. As part of the Florida cession, France gave Spain New Orleans and all of Louisiana west of the Mississippi.

CONSEQUENCES

Although Britain's victory appeared complete, the peace created a host of new problems. In Europe, Britain's wartime ally Frederick II of Prussia resented his abandonment on the eve of negotiations; Austria showed no interest after 1763 in reviving the alliance that had once been the centerpiece of British policy in Germany; and France and Spain sought revenge by rebuilding their empires and threatening British interests in Gambia, the Bahamas, Honduras Bay, and the Falkland Islands. Compounding this diplomatic isolation was a series of new obligations within the British Empire. In the Ohio Valley, the ill-advised decision to stop the practice of Indian gift giving triggered Pontiac's War (1763–1765). In response, the government issued the Royal Proclamation (1763), temporarily barring settlers from Indian lands west of the Appalachians, and decided to leave a permanent force of 10,000 regulars in the colonies. Britain also continued its wartime attempts to curtail illicit trade in North America and the West Indies, notably with the Sugar Act (1764). Finally, in an elaborate arrangement with the Mogul Emperor, the East India Company became the effective ruler of Bengal, raising the prospect of a new territorial British empire on the subcontinent.

The peace's domestic consequences were equally momentous. Although the British public welcomed the end of hostilities, the concessions to France and Spain gained the lasting enmity of William Pitt and his supporters, among whom was a hitherto obscure militia colonel named John Wilkes, whose *North Britain* no. 45 helped launch his own career as well as the myth that the Scottish Earl of Bute (whose ministry had handled the negotiations) was a closet Jacobite who had betrayed the English nation to its ancient enemies. More seriously, the magnitude of Britain's conquests fueled the popular press's enthusiasm for imperialism, creating fantasies of military invincibility and global hegemony. At the same time, the war raised taxation and military service to unprecedented levels, and its end coincided with a serious economic contraction, triggering unrest across England and prompting both Bute and his successor George Grenville to look for new sources of revenue without raising taxes at home.

One widely mooted solution to these fiscal problems was for Parliament to tax the colonies directly. Despite the objections of the Americans and their metropolitan friends, many Britons thought of the colonists as the main beneficiaries of the peace's North American provisions. The recent war had also encouraged the metropolitan public to think of Americans as fellow subjects in a greater British nation and to assume they possessed the same rights and responsibilities as British subjects in England, Scotland, and Wales. In addition, according to many observers, the tax burden in the individual colonies was comparatively light, meaning that a modest increase would do far less damage than in Britain proper. With these goals and assumptions in mind, Grenville persuaded Parliament to adopt the American Stamp Act in 1765.

Although the North American empire that the peace bequeathed to Britain lasted barely two decades, several of the peace's consequences were more enduring. By stripping France of Canada and Louisiana, the settlement all but ensured the Anglicization of the continent's northern and eastern half (whether under the auspices of the British Empire or the post-1783 United States). In India, the peace opened the way for another kind of English-speaking hegemony in the form of the British Raj. It is even possible to trace the origins of the modern humanitarian impulse to the sense of global responsibility felt by many Britons in the war's aftermath, with the movement to abolish slavery being only the most conspicuous. In a sense, the world we inhabit today is a legacy of the one created by the peace settlement of 1763. The taxation of the American colonies that followed with the 1764 Sugar Act and especially the 1765 Stamp Act marked the beginning of a constitutional crisis over the power of Parliament to rule the American colonies and over the rights of British citizens in America. The peace of 1763, which ended nearly a decade of imperial war, not only brought the British Empire to its height but also led to policies that caused Americans to protest what they considered British tyranny, and in 1775 to defend with arms what they felt were their rights and privileges.

BIBLIOGRAPHY

Anderson, Fred. *Crucible of War: The Seven Years' War and the Fate of Empire in British North America, 1754–1766.* New York: Knopf, 2000.

Brown, Christopher L. "Empire without Slaves: British Concepts of Emancipation in the Age of the American Revolution." *William and Mary Quarterly* (1999).

Gould, Eliga H. *The Persistence of Empire: British Political Culture in the Age of the American Revolution.* Chapel Hill: University of North Carolina Press, 2000.

Hinderaker, Eric. *Elusive Empires: Constructing Colonialism in the Ohio Valley, 1673–1800.* Cambridge, UK: Cambridge University Press, 1997.

Sosin, Jack. *Whitehall and the Wilderness: The Middle West in British Colonial Policy, 1760–1775.* Lincoln: University of Nebraska Press, 1961.

Eliga H. Gould

See also: Fort William Henry Massacre; Cultural Legacy; French and Indian War, Legacy of; Mobilization, French and Indian War; Sons of Liberty.

PIRATES AND THE BARBARY WAR

From the mid-eighteenth century until the early nineteenth century, pirate ships from the so-called Barbary States on the North African coast terrorized foreign shipping in the Mediterranean Sea. What are now the seaport cities of Tangiers (Morocco), Algiers (Algeria), Tunis (Tunisia), and Tripoli (Libya), as well as their surrounding areas, were recognized as separate states. Unless a foreign nation paid tribute to the leaders of these states, its ships were plundered and their crews sent into slavery. Even Great Britain, with its mighty navy, found it easier and cheaper to buy peace than to fight. The newly independent United States, with very little in the way of sea power, did likewise. However, in 1801 an infuriated President Thomas Jefferson surprised the Barbary pirates by sending ships into the Mediterranean. Although this brave show did not end the piracy, it did mark the beginning of recognized U.S. naval power. Another fourteen years would pass before the Barbary War came to an end.

THE BARBARY STATES

The Barbary States probably got their name from the Berbers, who were largely scattered in tribes across the North African coast. These tribes had been relatively independent until the twelfth century, when invading Bedouin Arabs destroyed their economy and sent many of them into a life of nomadic wandering.

By the sixteenth century, piracy along the Barbary Coast had become a relatively easy, publicly acclaimed way of making a living. The pirates were technically corsairs, meaning sailors who were given a government license to steal, and piracy was profitable to the beys, deys, and pashas who ruled these coastal cities. These rulers were under the nominal control of the Grand Turk, or sultan, at Constantinople, but in practice they were independent and absolute monarchs. They answered to no one and considered violence and the profits from piracy almost a tradition.

Barbary pirate raids were generally conducted by one ship only, and they were terrifying. The heavily-manned pirate ship would look as though it carried few passengers as it approached a foreign vessel, but as it drew alongside the pirate crew would spring over the side, screaming and brandishing swords. They stole everything in sight, including the seamen's clothes, and killed anybody who stood in their way. Even more terrifying was the taking of prisoners to be sold in the open marketplace, either to a private person or to some backbreaking government project. In either case, the captured seamen were not likely ever to be freed.

BRIBING THE PIRATES

By the time the United States gained its independence in the late 1700s, the Barbary States had come to regard the Mediterranean as their own private lake. Common piracy had grown into a sophisticated business. Great Britain had long before revived the ancient custom of paying tribute for the freedom to sail the Mediterranean, although the mighty British navy could easily have defeated the pirates. During the colonial period, the British had also paid tribute for any vessels from the colonies, and France had done so during the American Revolution. So it was a shock to the newly independent United States when one day in 1785 an American ship was seized and its crew jailed by a pirate ship in the employ of the dey of Algiers.

American ambassadors tried to free the sailors but were unsuccessful, and George Washington agreed, reluctantly, to pay tribute to Algiers and Tripoli in 1796 to stop the piracy. Congress authorized a cash payment plus a yearly tribute in naval supplies, which resulted in freedom for a number of American captives in Algiers.

DEFENDING NATIONAL HONOR

When Thomas Jefferson became the nation's third president in 1801, the country was still paying tribute. He soon discovered that the nation had paid an amount roughly equivalent to one-fifth of its annual income to the Barbary pirates. Congress had authorized the building of four frigates in 1794, including the *Constellation* and the *Constitution,* and Jefferson, although in principle against having a national navy, decided to put this new navy to use.

In 1801, Jefferson refused to negotiate a new arrangement with the pasha of Tripoli. This bravado seemed to amuse the pasha, who promptly declared war by chopping down the flagpole in front of the American consulate. In another show of bravado, Jefferson sent four ships into the Mediterranean. The lone success of the mission was the taking of a Tripolitan ship by the sloop *Enterprise,* which served to infuriate the pasha without accomplishing much else in the Mediterranean.

In 1803, the United States lost the ship *Philadelphia,* which was captured and held in the port of Tripoli. When it was rumored that pirates would refloat the vessel and use it against the Americans, Stephen Decatur from the *Enterprise* apprehended an enemy four-gun ketch and sailed into Tripoli harbor on February 15, 1804, killing many pirates, setting fire to the American ship, and escaping. Decatur, who was then twenty-five, was promoted to captain, then the highest rank in the U.S. Navy. He remains the youngest American seaman to have held that rank.

In July of that year, Captain Edward Preble led five attacks against Tripoli. His three vessels, one of them commanded by Decatur, plus three mortar boats and six gunboats faced twenty-four warships in a harbor defended by about 25,000 soldiers. The bombardment caused little damage, and the American fleet suffered the loss of the *Intrepid.*

The USS *Constitution* and the HMS *Guerriere* engage in battle during the War of 1812. The *Constitution* was one of four ships sent to the Mediterranean in 1802 to confront the pirates of the Barbary States. After the War of 1812, the United States declared war in 1815 on Algiers, during the Second Barbary War. In 1816 Algiers signed a peace treaty. © FRANCIS G. MAYER/CORBIS

The war with Tripoli did not end until March 1805, when the U.S. Navy and Marines, with the help of allied Arabs, took the Tripolitan port of Derna. This adventure is remembered in a line from the song of the U.S. Marines: "From the halls of Montezuma to the shores of Tripoli." The pasha of Tripoli signed a peace treaty in June for the return of his city.

But piracy resumed in 1807, when Algiers began harassing foreign shipping once again. Soon thereafter the United States turned its attention to the War of 1812, an inconclusive conflict with Great Britain over oppressive maritime practices, mainly the issue of impressment. The British boarded foreign ships to search for deserters and then impressed the foreign sailors into the Royal Navy. It was not until after the War of 1812 ended that the Americans declared war on Algiers in March 1815. Algiers signed a peace treaty in 1816.

Although it was a small war, America's conflict with the Barbary pirates was nevertheless significant. In addition to protecting American shipping, Jefferson's decision to build an American navy indicated the new nation's determination to use armed force to protect its sovereignty and commerce. The U.S.S. *Constitution*, or Old Iron Sides, remains the navy's oldest commissioned vessel and an enduring symbol of the nation's independence and identity.

BIBLIOGRAPHY

Chidsey, Donald Barr. *The Wars in Barbary: Arab Piracy and the Birth of the United States Navy.* New York: Crown, 1971.

Nash, Howard P., Jr. *The Forgotten Wars: The U.S. Navy in the Quasi-War with France and the Barbary Wars, 1798–1805.* New York: A. S. Barnes, 1968.

Tucker, Glenn. *Dawn Like Thunder: The Barbary Wars and the Birth of the U.S. Navy.* New York: Bobbs-Merrill, 1963.

Internet Resources

"Jefferson and the Barbary War." University of San Diego. Available from <http://history.sandiego.edu/gen/classes/diplo/barbarywar.html>.

Williams, Richard. "Another Forgotten War." Upper Mississippi Brigade. Available from <http://umbrigade.tripod.com/articles/forgotten.html>.

Corinne J. Naden and Rose Blue

See also: **Jefferson, Thomas; War of 1812.**

POLITICS AND EXPRESSIONS OF PATRIOTISM

The American Revolution bequeathed to the United States a legacy of liberty forged by bloodshed, and to reaffirm their patriotism Americans touted their identity as a freedom-loving people, enshrined the founding fathers, and commemorated Independence Day. John Adams's oft-quoted remark that Independence Day should be an annual holiday of "pomp and parade" distinguished by "solemn acts of devotion" underscored how some Americans thought the Revolution should be remembered (Butterfield, ed., p. 30). It does not, however, reveal the contested nature of this legacy. Americans might proclaim themselves patriots, yet they often disagreed on the definition of patriotism and about who warranted admission into the pantheon of Revolutionary icons.

CONFLICTING PATRIOTS

Evidence of this can be seen as early as the 1790s. With the development of the Federalist and Democratic-Republican parties, the Revolution's legacy became the subject of contentious debate. For the Federalists, the Revolution symbolized the restoration of constitutional rights previously denied Americans within the British Empire. It had not, strictly speaking, been a revolution. With the French Revolution spiraling out of control, drenched in blood and violence, Federalists preferred to champion an orderly image of the American Revolution. For the Democratic-Republicans, the Spirit of '76 meant something more than simple independence; it meant the continuing spread of liberty, and freedom from foreign and domestic foes—the last a not-so-subtle dig at Federalist policies. Increasingly, Democratic-Republicans challenged the Federalist message by appealing to ordinary people to protect their revolutionary heritage.

Both Federalists and Democratic-Republicans crafted symbols to inspire a sense of national unity and patriotism. Federalists saluted George Washington (and by extension his policies, since Washington was a Federalist) as the model of a Revolutionary icon. He became the father figure of the American Revolution. Democratic-Republicans did not dispute Washington's prominence, but they added other Revolutionary symbols, notably Thomas Jefferson; they hailed the Declaration of Independence and emphasized the importance of the common people.

Federalists and Democratic-Republicans clashed over their choice of Revolutionary symbols as well as their choice of heroes. The *Jersey* prison ship victims were one such source of contention. Incarcerated aboard British prison hulks in New York harbor during the Revolution, thousands of these patriots had died and received impromptu burials along Brooklyn's Wallabout Bay. While Federalists were applauding the construction of a George Washington statue in Manhattan, Democratic-Republicans bemoaned the lack of attention given the *Jersey* dead. The Tammany Society, a Democratic-Republican political club, pushed for a lavish reinterment of the bones; it organized a procession of artisans, officials, and veterans and ceremoniously reburied the remains in a display of patriotic splendor in 1808. Federalists denounced the efforts as a political ploy to capture votes. One Federalist paper even questioned the identity of the remains.

PATRIOTS: ICONS OR COMMONERS?

The disappearance of the Federalists after the War of 1812 ushered in a more inclusive patriotic ethos. Thomas Jefferson and John Adams, political rivals in the 1790s, came to be seen as equally worthy patriots by the 1820s, their political squabbles irrelevant to a new generation of Americans. Once criticized as hirelings, Continental soldiers now gained both recognition and pensions. A few veterans became celebrities. In the 1830s, George Robert Twelves Hewes, a shoemaker and one of the last survivors of the Boston Tea Party, won long-delayed recognition. Heroes could now be men of modest rank. Washington, Adams, and Jefferson were no longer the sole symbols of Revolutionary patriotism.

The issue of inclusion nonetheless foundered over questions of class, ethnicity, and race. Was it patriotic to include the contributions of commoners? The verdict remained mixed. Homage paid to commoners sometimes conflicted with the reverence rendered to the well-to-do. Uncertainties about John Paulding, Isaac Van Wart, and David Williams, the captors of the British major John André, Benedict Arnold's go-between, focused on their professed patriotism. Were they mercenaries or virtuous yeomen? Although Paulding and his comrades eventually won a measure of recognition in the 1820s, some Americans still lionized André. Cyrus Field, a prominent Gilded Age businessman, erected a monument to him in Tappan, New York, in 1879. Critics denounced the venture, and vandals toppled the monument in the 1880s.

André's fame also catapulted Nathan Hale into the public sphere, making Hale's enshrinement as a heroic American spy essential. As a consequence, Hale rated both monuments and statues before the end of the nineteenth century.

DEFINING AMERICAN PATRIOTISM AND IDENTITY

For some, patriotism hinged on the politics of identity. Immigrant groups sought Revolutionary heroes of their own, and Pulaski Day and Von Steuben Day parades satisfied Polish and German yearnings. A 1911 monument to John Barry, a Revolutionary naval captain, did the same for Philadelphia's Irish Catholics. Groups unable to locate a Revolutionary forbear could still display their patriotism (and their ethnicity—and gain political clout if they turned out in large numbers) by marching in Independence Day parades, and all Americans could salute the Liberty Bell, one of the defining symbols of Revolutionary patriotism, as it wended its way across the country on tours between 1885 and 1915.

African Americans faced more daunting obstacles. Black patriots had served bravely in the Revolution, but few Americans recognized their contributions. Nevertheless, Bostonians acknowledged the Boston Massacre's significance in 1888 with a monument to its five victims. What makes this noteworthy—aside from protests against the monument by the blue-blood Massachusetts Historical Society, which claimed the event did not merit enshrinement—is that one of the five, Crispus Attucks, was African American. The stone became popularly known as the Crispus Attucks monument and signified recognition of a sort, however belatedly, for black Americans.

The political expression of patriotism has served as a sounding board for debates among politicians and citizens alike. It also spurred people to identify appropriate individuals as icons of liberty. If Americans living in the age of counterterrorism believe that liberty defines America's patriotic heritage and celebrate it with speeches, parades, and barbecues, it remains an open question how they will honor this principle in practice. Will concerns about the nation's security trump its commitment to freedom? The answer remains uncertain.

BIBLIOGRAPHY

Bodnar, John. *Remaking America: Public Memory, Commemoration, and Patriotism in the Twentieth Century.* Princeton, NJ: Princeton University Press, 1992.

Butterfield, L. H., ed. *Adams Family Correspondence.* Cambridge, MA: Belknap Press of Harvard University Press, 1963–1993.

Cray, Robert E., Jr. "The John André Memorial: The Politics of Memory in Gilded Age New York." *New York History* 77 (1996): 5–32.

Cray, Robert E., Jr. "Commemorating the Prison Ship Dead: Revolutionary Memory and the Politics of Sepulture in the Early Republic, 1776–1808." *William and Mary Quarterly* 55 (1999): 565–590.

Cray, Robert E., Jr. "The Revolutionary Spy as Hero: Nathan Hale in the Public Memory, 1776–1846." *Connecticut History* 38 (1999): 85–104.

Mires, Charlene. *Independence Hall in American Memory.* Philadelphia: University of Pennsylvania Press, 2002.

Travers, Len. *Celebrating the Fourth: Independence Day and the Rites of Nationalism in the Early Republic.* Amherst: University of Massachusetts Press, 1997.

Young, Alfred F. *The Shoemaker and the Tea Party.* Boston: Beacon, 1999.

Robert E. Cray, Jr.

See also: **Fourth of July; Lafayette's Tour; Memory and Early Histories of the Revolution.**

QUASI-WAR AND THE RISE OF POLITICAL PARTIES

France was the United States' first friend. The 1778 Treaty of Alliance between the two nations secured French military support in the American War for Independence. Yet just two decades later, the nations stood at the brink of a formal war, battling each other in the halls of diplomacy and on the high seas. The Quasi-War (1797–1800) was America's first major international crisis and it precipitated a domestic political struggle that threatened to tear apart the new republic.

INTERNATIONAL CONFLICT

The first years of the new national government brought a rift among Americans over foreign policy, which corresponded to their divergent visions of political economy. These differences emerged in Congress between proto-parties, factions with similar voting records but lacking the formal organization of parties. Treasury Secretary Alexander Hamilton and fellow Federalists promoted a strong national commercial agenda, focused on extensive trade with England. Their opponents, most prominently Thomas Jefferson and James Madison, wanted to preserve an American economy centered on smaller agrarian interests. These Democratic-Republicans looked toward France, fearing that economic development on the English model could corrupt the fragile American republic. The Federalists took their name from the supporters of the federal Constitution in the ratification debates of the late 1780s; the term refers to the idea that the states and the new national government shared sovereignty. The name of the Democratic-Republicans, on the other hand, represented their more populist political philosophy.

Americans of both parties, grateful for France's earlier support, at first embraced the republican French Revolution of 1789. Yet its violent turn in 1792, and the renewal of the war between France and England for European hegemony, brought new urgency to the foreign policy debate in America. When the British refused to accept President George Washington's 1793 proclamation of neutrality, Washington dispatched John Jay to negotiate a treaty to avoid war with England. Controversy over the Jay Treaty highlighted the disagreement about foreign policy between the parties. Whereas Federalists supported the trade relationship with England that the new treaty heralded, Democratic-Republicans were outraged at England's refusal to accept the United States' rights of neutrality.

The French government was equally upset by the Jay Treaty. In 1797, France declared it would seize American ships carrying British goods and treat Americans serving on British ships as pirates. The French foreign minister refused to meet with American diplomats, and the unofficial French representatives who conducted the negotiations attempted to extort a $250,000 bribe and a $10 million loan from the Americans to prevent war. By March 1798, news of what became known as the XYZ Affair reached the United States, where it was met with popular outrage spurred on by the anti-French Federalists.

In 1798, President John Adams, a Federalist, considered a formal declaration of war against France but instead opted to pursue a sweeping legislative program to prepare the nation for war. Congress formally abrogated the 1778 Treaties of Alliance, the formal mechanism by which France and the United States had allied during the Revolutionary War, which stipulated that France would recognize the United States and provide military and economic assistance in that war. It established a Navy Department, increased the size of the navy, armed merchant ships, authorized vessels to seize French ships intending to capture American prizes, strengthened the defenses of American ports, and increased the manufacture of arms and munitions. Following these actions, the navy captured more than eighty French ships between 1798 and 1800. Federalists also enlarged the regular army and created a provisional army. Hamilton, named second-in-command of the army (behind only Washington), screened officers to ensure their political reliability.

DOMESTIC CONFLICT

In the summer of 1798, Federalists were not content to merely purge dissent from the army; they wanted it removed from the nation. Capitalizing on war fever, the Federalist Congress passed a series of four laws, known as the Alien and Sedition Acts, which were intended to crush the Democratic-Republican political opposition. Three dealt with aliens—immigrants who had yet to become naturalized American citizens and who overwhelmingly voted Democratic-Republican. The Act Concerning Aliens and the Alien Enemies Act established a registration and surveillance system for foreign nationals and allowed President Adams to arrest and deport aliens who might endanger the nation's security. The Naturalization Act increased the period of residence required to become a citizen, and thus to vote, from five to fourteen years.

The Sedition Act stifled the possibility and practice of opposition politics by prohibiting "scandalous and malicious" writing or speaking against the United States government, the president, or either house of Congress. Under a fiercely partisan application of the act, Federalist judges indicted fourteen Democratic-Republican editors and convicted and imprisoned ten of them. In an era when newspapers and their editors connected political leaders to their popular base, this constituted a major attack on the viability of the Democratic-Republican Party.

Democratic-Republicans looked to the states themselves to protect basic rights. Madison and Jefferson authored the Virginia and Kentucky Resolutions, which held that the states could declare null and void new federal laws they believed to be unconstitutional. Southerners would use similar arguments in the nineteenth century to defend secession. In 1798, Democratic-Republicans went so far as to suggest that Virginia prepare to defend itself militarily against the Federalist-controlled federal government's enforcement of the Alien and Sedition laws.

Some extreme Federalists were ready for a fight, but President Adams disappointed them, refusing to press war against Virginia or France. He reopened negotiations with France in 1799. Although the negotiations were initially deadlocked, in the final Convention of 1800 France agreed to allow the United States to break the Treaty of Alliance of 1778 in exchange for dropping $20 million in claims for France's seizures of American shipping. With the success of the negotiations, the Federalist program from the summer of 1798 began to collapse, mired by infighting between the moderate Adams and Hamilton's more extreme wing of the party. Adams dismantled Hamilton's army, the Alien and Sedition Acts began to expire and were not renewed, and Democratic-Republicans fared well in the national election of 1800.

The turmoil surrounding the Quasi-War has had long-lasting repercussions on American political life. The Quasi-War marked the high point of the decade-long conflict over foreign policy that solidified the first national party system. In that era of extreme political polarization, partisans on both sides denied the opposition's legitimacy, believing that their party alone could protect America's republican experiment. In an ironic encore to the Federalists' attempt to destroy the French-sympathizing Democratic-Republicans during the Quasi-War, the Federalists themselves were eliminated as a political force because of their support for England during the War of 1812. In spite of, or perhaps because of, these political battles to the death, the first parties democratized American politics by using print culture and public gatherings to connect ordinary citizens to leaders in the government. Most fundamentally, the Quasi-War introduced the nation to the difficulty of protecting civil liberties and open political debate during wartime. These issues would continue to challenge America in times of national emergency into the twenty-first century.

BIBLIOGRAPHY
Deconde, Alexander. *The Quasi-War: The Politics and Diplomacy of the Undeclared War with France, 1797–1801.* New York: Scribner, 1966.

Elkins, Stanley, and McKitrick, Eric. *The Age of Federalism: The Early American Republic, 1788–1800.* New York: Oxford University Press, 1993.

McCoy, Drew. *The Elusive Republic: Political Economy in Jeffersonian America.* Chapel Hill: University of North Carolina Press, 1980.

Sharpe, James Rogers. *American Politics in the Early Republic: The New Nation in Crisis.* New Haven, CT: Yale University Press, 1993.

Internet Resource

"The Quasi War with France, 1791–1800." Yale Law School Avalon Project. Available from <http://www.yale.edu/lawweb/avalon/quasi.htm>.

Justin Florence

See also: **Adams, John; Embargo; Fourth of July; Jefferson, Thomas; Pirates and the Barbary War.**

RELIGION AND REVOLUTION

Although the American War for Independence (1775–1783) was not a war of religion, religion played a significant though often subtle role in the events leading to that conflict, in sustaining the rebel cause against the British government, and in shaping the new nation. As Alexis de Tocqueville observed in 1831, "For Americans the ideas of Christianity and liberty are so completely mingled that it is almost impossible to get them to conceive of the one without the other" (*Democracy in America*, Book 1, Chapter 9). Many viewed the war as part of a universal struggle to secure human rights and liberty. With independence, they made new laws aimed at limiting the power of government over freedom of religion. Then as now, Americans used the legacy of that war and the principles from the Revolution to build their society and culture and to define the nation's ideals and identity.

WAR FOR INDEPENDENCE

In the decades prior to the battle of Lexington, April 1775, British colonists in North America represented a variety of religious denominations, including the Church of England (Anglican), Presbyterian, Congregationalist, Baptist, Methodist, Quaker, Catholic, German Reformed, and Jewish, to name only the most prominent. Most colonies had an established church, meaning that public taxes were used to pay ministers' salaries. Generally, taxpayers in the south supported the Anglican Church and those in New England, the Congregational Church, regardless of whether they were members. Prayers to God on behalf of the crown were part of the ritual observed by most colonists.

The outbreak of war in 1775 divided congregations, as it did most Americans, particularly those of the Church of England. Its ministers were bound by oath to defend the crown. With the Declaration of Independence nearly half the Anglican ministers resigned their posts rather than renounce their allegiance to the king. Religious division accentuated political division as congregations split between patriots and loyalists. Once independent, patriot congregations left the Church of England to form the Protestant Episcopal Church of the United States. They revised their Book of Common Prayer to replace prayers for the king and royal family with prayers for the president and "all in civil authority," and adopted a constitution and canons to conform to new democratic ideals.

In New England, on the other hand, while some congregations divided over the war, the combination of principles supporting civil and religious liberty created a powerful bond. In these instances religion fueled resistance and revolution. When the Reverend John Cleaveland of Chebacco, Maine, learned of the battle of Lexington and Concord he roused his congregation to oppose British rule. He declared that the king had "DISSOLVED OUR ALLEGIANCE" because he had failed to protect the colonists from "the oppressive, tyrannical and bloody measure of the British Parliament" (Jedrey, p. 138). Ministers supporting resistance and rebellion preached that Americans were fighting a righteous cause. Even pacifist denominations, such as the Quakers, were divided by the war. While the majority of Friends remained neutral, drawing the ire of both sides, a group called the Free Quakers renounced pacifism to fight against England.

POLITICAL REVOLUTION

More than a war to separate from Great Britain, the War for Independence created the opportunity to fashion a new political culture, in particular an altered relationship between government and religious institutions. Government-supported churches, religious loyalty oaths, and exclusion of non-Christians from political office were customary in most European nations and in most American colonies. Embracing the eighteenth-century Enlightenment ideal of individual freedom of conscience, Revolutionary leaders departed from that practice and rule. They rejected government use of taxes to fund religious institutions because they believed that political tyranny and religious repression went hand in hand. Between 1776 and 1784 most state constitutions disestablished tax-supported churches by incorporating a new principle of separation of church and government. Full religious freedom, in the form of removing religious tests and oaths aimed at keeping non-Christians and Catholics from holding political office and according equal protection of the law to people of all faiths, began in earnest after the adoption of the Virginia Statue for Religious Freedom in 1786.

Thomas Jefferson, a leading anticleric and drafter of the Declaration of Independence, wrote the Virginia Statue. That statute, drafted in 1779, was later incorporated in other state constitutions and its principles were applied in the Constitution of the United States. In the statue's preamble Jefferson declared that God "had created the mind free." He wrote that state-supported churches are based on the "impious presumption" that "fallible" legislators know the "true and infallible" faith and are empowered "to impose" it on others. Jefferson called this "sinful and tyrannical." Denouncing religious loyalty oaths and tests for holding political office, Jefferson concluded that civil rights should not be violated because of a person's religious belief. Attacking laws enforcing religious conformity and censorship, he stated that the truth will prevail if left to "free argument and debate." Virginia's law ensured that "no man" would be compelled to pay taxes to support a church or suffer infringement of civil rights "on account of his religious opinions or belief." Freedom of religion and opinion was declared one of the "natural rights of mankind."

The United States Constitution (1788) applied these principles to the federal government by banning religious tests for holding political office (Article VI). While not prohibiting states from supporting churches with tax money, in 1791 the first amendment in the Bill of Rights prohibited the federal government from doing so. The amendment declared that "Congress shall make no law respecting an establishment of religion, or prohibiting the free exercise thereof." When questioned in 1801 about the meaning of this provision, Jefferson wrote to the Danbury Baptist Association that the Constitution had built a "wall of separation between church and State," a concept that remains controversial. Created during a time of war and revolution, that wall and the principles it represents continue to be a defining feature of American society and culture.

BIBLIOGRAPHY

Bailyn, Bernard. *The Ideological Origins of the American Revolution.* Cambridge, MA: Belknap Press of Harvard University Press, 1992.

Gross, Robert A. *The Minutemen and Their World.* New York: Hill and Wang, 1976.

Hoffman, Ronald, and Albert, Peter J., eds. *Religion in a Revolutionary Age.* Charlottesville: University Press of Virginia, 1994.

Jedrey, Christopher M. *The World of John Cleaveland: Family and Community in Eighteenth-Century New England.* New York: Norton, 1979.

Marty, Martin E. *Religion and Republic: The American Circumstance.* Boston: Beacon Press, 1987.

Internet Resources

Jefferson, Thomas. "A Bill for Establishing Religious Freedom" (1779). Ashbrook Center for Public Affairs. Available from <http://teachingamericanhistory.org/library/index.asp?document=23>.

"Jefferson's Letter to the Danbury Baptists." Library of Congress. Available from <http://www.loc.gov/loc/lcib/9806/danpre.html>.

John P. Resch

See also: **Abolition; Constitution: Bill of Rights; Constitution: Creating a Republic; Jefferson, Thomas; Revolution and Radical Reform; Supreme Court.**

REPUBLICAN WOMANHOOD

The expanded political, economic, and social roles that many American women forged during the American Revolution generated postwar questions about the proper place of women in the new United States. One prominent ideology to emerge from this debate was Republican Womanhood, the idea that women could play an important yet indirect role in the political process by inculcating and maintaining the civic virtues of their husbands and sons, the present and future citizens of the republic.

WOMEN IN AND AFTER THE REVOLUTION

Even before armed hostilities began in 1775, American women were engaged in the growing conflict between Britain and her colonies. Politicizing domestic production and consumption, women boycotted merchants, pledged not to buy or use imported goods, and organized spinning and weaving bees to produce homespun cloth. During wartime (1775–1781), patriot women continued to support the war effort by making clothing and bandages. Some poorer women followed their soldier-husbands on campaign, cooking and washing for them or serving as nurses at camp.

When peace broke out, women seemed poised to reap the benefits of a revolution that had swept away patriarchal political authority and replaced it with a republican system of government. However, except in New Jersey where women were briefly given the right to vote, a similar revolution in gender relations never materialized. Rather, in the 1790s, a more moderate gender ideology emerged that seemed to recognize the changes wrought in the past decades of political protest and war while harnessing that momentum for essentially conservative purposes.

By the late 1780s, it had become apparent that the biggest threat to the new republic lay not in external military attack but in the hearts and minds of its own citizens. In a society in which government was conducted for and by the people, civic-mindedness—understood as a combination of self-sacrifice and disinterest—became the lynchpin of the republican experiment. Eager to recognize and reward women's contribution to the war effort and to enlist them in the construction and maintenance of the new republic, a generation of writers and theorists argued that women were, by virtue of their domestic responsibilities, ideally positioned to instill and endorse the civic-mindedness necessary to save the republic from ruin.

THE CONCEPT OF REPUBLICAN WOMANHOOD

Writing in Philadelphia and Boston, physician and reformer Benjamin Rush (1745–1813), playwright and essayist Judith Sargent Murray (1751–1820), and educator and dramatist Susanna Rowson (1762–1824) fashioned a new way of conceptualizing women's place in the home and the political sphere—a way that responded to the challenges of this changed world. All three worked in their writings to fuse the traditional attributes of the puritan goodwife—piety, virtue, wisdom, sobriety, industry, love, and fidelity—with the socializing, manners-shaping function recently envisioned by Scottish Enlightenment thinkers. This new set of responsibilities enjoined women of the republic to consider the performance of their domestic duties as important tools of politicization and socialization. In *Thoughts upon Female Education* (1787), Rush laid out the stakes in plain terms: "The equal share that every citizen has in the liberty and the possible share he may have in the government of our country make it necessary that our ladies should . . . concur in instructing their sons in the principles of liberty and government" (p. 28)—a sentiment that the spirit of the times extended to brothers and husbands as well.

Rush's pamphlet was soon supplemented by Murray's collection of essays, *The Gleaner* (1792–1794), and Rowson's *Slaves in Algiers* (1794). The authors used the ideology of republican womanhood to legitimate the relatively controversial expansion of female educational opportunities that they helped orchestrate in the decades following the Revolution. Rush had served as a founding trustee of the Young Ladies' Academy in Philadelphia (founded 1786) and in 1797 Rowson opened her Female Academy in Boston, quickly attracting a hundred new students a year. In a graduation oration delivered at Rowson's academy, P. W. Jackson of Boston explained how the curriculum brought glory to her sex: "A woman who is skilled in every useful art, who practices every domestic virtue . . . may, by her precept and example, inspire her brother, her husband, or her sons, with such a love of virtue, such just ideas of the true value of civil liberty . . . that future heroes and statesmen, who arrive at the summit of military or political fame, shall exaltingly declare, it is to my mother I owe this elevation" (quoted in Kerber 1974, p. 56). Couching the function of these academies in terms of preparing young ladies to dedicate themselves to a life of self-sacrificing domesticity soon silenced opponents of female education, who had argued that such establishments unsexed young women and threatened morality.

LEGACY OF THE REVOLUTION

How radical was this new model of female political participation? On the one hand, the movement institutionalized female higher education, implicitly credited women's moral and intellectual equality, and explicitly recognized the pseudopolitical role women have always assumed as domestic confidants, tutors, and counselors.

During the Revolution women supported the war effort by making clothing and bandages, and occassionally by following their soldier-husbands on campaign. After the war, though, the concept of republican womanhood suggested that women could help the emerging nation by dedicating themselves to a life of self-sacrificing domesticity in order to support their husbands and sons, the present and future citizens of the republic. © BETTMANN/CORBIS

By blurring the boundary between public and private and by politicizing the domestic sphere, it may also have defined the terms of the woman's rights movement that was christened at Seneca Falls, New York, in 1848. On the other hand, at a time when many women appeared to be testing the limits of patriarchy, it confined women to the domestic sphere by persuading them of the newfound importance of their traditional roles as wives, mothers, and homemakers, inaugurating the paradigm of Victorian sexuality that woman's rights activists would spend the next decades trying to undermine.

Ultimately, the ideology of republican womanhood offered women no new power; indeed, it served to highlight the limits of their domestic influence. As Rowson warned in *The Exemplary Wife* (1813), and as many women no doubt discovered for themselves, a virtuous example was no guarantee that a man would undergo a moral reformation. A successful moral makeover required susceptibility and compliance, but too often, Rowson suggested, men proved obstinate. In such standoffs, women as the inferior authorities were required to honor, obey, and concede to their husbands.

Although we may never know the extent to which women internalized this ideology, the currency it received, both in the early republic and in twentieth-century scholarly articles, seems to have had one lasting effect: It diverted attention from those women whose political influence was not circumscribed within the domestic sphere. Only recently have historians begun to recognize how many women circumvented prescriptions for their domestic confinement, taking leading roles in business and public political actions such as street protests and mob actions.

BIBLIOGRAPHY

Bloch, Ruth H. "American Feminine Ideals in Transition: The Rise of the Moral Mother, 1785–1815." *Feminist Studies* 4 (1978): 101–126.

Kerber, Linda K. "Daughters of Columbia: Educating Women for the Republic, 1787–1805." In *The Hofstadter Aegis: A Memorial*, edited by Stanley Elkins and Eric McKitrick. New York: Knopf, 1974.

Kerber, Linda K. "The Republican Mother: Women and the Enlightenment—An American Perspective." *American Quarterly* 28 (1976): 187–205.

Lewis, Jan. "The Republican Wife: Virtue and Seduction in the Early Republic." *William and Mary Quarterly* 44 (1987): 689–721.

Murray, Judith Sargent. *The Gleaner* [1792–1794; 1798]. Schenectady, NY: Union College Press, 1992.

Rowson, Susanna. *Slaves in Algiers; or, A Struggle for Freedom: A Play, Interspersed with Songs, in Three Acts*. Philadelphia: Wrigley and Berriman, 1794.

Rowson, Susanna. *Sarah, or the Exemplary wife*. Boston: C. Williams, 1813.

Rush, Benjamin. "Thoughts upon Female Education Accommodated to the Present State of Society, Manners, and Government in the United States of America." In *Essays on Education in the Early Republic*, edited by Frederick Rudolph. Cambridge, MA: Harvard University Press, 1965.

Zagarri, Rosemarie. "Morals, Manners, and the Republican Mother." *American Quarterly* 44, no. 2 (1992): 192–215.

Richard J. Bell

See also: **Brown, Charlotte: Diary of a Nurse; Families at War; Generals' Wives: Martha Washington, Katherine Greene, Lucy Knox; Warren, Mercy Otis.**

REPUBLICANISM AND WAR

When North American colonists protested British parliamentary measures in the 1760s and 1770s, they drew upon a rich tradition of political thought. One particularly virulent strand of opposition rhetoric informing their thinking came from a group of English writers known as Commonwealth men, who emphasized that concentrations of power in government were dangerous, especially the concentration that came from a standing army, which they warned could be used against the free subjects of a state. These ideas resonated powerfully in the colonies after the French and Indian War (1754–1763) as Parliament began reforming its imperial policies. Patriot leaders associated the British army with conspiracies and corruption and claimed that the army was at the center of a plot by Parliament to deprive Americans of their liberties and enslave them. When redcoats were stationed in Boston and civil-military conflicts increased, militant patriots saw it as evidence that their worst fears were coming true.

CITIZEN-SOLDIERS

Drawing on these same strands of political thought, patriot leaders emphasized the merits of a republican polity in opposition to what they saw as the tyranny of British rule. In theory at least, republicanism meant that the people would be the basis of all government and act for the common good. But under a republican government, the people also had the duty and obligation to maintain private and public virtue, social harmony, and vigilance against usurpations of power. In time, active participation in the militia by responsible—and property-owning—citizens acting for the common good came to be seen as the very embodiment of republicanism. If the colonies had citizens virtuous enough to defend themselves and their liberties through their active participation in the militia, they could achieve a truly republican government.

The Minute Men called to Arms by Jennie Brownescombe, ca. 1800. Active participation in the militia by responsible citizens acting for the common good came to be seen as the embodiment of republicanism. © BETTMANN/CORBIS

When New England militia scored important initial victories over the British army at Concord and Breed's Hill, the importance of the militia was underscored. Initially, patriot leaders tried to capitalize on these successes by creating a republican army—one composed of citizen-soldiers serving for short periods and paid no bounties—rather than a professional army such as the British army. However, militia would not stay in the field longer than they thought necessary, nor would they take orders from superior officers easily. In response, as early as 1776, Congress, under pressure from George Washington and other officers, made moves to create a much bigger, more professional army that looked remarkably like the one that political writers had excoriated. Offering large enlistment bounties in return for long periods of service, the patriots fell back on a familiar colonial tradition of paying professional soldiers to do the bulk of the fighting.

DISTRUST OF A STANDING ARMY

Republicanism and ideas about the importance of the militia continued to significantly affect mobilization, however. Although it is difficult to know just how widespread anti-standing army feeling was among the colonists, the division between the army and the militia

was clear. Some historians have concluded that few middle class colonists joined the army because of the stigma attached to soldiers in a professional force. That meant the army was filled with men from the lower classes—those who had little property of their own and were young, foreign-born, or African American. Yet because of popular opposition to professional armies, Washington never got what he wanted either—a fully professionalized force serving for the duration of the war. Ordinary Americans frustrated most attempts to conscript soldiers for anything but short terms of service.

There is little evidence to suggest a widespread wartime fear of the Continental army as an instrument of coercion. Congress, for example, never granted General Washington all the powers and measures he requested, but they were prepared to grant him virtually dictatorial authority for at least three brief periods. There were, however, civil-military tensions. Many citizens withheld or hid supplies and generally failed to support the army in time of need. In return, soldiers often stole from locals and officers seized and impressed needed goods and supplies from outraged citizens. In the end, the patriot cause came to rely almost wholly on the efforts of Washington to keep the army together and in the field, and the majority of Americans turned their backs on the army. Many turned out when needed as militia, but most had little to do with the army.

The persistent but inaccurate perception that the army was unnecessary to the winning of independence also shaped postwar policy toward a peacetime army. As the army began to demobilize at the end of the war, soldiers demanding full payment of their accounts mutinied, and officers demanding lifetime pensions in return for their wartime services (culminating in the so-called Newburgh conspiracy), helped reignite anti-standing army ideas. Although Washington himself advocated a small peacetime army, ideology and a poor economy meant that the army was fully demobilized. The lack of a standing army in the post-war period helped push some nationalists into supporting a constitutional convention, as they worried about the internal and external security of the Confederation in the 1780s.

LEGACY OF THE REVOLUTION

In the debate over the Constitution, both Federalists and anti-Federalists invoked republican principles in defending or opposing federal control over the military. In the end, the Constitution reflected Federalist arguments, giving Congress stronger powers and the exclusive right to declare war and raise and support an army and navy, and making the president the commander in chief when at war. Congress was also given control over a nationalized militia. These powers were tempered, however, by a provision that limited any appropriation for the army to two years, and by dividing power over the military between Congress and the executive branch. Anti-Federalists won concessions in the Bill of Rights, where the Second Amendment protected states and individuals against any misuse of a national army by affirming the importance of the militia and the Third Amendment protected citizens from home invasions by an army.

Almost immediately, Indian resistance in the western regions forced the federal government to raise a "legion" of 5,000 men, which was never fully disbanded. This was the beginning of a national standing army in peacetime. Almost at the same time, Congress passed the Uniform Militia Act of 1792, which put much of the responsibility for the state militias back into the hands of the state governments. Mirroring the Revolutionary War experience, America's military establishment would henceforth rest primarily on a regular army, supplemented by state militias. By the end of the War of 1812, and with the recent wars of the French Revolution in mind, most Americans agreed that only a professional military could meet the needs of national security during war and peace in the new world, although continued hostility to a regular army persisted, particularly from advocates of the militia, and the principle of civilian control

of the military remains a central feature of American culture.

BIBLIOGRAPHY

Carp, E. Wayne. "The Problem of National Defence in the Early Republic." In *The American Revolution: Its Character and Limits*, edited by Jack P. Greene. New York: New York University Press, 1987.

Cress, Lawrence Delbert. *Citizens in Arms: The Army and Militia in American Society to the War of 1812*. Chapel Hill: University of North Carolina Press, 1982.

Higginbotham, Don. *The War of American Independence: Military Attitudes, Policies, and Practice, 1763–1789*. New York: Macmillan, 1971.

Kohn, Richard H. *Eagle and Sword: The Beginnings of the Military Establishment in America*. New York: Free Press, 1975.

Mahon, John K. *History of the Militia and the National Guard*. New York: Macmillan, 1983.

Martin, James Kirby, and Lender, Mark Edward. *A Respectable Army: The Military Origins of the Republic, 1763–1789*. Arlington Heights, IL: Harlan Davidson, 1982.

Royster, Charles. *A Revolutionary People War: The Continental Army and American Character, 1775–1783*. Chapel Hill: University of North Carolina Press, 1979.

Shalhope, Robert E. *The Roots of Democracy: American Thought and Culture, 1760–1800*. Boston, MA: Twayne, 1990.

Watts, Steven. *The Republic Reborn: War and the Making of Liberal America, 1790–1820*. Baltimore, MD: Johns Hopkins University Press, 1987.

Michael A. McDonnell

See also: **Commonwealth Men; Mobilization, War for Independence.**

REVOLUTION AND RADICAL REFORM

How radical was the American Revolution? Historians are divided over this important question, taking varying positions on the extent and nature of change during the Revolutionary era. But most historians agree that the American Revolution did result in sweeping changes or radical reforms that had an enduring effect on American politics, culture, and society. These reforms can be divided into three categories: independence, constitutions and government, and social change.

INDEPENDENCE

The Declaration of Independence embodied the first radical reform of the American Revolution. But the American Revolution did not begin as an independence movement or as a movement for radical change. Quite the opposite was true: the earliest protests aimed at preserving the status quo in British America. For more than a century, colonial governments had administered the colonies as quasi-autonomous members of the British Empire. Historians identify this experience as salutary (or benign) neglect. Under this framework, England allowed a high degree of self government in the colonies as a way of encouraging maximum profitability.

Salutary neglect became less viable in the 1760s. Increased costs of empire and wartime debt following the Seven Years' War prompted Parliament to seek new sources of income. The result was tightened regulation of trade and a series of internal and external taxes. This was met with protests and resistance, which included boycotts, harassment of officials and destruction of property. The goals were conservative: restoration of the quasiautonomy of the colonies. But the results were far-reaching. After a decade of protest, the momentum shifted from protection of English rights to outright independence from Britain.

Inspired in part by Thomas Paine's radical treatise *Common Sense,* the colonies, assembled in congress, agreed on a formal Declaration of Independence. The Declaration was, in many ways, a pragmatic document. In declaring independence, the colonies also put into practice theories that had been promoted by philosophers of the Enlightenment. Liberty was redefined as inherent and universal, in contrast to the English understanding of rights granted selectively by the monarch and, later, by Parliament.

The Declaration of Independence also expressed four fundamental principles of modern republican societies in which sovereignty originates in the people, not the government. The first is the doctrine of equality—"that all men are created equal." While expressing the eighteenth-century idea of equality in the eyes of God, this doctrine became a catalyst for social conflict and cultural change. At the time of the Revolution citizens fought, and since then have continued to struggle, to implement the ideal by securing equal rights, equality before the law, and equal opportunity for personal advancement. The second is the assumption that people are born with "certain unalienable rights," which are expressed in the Declaration as "Life, Liberty, and the Pursuit of Happiness." The third is the precept that government gets its "just power" only from the "consent of the people" and by securing those unalienable rights. Finally, the Declaration proclaims the right of the people to "alter or abolish" their government should it no longer be based on the consent of the people or should it no longer secure their unalienable rights. This right of revolution, however, is tempered with "prudence," the acknowledgement that government should not be fundamentally "changed for light and transient causes."

CONSTITUTIONS AND GOVERNMENT

The Declaration was both the summary of American colonial ideals and the justification for the colonial war of independence from Great Britain. The newly independent colonies formed themselves into sovereign states in the immediate aftermath of the Declaration of Independence, employing constitutions to legitimize and organize their declarations of sovereignty. The process and methods of creating new governments varied, but the new state constitutions had one thing in common. Each of these constitutions was written and published, unlike the English constitution, which existed only in a vast body of laws and court rulings and in the imaginations of Englishmen.

The written constitution, an outgrowth of popular demands, was itself a radical reform. But these state constitutions incorporated additional reforms that were direct outgrowths of the American Revolution. Faced with an erosion of their rights as British colonists, Americans demanded guarantees from the new governments. Virginia led the way in June 1776 with a declaration or bill of rights: a written guarantee of individual liberties and restraints on government power. Most of the states followed Virginia's lead by incorporating bills of rights into their own constitutions.

In some cases, the bills of rights reflected existing grievances against Britain, including the quartering of troops and suppression of the press. But they also contained original demands, such as the guarantee of religious toleration (freedom of religion). In a few cases, religious toleration assumed a new and, for its time, radical form: separation of church and state. This was, in part, a concession to religious minorities, whose support was crucial to the success of the Revolution. But separation of church and state also reflected one step in a larger and broader rethinking of government and its role in society.

The most radical rethinking of government, at least from the perspective of contemporaries, was reflected in the Pennsylvania state constitution of 1776. Operating under the influence of radical patriots, the Pennsylvania legislature reduced government to its most basic form: a unicameral government (a single legislative body), elected annually and democratically by a broad male suffrage that virtually ended the traditional requirement that only property holders could vote.

Other states, including New York and Massachusetts, took more moderate approaches to government. Nevertheless, the resulting constitutions reflected a variety of radical changes. New York retained the English structure of government: a bicameral legislature (two houses) and an executive or governor. But New York's constitution, ratified in 1777, called for an elected governor; on the basis of this change, George Clinton became the first popularly elected executive in modern history. The Massachusetts state constitution, ratified in 1780, added an additional radical element by constructing an independent judiciary, freeing the courts from political entanglements. Massachusetts also made a sweeping change to the process of constitution-making. For the first time in modern history, a constitution was drafted by a special body of representatives elected for this purpose only and ratified by a popular vote.

The Massachusetts example was later followed in the adoption of the federal Constitution in 1787 and 1788. The long-term significance of this action cannot be overstated because it distinguished making fundamental law (a constitution) from passing legislation. That distinction has elevated the Constitution to a position of "higher law" by which all legislation and government acts can be judged.

Some of the state constitutions' radical reforms did not stand the test of time. Others evolved or returned in new forms, including term limits and limits on the number of offices an individual could hold. But the state experience of constitution-making had a direct and enduring effect, not only on the U.S. Constitution of 1788, but on constitution-making in the modern era.

SOCIAL CHANGE

Political reforms resulting from the American Revolution were indeed significant. But the Revolution unleashed a broader set of radical reforms that went to the heart of American society. Revolutionary ideology coupled with the demand for military forces and changes in government created new expectations among ordinary Americans. Many of these expectations were realized during and immediately following the Revolution. Other expectations developed and were realized in the decades and centuries that followed.

White males, in particular, expected much and gained significantly as a result of the American Revolution. Deference—the respect due an assumed superior—decreased considerably, resulting in broader assumptions of social equality. More important, however, was the incorporation of more of them into the body politic. Prior to the Revolution voting, office holding, and the right to serve on juries were restricted to those who owned a certain amount of property or controlled a certain level of wealth. In the wake of the Revolution, many states amended their voting qualifications to include most, if not all, white males over twenty-one years of age. This was the first step in what would become a continual demand in the United States for expanded suffrage and eligibility for office.

White females gained significantly less as a result of the Revolution, even though they had provided material support for the patriot cause. Protest and war forced many women to assume unaccustomed roles as boycotters, fund raisers, heads of households, artisans, farmers and laborers. Some women made their way to the front, where they served the needs of the army as nurses, cooks and laundresses. A few found themselves on the field of combat, including at least one woman—Deborah Sampson—who disguised herself as a man and served with distinction in the military.

For most women, participation in the war effort was an act of patriotism. Few if any of them expected to gain political rights. A small percentage of propertied women in New Jersey did, for a brief period, have the right to vote, although the loophole in the state constitution was quickly amended. Many women did, however, expect reforms within the household, particularly to women's economic roles and to divorce laws. This is what Abigail Adams meant in her often misinterpreted demand to her husband "to remember the ladies."

Women did not, in the end, gain much ground economically or legally as a result of the Revolution. Their gains were largely limited to newly-defined roles as mentors for the next generation of republican sons and daughters, what historian Linda Kerber identifies as "republican motherhood." Many women, particularly women from the upper strata of society, used this new responsibility to claim an education for themselves. In reaching for their own educations, these women benefited from a post-Revolutionary environment that was strongly in favor of education for American society as a whole.

Although the gains for women were limited, the American Revolution had a long-term effect on women's rights in the United States. The expectation of more freedom within marriage was, in itself, quite radical. The demand would gain momentum over the next two centuries, becoming an important element of the movement for women's suffrage and women's rights in general.

African Americans had a similar experience of limited gains with significant long-term effects. The Revolution raised important and challenging questions concerning the practice of slavery. In some cases, slaves and slave owners acted on their own. Some African Americans gained their freedom by serving in the British or American armies, or by running away in the confusion of war. A few individual slave owners, influenced by the ideology of the Revolution, voluntarily freed their slaves. Others included manumission in their wills. These routes to freedom, however, affected only a small fraction of enslaved African Americans.

A handful of leading patriots wrestled with the coexistence of democracy and slavery. A few hoped for general abolition. But that hope fell victim to the economic needs of the southern states and to the larger need for unity in the postwar period. Abolition in the post-revolutionary period was limited to northern states and was usually accomplished in a piecemeal or gradual manner. In any case, abolition and emancipation did not always guarantee economic, social or political equality for African Americans. But they did set an important precedent for the future, raising doubts among northerners about the racist assumptions of American society.

The American Revolution served as a catalyst for a wide variety of radical changes in the way nation-states are understood, governments are constructed, and people's roles in society are perceived and acted on. Some of these changes were immediate. Others took decades and centuries to come to fruition. Many continue to unfold. But the seeds can be traced to the Revolution: to an independence movement that unleashed more in the way of radical reforms than its authors originally imagined.

BIBLIOGRAPHY

Berkin, Carol. *A Brilliant Solution: Inventing the American Constitution.* New York: Harcourt, 2002.

Berlin, Ira and Ronald Hoffman, eds. *Slavery and Freedom in the Age of the American Revolution.* Charlottesville: University Press of Virginia, 1983.

Kerber, Linda. *Women of the Republic: Intellect and Ideology in Revolutionary America.* Chapel Hill: University of North Carolina Press, 1980.

Maier, Pauline. *American Scripture: Making the Declaration of Independence.* New York: Knopf, 1997.

Main, Jackson Turner. *The Sovereign States, 1775–1783.* New York: New Viewpoints, 1973.

Wood, Gordon S. *The Creation of the American Republic, 1776–1787.* Chapel Hill: University of North Carolina Press, 1969.

Wood, Gordon S. *The Radicalism of the American Revolution.* New York: Knopf, 1992.

Angelo T. Angelis

See also: Flags; Memory and Early Histories of the Revolution; Religion and Revolution.

REVOLUTIONARY WAR VETERANS

In 1783 William Alld was discharged from the Continental Army. The eight-year war, the longest in American history until the Vietnam War, was over. Like thousands of other veterans of the Revolutionary War, Alld made his way home alone. No parade, no public homecoming ceremony welcomed the veteran when he arrived at his father's house in Peterborough, New Hampshire. The country had tired of the long and costly war. Veterans like Alld received no benefits. These men were soon forgotten by the country they had liberated from Britain's empire. Proud veterans felt betrayed by the nation's ingratitude.

ANTI-ARMY SENTIMENT

The United States neglected its veterans because Americans were hostile toward regular armies. The lessons of history taught by Rome's Caesar and England's Cromwell were well known in Colonial America: generals used their armies to impose tyranny. Colonial experience with Britain also taught that regular armies were corrupt and dangerous because they were filled with mercenaries, men hired or forced into military service. Britain's soldiers were the dregs of society: uneducated, crude, and lawless, they preyed upon defenseless civilians.

Although British officers came from the upper classes, Americans viewed them as more dangerous than the British rank and file. Officers were notorious for their ambition and their willingness to use the army to extort payments and privileges from civilians and their governments. In King George's War (1744–1748) and the French and Indian War (1754–1763), British officers confirmed American hostility toward regular armies. They antagonized Colonial Americans with their aristocratic behavior and their conviction that the militia were rabble in need of the lash to discipline them into fighting men.

CITIZEN-SOLDIERS

In contrast to Britain's troops, Americans viewed themselves as citizen-soldiers. They treated military service as a form of voluntary, temporary employment in which soldiers retained their civil rights. When enlisting, Americans expected to be paid bounties in cash and land. Militiamen served short enlistments under officers who often were elected and who used persuasion rather than harsh discipline to lead troops. Soldiers had the right to return home when their enlistments expired even if in the middle of a campaign. Veterans resumed their place in society as ordinary citizens without additional rewards.

When the Revolution began in 1775, Americans believed that the war would be fought by its militia, that the war would be short, and that the natural courage of poorly trained citizen-soldiers would defeat harshly disciplined Britain regulars. British use of hired German troops reinforced American anti-army sentiment and reliance upon its militia. In 1777, however, because of defeats and the prospect of a long war, America created a regular army to win independence.

The Continental Army under George Washington recruited men for long enlistments and subjected them to discipline borrowed from European armies. Although they needed a regular army to fight the British, Americans retained their fear of it as a threat to civilian authority and liberty. Congress kept the army weak, undermanned, and undersupplied to prevent it from turning on its own government but strong enough to stalemate British forces. Despite the crucial role of the army, Americans lavished their praised on the militia and the patriotic people for winning independence. Anti-army sentiment shaped the Revolutionary generation's account of the war, which undervalued the Continental Army and overlooked veterans such as William Alld. That sentiment led to public rejection of the Society of Cincinnati, a hereditary organization formed by officers of the Continental Army—including Washington himself—because it was viewed as elitist and aristocratic.

VETERANS: FROM OUTCASTS TO IDOLS

Within forty years of independence a new generation changed how Americans viewed the Continental Army and its veterans. By 1825 the army, more than the militia, was credited with winning independence. The Continental Army, rather than being viewed as dangerous misfits led by ambitious and greedy officers, was celebrated as an army of patriotic warriors. Its veterans were regarded as idols rather than outcasts. No longer shunned, veterans became models of American character to be emulated by the younger generation.

This elevation of veterans to heroes and model citizens came about during the troubled period leading to the War of 1812. Americans needed heroes to unite a nation divided by slavery, partisan politics, sectionalism, and conflicts over foreign policy. Histories of the Revolution written at the turn of the nineteenth century helped to make Continental soldiers models of patriotism and courage. They praised soldiers for their devotion to liberty. Valley Forge, which Americans had all but forgotten, became a symbol of the soldiers' heroism and suffering in the accounts of the camp's hardships vividly portrayed by bloody footprints in the frozen snow.

The War of 1812 also required heroes. To arouse patriotism and unify a nation divided by war, Fourth of July orators celebrated Revolutionary War veterans for achievements that were regarded as surpassing those of mythical Greek warriors. In 1813, *Port Folio*, a national magazine, assured its readers that tributes to America's veterans would form a "new moral bond" that would unify the county. After the war, an outpouring of nationalism added to the stature of veterans. In Fourth of July speeches and newspapers, American were told that they should never forget the nation's gratitude owed its Revolutionary War veterans. The deaths of aging soldiers spurred the public to honor their memory in art, poetry, books, and monuments. In 1818 Congress approved service pensions to aid and reward Continental Army veterans.

VETERANS AND AMERICAN SOCIETY

In the early nineteenth century a new generation of Americans rewrote the history of the Revolutionary War. Rather than seeing the army as a necessary evil and as a threat to liberty, they idealized the soldiers as patriots and citizen-soldiers who deserved the nation's honor and gratitude. This younger generation treated veterans as models of national character and patriotism. The nation erected monuments to their glory and memorialized their achievements in art and literature to unite the country and to inspire future generations. Not only did Americans elevate the status of veterans as icons, they also set the precedent in public policy that continues today. By 1834 military pensions expanded to include militia and widows of veterans. This new way of remembering the Revolutionary War, through celebrations of its once maligned Continental Army and the honors, gratitude, and benefits bestowed upon its veterans, left a lasting imprint on the nation.

BIBLIOGRAPHY

Resch, John. *Suffering Soldiers: Revolutionary War Veterans, Moral Sentiment, and Political Culture in the Early Republic.* Amherst: University of Massachusetts Press, 1999.

Royster, Charles. *A Revolutionary People at War.* New York: Norton, 1979.

John P. Resch

See also: **Lafayette's Tour; Memory and Early Histories of the Revolution; Valley Forge; Veterans' Benefits.**

ROWLANDSON, MARY

(b. ca. 1637; d. 1710 or 1711) Author of a captivity narrative, the first book in English published by a woman in North America.

Mary White Rowlandson was born in England and moved with her family to the Salem, Massachusetts, area, where she married Joseph Rowlandson, a minister in Lancaster. They had three children. Lancaster, about fifty miles west of Boston, was a small British frontier community of approximately fifty families on the edge of what was the new English settlement and a number of Native American communities. On February 10, 1675, Native men attacked Lancaster. Mary Rowlandson and her children were among those captured. Her youngest daughter was killed. This was not merely an assault on a small population, but rather an event that marked the beginning of what became called King Philip's War.

Rowlandson was the first woman of British North America to publish a prose document in the English

A wood engraving of Mary Rowlanson and her children. On February 10, 1675, Mary and two of her three children were captured after an attack on their community Lancaster, Massachusetts. Her narrative of the attack and their captivity was the first book in English published by a woman in North America. COURTESY OF THE LIBRARY OF CONGRESS

language. Her account was both shocking and violent. Her first paragraph announced that on the morning of the assault "men's bodies" were "split open, houses and barns" were "in flames." Members of Lancaster's families were "fighting for their Lives, others wallowing in their Blood! Mothers and Children" were "crying out for themselves, and one another, *Lord, what shall we do!*"

Rowlandson, a highly literate woman, was a Puritan. The Puritans believed that incidents like Indian attacks did not simply happen. God determined them. They saw themselves as part of a new Israel, creators of a new community whose mission was to show the world a model of true Christian life. Rowlandson, her family, and Lancaster became part of not just another set of battles, but a struggle between the devil's world and a new Christian rebirth. In what was to become one of the shortest but most brutal wars in American history, Rowlandson became a witness of, participant in, and recorder of the furious encounters between the British and Native Americans.

Between her capture in February and her ransom and return eleven weeks later in May, Rowlandson experienced a major transformation in her life. From a leading member of her society, as the wife of Joseph Rowland-son, she became a servant of Narragansetts, Wampanoags, and Nipmucs who attacked Lancaster.

All of these Native groups objected to the increasing expansion of the English population and settlement in southern New England. In the forty years since the "Great Migration" of 1630 to the Boston area, a vast depopulation of natives occurred. Most of this was based on the spread of diseases, to which the native population was not immune. A series of incidents prompted disagreements, a death occurred, then the outbreak, and warfare began. Metacom, head of the Wampanoags, was called King Philip by the English, and the warfare was known as King Philip's War. Rowlandson and her family were caught up in these battles. In the process of her "removes," Rowlandson met with and admired Metacom.

Rowlandson's narrative, *The Sovereignty & Goodness of God*, also called *A True History of the Captivity & Restoration of Mrs. Mary Rowlandson*, was published first in London, then in Cambridge, Massachusetts, in 1682. It became what in our day would be called a best seller. Readers were fascinated by the fearsomeness of Indian warfare, the courage of a woman captured and victimized, and the sorrow of a mother who lost her youngest daughter in the attack. Rowlandson survived disaster by the power of her belief in God and by submitting to God's plan. The war and her trials demonstrated the ways which the new Zion and its people could fail in their mission to the new world, but how God graciously forgave them. Her writing and her traveling with various southern New England natives also showed how she learned to understand and sympathize with her native neighbors and enemies.

Mary Rowlandson became the founder of a significant literary and historical genre, the captivity narrative, which influenced later writers. The wartime and border experiences of capture from the late seventeenth through the nineteenth centuries became a consistent theme of early American life and writing, ministerial sermons, journals, newspapers, and novels. In the twentieth century captivity became a popular theme in films such as John Ford's *The Searchers*, with John Wayne as the uncle and Natalie Wood as his captive niece (1956). In the 1991 film *Dances with Wolves*, Kevin Costner's lover is really a white captive turned Lakota.

Like Rowlandson's account, many of these later stories portray Native Americans as the savage enemy. Many involve mindless Indians running off with young Anglo-American women and children. White male captives like John Smith and Daniel Boone were often portrayed as heroes able to defeat the savage, thus making way for the new Anglo-America. Mary Rowlandson's is an affecting story of her experiences. It remains a most powerful account of her life in early America. The legacy of the captivity narrative, beginning with Rowlandson, continues to influence how Americans view their own culture as well as that of the native peoples.

BIBLIOGRAPHY

Axtell, James. *The European and the Indian: Essays in the Ethnohistory of Colonial North America.* New York: Oxford University Press, 1981.

Axtell, James. *The Invasion Within: The Contest of Cultures in Colonial America.* New York: Oxford University Press, 1985.

Namias, June. *White Captives: Gender and Ethnicity on the American Frontier.* Chapel Hill and London: University of North Carolina Press, 1993.

Rowlandson, Mary. *Sovereignty and Goodness of God, Together with the Faithfulness of His Promises Displayed: Being a Narrative of the Captivity and Restoration of Mrs. Mary Rowlandson and Related Documents.* Edited by Neal Salisbury. Boston and New York: Bedford/St. Martin's, 1997. Originally published as *A True History of the Captivity & Restoration of Mrs. Mary Rowlandson*, vol. 1 (1682). New York: Garland Publishers, 1977.

Sayre, Gordon F., ed. *American Captivity Narratives: Selected Narratives with Introductions.* Boston: Houghton Mifflin, 2000.

Slotkin, Richard. *Regeneration through Violence: The Mythology of the American Frontier, 1600–1860.* Middletown, CT: Wesleyan University Press, 1973.

Vaughan, Alden T., and Clark, Edward W., eds. *Puritans among the Indians: Accounts of Captivity and Redemption 1676–1724.* Cambridge, MA: Harvard University Press, 1981.

Washburn, Wilcomb E., ed. *The Garland Library of Narratives of North American Captivities,* 111 vols. New York: Garland Publishers, 1976–1983.

June Namias

See also: **King Philip's War, Legacy of; Legacies of Indian Warfare; Native Americans: Images in Popular Culture; Sampson, Deborah.**

SAMPSON, DEBORAH

(b. December 17, 1760; d. April 29, 1827) Soldier during the American Revolution.

During the American Revolution, a young woman named Deborah Sampson disguised herself as a man, enlisted in the Continental Army, and served with apparent valor for one and a half years before being discharged. Sampson's story became widely known only in later years, when she published an account of her life and traversed the country on a speaking tour in an effort to raise funds for her family. Sampson's adventures reveal both the limitations on women's roles during the Revolutionary era and the lengths to which one woman would go to serve her country.

Born to a poor family in Plympton, Massachusetts, Sampson lost her father, a sailor, at sea when she was five years old. Her mother, unable to support her six children, sent her to live with family friends and acquaintances; eventually she was bound out as an indentured servant to the family of Jeremiah Thomas in Middleborough. During this time, Sampson taught herself to read. After her indenture ended at age eighteen, she continued to work for the Thomas family while she attended school. Soon she began to teach school.

By this time, the War for Independence raged around her. Massachusetts was a hotbed of resistance against Britain. She learned that the Continental Army faced a shortage of recruits. Inspired by a fierce patriotism, she tried to enlist. Standing five feet seven inches tall, she realized that if she bound her chest with cloth and dressed in male clothing, she could pass as a man. As she later explained, "Wrought upon at length by an enthusiasm and frenzy that could brook no control, I burst the tyrant bonds which *held my sex in awe,* and clandestinely, or by stealth, grasped an opportunity which custom and the world seemed to deny, as a natural privilege." Throwing off "the soft habiliments of *my sex,*" she said, she "assumed those of the *warrior,* already prepared for battle" (as quoted in Gustafson, p. 253).

Although her first attempt to enlist resulted in her unmasking as a woman, she did not give up. In May 1782, using the name Robert Shurtlieff (spelled, at various times, as Shirtliff, Shurtleff, or Shirtlief), she signed up with the Fourth Massachusetts Regiment at Uxbridge, Massachusetts. During the summer of 1782, she saw action during various battles in upstate New York. At one point she received a wound from a sword. In another incident, a musket ball lodged in her thigh. In order to

Northeast. In her performances on stage, she dressed in her soldier's uniform, displayed her musket, and recounted her wartime experiences. Although it was highly unusual for a woman to speak to audiences of men and women, people flocked to hear her curious tale. Finally in 1805, after a personal intervention by Paul Revere, Sampson Gannett received a pension of four dollars per month, retroactive to 1803. Congress passed additional legislation in 1818 that allotted her eight dollars more per month. After her death on April 29, 1827, her heirs received the full pension. Although Deborah Sampson Gannett is not the only woman known to have fought in the American Revolution, her case is by far the best known and best documented.

BIBLIOGRAPHY

Gustafson, Sandra M. *Eloquence Is Power: Oratory and Performance in Early America.* Chapel Hill: University of North Carolina Press, 2000.

Purcell, Sarah J. *Sealed with Blood: War, Sacrifice, and Memory in Revolutionary America.* Philadelphia: University of Pennsylvania Press, 2002.

Young, Alfred F. *Masquerade: The Life and Times of Deborah Sampson, Continental Soldier.* New York: Alfred A. Knopf, 2004.

Rosemarie Zagarri

See also: **Adams, Abigail; Brown, Charlotte: Diary of a Nurse; Camp Followers: War and Women; Generals' Wives: Martha Washington, Catherine Greene, Lucy Knox; Madison, Dolley.**

Painting of Deborah Sampson by Joseph Stone.

avoid exposure, she reportedly treated the wound herself. In 1783 she was transferred to Philadelphia, where she contracted a high fever. The physician who treated her, Doctor Barnabas Binney, discovered her secret but did not expose her. Subsequently, she returned to service and journeyed with the Eleventh Massachusetts Regiment on a surveying expedition to the Ohio River Valley. On October 23, 1783, she received an honorable discharge at West Point, when she revealed her true identity.

Although she continued to pose as a man for some time thereafter, in 1784 she married Benjamin Gannett, moved to Sharon, Massachusetts, and bore three children. Her family was poor and their life difficult. Her war wounds never healed properly and gave her chronic pain. In an effort to help her family, in 1792 she petitioned the Massachusetts General Court for a pension, but was awarded only thirty-four pounds in back pay. Although there was no dispute as to whether she had served in the army, there was controversy over whether she should receive the same benefits as male veterans. To publicize her plight, she collaborated in 1797 with Herman Mann to publish an account of her wartime service called *The Female Review: or, Memoirs of an American Young Lady.*

In 1802 she began to campaign publicly for her pension by undertaking a speaking tour throughout the

SHAYS'S AND WHISKEY REBELLIONS

Two short-lived armed uprisings, Shays's Rebellion and the Whiskey Rebellion, took place just before and shortly after the creation of the federal Constitution. The first, named after its nominal leader, Daniel Shays, erupted in western Massachusetts in the winter of 1786 and continued into the early months of 1787. The Whiskey Rebellion occurred in western Pennsylvania in 1794 and ended that same year. Neither uprising presented a serious military threat, but they both raised troubling questions throughout the new United States concerning the stability of republican governments.

SHAYS'S REBELLION: CAUSES

The causes of Shays's Rebellion were rooted in the economic and social dislocations accompanying the end of the Revolution. An economic depression followed the war, as the new United States was now excluded from its former markets in the British empire. A bewildering tangle of debts, public and private, added to America's economic woes, complicated by a scarcity of hard currency that tended to be drained off to pay for European imports.

Some states, notably Rhode Island, issued large amounts of paper currency to stimulate the local economy, earning that state the dubious nickname of "Rogues Island" by merchant creditors who viewed paper money as immoral. That did not happen in Massachusetts where conservative eastern merchant-politicians dominated the state's new government. Despite the hard times, the Massachusetts legislature sought to meet its financial obligations with ever more oppressive taxes, payable only in hard currency. Unable to pay their state taxes and private debts in so depressed an economy, many farmers were hauled into court to face not only exorbitant court costs, but the all too real threat of losing their property at public auction to pay their creditors. To the losers in this legal process, it seemed that there must exist a conspiracy among eastern politicians and merchants, many of whom were holders of the state debt that the farmers were suffering to pay off.

SHAYS'S REBELLION: SIGNS OF UNREST

Rumblings of discontent sounded early in the 1780s, even before the Revolution had officially ended. An itinerant evangelistic preacher, Samuel Ely, rallied disgruntled farmers in western Massachusetts to block the sitting of the civil courts. Ely eventually turned up in the eastern district of Massachusetts, now called Maine, where he joined backcountry squatters fighting against the great landed proprietors—a struggle similar to the one in the western parts of the state.

During 1785 and 1786, throughout the western counties of Berkshire, Hampshire, and Worcester, conventions met to draw up petitions to the state legislature in Boston. They voiced popular demands for lower taxes, paper money, lower court fees and lower government salaries, the relocation of the state capitol from Boston to Worcester, and even the abolition of the entire state senate as too aristocratic. The state legislature was not unresponsive, but its remedies were too limited and too late.

During the fall of 1786, armed crowds in the three western counties again shut down the civil courts. Violent unrest reached eastward and southward in Massachusetts and spread into the neighboring state of New Hampshire. So far, no blood had been shed; armed crowds had protested, intimidated, and then disbanded, having accomplished little more than their Revolutionary-era predecessors in pressing demands upon an unresponsive government. But Governor James Bowdoin and his eastern mercantile associates imagined something far more sinister: they envisioned open rebellion fomented by British sympathizers and spies against a legally constituted republican government.

PROTEST BECOMES REBELLION

Because the national government under the Articles of Confederation possessed neither an army nor the money to raise one, Massachusetts was left on its own to reassert its authority. Terrified eastern merchants contributed funds to raise a state army of 4,400 men under General Benjamin Lincoln, which set out in late January to crush the "rebels." In the western part of the state, supporters of the protest began organizing in bands under former army officers. The climax, or anti-climax, came on January 25, 1787. Insurgents led by Luke Day, Eli Parsons, and Daniel Shays surrounded the town of Springfield where General William Shepard guarded the arsenal with loyal militia and toward which General Lincoln was hurrying his merchant's army. Owing to confused communications, neither Parsons nor Day supported Shays when he initiated an attack. Shepard's militia responded by discharging cannon directly into the advancing "Shaysites," killing four and wounding twenty; the remaining insurgents turned and fled. State troops spent the next several weeks hunting down and arresting those fugitives who did not immediately surrender. Others sought anonymity in Vermont or, like Daniel Shays, in northern New York, where Shays died in 1825.

In the spring of 1787, a newly elected state legislature with John Hancock as the new governor, remedied the insurgents' most immediate grievances, and wisely pardoned the offenders, eventually even the leaders, including Daniel Shays himself. Shays's Rebellion produced no martyrs, but the insurrection left a legacy in both the shaping and adoption of the federal Constitution.

SHAYS'S REBELLION AND THE FEDERAL CONSTITUTION

The convention that met at Philadelphia in May 1787 evolved from several earlier such gatherings to consider revising the Articles of Confederation. The fact that all the states except Rhode Island sent delegates is evidence of a widespread sense of crisis as to whether republican government, state or national, could survive. News of Shays's Rebellion heightened this concern.

The convention's solution was to construct an entirely new, more highly centralized frame of government which included the powers to raise direct taxes, maintain a national army, call up the state militia in time of national emergency, and guarantee each state a republican form of government. These, along with other powers and procedures strengthening government, provoked heated debate when the new federal Constitution was submitted to the states for ratification. Supporters and opponents everywhere drew on the legacy of Shays's Rebellion to support their respective arguments concerning the new frame of government. In Massachusetts, opposition was so strong, especially in the western counties, that proponents narrowly won the vote for ratification only by promising to promote a series of amendments protecting individual rights. This process of "conditional ratification" provided a model for approval of the Constitution in other conflicted states, such as Virginia, and laid the basis for the first ten amendments, or the Bill of Rights, adopted in 1791.

THE WHISKEY REBELLION: CAUSES

The government under the new Constitution soon had an opportunity to demonstrate its ability to deal with the threat of insurrection, this time in western Pennsylvania. Beyond the Allegheny Mountains, backcountry farmers raised grain from which they distilled liquor for export and for use as a medium of exchange. They had long defied the state's efforts to collect an excise, or luxury tax, on their liquor, but starting in 1791, the new federal government took up the challenge with a national excise tax to help pay the national debt. An additional burden required those indicted under the act to be tried in federal court in far-off Philadelphia, rather than in the courts in their home districts as guaranteed by the new Bill of Rights. Congress soon redressed the act's judicial provisions, but not soon enough.

THE WHISKEY PROTESTS

Western farmers responded with techniques perfected during the Revolution. They gathered in conventions, petitioned legislatures both national and state, terrorized federal collectors, burned their property, and in short nullified the federal tax, just as they had the state tax, and just as colonists had parliamentary taxes. The only blood shed occurred in July 1794, when those defending the home of Excise Inspector John Neville fired upon a menacing crowd. The protestors themselves did not seek to take lives, only to demonstrate against an unpopular law imposed by a distant government. The anti-excise movement reached its culmination on August 1, 1794 at Braddock's Field. There, a large crowd of rural protestors threatened to march upon the nearby town of Pittsburgh, the regional symbol of urban oppression. The townspeople, however, escaped their fate by voting to join the insurgents rather than resist them. Deprived of its physical objective and lacking any clearly defined organization, program, or leadership, the excise protest lost its momentum.

PROTESTS BECOME REBELLION

The federal government, however, could not ignore this challenge to its authority. To President George Washington and Secretary of the Treasury Alexander Hamilton, the threat did not come merely from insurgent farmers in backcountry Pennsylvania, or from the frontiers of Maryland and Virginia to which the unrest had spread. More insidiously, it appeared, once again, to be the results of a foreign conspiracy by agents working, not for the British, but on behalf of revolutionary France seeking to spread its radical revolutionary ideology. In the United States, numerous Democratic Clubs sympathetic to the French Revolution had sprung up. Several were in western Pennsylvania, where members had participated in the protests, yielding enough evidence of a plot.

On August 7, 1794, Washington issued a proclamation condemning "combinations" to prevent the execution of federal laws and accusing the insurgents of treason for levying war against the United States. The president then used his authority under the new constitution to call up 15,000 state militia that Washington himself briefly commanded before yielding to more youthful leadership. Confronted with such a military force, all opposition in western Pennsylvania simply evaporated. Two obscure individuals were eventually arrested and convicted of high treason, but President Washington pardoned both on the grounds that one was simple minded and the other insane. As in the case of Shays's Rebellion, the Whiskey Rebellion created no martyrs.

It was now clear to almost everyone that armed violence against republican government, national or state, was an unacceptable means of protest. But what if republican government itself became oppressive? The overwhelming display of federal military power in western Pennsylvania alarmed those already concerned with such a possibility. Out of the sharpening debate over the proper exercise of national power evolved two political parties. The Democratic Republicans advocated states' rights and a narrow interpretation of the Constitution as essential to liberty, and the Federalists emphasized the importance of order and a strong, flexible central government. The vigorous but peaceful competition between these two national political parties, and their successors, replaced armed protest as a tool of political change—until the Civil War.

BIBLIOGRAPHY

Baldwin, Leland D. *Whiskey Rebels: The Story of a Frontier Uprising* (1939). Revised edition, Pittsburgh, PA: University of Pittsburgh Press, 1968.

Boyd, Steven R., ed. *The Whiskey Rebellion: Past and Present Perspectives.* Westport, CT: Greenwood Press, 1985.

Chambers, William Nisbet. *Political Parties in a New Nation: The American Experience, 1776–1809.* New York: Oxford University Press, 1963.

Cunningham, Nobel E., ed. *The Making of the American Party System, 1789–1809.* Englewood Cliffs, NJ: Prentice-Hall, 1965.

Gross, Robert A., ed. *In Debt to Shays: The Bicentennial of an Agrarian Rebellion.* Charlottesville: University Press of Virginia, 1993.

Richards, Leonard L. *Shays's Rebellion: The American Revolution's Final Battle.* Philadelphia: University of Pennsylvania Press, 2002.

Slaughter, Thomas P. *The Whiskey Rebellion: Frontier Epilogue to the American Revolution.* New York: Oxford University Press, 1986.

Szatmary, David P. *Shays' Rebellion: The Making of an Agrarian Insurrection.* Amherst: University of Massachusetts Press, 1980.

Taylor, Robert J. *Western Massachusetts in the Revolution.* Providence, RI: Brown University Press, 1954.

James S. Leamon

See also: Articles of Confederation; Constitution: Creating a Republic; Federalist Papers.

SLAVERY AND THE HOMEFRONT, 1775–1783

No African-American colonist signed the Declaration of Independence. Indeed, despite the Patriots' common use of the words *slavery, tyranny,* and *oppression* in making a case for separation from Great Britain, the signers of the Declaration did not consider the slavery as it was lived by African-American colonists a cause for revolution. Holding no promise for freedom for the men and women in bondage, the American Revolution posed difficult choices for black colonists. For some, the Revolution's rhetoric of freedom raised the hope that the ideals of the Revolution would mean freedom for all Americans. Despite the lack of a clear statement from the Patriots on how the Revolution could benefit African Americans, black militiamen took part in the Revolution's initial skirmishes at Lexington and Concord, and by the end of the conflict an estimated 5,000 African-American colonists had served the Patriot cause on land and sea. However, not all African-American colonists supported the fight for independence. As Benjamin Quarles writes in his classic *The Negro in the American Revolution,* many were likely "to join the side that made [them] the quickest and best offer in terms of those inalienable rights'" (p. vii). Still others fled the colonies altogether, settling in Canada or Florida or on Indian land.

SLAVERY IN THE AMERICAN COLONIES

An estimated one-fifth of the population in the American colonies before the Revolution were slaves—more than a half million individuals. Slavery was dispersed unevenly across the colonies, but few white colonists, North or South, could escape knowledge of the institution. Even in the North, slaves (often called servants, which tended to disguise their real status) were part of many house-holds. Among the Patriots, it was not just George Washington and Thomas Jefferson who owned slaves; so did the early Whig leader John Dickinson of Philadelphia. New England families (including the family of Boston Patriot Samuel Adams) often included a slave member. Slaves were sold at auction in Northern ports such as Philadelphia and Newport, Rhode Island; advertisements of slaves for sale (in Boston, unwanted slave children were simply given away) and calls for the return of so-called runaway, or escaped, slaves were regular parts of local newspapers.

This widespread awareness of real, not metaphorical, slavery in colonial America provided a compelling although not always recognized impetus to Revolutionary slogans. White American colonists did not have to imagine what slavery might mean; it was demonstrated daily. However, the Patriot call to end American slavery to Great Britain with no corollary promise to end slavery at home did not go unnoticed by African Americans. Phillis Wheatley, a former slave and Boston poet, wrote:

> O might God! Let conscience seize the mind
> Of inconsistent man, who wish to find
> A partial god to vindicate their cause
> And plead their freedom while they
> break its laws.

(quoted in Bradley, 106)

encouraged African-American colonists to take up the call of liberty and unalienable rights for all. Free black colonists Prince Hall and Paul Cuffee were among the signers of slave petitions for the freedom that Revolutionary rhetoric encouraged. Lemuel Haynes, a Patriot soldier and an African-American Congregational minister, preached that slavery was an affront to God. In a 1773 petition to the Massachusetts legislature, a Boston man, whom we know only as Felix, called for liberty in the emotional language of the time: "We have no Property! We have no Wives! No Children! We have no City! No Country!" (Aptheker, p. 6). In an essay in the *Essex Journal,* a former slave, Caesar Sarter, asked white readers to put themselves in the place of a family sold the auction block: "Suppose you were trepanned [kidnapped] away, the husband from the dear wife of his bosom—the wife from her affectionate husband—children from their fond parents—or parents from their beloved offspring."

THE REVOLUTION AND ANTISLAVERY SENTIMENT

The Revolutionary period also produced considerable activity by white antislavery advocates, many of them Quakers who opposed not only slavery but also all war, including the Revolution, and were thus not part of the Patriot leadership. Other antislavery advocates were influenced by the conservative New Divinity stream of Congregationalism, which saw slavery as a sin against

God. However, Congregationalist ministers were not generally influential in the Revolutionary period, when American colonists became increasingly secular or, in the case of Southern Patriots, had little connection to formal churches.

Most Northern Patriots were not willing to jeopardize the support of the Southern colonies by adopting an antislavery stance. A few exceptions should be noted. Thomas Paine and Benjamin Rush, both important Patriots, sought unsuccessfully to have the Patriot message include opposition to slavery. As president of the Pennsylvania Society Promoting the Abolition of Slavery, Franklin called slavery "an atrocious debasement of human nature," but that was after the Revolution was won.

AFRICAN AMERICANS IN THE MILITARY

The willingness of African-American Patriots to serve the cause did not always translate into the opportunity to do so. Military recruiters for the Continental Army at first excluded slave and nonwhite Americans, for several reasons—suspicions of Toryism, fear that armed slaves would turn on white Americans, and the belief that African Americans would lack courage under fire. As white volunteers dwindled, however, Northern recruiters ignored policy, sometimes with the encouragement of masters who enlisted their slaves for the land bounty they would receive.

The fear of allowing African Americans to serve in the military was particularly strong in the South, and a proposal by South Carolina's John Laurens, the son of a planter, to supply the Continental Army with 3,000 black South Carolinians was strongly rejected. Still, Southern slave masters were willing to turn over slaves to the army (for a price) for use in the laborious tasks of backing up frontline troops. In both North and South, black soldiers typically served as non-arms-bearing infantrymen. Others were guides, messengers, and orderlies. Yet stories of African-American heroism emerged, including the story of Jack Sisson, who was credited with taking part in the capture of General Richard Prescott in 1777 and became the subject of a popular song. The American navy was less resistant to black enlistment, and African Americans served there with distinction. One example is James Forten, who survived British capture to become a wealthy and famous Philadelphian.

The British took advantage of the Patriots' reluctance to accept black soldiers. Indeed, the British general John Burgoyne expressed the view that the British could not win the war unless discontented slaves and Indians could be attracted to the British side. His theory was put to the test in 1775, when Virginia's royal governor, Lord Dunmore, promised freedom to any American slave (that is, a slave owned by an American rebel; British slave owners were protected) who would fight for the British. Despite a virtual lockdown of the colony, some 2,000 Virginia slaves, courting capture and death, found their way to the Dunmore fleet, where they were armed and fitted out with British uniforms, which had sashes emblazoned with the words "Freedom for Slaves." They participated in military actions on land and sea, but the British were slow to follow Dunmore's example and his proclamation was not repeated until it was picked up in 1779 by Sir Henry Clinton—a lag time that may have cost the British the war. Exact numbers are unknown, but Quarles estimates the "number of Negroes who fled to the British [to be] into the tens of thousands" (p. 119). However, slaves who joined the British usually found they had exchanged one master for another; they served British officers as personal servants and worked as laborers, spies, drummers, couriers, guides, and seamen, but seldom as combatants. Slaves were also occasionally plundered by the British from American masters and given to Loyalists to make up for slaves who had escaped.

When hostilities ceased, the American military sought to reestablish slavery along prewar lines. The return of captured African Americans to their former Patriot masters was including in the terms of the Yorktown surrender, setting off a new wave of flight to the British as black Americans sought places on departing British warships, escaping to problematical futures.

THE CONSTITUTIONAL CONVENTION

Even as many white Americans sought to reestablish the prewar slave society, the rhetoric of the Revolution, the discussion it engendered among blacks and whites, and the service of African Americans in the war itself prompted six Northern states to outlaw slavery within a few years of the war's conclusion. But at the Constitutional Convention delegates could not even agree to abolish the slave trade, much less slavery itself. The discussion of slavery at the convention turned not on its existence, but rather on how slaves were to be counted. In the resulting Three-Fifths Compromise, the Southern states agreed to federal taxation in exchange for an agreement that slaves would be counted as three-fifths of a person for the purposes of (white) representation in the Congress. As it turned out, Congress did not levy taxes on the states before the Civil War, but the inclusion of slaves in the population count helped maintain Southern legislative power. The Bill of Rights that came to accompany the Constitution and made its approval possible has come to represent the meaning of the nation, but none of its ten amendments abolished slavery. It was not until after the Civil War that the Thirteenth Amendment began the process of fulfilling the American Revolution's promise of freedom.

BIBLIOGRAPHY

Aptheker, Herbert, ed. *A Documentary History of the Negro People in the United States*, vol. 1. Secaucus, NJ: Citadel. 1973.

Bailyn, Bernard. *The Ideological Origins of the American Revolution*. Cambridge, MA: Harvard University Press, 1967.

Bradley, Patricia. *Slavery, Propaganda, and the American Revolution*. Jackson: University Press of Mississippi, 1998.

Davis, David Brion. *The Problem of Slavery in the Age of Revolution, 1770–1823*. Ithaca, NY: Cornell University Press, 1975.

Quarles, Benjamin. *The Negro in the American Revolution*. Chapel Hill: University of North Carolina Press, for the Institute of Early American History and Culture, Williamsburg, VA, 1961.

Internet Resources

"Africans in America's Journey through Slavery." Public Broadcasting System. Available from <http://www.pbs/wgbh/aia>.

Digital History; Gilder Lehrman Institute of American History. Available from <http://www.digitalhistory.uh.edu>.

Patricia Bradley

See also. Slavery in America.

SLAVERY IN AMERICA

European explorers first enslaved individuals and groups native to the American continent during the late fifteenth and early sixteenth centuries in a drive for the accumulation of capital wealth. When indigenous slavery failed, systematically organized African slave-labor became integral to the complex economic systems of British mercantilism and Western capitalism. The voyages of European explorers made the trade in Africans, and the staples of their labor, top priorities in the exchange and development of European markets and wealth. Hence slavery emerged in the thirteen American colonies in relation to the development of the Western world. As W. E. B. DuBois notes in *The Suppression of the Slave Trade to the United States, 1638–1870* (1965 [1898]), the colonies played a vital role in the Triangular Trade between Europe, North America, and Africa during the eighteenth century. The British maintained that the slave trade was the "very life of the colonies."

Africans themselves participated in trading other Africans who were enslaved, usually as a result of tribal wars on the continent. African slavery was not benign, but European and North American slavery were wholly different from what Africans understood slavery to be. American slavery was permanent rather than indentured; it could be inherited and passed from generation to generation; it was based on racial oppression; and it deemed its subjects to be the subhuman property of others.

After more than a century of Spanish domination, an unnamed Dutch man-of-war arrived at Jamestown, Virginia, in 1619 with a cargo that included nearly two dozen Africans, commencing the slavery epoch in the British colonies. At best there are only estimates of the total number of African slaves imported through the tumultuous, one-way journey from Africa called the Middle Passage. The British alone imported roughly 300,000 Africans to the Americas between 1713 and 1733 after they were permitted by the Spanish to monopolize the colonial slave trade. Although the impact of the American Revolution brought the trade to a near halt, approximately 700,000 African slaves were imported to the United States by 1790. Aboard thousands of ships known as slavers, major shipping corporations from England, such as the Royal African Company, and independent ship merchants from various parts of Europe and North America imported two million African slaves to America between 1680 and 1790. And the slave population would increase significantly in the coming century. In 1781 there were about 575,000 slaves out of a total population of 3.5 million people in the United States.

The violence and trauma of the Middle Passage resulted in millions of Africans dying en route. Individuals were chained to each other by neck, hand, and foot in close quarters and crammed together in intolerable surroundings where they contracted fatal diseases, starved, and slept in human waste. The sick, including pregnant women, were routinely thrown in the Atlantic and drowned. Two of every five Africans died before boarding the slavers in the 1,000-mile marches from the interior of Africa to its coasts, and one in three died en route aboard them. Altogether, between the seventeenth and nineteenth centuries about twelve million Africans were taken from the African continent by force.

SLAVERY IN THE NEW NATION

Slavery was a national institution in the new nation. However, many American leaders, including the framers of the U.S. Constitution and Thomas Jefferson, thought of slavery as an increasingly obsolete institution that would become unnecessary with the passing of a generation or two. After the American Revolution, slavery was dying in the Northern colonies and was presumably weakening in the middle and Southern colonies. The framers compromised, mainly in deference to political leaders from the Carolinas and Georgia, to prohibit the abolition of the slave trade before 1808 (Article I, Section 9; Article V). This suggests that of all the areas of interstate commerce that the new Congress was empowered to regulate, the Constitution did not permit the

TIMELINE OF EVENTS

1619 The first African slave imports arrive in Jamestown, Virginia.

1688 The Society of Friends/Quakers in Pennsylvania oppose slavery.

1698 South Carolina encourages the importation of white laborers as the proportion of imported blacks heightened concerns of public safety.

1712 Pennsylvania enacts a prohibition against the importation of blacks and Native Americans as a result of the discovery of "divers plots and insurrections." The state also charged twenty pounds per head for every imported Black person or Native American—Blacks from the West Indies excluded.

1776 The Declaration of Independence.

1787 Eighty black individuals petition the Massachusetts legislature to be returned to Africa.

1787 England relocates slaves from London to Sierra Leone in Africa for the purpose of introducing the Christian religion to the continent.

1787 The Northwest Ordinance prohibits slavery north of the Ohio River territories.

1787 The Constitutional Convention in Philadelphia establishes slavery as a legally protected institution.

1789 The French Revolution occurs.

1791 Eli Whitney develops the Cotton Engine.

1791–1803 The Haitian Revolution occurs.

1800 The plot of Gabriel Prosser and one thousand others is aborted in Richmond, Virginia.

1803 The Louisiana Purchase results in part from the slave uprising in Hispaniola (Haiti).

1807–1808 Congress abolishes the slave trade in the United States. It continues illegally until slavery is abolished in the 1860s.

1811 Several hundred Louisiana slaves participate in attacks across several New Orleans plantations.

1812 The War of 1812 occurs between the United States and England.

1817 The American Colonization Society promotes relocating free blacks to Africa in order to strengthen slavery by depriving the slaves of potential anti-slavery leadership.

1820 The Missouri Compromise line divides the nation into slave and free states. This formula would settle most sectional hostilities until the decade before the Civil War.

1822 Denmark Vesey and as many as 9,000 individuals organize an attempt to take Charleston, South Carolina before it is betrayed and aborted.

1822 The American Colonization Society relocates free blacks to Liberia in Africa. Liberia is recognized as a country in 1840.

James Lance Taylor

---

regulation of slave trading for a generation. Some scholars estimate that as many as 250,000 people may have been illegally imported as slaves between 1808 and the Civil War. More conservative estimates suggest roughly 35,000.

Slavery was a major concern at the Constitutional Convention, especially for the two-dozen framers who actually owned slaves, including George Washington (with 200) and Virginia's George Mason (with more than 300). When Thomas Jefferson and Benjamin Franklin authored the Declaration of Independence in 1776, Jefferson owned 175 people. Ironically, at the behest of the elder Franklin and in deference to Southern interests, Jefferson removed an antislavery paragraph accusing King George III of waging "cruel war against human nature itself," and

of "violating its most sacred rights of life and liberty in the persons of a distant people who never offended him, captivating and carrying them into slavery in another hemisphere or to incur miserable death in their transportation thither." Jefferson did not clarify his own participation in the "cruel war" against the Africans by means of their enslavement, but unlike John Adams and his son John Quincy Adams (who later represented the *L'Amistad* Africans), Jefferson, like most American presidents between 1787 and 1836, participated in slaveholding and trading. The framers also compromised by including a fraction of the Southern slave population (also known as the three-fifths clause) in the apportioning of congressional representatives and in the Electoral College (Article I, Sections 2 and 9); it also provided a fugitive slave clause requiring the return of runaway slaves (Article V, Section 2); it based taxing of slaves in a given state on the three-fifths criterion (Article I, Section 9); and it obligated the federal government to aid the Southern states in the event of slave uprisings and insurrections (Article I, Section 8; Article IV, Section 4). A concern with potential slave insurrections is implicated in the Preamble to the U.S. Constitution, explicitly stating that among its primary functions is to "insure domestic tranquility," and "provide for the common defense." Thus the American Constitution recognized the legality of slavery and compelled the federal government to defend it. This proved to be one of the major legacies of the Revolutionary War. The conflict over legalized slavery was to shape American identity and culture through the Civil War.

The slavery question was a highly contentious issue, and the factions were not strictly drawn along North and South sectional lines, as is commonly thought. Only after the publication of James Madison's notes on the Constitutional Convention was it revealed how this single issue almost prevented the nation from forming into a federal republic. The equalitarian implications of the American Revolution led states such as New York (in 1799) and New Jersey (1804) to implement gradual abolition plans. They were soon joined by Virginia and North Carolina, but the trend did not extend as readily into the cotton colonies.

THE VALUE OF SLAVES

The invention of the cotton engine (known more commonly as the cotton 'gin) by northern inventor Eli Whitney in 1793 increased average annual bales (one thousand pounds) of cotton production from three thousand in 1791 to more than five million in 1860, to be sold on the European markets. The slave population would increase exponentially with annual cotton production. The surplus populations of African slaves in Virginia and South Carolina would increase the value of an individual slave who might be sold in other states and territories. Generally, an individual slave was valued at $200 in 1800 and increased to a value between $1,400 and $2,000 in 1860. Slavery and the slave trade were maintained in the U.S. to satisfy the planters and slaveholders' demands to increase the productivity in tobacco in Virginia, North Carolina and Kentucky, rice and indigo in South Carolina, and especially cotton in Georgia, Mississippi, and Alabama.

There was ongoing anxiety over the potential for slave violence and insurrections, especially from the earliest African imports who continued to long for and view Africa as their homeland. In turn the treatment of these slaves in the large plantations of the Deep South states became increasingly brutal and violent. In the northern states, Africans were used mainly as domestics because

the topography and environment were not conducive to the crops that thrived in the Chesapeake region and Deep South states. Exploited low-wage immigrant white workers, who had to compete with free labor, mostly despised northern slaves. New York had roughly 20,000 imported slaves in the late eighteenth century and incrementally continued to permit their importation until the Civil War. Pennsylvania was the seat of the earliest opposition to slavery as expressed by the Quaker Society of Friends, who in 1688 opposed the "traffic" in humans; it expressed continued opposition in 1712 after the discovery of slave insurrection plots in other Northern Colonies.

ABOLITION BY ANY MEANS

In the decades before the Civil War, many of the four million African slaves and the 300,000 nominally free blacks adopted different methods and approaches in support of abolition. As early as 1787 a group of eighty blacks petitioned the Massachusetts legislature for the right to return to Africa. In that same year, England relocated some of its ex-slaves to Sierra Leone in order to do missionary work there; in turn, an African-American ship captain named Paul Cuffee of New Bedford, Massachusetts, promoted emigration to Africa until his plan was interrupted by the War of 1812. Cuffee was able to relocate thirty-eight people to Sierra Leone in 1815. At the risk of bodily harm (thirty-nine whip lashes was the custom), some slaves deprived the planters and slaveholders of their labor through work slowdowns and stoppages, and others became fugitives. At least 300, led by Harriet Tubman, escaped through the Underground Railroad to the North and Canada, while others purchased their own freedom. Very few supported the American Colonization Society, which Kentucky congressman Henry Clay and others created in 1817. This society of prominent Americans was committed to relocating only free blacks to Liberia because of their militant antislavery activism. Established in 1822, with its capital Monrovia named after U.S. president James Monroe, 13,000 free blacks relocated to Liberia before the Civil War.

In 1827 individual African Americans such as Samuel Cornish and John Russwurm published the first African-American newspaper called *Freedom's Journal*, demanding that black people be allowed to make their case against slavery. The Abolitionist movement would emerge among white Bostonians in the 1830s after its leader William Lloyd Garrison read the incendiary *Appeal to the Colored Citizens of the World* (1829) by David Walker, which called for abolition through insurrectionist violence if necessary. Garrison preferred the use of moral persuasion over violence. In his early public career, former slave Frederick Douglass aligned with Garrison and the Abolitionists, only later to support political abolitionism including voting, agitation, and, like Walker, violence if necessary. The impending civil war would prove that abolition required more than legal remedies.

SLAVERY AND SOCIETY

The promise of "domestic tranquility" was an ongoing concern in those states and territories that had majority or near-majority slave populations. At times, slave leaders rejected gradualist approaches to abolition, initiating hundreds of slave plots and near and actual insurrections. David Walker and most of the militant individuals (slave and free) who led insurrections used religious justifications in their calls to arms. Because of American blacks' numerical minority status and their Protestantism, systematic rebellions were less likely to occur in the United States than in other parts of the Americas and the Caribbean. The rarity of slave rebellions in the United States did little to ease concerns, however; in fact it was their potential to occur that constantly disturbed the South. From the time of the "French and Indian/Seven Years War" through the American Revolution, the Haitian Revolution and the War of 1812, the Southern and Middle colonies were often paralyzed by the fear of real or rumored slave rebellions. During the "French and Indian" war against the British on the American continent between 1754 and 1756 (it spread to Europe until 1763), colonial officials such as Virginia's Lieutenant Governor Robert Dinwiddie felt compelled to leave troops throughout Maryland, Virginia, and South Carolina out of concern for the part which blacks played in aiding the French in their few victories in the region. In 1763, Virginia's slave population was 170,000, constituting half its population, and later increasing to sixty percent. By 1778, Virginia passed an "Act to prevent the further importation of slaves." At the time of the American Revolution, South Carolina was unable to deploy its militia against the British out of fear that its slaves would rebel with the expectation that they would be manumitted by the British. The slaves were considered a domestic threat to the Southern states in every major military action leading up to the Civil War.

No single event created more fear among slaveholders and traders than the uprising of slaves in Haiti (French-ruled Hispaniola/Santo Domingo) against tens of thousands of French, Spanish, and British troops between 1791 and 1803. The success of this insurrection rendered the French-owned Louisiana Territory useless as a trading post from which Haiti's coveted banana crops could be imported and sold. In 1803, during Jefferson's administration, the purchase of the Louisiana Territory from Napoleon doubled its size and boundaries. The Haitian Revolution became a signal event that spread fear throughout the nation, especially as many of the French colonists and slaveholders fled from Haiti to South Carolina, spreading accounts of its violence. Leaders such as George Washington and a group of Southern Congressmen expressed serious concern that the Haitian rebels would next move to Jamaica and eventually, by way of Florida, to the American South.

The Haitian revolution inspired the famous aborted plots of "Black" Gabriel Prosser, of Richmond, Virginia, in 1800. In 1811 Louisiana witnessed a series of violent confrontations between local militia and rebellious slaves. The most notable of these occurred when between 400 and 500 armed individuals moved from plantation to plantation, killing the son of a slaveholder named Andry along the way, before being stopped by the U.S. army and local militia. Between 82 and 120 were executed onsite and after brief trials. Some of their bloodied bodies were put on display at the Andry plantation to ward off any future attempts at rebellion.

By 1819 half of the twenty-two states in the union were slave states and half free. Agitation among black people increased after 1820 because many of them understood the Missouri Compromise, which divided the free and slave states at the 36°30' parallel, to be the end of slavery as a national system. In 1822 a plot by Denmark Vesey in South Carolina to create an army of slaves, said to number 9,000, was thwarted. Nine years later, Nat Turner led a bloody insurrection in Southampton, Virginia. The Vesey plot and Nat Turner's massacre of his master and fifty-four other whites confirmed the rebellious antislavery mood of African Americans during the first half of the nineteenth century. They were willing to align militantly and militarily with any force, foreign or domestic, that would reward them with freedom.

CONCLUSION

Widely practiced in the Caribbean and South America by Europeans prior to the English settlement of North America, slavery was introduced in Virginia in 1619 as a source of labor. Thus began an institution that would have profound effects on American society and culture from its founding, through the War for Independence, the creation of the Constitution, and early years as a nation. At the beginning of the Revolution, slavery existed in all thirteen colonies. Its presence created a moral and philosophical dilemma for Americans who rebelled against English rule to prevent, as they proclaimed, being "enslaved" by British tyranny, and to secure their liberty.

During the Revolution slavery was a contentious issue, heightened by the need to recruit slaves and former slaves into the Continental Army. Whereas some Northern states abolished slavery during the Revolution, Southern states, which had large slave populations, did not. In order to create the Federal Union, the founders compromised on slavery by regarding slaves as property and by protecting the rights of owners of this property. On the

The discovery of Nat Turner. In 1831 Nat led an insurrection in which he and seven other slaves killed his master, Joseph Travis, and the Travis family. © BETTMANN/CORBIS

other hand, the new nation also outlawed the extension of slavery to the Northwest Territory and provided for Congress's abolition of the African slave trade in 1807.

Slavery continued to create a moral dilemma for the new nation, which professed the ideals of natural rights and individual liberty while expanding the institution of slavery as more states were added to the Union following the Missouri Compromise of 1820. Slave conspiracies and uprisings required Southern states to maintain military readiness to defeat rebels. States implemented increasingly oppressive laws to deter rebellions. Slavery festered and divided the nation. While not a source of foreign wars, slavery remained a cause of sectional tension and conflict between slave and non-slave states, especially in the 1830s as antislavery sentiment grew into a fervent campaign by a small group of radicals to abolish slavery. The Civil War (1861–1865) provided the opportunity to do what the Founders had considered but failed to do abolish slavery (through the Thirteenth Amendment), and to extend equal rights to freed slaves

(Fourteenth and Fifteenth Amendments). Victory over slavery marked the end of one era and also the beginning of another—the struggle to overcome inequalities and racism that are the legacies of slavery.

BIBLIOGRAPHY

Aptheker, Herbert. *To Be Free.* New York: International Publishers, 1968.

Aptheker, Herbert. *American Negro Revolts.* New York: International Publishers, 1974.

Du Bois, W. E. Burghardt. *The Suppression of the African Slave-Trade to the United States, 1638–1870* [1898]. New York: Russell and Russell, 1965.

Du Bois, W. E. Burghardt. *The World and Africa* [1946]. New York: International Publishers, 2003.

Finkelman, Paul. *Slavery and the Founders: Race and Liberty in the Age of Jefferson.* Armonk, NY: M. E. Sharpe, 2001.

Zinn, Howard. *A People's History of the United States.* New York: New Press, 1997.

James Lance Taylor

See also: **Armed Conflicts in America, 1587–1815; Legacies of Indian Warfare; Revolution and Radical Reform; Slavery and the Homefront, 1775–1783; Stono Rebellion; War of 1812.**

Samuel Adams.

SONS OF LIBERTY

Disregarding American protests that the colonists could not be taxed because they were not represented in Parliament, in March 1765 the British government enacted a stamp tax to take effect in the American colonies on November 1, 1765. Speaking against the proposed Stamp Act in the House of Commons, Isaac Barré had described the Americans as "Sons of Liberty" who would steadfastly resist any assault on their liberties.

PROTESTING THE STAMP ACT

Although the term "Sons of Liberty" did not become commonplace until December 1765 and although not all Americans actively opposed Britain's new imperial policies, Barré was right about the general colonial response to the Stamp Act. Open defiance started in Boston when nine men, most of whom were middle-class shopkeepers or manufacturers, devised a plan to force the designated stamp distributor, Andrew Oliver, to resign. If Oliver resigned, the Stamp Act could not be implemented. Having gotten usually antagonistic working-class groups to unite, the Loyal Nine—who formed the nucleus of what became the city's Sons of Liberty—fashioned effigies, including one of Oliver. On August 14, 1765, Bostonians awoke to see those effigies hanging from a large old elm christened the Liberty Tree. Thereafter, it became a stag-

ing area for Sons of Liberty activities. That evening a huge crowd of perhaps 3,000 people paraded the effigies through the streets. Coming upon a small building that Oliver reportedly would use as the stamp distribution office, the crowd demolished it. Later the crowd beheaded the Oliver figure and burned the other effigies. After the Loyal Nine left the scene, members of the crowd, acting on their own, slightly damaged Oliver's home. He resigned his stamp distributorship the next day. Neither the Loyal Nine nor Samuel Adams, who soon began working with them, saw any reason for further crowd action. Nevertheless, on August 26, crowds, not led by the Loyal Nine or other middle-class persons, spent the night tearing apart the mansion of Thomas Hutchinson, the colony's wealthy lieutenant governor. The Loyal Nine, and their new ally Samuel Adams, were horrified by this rioting.

Violent crowd actions attributed to Sons of Liberty also occurred in Newport, Rhode Island at the end of August. By threatening more violence and staging public protests at their own local Liberty Trees, Sons of Liberty groups in other colonies effectively stopped the Stamp Act from being implemented. By late 1765, the term Sons of Liberty—as well as "Liberty Boys"—had come to signify those Americans who secretly banded together and used extralegal means and public demonstrations—ranging from parading with effigies to destructive rioting—to stop the implementation of the Stamp Act.

In December 1765, with New York City Sons initiating the effort, plans were formulated to coordinate the Sons' resistance to Britain's intrusive imperial policies. By February 1766, the New York Sons were developing a committees of correspondence system to link Sons of Liberty organizations in the colonies as far away as Maryland. During this same period, many Sons of Liberty groups regularized their meetings and opened them to anyone who supported the American cause. The repeal of the Stamp Act in March 1766 marked the key triumph and, ironically, the start of the decline of the Sons' influence. Individual groups of Sons continued to meet, and Sons of Liberty often held public meetings to celebrate significant anniversaries in the fight against the Stamp Act. Internal fissures, however, soon developed. In New York City, for example, the Sons split into competing groups that backed different local political parties; only the threat of the Townshend duties forced a truce in which a group calling itself "The United Sons of Liberty" pledged in July 1769 steadfastly to support a non-importation agreement against the duties. Moreover, into the 1770s, groups and individuals calling themselves Sons of Liberty issued propaganda statements attacking British taxing policies and other efforts to tighten Britain's control over the colonies. But by the eve of the revolution, few groups used the term Sons of Liberty, and when the term was employed it had come to stand for virtually any American "patriot."

DECLINE OF SONS OF LIBERTY

There were many reasons why the Sons' influence declined. Communities—especially urban communities—that had readily joined in opposition to the Stamp Act were not so united when it came to using economic boycotts as a weapon after 1766. The systematic opposition to the 1767 Townshend duties took over a year to materialize. Worse yet, the response to the 1770 repeal of all the Townshend duties except the one on tea revealed how fractured the resistance movement was. In city after city, an unbridgeable gulf appeared between manufacturers and merchants. In no small part to further their own economic position, manufacturers advocated maintaining the boycott until all the Townshend duties were repelled; most merchants, though, opposed continuing the boycott or undertaking any new economic warfare because it undermined their immediate economic interests. The rise of government sanctioned committees of correspondence to unify resistance against British policies also undercut the need for the kinds of activities that Sons of Liberty had undertaken in 1765 to 1766. And the crucial protests against the Tea Act of 1773 were usually based on mass

gatherings such as those held in Philadelphia and Boston. These meetings created their own committees to force everyone in the community to comply with the publicly expressed will. Finally, once the Continental Congress created the Continental Association in October 1774, elected committees of inspection and observation provided the political muscle and engaged in the kind of pressure tactics associated with the Sons of Liberty.

Although the role of the Sons of Liberty declined sharply after 1766, their actions were essential in thwarting the Stamp Act. And the defeat of the Stamp Act stiffened the resolve of both Americans and the British Parliament to hold fast to their very different views of Parliament's powers. Had the Sons of Liberty not conducted vigorous extra legal actions, especially in 1765, the revolutionary movement surely would have unfolded in a very different way—if it unfolded at all.

BIBLIOGRAPHY

Alexander, John K. *Samuel Adams: America's Revolutionary Politician.* Lanham, MD: Rowman & Littlefield, 2002.

Becker, Carl L. *The History of Political Parties in the Province of New York, 1760–1776.* Madison: University of Wisconsin Press, 1960 (originally published 1909).

Bridenbaugh, Carl. *Silas Downer: Forgotten Patriot—His Life and Writings.* Providence: Rhode Island Bicentennial Foundation, 1974.

Copeland, David A. *Debating the Issues in Colonial Newspapers: Primary Documents on Events of the Period.* Westport, CT: Greenwood Press, 2000.

Davidson, Philip. *Propaganda and the American Revolution, 1763–1783.* Chapel Hill: University of North Carolina Press, 1941.

Morgan, Edmund S., ed. *Prologue to Revolution: Sources and Documents on the Stamp Act Crisis, 1764–1766.* Chapel Hill: University of North Carolina Press, 1959.

Morgan, Edmund S., and Morgan, Helen M. *The Stamp Act Crisis: Prologue to Revolution,* 3d edition. Chapel Hill: University of North Carolina Press, 1995.

Walsh, Richard. *Charleston's Sons of Liberty: A Study of the Artisans 1763–1789.* Columbia: University of South Carolina Press, 1959.

John K. Alexander

See also: Boston Massacre: Pamphlets and Propaganda; *Common Sense*; Paine, Thomas.

THE SPY: FIRST AMERICAN WAR NOVEL

When James Fenimore Cooper decided to write *The Spy* (1821), a narrative of manners set in the America of the Revolutionary War, he was certainly conscious of the fact that nothing of the kind already existed.

CREATING AN AMERICAN LITERATURE

Cooper justified his undertaking explicitly in his preface. He points out first off that the best reason in favor of an American trying to write a novel set in this country is that the ground is "untrodden." Significantly, he adds that this may in fact help the book to gain notice abroad; at least critics there would find it new. Perhaps he felt that the British market would account for an important share of sales; such thoughts can't have been beneath him. After all, Cooper also points out immediately that such a book can't fail to appeal at home, where "patriotic ardor will ensure a sale."

In the immediate aftermath of another war, that of 1812, in which the young nation had bested Great Britain in what could be termed as the "rematch" of the Revolution, national sentiment was riding high in the United States. Cooper had written one novel, *Precaution* (1820), purportedly at his young wife's instigation. It was competently written, but it was not seen as likely to inspire much public enthusiasm at home for a number of reasons. *Precaution* was a weak attempt to create a novel in the style of Jane Austen, and it had none of the qualities which we have come to expect in his own work. It was set in England, featured characters and concerns which were fashionable in British literature of the time, and was in fact even presented as being the work of an Englishman. But Cooper seems to have learned quickly from the experience.

LITERATURE AND THE AMERICAN REVOLUTION

His second book, *The Spy*, appeared scarcely a year later, and was pretty close to right on target; a rewrite in 1831 cleared up some problems attributed to hasty writing. *The Spy* presents a cast of real Americans, the Wharton family, living in Westchester County, just north of New York City in 1780, when the Revolution had turned their neighborhood into a hostile, if neutral, ground. One of the engagements described in the book took place in what is today the Bronx; the events in the novel otherwise occur in Westchester, Dutchess and Putnam counties. Much curious local history, which apparently fascinated Cooper, is also related about local brigands called "Skinners" and "Cow Boys." The story of a legendary local peddler and alleged spy is skillfully woven into the novel, as is the story of the very true betrayal of the American cause by a one-time war hero, General Benedict Arnold. With all of this material, Cooper creates mystery characters, including George Washington (who appears incognito), and the eponymous spy Harvey Birch himself; narrates plenty of military goings on; and pens colorful portraits of delightful American characters such as the African-American house servant Caesar, and the barmaid and camp-follower Betsy Flanagan, to name but a few.

There is a fine courtroom scene at the climax of the story, when young Henry Wharton, who is serving as an officer on the side of the British, is convicted of spying (which he did not). Henry's sister, Frances, pleads movingly for her brother's life: yes, he was out of uniform behind American lines but only to return home to visit his aging father. But she lets slip the fact that he indeed saw Birch, thus certainly condemning him by association. Frances's fiancé, (and Henry's dear friend), Major Dunwoodie, is in the American army, and he must ride to obtain a pardon for Henry in extremis.

The trope of the American family riven by domestic warfare would have to wait until the Civil War to become a cliché. The drama is superbly offset by detailed descriptions of the beauty of the American countryside, all of it most entertaining, while at the same time, stirring fine patriotic sentiment; all of it was just right for the times.

The book was an immediate success in the United States. A British edition took two years to reach that market, but thereafter the book did extremely well abroad and was translated widely in Europe before ten years had passed. This seems to confirm Cooper's every hope for his book, in retrospect.

What he could not have predicted was that he was also inventing a new genre entirely, that of the American war novel. Cooper wrote over two dozen more novels over the next thirty years, many of them involving military action on land and sea, and many which involved combat with and alongside native populations in New York and New England. Echoes of his work in the new genre can be found in American writing from Melville (*Israel Potter*) to the work of such contemporary writers as W.E.B. Griffin.

Charles B. Potter

See also: **Bunker Hill Monument; Cooper, James Fenimore; Flags; Fourth of July; Revolutionary War Veterans; Valley Forge.**

STAMP ACT CONGRESS

The Stamp Act Congress, which met in New York City from October 7 to 25, 1765, was the first gathering of representatives from several American colonies to devise a unified protest against British taxation. The congress adopted petitions to the British government spelling out the colonial grievances that would eventually lead to the Revolution while simultaneously laying the groundwork for future cooperation between the colonies. It was the forerunner of the Continental Congresses that would meet nearly a decade later to coordinate resistance to British policies.

The costs of fighting the French and Indian War (1754–1763) had left Great Britain burdened with an immense debt. British officials believed that the American colonists, who had benefited from the war by the expulsion of the French from Canada, and who were being protected from their Native American neighbors by British troops, should pay part of the expenses.

The first measure designed to increase revenues from the colonies, the Sugar Act of 1764, imposed import duties on foreign molasses while tightening enforcement of customs laws to reduce smuggling. Although many Americans disliked the Sugar Act, opposition was limited because the colonists accepted the British government's right to impose trade duties. But the next colonial revenue law, the Stamp Act, provoked fierce opposition.

The Stamp Act, passed in February 1765 and modeled on a tax already collected in Britain, required colonists to pay a small fee for newspapers, diplomas, wills, and other items. Unlike customs duties, which the colonists considered external taxes levied throughout the British Empire, the Stamp Act was an internal tax, to be levied within the colonies themselves. Americans believed that only their own elected legislatures could impose internal taxes.

By stepping beyond what Americans considered its legal limits, the British government's actions aroused fears that colonial liberties were in danger. Most colonists believed that corrupt government officials might next attempt to deprive the people of their rights and property, and that the first step in such a conspiracy would be unjust taxation. Frightened by the possibility that the Stamp Act was part of such a plan, angry colonists protested in a variety of ways.

Colonial legislatures petitioned the king and Parliament, declaring their loyalty but insisting that the stamp duties violated Americans' right to be taxed only through their own legislatures. Other forms of protest included boycotts of imported British goods; appeals to the public, through newspaper essays and pamphlets, to resist the Stamp Act; and eventually violence. The act was scheduled to take effect on November 1, 1765, and as that date approached the colonists held mock funerals for liberty, demanded the resignation of the officials appointed to collect the tax, and sometimes burned them in effigy. Many stamp agents promptly resigned; some of those who showed reluctance were threatened and their property was attacked by mobs. The most violent protests occurred in Boston, where a crowd devastated the home of Lieutenant Governor Thomas Hutchinson in retaliation for his support of the act.

The Massachusetts legislature took the lead in organizing the Stamp Act Congress by inviting other colonial legislatures to send representatives to meet and formulate a common policy of opposition. The congress convened in New York City on October 7, 1765, with delegates from nine of the thirteen colonies attending; Virginia, North Carolina, Georgia, and New Hampshire did not participate. The delegates chose Timothy Ruggles of Massachusetts as president and spent over two weeks discussing colonial rights and taxation. They produced petitions to the king and Parliament in which they clearly laid out the colonial position on these issues. The petitions stated that the colonists could only be taxed by their own consent, given through their elected representatives in the colonial legislatures. Since they were not represented in Parliament, and since their distance from London made such representation impractical, Parliament had no authority to tax the colonies. The congress also eliminated the distinction between internal and external taxation and asserted the colonists' right to tax themselves in all circumstances.

Protests from British merchants hurt by the American boycott and from the West Indies colonies, where the tax was also unpopular, together with the unrest in America, convinced Parliament to abolish the Stamp Act early in 1766. Colonial opposition had been so strong that officials had not been able to collect the tax in any of the thirteen colonies except Georgia. Parliament, however, passed the Declaratory Act at the same time it repealed the Stamp Act. This repudiated the claims of the Stamp Act Congress by asserting that Parliament had the authority to pass laws binding on the colonies in all possible cases.

The Stamp Act Congress had summarized the colonists' beliefs in their political rights while uniting them in opposition to British policy. Parliament had replied with its own assertion of supremacy. Thus the lines of argument were drawn, and they would produce a decade of disputes and eventually a colonial revolt against the British government.

BIBLIOGRAPHY

Morgan, Edmund S., and Morgan, Helen M. *The Stamp Act Crisis: Prologue to Revolution.* Chapel Hill: University of North Carolina Press, for the Institute of Early American History and Culture, 1995.

Proceedings of the Congress at New York (1766). Boston: John Carter Brown Library, 1938.

Jim Piecuch

See also: **Commonwealth Men; Peace of Paris, 1763.**

STATES AND NATION BUILDING, 1775–1783

The American Revolution represents a culmination of conflicting social, political and economic forces. Colonies became states and colonial charters often became state constitutions that gave most governmental power to the legislatures. Nevertheless, as the Revolution proceeded the states became building blocks for the nation within which Americans experimented in forming governments based on their experience, as well as on democratic and republican principles.

STATE CONSTITUTIONS

The creation of state constitutions was a significant achievement because, unlike charters, written constitutions were intended to explicitly limit the powers of government, rather than allow it to rely on custom and tradition. Moreover, state constitutions incorporated the republican principle that political power came from the people. Most state constitutions specified the separation of powers—executive, legislative, and judicial—in contrast to the British practice of mixing these powers on the basis of distinct social ranks: commons, aristocracy, and royalty. Furthermore, the 1780 Massachusetts constitution set a precedent of dividing the legislature into two houses, one representing ordinary people and the other the wealthy property holders of the state. The adoption of this constitution, written by John Adams, set another precedent that further entrenched the principle of "constitutionalism" in American culture. Instead of being approved by a legislature, the Massachusetts constitution was submitted to the voters, thereby making it in principle a fundamental law derived from the people and superior to legislative law; laws passed by the legislature had to conform to the constitution.

The Virginia constitution approved in 1776 incorporated a Bill of Rights that stated that government should protect the liberties of its citizens. In 1786, Virginia adopted a law of religious tolerance that separated church and state, a precedent followed by other states and incorporated in the federal Constitution. Pennsylvania had the most radical experiment. Its 1776 constitution was the most democratic of any state's. It allowed all adult males to vote, while other states restricted voting to males who owned property. Pennsylvania also eliminated the executive branch and reduced its legislature to one house.

The states began the abolition of slavery. In 1780 Pennsylvania passed a law emancipating slaves at age twenty-eight. Other states followed this example of legalizing gradual emancipation. In 1781, after the Massachusetts Bill of Rights declared all men free and equal and a slave won her freedom in a court case, slavery ended

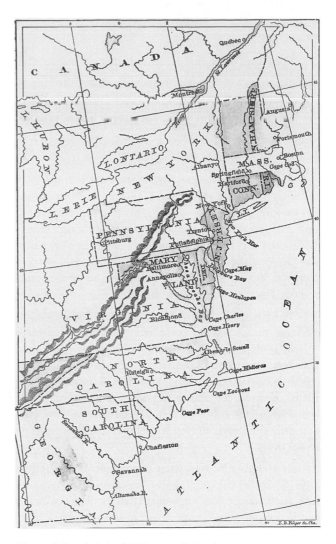

Map of the Original Thirteen Colonies. © BETTMANN/CORBIS

as institution in that state. Thus the states became laboratories for republicanism and their experiments in democracy affirmed the value of federalism, besides providing a foundation for the Constitution adopted in 1788.

STATES' RIGHTS AND THE REVOLUTIONARY WAR

The military necessity of unity and coordinated collective action made the war a force for national identity, but the distinctive political culture, history, and economy of each state determined the primary political identity of that state. And the ongoing struggle between national unity and states' rights has continued this fundamental constitutional tension throughout American history.

The American Revolution represents a period in U.S. history when the states' rights view was the dominant paradigm for governance; it was the revolution that brought cause for the states to confederate in the interest of their collective defense. Independent state militias had been the norm prior to the Continental Congress taking over the "troops of the United Provinces of North America" on July 4, 1775. The role of the states in providing soldiers for the Continental Army and militias was essential, yet the states varied significantly in their contribution to the cause: Massachusetts and Virginia provided fifteen battalions each, some others as few as one or two. [See figure 1.] The states, not the Continental Congress, bore the expenses of the soldiers' wages and pensions. Each soldier was clothed at the state's expense, and was provided with arms if not able to provide his own—these items were deducted from soldiers' monthly pay. The states had significant difficulty in recruiting the allotted number of soldiers, and they were forced to raise additional bounties.

FEDERALISM: LEGACY OF STATES' RIGHTS

The influence of the revolutionary era has left a long-standing legacy in American history, particularly with respect to the states' rights doctrine. The states maintained provincial authority before they confederated as the United States. The Articles of Confederation (1781) was the first U.S. constitution. Under the Articles, the United States successfully fought and won the war for independence from Great Britain, but there were weaknesses in the instruments of federal power needed to deal with emerging national issues. The Articles required amendment, but any changes required unanimity of the sovereign states and obtaining it proved a complex and daunting task.

The two sides in the debate over the scope and manner of changes were Federalist (nationalistic) and anti-Federalist (states' rights) views on war and the experiences during the revolutionary period. Even under the Constitution (1788), states retain powers not given the national government. The events during and after the revolution demonstrate state sovereignty in action, and foreshadow disputes to follow throughout U.S. history.

The Alien and Sedition Acts (1798) were a Federalist policy viewed by many southerners as a subversion of state authority, and their passage led to the Kentucky and Virginia Resolutions (penned by the Anti-Federalists Thomas Jefferson and James Madison, respectively)—the first firm statements interpreting the Constitution as defining a compact between the states and refuting federal authority over state issues. These works provide the foundation upon which the concepts of nullification (right of a state to declare a federal law null and void within its boundaries), and later secession, were based. The regional distinction, based largely on differences between urban and rural needs, later played out in the conversion of South Carolinian John C. Calhoun from a

FIGURE 1.

Proportion of contribution to war, September 16, 1776

State	Battalions	State	Battalions
New Hampshire	3	Delaware	1
Massachusetts	15	Maryland	8
Rhode Island	2	Virginia	15
Connecticut	8	North Carolina	9
New York	4	South Carolina	6
New Jersey	4	Georgia	1
Pennsylvania	12		

SOURCE: Bolton, pp. 49.

nationalist to a states' rights advocate, leading him to resign as vice president in 1832. The Nullification Crisis of that year came about as southern states felt more and more that northern policies no longer represented their interests or supported their rights.

Today, conflict over the balance between federal and states' rights endures. Whereas the national government has gradually increased its power over time, the modern Republican Party in the 1980s, under the leadership of Ronald Reagan, embraced the goal of returning authority to the states and decreasing the overall size of the federal government. The ideals of the Anti-Federalists continue to be expressed in twenty-first-century policy discussions—for example, on the issue of gay marriage—as states seek to retain their roles as crucibles of experiments in democracy.

BIBLIOGRAPHY

Bolton, Charles Knowles. *The Private Soldier Under Washington*. New York: Scribners, 1902.

Main, Jackson Turner. *The Sovereign States: 1775–1783*. New York: New Viewpoints, 1973.

Michael W. Hail and Jeremy L. Hall

See also: **Articles of Confederation; Constitution: Creating a Republic; Declaration of Independence; Stamp Act Congress.**

STONO REBELLION

Claiming roughly eighty black and white lives and involving as many as one hundred slaves and perhaps as many whites, the Stono Rebellion of September 1739 was one of the most significant and violent slave uprisings in colonial America. Although the rebels failed in their attempt to reach St. Augustine and claim freedom under Spanish rule, the revolt shaped South Carolina slave society in some important ways and its legacy lingered for years after the event.

The rebellion began at the Stono River in St. Paul's Parish, near Charleston, South Carolina. Several factors played a role in the timing of the rebellion. It is likely that the slaves organized their revolt to take place before September 29, when a certain provision was to go into effect requiring all white men to carry firearms to Sunday church services. It is also probable that many of the rebels were recently imported from the Kingdom of Kongo and that their religious beliefs (a syncretic form of Catholicism) influenced the uprising's timing. Contemporaries thought that the revolt was inspired in part by a visit to Charleston by a priest who relayed the Spanish offer of freedom in Florida. It is also likely that the slaves viewed a yellow fever epidemic that swept the area in August and September and rumors of war between Spain and England as fortuitous to their timing of the insurrection.

From Stono River, the rebels moved to Stono Bridge, where they equipped themselves with guns, killed five whites, and burned a house. Turning southward, they reached a tavern before sunup, sparing the innkeeper because they considered him "a good man and kind to his slaves" but killing his neighbors (Wood, p. 315). Other slaves joined the rebellion and, in Kongolese military fashion, the insurgents used drums, flags, and songs to inspire and fortify the group and coordinate their march southward.

South Carolina's Lieutenant Governor, William Bull, and four companions encountered the insurgents before noon, but managed to escape and warned other whites of the revolt. The rebels continued their march, pausing at the Edisto River to rest and also to draw more slaves to their ranks. At four P.M., up to one hundred armed planters and militiamen, possibly alerted by Bull, confronted the rebels. Even in the eyes of their enemies, the insurgents fought bravely. White firepower won the day, however. A few slaves were released but others were shot and some were decapitated, their heads displayed conspicuously on posts. About thirty rebels escaped, although most of them were captured the following week. But the revolt was not yet over and fighting continued in piecemeal fashion at least until the following Sunday, when militiamen encountered and defeated a group of disbanded rebels. White fears lingered and the militia remained on guard. Some of the insurgents were rounded up in the spring of 1740, with one leader eluding capture until 1742.

LEGACY OF SLAVE UPRISING

The Stono Rebellion reminded whites that although they had successfully discovered conspiracies in 1714 and 1720, not all plots could be detected. The ferocity of the revolt led authorities to try to increase the number of whites in the predominately black colony and beef up rules concerning the surveillance and regulation of slaves. On November 8, 1739 the South Carolina General Assembly appointed a committee to consider how to safeguard against future insurrections. The principal outcome of the committee's deliberations was the so-called Negro Act of 1740; in historian Darold D. Wax's estimation, "a thorough revision of the South Carolina slave code that survived into the nineteenth century" (Wax, p. 139). Designed to regulate more closely the activities of slaves and free blacks, the Act restricted the manumission of slaves and mandated patrol service for militiamen. The colony also imposed a prohibitive duty on the importation of new slaves in 1741 in an effort to stem the growth of South Carolina's slave population. A system of rewards for slaves who betrayed plots and imminent revolts was initiated, and finally, South Carolina tried to inspire loyalty to their owners by introducing slaves to a slanted form of Christianity.

Although these provisions placed tighter controls on slaves, they were not wholly effectual in regulating slave behavior. South Carolina slaves continued to revolt and conspire periodically throughout the colonial and antebellum period. Moreover, the drive for profit ensured that the moratorium on the slave trade lasted only three years, and by the mid 1740s, African slaves were again being imported at a rate and level that ensured that South Carolina's black population would remain large. However, the ferocity of the Stono Rebels heightened the anxieties of whites over internal security in South Carolina slaveholding society for years to come. The example of the Stono insurrection inspired some northern abolitionist literature in the antebellum period and remained in the memories of African Americans well into the twentieth century.

BIBLIOGRAPHY

Olwell, Robert. *Masters, Slaves, and Subjects: The Culture of Power in the South Carolina Low Country 1740–1790*. Ithaca, NY: Cornell University Press, 1998.

Pearson, Edward A. "'A Countryside Full of Flames': A Reconsideration of the Stono Rebellion and Slave Rebelliousness in the Early Eighteenth-Century South Carolina Lowcountry." *Slavery and Abolition* 17, no. 2 (1996): 22–50.

Smith, Mark M. "Remembering Mary, Shaping Revolt: Reconsidering the Stono Rebellion." *Journal of Southern History* 67, no. 3 (2001): 513–534.

Thornton, John K. "African Dimensions of the Stono Rebellion." *American Historical Review* 96, no. 4 (1991): 1101–1113.

Wax, Darold D. "'The Great Risque We Run': The Aftermath of Slave Rebellion at Stono, South Carolina, 1739–1745." *Journal of Negro History* 67, no. 2 (1982): 136–147.

Wood, Peter H. *Black Majority: Negroes in Colonial South Carolina From 1670 through the Stono Rebellion.* New York: Norton and Co., 1975.

Mark M. Smith

See also: **Bacon Rebellion; Revolution and Radical Reform; Slavery and the Homefront, 1775–1783; Slavery in America.**

SUPREME COURT

The War for Independence created a new nation, which the Supreme Court helped to shape. Authorized by the federal Constitution (ratified in 1788) and formed by the Judiciary Act of 1789, the Court was expected by some to be the weakest of the three branches of government. In the next forty years, however, as it dealt with the legacies of the Revolutionary War, the nation's territorial expansion, and issues of diplomacy, war, trade, and economic development, the Court played a key role in establishing the foundations for American society and culture.

LEGACIES OF THE REVOLUTION

One of the tasks resulting from the War for Independence and facing the Supreme Court was the definition of American citizenship, which was essential for resolving litigation involving the prosecution of treason and the confiscation of property during that war. Looking to state procedures, the Court determined the date at which residents of a state were required to choose between loyalty to Great Britain and adherence to their revolutionary state government. After that date, individuals who remained in the state and accepted its protection would be considered citizens and thus subject to prosecution for treason if they joined in warfare against their state. However, some property rights, such as a married woman's right to dower in her husband's real estate, were not affected by a spouse's treasonable or disloyal actions.

During the American Revolution, most state governments enacted laws seizing the real or personal property of inhabitants who remained loyal to the British crown, and other state legislation canceled the debts Americans owed to British mercantile firms, but the Peace Treaty of 1783, as subsequently strengthened by the Jay Treaty of 1794, raised serious questions about the validity of these state actions. The debt cancellation issue was resolved by the U.S. Supreme Court in 1796, when it held that the states could not impede the collection of debts owed to British merchants when the fed-

eral government had by treaty guaranteed that these obligations would be paid (*Ware v. Hylton,* 1796). However, for over thirty years after the end of the Revolution the seizure of real property and the attempted forfeiture of land by state inheritance laws remained in litigation until the Supreme Court's decisions in 1812 and 1816 (*Fairfax's Devisee v. Hunter's Lessee,* 1812; *Martin v. Hunter's Lessee,* 1816). After closely examining the treaty provisions and state confiscation procedures, the Court held that when the transfer of title had been completed prior to the ratification of the peace treaty the state's action would be irrevocable; however, if the seizure was still in process at the time the treaty came into effect, the state's action was contrary to international law and hence invalid.

EXPANSION, WAR, AND FEDERAL AUTHORITY

During John Marshall's tenure as chief justice of the Supreme Court (1801–1835), the United States embarked on what was then often described as its Manifest Destiny: to expand across the North American continent through the acquisition of new territories by purchase and conquest. The most notable and largest acquisition before 1824 was the Louisiana Purchase (1803). Although the Constitution authorized Congress to make rules for the administration of federal territories, it was silent concerning the legal and constitutional requirements for annexation except to the extent that treaties were perhaps authorized for this purpose. Although the Louisiana Purchase's constitutionality was never presented to the Court, the 1819 treaty acquiring Florida from Spain required the Court to rule on the issue. In *American and Ocean Insurance v. Canter* (1829), the Court indirectly approved of the annexation of Florida, giving judicial sanction to the purchase. Increasingly, the duty to protect settlers, maintain order, and govern territories fell to the military and naval departments of the federal government.

In the first three decades after the Constitution was ratified, the Napoleonic Wars resulted in American commercial ships being seized by both England and France, triggering a quasi-war with France (1797–1800) and outright war with Britain (1812–1815). The Supreme Court became heavily involved in establishing an American law concerning prize cases—the capture and forfeiture of enemy vessels as a result of economic warfare between warring nations. Under international law, the existence of hostilities justified the capture of enemy vessels. Hostilities also validated the seizure of neutral merchant ships that violated international law by trading illegally or violating an established naval blockade. Admiralty courts could declare both the goods in the ship and the ship itself forfeit to the capturing vessel and

John Marshall, Chief Justice of the United States Supreme Court (1801–1835).

courts were required to enforce the decrees of the old federal court of appeals. This ruling confirmed the supremacy of the federal government in admiralty and maritime matters and validated the authority of the central government in the adjudication of prize cases.

Prior to the Civil War (1861–1865), the federal government maintained an extremely small military establishment, a situation based in part upon a distrust of standing armies inherited from the seventeenth-century English experience of government by Oliver Cromwell's major generals. The U.S. Constitution and supplementary legislation provided for state militia units, which under specified circumstances might be called into federal service to repel invasion or suppress riots. A 1795 congressional statute began the process of training militia units to meet federal standards, but the division of state and federal authority remained unclear. Some of the difficulties are shown by the U.S. Supreme Court decision in *Houston v. Moore* (1820), which dealt with a Pennsylvania militia private who refused to appear for his unit's rendezvous during the War of 1812. For this offense he was court-martialed, convicted, and fined by the state. Houston argued that the state court-martial did not have jurisdiction because under the U.S. Constitution he was part of the military forces of the United States. The Supreme Court reasoned that the state and federal courts had concurrent jurisdiction in this situation and that an offense might be subject to punishment by both the federal and state governments. The *Houston* case represents the beginning of a long line of cases that grew out of the dual and interconnected authority of the federal government and the states in militia command, training, and administration.

In its constitutional decisions, the Marshall Court made a major contribution in delineating the central government's authority. Foremost in this regard is the opinion in *McCulloch v. Maryland* (1819), which advanced the principle that although the federal government was limited in its scope it was supreme in areas where it exercised constitutional authority. Furthermore, Marshall pointed out that in addition to its enumerated powers the central government had all the constitutional authority that was "necessary and proper" to effectuate its exercise of the Constitution's enumerated powers. In the areas of war powers and the conduct of international diplomacy, the Marshall Court and its successors have tended to be deferential to the policy decisions made by the president and Congress.

its crew. The practice was expanded by governmental commissions authorizing private ship owners to capture enemy ships and bring them into port for trial in admiralty courts. These entrepreneurs were called privateers, and wartime provided an excellent opportunity to establish a fortune through privateering.

An appeal caused Chief Justice John Marshall and his colleagues to review the prize cases decisions of lower federal courts. This jurisdiction in federal tribunals predated the Constitution's ratification (1788), and during the Confederation period had been exercised by a committee of the Continental Congress and after 1781 by a federal Court of Appeals in Cases a of Prize and Capture. It was a decision of the old federal court of appeals that almost resulted in military conflict between the Commonwealth of Pennsylvania and the U.S. government; however, the Supreme Court resolved the conflict by its decision in *U.S. v. Peters* (1809). In its decree, the Marshall Court held that under the Articles of Confederation the federal court of appeals was empowered to review the decisions of the state admiralty courts. Furthermore, under the Constitution the new federal

ECONOMIC GROWTH AND PROPERTY RIGHTS

The decisions of the Marshall Court made significant changes in the nation's economic life. Essentially, the Court laid the legal and constitutional basis for a stable capitalist economy through the contract clause decisions (*Fletcher v. Peck,* 1810; *Dartmouth College v. Woodward,* 1819), thereby encouraging foreign investment. Stability and respect for private property rights were critical to the prosperity of the new nation. The Constitution's introduction of a nationwide common market, greatly advanced by the Marshall Court's broad construction of interstate commerce (*Gibbons v. Ogden,* 1824), lessened dependence upon foreign imports and also made the United States a desirable trading partner in the Atlantic world. Economic growth based on commerce and industrialization began the process of America's rise to world power and increased the need for military and naval organizations to defend expanding territorial limits and protect American national interests throughout the world.

The magnitude of the Marshall Court's achievements made the court an important branch of the federal government. At the same time that the Court grew in stature, it also enhanced federal power in matters of military, naval, and international concern. Although most of the legal and constitutional aspects of waging war were left for future Supreme Courts to resolve, the Court under Marshall made it clear that issues of federalism and separation of powers were to be resolved by the Supreme Court of the United States. As the military and naval forces of the United States grew in size and function, the Court would exercise growing authority concerning the war powers of the United States government.

BIBLIOGRAPHY

Currie, David P. *The Constitution in the Supreme Court: The First Hundred Years, 1789–1888.* Chicago: University of Chicago Press, 1985.

Hawkins, George L., and Johnson, Herbert A. *Foundations of Power: John Marshall, 1801–1815,* vol. 2: *History of the Supreme Court of the United States.* New York: Macmillan, 1981.

Hobson, Charles F. *The Great Chief Justice: John Marshall and the Rule of Law.* Lawrence: University Press of Kansas, 1996.

Johnson, Herbert A. *The Chief Justiceship of John Marshall, 1801–1835.* Columbia: University of South Carolina Press, 1997.

Kuttner, James H. *The Development of American Citizenship, 1608–1970.* Chapel Hill: University of North Carolina Press, 1978.

White, G. Edward. *The Marshall Court and Cultural Change, 1815–1835,* vols. 3 and 4 in one: *History of the Supreme Court of the United States.* New York: Macmillan, 1988.

Herbert A. Johnson

See also: **Supreme Court and War Powers; War of 1812.**

SUPREME COURT AND WAR POWERS

Throughout the nineteenth century the U.S. Supreme Court had little direct involvement in the administration of military or naval forces. However, as the ultimate authority on international law in the United States, and as an appellate court dealing with property issues decided either in the subordinate federal courts or in the highest courts of the states having jurisdiction, the Court had a small but measurable impact on military policy. Before John Marshall became chief justice in 1801, the small number of litigated cases and the lack of extensive international warfare prior to 1797 limited the Court's influence in military and naval affairs. However, the outbreak of the quasi-war with France (1798–1800) directed the justices' attention to military matters. Eventually, the American law of warfare would become a point of major concern and a great deal of disagreement, as complex legal and constitutional issues arose concerning the consequences of the American Revolution and the conduct of the War of 1812.

THE SUPREME COURT AND THE AMERICAN REVOLUTION

During the Revolution most state governments enacted laws seizing the real or personal property of their residents who remained loyal to the British crown. One of the fundamental tasks facing the Marshall Court was the definition of American citizenship, which was essential for resolving litigation involving the prosecution of treason and the resolution of related property issues. Looking to state procedures, the Court determined the date by which residents of the state were required to choose between loyalty to Great Britain or adherence to their revolutionary state governments. Beyond that date, individuals who remained in the state and accepted its protection would be considered citizens and thus subject to treason prosecutions if they joined in warfare against their state. However, some property rights, such as a married woman's right to dower in her husband's real estate, were not affected by her spouse's treasonable or disloyal actions. Citizenship also played a role in the adjudication of prize cases, or cases resulting from economic warfare between warring nations. Ships and goods owned by American merchants and captured on the high seas by U.S. warships during time of war were protected from forfeiture. On the other hand, an American merchant who continued to reside in enemy territory after war was declared might be considered to have so incorporated himself into the nation of his residence that he could no longer claim American character for his property.

Other state legislation passed during the Revolution purported to cancel the debts Americans owed to British mercantile firms. The Peace Treaty of 1783, as subsequently strengthened by the Jay Treaty of 1794, raised serious questions about the validity of states' canceling such debts as well as seizing loyalists' property during the Revolution. The debt cancellation issue was resolved by the U.S. Supreme Court under the leadership of John Jay in 1796, where the Court held that the states could not impede the collection of debts when the federal government had by treaty guaranteed that these obligations would be subject to collection by the British merchants (*Ware v. Hylton*, 1796). However, the seizure of real property and the attempted forfeiture of land by state inheritance laws remained in litigation until 1816 (*Fairfax's Devisee v. Hunter's Lessee*, 1812; *Martin v. Hunter's Lessee*, 1816). Closely examining the treaty provisions and the nature of the state procedures for seizure, the Court ultimately held that when the transfer of title had been completed prior to the ratification of the Peace Treaty, the state's action would be irrevocable. However, if the seizure was still in process at the time the treaty came into effect, the state action was contrary to international law and hence invalid.

These war-related issues led to the development of rules in the U.S. Constitution concerning the impact of international law on the new American Union. Article 6 of the Constitution mandated that treaties made under the authority of the United States, even if entered into prior to the ratification of the Constitution (1788), were the supreme law of the land. The constitutional authority to enter into treaties was securely vested in the president, who would conduct the foreign relations of the United States and ratify treaties after receiving the consent of the Senate. Although the Supreme Court has been called upon to resolve questions concerning the treaty-making process and the resulting private rights, beginning in the Marshall era the resolution of international relations questions has traditionally rested with the president and Congress.

THE MARSHALL COURT: INTERNATIONAL CONFLICT AND THE WAR OF 1812

John Marshall and his judicial colleagues were required by the Constitution to review on appeal decisions by the lower federal courts on prize cases, which resulted from economic warfare. This jurisdiction in federal tribunals pre-dated the Constitution's ratification and had been exercised during the American Revolution by a committee of the Continental Congress; after 1781, a Federal Court of Appeals in Cases of Prize and Capture oversaw such cases. Under international law, the existence of hostilities between warring nations justified the forcible capture of enemy vessels as well as those neutral ships that violated international law by trading illegally or violating an established naval blockade. Admiralty courts in appropriate cases could declare both the goods in the ship, and

the ship itself, to be forfeited to the capturing vessel and its crew. This practice was enhanced by governmental commissioners, who could authorize private ship owners, called privateers, to capture ships of the enemy and bring them into port for trial in admiralty courts. Wartime provided an excellent opportunity to establish a family fortune through privateering.

During the American Revolution the United States relied heavily on neutral shipping to supply its commercial needs and equip its armies. As a consequence, it had adopted a policy of armed neutrality. This policy significantly benefited neutral commercial nations but was rejected out of hand by Britain, which dominated the seas with its powerful navy. During the War of 1812 the Supreme Court, along with the lower federal courts, found itself engaged in the establishment of a law concerning prize cases. This was an area in which the justices differed sharply among themselves. Justice Joseph Story and the majority favored the adoption of British rules concerning prize cases; Chief Justice Marshall objected to this, pointing out that most English prize decisions were unduly favorable to the capturing vessel and crew. These disagreements ultimately shattered the seeming unanimity, from 1801 through 1810, of the Marshall Court. As the War of 1812 progressed, the Supreme Court became more suspicious of British and neutral practices that made it difficult to determine whether the vessel or goods were truly neutral in character.

The case *U.S. v. Peters* (1809) almost resulted in military conflict between Pennsylvania and the U.S. government. In December 1778 the Federal Court of Appeals in Cases of Prize and Capture had reversed a Pennsylvania state admiralty court's prize decree. But U.S. District Judge Richard Peters refused to accept the reversal, arguing that the jury verdict was final as a matter of state law. Because of this deadlock, the property involved was sold at auction and the proceeds were held in an escrow account. Judge Peters refused to order the estate of the stakeholder to pay over the escrowed amount, and the U.S. Supreme Court was asked to direct Peters to follow the Federal Court of Appeals order.

Pointing out that the state of Pennsylvania was not a party, Marshall rejected the argument that the Eleventh Amendment to the Constitution nullified the authority of the federal district courts. He then held that the old Federal Court of Appeals had full authority to review and in appropriate cases to revise or reverse the orders of state admiralty courts. The Peters case highlights the primacy of federal court jurisdiction in all matters of prize and capture. This overriding authority of the federal court is necessary to support the diplomatic and military initiatives of the U.S. government, and to ensure that international law is enforced in a uniform manner throughout the United States.

THE SUPREME COURT AND MILITARY SERVICE

Prior to the Civil War (1861–1865) the federal military establishment was extremely small. The nation still maintained a distrust of standing armies, in part because of England's seventeenth-century experience of government by Oliver Cromwell's major generals. The U.S. Constitution and supplementary legislation provided for state militia units that, under specified circumstances, might be called into federal service to repel invasion or suppress riots. A 1795 congressional statute began the process of training militia units to meet federal standards, but the division of state and federal authority remained unclear.

The U.S. Supreme Court decision in *Houston v. Moore* (1820) illustrates the problem the nation faced regarding authority over the military. A Pennsylvania militia private who refused to appear at the place of his unit's rendezvous during the War of 1812 had been tried and convicted by court-martial. A Pennsylvania state marshal then levied against Private Houston's property to collect the fine imposed by the court-martial. Houston brought a civil case against the Pennsylvania marshal, arguing that the state court-martial did not have jurisdiction because, under the U.S. Constitution, he was part of the military forces of the United States. In the Supreme Court's decision, Justice William Johnson reasoned that the state and federal courts had concurrent jurisdiction in this situation, and that an offense might be subject to punishment by both the federal and state governments. Furthermore, the states might use their tribunals to enforce U.S. law as well as their own statutes. Johnson made a distinction between being "called forth" and actually being in "active service." It was the state of being in service that made a militiaman a member of the federal forces. The *Houston* case represents the beginning of a long line of cases involving the dual and interconnected authority of the federal government and the states in militia command, training, and administration.

In its constitutional decisions the Marshall Court made a major contribution to the law of war by clarifying the central government's authority. The most important case in this regard is *McCulloch v. Maryland* (1819) The Court's opinion advanced the principle that, although the federal government was limited in its scope, it was supreme in areas where it exercised constitutional authority. Furthermore, Marshall pointed out that, in addition to its enumerated powers, the central government had all the constitutional authority that was "necessary and proper" to effectuate its exercise of the Constitution's enumerated powers. On the matters of war powers and the conduct of international diplomacy, the Marshall Court and its successors have tended to defer to the policy decisions made by the president or congress, or both.

WAR AND SOCIETY: LEGACY OF THE MARSHALL COURT

During the Marshall era the United States embarked on its Manifest Destiny—to expand across the North American continent through the acquisition and settlement of new territories. The largest and most notable acquisition before 1824 was the Louisiana Purchase (1803) and portions of Florida (1812–1819). Although the Constitution authorized Congress to make rules for the administration of federal territories, it was silent concerning the legal and constitutional process for annexations (except to the extent that peace treaties were perhaps authorized for this purpose). In *American and Ocean Insurance v. Canter*, the Court indirectly approved of the annexation of Florida in the 1819 Treaty of Washington, thereby giving judicial sanction to the extension of American territory through purchase. Increasingly, the duty to protect settlers, maintain order, and govern territories fell within the responsibilities of the military and naval departments of the federal government.

The economic decisions of the Marshall Court have also shaped national life. The Court, through decisions that encouraged foreign investment, laid the legal and constitutional basis for a stable capitalist economy. Had the United States instead remained an agricultural nation, the nation's military needs would have developed differently. Furthermore, stability and respect for private property rights were critical to the prosperity of the new nation. The U.S. Constitution's introduction of the concept of a nationwide common market, greatly advanced by the Marshall Court's broad construction of interstate commerce, lessened dependence on foreign imports and also made the United States a desirable trading partner in the Atlantic world. Economic growth based on commerce and industrialization began the process of America's rise to world power. This increasing power in turn increased the need for military and naval organizations to defend the expansion of territory and protect American national interests throughout the world.

BIBLIOGRAPHY

Currie, David P. *The Constitution in the Supreme Court: The First Hundred Years, 1789–1888*. Chicago: University of Chicago Press, 1985.

Haskins, George L., and Johnson, Herbert A. *History of the Supreme Court of the United States*, Vol. 2: *Foundations of Power: John Marshall, 1801–15*. New York: Macmillan, 1981.

Hobson, Charles F. *The Great Chief Justice: John Marshall and the Rule of Law*. Lawrence: University Press of Kansas, 1996.

Johnson, Herbert A. *The Chief Justiceship of John Marshall, 1801–1835*. Columbia: University of South Carolina Press, 1997.

Kettner, James H. *The Development of American Citizenship, 1608–1970*. Chapel Hill: University of North Carolina Press, 1978.

White, G. Edward. *History of the Supreme Court of the United States*, Vols. 3 and 4 in one: *The Marshall Court and Cultural Change, 1815–35*. New York: Macmillan, 1988.

Herbert A. Johnson

See also: Constitution: Creating a Republic; Federalist Papers; Federalist Party; Hamilton, Alexander; Jefferson, Thomas; Madison, James; Memory and Early History of the Revolution; Monroe, James; Supreme Court.

VALLEY FORGE

Between December 19, 1777, and June 19, 1778, the American Continental Army camped on about 2,000 acres of ground in a Pennsylvania community called Valley Forge, approximately twenty miles northwest of Philadelphia. While there, approximately 11,000 men under the command of General George Washington constructed light shelters and defensive earthworks, endured a harsh winter, trained, and executed rigorous military drills. Initially ignored by historians, the Valley Forge story was "rediscovered" during the mid-nineteenth century. Romantic Era authors emphasized the hardships of the encampment and caused it to be adopted as a national symbol of perseverance and sacrifice resulting in eventual triumph. Citizens joined efforts to preserve the campground where monuments and reconstructions were built during the late nineteenth and early twentieth centuries to interpret the story.

DEPRIVATION AND RENEWAL

No battles were fought at Valley Forge, but historians acknowledged the encampment as a turning point in the American Revolution because the troops overcame many deprivations and went on to fight. Documentary records indicate that the winter was not particularly severe, but exposure to the elements combined with the camp's poor sanitation led to significant losses from disease. Certain regiments were also poorly clothed, making many men unfit for duty. In one letter, George Washington mentioned a lack of shoes so severe that the men's "marches might be tracked by the blood from their feet," a phrase that permanently linked the powerful image of bloody footprints to the Valley Forge encampment (Washington to Barrister, pp. 284–293).

Just days after his men marched into Valley Forge, it seemed to Washington that mutiny was imminent when the soldiers, faced with short supplies, began chanting "no meat," and "no bread, no soldier." Washington intentionally invoked the strongest possible language in his most famous letter from Valley Forge, warning Congress that his army would "starve, dissolve, or disperse" if the politicians failed to adequately supply it. A committee appointed by Congress to inspect conditions at the camp arrived during another supply crisis in February, and Washington succeeded in achieving the military supply system reforms he desired.

Another reason historians consider Valley Forge a military turning point is the transformation made by In-

George Washington at Valley Forge. During the harsh winter of 1777–1778, approximately 11,000 men trained and executed rigorous military drills.

spector General Friedrich von Steuben. He drafted a training manual and initiated a system of standardized military training that turned a group of diversely trained men into a more efficient fighting force. In 1777 Washington had essentially taken command of a new army because some men's terms expired and new recruits arrived, leaving him with only a small core of veterans. Washington began their training, but von Steuben took over in March 1778, introducing drills to a small model unit before imposing them on the entire army. The army's heroic suffering, its perseverance, and its renewed strength made Valley Forge a legendary symbol of American character.

PRESERVING THE LEGEND

Most Americans of the late eighteenth and early nineteenth centuries tended to be rather indifferent to their Revolutionary War history. Only when veterans of this conflict began dying off, and later, during the Romantic Era of the mid-nineteenth century, Americans transformed the mundane tale of soldiers suffering and surviving the rigors of the winter camp at Valley Forge into

an inspiring legend in which virtue triumphed after sacrifices were made. The American fascination with Valley Forge intensified in the late nineteenth and early twentieth centuries when an increasingly industrialized society populated by a growing number of foreigners seemed to threaten American values. The resulting Colonial Revival Movement was a period of artistic and cultural renewal lasting approximately from 1880 to 1940 when Americans looked nostalgically back to the Colonial and Revolutionary periods of the nation's history and were inspired to collect and reproduce antiques and preserve and restore old buildings and places of historic importance, such as Valley Forge.

In 1850 Henry Woodman wrote a series of letters for a regional newspaper about his youth at Valley Forge that helped spread the encampment's fame. In 1877, interested citizens formed an organization to celebrate on a grand scale the centennial of the army's exit from Valley Forge and to preserve the modest house that had served as Washington's headquarters. A Pennsylvania state legislator lobbied to establish a state park at Valley Forge, resulting in the creation of the Valley Forge Park

Commission in 1893. This committee researched the encampment and used appropriated funds to purchase the land where the army had camped and the soldiers had constructed their earthworks. Governor Samuel Pennypacker appropriated additional funds for roads and historic markers early in the twentieth century.

States and patriotic organizations soon decorated the grounds with monuments, a trend culminating with the 1917 dedication of the National Memorial Arch funded by the U.S. Congress, making it the nation's gift honoring the historic importance of Valley Forge. Later in the twentieth century, when the popularity of Williamsburg inspired other historical reconstructions, the Valley Forge Park Commission instituted a project intended to evoke the military encampment at Valley Forge with a number of restorations and reconstructions, most notably replica log huts representing the structures that had housed the soldiers. On July 4, 1976, President Gerald Ford signed a bill into law making Valley Forge a national park. In the early years of the twenty-first century, the park service began working with a private organization to form a model public/private partnership to build the Center for the American Revolution at Valley Forge.

SYMBOL OF PATRIOTISM

While visiting Valley Forge in 1828, antiquarian John Fanning Watson wrote, "On those hills, were miserably hutted the forlorn hope of the country in its day of most gloomy peril." In his 1860 book titled *The Pictorial Field-Book of the Revolution*, Benson Lossing opens his chapter on Valley Forge by stating, "There, in the midst of frost and snows, disease and destitution, Liberty erected her altar; and in all the world's history we have no record of purer devotion, holier sincerity, or more pious self-sacrifice, than was there exhibited" (vol. 2, p. 125). Valley Forge has come to symbolize American perseverance, faith, courage in adversity, and willingness to sacrifice for freedom, aspects of the national character poignantly illustrated by war.

BIBLIOGRAPHY

Bodle, Wayne. *The Valley Forge Winter: Civilians and Soldiers in War*. University Park, PA: The Pennsylvania State University Press, 2002.

Lossing, Benson J. *The Pictorial Field-Book of the Revolution*, 2 vols. New York: Harper & Brothers, Publishers, 1860.

Treese, Lorett. *Valley Forge: Making and Remaking a National Symbol*. University Park, PA: The Pennsylvania State University Press, 1995.

Trussell, John B.B., Jr. *Birthplace of an Army: A Study of the Valley Forge Encampment*. Harrisburg, PA: Pennsylvania Historical and Museum Commission, 1976.

Washington to John Banister, April 22, 1778, in *The Writings of George Washington from the Original Manuscript Sources, 1745–1799*, vol. 11, ed. John C. Fitzpatrick. Washington, DC: Government Printing Office, 1934.

Watson, John Fanning. *Trip to Valley Forge and the Camp Hills*. Philadelphia: Historical Society of Pennsylvania, 1928.

Lorett Treese

See also: **Bunker Hill Monument; Flags; Lafayette's Tour; Monroe's Tour of New England; Revolutionary War Veterans; Washington, George.**

VETERANS' BENEFITS

Veterans' benefits played a vital role in the development of the nation and its institutions and contributed significantly to the welfare of many citizens. In addition to salary and enlistment bonuses paid to men fighting in American forces, four basic kinds of public benefits were created in recognition of their service and its consequences: pensions for veterans disabled in combat; pensions for the widows and orphans of men killed in combat; grants of land in western regions of the country; and pensions for men based on service alone, or on service combined with poverty.

EARLY AMERICAN ORIGINS

The earliest American veterans' benefits were pensions established by individual colonies for men who were disabled in combat and rendered incapable of earning a living. These "invalid" pensions reflected the English practice of supporting poor, wounded, and disabled soldiers. As early as 1624, the general assembly of Virginia voted to create pension benefits for Englishmen injured in wars against Native Americans and colonists from other countries. In 1636, Massachusetts authorities resolved that any man disabled in the service of the Plymouth Colony would be adequately cared for at the public's expense for life. Some of the colonies also established survivors' pensions for the widows and orphans of men killed in combat. In order to qualify for survivors' benefits, veterans' widows and orphans typically had to be poor and in need of public support.

The outbreak of war with Great Britain required Americans to consider how to provide for men maimed in the war for independence and the survivors of those killed. Despite its limited authority, the Continental Congress enacted disability pension legislation in 1776, promising half pay for life (or during disability) to officers, soldiers, and sailors of the Continental Army or Navy who lost limbs in combat or were otherwise rendered incapable of earning a living. In 1780, the Continental Congress also created the first national-level pensions for widows and orphans in the United States, granting the survivors of Continental Army officers half pay for seven years. It was left to the individual states to supply these benefits and to provide for men serving in the militia and other state-level forces.

U.S. DISABILITY AND SURVIVORS' PENSIONS

After the Constitution was ratified, the newly-established Congress of the United States voted to make the payment of Revolutionary War disability and survivors' benefits a federal responsibility and vested the authority for program administration with the Secretary of War. Between 1792 and 1828, Congress repeatedly extended the deadline for establishing Revolutionary War disability claims. The law providing pensions to the Continental officers' survivors was allowed to expire in the mid-1790s. Much broader legislation was passed in 1836, granting half pay for life to the widows and orphans of Revolutionary War veterans who had died (or would die) from wounds received in the service of the United States.

These benefits were a vital source of public assistance for disabled veterans and veterans' survivors. They provided an honorable source of income for persons harmed by war—a source that was distinct from poor relief. They also forged tangible and psychic links between citizens and national authorities at a time when the U.S. government played a minimal role in the everyday lives of the American people. The last federal law specifically benefiting Revolutionary War widows was enacted in 1878, over a century after the nation's formative war began. Because young women marrying aged veterans were eligible for survivors' benefits, widows remained on the Revolutionary War pension list until the last one died in 1906.

The Revolutionary War pensions served as policy precedents in later wars. The establishment of disability and survivors' benefits was vital to the U.S. government's efforts to raise troops to fight the War of 1812, the Mexican War, and the Civil War. With the Act of 1862, Congress established pensions for those killed or disabled in the service of the United States in the Civil War and all subsequent wars, acknowledging both the government's obligation to provide and the likelihood of future military conflict. Rebels injured or killed in the service of the Confederacy were not entitled to federal veterans' benefits, even after the nation was reunited and the federal pension system grew to unprecedented proportions.

LAND GRANTS FOR VETERANS

In 1776, the Continental Congress devised the nation's first program of veterans' land entitlements, promising land to officers and soldiers serving in the Continental Army for the duration of the Revolution. Acreage was determined by military rank, and claims had to be located in western military districts established by the government. George Washington and other leaders believed that sending veterans to settle the frontier would encourage Native Americans to relinquish their territory and migrate to the far west. However, many Revolutionary veterans eager to realize their benefits sold their land certificates to speculators for cash long before 1796, when the Fourth U.S. Congress finally established a military district in Ohio.

The failure of military land warrants to bring about western settlement did not deter Congress from creating new veterans' land entitlements before, during, and after subsequent wars. Laws enacted in 1811 and 1814 created (and then increased the size of) land grants for soldiers and noncommissioned army officers serving in the War of 1812.

That men enlisting late in the war received more land than those who served longer was a source of conflict, as was the fact that the army's officers (and naval veterans) were not entitled to land at all. The officers lobbied Congress intensely into the 1830s but could not convince a majority that they were deserving of benefits, even when disability and poverty were added as qualifying criteria. Army officers were again passed over when Congress voted to offer land grants to veterans of the Mexican War. However, in laws enacted between 1850 and 1855, Congress gradually entitled all men (including officers) who had served for a minimum of fourteen days in any American war since 1775, and their survivors, to 160 acres of the public domain. Men who served in Union forces in the Civil War believed themselves deserving of military land grants, but they received only the same acreage promised to ordinary citizens under the Homestead Act of 1862.

SERVICE PENSIONS

Pensions granted primarily on the basis of service, in the absence of injury or disability, were the most controversial of early U.S. veterans' benefits. At the time of the nation's founding, many believed that such pensions violated core American values. Military leaders convinced the Continental Congress that granting Continental Army officers half pay for life (and soldiers a one-time grant of $80) was necessary to the success of the Revolution, but its decision was extremely unpopular, and the nation lacked the resources to provide the pensions at war's end. Not until 1818, after victory in the War of 1812, would Congress create a service pension program for men who had served for a minimum of nine months in the Continental Army or Navy and who also were poor and willing to ask for their country's support.

The 1818 service pension law reflected the aged Revolutionary War veterans' increasingly positive image.

However, many members of Congress and the public objected to certain aspects of the law, including its exclusion of many Revolutionary War veterans (especially the militia) and its requirement that surviving patriots be poor in order to qualify for benefits. Still others criticized the pension program's cost and argued for retrenchment as national economic conditions deteriorated with the Panic of 1819. Remedial legislation passed in 1820 cut many veterans from the pension rolls, but afterward the program expanded greatly. Congress voted to restore certain benefits to Continental officers in 1828, and in 1832 granted service pensions to militia officers and soldiers, volunteers, and state troops. Despite intense pressure, Congress would not enact service pensions for War of 1812 veterans until 1871. Many Union veterans of the Civil War received pensions because of generous interpretations of the disability benefit laws, but strictly speaking Congress never created a true service pension program for Civil War veterans.

The pensions and land grants created for veterans and their survivors constituted America's original system of public social benefits. In addition to enhancing the economic welfare of individuals and families, they encouraged enlistment, giving shape to the militia and to national-level military forces. They also fostered a sense of public purpose through the expenditure of common resources. Although they were sometimes controversial, early pensions and land grants bound citizens together as a people, turning their imaginations and energies toward the conquest of a continent through war, the extermination of native peoples, and westward migration and settlement.

BIBLIOGRAPHY

Glasson, William H. *Federal Military Pensions in the United States*, edited by David Kinley. New York: Oxford University Press, 1918.

Jensen, Laura. *Patriots, Settlers, and the Origins of American Social Policy.* Cambridge, UK: Cambridge University Press, 2003.

McConnell, Stuart. *Glorious Contentment: The Grand Army of the Republic, 1865–1900.* Chapel Hill: University of North Carolina Press, 1992.

Resch, John. *Suffering Soldiers: Revolutionary War Veterans, Moral Sentiment, and Political Culture in the Early Republic.* Amherst: University of Massachusetts Press, 1999.

Laura S. Jensen

See also: **Republicanism and War; Revolutionary War Veterans; Widows and Orphans.**

WAR OF 1812

The War of 1812 was the first major war fought by the United States under the Constitution. It was also the second and last time that the nation waged war against Great Britain. The contest was a direct outgrowth of the Napoleonic Wars (1803–1815). The United States went to war to force the British to give up the Orders-in-Council, which regulated American trade with the European Continent, and impressment, which was the Royal Navy's practice of removing seamen from American merchant ships on the high seas.

The United States declared war on June 18, 1812, after little preparation. The congressional vote was relatively close: 79 to 49 in the House and 19 to 13 in the Senate. Declaring war against a major power after such limited preparation and against the wishes of a large minority of the American people was decidedly risky. Jeffersonian Republicans were willing to take this risk because they were confident that if the British did not cave into their demands, the conquest of Canada would be, in the words of former president Thomas Jefferson, "a mere matter of marching" (Letter to William Duane, August 4, 1812). Once conquered, Canada would be held as ransom for concessions on the maritime issues. If the British refused to make concessions, then presumably Canada would be permanently annexed.

The British repealed the Orders-in-Council five days after the declaration of war but were unwilling to give up impressment because they considered the practice essential to maintaining their naval power and thus their war effort against Napoleon. Hence, despite the interest that both sides showed in terminating the war quickly, it dragged on for two and a half years.

BATTLE AND CAMPAIGNS

In the campaign of 1812, the United States launched a three-pronged assault against Canada that ended in disaster. One army surrendered at Detroit when Major General William Hull lost his nerve; a second U.S. army under Lieutenant Colonel Winfield Scott surrendered on the Niagara frontier when American militia refused to cross the border to reinforce the regulars who had established a beachhead on the Canadian side; and a third army under Brigadier General Henry Dearborn conducted little more than a demonstration on the St. Lawrence front before returning to the United States.

The United States launched another three-pronged campaign in 1813, and this time it was more successful, but only in the West. Commodore Oliver H. Perry defeated a British fleet on Lake Erie, which enabled Major General William Henry Harrison to crush an Anglo-Indian army in the Battle of the Thames fifty miles east of Detroit. The great Indian leader and British ally, Tecumseh, was killed in this battle. Perry added more luster to his name by sending Harrison a message that read: "We have met the enemy and they are ours." Further east, however, the United States made no headway, and after two years of campaigning, Canada remained in British hands.

In 1814 the initiative in the war shifted to the British because Napoleon's defeat in spring had ended the war in Europe, thus enabling Great Britain to concentrate on the American war. The United States launched a bloody but inconclusive offensive on the Niagara frontier, but elsewhere the British took the offensive. One British army retreated from New York when a spectacular American naval victory by Commodore Thomas Macdonough on Lake Champlain gave the United States command of this crucial waterway. A second British army successfully occupied eastern Maine.

A third British army achieved mixed results in the Chesapeake, occupying Washington and burning the public buildings there but then giving up an attack on Baltimore because the American defenses were too formidable. A British naval bombardment of Fort McHenry at Baltimore prompted Georgetown lawyer Francis Scott Key to write "The Star-Spangled Banner," describing the artillery barrage. A final British assault on the Gulf Coast in early 1815 was rebuffed by Major General Andrew Jackson's forces at New Orleans in one of the most lopsided defeats in British military history.

Both sides in this war had trouble mounting successful offensive operations. Waging war in remote wilderness areas posed such difficult logistical problems that fate usually favored the defending side. Hence, on the battlefield the War of 1812 ended in a draw.

In the war at sea, the United States won a series of impressive frigate duels early in the war, but thereafter an ever tightening British naval blockade kept most American warships in port. American privateers did considerable damage to British trade, although getting prizes to a friendly port was always problematical. Moreover, British warships and privateers took a heavy toll on those American merchantmen that ventured to sea. In the end, British naval power triumphed in the war at sea, although the United States made a much better showing than anyone had anticipated.

MEN AND MONEY

The United States faced persistent problems raising men and money to fight and finance this war. Despite offering princely bounties (which by the end of the war amounted to two or three times the annual income of an unskilled civilian laborer), recruitment for the U.S. Army always lagged behind need. At the end of the war, army strength was only at around two-thirds of its authorized level.

The United States found it no easier to raise money to finance the war. When a major war loan failed in the summer of 1814, public credit collapsed. The government defaulted on the national debt and was forced to rely increasingly on treasury notes, a form of short-term, interest-bearing paper money that banks and army contractors were increasingly reluctant to accept, even at a steep discount. Had the war lasted much longer, the popular phrase from the American Revolution, "not worth a Continental," might have been replaced by "not worth a treasury note." The government's financial problems were compounded by a weak economy. Unlike most American wars, the War of 1812 did not stimulate prosperity. Although the middle Atlantic and western states profited from large war contracts and a surge in manufacturing, New England and the southern states suffered from the British naval blockade, which made it risky to send ships and commodities to sea. The nation's primitive road system made it costly to ship goods overland, and in the coastal trade only short voyages in shallow waters were likely to be safe.

FEDERALIST OPPOSITION

Compounding the U.S. government's problems in waging this war was the opposition of the Federalists, which was more determined and partisan than the nation has experienced in any other foreign war. Federalists voted unanimously against the declaration of war in Congress, and thereafter they presented a united front against most war measures. They opposed all bills to raise men and money, to authorize privateering, or to restrict trade with the enemy, although they supported proposals to increase the navy and coastal fortifications because they considered these measures defensive in character.

Even though Federalists everywhere opposed the war, the opposition was stiffest in New England, where the unpopularity of the war enabled the party to win control of all five states. Federalists in this section wrote, spoke, and preached against the war; they refused to enlist in the army and discouraged subscriptions to the war loans; and on occasion their governors withheld their militia from federal service.

The climax of New England's opposition was the Hartford Convention, a regional conference held in the winter of 1814 to 1815 to protest the war and other Republican policies, provide for the defense of the region, and propose amendments to the Constitution to protect New England's position in the Union. The war ended

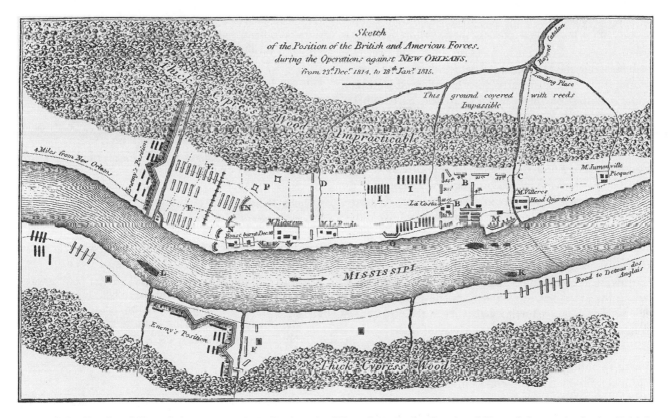

Map of the Battle of New Orleans, ca. 1815. During the War of 1812, the Battle of New Orleans dealt the British one of their most lopsided defeats, 2,036 men killed versus 71 Americans, and made Andrew Jackson a hero.
© BETTMANN/CORBIS

before any action could be taken on these proposals, and their effect was to further discredit the Federalist party in other parts of the Union.

THE TREATY OF GHENT

Peace feelers sent out by the United States in 1812 produced no agreement, and the British refused a Russian mediation offer the following year. The two sides met for direct negotiations in summer of 1814 in Ghent in modern-day Belgium. The United States was represented by a strong delegation that was headed by John Quincy Adams and included rising congressional star Henry Clay and former secretary of the treasury Albert Gallatin.

By the time the negotiations got under way in August, the United States had dropped its impressment demands, but the British, now in the driver's seat in the war, laid out their own terms. They demanded the establishment of an Indian barrier state in the Old Northwest, the surrender of territory in northern Minnesota and Maine, the unilateral demilitarization of the Great Lakes, and an end to American fishing privileges in Canadian waters. The American delegation adamantly refused to make any concessions, and gradually the British dropped their demands.

On December 24, 1814, the two nations signed the Treaty of Ghent (also known as the Peace of Christmas Eve). This agreement provided for ending the war and returning to the *status quo ante bellum* (the state that existed before the war) as soon as both governments had ratified. The British ratified the treaty on December 27; the United States on February 16, 1815. Both sides immediately proclaimed an end to hostilities, although desultory fighting continued in remote parts of the world for several months. The last engagement took place in the Indian Ocean on June 30, 1815, when the USS *Peacock* (carrying 22 guns) compelled the surrender of the East Indian cruiser *Nautilus* (14 guns).

CONSEQUENCES

The War of 1812 ended in a draw, and the maritime issues that United States had fought for were not mentioned in the peace treaty. Although the American people might have blamed the Republicans for a failed war policy, they chose instead to focus on the great victory at New Orleans and to view the war as a success. As a result, a number of Americans leaders (such as Andrew Jackson, William Henry Harrison, James Monroe, Henry Clay, and John Quincy Adams) were able to capitalize on their service during the war to advance their public careers. The Federalists, on the other hand, saw their wartime popularity vanish. Opposition to the war, so popular while the conflict raged, suddenly seemed unpatriotic. The Federalist party quickly collapsed as a national organization and survived as a viable party only in New England.

The war affected other people as well. Some four thousand runaway slaves, mainly from the Chesapeake, found sanctuary and freedom with the British. Other black Americans capitalized on manpower shortages to make a mark for themselves in the army, navy, and privateers. American Indians, on the other hand, were the heaviest losers in the war. The relentless drive to dispossess them of their lands gained momentum as a result of Harrison's victories in the Northwest and Jackson's in the Southwest. Never again would Native Americans pose a serious threat to the United States, and never again would they be able to secure foreign assistance in their campaign to hold on to their lands and their way of life.

The war had other lasting effects. It promoted nationalism and patriotism and produced several enduring national symbols: Uncle Sam (who was probably named after a Troy, New York, army contractor named Samuel Wilson); the Fort McHenry flag, which is now in the Smithsonian and is the nation's most revered and tangible link to the war; and "The Star-Spangled Banner," which gradually surpassed other patriotic songs and was designated the national anthem by Congress in 1931. Defense spending received a boost as a result of the war. The navy's wartime victories against the acknowledged Mistress of the Seas gave notice to the world of a rising naval power, and this service won a special claim on the nation's resources that even penny-pinching, land-locked congressmen acknowledged. The United States acquired part of West Florida during the war, although this acquisition came at the expense of the hapless Spanish rather than the enemy. In Europe, Americans enjoyed a new-found respect. Even the British were careful not to alienate the young republic in the postwar era, frequently subordinating other interests to promote Anglo-American accord.

At the time, Republicans claimed that the War of 1812 was a second war of independence. Although the nation's independence was never really at stake, there is no denying the this inconclusive war shaped the future of the young republic in a host of ways that reverberated across the Atlantic and through history.

BIBLIOGRAPHY

Altoff, Gerard T. *Amongst My Best Men: African Americans and the War of 1812*. Put-in-Bay, OH: Perry Group, 1996.

Benn, Carl. *The Iroquois in the War of 1812*. Toronto: University of Toronto Press, 1998.

Engelman, Fred L. *The Peace of Christmas Eve*. New York: Harcourt, Brace and World, 1962.

Hickey, Donald R. *The War of 1812: A Forgotten Conflict*. Urbana: University of Illinois Press, 1989.

Hitsman, J. Mackay. *The Incredible War of 1812: A Military History* [1965]. Revised edition by Donald E. Graves. Toronto: Robin Brass Studio, 1999.

Horsman, Reginald. *The Causes of the War of 1812*. Philadelphia: University of Pennsylvania Press, 1962.

Perkins, Bradford. *Prologue to War: England and the United States, 1805–1812*. Berkeley: University of California Press, 1961.

Quimby, Robert S. *The U.S. Army in the War of 1812: An Operational and Command Study*, 2 vols. East Lansing: Michigan State University Press, 1997.

Roosevelt, Theodore. *The Naval War of 1812*. New York: Putnam's Sons, 1882.

Skeen, C. Edward. *Citizen Soldiers in the War of 1812*. Lexington: University Press of Kentucky, 1999.

Stagg, J.C.A. *Mr. Madison's War: Politics, Diplomacy, and Warfare in the Early American Republic, 1783–1830*. Princeton, NJ: Princeton University Press, 1983.

Donald R. Hickey

See also: **Federalist Party; Flags; Jackson, Andrew; Monroe, James.**

WARREN, MERCY OTIS

(b. September 5, 1728; d. October 19, 1814) Dramatist, Historian, and Poet.

Mercy Otis Warren was the first American woman to publish poems, plays, and nonfiction about politics and war, subjects that had traditionally been considered the exclusive province of men. During the crisis leading up to the American Revolution, her satirical pieces attacked the tyrannical injustice of British government in the colonies. After the war, her scathing critique of the proposed U.S. Constitution and a three-volume history of the Revolution secured her reputation as an astute political commentator. Yet throughout her career, questions about the appropriateness of a woman writing about quintessentially masculine affairs continued to haunt her.

Born in Barnstable, Massachusetts, to a politically active family, Warren received a more sophisticated education than most girls of her day. Tutored along with her brother, James Otis, she not only learned to read and write, but became familiar with the great works of history, literature, and philosophy. James went off to Harvard and then began a career as a lawyer and politician, while she continued to educate herself and started to write poetry, mostly on nonpolitical matters. In 1754 she married James Warren, a wealthy trader and farmer from a nearby town. Over the next twelve years, she gave birth to five sons. During this same period, Mercy's husband, brother, and father all assumed leadership roles in the resistance against Great Britain. By the early 1770s, John Adams, a family friend who knew of Mercy's talent for writing verse, encouraged her to use her pen in support of the patriot cause. She did so with great success.

Warren's earliest political writings assailed royal officials in Massachusetts for their attempts to deprive colonists of their freedom. In 1772 Warren published a political satire, a play called *The Adulateur*, followed in 1773 by another play, *The Defeat* and in 1775 by *The Group*. In each piece she attacked the corruption and cowardice of Lieutenant Governor Thomas Hutchinson and his cronies for currying favor with the Crown at the colonists' expense. At the same time, she published poems in Boston newspapers that urged Americans to assert their virtue, resist British taxes, and boycott British tea and other goods. Especially after the closing of the Boston Port in 1774, she warned that stronger measures might be necessary. Reprinted in newspapers in New York and Philadelphia, her works helped prepare Americans to take up arms against British tyranny.

Warren published these works anonymously. Like male political satirists at the time, she sought to elude harsh British libel laws as well as avoid personal retribution from those she had attacked. She may also have feared that people would not take a woman's ideas seriously. Yet a close-knit circle of Massachusetts patriots did know that a woman had authored the works. Although they supported Warren's endeavors, they did so only because she was useful to their cause. They did not believe that women in general should express their political views publicly, much less be able to vote or hold public office. Warren was the exception, not the rule.

During the War for Independence, Warren began to compose another kind of work, a *History of the Rise, Progress, and Termination of the American Revolution*. Drawing on public papers, private correspondence, and her own knowledge, she published the monumental, three-volume work in 1805—this time under her own name. She was well aware that she was making herself vulnerable by writing about traditionally male subjects. Although she noted that she shied away from recounting "the blood-stained field and . . . the story of slaughtered armies," she believed that women had as much at stake in the country's history and future as did men. "Every domestic enjoyment," she said, "depends on the unimpaired possession of civil and religious liberty" (Warren, p. xlii).

Unlike her Revolutionary era propaganda, however, the *History* attracted more criticism than praise. Over time, Warren had grown disaffected with the course of American society. She had publicly opposed the ratification of the U.S. Constitution in a tract signed "A Columbian Patriot." Her *History* lamented America's path after the Revolution: the decline in public virtue, the growing distance between people and their government, and the increasing concentration of power in an aristocratic elite. The presidencies of George Washington and John Adams, she believed, betrayed the Revolutionary cause and put America on a path toward self-destruction. Thus, despite its detailed accounting and factual accuracy, her work did not find a large or receptive audience at the time. In fact, John Adams, stunned by her negative portrayal of him, dismissed the project, saying, "History is not the Province of the Ladies" (Zagarri, p. 159). Only in retrospect does the work's grandeur—and the full scope of Warren's achievements—appear in plain view.

BIBLIOGRAPHY

Anthony, Katharine S. *First Lady of the Revolution: The Life of Mercy Otis Warren*. New York: Doubleday, 1958.

Franklin, Benjamin, V., ed. *The Plays and Poems of Mercy Otis Warren*. Delmar, NY: Scholars' Facsimiles and Reprints, 1980.

Richards, Jeffrey H. *Mercy Otis Warren*. New York: Twayne Publishers, 1995.

Warren, Mercy Otis. *History of the Rise, Progress and Termination of the American Revolution* [1805], 2 vols., edited by Lester Cohen. Indianapolis, IN: Liberty Classics, 1988.

Zagarri, Rosemarie. *A Woman's Dilemma: Mercy Otis Warren and the American Revolution*. Wheeling, IL: Harlan Davidson, 1995.

Rosemarie Zagarri

See also: **Drinker, Elizabeth; Madison, Dolley; Memory and Early Histories of the Revolution; Republican Womanhood. Sampson, Deborah.**

WASHINGTON, GEORGE

(b. February 22, 1732; d. December 14, 1799) Revolutionary War general and statesman, first president of the United States (1789–1797).

"First in war, first in peace, and first in the hearts of his countrymen" were the words spoken of George Washington when he died. Long before the American Revolution, George Washington was a military hero. Leading a small militia unit and American Indian allies, he ambushed a detachment of Frenchmen thus provoking the French and [American] Indian War. At the age of twenty-two,

Washington became commander in chief of the Virginia militia. He served as a special adviser to General Edward Braddock in the ill-fated campaign that ended in disaster near the Monongahela River in 1755. Washington escaped unscathed from this battle and courageously led the badly defeated troops to safety. His experiences in the war were invaluable and his exploits became legendary.

After unsuccessfully applying for a commission in the British army, Washington retired to private life and after 1763 became active in the colonial opposition to Britain's new imperial policy. As a member of the Virginia House of Burgesses, Washington gained recognition for an eloquent speech in which he denounced the Intolerable Acts and vowed that if the British attacked Boston, he would march to their relief at the head of a thousand men at his own expense.

Elected to the Second Continental Congress by Virginia, Washington alone arrived in Philadelphia wearing a military uniform. On June 15, 1775, the Continental Congress elected him commander in chief of the colonial forces.

On his way to take command of the New England army bottling up the British forces in Boston, Washington was feted by the New York Provincial Congress. Remembering Oliver Cromwell's perfidy in ruling Commonwealth England with his army, a New Yorker asked Washington if he and his officers would promise to surrender their commissions at the end of hostilities. Washington responded that when he and his officers put on their military uniforms, they never ceased to be citizens. They were citizens first and soldiers second. They surely would surrender their commissions.

Washington served as commander in chief for the entire Revolutionary War. His achievements were remarkable. He kept a citizen's army in the field for over eight years even though it was outnumbered by the enemy, ill-provisioned, and unpaid by Congress. He withstood intrigues against him by fellow officers and Congressmen, periodic mutinies, and ineffective and unreliable state militias. Washington's charismatic leadership kept the army intact despite terrible hardships.

During the last year of the war, Washington defeated a potential military coup (March 1783), and in a June 1783 circular to the states, he announced that he would retire at the end of the war. In this first farewell address, Washington called for continuing the Union, strengthening Congress, replacing the militias with an effective military establishment, and paying the war debt and back pay of the army, the officers' pensions, and benefits for widows and orphans of soldiers. When the British evacuated, Washington fulfilled his promise by surrendering his commission to the [Continental] Confederation Congress in December 1783.

Because of the crisis in American affairs, Washington was called out of retirement and served in the Constitutional Convention from May to September 1787. The confidence that Washington would serve as the first president under the new Constitution led the Convention to give the president significant powers and contributed greatly to the willingness of Americans to ratify the Constitution.

Washington was unanimously elected president in 1789. He depended upon great statesmen for advice—Thomas Jefferson as secretary of state, Alexander Hamilton as secretary of the treasury, and James Madison as the leader of the House of Representatives. As political parties formed over policy disagreements, Washington stood above party. As president, Washington's goals were to persuade the American public to accept the new Constitution and the federal government, to revive American finances and commerce, to keep America out of the maelstrom of European politics and war, to enter into treaties with neighboring American Indian tribes, to remove the British from their old Revolutionary War forts located on American soil near the Great Lakes, and to obtain Spanish permission for Americans to navigate the full length of the Mississippi River. All of these goals were accomplished. Washington's every act as president set precedent as he gave the new government a chance to survive in a dangerous world unfriendly to republican forms of government.

After two terms in office, Washington retired, setting a precedent for future presidents. Years after Washington's death, Jefferson said of him that it was his "singular destiny and merit" to lead "the armies of his country successfully through an arduous war, for the establishment of its independence; of conducting its councils through the birth of a government, new in its forms and principles, until it had settled down into a quiet and orderly train; and of scrupulously obeying the laws through the whole of his career, civil and military, of which the history of the world furnishes no other example" (Letter to Walter Jones, January 2, 1814).

BIBLIOGRAPHY

Ferling, John E. *The First of Men: A Life of George Washington.* Knoxville: The University of Tennessee Press, 1988.

Flexner, James Thomas. *Washington: The Indispensable Man.* Boston: Little, Brown and Company, 1969.

Grizzard, Frank E., Jr. *George Washington: A Biographical Companion.* Santa Barbara, CA: ABC-CLIO, 2002.

Higginbotham, Don. *George Washington: Uniting a Nation.* Lanham, MD: Rowman & Littlefield, 2002.

Kaminski, John P., and McCaughan, Jill Adair, eds. *A Great and Good Man: George Washington in the Eyes of His Contemporaries.* Madison, WI: Madison House, 1989.

Smith, Richard Norton. *Patriarch: George Washington and the New American Nation.* Boston: Houghton Mifflin Company, 1993.

Wills, Garry. *Cincinnatus: George Washington & the Enlightenment.* Garden City, NY: Doubleday, 1984.

John P. Kaminski

See also: **Jefferson, Thomas; Madison, James; Monroe, James; Marshall, John.**

WASHINGTON'S FAREWELL ADDRESS

Near the end of his second term as president, George Washington decided not to seek reelection. With Alexander Hamilton's assistance, he crafted an address that offered his wisdom and advice to the nation. Washington's 1796 farewell address, which reflected the president's experiences in war and peace, has become a reference point for American identity and relations with the world.

The first goal of the address was to inform the nation he would not seek office again: "I should now apprise you of the resolution I have formed, to decline being considered among the number of those out of whom a choice is made." He went on to explain that he had originally hoped to retire in 1783, but at the time felt his country still needed him. He expressed gratitude to the country and assured the people he still cared a great deal about the nation's future. Washington's decision not to seek a third term set a precedent expressing the Revolution's republican ideal that public officials were servants of the people rather than rulers for life. The two-term limit was later incorporated into the Constitution in the Twenty-second Amendment.

Washington next stressed the importance of unity and explained that the nation was truly the sum of all its parts. In his view, North and South, East and West, engaged in a relationship in which all benefited from being together. He also stressed the importance of unities among the different political factions within the country. He was speaking from direct experience of the time, when the followers of Jefferson were at odds with the followers of Hamilton. Washington also pointed out that only in unity was there strength against "external danger."

The speech then discussed foreign policy. Washington asked people to "observe good faith and justice towards all nations; cultivate peace and harmony with all." He urged the young nation not to play favorites with other nations. Having sympathy for a favored nation clouded judgment and would lead America to participate in the wars and disputes of a favorite nation without just cause. This type of favoritism, Washington stated, also inspired jealousy among the countries that had not been favored.

Washington was clearly drawing on his past experiences. During his military service, he saw the immense toll of war, both in the French and Indian War and the Revolution. Later, as president, he understood even further the difficulties of foreign entanglements. The year of Washington's inauguration was the year of the French Revolution. At first, Americans remembered the kindness of the French during the American Revolution, and hoped for the best outcome. But when France declared war on England in 1793, the Hamiltonians sided with the English and the Jeffersonians sided with the French. Washington was wary of any commitment to France and pushed for neutrality.

Washington's farewell address argued that foreign influence was "insidious" and "one of the most baneful woes of republican government." In one place the government might see danger, but in another place danger and undue influence might be concealed by an alliance. He saw no reason for the United States to interweave its destiny with Europe's, to "entangle our peace and prosperity in the toils of European ambition, rivalship, interest, humor or caprice." Any existing alliances should be honored, he believed, but it was wise to stay away from permanent alliances with any foreign nations.

In truth, there was only one course of action the nation could take with regard to foreign policy—to have "as little political connection as possible" while still maintaining fair and regulated trade. In Washington's view, Europe's interests and internal quarrels belonged in Europe, and it would have been unwise to implicate our country in those foreign struggles. His suggested course for the future was for the United States to remain distant and detached from Europe. Neutrality would bring a universal respect from all nations and would make anyone think twice about provoking the United States.

Still, harmony toward nations and impartial limited dealings with them were acceptable, so long as the United States remembered that favors were not free and came at a price; the nation "must pay with a portion of its independence."

The words of the president went a long way in forming a general political philosophy for the nation. The Alien and Sedition Laws of 1798 continued in this spirit, and went as far as to allow the government to expel any foreigner whom it considered dangerous. Washington's words were also echoed in the so-called Monroe Doctrine of 1823 that warned all foreign nations not to interfere in American territory. Over the next 140 years, only when pushed or provoked to the very limit of its patience—in 1812, 1917, and 1941, most notably—did the United States enter into a war.

America's entry into World War II in 1941 marked a new era in the nation's foreign policy. As a result of events more than ambition, the United States became a world power. The war against totalitarianism, the Cold War, and the War on Terror have fundamentally reversed the advice given by Washington in his farewell address. To remain at peace and to ensure trade and prosperity, the nation has abandoned neutrality and detachment from alliances to embrace diplomatic, economic, and military globalism. These changes profoundly affected American identity, society, and culture in the last half of the twentieth century and will continue to do so in the twenty-first.

BIBLIOGRAPHY

Burns, James MacGregor, and Dunn, Susan. *George Washington.* New York: Times Books, 2004.

Flexner, James Thomas. *George Washington: Anguish and Farewell (1793–1799).* Boston: Little, Brown and Company, 1972.

Gordy, Wilbur F. *A History of the United States.* New York: Charles Scribner's Sons, 1920.

Internet Resource

"The Papers of George Washington." Available at <http://www.gwpapers.virginia.edu/index>.

Richard Panchyk

See also: **Lafayette's Tour; Memory and Early Histories of the Revolution; Washington, George.**

WYOMING VALLEY CONFLICT

On Christmas Day in 1775, six months before the outbreak of the war that would make the United States a nation, Americans in the Wyoming Valley of the Susquehanna River, in what is now Pennsylvania, were already engaged under arms in a bitter fight among themselves. This little-known conflict is sometimes referred to as the Pennamite Wars.

The dispute had been growing since 1754 when an association of Connecticut residents purchased a parcel of land, which they intended to settle and farm, from the Six Nations at a tribal council in Albany "for 2,000 pounds of current money in New York." The association, calling itself the Susquehanna Company, at that time numbered fewer than six hundred souls. It was not for another ten years that they would begin to settle their land. By then, the Pennsylvania colony, which claimed the land as its own, and the Connecticut colony, with an equally valid claim extending back to the British Crown

itself, had entered the fray. The fighting began as early as 1769, when a faction of local Pennsylvanians known as Pennamites began harassing and driving off Yankee settlers from their homes on the eastern bank of the Susquehanna near Jacob's Plains. Most returned right away. By 1775 violent skirmishes between the two parties were common. On Christmas in 1775 a bloody confrontation took place at Forty Fort, claiming lives and leaving many wounded. This period is known as the First Pennamite War.

The Revolutionary War put a halt to the fighting, but added its own dose of bitter feeling to the brew. The British induced the Six Nations to take up arms against the Americans. Colonel John Butler accompanied the American Indians along with a party of Tories and a troop of British soldiers down the Susquehanna to destroy settlements in the Wyoming Valley. A few old men and some soldiers on leave from the Continental Army were defeated, and the survivors of the fight were put to the tomahawk. In all, some four hundred were massacred, an event that was immortalized in Thomas Campbell's 1809 narrative poem *Gertrude of Wyoming.* The Native Americans were punished for their role by the Continental Army under General Sullivan in 1779, but rancor in the valley remained.

When the Revolutionary War ended in 1783, the old dispute resurfaced. In 1782 the Decree of Trenton had been passed, assigning the right of jurisdiction and preemption to Pennsylvania, but as spring planting began in 1783 the Yankee settlers were still in the Susquehanna Valley. Pennamite sentiment flared once again; settlers were attacked, men were rounded up and whipped with rifle rods and made to lie in pens on the muddy ground. A rule that no more than two Yankee men could congregate in any place was put into effect, and on May 14 soldiers from Pennsylvania arrived with orders to drive the settlers out. Some five hundred took to the Lackawaxen Road headed back toward Connecticut. But they did not give up. Appeals were made to the Connecticut legislature, but many settlers did not wait for a decision to be reached and returned directly to their homes.

In the fall of 1785 there was a skirmish between Pennamites and Yankees in a piece of woods called Plymouth in which two were killed and several wounded. The Pennamites were driven back, but soldiers were again sent and there began a prolonged struggle. This period is known as the Second Pennamite War. The Yankees were defeated, but still refused to leave. In 1786 the Pennsylvania legislature took up the matter and both Pennamites and Yankees were expelled from Forty Fort, but it would take years before the Compromise Act (1799) settled all claims and peace finally came to the region, now known as Luzerne County in Pennsylvania.

These conflicts in the Wyoming Valley represent a feature of American society that has been overlooked and overwhelmed by attention given to the war with England. Before and during the Revolution, Americans were often at war with each other, and with American Indians, over land, and in some cases combatants used the Revolutionary War as a pretext to engage in vicious frontier warfare for their own ends, including revenge killings.

Charles B. Potter

Abolitionist: In the United States, anyone who campaigned against the continued practice of slavery during the eighteenth and nineteenth centuries.

Allies: The nations, including Great Britain, France, and the United States, among others, aligned against the Central Powers during World War I and against the Axis during World War II.

American Anti-Slavery Society: Abolitionist organization found in 1833 by William Lloyd Garrison and Arthur Tappan. Frederick Douglass was one of the group's most prominent members.

Americanization Movement: During the early part of the twentieth century, a social trend, partly driven by fear, towards pressuring recent immigrants to adopt American styles, values, and language.

(Anti)Rent War: An uprising in New York state in which disgruntled tenants resisted attempts by local sheriffs to evict them. Governor Silas Wright involved the state militia in 1845, and the violent phase of the anti-rent movement came to an end.

Antisuffragist: Anyone who opposed the right of women to vote.

Baltimore Riots: On April 19, 1861, a pitched battle between a mob of secessionists and a group of Union soldiers on its way through Baltimore. Four soldiers and twelve civilians were killed. Scores more were wounded. The encounter is often considered to be the first blood drawn in the American Civil War.

Barbary Coast: Common name for the waterfront area of San Francisco, California, in the years following the Gold Rush of 1849, when the area was famous for prostitution, gambling, crime, and a surfeit of notorious characters.

Barbary States: From the sixteenth to the nineteenth century, collective name of the North African countries of Morocco, Tunisia, Algeria, and Tripoli, and used especially to denote a time and an area in which ocean piracy was common.

Bedouin: A desert nomad, especially an Arab in the Middle East or North Africa.

Berber: Of or belonging to any of a number of Muslim North African tribes. Also, the language of those tribes.

Berlin airlift: In 1948 and 1949, the massive air transport into post-war Berlin of food, fuel, and other necessities by the Allies in response to a Soviet blockade of the divided city. By the end of the operation, more than two million tons of goods had been delivered.

Berlin blockade: In 1948, an attempt by the Soviet Union to force the United States and its allies out of Berlin by blocking access to their occupied territories. Following the success of the Berlin airlift, however, the Soviets were forced to abandon their plan and reopen the borders in May 1949.

Berlin Wall: Constructed in 1961 by the East German government, a wall to separate West Berlin from East Berlin. Among the most visible symbols of the Cold War, the Berlin Wall kept East Germans from crossing over into the west until November 1989 when a series of bureaucratic miscommunications led the government of East Germany to once again begin issuing visas. The wall was soon demolished.

Bey: In the Ottoman Empire, a denotation of rank or superior status. A provincial governor there.

Black Codes: Laws passed by former Confederate states to restrict the personal freedoms of recently freed slaves. Among their many notorious proscriptions were the segregation of places of public access and restrictions on the right to own property.

British Crown: The monarchy of Great Britain and the United Kingdom.

Bumppo, Natty: The hero of the so-called Leatherstocking Tales by James Fenimore Cooper (1789–1851), Bumppo was a tracker, a trapper, and an all-around outdoorsman. A voluntary outcast from his own society, Bumppo lived among Native Americans and was known by several nicknames, among them Hawkeye, Pathfinder, Leatherstocking, and Deerslayer.

Carte De Visite: Literally, a visiting card. One's photographic likeness, printed on a card for use as proof of identity.

Central Powers: During World War I, Germany and its military allies, including Bulgaria and the Ottoman Empire.

Civil Rights Movement: In the United States, the popular movement among African Americans and their supporters during the 1950s and 1960s to secure equal treatment under the law and to defeat segregation and other forms of institutionalized racism.

Committee On Public Information: Established in 1917 during World War I, the Committee spread propaganda to help increase support for the war in the United States.

Communism: A political ideology in which property and industry belong to the citizenry, rather than to individuals.

Constitution: Established in 1707 at the constitutional convention in Philadelphia, the foundational document of the United States. Originally consisting of a preamble and seven articles, the Constitution has been amended twenty-seven times.

Defense Plant Corporation: Organized in 1940, a government agency responsible for overseeing the production and finance of the facilities utilized by private defense contractors and manufacturers.

Department of the Treasury: Established in 1789, an arm of the federal executive branch charged with minting currency, advising the President on fiscal matters, and collecting taxes. The treasury department also administers the Secret Service.

Détente: A period or state of relaxed tensions between two military powers.

Dey: During the reign of the Ottoman Empire, the title given to the governor of Algiers.

Don't Ask, Don't Tell: Adopted in 1993 during the administration of President Bill Clinton, a policy on homosexuals in the United States military in which commanders agree to not attempt to learn a soldier's sexual orientation ("don't ask") as long as the soldier does not volunteer it ("don't tell").

Dred Scott Case: In 1857, a case before the United States Supreme Court. Dred Scott, a slave, argued that since he had lived for four years in a free territory that he should be declared free. The court disagreed, declaring that Scott was property and therefore could not seek status as a citizen of the United States.

E-mail: A method of communication whereby correspondence is instantaneously transmitted from one computer to another. Also, a communication sent or received by this method.

Euro-American: A citizen of the United States of European descent.

Federal: Denotes a system of government in which several regions or states agree to defer certain rights and responsibilities to a centralized authority.

First Lady: The wife of the president of the United States or of one of its state governors.

Founding Fathers: A collective name for the men who signed the Declaration of Independence and who helped to compose the Constitution of the United States.

Freedpeople: Slaves freed after or during the American Civil War.

G.I.: In military parlance, general issue, or that provided by the United States military to its soldiers. By extension, a soldier in that military.

Gorbachev, Mikhail: Soviet political leader (b. 1931), responsible for many pro-democratic reforms and the liberalization of Soviet society, Gorbachev was instrumental in improving relations with the United States and in helping to end the Cold War. Gorbachev resigned in 1991.

Gross National Product (GNP): The accumulated value of goods and services produced by the citizenry of a country within a year. Often used as an indicator of a country's economic health.

Gulf War: From January to February 1991, a military conflict between Iraq and a United States-led coalition of more than thirty countries. The war erupted after Iraq invaded Kuwait, its oil-rich neighbor, on 2 August 1990. Hostilities came to an end on 28 February with the rout of Iraqi forces during a short-lived ground war.

Habeas Corpus: A legal writ issued to order the physical production of a detained person as well as appropriate evidence of the necessity of continued detention. Literally, you should have the body.

House of Representatives: In the United States, the lower house of Congress.

Image-Maker: An individual or organization employed to help create a positive public image for another individual or organization, especially in politics and the entertainment industry.

Indian Wars: Collective term for a number of violent clashes between Native Americans and Europeans or people of European descent at various times during American history.

Internet: A global network connecting computers for the purpose of information exchange and communication through a variety of specialized servers, such as e-mail, bulletin boards, and the World Wide Web of on-line sites, magazines, newspapers, stores, and entertainment venues.

Jamestown colony: Founded in 1607, the first English settlement in North America. Jamestown was named for King James I.

Kansas–Nebraska Act: A law passed by Congress in 1854 that created the western territories of Kansas and Nebraska. In the end, the Act, which legalized slavery in the new territories in defiance of the Missouri Compromise, led to the rise of the Republican party.

Know-Nothings: During the 1850s, nickname for members of the American Party, nativists who opposed the holding of public office by immigrants and Roman Catholics. The name derived from the party's notorious secrecy and its unwillingness to answer questions about its activities.

Lame Duck: An elected official serving out his or her term after having been defeated or having decided not to seek another term. A figure of powerlessness.

Lend-Lease Act: Legislation passed in 1941 by the Congress, the Lend-Lease Act gave the president the discretion to sell, lease, or lend supplies and necessities during wartime to countries believed to be vital to the security of the United States.

Lopez de Santa Anna: General of the Armies of Mexico, politician, dictator, and twice President. Santa Anna (1794–1876) had a remarkable, often brutal, capricious, and mystifying career in his various roles. His most infamous military achievement was the capture of the Alamo and the slaughter of Texas revolutionaries in 1836. In and out of public favor his entire life, Santa Anna was twice exiled from Mexico, but at last allowed to return in 1874.

Lost Cause: During the American Civil War, another name for the cause of the Confederate states.

Manifest Destiny: A belief among many Americans of the nineteenth century, whereby the United States was thought to possess, by the grace of God, the right to expand to fill the whole of the North American continent.

Mexican War: From 1846 to 1848, military conflict between the United States and Mexico. Growing tensions between the two nations erupted into war with the United States' decision to annex Texas in December of 1845. In the negotiated peace, the United States won some two-fifths of Mexico's territory as well as $15 million in compensation.

Military-Industrial Complex: So called by President Dwight D. Eisenhower (1890–1969), a cautionary description of the relationship between the military and the industrial forces responsible for manufacturing military equipment. Eisenhower warned that such a collaboration might one day endanger the republic.

Militia: An army of civilians with military training who can be called upon to serve in time of war or national emergency.

Naiveté: A quality of excessive trustworthiness or belief in the fundamental goodness of human nature, often among the very young or inexperienced.

National American Woman's Suffrage Association: Organization of suffragettes that in 1920 became the League of Women Voters.

National Security Council Paper 68 (NSC #68): Ordered by President Harry S. Truman (1884–1972), an examination and reassessment of both the relative strengths of the Soviet Union and of the United States' strategy in containing or stopping the spread of Communism. Considered a seminal Cold War document, NSC #68 led to a massive military buildup and to increased tensions between the two global superpowers.

National Women's Party: Organization of suffragettes founded in 1916.

Nativists: Members of the American Party, known for its anti-immigration, anti-Catholic positions, and its belief that only "native born" Americans had the right to hold public office.

Nemattanew: Powhatan warrior and mystic. His murder by the English in 1622 led the Powhatan chief Opechancanough to make war against the English colonies, killing more than three hundred of the colonists.

Newburgh Conspiracy: In 1783, a plot by members of the Continental Army of the United States, stationed in Newburgh, New York, to overthrow the Congress by coup. A speech given by George Washington was instrumental in convincing the officers to set aside their plans.

Neoconservative: A political ideology in the United States that embraced the conservative policies and ideas of the Republican party, favored an active and robust military, and believed in the spread of democracy through armed intervention in undemocratic societies.

Opechancanough: Native American chief, and brother to Powhatan, Opechancanough (c. 1545–1644) was responsible for the capture of the English Captain, John Smith, and, indirectly, for Captain Smith's introduction to Opechancanough's niece, Pocahontas.

Pasha: Title used in Turkey and various Middle Eastern countries during the reign of the Ottoman Empire to denote a high-ranking official.

Patriot Missiles: A guided surface-to-air missile designed primarily to shoot down incoming missiles before they reach their targets. First widely deployed during the Gulf War in 1991, the Patriot Missile system, though at first reported to be successful, in fact shot down none of its intended targets and may have been responsible for firing on friendly Coalition aircraft.

Patriots: Before and during the Revolutionary War, the colonists who supported independence from Great Britain. Generally, anyone who proudly defends the actions or culture of his or her own country.

Policymakers: Those responsible for creating or crafting public policy, as legislators, politicians, or other elected or appointed officials.

Postwar: The period following the end of a military conflict.

Progressives: From 1900 to 1920, a political and social movement inside the United States that called for, among other things, a graduated income tax, direct election of the United States Senate, and government action to break up industrial monopolies.

Radical Republicans: Members of the Republican party during and after the American Civil War who advocated harsh Reconstruction measures as a way of punishing the former Confederate states.

Reconstruction Acts: Passed on May 31, 1870, February 28, 1870, and April 20, 1871, laws designed to curb illegal activity, such as that perpetrated by the Ku Klux Klan, in parts of the South after the end of hostilities in the Civil War. Among other things, the Reconstruction Acts levied harsh penalties against anyone who attempted to prevent recently freed slaves from voting.

Redcoats: Informal or derisive name given to British soldiers, especially those in the colonies before and during the American Revolutionary War.

Red Scare: Following the end of World War I and brought about largely by the onset of the Russian Revolution, a period of general suspicion and paranoia regarding the political beliefs of recent immigrants, a few hundred who were arrested and deported. A second scare occurred in the late 1940s as Americans began to fear that communists had infiltrated the highest levels of government and the entertainment industry.

Revolutionary War: From 1775 to 1781, the war of American independence, fought between the colonies in the New World and the forces of the British Crown.

SCUD Missiles: Short-range ballistic missiles used by the Iraqi military, especially during the Gulf War of 1991.

Senate: In the United States, the highest house of Congress.

Slaughterhouse Cases: A number of cases heard by the United States Supreme Court in 1873 involving the legality of a twenty-five year monopoly granted by the Louisiana state legislature to a single slaughterhouse operator in New Orleans for the purpose of protecting the public health. The court ruled that the state had not violated the 14th amendment, as had been charged.

Slave-Power Conspiracy: Before the American Civil War, a belief among many northerners, to some degree perpetuated by the Republican Party and abolitionist groups, that the South planned to marginalize the North by extending slavery into the western territories and Central America.

Spanish American War: In 1898, a military conflict between the United States and Spain on behalf of Cuba. Its victory increased the standing of the United States as a legitimate world power.

Sunset Laws: Laws designed with a specific date of termination.

Supreme Court: The highest federal court in the United States, composed of a chief justice and eight associate judges. The Supreme Court was established by Article 3 of the United States Constitution. Its justices are appointed by the President and serve for life.

Texas Revolution: Beginning in 1835, Texas' war of independence from Mexico. The conflict involved the famous battle at the Alamo and ended in 1836 when Samuel Houston defeated Santa Anna and forced him to recognize the independence of Texas.

Three-Fifths Compromise: An agreement reached during the Constitutional Convention of 1787. As proposed by James Madison, the Three-Fifths Compromise sought to solve the divisive issue of how to count the slaves for the purpose of establishing representation in the new Congress. Madison's compromise was that each slave would be counted as three-fifths of a free white. The 14th Amendment to the United States Constitution later repealed the Compromise.

Unionist: One who supported the Northern or Union cause during the Civil War.

Vietcong: Any supporter or member of the Communist-supported armed forces of the so-called National Liberation Front, which fought to reunite South Vietnam with North Vietnam during the Vietnam War (1954–1976).

Whig Party: Political party founded in the 1830s to oppose the Democrats. Notable Whigs include Daniel Webster (1782–1852) and William Henry Harrison (1773–1841).

Women's Rights Movement: The populist activity that aimed to secure social, economic, and political equality for women.

Zacatecas: A state in north central Mexico. Also, the capital of that state.

PRIMARY SOURCE DOCUMENTS

ACTS OF CONGRESS AND PROCLAMATIONS

Stamp Act of 1765

Commentary

The Stamp Act prescribed taxes for legal and commercial transactions and documents used in court proceedings (including the licenses of attorneys), the papers used in clearing ships from harbors, college diplomas, appointments to public office, bonds, grants and deeds for land, mortgages, indentures, leases, contracts, bills of sale, articles of apprenticeship, liquor licenses, playing cards, and dice. It taxed a printer's entire business: pamphlets, almanacs, newspapers, and newspaper advertisements. The law required these documents to be written or printed on paper carrying a stamp embossed by the Treasury Office in England which was sold only by the stamp commissioners. This legislation hurt printers even more because many of them manufactured their own paper.

Prime Minister George Grenville (1712–1770) did not think he had asked for anything unreasonable. If a merchant did not consider it worth the price of a stamp to clear a ship from a colonial harbor, then he should not have it make the voyage, Grenville thought. Similarly, if a wife was not worth the price of the stamp required on a marriage license, a man should remain a bachelor.

An act for granting and applying certain stamp duties, and other duties, in the British colonies and plantations in; America, towards further defraying the expenses of defending, protecting, and securing the same; and for amending such parts of the several acts of parliament relating to the trade and revenues of the said colonies and plantations, as direct the manner of determining and recovering the penalties and forfeitures therein mentioned.

Whereas by an act of the last session of parliament, several duties were granted, continued, and appropriated, towards defraying the expenses of defending, protecting, and securing, the British colonies and plantations in America: and whereas it is just and necessary, that provision be made for raising a further revenue within your Majesty's dominions in America, towards defraying the said expenses: we, your Majesty's most dutiful and loyal subjects, the commons of Great Britain in parliament assembled, have therefore resolved to give and grant unto your Majesty the several rates and duties herein after mentioned; and do most humbly beseech your Majesty that it may be enacted, and be it enacted by the King's most excellent majesty, by and with the advice and consent of the lords spiritual and temporal, and commons, in this present parliament assembled, and by the authority of the same, That from and after the first day of November, one thousand seven hundred and sixty five, there shall be raised, levied, collected, and paid unto his Majesty, his heirs, and successors, throughout the colonies and plantations in America which now are, or hereafter may be, under the dominion of his Majesty, his heirs and successors,

For every skin or piece of vellum or parchment, or sheet or piece of paper, on which shall be engrossed, written or printed, any declaration, plea, replication, rejoinder, demurrer, or other pleading, or any copy thereof, in any court of law within the British colonies and plantations in America, a stamp duty of three pence.

For every skin or piece of vellum or parchment, or sheet or piece of paper, on which shall be engrossed, written or printed, any special bail and appearance upon such bail in any such court, a stamp duty of two shillings.

For every skin or piece of vellum or parchment, or sheet or piece of paper, on which shall be engrossed, written or printed, any petition, bill, answer, claim, plea, replication, rejoinder, demurrer, or other pleading in any court of chancery or equity within the said colonies and plantations, a stamp duty of one shilling and six pence.

For every skin or piece of vellum or parchment, or sheet or piece of paper, on which shall be engrossed, written or printed, any copy of any petition, bill, answer, claim, plea, replication, rejoinder, demurrer, or other pleading in any such court, a stamp duty of three pence.

For every skin or piece of vellum or parchment, or sheet or piece of paper, on which shall be engrossed, written, or printed, any monition, libel, answer, allegation, inventory, or renunciation in ecclesiastical matters in any court of probate, court of the ordinary, or other court exercising ecclesiastical jurisdiction within the said colonies and plantations, a stamp duty of one shilling.

For every skin or piece of vellum or parchment, or sheet or piece of paper, on which shall be engrossed, written, or printed, any copy of any will (other than the probate thereof) monition, libel, answer, allegation, inventory, or renunciation in ecclesiastical matters in any such court, a stamp duty of six pence.

For every skin or piece of vellum or parchment, or sheet or piece of paper, on which shall be engrossed, written, or printed, any donation, presentation, collation, or institution of or to any benefice, or any writ or instrument for the like purpose, or any register, entry, testimonial, or certificate of any degree taken in any university, academy, college, or seminary of learning, within the said colonies and plantations, a stamp duty of two pounds.

For every skin or piece of vellum or parchment, or sheet or piece of paper, on which shall be engrossed, written, or printed, any monition, libel, claim, answer,

allegation, information, letter of request, execution, renunciation, inventory, or other pleading, in any admiralty court within the said colonies and plantations, a stamp duty of one shilling.

For every skin or piece of vellum or parchment, or sheet or piece of paper, on which any copy of any such monition, libel, claim, answer, allegation, information, letter of request, execution, renunciation, inventory, or other pleading shall be engrossed, written, or printed, a stamp duty of six pence.

For every skin or piece of vellum or parchment, or sheet or piece of paper, on which shall be engrossed, written, or printed, any appeal, writ of error, writ of dower, Ad quod damnum, certiorari, statute merchant, statute staple, attestation, or certificate, by any officer, or exemplification of any record or proceeding in any court whatsoever within the said colonies and plantations (except appeals, writs of error, certiorari, attestations, certificates, and exemplifications, for or relating to the removal of any proceedings from before a single justice of the peace) a stamp duty of ten shillings.

For every skin or piece of vellum or parchment, or sheet or piece of paper, on which shall be engrossed, written, or printed, any writ of covenant for levying of fines, writ of entry for suffering a common recovery, or attachment issuing out of, or returnable into, any court within the said colonies and plantations, a stamp duty of five shillings.

For every skin or piece of vellum or parchment, or sheet or piece of paper, on which shall be engrossed, written, or printed, any judgment, decree, sentence, or dismission, or any record of Nisi Prius or Postea, in any court within the said colonies and plantations, a stamp duty of four shillings.

For every skin or piece of vellum or parchment, or sheet or piece of paper, on which shall be engrossed, written, or printed, any affidavit, common bail or appearance, interrogatory deposition, rule, order, or warrant of any court, or any Dedimus, Potestatem, Capias, Subpoena, summons, compulsory citation, commission, recognizance, or any other writ, process, or mandate, issuing out of, or returnable into, any court, or any office belonging thereto, or any other proceeding therein whatsoever, or any copy thereof, or of any record not herein before charged, within the said colonies and plantations (except warrants relating to criminal matters, and proceeding thereon or relating thereto) a stamp duty of one shilling.

For every skin or piece of vellum or parchment, or sheet or piece of paper, on which shall be engrossed, written, or printed, any licence, appointment, or admission of any counselor, solicitor, attorney, advocate, or proctor, to practice in any court, or of any notary within the said colonies and plantations, a stamp duty of ten pounds.

For every skin or piece of vellum or parchment, or sheet or piece of paper, on which shall be engrossed, written, or printed, any note or bill of lading, which shall be signed for any kind of goods, wares, or merchandize, to be exported from, or any cocket or clearance granted within the said colonies and plantations, a stamp duty of four pence.

For every skin or piece of vellum or parchment, or sheet or piece of paper, on which shall be engrossed, written, or printed, letters of mart, or commission for private ships of war, within the said colonies and plantations, a stamp duty of twenty shillings.

For every skin or piece of vellum or parchment, or sheet or piece of paper, on which shall be engrossed, written or printed, any grant, appointment, or admission of or to any public beneficial, office or employment, for the space of one year, or any lesser time, of or above the value of twenty pounds per annum sterling money, in salary, fees, and perquisites, within the said colonies and plantations, (except commissions and appointments of officers of the army, navy, ordnance, or militia, of judges, and of justices of the peace) a stamp duty of ten shillings.

For every skin or piece of vellum or parchment, or sheet or piece of paper, on which any grant of any liberty, privilege, or franchise, under the seal of any of the said colonies or plantations, or under the seal or sign manual of any governor, proprietor, or public officer alone, or in conjunction with any other person or persons, or with any council, or any council and assembly, or any exemplification of the same, shall be engrossed, written, or printed, within the said colonies and plantations, a stamp duty of six pounds.

For every skin or piece of vellum or parchment, or sheet or piece of paper, on which shall be engrossed, written, or printed, any licence for retailing of spirituous liquors, to be granted to any person who shall take out the same, within the said colonies and plantations, a stamp duty of twenty shillings.

For every skin or piece of vellum or parchment, or sheet or piece of paper, on which shall be engrossed, written, or printed, any licence for retailing of wine, to be granted to any person who shall not, take out a licence for retailing of spirituous liquors, within the said colonies and plantations, a stamp duty of four pounds.

For every skin or piece of vellum or parchment, or sheet or piece of paper, on which shall be engrossed, written, or printed, any licence for retailing of wine, to be granted to any person who shall take out a licence for retailing of spirituous liquors, within the said colonies and plantations, a stamp duty of three pounds.

For every skin or piece of vellum or parchment, or sheet or piece of paper, on which shall be engrossed, written, or printed, any probate of a will, letters of administration, or of guardianship for any estate above the value of twenty pounds sterling money; within the British colonies and plantations upon the continent of America, the islands belonging thereto, and the Bermuda and Bahama islands, a stamp duty of five shillings.

For every skin or piece of vellum or parchment, or sheet or piece of paper on which shall be engrossed, written or printed, any such probate, letters of administration or of guardianship, within all other parts of the British dominions in America, a stamp duty of ten shillings.

For every skin or piece of vellum or parchment, or sheet or piece of paper on which shall be engrossed, written, or printed, any bond for securing the payment of any sum of money not exceeding the sum of ten pounds sterling money, within the British colonies and plantations upon the continent of America, the islands belonging thereto, and the Bermuda and Bahama islands, a stamp duty of six pence.

For every skin or piece of vellum or parchment, or sheet or piece of paper on which shall be engrossed, written, or printed, any bond for securing the payment of any sum of money above ten pounds, and not exceeding the sum of twenty pounds sterling money, within such colonies, plantations, and islands, a stamp duty of one shilling.

For every skin or piece of vellum or parchment, or sheet or piece of paper on which shall be engrossed, written, or printed, any bond for securing the payment of any sum of money above twenty pounds, and not exceeding forty pounds sterling money, within such colonies, plantations, and islands, a stamp duty of one shilling and six pence.

For every skin or piece of vellum or parchment, or sheet or piece of paper on which shall be engrossed, written, or printed, any bond for securing the payment of any order or warrant for surveying or setting out any quantity of land not exceeding one hundred acres, issued by any governor, proprietor or any public officer alone, or in conjunction with any other person or persons, or with any council, or any council and assembly, within the British colonies and plantations in America, a stamp duty of six pence.

For every skin or piece of vellum or parchment, or sheet or piece of paper on which shall be engrossed, written, or printed, any such order or warrant for surveying or setting out any quantity of land above one hundred, and not exceeding two hundred acres, within the said colonies and plantations, a stamp duty of one shilling.

For every skin or piece of vellum or parchment, or sheet or piece of paper on which shall be engrossed, written, or printed any such order or warrant for surveying or setting out any quantity of land above two hundred, and not exceeding three hundred and twenty acres, and in proportion for every such order or warrant for surveying or setting out every other three hundred and twenty acres, within the said colonies and plantations, a stamp duty of one shilling and six pence.

For every skin or piece of vellum or parchment, or sheet or piece of paper on which shall be engrossed, written, or printed any original grant, or any deed, mesne conveyance, or other instrument whatsoever, by which any quantity of land not exceeding one hundred acres shall be granted, conveyed, or assigned, within the British colonies and plantations upon the continent of America, the islands belonging thereto, and the Bermuda and Bahama islands (except leases for any term not exceeding the term of twenty one years) a stamp duty of one shilling and six pence.

For every skin or piece of vellum or parchment, or sheet or piece of paper on which shall be engrossed, written, or printed any such original grant, or any such deed, mesne conveyance, or other instrument whatsoever, by which any quantity of land above one hundred, and not exceeding two hundred acres shall be granted, conveyed, or assigned, within such colonies, plantations and islands, a stamp duty of two shillings.

For every skin or piece of vellum or parchment, or sheet or piece of paper on which shall be engrossed, written, or printed any such original grant, or any such deed, mesne conveyance, or other instrument whatsoever, by which any quantity of land above two hundred, and not exceeding three hundred and twenty acres shall be granted, conveyed, or assigned, and in proportion for every such grant, deed, mesne conveyance, or other instrument, granting, conveying, or assigning, every other three hundred and twenty acres, within such colonies, plantations and islands, a stamp duty of two shillings and six pence.

For every skin or piece of vellum or parchment, or sheet or piece of paper on which shall be engrossed, written, or printed any such original grant, or any such deed, mesne conveyance, or other instrument whatsoever, by which any quantity of land not exceeding one hundred acres shall be granted, conveyed, or assigned within all other parts of the British dominions in America, a stamp duty of three shillings.

For every skin or piece of vellum or parchment, or sheet or piece of paper on which shall be engrossed, written, or printed any such original grant, or any such deed, mesne conveyance, or other instrument whatsoever, by

which any quantity of land above one hundred and not exceeding two hundred acres, shall be granted, conveyed, or assigned within the same parts of the said dominions, a stamp duty of four shillings.

For every skin or piece of vellum or parchment, or sheet or piece of paper on which shall be engrossed, written, or printed any such original grant, or any such deed, mesne conveyance, or other instrument whatsoever, whereby any quantity of land above two hundred and not exceeding three hundred and twenty acres, within the same parts of the said dominions, a stamp duty of five shillings.

For every skin or piece of vellum or parchment, or sheet or piece of paper on which shall be engrossed, written, or printed any grant, appointment or admission, of or to any public beneficial office or employment, not herein before charged, above the value of twenty pounds per annum sterling money in salary, fees, and perquisites, or any exemplification of the same, within the British colonies and plantations upon the continent of America, the islands belonging thereto, and the Bermuda and Bahama islands (except commissions of officers of the army, navy, ordnance, or militia, and of justices of the peace) a stamp duty of four pounds.

For every skin or piece of vellum or parchment, or sheet or piece of paper, on which shall be engrossed, written, or printed, any such grant, appointment, or admission, of or to any such public beneficial office or employment, or any exemplification of the same, within all other parts of the British dominions in America, a stamp duty of six pounds.

For every skin or piece of vellum or parchment, or sheet or piece of paper, on which shall be engrossed, written, or printed, any indenture, lease, conveyance, contract, stipulation, bill of sale, charter party, protest, articles of apprenticeship, or covenant (except for the hire of servants not apprentices, and also except such other matters as are herein before charged) within the British colonies and plantations in America, a stamp duty of two shillings and six pence.

For every skin or piece of vellum or parchment, or sheet or piece of paper, on which any warrant or order for auditing any public seal, or under the seal or sign manual of any governor, proprietor, or public officer alone, or in conjunction with any other person or persons, or with any council, or any council and assembly, not herein before charged, or any passport or let-pass, surrender of office, or policy of assurance, shall be engrossed, written, or printed, within the said colonies and plantations (except warrants or orders for the service of the navy, army, ordnance, or militia, and grants of offices under twenty pounds per annum in salary, fees, and perquisites) a stamp duty of five shillings.

For every skin or piece of vellum or parchment, or sheet or piece of paper, on which shall be engrossed, written, or printed, any notorial act, bond, deed, letter of attorney, procuration, mortgage, release, or other obligatory instrument, not herein before charged, within the said colonies and plantations, a stamp duty of two shillings and three pence.

For every skin or piece of vellum or parchment, or sheet or piece of paper, on which shall be engrossed, written, or printed, any register, entry, or enrollment of any grant, deed or other instrument whatsoever herein before charged, within the said colonies and plantations, a stamp duty of three pence.

For every skin or piece of vellum or parchment, or sheet or piece of paper, on which shall be engrossed, written, or printed, any register, entry, or enrollment of any grant, deed or other instrument whatsoever not herein before charged, within the said colonies and plantations, a stamp duty of two shillings.

And for and upon every pack of playing cards, and all dice, which shall be sold or used within the said colonies and plantations, the several stamp duties following (that is to say)

For every pack of such cards, the sum of one shilling.

And for every pair of such dice, the sum of ten shillings.

And for and upon every paper, commonly called a pamphlet, and upon every news paper, containing public news, intelligence, or occurrences, which shall be printed, dispersed, and made public, within any of the said colonies and plantations, and for and upon such advertisements as are herein after mentioned, the respective duties following (that is to say)

For every such pamphlet and paper contained in half a sheet, or any lesser piece of paper, which shall be so printed, a stamp duty of one halfpenny, for every printed copy thereof.

For every such pamphlet and paper (being larger than half a sheet, and not exceeding one whole sheet) which shall be so printed, a stamp duty of one penny, for every printed copy thereof.

For every pamphlet and paper being larger than one whole sheet, and not exceeding six sheets in octavo, or in a lesser page, or not exceeding twelve sheets in quarto, or twenty sheets in folio, which shall be so printed, a duty after the rate of one shilling for every sheet of any kind of paper which shall be contained in one printed copy thereof.

For every advertisement to be contained in any gazette, news paper, or other paper, or any pamphlet which shall be so printed, a duty of two shillings.

For every almanac or calendar, for, any one particular year, or for any time, less than a year, which shall be written or printed on one side only of any one sheet, skin, or piece of paper parchment, or vellum, within the said colonies and plantations, a stamp duty of two pence.

For every other almanac or calendar for any one particular year, which shall be written or printed within the said colonies and plantations, a stamp duty of four pence.

And for every almanac or calendar written or printed within the said colonies and plantations, to serve for several years, duties to the same amount respectively shall be paid for every such year.

For every skin or piece of vellum or parchment, or sheet or piece of paper, on which any instrument, proceeding, or other matter or thing aforesaid, shall be engrossed, written, or printed, within the said colonies and plantations, in any other than the English language, a stamp duty of double the amount of the respective duties before charged thereon.

And there shall be also paid in the said colonies and plantations, a duty of six pence for every twenty shillings, in any sum not exceeding fifty pounds sterling money, which shall be given, paid, contracted, or agreed for, with or in relation to any clerk or apprentice, which shall be put or placed to or with any master or mistress to learn any profession, trade or employment.

II. And also a duty of one shilling for every twenty shillings, in any sum exceeding fifty pounds, which shall be given, paid, contracted, or agreed, for, with, or in relation to any such clerk, or apprentice.

III. And be it further enacted by the authority aforesaid, That every deed, instrument, note, memorandum, letter, or other minument or writing, for or relating to the payment of any sum, of money, or for making any valuable consideration for or upon, the loss of any ship, vessel, goods, wages, money, effects, or upon any loss by fire, or for any other loss whatsoever, or for or upon any life or lives, shall be construed, deemed, and adjudged to be policies of assurance, within the meaning of this act: and, if any such deed, instrument, note, memorandum, letter, or other minument or writing, for insuring, or tending to insure, any more than one ship or vessel for more than any one voyage, or any goods, wages, money, effects, or other matter or thing whatsoever, for more than one voyage, or in more than one ship or vessel, or being the property of, or belonging to, any more than, one person or any particular number of persons in general partnership, or any more than one body politick or corporate, or for more than one risque; then, in every such case, the money insured thereon, or the valuable consideration thereby agreed to be made, shall become the absolute property of the insured, and the insurer shall also forfeit the premium given for such insurance, together with the sum of one hundred pounds.

IV. And be it further enacted by the authority aforesaid, That every deed, instrument, note, memorandum, letter, or other minument or writing, between the captain or master or owner of any ship or vessel, and any merchant, trader, or other person, in respect to the freight or conveyance of any money, goods, wares, merchandises, or effects, laden or to be laden on board of any such ship or vessel, shall be deemed and adjudged to be a charter party within the meaning of this act.

V. And be it further enacted by the authority aforesaid, That all books and pamphlets serving chiefly for the purpose of an almanac, by whatsoever name or names entitled or described, are and shall be charged with the duty imposed by this act on almanacs, but not with any of the duties charged by this act on pamphlets, or other printed papers; any thing herein contained to the contrary notwithstanding.

VI. Provided always, That this act shall not extend to charge any bills of exchange, accompts, bills of parcels, bills of fees, or any bills or notes nor sealed for payment of money at sight or upon demand, or at the end of certain days of payment.

VII. Provided, That nothing in this act contained shall extend to charge the probate of any will, or letters of administration to the effects of any common seaman or soldier, who shall die in his Majesty's service; a certificate being produced from the commanding officer of the ship or vessel, or troop or company in which such seaman or soldier served at the time of his death, and oath, or if by a quaker a solemn affirmation, made of the truth thereof, before the proper judge or officer by whom such probate or administration ought to be granted; which oath or affirmation such judge or officer is hereby authorized and required to administer, and for which no fee or reward shall be taken.

VIII. Provided always, and be it enacted, That until after the expiration of five years from the commencement of the said duties, no skin or piece of vellum or parchment, or sheet or piece of paper, on which any instrument, proceeding or other matter or thing shall be engrossed, written, or printed, within the colonies of Quebec or Granada, in any other than the English language, shall be liable to be charged with any higher stamp duty than if the same had been engrossed, written or printed in the English language.

IX. Provided always, That nothing in this act contained shall extend to charge with any duty, any deed, or other instrument, which shall be made between any Indian nation and the governor, proprietor of any colony, lieutenant governor, or commander in chief alone, or in conjunction with any other person or persons, or with any council, or any council and assembly of any of the said colonies or plantations, for or relating to the granting, surrendering, or conveying, any lands belonging to such nation, to for, or on behalf of his Majesty, or any such proprietor, or to any colony or plantation.

X. Provided always, That this act shall not extend to charge any proclamation, forms of prayer and Thanksgiving, or any printed votes of any house of assembly in any of the said colonies and plantations, with any of the said duties on pamphlets or news papers; or to charge any books commonly used in any of the schools within the said colonies and plantations, or any books containing only matters of devotion or piety; or to charge any single advertisement printed by itself, or the daily accounts or bills of goods imported and exported, so as such accounts or bills do contain no other matters than what have been usually comprised therein; any thing herein contained to the contrary notwithstanding.

XI. Provided always, That nothing in this act contained shall extend to charge with any of the said duties, any vellum, parchment, or paper, on which shall only be engrossed, written, or printed, any certificate that shall be necessary to in title any person to receive a bounty granted by act of parliament.

XII. And be it further enacted by the authority aforesaid, That the said several duties shall be under the management of the commissioners, for the time being, of the duties charged on, stamped vellum, parchment, and paper, in Great Britain: and the said commissioners are hereby empowered and required to employ such officers under them, for that purpose, as they shall think proper; and to use such stamps and marks, to denote the stamp duties hereby charged, as they shall think fit; and to repair, renew, or alter the same, from time to time, as there shall be occasion; and to do all other acts, matters, and things, necessary to be done, for putting this act in execution with relation to the duties hereby charged.

XIII. And be it further enacted by the authority aforesaid, That the commissioners for managing the said duties, for the time being, shall and may appoint a fit person or persons to attend in every court or public office within the said colonies and plantations, to take notice of the vellum, parchment, or paper, upon which any the matters or things hereby charged with a duty shall be engrossed, written, or printed, and of the stamps or marks thereupon, and of all other matters and things tending to secure the said duties; and that the judges in the several courts, and all other persons to whom it may appertain shall, at the request of any such officer, make such orders, and do such other matters and things, for the better securing of the said duties, as shall be lawfully or reasonably desired in that behalf: and every commissioner and other officer, before he proceeds to the execution of any part of this act, shall take an oath in the words, or to the effect following (that is to say)

I A. B. do swear, That I will faithfully execute the trust reposed in my, pursuant to an act of parliament made in the fifth year of the reign of his majesty King George the Third, for granting certain stamp duties, and other duties, in the British colonies and plantations in America, without fraud or concealment; and will from time to time true account make of my doing therein, and deliver the same to such person or persons as his Majesty, his heirs, or successors, shall appoint to receive such account; and will take no fee, reward, or profit, for the execution or performance of the said trust, or the business relating thereto, from any person or persons, other than such as shall be allowed by his Majesty, his heirs, and successors, or by some other person or persons under him or them to that purpose authorized.

Or if any such officer shall be of the people commonly called Quakers, he shall take a solemn affirmation to the effect of the said oath; which oath or affirmation shall and may be administered to any such commissioner or commissioners by any two or more of the same commissioners, whether they have or have not previously

taken the same: and any of the said commissioners, or any justice of the peace, within the kingdom of Great Britain, or any governor, lieutenant governor, judge, or other magistrate, within the said colonies or plantations, shall and may administer such oath or affirmation to any subordinate officer.

XIV. And be it further enacted by the authority aforesaid, That the said commissioners, and all officers to be employed or entrusted by or under them as aforesaid, shall, from time to time, in and for the better execution of their several places and trusts, observe such rules, methods, and orders, as they respectively shall, from time to time, receive from the high treasurer of Great Britain, or the commissioners of the treasury, or any three or more of such commissioners for the time being; and that the said commissioners for managing the stamp duties shall take especial care, that the several parts of the said colonies and plantations shall, from time to time, be sufficiently furnished with vellum, parchment, and paper, stamped or marked with the said respective duties.

XV. And be it further enacted by the authority aforesaid, That if any person or persons shall sign, engross, write, print, or sell, or expose to sale, or cause to be signed, engrossed, written, printed, or sold, or exposed to sale, in any of the said colonies of plantations, or in any other part of his Majesty's dominions, any matter or thing, for which the vellum, parchment, or paper, is hereby charged to pay any duty, before the same shall be marked or stamped with the marks or stamps to be provided as aforesaid, or upon which there shall not be some stamp or mark resembling the same; or shall sign, engross, write, print, or sell, or expose to sale, or cause to be signed, engrossed, written, printed, or sold, or exposed to sale, any matter or thing upon any vellum, parchment, or paper, that shall be marked or stamped for any lower duty than the duty by this act made payable in respect thereof; every such person so offending shall, for every such offence, forfeit the sum of ten pounds.

XVI. And be it further enacted by the authority aforesaid, That no matter or thing whatsoever, by this act charged with the payment of a duty, shall be pleaded or given in evidence, or admitted in any court within the said colonies and plantations, to be good, useful, or available in law or equity, unless the same shall be marked or stamped, in pursuance of this act, with the respective duty hereby charged thereon, or with an higher duty.

XVII. Provided, nevertheless, and be it further enacted by the authority aforesaid, That if any vellum, parchment, or paper, containing any deed, instrument, or other matter or thing, shall not be duly stamped in pursuance of this act, at the time of the signing, sealing, or other execution, or the entry or enrollment thereof, any person interested therein, or any person on his or her behalf, upon producing the same to any one of the chief distributors of stamped vellum, parchment, and paper, and paying to him the sum of ten pounds for every such deed, instrument, matter, or thing, and also double the amount of the duties payable in respect thereof, shall be entitled to receive from such distributor, vellum, parchment, or paper, stamped pursuant to this act, to the amount of the money so paid a certificate being first written upon every such piece of vellum, parchment, or paper, expressing the name and place of abode of the person by or on whose behalf such payment is made, the general purport of such deed, instrument, matter, or thing, the names of the parties therein, and of the witnesses (if any) thereto, and the date thereof, which certificate shall be signed by the said distributor; and the vellum, parchment, or paper, shall be then annexed to such deed, instrument, matter, or thing, by or in the presence of such distributor, who shall impress a seal upon wax, to be affixed on the part where such annexation shall be made, in the presence of magistrate, who shall attest such signature and sealing; and the deed, instrument, or other matter or thing, from thenceforth shall and may, with the vellum, parchment, or paper so annexed, be admitted and allowed in evidence in any court whatsoever, and shall be as valid and effectual as if the proper stamps had been impressed thereon at the time of the signing, sealing or other execution, or entry or enrollment thereof: and the said distributor shall, once in every six months, or oftener if required by the commissioners for managing the stamp duties, send to such commissioners true copies of all such certificates, and an account of the number of pieces of vellum, parchment, and paper, so annexed, and of the respective duties impressed upon every such piece.

XVIII. And be It further enacted by the authority aforesaid, That if any person shall forge, counterfeit, erase, or alter, any such certificate, every such person so offending shall be guilty of felony, and shall suffer death as in cases of felony without the benefit of clergy.

XIX. And be it further enacted by the authority aforesaid, That if any person or persons shall, in the said colonies or plantations, or in any other part of his Majesty's dominions counterfeit or forge any seal, stamp, mark, type, device, or label, to resemble any seal, stamp, mark, type, device, or label, which shall be provided or made in pursuance of this act; or shall counterfeit or resemble the impression of the same upon any vellum parchment, paper, cards, dice or other matter or thing, thereby to evade the payment of any duty hereby granted; or shall make, sign, print, utter, vend, or sell, any vellum, parchment, or paper, or other matter or thing, with such counterfeit mark or impression thereon, knowing such mark or impression to be counterfeited; then every person so offending shall be adjudged a felon, and shall suffer death as in cases of felony without the benefit of clergy.

XX. And it is hereby declared, That upon any prosecution or prosecutions for such felony, the dye, tool, or other instrument made use of in counterfeiting or forging any such seal, stamp, mark, type, device, or label, together with the vellum, parchment, paper, cards, dice, or other matter, or thing having such counterfeit impression, shall, immediately after the trial or conviction of the party or parties accused, be broke, defaced, or destroyed, in open court.

XXI. And be it further enacted by the authority aforesaid, That if any register, public officer, clerk, or other person in any court registry, or office within any of the said colonies or plantation, shall, at any time after the said first day of November, one thousand seven hundred and sixty five, enter, register, or enroll, any matter or thing hereby charged with a stamp duty unless the same shall appear to be duly stamped; in every such case such register, public officer, clerk, or other person, shall for every such offence, forfeit the sum of twenty pounds.

XXII. And be it further enacted by the authority aforesaid, That from and after the said first day of November, one if any counselor, clerk, officer, attorney, or other person, to whom it shall appertain, or who shall be employed or intrusted, in the said colonies or plantations, to enter or file any matter or thing in respect whereof any duty shall be payable by virtue of this act, shall neglect to enter, file, or record the same, as by law the same ought to be entered, filed, or recorded, within the space of four months after he shall have received any money for or in respect of the same, or shall have promised or undertaken so to do; or shall neglect to enter, file, or record, any such matter or thing, before any subsequent, further or other proceeding, matter, or thing, in the same suit, shall be had, entered, filed, or recorded; that then every such counselor, clerk, officer, attorney, or other person so neglecting or offending, in each of the cases aforesaid, shall forfeit the sum of fifty pounds for every such offence.

XXIII. And be it further enacted by the authority aforesaid, That if any person or persons, at any time after the said first day of November, one thousand seven hundred and sixty five, shall write, engross, or print, or cause to be written, engrossed, or printed, in the said colonies or plantations, or any other part of his said Majesty's dominions, either the whole or any part of any matter or thing whatsoever in respect whereof any duty is payable by this act, upon any part of any piece of vellum, parchment, or paper, whereon there shall have been before written any other matter or thing in respect whereof any duty was payable by this act; or shall fraudulently erase, or cause to be erased, the name or names of any person or persons, or any sum, date, or other thing, engrossed, written, or printed, in such matter or thing as aforesaid; or fraudulently cut, tear, or get off, any mark or stamp from any piece of vellum, parchment, or paper, or any part thereof, with intent to use such stamp or mark for any other matter or thing in respect whereof any duty shall be payable by virtue of this act; that then, and so often, and in every such case, every person so offending shall, for every such offence, forfeit the sum of fifty pounds.

XXIV. And be it further enacted by the authority aforesaid, That every matter and thing, in respect whereof any duty shall be payable in pursuance of this act, shall be engrossed, written, or printed, in such manner, that some part thereof shall be either upon, or as

near as conveniently may be, to the stamps or marks denoting the duty; upon pain that the person who shall engross, write, or print, or cause to be engrossed, written, or printed, any such matter or thing in any other manner, shall, for every such offence, forfeit the sums of five pounds.

XXV. And be it further enacted by the authority aforesaid, That every officer of each court, and every justice of the peace or other person within the said colonies and plantations, who shall issue any writ or process upon which a duty is by this act payable, shall, at the issuing thereof, set down upon such writ or process the day and year of his issuing the same, which shall be entered upon a remembrance, or in a book to be kept for that purpose, setting forth the abstract of such writ or process; upon pain to forfeit the sum of ten pounds for every such offence.

XXVI. And, for the better collecting and securing the duties hereby charged on pamphlets containing more than one sheet of paper as aforesaid, be it further enacted by the authority aforesaid, That from and after the said first day of November, one thousand seven hundred and sixty five, one printed copy of every pamphlet which shall be printed or published within any of the said colonies or plantations, shall within the space of fourteen days after the printing thereof, be brought to the chief distributor in the colony or plantation where such pamphlet shall be printed, and the title thereof, with the number of the sheets contained therein, and the duty hereby charged thereon, shall be registered or entered in a book to be there kept for that purpose; which duty shall be thereupon paid to the proper officer or officers appointed to receive the same, or his or their deputy or clerk, who shall thereupon forthwith give a receipt for the same on such printed copy, to denote the payment of the duty hereby charged on such pamphlet; and if any such pamphlet shall be printed copy, to denote the payment of the duty thereon shall not be duly paid, and the title and number of sheets shall not be registered, and a receipt for such duty given on one copy, where required so to be, within the time herein before for that purpose limited; that then the author, printer, and publisher, and all other persons concerned in or about the printing or publishing of such pamphlet, shall, for every such offence, forfeit the sum of ten pounds, and shall lose all property therein, and in every other copy thereof, so as any person may freely print and publish the same, paying the duty payable in respect thereof by virtue of this act, without being liable to any action, prosecution, or penalty for so doing.

XXVII. And it is hereby further enacted by the authority aforesaid, That no person whatsoever shall sell or expose to sale any such pamphlet, or any new paper, without the true respective name or names, and place or places of abode, of some known person or persons by or for whom the same was really and truly printed or published, shall be written or printed thereon; upon pain that every person offending therein shall, for every such offence, forfeit the sum of twenty pounds.

XXVIII. And be it further enacted by the authority aforesaid, That no officer appointed for distributing stamped vellum, parchment, or paper, in the said colonies or plantations, shall sell or deliver any stamped paper for printing any pamphlet, or any public news, intelligence, or occurrences, to be contained in one sheet, or any lesser piece of paper, unless such person shall give security to the said officer, for the payment of the duties for the advertisements which shall be printed therein or thereupon.

XXIX. And whereas it may be uncertain how many printed copies of the said printed news papers or pamphlets, to be contained in one sheet or in a lesser piece of paper, may be sold; and to the intent the duties hereby granted thereupon any not be lessened by printing a less number than may be sold, out of a fear of a loss thereby in printing more such copies than will be sold; it is hereby provided, and be it further enacted by the authority aforesaid, That the proper officer or officers appointed for managing the said stamp duties, shall and may cancel, or cause to be cancelled, all the stamps upon the copies of any impression of any new paper or pamphlet contained in one sheet, or any lesser piece of paper, which shall really and truly remain unfold, and of which no profit or advantage has been made; and upon oath, or if by a quaker, upon solemn affirmation, made before a justice of the peace, or other proper magistrate, that all such copies, containing the stamps so tendered to cancelled, are really and truly remaining unfold, and that none of the said copies have been fraudulently returned or rebought, or any profit or advantage made thereof; which oath or affirmation such magistrate is hereby authorized or administer, and to examine upon oath or affirmation into all circumstances relating to the selling or disposing of such printed copies, shall and map deliver, or cause to be delivered, the like number of other sheets, half sheets, or less pieces of paper, properly stamped with the same respective stamps, upon payment made for such paper, but no duty shall be taken for the stamps thereon; any thing herein contained to the contrary notwithstanding; and the said commissioners for managing the stamp duties for the time being are hereby empowered, from time to time, to make such rules and orders for regulating the methods, and limiting the times, for such cancelling and allowance as aforesaid, with respect to such news papers and pamphlets, as they shall, upon experience and consideration of the several circumstances, find necessary or convenient, for the effectual securing the duties thereon, and doing justice to the persons concerned in the printing and publishing thereof.

XXX. Provided always, and be it further enacted by the authority aforesaid, That if any officer or officers employed by the said commissioners for managing the stamp duties, shall and may deliver to any person, by or for whom any almanac or almanacs shall have been printed, paper marked or stamped according to the true intent and meaning hereof, for the printing such almanac or almanacs, upon his or her giving sufficient security to pay the amount of the duty hereby charged thereon, within the space of three months after such delivery; and that the said officer or officers, upon bringing to him or them any number of the copies of such almanacs, within the space of three months from the said delivery and request to him or them in that behalf made, shall cancel all the stamps upon such copies, and abate to every such person so much of the money due upon such security as such cancelled stamps shall amount to.

XXXI. Provided always, That where any almanac shall contain more than one sheet of paper, it shall be sufficient to stamp only one of the sheets or pieces of paper upon which such almanac shall be printed, and to pay the duty accordingly.

XXXII. And it is hereby further enacted by the authority aforesaid, That from and after the said first day of November, one thousand seven hundred and sixty five, in case any person or persons, within any of the said colonies or plantations, shall sell, hawk, carry about, utter, or expose to sale, any almanac, or calendar, or any news paper, or any book, pamphlet, or paper, deemed or construed to be, or serving the purpose of, an almanac or news paper, within the intention and meaning of this act, not being stamped or marked as by this act is directed; every such person, shall for every such offence, forfeit the sum of forty shillings.

XXXIII. And be it further enacted by the authority aforesaid, That from and after the said first day of November, one thousand seven hundred and sixty five, the full sum or sums of money, or other valuable consideration received, or in any wise directly or indirectly given, paid, agreed, or contracted, for, with, or in relation to any clerk or apprentice, within any of the said colonies or plantations, shall be truly inserted, or written in words at length, in some indenture or other writing which shall contain the covenants, articles, contracts, or agreements, relating to the service of such clerk or apprentice; and shall bear date upon the day of the signing, sealing, or other execution of the same, upon pain that every master or mistress to or with whom, or to whose use, any sum of money, or other valuable consideration whatsoever, shall be given, paid, secured, or contracted, for or in respect of any such clerk or apprentice, which shall not be truly and fully so inserted and specified in some such indenture, or other writing, shall, for every such offence, forfeit double the sum, or double the amount of any other valuable consideration so given, paid, agreed, secured, or contracted for; to be sued for and recovered at any time, during the term specified in the indenture or writing for the service of such clerk or apprentice, or within one year after the determination thereof; and that all such indentures, or other writings, shall be brought, within the space of three months, to the proper officer or officers, appointed by the said commissioners for collecting the said duties within the respective colony or plantation; and the duty hereby charged for the sums, or other valuable consideration inserted therein, shall be paid by the master or mistress of such clerk or apprentice to the said officer or officers, who shall give receipts for such duty on the back of such indentures or other writings; and in case the duty shall not be paid within the time before limited, such master or mistress shall forfeit double the amount of such duty.

XXXIV. And be it further enacted by the authority aforesaid, That all indentures or writings within the said colonies and plantations, relating to the service of clerks or apprentices, wherein shall not be truly inserted or written the full sum or sums of money, or other valuable consideration, received, or in any wise directly or indirectly given, paid, agreed, secured, or contracted for, with, or in relation to any such clerk or apprentice, and a receipt given for the same by the officer or officers aforesaid, or whereupon the duties payable by this act shall not be duly paid or lawfully tendered, according to the tenor and true meaning of this act, within the time herein for that purpose limited, shall be void and not available in any court or place or to any purpose whatsoever.

XXXV. And be it further enacted by the authority aforesaid, That if any master or mistress of any clerk or apprentice shall neglect to pay the said duty, within the time herein before limited, and any such clerk or apprentice shall in that case pay, or cause to be paid, to the amount of double the said duty, either during the term of such clerkship or apprenticeship, or within one year after the determination thereof, such master or mistress not having then paid the said double duty although required by such clerk or apprentice so to do; then, and in such case, it shall and may be lawful to and for any such clerk or apprentice, within three months after such payment of the said double duty, to demand of such master or mistress, or his or her executors or administrators, such sum or sums of money, or valuable consideration, as was or were paid to such master or mistress, for or in respect of such clerkship or apprenticeship; and in case such sum or sums of money, or valuable consideration, shall not be paid within three months after such demand thereof made, it paid within three months after such demand thereof made, it shall and may be lawful to and for any such clerk or apprentice, or any other person or persons on his or her behalf, to sue for and recover the same, in such manner as any penalty hereby inflicted may be sued for and recovered; and such clerks or apprentices shall, immediately after payment of such double duty, be and are hereby discharged from their clerkships or apprenticeships, and from all actions, penalties, forfeitures, and damages, for not serving the time for which they were respectively bound, contracted for, or agreed to serve, and shall have such and the same benefit and advantage of the time they shall respectively bound, contracted for, or agreed to serve, and shall have such and the same benefit and advantage of the time they shall respectively have continued with and served such master or mistress, as they would have been entitled to in case such duty has been paid by such master or mistress, within the time herein before limited for that purpose.

XXXVI. And be it further enacted by the authority aforesaid, That all printed indentures, or contacts for binding clerks or apprentices, after the said first day of November, one thousand seven hundred and sixty five, with the said colonies and plantations, shall have the following notice or memorandum printed under the same, or added thereto, videlicet,

The indenture must bear date the day it is executed and the money or other thing, given or contracted for with the clerk or apprentice, must be inserted in words at length, and the duty paid, and a receipt given on the back of the indenture, by the distributor of stamps, or his substitute, within three months after the execution of such indenture, under the penalties inflicted by law.

And if any printer, stationer, or other person or persons, within any of the said colonies or plantations, or any other part of his Majesty's dominions, shall fell, or cause to be sold, any such indenture or contract, without such notice or memorandum being printed under the same, or added thereto; then, and in every such case, such printer, stationer, or other person or persons, shall, for every such offence, forfeit the sum of ten pounds.

XXXVII. And, for the better securing the said duty on playing cards and dice; be it further enacted by the authority aforesaid, That from and after the said first day of November, one thousand seven hundred and sixty five, no playing cards or dice shall be sold, exposed to sale, or used in play, within the said colonies and plantations, unless the paper and thread inclosing, or which shall have inclosed, to same, shall be or shall have been respectively sealed and stamped, or marked, and unless one of

the cards of each pack or parcel of cards, so sold, shall be also marked or stamped on the spotted or painted side thereof with such mark or marks as shall have been provided in pursuance of this act, upon pain that every person who shall sell, or expose to sale, any such cards or dice which shall not have been so respectively sealed, marked, or stamped, as hereby is respectively required, shall forfeit for every pack or parcel of cards, and every one of such dice so sold or exposed to sale, the sum of ten pounds.

XXXVIII. And be it further enacted by the authority aforesaid, That if any person within the said colonies and plantations, or any other part of his Majesty's dominions, shall sell or buy any cover or label which has before been made use of for denoting the said duty upon cards, in order to be made use of for the inclosing any pack or parcel of cards; every person so offending shall, for every such offence, forfeit twenty pounds.

XXXIX. Provided always, and be it further enacted by the authority aforesaid, That if either the buyer or seller of any such cover or label shall inform against the other party concerned in buying or selling such cover or label, the party so informing shall be admitted to give evidence against the party informed against, and shall be indemnified against the said penalties.

XL. And be it further enacted by the authority aforesaid, That if any person or persons shall fraudulently inclose any parcel or pack of playing cards in any outside paper so sealed and stamped as aforesaid, the same having been made use of for the purpose aforesaid; then, so often, and in every such case, every person so offending in any of the particulars before-mentioned shall, for every such offence, forfeit the sum of twenty pounds.

XLI. And be it further enacted by the authority aforesaid, That from and after the said first day of November, one thousand seven hundred and sixty five, every clerk, officer, and other person employed or concerned in granting, making out, or delivering licences for retailing spirituous liquors or wine within any of the said colonies or plantations, shall, and he is hereby required and directed, within two months after delivering any such licences, to transmit to the chief distributor of stamped vellum, parcmen, and paper, a true and exact list or account of the number of licences so delivered, in which shall be inserted. the names of the persons licensed, and the places where they respectively reside; and if any such clerk, officer, or other person shall refuse or neglect to transmit any such list or account to such distributor, or shall transmit a false or untrue one, then, and in every such case, such clerk, officer, or other person, shall, for every such offence, forfeit fifty pounds.

XLII. And be it further enacted by the authority aforesaid, That licences for selling or uttering by retail spirituous liquors or wine within the said colonies and plantations, shall be in force and serve for no longer than one year from the date of each licence respectively.

XLIII. Provided nevertheless, and be it enacted by the authority aforesaid, That if any person licenced to sell spirituous liquors or wines, shall die or remove from the house or place wherein such spirituous liquors or wine shall, by virtue of such licence, be sold, it shall and may be lawful for the executors, administrators, of assigns of such person so dying or removing, who shall be possessed of such house or place, or for any occupier of such house or place, to sell spirituous liquors or wine therein during the residue of the term for which such licence shall have been granted, without any new licence to be had or obtained in that behalf; any thing to the contrary thereof in any wise notwithstanding.

XVIV. And it is hereby enacted by the authority aforesaid, That if any person or persons shall sell or utter by retail, that is to say, in any less quantity than one gallon at any one time, any kind of wine, or any liquor called or reputed wine, or any kind of spirituous liquors, in the said colonies or plantations, without taking out such licence yearly and every year, he, she, or they so offending shall, for every such offence, forfeit the sum of twenty pounds.

XLV. And be it further enacted by the authority aforesaid, That every person who shall retail spirituous liquors or wine in any prison or house of correction, or any workhouse appointed or to be appointed for the reception of poor persons within any of the said colonies or plantations, shall be deemed a retailer of spirituous liquors or wine within this act.

XLVI. Provided always, and be it further enacted by the authority aforesaid, That if at any time after the said first day of November, one thousand seven hundred and sixty five, there shall not be any provision made for licensing the retailers of wine or spirituous liquors, within any of the said colonies or plantations; then, and in every such case, and during such time as no provision shall be made, such licences shall and may be granted for the space of one year, and renewed from time to time by the governor or commander in chief of every such respective colony or plantation.

XLVII. And it is hereby further enacted by the authority aforesaid, That every person who shall at any one time buy of any chief distributor within any of the said colonies or plantations, who shall from time to time have in their custody any public books, or other matters or things hereby charged with a stamp duty, shall, at any seasonable time or times, permit any officer or officers thereunto authorized by the said commissioners for managing the stamp duties, to inspect and view all such public books, matters, and things, and to take thereout such notes and memorandums as shall be necessary for the purpose of ascertaining or securing the said duties, without fee or pose or reward; upon pain that every such clerk or other officer who shall refuse or neglect so to do, upon reasonable request in that behalf made, shall, for every such refusal or neglect, forfeit the sum of twenty pounds.

XLIX. And be it further enacted by the authority aforesaid, That the high treasurer of Great Britain, or the commissioners of his Majesty's treasury, or any three or more of such commissioners, for the time being, shall once in every year at least, set the prices at which all sorts of stamped vellum, parchment, and paper, shall be sold by the said commissioners for managing the stamp duties, and their officers; and that the said commissioners for the said duties shall cause such prices to be marked upon every such skin and piece of vellum and parchment, and sheet and piece paper: and if any officer or distributor to be appointed by virtue of this act, shall sell, or cause to be sold, any vellum, parchment, or paper, for a greater or higher price or sum, than the price or sum so set or affixed thereon; every such officer distributor shall, for every such offence, forfeit the sum of twenty pounds.

L. And be it also enacted by the authority aforesaid, That the several officers who shall be respectively employed in the raising, receiving, collecting, or paying, the several duties hereby charged, within the said colonies and plantations, shall every twelve months, or of-tener, if thereunto required by the said com-missioners for managing for the said duties, exhibit his and their respective account and accounts of the said several duties upon oath, or if a quaker upon affirmation, in the pres-ence of the governor, or commander in chief, or principal judge of the colony or plantation where such officers shall be respectively res-ident, in such manner as the high treasurer, or the commissioners of the treasury, or any three or more of such commissioners for the time being, shall, from time to time, direct and appoint, in order that the same may be immediately afterwards transmitted by the said officer or officers to the commissioners for managing the said duties, to be comp-trolled and audited according to the usual course and form of comptrolling and audit-ing the accounts of the stamp duties arising within this kingdom: and if any of the said officers shall neglect or refuse to exhibit any such account, or to verify the same upon oath or affirmation, or to transmit any such ac-count so verified to the commissioners for managing the said duties, in such manner, and within such time, as shall be so appointed or directed; or shall neglect or refuse to pay, or cause to be paid, into the hands of the re-ceiver general of the stamp duties in Great Britain, or to such other person or persons as the high treasurer, or commissioners of the treasury, or any three or more of such com-missioners for the time being, shall, form time to time, nominate or appoint, the monies respectively raised, levied, and re-ceived, by such officers under the authority of this act, at such times, and in such man-ner, as they shall be respectively required by the said high treasurer, or commissioners of the treasury; or if any such officers shall di-vert, detain, or misapply, all or any part of the said monies so by them respectively raised, levied, and received, or shall know-ingly return any person or persons insurer for any monies or other things duly answered, paid, or accounted for, by such person or per-sons, whereby he or they shall sustain any damage or prejudice; in every such case, every such officer shall be liable to pay treble the value of all and every sum and sums of money so diverted or misapplied; and shall also be liable to pay treble damages to the party grieved, by returning him insurer.

LI. And be it further enacted by the authority aforesaid, That the commissioners, receiver or receivers general, or other person or per-sons, who shall be respectively employed in Great Britain, in the directing, receiving, or paying, the monies arising by the duties hereby granted, shall, and are hereby re-quired, between the tenth day of October and the fifth day of January following, and so from year to year, yearly, at those times, to exhibit their respective accounts thereof to his Majesty's auditors of the imprest in Eng-land for the time being, or one of them, to be declared before the high treasurer, or commissioners of the treasury and chancellor of the exchequer for the time being, accord-ing to the course of the exchequer.

LII. And be it further enacted by the authority aforesaid, That if the said commissioners for managing the said duties, or the said receiver or receivers general, shall neglect or refuse to pay into the exchequer all or any of the said monies, in such manner as they are required by this act to pay the same, or shall divert or misapply any part thereof; then they, and every of them so offending, shall be liable to pay double the value of all and every sum and sums of money so diverted or misapplied.

LIII. And be it further enacted by the authority aforesaid, That the comptroller or comptrol-lers for the time being of the duties hereby imposed, shall keep perfect and distinct ac-counts in books fairly written of all the monies arising by the said duties; and if any such comptroller or comptrollers shall neglect his or their duty therein, then he or they, for every such offence, shall forfeit the sum of one hundred pounds.

LIV. And be it further enacted by the authority aforesaid, That all the monies which shall arise by the several rates and duties hereby granted (except the necessary charges of rais-ing, collecting, recovering, answering, pay-ing, and accounting for the same, and the necessary charges from time to time incurred in relation to this act, and the execution thereof) shall be paid into the receipt of his Majesty's exchequer, and shall be entered separate and apart from all other monies, and shall be there reserved to be from time to time disposed of by parliament, towards further defraying the necessary expenses of defend-ing, protecting, and securing, the said colonies and plantations.

LVI. And it is hereby further enacted and deal red, That all the powers and authorities by this act granted to the commissioners for managing the duties upon stamped vellum, parchment, and paper, shall and may be fully and effectually carried into execution by any three or more of the said commissioners; any thing herein before contained to the contrary notwithstanding.

LVII. And be it further enacted by the authority aforesaid, That all forfeitures and penalties incurred after the twenty ninth day of September, one thousand seven hundred and sixty five, for offences committed against an act passed in the fourth year of the reign of his present Majesty, entitled, An act for granting certain duties in the British colonies and plantations in America; for continuing, amending, and making perpetual, an act passed in the sixth year of the reign of his late majesty King George the Second entitled, And act for the better securing and encouraging the trade of his Majesty's sugar colonies in America; or applying the produce of such duties, and of the duties to arise by virtue of the said act, towards defraying the expenses of defending, protecting, and securing, the said colonies and plantations; for explaining an act made in the twenty fifth year of the reign of King Charles the Second entitled, And act for the encouragement of the Greenland and Eastland trades, and for the better securing the plantation trade; and for altering and disallowing several drawbacks on exports form this kingdom, and more effectually preventing the clandestine conveyance this kingdom, and more effectually preventing the clandestine conveyance of goods to and form the said colonies and plantations, and improving and securing the trade between the same and Great Britain, and for offences committed against any other act or acts of parliament relating to the trade or revenues of the said colonies and plantations; shall and may be prosecuted, sued for and recovered, in any court of record, or in any court of admiralty, in the respective colony or plantation where the offence shall be committed, or in any court of vice admiralty appointed or to be appointed, and which shall have jurisdiction within such colony, plantation, or place, (which courts of admiralty or vice admiralty are hereby respectively authorized and required to proceed, hear, and determine

the same) at the election of the informer or prosecutor.

LVIII. And it is hereby further enacted and declared by the authority aforesaid, That all sums of money granted and imposed by this act as rates or duties, and also all sums of money imposed as forfeitures or penalties, and all sums of money required to be paid, and all other monies herein mentioned, shall be deemed and taken to be sterling money of Great Britain, and shall be collected, recovered, and paid, to the amount of the value which such nominal sums bear in Great Britain; and shall and may be received and taken, according to the proportion and value of five shillings and six pence the ounce in silver; and that all the forfeitures and penalties hereby inflicted, and which shall be incurred, in the said colonies and plantations, shall and may be prosecuted, sued for, and recovered, in any court of record, or in any court of admiralty, in the respective colony or plantation where the offence shall be committed, or in any court of vice admiralty appointed or to be appointed, and which shall have jurisdiction within such colony, plantation, or place, (which courts of admiralty or vice admiralty are hereby respectively authorized and required to proceed, hear, and determine the same,) at the election of the informer or prosecutor; and that from and after the twenty ninth day of September, one thousand seven hundred and sixty five, in all cases, where any suit or prosecution shall be commenced and determined for any penalty or forfeiture inflicted by this act, or by the said act made in the fourth year of his present Majesty's reign, or by any other act of parliament relating to the trade or revenues of the said colonies or plantations, in any court of admiralty in the respective colony or plantation where the offence shall be committed, either party, who shall think himself aggrieved by such determination, may appeal from such determination to any court of vice admiralty appointed or to be appointed and which shall have jurisdiction within such colony, plantation, or place, (which court of vice admiralty is hereby authorized and required to proceed, hear, and determine such appeal) any law, custom, or usage, to the contrary notwithstanding; and the forfeitures and penalties hereby inflicted, which shall be incurred in any other part of his Majesty's dominions, shall and may be prosecuted, sued for, and recovered, with full costs of suit, in any court of record within the kingdom, territory, or place, where the offence shall be committed, in such and the same manner as any debt or damage, to the amount of such forfeiture or penalty, can or may be sued for and recovered.

LIX. And it is hereby further enacted, That all forfeitures and penalties hereby inflicted shall be divided, paid, and applied, as follows: (that is to say) one third part of all such forfeitures and penalties recovered in the said colonies and plantations, shall be paid into the hands of one of the chief distributors of stamped vellum, parchment, and paper, residing in the colony or plantation wherein the offender shall be convicted, for the use of his Majesty, his heirs, and successors; one third part of the penalties and forfeitures, so recovered, to the governor or commander in chief of such colony or plantation; and the other third part thereof, to the person who shall inform or sue for the same; and that one moiety of all such penalties and forfeitures recovered in any other part of his Majesty's dominions, shall be to the use of his Majesty, his heirs, and successors, and the other moiety thereof, to the person who shall inform or sue for the same.

LX. And be it further enacted by the authority aforesaid, That all the offences which are by this act made felony [counterfeiting or forging a stamped paper], and, shall be committed within any part of his Majesty's dominions, shall and may be heard, tried, and determined, before any court of law within the respective kingdom, territory, colony, or plantation, where the offence shall be committed, in such and the same manner as all other felonies can or may be heard, tried, and determined, in such court.

LXI. And be it further enacted by the authority aforesaid, That all the present governors or commanders in chief of any British colony or plantation, shall, before the said first day of November, one thousand seven hundred and sixty five, and all who hereafter shall be made governors or commanders in chief of the said colonies or plantations, or any of them, before their entrance into their government, shall take a solemn oath to do their utmost, that all and every the clauses contained in this present act be punctually and bona fide observed, according to the true intent and meaning thereof, so far as appertains unto the said governors or commanders in chief respectively, under the like penalties, forfeitures, and disabilities, either for neglecting to take the said oath, or wittingly neglecting to do their duty accordingly, as are mentioned and expressed in an act made in the seventh and eighth year of the reign of King William the Third, entitled, An act for preventing frauds, and regulating abuses, in the plantation trade; and the said oath hereby required to be taken, shall be administered by such person or persons as hath or have been, or shall be, appointed to administer the oath required to be taken by the said act made in the seventh and eighth year of the reign of King William the Third.

LXII. And be it further enacted by the authority aforesaid, That all records, writs, pleadings, and other proceedings in all courts whatsoever, and all deeds, instruments, and writings whatsoever, hereby charged, shall be engrossed and written in such manner as they have been usually accustomed to be engrossed and written, or are now engrossed and written within the said colonies and plantations.

LXIII. And it is hereby further enacted, That if any person or persons shall be sued or prosecuted, either in Great Britain or America, for any thing done in pursuance of this act, such person and persons shall and may plead the general issue, and give this act and the special matter in evidence; and it shall appear so to have been done, the jury shall find for the defendant or defendants: and if the plaintiff or plaintiffs shall become non-suited or discontinue his or their action after the defendant or defendants shall recover treble costs and have the like remedy for the same as defendants have in other cases by law.

Proclamation by the King for Suppressing Rebellion and Sedition (1775)

Commentary

News of American resistance to British troops at Lexington and Concord provoked King George III to proclaim the colonies in a state of rebellion on August 23, 1775. News of this proclamation arrived in America on October 31 of that year.

Whereas many of our subjects in divers parts of our Colonies and Plantations in North America, misled by dangerous and ill designing men, and forgetting the allegiance which they owe to the power that has protected and supported them; after various disorderly acts committed in disturbance of the publick peace, to the obstruction of lawful commerce, and to the oppression of our loyal subjects carrying on the same; have at length proceeded to open and avowed rebellion, by arraying themselves in a hostile manner, to withstand the execution of the law, and traitorously preparing, ordering and levying war against us: And whereas, there is reason to apprehend that such rebellion hath been much promoted and encouraged by the traitorous correspondence, counsels and comfort of divers wicked and desperate persons within this realm: To the end therefore, that none of our subjects may neglect or violate their duty through ignorance thereof, or through any doubt of the protection which the law will afford to their loyalty and zeal, we have thought fit, by and with the advice of our Privy Council, to issue our Royal Proclamation, hereby declaring, that not only all our Officers, civil and military, are obliged to exert their utmost endeavours to suppress such rebellion, and to bring the traitors to justice, but that all our subjects of this Realm, and the dominions thereunto belonging, are bound by law to be aiding and assisting in the suppression of such rebellion, and to disclose and make known all traitorous conspiracies and attempts against us, our crown and dignity; and we do accordingly strictly charge and command all our Officers, as well civil as military, and all others our obedient and loyal subjects, to use their utmost endeavours to withstand and suppress such rebellion, and to disclose and make known all treasons and traitorous conspiracies which they shall know to be against us, our crown and dignity; and for that purpose, that they transmit to one of our principal Secretaries of State, or other proper officer, due and full information of all persons who shall be found carrying on correspondence with, or in any manner or degree aiding or abetting the persons now in open arms and rebellion against our Government, within any of our Colonies and Plantations in North America, in order to bring to condign punishment the authors, perpetrators, and abetters of such traitorous designs.

Given at our Court at St. James's the twenty-third day of August, one thousand seven hundred and seventy five, in the fifteenth year of our reign.

God save the King.

Declaration of Independence (1776)

The Commentary

The Declaration of Independence was written by Thomas Jefferson and ratified shortly after by the Second Continental Congress on 4 July 1776, two days after that body had officially severed its ties to Great Britain.

In composing this greatest, most famous of legal documents, Jefferson, already well regarded as an essayist, drew heavily not only on the ideas of his fellow patriots, but also on the natural-rights theories of John Locke and the Swiss legal philosophy of Emerich de Vattel. Although Jefferson's bitter attack on the institution of slavery was rejected by the convention in deference to South Carolina and Georgia, the principles set forth in the Declaration, among them the revolutionary notion that human beings had rights which even governments and kings could not take from them, would nevertheless become a rallying cry not only for Jefferson and his New World contemporaries, but also for many people at all times in the United States and around the world.

In Congress, July 4, 1776
The Unanimous Declaration of The Thirteen United States of America

When in the Course of human events, it becomes necessary for one people to dissolve the political bands which have connected them with another, and to assume among the Powers of the earth, the separate and equal station to which the Laws of Nature and of Nature's God entitle them, a decent respect to the opinions of mankind requires that they should declare the causes which impel them to the separation. We hold these truths to be self-evident, that all men are created equal, that they are endowed by their Creator with certain unalienable Rights, that among these are Life, Liberty and the pursuit of Happiness. That to secure these rights, Governments are instituted among Men, deriving their just powers from the consent of the governed, That whenever any Form of Government becomes destructive of these ends, it is the Right of the People to alter or to abolish it, and to institute new Government, laying its foundation on such principles and organizing its powers in such form, as to them shall seem most likely to effect their Safety and Happiness. Prudence, indeed, will dictate that Governments long established should not be changed for light and transient causes; and accordingly all experience hath shown, that mankind are more disposed to suffer, while evils are sufferable, than to right themselves by abolishing the forms to which they are accustomed. But when a long train of abuses and usurpations, pursuing invariably the same Object evinces a design to reduce them under absolute Despotism, it is their right, it is their duty, to throw off such Government, and to provide new Guards for their future security. Such has been the patient sufferance of these Colonies; and such is now the necessity which constrains them to alter their former Systems of Government. The history of the present King of Great Britain is a history of repeated injuries and usurpations, all having in direct object the establishment of an absolute Tyranny over these States. To prove this, let Facts be submitted to a candid world.

He has refused his Assent to Laws, the most wholesome and necessary for the public good.

He has forbidden his Governors to pass Laws of immediate and pressing importance, unless suspended in their operation till his Assent should be obtained; and when so suspended, he has utterly neglected to attend to them.

He has refused to pass other Laws for the accommodation of large districts of people, unless those people would relinquish the right of Representation in the Legislature, a right inestimable to them and formidable to tyrants only.

He has called together legislative bodies at places unusual, uncomfortable, and distant from the depository or their public Records, for the sole purpose of fatiguing them into compliance with his measures.

He has dissolved Representative Houses repeatedly, for opposing with manly firmness his invasions on the rights of the people.

He has refused for a long time, after such dissolutions, to cause others to be elected; whereby the Legislative powers, incapable of Annihilation, have returned to the People at large for their exercise; the State remaining in the mean time exposed to all the dangers of invasion from without, and convulsions within.

He has endeavoured to prevent the population of these States; for that purpose obstructing the Laws for Naturalization of Foreigners; refusing to pass others to encourage their migration hither, and raising the conditions of new Appropriations of Lands.

He has obstructed the Administration of Justice, by refusing his Assent to Laws for establishing Judiciary powers.

He has made Judges dependent on his Will alone, for the tenure of their offices, and the amount and payment of their salaries.

He has erected a multitude of New Offices, and sent hither swarms of Officers to harrass our people, and eat out their substance.

He has kept among us, in times of peace, Standing Armies, without the Consent of our legislatures.

He has affected to render the Military independent of and superior to the Civil power.

He has combined with others to subject us to a jurisdiction foreign to our constitution, and unacknowledged by our laws; giving his Assent to their Acts of pretended Legislation:

For quartering large bodies of armed troops among us:

For protecting them, by a mock Trial, from Punishment for any Murders which they should commit on the Inhabitants of these States:

For cutting off our Trade with all parts of the world:

For imposing Taxes on us without our Consent:

For depriving us in many cases, of the benefits of Trial by Jury:

For transporting us beyond Seas to be tried for pretended offenses:

For abolishing the free System of English Laws in a neighboring Province, establishing therein an Arbitrary government, and enlarging its Boundaries so as to render it at once an example and fit instrument for introducing the same absolute rule into these Colonies:

For taking away our Charters, abolishing our most valuable Laws, and altering fundamentally the Forms of our Governments:

For suspending our own Legislatures, and declaring themselves invested with power to legislate for us in all cases whatsoever.

He has abdicated Government here, by declaring us out of his Protection and waging War against us.

He has plundered our seas, ravaged our Coasts, burnt our towns, and destroyed the lives of our people.

He is at this time transporting large Armies of foreign Mercenaries to compleat the works of death, desolation and tyranny, already begun with circumstances of Cruelty & perfidy scarcely paralleled in the most barbarous ages, and totally unworthy the Head of a civilized nation.

He has constrained our fellow Citizens taken Captive on the high Seas to bear Arms against their Country, to become the executioners of their friends and Brethren, or to fall themselves by their Hands.

He has excited domestic insurrections amongst us, and has endeavoured to bring on the inhabitants of our frontiers, the merciless Indian Savages, whose known rule of warfare, is an undistinguished destruction of all ages, sexes and conditions.

In every state of these Oppressions We have Petitioned for Redress in the most humble terms: Our repeated Petitions have been answered only by repeated injury. A Prince, whose character is thus marked by every act which may define a Tyrant, is unfit to be the ruler of a free people.

Nor have We been wanting in attentions to our British brethren. We have warned them from time to time of attempts by their legislature to extend an unwarrantable jurisdiction over us. We have reminded them of the circumstances of our emigration and settlement here. We have appealed to their native justice and magnanimity, and we have conjured them by the ties of our common kindred to disavow these usurpations, which, would inevitably interrupt our connections and correspondence. They too have been deaf to the voice of justice and of consanguinity. We must, therefore, acquiesce in the necessity, which denounces our Separation, and hold them, as we hold the rest of mankind, Enemies in War, in Peace Friends.

We, Therefore, the Representatives of the United States of America, in General Congress, Assembled, appealing to the Supreme Judge of the world for the rectitude of our intentions, do, in the Name, and by Authority of the good People of these Colonies, solemnly publish and declare, That these United Colonies are, and of Right ought to be Free and Independent States; that they are Absolved from all Allegiance to the British Crown, and that all political connection between them and the State of Great Britain, is and ought to be totally disolved; and that as Free and Independent States, they have full Power to levy War, conclude Peace, contract Alliances, establish Commerce, and to do all other Acts and Things which Independent States may of right do. And for the support of this Declaration, with a firm reliance on the protection of Divine Providence, we mutually pledge to each other our Lives, our Fortunes and our sacred Honor. John Adams, Samuel Adams, Josiah Bartlett, Carter Braxton, Charles Carroll, Samuel Chase, Abraham Clark, George Clymer, William Ellery, William Floyd, Benjamin Franklin, Elbridge Gerry, Button Gwinnett, Lyman Hall, John Hancock, Benjamin Harrison, John Hart, Richard Henry Lee, Joseph Hewes, Thomas Heyward, Jr., William Hooper, Stephen Hopkins, Fras. Hopkinson, Samuel Huntington, Thomas Jefferson, Frans. Lewis, Francis Lightfoot Lee, Phil. Livington, Thomas Lynch, Jr., Thomas M'Kean, Arthur Middleton, Lewis Morris, Robert Morris, John Morton, Thomas Nelson, Jr., William Paca, John Penn, George Read, Caesar Rodney, George Ross, Benjamin Rush, Edward Rutledge, Roger Sherman, Jason Smith, Richard Stockton, Thomas Stone, George Taylor, Matthew Thornton, Robert Treat Paine, George Walton, William Whipple, William Williams, James Wilson, Johnothan Witherspoon, Oliver Wolcott, George Wythe.

Formation of African-American Regiment (1778)

Commentary

In 1778, faced with the difficulties of recruiting soldiers, Rhode Island and Massachusetts voted to recruit African-American regiments. Rhode Island was the first to do so in February of that year, when it voted to enlist African Americans in the Continental army and to free those who passed muster. No records exist of the debates in the General Assembly over their recruitment, but the important point is that the legislators decided to free African Americans before enlisting them in the militia.

Not everyone agreed to arm African Americans. Some members of the assembly signed a "Protest Against Enlisting Slaves to Serve in the Army." They argued that the state did not have enough slaves who would be likely to enlist and the project should be abandoned. They may also have feared that creating an African-American regiment might also give the British the idea of doing the same against the Whigs or that it might appear that the state had purchased a band of slaves to defend the country.

Three months after the Rhode Island General Assembly voted to enlist slaves in the Continental army, it rescinded its order. It voted in May 1778 not to allow slaves to join the army after June 10, 1778, stating, "it is necessary for answering the purposed intend by said act that the same should be temporary." Even though the Assembly reversed itself, African Americans continued to enlist after the June 10 deadline. Records of the state treasurer indicate that forty-four slaves enrolled in the regiment between June 12 and October 13.

Whereas, for the preservation of the rights and liberties of the United States, it is necessary that the whole power of Government should be exerted in recruiting the Continental battalions; and, whereas, His Excellency, General Washington, hath inclosed to this State a proposal made to him by Brigadier General Varnum, to enlist into the two battalions raising by this State such slaves as should be willing to enter into the service; and, whereas, history affords us frequent precedents of the wisest, the freest and bravest nations having liberated their slaves and enlisted them as soldiers to fight in defence of their country; and also, whereas the enemy have, with great force, taken possession of the capital and of a great part of this State, and this State is obliged to raise a very considerable number of troops for its own immediate defence, whereby it is in a manner rendered impossible for this State to furnish recruits for the said two battalions without adopting the said measures so recommended, —

It is Voted and Resolved, That every able-bodied negro, mulatto, or Indian man-slave in this State may enlist into either of the said two battalions, to serve during the continuance of the present war with Great Britain; That every slave so enlisting shall be entitled to and receive all the bounties, wages and encouragements allowed by the Continental Congress to any soldiers enlisting into this service.

It in further Voted and Resolved, That every slave so enlisting shall, upon his passing muster by Col. Christopher Greene, be immediately discharged from the service of his master or mistress, and be absolutely free, as though he had never been incumbered and be incumbered with any kind of servitude or slavery. And in case such slave shall, by sickness or otherwise, be rendered unable to maintain himself, he shall not be chargeable to his master or mistress, but shall be supported at the expense of the State.

And, whereas, slaves have been by the laws deemed the property of their owners, and therefore compensation ought to be made to the owners for the loss of their service,—

It is further Voted and Resolved, That there be allowed and paid by this State to the owners, for every such slave so enlisting, a sum according to his worth, at a price not exceeding one hundred and twenty pounds for the most valuable slave, and in proportion for a slave of less value, — provided the owner of said slave shall deliver up to the officer who shall enlist him the clothes of the said sum.

And for settling and ascertaining the value of such slaves, — It is further Voted and Resolved, that a committee of five shall be appointed, to wit, — one from each county, any three of whom to be a quorum, — to examine the slaves who shall be so enlisted, after they shall have passed muster, and to set a price upon each slave, according to his value as aforesaid.

It is further Voted and Resolved, That upon any able-bodied negro, mulatto or Indian slave enlisting as aforesaid, the officer who shall so enlist him, after he has passed muster as aforesaid, shall deliver a certificate thereof to the master or mistress of said negro, mulatto or Indian slave, which shall discharge him from the service of said master or mistress.

It is further Voted and Resolved, That the committee who shall estimate the value of the slave aforesaid, shall give a certificate of the sum at which he may be valued to the owner of said slave, and the general treasurer of this State is hereby empowered and directed to give unto the owner of said slave his promissory note for the sum of money at which he shall be valued as aforesaid, payable on demand, with interest, — which shall be paid with the money from Congress.

A true copy, examined, HENRY WARD, Sec'y

Constitution of the United States (1791)

Commentary

Delegates sent to Philadelphia from the thirteen states to discuss changes to the existing Confederation government formed the Constitution during the summer of 1787. The delegates tended to be well-educated, wealthy conservatives who worried about the economic and diplomatic problems facing the young United States. Shortly after the beginning of the proceedings, the delegates adopted a rule of debate behind closed doors, so that views could be expressed without fear of repercussions at home. James Madison (1751–1836) of Virginia used this opportunity to introduce his plan for revising the government of the United States. Madison's Virginia Plan scrapped the Articles of Confederation, replacing it with a highly centralized government based on *federalism*. The delegates, realizing that Madison's plan answered their desire for a government that would protect liberty while ensuring order, began in earnest to create a new government for the United States.

The heart of Madison's proposal balanced and separated the three most important functions of government: a bicameral legislature, a strong executive, and an independent judiciary. The Constitution models itself on past successful republics in creating a lower house, the members of which are elected according to the respective population of the states, with authority over how money is raised and spent; and an upper house, restricted to two representatives from each state, with functions resembling that of a general court. Executive power is modeled on the consuls of the ancient Roman Republic, who had two general powers: to serve as commander in chief and to execute the laws passed by the legislative power. Madison, who realized the importance of freeing judges from the influence of significant others, created a judicial system independent of the legislative and executive branches. The resulting Constitution balances power among the varying functions of the federal government while creating a method for local, state, and federal governments to share power. The proposal to include a Bill of Rights, as the first ten amendments are now known, came to the fore during the ratification campaign for the Constitution. They became law in December 1791, but their interpretation and impact on the rights of citizens continue to evolve into the twenty-first century.

The text of the thirteenth through fifteenth amendments can be found in the appendix of Volume 2.

PREAMBLE

WE THE PEOPLE of the United States, in Order to form a more perfect Union, establish Justice, insure domestic Tranquility, provide for the common defence, promote the general Welfare, and secure the Blessings of Liberty to ourselves and our Posterity, do ordain and establish this Constitution for the United States of America.

ARTICLE I

Sec. 1. All legislative Powers herein granted shall be vested in a Congress of the United States, which shall consist of a Senate and House of Representatives.

Sec. 2. The House of Representatives shall be composed of Members chosen every second Year by the People of the several States, and the Electors in each State shall have the qualifications requisite for Electors of the most numerous Branch of the State Legislature. No Person shall be a Representative who shall not have attained to the age of twenty five Years, and been seven Years a Citizen of the United States, and who shall not, when elected, be an Inhabitant of that State in which he shall be chosen.

Representatives and direct Taxes shall be apportioned among the several States which may be included within this Union, according to their respective Numbers, which shall be determined by adding to the whole Number of free Persons, including those bound to Service for a Term of Years, and excluding Indians not taxed, three fifths of all other Persons. The actual Enumeration shall be made within three Years after the first Meeting of the Congress of the United States, and within every subsequent Term of ten Years, in such Manner as they shall by Law direct. The Number of Representatives shall not exceed one for every thirty Thousand, but each State shall have at Least one Representative; and until such enumeration shall be made, the State of New Hampshire shall be entitled to chuse three, Massachusetts eight, Rhode Island and Providence Plantations one, Connecticut five, New York six, New Jersey four, Pennsylvania eight, Delaware one, Maryland six, Virginia ten, North Carolina five, South Carolina five and Georgia three.

When vacancies happen in the Representation from any State, the Executive Authority thereof shall issue Writs of Election to fill such Vacancies.

The House of Representatives shall chuse their Speaker and other officers; and shall have the sole Power of Impeachment.

Sec. 3. The Senate of the United States shall be composed of two Senators from each State, chosen by the Legislature thereof, for six Years; and each Senator shall have one Vote.

Immediately after they shall be assembled in Consequence of the first Election, they shall be divided as equally as may be into three Classes. The Seats of the Senators of the first class shall be vacated at the Expiration of the second Year, of the second Class at the Expiration of the fourth Year, and of the third Class at the Expiration of the sixth Year, so that one third may be chosen every second Year; and if Vacancies happen by Resignation, or otherwise, during the Recess of the Legislature of any State, the Executive thereof may make temporary Appointments until the next Meeting of the Legislature, which shall then fill such Vacancies.

No Person shall be a Senator who shall not have attained to the Age of thirty Years, and been nine Years a Citizen of the United States, and who shall not, when elected, be an Inhabitant of that State for which he shall be chosen.

The Vice President of the United States shall be President of the Senate, but shall have no Vote, unless they be equally divided.

The Senate shall chuse their other Officers, and also a President pro tempore, in the Absence of the Vice President, or when he shall exercise the Office of President of the United States.

The Senate shall have the sole Power to try all Impeachments. When sitting for that Purpose, they shall be on Oath or Affirmation. When the President of the United States is tried, the Chief Justice shall preside: and no Person shall be convicted without the Concurrence of two thirds of the Members present.

Judgment in Cases of Impeachment shall not extend further than to removal from Office, and disqualification to hold and enjoy any Office of honor, Trust or Profit under the United States: but the Party convicted shall nevertheless be liable and subject to Indictment, Trial, Judgment and Punishment, according to Law.

Sec. 4. The Times, Places and Manner of holding Elections for Senators and Representatives, shall be prescribed in each State by the Legislature thereof; but the Congress may at any time by Law make or alter such Regulations, except as to the Places of chusing Senators.

The Congress shall assemble at least once in every Year, and such Meeting shall be on the first Monday in December, unless they shall by Law appoint a different Day.

Sec. 5. Each House shall be the Judge of the Elections, returns and Qualifications of its own Members, and a Majority of each shall constitute a Quorum to do Business; but a smaller Number may adjourn from day to day, and may be authorized to compel the Attendance of absent Members, in such Manner, and under such Penalties as each House may provide.

Each House may determine the Rules of its Proceedings, punish its Members for disorderly Behavior, and, with the Concurrence of two thirds, expel a Member.

Each House shall keep a Journal of its Proceedings, and from time to time publish the same, excepting such Parts as may in their Judgment require Secrecy; and the Yeas and Nays of the Members of either House on any question shall, at the Desire of one-fifth of those Present, be entered on the Journal.

Neither House, during the Session of Congress, shall, without the Consent of the other, adjourn for more than three days, nor to any other Place than that in which the two Houses shall be sitting.

Sec. 6. The Senators and Representatives shall receive a Compensation for their Services, to be ascertained by Law, and paid out of the Treasury of the United States. They shall in all Cases, except Treason, Felony and Breach of the Peace, be privileged from Arrest during their Attendance at the Session of their respective Houses, and in going to and returning from the same; and for any Speech or Debate in either House, they shall not be questioned in any other Place.

No Senator or Representative shall, during the Time for which he was elected, be appointed to any civil Office under the Authority of the United States which shall have been created, or the Emoluments whereof shall have been increased during such time; and no Person holding any Office under the United States, shall be a member of either House during his Continuance in Office.

Sec. 7. All Bills for raising Revenue shall originate in the House of Representatives; but the Senate may propose or concur with Amendments as on other Bills.

Every Bill which shall have passed the House of Representatives and the Senate, shall, before it become a Law, be presented to the President of the United States; If he approve he shall sign It, but If not he shall return It, with his Objections to that House in which it shall have originated, who shall enter the Objections at large on their Journal, and proceed to reconsider it. If after such Reconsideration two thirds of that House shall agree to pass the Bill, it shall be sent, together with the Objections, to the other House, by which it shall likewise be reconsidered, and if approved by two thirds of that House, it shall become a Law. But in all such Cases the Votes of both Houses shall be determined by yeas and Nays, and the Names of the Persons voting for and against the Bill shall be entered on the Journal of each House respectively. If any Bill shall not be returned by the President within ten Days (Sundays excepted) after it shall have been presented to him, the Same shall be a Law, in like Manner as if he had signed it, unless the Congress by their Adjournment prevent its Return, in which Case it shall not be a Law.

Every Order, resolution, or Vote to which the Concurrence of the Senate and House of Representatives may be necessary (except on a question of Adjournment) shall be presented to the President of the United States; and before the Same shall take Effect, shall be approved by him, or being disapproved by him, shall be repassed by two thirds of the Senate and House of Representatives, according to the Rules and Limitations prescribed in the Case of a Bill.

Sec. 8. The Congress shall have Power

To lay and collect Taxes, Duties, Imposts and Excises, to pay the Debts and provide for the common Defence and general Welfare of the United States; but all Duties, Imposts and Excises shall be uniform throughout the United States;

To borrow Money on the credit of the United States; To regulate Commerce with foreign Nations, and among the several States, and with the Indian Tribes;

To establish a uniform Rule of Naturalization, and uniform Laws on the subject of Bankruptcies throughout the United States;

To coin Money, regulate the Value thereof, and of foreign coin, and fix the Standard of Weights and Measures;

To provide for the Punishment of counterfeiting the Securities and current Coin of the United States;

To establish Post-Offices and post-Roads;

To promote the Progress of Science and useful Arts, by securing for limited Times to Authors and Inventors the exclusive Right to their respective Writings and Discoveries;

To constitute Tribunals inferior to the Supreme Court;

To define and punish Piracies and Felonies committed on the high Seas, and Offenses against the Law of Nations;

To declare War, grant Letters of Marque and Reprisal, and make Rules concerning Captures on Land and Water;

To raise and support Armies, but no Appropriation of Money to that Use shall be for a longer Term than two Years;

To provide and maintain a Navy;

To make Rules for the Government and Regulation of the land and naval Forces;

To provide for calling forth the Militia to execute the Laws of the Union, suppress insurrections and repel invasions;

To provide for organizing, arming, and disciplining, the Militia, and for governing such Part of them as may be employed in the Service of the United States, reserving to the States respectively, the Appointment of the Officers, and the Authority of training the Militia according to the discipline prescribed by Congress;

To exercise exclusive Legislation in all Cases whatsoever, over such District (not exceeding ten Miles square) as may, by Cession of particular States, and the Acceptance of Congress, become the Seat of the Government of the United States, and to exercise like Authority over all Places purchased by the Consent of the Legislature of the State in which the Same shall be, for the erection of Forts, Magazines, arsenals, dock-Yards, and other needful Buildings; and

To make all Laws which shall be necessary and proper for carrying into Execution the foregoing Powers, and all other Powers vested by this Constitution in the Government of the United States, or in any Department or Officer thereof.

Sec. 9. The Migration or Importation of such Persons as any of the States now existing shall think proper to admit, shall not be prohibited by the Congress prior to the Year one thousand eight hundred and eight, but a Tax or duty may be imposed on such Importation, not exceeding ten dollars for each Person.

The Privilege of the Writ of Habeas Corpus shall not be suspended, unless when in Cases of Rebellion or Invasion the public Safety may require it.

No bill of Attainder or ex post facto Law shall be passed.

No Capitation, or other direct Tax shall be laid, unless in Proportion to the Census or Enumeration herein before directed to be taken.

No Tax or Duty shall be laid on Articles exported from any State.

No Preference shall be given by any Regulation of Commerce or Revenue to the Ports of one State over those of another: nor shall Vessels bound to, or from, one State, be obliged to enter, clear, or pay Duties in another.

No Money shall be drawn from the Treasury, but in Consequence of Appropriations made by Law; and a regular Statement and Account of the Receipts and Expenditures of all public Money shall be published from time to time.

No Title of Nobility shall be granted by the United States: And no Person holding any Office of Profit or Trust under them, shall, without the Consent of the Congress, accept of any present, Emolument, Office, or Title, of any kind whatever, from any King, Prince or Foreign State.

Sec. 10. No State shall enter into any Treaty, Alliance, or Confederation; grant Letters of Marque and Reprisal; coin Money; emit Bills of Credit; make any Thing but gold and silver Coin a Tender in Payment of Debts; pass any Bill of Attainder, ex post facto Law, or Law impairing the Obligation of Contracts, or grant any Title of Nobility.

No State shall, without the Consent of the Congress, lay any Imposts or Duties on Imports or Exports, except what may be absolutely necessary for executing it's inspection Laws: and the net Produce of all Duties and Imposts, laid by any State on Imports or Exports, shall be for the use of the Treasury of the United States; and all such Laws shall be subject to the Revision and Controul of the Congress.

No State shall, without the Consent of Congress, lay any Duty of Tonnage, keep Troops, or Ships of War in time of Peace, enter into any Agreement or Compact with another State, or with a foreign Power, or engage in War, unless actually invaded, or in such imminent Danger as will not admit of delay.

ARTICLE II

Sec. 1. The executive Power shall be vested in a President of the United States of America. He shall hold his Office during the Term of four Years, and, together with the Vice President chosen for the same Term, be elected, as follows:

Each State shall appoint, in such Manner as the Legislature thereof may direct, a Number of Electors, equal to the whole Number of Senators and Representatives to which the State may be entitled in the Congress: but no Senator or Representative, or person holding an Office of Trust or Profit under the United States, shall be appointed an elector.

The Electors shall meet in their respective States, and vote by Ballot for two Persons, of whom one at least shall not be an Inhabitant of the same State with themselves. And they shall make a List of all the persons voted for, and of the Number of Votes for each; which List they shall sign and certify, and transmit sealed to the Seat of the Government of the United States, directed to the President of the Senate. The President of the Senate shall, in the Presence of the Senate and House of Representatives, open all the Certificates, and the Votes shall then be counted. The Person having the greatest Number of Votes shall be the President, if such Number be a Majority of the whole Number of Electors appointed; and if there be more than one who have such Majority, and have an equal Number of Votes, then the House of Representatives shall immediately chuse by Ballot one of them for President; and if no person have a Majority, then from the five highest on the List the said House shall in like Manner chuse the President. But in chusing the President, the Votes shall be taken by States, the representation from each State having one Vote; a quorum for this Purpose shall consist of a Member or Members from two thirds of the States, and a Majority of all the States shall be necessary to a Choice. In every Case, after the Choice of the President, the Person having the greatest number of votes of the electors shall be the Vice President. But if there should remain two or more who have equal Votes, the Senate shall chuse from them by Ballot the Vice President.

The Congress may determine the time of chusing the Electors, and the Day on which they shall give their Votes; which Day shall be the same throughout the United States.

No Person except a natural born Citizen, or a Citizen of the United States, at the time of the Adoption of this Constitution, shall be eligible to the Office of President; neither shall any person be eligible to that Office who shall not have attained to the Age of thirty five Years, and been fourteen Years a Resident within the United States.

In Case of the Removal of the President from Office, or of his Death, Resignation, or Inability to discharge the Powers and Duties of the said Office, the Same shall devolve on the Vice President, and the Congress may by Law provide for the Case of Removal, Death, Resignation or Inability, both of the President and Vice President, declaring what Officer shall then act as President, and such Officer shall act accordingly, until the Disability be removed, or a President shall be elected.

The President shall, at stated Times, receive for his Services, a Compensation, which shall neither be increased nor diminished during the Period for which he shall have been elected, and he shall not receive within that Period any other Emolument from the United States, or any of them.

Before he enter on the Execution of his Office, he shall take the following Oath or Affirmation:

> "I do solemnly swear (or affirm) that I will faithfully execute the Office of President of the United States, and will to the best of my Ability, preserve, protect and defend the Constitution of the United States."

Sec. 2. The President shall be Commander in Chief of the Army and Navy of the United States, and of the Militia of the several States, when called into the actual service of the United States; he may require the Opinion, in writing, of the principal Officer in each of the executive Departments, upon any Subject relating to the Duties of their respective Offices, and he shall have Power to grant Reprieves and Pardons for Offenses against the United States, except in Cases of Impeachment.

He shall have Power, by and with the Advice and Consent of the Senate, to make Treaties, provided two thirds of the Senators present concur; and he shall nominate, and by and with the Advice and Consent of the Senate, shall appoint Ambassadors, other public Ministers and Consuls, Judges of the supreme Court, and all other Officers of the United States, whose appointments are not herein otherwise provided for, and which shall be established by law: but the Congress may by law vest the appointment of such inferior officers, as they think proper, in the President alone, in the Courts of Law, or in the Heads of Departments.

The President shall have Power to fill up all Vacancies that may happen during the Recess of the Senate, by granting Commissions which shall expire at the End of their next session.

Sec. 3. He shall from time to time give to the Congress Information of the State of the Union, and recommend to their consideration such Measures as he shall judge necessary and expedient; he may, on extraordinary Occasions, convene both Houses, or either of them, and in Case of Disagreement between them, with Respect to the Time of Adjournment, he may adjourn them to such Time as he shall think proper; he shall receive Ambassadors and other public Ministers; he shall take Care that the Laws be faithfully executed, and shall Commission all the Officers of the United States.

Sec. 4. The President, Vice President and all civil Officers of the United States, shall be removed from Office on Impeachment for, and Conviction of, Treason, Bribery, or other high Crimes and Misdemeanors.

ARTICLE III

Sec. 1. The judicial Power of the United States, shall be vested in one supreme Court, and in such inferior Courts as the Congress may from time to time ordain and establish. The Judges, both of the supreme and inferior courts, shall hold their Offices during good Behavior, and shall, at stated times, receive for their Services, a Compensation, which shall not be diminished during their Continuance in Office.

Sec. 2. The judicial Power shall extend to all Cases, in Law and Equity, arising under this Constitution, the Laws of the United States, and Treaties made, or which shall be made, under their Authority; to all Cases affecting Ambassadors, other public Ministers and Consuls; to all Cases of admiralty and maritime Jurisdiction; to Controversies to which the United States shall be a Party; to Controversies between two or more States; between a State and Citizens of another State; between Citizens of different States; between Citizens of the same State claiming Lands under Grants of different States, and between a State, or the Citizens thereof, and foreign States, Citizens or Subjects.

In all Cases affecting Ambassadors, other public Ministers and Consuls, and those in which a State shall be party, the supreme Court shall have original Jurisdiction. In all the other Cases before mentioned, the supreme Court shall have appellate Jurisdiction, both as to Law and Fact, with such Exceptions, and under such Regulations as the Congress shall make.

The trial of all Crimes, except in Cases of Impeachment, shall be by Jury; and such trial shall be held in the State where the said Crimes shall have been committed; but when not committed within any State, the Trial shall be at such Place or Places as the Congress may by Law have directed.

Sec. 3. Treason against the United States, shall consist only in levying War against them, or in adhering to their Enemies, giving them Aid and Comfort. No Person shall be convicted of Treason unless on the Testimony of two Witnesses to the same overt Act, or on Confession in open court.

The Congress shall have Power to declare the Punishment of Treason, but no Attainder of Treason shall work Corruption of Blood, or Forfeiture except during the Life of the Person attainted.

ARTICLE FOUR

Sec. 1. Full Faith and Credit shall be given in each State to the public Acts, Records, and judicial Proceedings of every other State. And the Congress may by general Laws prescribe the Manner in which such Acts, Records and Proceedings shall be proved, and the Effect thereof.

Sec. 2. The Citizens of each State shall be entitled to all Privileges and Immunities of Citizens in the several States.

A person charged in any State with Treason, Felony, or other Crime, who shall flee from Justice, and be found in another State, shall on Demand of the Executive Authority of the State from which he fled, be delivered up, to be removed to the State having Jurisdiction of the Crime.

No Person held to Service or Labour in one State, under the Laws thereof, escaping into another, shall, in Consequence of any Law or Regulation therein, be discharged from such Service or Labour, but shall be delivered up on Claim of the Party to whom such Service or Labour may be due.

Sec. 3. New States may be admitted by the Congress into this Union; but no new States shall be formed or erected within the Jurisdiction of any other State; nor any State be formed by the Junction of two or more States, or Parts of States, without the Consent of the Legislatures of the States concerned as well as of the Congress.

The Congress shall have Power to dispose of and make all needful Rules and Regulations respecting the Territory or other Property belonging to the United States; and nothing in this Constitution shall be so construed as to Prejudice any Claims of the United States, or of any particular State.

Sec. 4. The United States shall guarantee to every State in this Union a Republican Form of government, and shall protect each of them against Invasion; and on Application of the Legislature, or of the Executive (when the legislature cannot be convened) against domestic Violence.

ARTICLE V

The Congress, whenever two thirds of both Houses shall deem it necessary, shall propose Amendments to this Constitution, or, on the Application of the Legislatures of two thirds of the several States, shall call a Convention for proposing Amendments, which, in either Case, shall be valid to all intents and purposes, as part of this Constitution, when ratified by the Legislatures of three fourths of the several States, or by Conventions in three fourths thereof, as the one or the other Mode of Ratification may be proposed by the Congress; Provided that no Amendment which may be made prior to the Year One thousand eight hundred and eight shall in any Manner affect the first and fourth Clauses in the Ninth Section of the first Article; and that no State, without its Consent, shall be deprived of its equal Suffrage in the Senate.

ARTICLE VI

All Debts contracted and Engagements entered into, before the Adoption of this Constitution, shall be as valid against the United States under this Constitution, as under the Confederation.

This Constitution, and the Laws of the United States which shall be made in Pursuance thereof; and all Treaties made, or which shall be made, under the Authority of the United States, shall be the supreme Law of the Land; and the Judges in every State shall be bound thereby, any Thing in the Constitution or Laws of any State to the Contrary notwithstanding.

The Senators and Representatives before mentioned, and the Members of the several State Legislatures, and all executive and judicial Officers, both of the United States and of the several States, shall be bound by Oath or Affirmation, to support this Constitution; but no religious Test shall ever be required as a Qualification to any Office or public Trust under the United States.

ARTICLE VII

The Ratification of the Conventions of nine States, shall be sufficient for the establishment of this Constitution between the States so ratifying the Same.

Done in Convention by the Unanimous Consent of the States present the Seventeenth day of September in the Year of our Lord one thousand seven hundred and Eighty-seven and of the Independence of the United States of America the Twelfth, In witness whereof We have hereunto subscribed our Names,

GEORGE WASHINGTON, President and deputy from Virginia

New Hampshire. John Langdon, Nicholas Gilman

Georgia. William Few, Abraham Baldwin

Massachusetts. Nathaniel Gorham, Rufus King

Connecticut. William Samuel Johnson, Roger Sherman

New Jersey. William Livingston, David Brearley, William Paterson, Jonathan Dayton

New York. Alexander Hamilton

Maryland. James McHenry, Daniel Carrol, Daniel of St. Thomas Jenifer

Pennsylvania. Benjamin Franklin, Robert Morris, Thomas FitzSimons, James Wilson, Thomas Mifflin, George Clymer, Jared Ingersoll, Gouverneur Morris

Virginia. John Blair, James Madison Jr.

North Carolina. William Blount, Hugh Williamson, Richard Dobbs Spaight

Delaware. George Read, John Dickinson, Jacob Broom, Gunning Bedford Jr., Richard Bassett

South Carolina. John Ruttledge, Charles Pinckney, Charles Cotesworth Pinckney, Pierce Butler

Attest: William Jackson, Secretary

BILL OF RIGHTS

Amendment I Congress shall make no law respecting an establishment of religion, or prohibiting the free exercise thereof; or abridging the freedom of speech, or of the press; or the right of the people peaceably to assemble, and to petition the government for a redress of grievances.

Amendment II A well regulated militia, being necessary to the security of a free State, the right of the people to keep and bear arms, shall not be infringed.

Amendment III No soldier shall, in time of peace, be quartered in any house, without the consent of the owner, nor in time of war, but in a manner to be prescribed by law.

Amendment IV The right of the people to be secure in their persons, houses, papers, and effects, against unreasonable searches and seizures, shall not be violated, and no warrants shall issue, but upon probable cause, supported by Oath or affirmation, and particularly describing the place to be searched, and the persons or things to be seized.

Amendment V No person shall be held to answer for a capital, or otherwise infamous crime, unless on a presentment or indictment of a Grand Jury, except in cases arising in the land or naval forces, or in the militia, when in actual service in time of war or public danger; nor shall any person be subject for the same offence to be twice put in jeopardy of life or limb; nor shall be compelled in any criminal case to be a witness against himself, nor be deprived of life, liberty, or property, without due process of law; nor shall private property be taken for public use, without just compensation.

Amendment VI In all criminal prosecutions, the accused shall enjoy the right to a speedy and public trial, by an impartial jury of the State and district wherein the crime shall have been committed, which district shall have been previously ascertained by law, and to be informed of the nature and cause of the accusation; to be confronted with the witnesses against him; to have compulsory process for obtaining witnesses in his favor, and to have the assistance of counsel for his defence.

Amendment VII In suits at common law, where the value in controversy shall exceed twenty dollars, the right of trial by jury shall be preserved, and no fact tried by a jury, shall be otherwise re-examined in any court of the United States, than according to the rules of the common law.

Amendment VIII Excessive bail shall not lie required, nor excessive fines imposed, nor cruel and unusual punishments inflicted.

Amendment IX The enumeration in the Constitution, of certain rights, shall not be construed to deny or disparage others retained by the people.

Amendment X The powers not delegated to the United States by the Constitution, nor prohibited by it to the States, are reserved to the States respectively, or to the people.

An Act Concerning Aliens (1798)

Commentary

By the 1790s, some Americans began to reconsider the tolerant attitude toward immigrants demonstrated by the Constitution and the Naturalization Act of 1790. Leaders among the recent immigrants from France and Ireland not only spoke on behalf of French revolutionaries, but also lobbied against strengthening and renewing social, economic, and political ties between America and England. As war with the French seemed likely in the late 1790s, such activities were perceived by some as traitorous or un-American.

Members of the Federalist party cherished America's Anglo-dominated culture and viewed the pro-revolution, anti-English sentiment of immigrants as evidence of the disloyalty of foreigners. The participation by French and Irish immigrants in the opposing Republican party offered final proof to Federalists of foreigners' treasonous nature. Federalists pushed through Congress three Aliens Acts, which increased the residency requirement for citizenship from two to fourteen years, required that aliens declare their intention to apply for naturalization five years before doing so, and made some immigrants from "enemy" nations ineligible for citizenship and subject to deportation.

Excerpt of Fifth Congress: 1

June 25, 1798.

Chap. LVIII.—*An Act concerning Aliens.*

Sec. 1. *Be it enacted by the Senate and House of Representatives of the United States of America in Congress assembled,* That it shall be lawful for the President of the United States at any time during the continuance of this act, to order all such aliens as he shall judge dangerous to the peace and safety of the United States, or shall have reasonable grounds to suspect are concerned in any treasonable or secret machinations against the government thereof, to depart out of the territory of the United States, within such time as shall be expressed in such order, which order shall be served on such alien by delivering him a copy thereof, or leaving the same at his usual abode, and returned to the office of the Secretary of State, by the marshal or other person to whom the same shall be directed. And in case any alien, so ordered to depart, shall be found at large within the United States after the time limited in such order for his departure, and not having obtained a *license* from the President to reside therein, or having obtained such license shall not have conformed thereto, every such alien shall, on conviction thereof, be imprisoned for a term not exceeding three years, and shall never after be admitted to become a citizen of the United States. *Provided always, and be it further enacted*, that if any alien so ordered to depart shall prove to the satisfaction of the President, by evidence to be taken before such person or persons as the President shall direct, who are for that purpose hereby authorized to administer oaths, that no injury or danger to the United States will arise from suffering such alien to reside therein the President may grant a *license* to such alien to remain within the United States for such time as he shall judge proper, and at such place as he may designate. And the President may also require of such alien to enter into a bond to the United States, in such penal sum as he may direct, with one or more sufficient sureties to the satisfaction of the person authorized by the President to take the same, conditioned for the good behavior of such alien during his residence in the United States, and not violating his license, which license the President may revoke, whenever he shall think proper.

Sec. 2. *And be it further enacted*, That it shall be lawful for the President of the United States, whenever he may deem it necessary for the public safety, to order to be removed out of the territory thereof, any alien who may or shall be in prison in pursuance of this act; and to cause to be arrested and sent out of the United States such of those aliens as shall have been ordered to depart therefrom and shall not have obtained a license as aforesaid, in all cases where, in the opinion of the President, the public safety requires a speedy removal. And if any alien so removed or sent out of the United States by the President shall voluntarily return thereto, unless by permission of the President of the United States, such alien on conviction thereof, shall be imprisoned so long as, in the opinion of the President, the public safety may require.

Sec. 3. *And be it further enacted*, That every master or commander of any ship or vessel which shall come into any port of the United States after the first day of July next, shall immediately on his arrival make report in writing to the collector or other chief officer of the customs of such port, of all aliens, if any, on board his vessel, specifying their names, age, the place of nativity, the country from which they shall have come, the nation to which they belong and owe allegiance, their occupation and a description of their persons, as far as he shall be informed thereof, and on failure, every such master and commander shall forfeit and pay three hundred dollars, for the payment whereof on default of such master or commander, such vessel shall also be holden, and may by such collector or other officer of the customs be detained. And it shall be the duty of such collector or other officer of the customs, forthwith to transmit to the office of the department of state true copies of all such returns.

Sec. 4. *And be it further enacted*, That the circuit and district courts of the United States, shall respectively have cognizance of all crimes and offences against this act. And all marshals and other officers of the United States are required to execute all precepts and orders of the President of the United States issued in pursuance or by virtue of this act.

Sec. 5. *And be it further enacted*, That it shall be lawful for any alien who may be ordered to be removed from the United States, by virtue of this act, to take with him such part of his goods, chattels, or other property, as he may find convenient; and all property left in the United States by any alien, who may be removed, as aforesaid, shall be, and remain subject to his order and disposal, in the same manner as if this act had not been passed.

Sec. 6. *And be it further enacted*, That this act shall continue and be in force for and during the term of two years from the passing thereof.

Approved, June 25, 1798.

FIRST PERSON NARRATIVES

Remonstrance of Distressed Frontier Inhabitants (1764)

Source: *Minutes of the Provincial Council of Pennsylvania*, vol. 9. Philadelphia: J. Severns and Co., 1852.

Commentary

Though disagreements with the king of England dominated much of American politics on the eve of the Revolution, many colonies were also troubled by internal disputes which pitted Americans against one another. Here, too, many issues arose from settlement of the western frontier. When colonial governments attempted to regulate the pace of settlement, they discovered that the western pioneers resented interference from fellow Americans just as much as they resented the interference of the king himself.

Such disputes had recurred throughout colonial history, but the end of the Seven Years War (1756–1763) caused them to break out with renewed force in many colonies, including Pennsylvania. Concerned by the worsening of relations between the king and the colonies, political leaders in eastern Pennsylvania were eager to demonstrate that they themselves could effectively regulate the western frontier, and hence put to rest one of the issues which preoccupied the king's ministers. In addition, Philadelphia Quakers who dominated the Pennsylvania Assembly were sympathetic to the rights of Native American tribes and were troubled by reports of violence by settlers against peaceful Indians which reached them from the western frontier. In response, the assembly took several actions to try to restrain the western settlers and enforce good relations with the tribes.

To settlers living on the frontier, these actions represented a betrayal. This letter, more like a petition, illustrates both the reasons for and the depth of the westerners' anger. The petitioners remonstrated, or protested, against their underrepresentation in the assembly. They raged against the Indians and served notice that they viewed all Indians as implacable foes—even those "peaceful Indians" who enjoyed the protection of the Pennsylvania government. They begged for help in fighting the tribes, and demanded that the government post bounties for Indian scalps. So frustrated were the frontiersmen that they sound as though they are ready to take up arms against their own colonial government. In the end, such threats came to nothing. Nevertheless, the establishment of self-government after the Revolution did not end disputes between western settlers and eastern governments that seemed oppressive and unresponsive to their concerns.

To the Honourable John Penn, Esquire, Governor of the Province of Pennsylvania, & of the Counties of New Castle, Kent, and Sussex, on Delaware, and to the Representatives of the Freemen of the said Province, in General Assembly met:

We Matthew Smith and James Gibson, in behalf of ourselves and His Majesty's faithful and loyal Subjects, the Inhabitants of the Frontier Counties of Lancaster, York, Cumberland, Berks, and Northampton, humbly beg leave to remonstrate and to lay before you the following Grievances, which we submit to your Wisdom for Redress.

First. We apprehend that as Freemen and English Subjects, we have an indisputable Title to the same Privileges & immunities with His Majesty's other Subjects who reside in the interior Counties of Philadelphia, Chester, and Bucks, and therefore ought not to be excluded from an equal share with them in the very important Privilege of Legislation; nevertheless, contrary to the Proprietor's Charter and the acknowledged principles of common Justice & Equity, our five counties are restrained from electing more than ten Representatives, viz: four for Lancaster, two for York, two for Cumberland, one for Berks, and one for Northampton; while the three Counties and City of Philadelphia, Chester, and Bucks, elect Twenty-Six. This we humbly conceive is oppressive, unequal, and unjust, the cause of many of our Grievances, and an infringement of our Natural privileges of Freedom & Equality; wherefore we humbly pray that we may be no longer deprived of an equal number with the three aforesaid Counties, to represent us in Assembly.

Secondly. We understand that a Bill is now before the House of Assembly, wherein it is provided that such Persons as shall be charged with killing any Indians in Lancaster County, shall not be tried in the County where the Fact was committed, but in the Counties of Philadelphia, Chester, or Bucks. This is manifestly to deprive British Subjects of their known Privileges, to cast an eternal Reproach upon whole Counties, as if they were unfit to serve their Country in the quality of Jurymen, and to contradict the well-known Laws of the British Nation in a point whereon Life, Liberty, and security essentially depend, namely, that of being tried by their equals in the neighborhood where their own, their Accusers', and the Witnesses' Character and Credit, with the Circumstances of the Fact, are best known, & instead thereof putting their Lives in the hands of Strangers who may as justly be suspected of partiallity to, as the Frontier Counties can be of prejudices against Indians; and this, too, in favour of Indians only, against His Majesty's faithful & loyal subjects.

Thirdly. During the late and present Indian War, the Frontiers of this Province have been repeatedly attacked and ravaged by Skulking parties of the Indians, who have with the most Savage Cruelty murdered Men, Women, and Children without distinction, and have reduced near a thousand Families to the most extream distress. It grieves us to the very heart to see such of our Frontier Inhabitants as have escaped Savage Fury with the loss of their parents, their Children, their Wives or Relatives, left destitute by the public, and exposed to the most cruel Poverty and Wretchedness while upwards of an Hundred and twenty of these Savages, who are with great reason suspected of being guilty of these horrid Barbarities under the Mask of Friendship, have procured themselves to be taken under the protection of the Government, with a view to elude the Fury of the brave Relatives of the murdered, and are now maintained at the public Expence. Some of these Indians now in the Barracks of Philadelphia, are confessedly a part of the Wyalusing Indians, which Tribe is now at war with us, and the others are the Moravian Indians, who, living amongst us under the Cloak of Friendship, carried on a Correspondence with our known Enemies on the Great Island. We cannot but observe with sorrow & indignation that some Persons in this Province are at pains to extenuate the barbarous Cruelties practised by these Savages on our murdered Brethren & Relatives, which are shocking to human Nature, and must pierce every Heart but that of the hardened perpetrators or their Abettors; Nor is it less distressing to hear others pleading that although the Wyalusing Tribe is at War with us, yet that part of it which is under the Protection of the Government may be friendly to the English and innocent. In what nation under the Sun was it ever the custom that when a neighboring Nation took up Arms, not an individual should be touched but only the Persons that offered Hostilities? Who ever proclaimed War with a part of a Nation, and not with the Whole? Had these Indians disapproved of the Perfidy of their Tribe, & been willing to cultivate and preserve Friendship with us, why did they not give notice of the War before it happened, as it is known to be the Result of long Deliberations, and a preconcerted Combination amongst them? Why did they not leave their Tribe immediately, and come amongst us before there was Ground to suspect them, or War was actually waged with their Tribe? No, they stayed amongst them, were privy to their murders & Ravages, until we had destroyed their Provisions; and when they could no longer subsist at home, they come not as Deserters, but as Friends to be maintained through the Winter, that they may be able to Scalp and butcher us in the Spring.

And as to the Moravian Indians, there are strong Grounds at least to suspect their Friendship, as it is known they carried on a Correspondence with our Enemies on the Great Island. We killed three Indians going from Bethlehem to the Great Island with Blankets, Ammunition, & Provisions, which is an undeniable Proof that the Moravian Indians were in confederacy with our open Enemies; And we cannot but be filled with Indignation to hear this action of ours painted in the most odious and detestable Colours, as if we had inhumanly murdered our Guides who preserved us from perishing in the Woods, when we only killed three of our known Enemies, who attempted to shoot us when we surprised them. And besides all this, we understand that one of these very Indians is proved by the oath of Stinton's Widow, to be the very Person that murdered her Husband. How then comes it to pass that he alone, of all the Moravian Indians, should join with the enemy to murder that family? Or can it be supposed that any Enemy Indians, contrary to their known custom of making War, should penetrate into the Heart of a settled Country to burn, plunder and murder the Inhabitants, and not molest any Houses in their return, or ever be seen or heard of? Or how can we account for it, that no ravages have been committed in Northampton County, since the removal of the Moravian Indians, when the Great Cove has been struck since? These things put it beyond doubt with us that the Indians now at Philadelphia are His Majesty's Perfidious Enemies, & therefore to protect and maintain them at the Public Expence, while our suffering Brethren on the Frontiers are almost destitute of the necessaries of Life and are neglected by the Public, is sufficient to make us mad with rage, and tempt us to do what nothing but the most violent necessity can vindicate. We humbly and earnestly pray, therefore, that those Enemies of His Majesty may be removed as soon as possible out of the Province.

Fourthly. We humbly conceive that it is contrary to the maxims of good Policy, and extreamly dangerous to our Frontiers, to suffer any Indians of what tribe soever to live within the Inhabited parts of this Province while we are engaged in an Indian War, as Experience has taught us that they are all perfidious, and their claim to Freedom & Independency, puts it in their power to act as Spies, to entertain & give intelligence to our Enemies, and to furnish them with Provisions and Warlike Stores. To this fatal intercourse between our pretended Friends and open Enemies, we must ascribe the greatest of the Ravages and Murders that have been committed in the course of this and the last Indian War. We therefore pray that this grievance be taken under consideration and remedied.

Fifthly. We cannot help lamenting that no Provision has been hitherto made, that such of our Frontier Inhabitants as have been wounded in defence of the Province, their Lives and Liberties, may be taken care of and cured of their Wounds at the publick Expence. We therefore pray that this Grievance may be redressed.

Sixthly. In the late Indian war this Province, with others of His Majesty's Colonies, gave rewards for Indian Scalps, to encourage the seeking them in their own Country, as the most likely means of destroying or reducing them to reason; but no such Encouragement has been given in this War, which has damped the Spirits of many brave Men who are willing to venture their Lives in parties against the Enemy. We therefore pray that public rewards may be proposed for Indian Scalps, which may be adequate to the Dangers attending Enterprizes of this nature.

Seventhly. We daily lament that numbers of our nearest & dearest relatives are still in Captivity among the Savage Heathen, to be trained up in all their Ignorance & Barbarity, or to be tortured to death with all the contrivances of Indian Cruelty, for attempting to make their escape from Bondage; We see they pay no regard to the many solemn Promises which they have made to restore our Friends who are in Bondage amongst them. We therefore earnestly pray that no trade may hereafter be permitted to be carried on with them, until our Brethren and Relatives are brought home to us.

Eightly. We complain that a certain Society of People in this Province, in the late Indian War, & at several Treaties held by the King's representatives, openly loaded the Indians with Presents, and that J. P., a leader of the said Society, in Defiance of all Government, not only abetted our Indian Enemies, but kept up a private intelligence with them, and publickly received from them a Belt of Wampum, as if he had been our Governor or authorized by the King to treat with his Enemies. By this means the Indians have been taught to despise us as a weak and disunited people, and from this fatal Source have arose many of our Calamities under which we groan. We humbly pray therefore that this Grievance may be redressed, and that no private subject be hereafter permitted to treat with, or carry on a Correspondence with our Enemies.

Ninthly. We cannot but observe with sorrow that Fort Augusta, which has been very expensive to this Province, has afforded us but little assistance during this or the last War. The men that were stationed at that place neither helped our distressed Inhabitants to save their Crops, nor did they attack our Enemies in their Towns, or patrole on our Frontiers. We humbly request that proper measures may be taken to make that Garrison more serviceable to us in our Distress, if it can be done.

N.B. We are far from intending any Reflection against the Commanding Officer stationed at Augusta, as we presume his Conduct was always directed by those from whom he received his Orders.

SIGNED on Behalf of ourselves, and by appointment of a great number of the Frontier Inhabitants.

MATTHEW SMITH.

JAMES GIBSON.

February 13th, 1764.

Account of the Battle of Lexington (1775)

Source: Thomas, Isaiah. *The Massachusetts Spy* (May 3, 1775).

Commentary

When fighting broke out at Lexington, Massachusetts on April 19, 1775, word spread quickly throughout the colonies, primarily through the publication in newspapers of letters and accounts of the battle. Most of the letters, in particular, those written on the day of battle or shortly thereafter, expressed surprise and shock at the actions of the British. However, the authors of the letters generally described the events as best they could without making many comments. Isaiah Thomas editorialized more in his account. He had fled from Boston to Worcester following the skirmishes at Lexington and Concord. His report began with a verbal attack on the British for their uncalled-for attack on the Americans. He continued with an account of the skirmish, emphasizing the death and destruction caused by the redcoats.

Throughout the war, Thomas proved to be one of the most vocal printers. He continually used the pages of his newspaper, the *Massachusetts Spy*, to print propaganda designed to urge Americans to defy the British and to fight on until final victory and independence were achieved. His report of the Battle of Lexington was only the first of many such slanted reports which praised the Americans and condemned the British.

The Massachusetts Spy, May 3, 1775.

Americans! Forever bear in mind the Battle of Lexington! where British troops, unmolested and unprovoked, wantonly and in a most inhuman manner, fired upon and killed a number of our countrymen, then robbed, ransacked, and burnt their houses! nor could the tears of defenseless women, some of whom were in the pains of childbirth, the cries of helpless babes, nor the prayers of old age, confined to beds of sickness, appease their thirst for blood!—or divert them from their Design of Murder and Robbery!

The particulars of this alarming event will, we are credibly informed, be soon published by authority, as a Committee of the Provincial Congress have been appointed to make special inquiry and to take the depositions, on oath, of such as are knowing in the matter. In the meantime, to satisfy the expectations of our readers, we have collected from those whose veracity is unquestioned the following account, viz.

A few days before the battle, the Grenadier and Light-Infantry companies were all drafted from the several regiments in Boston; and put under the command of an officer, and it was observed that most of the transports and other boats were put together, and fitted for immediate service. This maneuver gave rise to a suspicion that a more formidable expedition was intended by the soldiery, but what or where the inhabitants could not determine. However, town watches in Boston, Charlestown, Cambridge, etc., were ordered to look well to the landing place.

About ten o'clock on the night of the eighteenth of April, the troops in Boston were disclosed to be on the move in a very secret manner, and it was found they were embarking on boats (which they had privately brought to the place in the evening) at the bottom of the Common; expresses set off immediately to alarm the country, that they might be on their guard. When the expresses got about a mile beyond Lexington, they were stopped by about fourteen officers on horseback, who came out of Boston in the afternoon of that day, and were seen lurking in by-places in the country till after dark. One of the expresses immediately fled, and was pursued two miles by an officer, who when he had got up with him presented a pistol, and told him he was a dead man if he did not stop, but he rode on till he came up to a house, when stopping of a sudden his horse threw him off, having the presence of mind to holler to the people in the house,

"Turn out! Turn out! I have got one of them!"

The officer immediately retreated and fled as fast as he had pursued. The other express, after passing through a strict examination, by some means got clear.

The body of the troops, in the meantime, under the command of Lieutenant Colonel Smith, had crossed the river and landed at Phipp's Farm. They immediately, to the number of 1,000, proceeded to Lexington, about six miles below Concord, with great silence. A company of militia, of about eighty men, mustered near the meetinghouse; the troops came in sight of them just before sunrise. The militia, upon seeing the troops, began to disperse. The troops then set out upon the run, hallooing and huzzaing, and coming within a few rods of them the commanding officer accosted the militia, in words to this effect,

"Disperse, you damn'd rebels!—Damn you, disperse!"

Upon which the troops again huzzaed and immediately one or two officers discharged their pistols, which were instantaneously followed by the firing of four or five of the soldiers; and then there seemed to be a general discharge from the whole body. It is to be noticed they fired on our people as they were dispersing, agreeable to their command, and that we did not even return the fire. Eight of our men were killed and nine wounded. The troops then laughed, and damned the Yankees, and said they could not bear the smell of gunpowder.

A little after this the troops renewed their march to Concord, where, when they arrived, they divided into parties, and went directly to several places where the province stores were deposited. Each party was supposed to have a Tory pilot. One party went into the jailyard and spiked up and otherwise damaged two cannon, belonging to the province, and broke and set fire to the carriages. Then they entered a store and rolled out about a hundred barrels of flour, which they unheaded and emptied about forty into the river. At the same time others were entering houses and shops, and unheading barrels, chests, etc., the property of private persons. Some took possession of the town house, to which they set fire, but was extinguished by our people without much hurt. Another party of the troops went and took possession of the North Bridge. About 150 provincials who mustered upon the alarm, coming toward the bridge, the troops fired upon them without

ceremony and killed two on the spot! (Thus had the troops of Britain's king fired First at two separate times upon his loyal American subjects, and put a period to two lives before one gun was fired upon them.) Our people Then fired and obliged the troops to retreat, who were soon joined by their other parties, but finding they were still pursued the whole body retreated to Lexington, both provincials and troops firing as they went.

During this time an express from the troops was sent to General Gage, who thereupon sent out a reinforcement of about 1400 men, under the command of Earl Percy, with two fieldpieces. Upon the arrival of this reinforcement at Lexington, just as the retreating party had got there, they made a stand, picked up their dead, and took all the carriages they could find and put their wounded thereon. Others of them, to their eternal disgrace be it spoken, were robbing and setting houses on fire, and discharging their cannon at the meetinghouse.

The enemy, having halted about an hour at Lexington, found it necessary to make a second retreat, carrying with them many of their dead and wounded. They continued their retreat from Lexington to Charlestown with great precipitation. Our people continued their pursuit, firing till they got to Charlestown Neck (which they reached a little after sunset), over which the enemy passed, proceeded up Bunker's Hill, and the next day went into Boston, under the protection of the Somerset, man-of-war of sixty-four guns.

A young man, unarmed, who was taken prisoner by the enemy, and made to assist in carrying off their wounded, says that he saw a barber who lives in Boston, thought to be one Warden, with the troops and that he heard them say he was one of their pilots. He likewise saw the said barber fire twice upon our people and heard Earl Percy give the order to fire the houses. He also informs that several officers were among the wounded who were carried into Boston, where our informant was dismissed. They took two of our men prisoners in battle, who are now confined in barracks.

Immediately upon the return of the troops to Boston, all communication to and from the town was stopped by General Gage. The provincials, who flew to the assistance of their distressed countrymen, are posted in Cambridge, Charlestown, Roxbury, Watertown, etc., and have placed a guard on Roxbury Neck, within gunshot of the enemy. Guards are also placed everywhere in view of the town, to observe the motions of the King's troops. The Council of War and the different Committees of Safety and Supplies sit at Cambridge, and the Provincial Congress at Watertown. The troops in Boston are fortifying the place on all sides, and a frigate of war is stationed at Cambridge River, and a sixty-four-gun ship between Boston and Charlestown.

Deacon Joseph Loring's house and barn, Mrs. Mulliken's house and shop, and Mr. Joshua Bond's house and shop, in Lexington, were all consumed. They also set fire to several other houses, but our people extinguished the flames. They pillaged almost every house they passed by, breaking and destroying doors, windows, glass, etc., and carrying off clothing and other valuable effects. It appeared to be their design to burn and destroy all before them, and nothing but our vigorous pursuit prevented their infernal purposes from being put into execution. But the savage barbarity exercised upon the bodies of our unfortunate brethren who fell is almost incredible. Not content with shooting down the unarmed, aged, and infirm, they disregarded the cries of the wounded, killing them without mercy, and mangling their bodies in the most shocking manner.

We have the pleasure to say that notwithstanding the highest provocations given by the enemy, not one instance of cruelty that we have heard of was committed by our militia; but, listening to the merciful dictates of the Christian religion, they "breathed higher sentiments of humanity."

The public most sincerely sympathize with the friends and relations of our deceased brethren, who sacrificed their lives in fighting for the liberties of their country. By their noble intrepid conduct, in helping to defeat the force of an ungrateful tyrant, they have endeared their memories to the present generation, who will transmit their names to posterity with the highest honor.

LETTERS AND SPEECHES

Letter from Abigail Adams Regarding Price Gouging (1777)

Source: Adams, Charles Francis, ed. *Familiar Letters of John Adams and His Wife Abigail Adams During the Revolution* (1876). Freeport, NY: Books for Libraries Press, 1970.

Commentary

In this excerpt from a 1777 letter, Abigail Adams (1744–1818) describes for her husband, John Adams (1735–1826), how a group of women nearly rioted when they learned that a merchant tried to profit from the scarcity of goods during the trade embargo with England. Passive resistance became increasingly effective as the women colonists enacted boycotts of British goods.

Although tea was a very popular beverage in the colonies, as in England, America changed from a tea-drinking to a coffee-drinking nation in opposition to the tax on it. Women of the Revolutionary era refused to serve tea to their families or friends, usually substituting coffee, imported with no assistance—or tax—from England.

July 31 [1777]

I have nothing new to entertain you with, unless it is an account of a New Set of Mobility which have lately taken the Lead in B[osto]n. You must know that there is a great Scarcity of Sugar and Coffe, articles which the Female part of the State are very loth to give up, especially whilst they consider the Scarcity occasiond by the merchants having secreted a large Quantity. There has been much rout and Noise in the Town for several weeks. Some Stores had been opend by a number of people and the Coffe and Sugar carried into the Market and dealt out by pounds. It was rumourd that an eminent, wealthy, stingy Merchant (who is a Batchelor) had a Hogshead of Coffe in his Store which he refused to sell to the committee under 6 shillings per pound. A Number of Females some say a hundred, some say more assembled with a cart and trucks, marchd down to the Ware House and demanded the keys, which he refused to deliver, upon which one of them seazd him by his Neck and tossd him into the cart. Upon his finding no Quarter he deliverd the keys, when they tipd up the cart and dischargd him, then opend the Warehouse, Hoisted out the Coffe themselves, put it into the trucks and drove off.

It was reported that he had a Spanking among them, but this I believe was not true. A large concourse of Men stood amazd silent Spectators of the whole transaction.

Letter to the Editor (1778)

Source: *Pennsylvania Evening Post* (May 8, 1778).

Commentary

During the Revolutionary era, marrying a successful and respected spouse was of great importance to young women and their families. In North Carolina, women of prominent families promised not to marry anybody who refused to serve in the military. Sometimes men, using female pseudonyms, published such advice in newspaper columns, which may have influenced these women. Governor William Livingston of New Jersey wrote this article in the Pennsylvania Evening Post of May 8, 1778, under the name "Belinda." The pressure to serve also may have influenced otherwise indifferent young men who wished to impress young ladies and others in their social circle with their patriotism and bravery.

I do not remember whether your gazette has hitherto given us the production of any woman correspondent. Indeed nothing but the most pressing call of my country could have induced me to appear in print. But rather than suffer your sex to be caught by the bait of that archfoe to American liberty, Lord North, I think ours ought, to a woman, to draw their pens, and to enter our solemn protest against it. Nay the fair ones in our neighborhood have already entered into a resolve for every mother to disown her son, and refuse the caresses of her husband, and for every maiden to reject the addresses of her gallant, where such husband, son, or gallant, shows the least symptoms of being imposed upon by this flimsy subterfuge, which I call the dying speech, and last refuge of Great Britain, pronounced and grunted out by her great oracle, and little politician, who now appears ready to hang himself, for having brought the nation to the brink of that ruin from which he cannot deliver her. You will be kind enough to correct my spelling, a part of my education in which I have been much neglected. I am your sincere friend. BELINDA.

Letters of Eliza Wilkinson (1781)

Source: Wilkinson, Eliza. *Letters During the Invasion and Possession of Charleston, S.C., by the British in the Revolutionary War*. New York: S. Colman, 1839.

Commentary

South Carolina matron Eliza Wilkinson experienced one of the most humiliating defeats suffered by the Americans during the Revolutionary War. British strategy in the South paid off with victories in South Carolina, including the spectacular fall of Charleston in the spring of 1780. In the aftermath, British soldiers and American Tories (the Loyalists, or as Wilkinson called them, "liars") taunted and abused the South Carolinians and looted their homes. Their avariciousness knew no bounds, according to the story related by Wilkinson in the first letter. What was worse, the Tories had no respect for elderly Americans (the "grey hairs"), and stole from them and humiliated them at will.

I seem to have an inexhaustible fund just now for letter writing; but it will amuse your leisure hours, and that hope encourages me to proceed. Without further preamble, I will present you with another scene, where my Father noted Mother were spectators, and also sufferers. It was likewise on the 3d of June that my Father, with an old man who lived a few miles from him, and whose head was silvered o'er with age, (one Mr. Byrant,) was sitting in the Piazza, when they saw a liar party of men—some in red, others in green, coming up to the house furiously; the moment they arrived, they jumped from their horses, and ran into the house with drawn swords and pistols, and began to curse and abuse Father and the other man very much; indeed, took his buckles from his shoes, searched his pockets, and took all they found there; they then went to search Mr. Bryant's pockets; he threw his top jacket aside, and producing his under-one, "Here," said he, "I'm a poor old man," (he was so, sure enough.) They searched but I believe found nothing, for by a lucky thought the "poor old man" saved several hundred pounds, by carelessly casting aside his top jacket, as if it had no pockets in it. They then went in the rooms up and down stairs, demolished two sets of drawers, and took all they could conveniently carry off. One came to search Mother's pockets too, (audacious fellow!) but she resolutely threw his hand aside. "If you must see what's in my pocket, I'll show you myself," and she took out a threadcase, which had thread, needles, pins, tape, &c. &c. The mean wretch took it from her. They even took her two little children's caps, hats, &c. &c.; and when they took Mother's thread, &c. she asked them what they did with such things, which must be useless to them? "Why, Nancy would want them." They then began to insult Father again in the most abusive manner. "Aye," says one, "I told you yesterday how you'd be used if you did not take a protection! But you would not hear me; you would not do as I told you, now you see what you have got by it." "Why," said Mother, in a jeering way, "is going about plundering women and children, taking the State?" "I suppose you think you are doing your king a great piece of service by these actions, which are very noble, to be sure; but you are mistaken—'twill only enrage the people; I think you'd much better go and fight the men, than go about the country robbing helpless women and children; that would be doing something." "O! you are all, every one of you, rebels! and, old fellow," (to Father,) "I have a great mind to blow my pistol through your head." Another made a pass at him, (inhuman monsters—I have no patience to relate it,) with his sword, swearing he had "a great mind," too, to run him through the body.

What callous-hearted wretches must these be, thus to treat those who rather demanded their protection and support. Grey hairs have always commanded respect and reverence until now; but these vile creatures choose the aged and helpless for the objects of their insults and barbarity. But what, think you, must have been my Father's feelings at the time! used in such a manner. and not having it in his power to resent it; what a painful conflict must at that instant have filled his breast. He once or twice, (I heard him say afterwards,) was on the verge of attempting to defend himself and property; his breast was torn with the most violent agitations; but when he considered his helpless situation, and that certain death must ensue, he forbore, and silently submitted to their revilings and insults. It reminds me of poor old Priam, King of Troy, when he says,

> As for my sons! I thank ye, Gods—'twas well—
> Well—they have perished, for in fight they fell.
> Who dies in youth and vigor, dies the best,
> Cover'd with wounds, all honest, on the breast,
> But when the Fates, in fury of their rage,
> Spurn the hoar head of *unresisting age*,

This, this is misery, the last, the worst,
That man can feel—man fated to be curst.

I think those are the lines; it is a great while since I read them

But to proceed. After drinking all the wine, rum, &c. they could find, and inviting the negroes they had with them, who were very insolent, to do the same; they went to their horses, and would shake hands with Father and Mother before their departure. Did you ever hear the like? Fine amends, to be sure! a bitter pill covered with gold, and so a shake of the hand was to make them ample satisfaction for all their sufferings! But the "iron hand of Justice" will overtake them sooner or later. Though *slow*, it is *sure*.

After they were gone, poor old Bryant began to bless his stars for saving his money, and to applaud himself for his lucky invention; he was too loud with it; Father admonished him to speak lower, for, should any of the servants about the house hear him, and another party come, he might stand a chance to lose it after all; but still the old man kept chatting on, when lo! another company of horsemen appeared in view: the poor soul was panic-struck, he looked aghast, and became mute: these were M'Girth's men, who had just left *us*. They did not behave quite so civil to Mother as they did to us; for they took sugar, flour, butter, and such things from her; but not much. These particulars I had from Mother. And now, my dear, I'll conclude here; I expect company to spend the day, so will defer ending my long story till the next leisure hour, and will then bare another epistolary chat with you. Adieu.

Eliza.

Mount Royal, May 19, 1781.

Washington and Cornwallis's Correspondence Concerning Surrender (1781)

Commentary

On October 17, 1781, the very day that Admiral Graves set sail from New York with a reinforced fleet and 7,000 troops for the relief of Yorktown, Virginia, General Charles Cornwallis (1735–1805) sent General George Washington (1732–1799) a letter requesting a cease-fire and an armistice. Washington accepted and the two agreed to meet at the Moore house to set the terms. It took two days to finalize the terms of surrender after the cease-fire. Graves arrived five days too late.

Sir,

I propose a cessation of hostilities for twenty-four hours, and that two officers may be appointed by each side, to meet at Mr. Moore's house, to settle terms for the surrender of the posts of York and Gloucester.

*I have the honor to be, &c
Cornwallis*

My Lord,

I have had the honor of receiving your Lordship's letter of this date. An ardent desire to spare the further effusion of blood will readily incline me to listen to such terms for the surrender of your posts of York and Gloucester, as are admissible.

I wish, previously to the meeting of commissioners, that your Lordship's proposals in writing may be sent to the American lines, for which purpose a suspension of hostilities, during two hours from the delivery of this letter, will be granted.

*I have the honor to be, &c
George Washington*

Washington's Farewell Address (1796)

Source: Ford, Worthington C., ed. *The Writings of George Washington.* New York: Putnam, 1889-1983.

Commentary

When George Washington was unanimously elected by the Constitutional Convention as the first president of the United States in 1789, the newly forged nation was still deeply uncertain of its own survival. Washington, a towering figure, legendary even in his own time, served two terms as president, but grew weary at last of public service and longed to return to his beloved farm at Mount Vernon, determined not to seek a third. No provisions for term limits had yet been considered, and Washington could almost certainly have remained president for the rest of his life. What followed, however, was perhaps as astonishing as the Revolution itself. The ruler of a nation, and its greatest military hero, voluntarily surrendered his office. For Washington, this act was the very fulfillment of the promise of the War of Independence and a sign to the rest of the world that the Revolution had not been in vain. Among its other subjects, Washington's masterful "Farewell Address," published in newspapers in 1796, warned against close alliances with foreign powers and gave birth to the sometimes controversial American tradition of Isolationism.

United States, September 17, 1796
Friends and Fellow-Citizens:

The period for a new election of a citizen to administer the Executive Government of the United States being not far distant, and the time actually arrived when your thoughts must be employed in designating the person who is to be clothed with that important trust, it appears to me proper, especially as it may conduce to a more distinct expression of the public voice, that I should now apprise you of the resolution I have formed to decline being considered among the number of those out of whom a choice is to be made. . . .

The impressions with which I first undertook the arduous trust were explained on the proper occasion. In the discharge of this trust I will only say that I have, with good intentions, contributed toward the organization and administration of the Government the best exertions of which a very fallible judgment was capable. Not unconscious in the outset of the inferiority of my qualifications, experience in my own eyes, perhaps still more in the eyes of others, has strengthened the motives to diffidence of myself; and every day the increasing weight of years admonishes me more and more that the shade of retirement is as necessary to me as it will be welcome. Satisfied that if any circumstances have given peculiar value to my services they were temporary, I have the consolation to believe that, while choice and prudence invite me to quit the political scene, patriotism does not forbid it. . . .

Here, perhaps, I ought to stop. But a solicitude for your welfare which can not end with my life, and the apprehension of danger natural to that solicitude, urge me on an occasion like the present to offer to your solemn contemplation and to recommend to your frequent review some sentiments which are the result of much reflection, of no inconsiderable observation, and which appear to me all important to the permanency of your felicity as a people. . . .

Interwoven as is the love of liberty with every ligament of your hearts, no recommendation of mine is necessary to fortify or confirm the attachment.

The unity of government which constitutes you one people is also now dear to you. It is justly so, for it is a main pillar in the edifice of your real independence, the support of your tranquillity at home, your peace abroad, of your safety, of your prosperity, of that very liberty which you so highly prize. But as it is easy to foresee that from different causes and from different quarters much pains will be taken, many artifices employed, to weaken in your minds the conviction of this truth, as this is the point in your political fortress against which the batteries of internal and external enemies will be most constantly and actively (though often covertly and insidiously) directed, it is of infinite moment that you should properly estimate the immense value of your national union to your collective and individual happiness; that you should cherish a cordial, habitual, and immovable attachment to it; accustoming yourselves to think and speak of it as of the palladium of your political safety and prosperity; watching for its preservation with jealous anxiety; discountenancing whatever may suggest even a suspicion that it can in any event be abandoned, and in-

dignantly frowning upon the first dawning of every attempt to alienate any portion of our country from the rest or to enfeeble the sacred ties which now link together the various parts.

For this you have every inducement of sympathy and interest. Citizens by birth or choice of a common country, that country has a right to concentrate your affections. The name of American, which belongs to you in your national capacity, must always exalt the just pride of patriotism more than any appellation derived from local discriminations. With slight shades of difference, you have the same religion, manners, habits, and political principles. You have in a common cause fought and triumphed together. The independence and liberty you possess are the work of joint councils and joint efforts, of common dangers, sufferings, and successes.

But these considerations, however powerfully they address themselves to your sensibility, are greatly outweighed by those which apply more immediately to your interest. Here every portion of our country finds the most commanding motives for carefully guarding and preserving the union of the whole.

The *North*, in an unrestrained intercourse with the *South*, protected by the equal laws of a common government, finds in the productions of the latter great additional resources of maritime and commercial enterprise and precious materials of manufacturing industry. The *South*, in the same intercourse, benefiting by the same agency of the *North*, sees its agriculture grow and its commerce expand. Turning partly into its own channels the seamen of the *North*, it finds its particular navigation invigorated; and while it contributes in different ways to nourish and increase the general mass of the national navigation, it looks forward to the protection of a maritime strength to which itself is unequally adapted. The *East*, in a like intercourse with the *West*, already finds, and in the progressive improvement of interior communications by land and water will more and more find, a valuable vent for the commodities which it brings from abroad or manufactures at home. The *West* derives from the *East* supplies requisite to its growth and comfort, and what is perhaps of still greater consequence, it must of necessity owe the *secure* enjoyment of indispensable *outlets* for its own productions to the weight, influence, and the future maritime strength of the Atlantic side of the Union, directed by an indissoluble community of interest as *one nation*. Any other tenure by which the *West* can hold this essential advantage, whether derived from its own separate strength or from an apostate and unnatural connection with any foreign power, must be intrinsically precarious.

While, then, every part of our country thus feels an immediate and particular interest in union, all the parts combined can not fail to find in the united mass of means and efforts greater strength, greater resource, proportionably greater security from external danger, a less frequent interruption of their peace by foreign nations, and what is of inestimable value, they must derive from union an exemption from those broils and wars between themselves which so frequently afflict neighboring countries not tied together by the same governments, which their own rivalships alone would be sufficient to produce, but which opposite foreign alliances, attachments, and intrigues would stimulate and imbitter. Hence, likewise, they will avoid the necessity of those overgrown military establishments which, under any form of government, are inauspicious to liberty, and which are to be regarded as particularly hostile to republican liberty. In this sense it is that your union ought to be considered as a main prop of your liberty, and that the love of the one ought to endear to you the preservation of the other. . . .

Is there a doubt whether a common government can embrace so large a sphere? Let experience solve it. To listen to mere speculation in such a case were criminal. It is well worth a fair and full experiment. With such powerful and obvious motives to union affecting all parts of our country, while experience shall not have demonstrated its impracticability, there will always be reason to distrust the patriotism of those who in any quarter may endeavor to weaken its bands.

In contemplating the causes which may disturb our union it occurs as matter of serious concern that any ground should have been furnished for characterizing parties by *geographical* discriminations—*Northern* and *Southern, Atlantic* and *Western*—whence designing men may endeavor to excite a belief that there is a real difference of local interests and views. One of the expedients of party to acquire influence within particular districts is to misrepresent the opinions and aims of other districts. You cannot shield yourselves too much against the jealousies and heartburnings which spring from these misrepresentations; they tend to render alien to each other those who ought to be bound together by fraternal affection. . . .

To the efficacy and permanency of your union a government for the whole is indispensable. No alliances, however strict, between the parts can be an adequate substitute. They must inevitably experience the infractions and interruptions which all alliances in all times have experienced. Sensible of this momentous truth, you have improved upon your first essay by the adoption of a Constitution of Government better calculated than your former for an intimate union and for the efficacious management of your common concerns. This Government, the offspring of our own choice, uninfluenced and unawed, adopted upon full investigation and mature de-

liberation, completely free in its principles, in the distribution of its powers, uniting security with energy, and containing within itself a provision for its own amendment, has a just claim to your confidence and your support. Respect for its authority, compliance with its laws, acquiescence in its measures, are duties enjoined by the fundamental maxims of true liberty. The basis of our political systems is the right of the people to make and to alter their constitutions of government. But the constitution which at any time exists till changed by an explicit and authentic act of the whole people is sacredly obligatory upon all. The very idea of the power and the right of the people to establish government presupposes the duty of every individual to obey the established government. . . .

Toward the preservation of your Government and the permanency of your present happy state, it is requisite not only that you steadily discountenance irregular oppositions to its acknowledged authority, but also that you resist with care the spirit of innovation upon its principles, however specious the pretexts. One method of assault may be to effect in the forms of the Constitution alterations which will impair the energy of the system, and thus to undermine what cannot be directly overthrown. In all the changes to which you may be invited remember that time and habit are at least as necessary to fix the true character of governments as of other human institutions; that experience is the surest standard by which to test the real tendency of the existing constitution of a country; that facility in changes upon the credit of mere hypothesis and opinion exposes to perpetual change, from the endless variety of hypothesis and opinion; and remember especially that for the efficient management of your common interests in a country so extensive as ours a government of as much vigor as is consistent with the perfect security of liberty is indispensable. Liberty itself will find in such a government, with powers properly distributed and adjusted, its surest guardian. It is, indeed, little else than a name where the government is too feeble to withstand the enterprises of faction, to confine each member of the society within the limits prescribed by the laws, and to maintain all in the secure and tranquil enjoyment of the rights of person and property.

I have already intimated to you the danger of parties in the State, with particular reference to the founding of them on geographical discriminations. Let me now take a more comprehensive view, and warn you in the most solemn manner against the baneful effects of the spirit of party generally.

This spirit, unfortunately, is inseparable from our nature, having its root in the strongest passions of the human mind. It exists under different shapes in all governments, more or less stifled, controlled, or repressed; but in those of the popular form it is seen in its greatest rankness and is truly their worst enemy. . . .

It serves always to distract the public councils and enfeeble the public administration. It agitates the community with ill-founded jealousies and false alarms; kindles the animosity of one part against another; foments occasionally riot and insurrection. It opens the door to foreign influence and corruption, which find a facilitated access to the government itself through the channels of party passion. Thus the policy and the will of one country are subjected to the policy and will of another.

There is an opinion that parties in free countries are useful checks upon the administration of the government, and serve to keep alive the spirit of liberty. This within certain limits is probably true; and in governments of a monarchical cast patriotism may look with indulgence, if not with favor, upon the spirit of party. But in those of the popular character, in governments purely elective, it is a spirit not to be encouraged. From their natural tendency it is certain there will always be enough of that spirit for every salutary purpose; and there being constant danger of excess, the effort ought to be by force of public opinion to mitigate and assuage it. A fire not to be quenched, it demands a uniform vigilance to prevent its bursting into a flame, lest, instead of warming, it should consume.

It is important, likewise, that the habits of thinking in a free country should inspire caution in those intrusted with its administration to confine themselves within their respective constitutional spheres, avoiding in the exercise of the powers of one department to encroach upon another. The spirit of encroachment tends to consolidate the powers of all the departments in one, and thus to create, whatever the form of government, a real despotism. . . . If in the opinion of the people the distribution or modification of the constitutional powers be in any particular wrong, let it be corrected by an amendment in the way which the Constitution designates. But let there be no change by usurpation; for though this in one instance may be the instrument of good, it is the customary weapon by which free governments are destroyed. The precedent must always greatly overbalance in permanent evil any partial or transient benefit which the use can at any time yield.

Of all the dispositions and habits which lead to political prosperity, religion and morality are indispensable supports. In vain would that man claim the tribute of patriotism who should labor to subvert these great pillars of human happiness—these firmest props of the duties of men and citizens. The mere politician, equally with the pious man, ought to respect and to cherish them. A volume could not trace all their connections with private and public felicity. Let it simply be asked, Where is the

security for property, for reputation, for life, if the sense of religious obligation *desert* the oaths which are the instruments of investigation in courts of justice? And let us with caution indulge the supposition that morality can be maintained without religion. Whatever may be conceded to the influence of refined education on minds of peculiar structure, reason and experience both forbid us to expect that national morality can prevail in exclusion of religious principle.

It is substantially true that virtue or morality is a necessary spring of popular government. The rule indeed extends with more or less force to every species of free government. Who that is a sincere friend to it can look with indifference upon attempts to shake the foundation of the fabric? Promote, then, as an object of primary importance, institutions for the general diffusion of knowledge. In proportion as the structure of a government gives force to public opinion, it is essential that public opinion should be enlightened.

As a very important source of strength and security, cherish public credit. One method of preserving it is to use it as sparingly as possible, avoiding occasions of expense by cultivating peace, but remembering also that timely disbursements to prepare for danger frequently prevent much greater disbursements to repel it; avoiding likewise the accumulation of debt, not only by shunning occasions of expense, but by vigorous exertions in time of peace to discharge the debts which unavoidable wars have occasioned, not ungenerously throwing upon posterity the burthen which we ourselves ought to bear. . . .

Observe good faith and justice toward all nations. Cultivate peace and harmony with all. Religion and morality enjoin this conduct. And can it be that good policy does not equally enjoin it? It will be worthy of a free, enlightened, and at no distant period a great nation to give to mankind the magnanimous and too novel example of a people always guided by an exalted justice and benevolence. Who can doubt that in the course of time and things the fruits of such a plan would richly repay any temporary advantages which might be lost by a steady adherence to it? Can it be that Providence has not connected the permanent felicity of a nation with its virtue? The experiment, at least, is recommended by every sentiment which ennobles human nature. Alas! is it rendered impossible by its vices?

In the execution of such a plan nothing is more essential than that permanent, inveterate antipathies against particular nations and passionate attachments for others should be excluded, and that in place of them just and amicable feelings toward all should be cultivated. The nation which indulges toward another an habitual hatred or an habitual fondness is in some degree a slave. It is a slave to its animosity or to its affection, either of which is sufficient to lead it astray from its duty and its interest. Antipathy in one nation against another disposes each more readily to offer insult and injury, to lay hold of slight causes of umbrage, and to be haughty and intractable when accidental or trifling occasions of dispute occur.

So, likewise, a passionate attachment of one nation for another produces a variety of evils. Sympathy for the favorite nation, facilitating the illusion of an imaginary common interest in cases where no real common interest exists, and infusing into one the enmities of the other, betrays the former into a participation in the quarrels and wars of the latter without adequate inducement or justification. It leads also to concessions to the favorite nation of privileges denied to others, which is apt doubly to injure the nation making the concessions by unnecessarily parting with what ought to have been retained, and by exciting jealousy, ill will, and a disposition to retaliate in the parties from whom equal privileges are withheld; and it gives to ambitious, corrupted, or deluded citizens (who devote themselves to the favorite nation) facility to betray or sacrifice the interests of their own country without odium, sometimes even with popularity, gilding with the appearances of a virtuous sense of obligation, a commendable deference for public opinion, or a laudable zeal for public good the base or foolish compliances of ambition, corruption, or infatuation. . . .

Against the insidious wiles of foreign influence (I conjure you to believe me, fellow-citizens) the jealousy of a free people ought to be *constantly* awake, since history and experience prove that foreign influence is one of the most baneful foes of republican government. But that jealousy, to be useful, must be impartial, else it becomes the instrument of the very influence to be avoided, instead of a defense against it. Excessive partiality for one foreign nation and excessive dislike of another cause those whom they actuate to see danger only on one side, and serve to veil and even second the arts of influence on the other. Real patriots who may resist the intrigues of the favorite are liable to become suspected and odious, while its tools and dupes usurp the applause and confidence of the people to surrender their interests.

The great rule of conduct for us in regard to foreign nations is, in extending our commercial relations to have with them as little *political* connection as possible. So far as we have already formed engagements let them be fulfilled with perfect good faith. Here let us stop.

Europe has a set of primary interests which to us have none or a very remote relation. Hence she must be engaged in frequent controversies, the causes of which are essentially foreign to our concerns. Hence, therefore, it must be unwise in us to implicate ourselves by artificial ties in the ordinary vicissitudes of her politics or the ordinary combinations and collisions of her friendships or enmities.

Our detached and distant situation invites and enables us to pursue a different course. If we remain one people, under an efficient government, the period is not far off when we may defy material injury from external annoyance; when we may take such an attitude as will cause the neutrality we may at any time resolve upon to be scrupulously respected; when belligerent nations, under the impossibility of making acquisitions upon us, will not lightly hazard the giving us provocation; when we may choose peace or war, as our interest, guided by justice, shall counsel.

Why forego the advantages of so peculiar a situation? Why quit our own to stand upon foreign ground? Why, by interweaving our destiny with that of any part of Europe, entangle our peace and prosperity in the toils of European ambition, rivalship, interest, humor, or caprice?

It is our true policy to steer clear of permanent alliances with any portion of the foreign world, so far, I mean, as we are now at liberty to do it; for let me not be understood as capable of patronizing infidelity to existing engagements. I hold the maxim no less applicable to public than to private affairs that honesty is always the best policy. I repeat, therefore, let those engagements be observed in their genuine sense. But in my opinion it is unnecessary and would be unwise to extend them.

Taking care always to keep ourselves by suitable establishments on a respectable defensive posture, we may safely trust to temporary alliances for extraordinary emergencies.

Harmony, liberal intercourse with all nations are recommended by policy, humanity, and interest. But even our commercial policy should hold an equal and impartial hand, neither seeking nor granting exclusive favors or preferences; consulting the natural course of things; diffusing and diversifying by gentle means the streams of commerce, but forcing nothing; establishing with powers so disposed, in order to give trade a stable course, to define the rights of our merchants, and to enable the Government to support them, conventional rules of intercourse, the best that present circumstances and mutual opinion will permit, but temporary and liable to be from time to time abandoned or varied as experience and circumstances shall dictate; constantly keeping in view that it is folly in one nation to look for disinterested favors from another; that it must pay with a portion of its independence for whatever it may accept under that character; that by such acceptance it may place itself in the condition of having given equivalents for nominal favors, and yet of being reproached with ingratitude for not giving more. There can be no greater error than to expect or calculate upon real favors from nation to nation. It is an illusion which experience must cure, which a just pride ought to discard. . . .

Though in reviewing the incidents of my Administration I am unconscious of intentional error, I am nevertheless too sensible of my defects not to think it probable that I may have committed many errors. Whatever they may be, I fervently beseech the Almighty to avert or mitigate the evils to which they may tend. I shall also carry with me the hope that my country will never cease to view them with indulgence, and that, after forty five years of my life dedicated to its service with an upright zeal, the faults of incompetent abilities will be consigned to oblivion, as myself must soon be to the mansions of rest.

Relying on its kindness in this as in other things, and actuated by that fervent love toward it which is so natural to a man who views in it the native soil of himself and his progenitors for several generations, I anticipate with pleasing expectation that retreat in which I promise myself to realize without alloy the sweet enjoyment of partaking in the midst of my fellow-citizens the benign influence of good laws under a free government—the ever-favorite object of my heart, and the happy reward, as I trust, of our mutual cares, labors, and dangers.

LITERATURE AND ARTICLES

"Female Patriots, Address'd to the Daughters of Liberty in America" (1768)

Source: "The Female Patriots." Moore, Milcah Martha. 1768.

Commentary

If men had grown accustomed to their unusual freedoms in the colonies, women had also, and one of those freedoms was making their feelings and opinions known. The "female patriots" mentioned in this poem vowed their willingness to boycott English goods like stamped paper or tea if they could help the cause of liberty. When this poem first appeared in the *Pennsylvania Gazette* in 1768, its then-anonymous author hoped it would contribute "to the entertainment or reformation of your male readers." The poem's author was Milcah Martha Moore, a Philadelphia Quaker whose moral and instructive poems were published, along with this one, in England and Ireland as well as in America. As this lively poem suggests, her moral lessons were not devoid of humor and good sense.

Since the men, from a party or fear of a frown,
Are kept by a sugar-plum quietly down,
Supinely asleep—and depriv'd of their sight,
Are stripp'd of their freedom, and robb'd of their
    right;
If the sons, so degenerate! the blessings despise,
Let the Daughters of Liberty nobly arise;
And though we've no voice but a negative here,

The use of the taxables, let us forbear:—
  (Then merchants import till your stores are all full,
May the buyers be few, and your traffic be dull!)
Stand firmly resolv'd, and bid Grenville to see,
That rather than freedom we part with our tea,
And well as we love the dear draught when a dry,
As American Patriots our taste we deny—
Pennsylvania's gay meadows can richly afford
To pamper our fancy or furnish our board;
And paper sufficient at home still we have,
To assure the wiseacre, we will not sign slave;
When this homespun shall fail, to remonstrate our
    grief,
We can speak viva voce, or scratch on a leaf;
Refuse all their colors, though richest of dye,
When the juice of a berry our paint can supply,
To humor our fancy—and as for our houses,
They'll do without painting as well as our spouses;
While to keep out the cold of a keen winter morn,
We can screen the north-west with a well polished
    horn;
And trust me a woman, by honest invention,
Might give this state-doctor a dose of prevention.
Join mutual in this and but small as it seems,
We may jostle a Grenville, and puzzle his schemes;
But a motive more worthy our patriot pen,
Thus acting—we point out their duty to men;
And should the bound-pensioners tell us to hush,
We can throw back the satire, by biding them
    blush.

Excerpt from "New Song for American Freedom" (1768)

Source: Dickinson, John. "The New Song for American Freedom." 1768.

Commentary

Before the Revolutionary War, the influential Philadelphian writer John Dickinson (1732–1808) had mixed feelings about the course of action the colonies should take toward Great Britain. As a conscientious lawyer, he was appalled that the British did not abide by their own laws; at the same time, he admired British principles and thus supported reconciliation with Britain. These two views come across very clearly in his important pre-Revolutionary work *Letters from a Farmer in Philadelphia* (1768). Ironically, given Dickinson's ambivalent feelings, another of his works from 1768 became a favorite patriot drinking song and rallying cry "A New Song for American Freedom," better known as the Liberty Song, rousingly reminded all Americans of their tradition of freedoms. Not surprisingly, patriot singers usually omitted the last, pro-British verse, which asked them to drink the king's health. Instead, they stressed Dickinson's specifically American message, to join together for their right to self-direction and liberty: "By uniting we stand, by dividing we fall."

Come join Hand in Hand, brave Americans all,
And rouse your bold Hearts at fair Liberty' Call;
No tyrannous Acts shall suppress your just Claim
Or stain with Dishonor America's Name

Chorus:
In Freedom we're Born, and in Freedom we'll Live,
Our Purses are ready,
Steady, Friends, Steady,
Not as Slaves, but as Freemen our Money we'll give.

Then join Hand in Hand brave Americans all,
By uniting We stand, by dividing We fall,
In So Righteous A Cause let us hope to succeed,
For Heaven approves of each generous Deed

Chorus

All Ages shall speak with Amaze and Applause,
Of the Courage we'll shew In Support Of Our
    Laws;
To Die we can bear,—but, to Serve we disdain—
For Shame is to Freemen more dreadful than Pain

Chorus

Excerpt from Common Sense *(1776)*

Source: Paine, Thomas. *Common Sense*. Philadelphia: self-published pamphlet, 1776.

Commentary

In January 1776, Thomas Paine (1737–1809) anonymously published *Common Sense*. It sold 120,000 copies within the first three months at two shillings each. It attained total sales of about half a million copies during the Revolutionary period—an astounding number, given the small population of the colonies at that time. Paine's ideas had a strong appeal and went a long way to foster the climate for independence. Had it not been published and read throughout the colonies, there may not have been a movement toward independence. George Washington (1732–1799) commended it, saying it contained "sound logic and unanswerable reasoning."

Leaving the moral part to private reflection, I shall chiefly confine my further remarks to the following heads:

First, That it is the interest of America to be separated from Britain.

Secondly, Which is the easiest and most practicable plan, reconciliation or independence? with some occasional remarks.

In support of the first, I could, if I judged it proper, produce the opinion of some of the ablest and most experienced men on this continent; and whose sentiments, on that head, are not yet publicly known. It is in reality a self-evident position: For no nation, in a state of foreign dependence, limited in its commerce, and cramped and fettered in its legislative powers, can ever arrive at any material eminence. America does not yet know what opulence is; and although the progress which she has made stands unparalleled in the history of other nations,

it is but childhood, compared with what she would be capable of arriving at, had she, as she ought to have, the legislative powers in her own hands. England is, at this time, proudly coveting what would do her no good, were she to accomplish it; and the continent hesitating on a matter, which will be her final ruin if neglected. It is the commerce, and not the conquest of America, by which England is to be benefited, and that would in a great measure continue, were the countries as independent of each other as France and Spain; because in many articles, neither can go to a better market. But it is the independence of this country on Britain or any other, which is now the main and only object worthy of contention, and which, like all other truths discovered by necessity, will appear clearer and stronger every day.

First. Because it will come to that one time or other.

Secondly. Because the longer it is delayed, the harder it will be to accomplish.

I have frequently amused myself both in public and private companies, with silently remarking the specious errors of those who speak without reflecting. And among the many which I have heard, the following seems the most general, viz. that had this rupture happened forty or fifty years hence, instead of now, the Continent would have been more able to have shaken off the dependence. To which I reply, that our military ability at this time, arises from the experience gained in the late war, and which in forty or fifty years time, would have been totally extinct. . . .

Should affairs be patched up with Britain, and she to remain the governing and sovereign power of America, (which as matters are now circumstanced, is giving up the point entirely) we shall deprive ourselves of the very means of sinking the debt we have, or may contract. The value of the back lands, which some of the provinces are clandestinely deprived of, by the unjust extension of the limits of Canada, valued only at five pounds sterling per hundred acres, amount to upwards of twenty-five millions, Pennsylvania currency; and the quit-rents at one penny sterling per acre, to two millions yearly. . . .

I proceed now to the second head, viz. Which is the easiest and most practicable plan, Reconciliation or Independence; with some occasional remarks.

He who takes nature for his guide, is not easily beaten out of his argument, and on that ground, I answer generally, that independence being a single simple line, contained within ourselves; and reconciliation, a matter of exceedingly perplexed and complicated, and in which, a treacherous capricious court is to interfere, gives the answer without a doubt.

The present state of America is truly alarming to every man who is capable of reflection. Without law, without government, without any other mode of power than what is founded on, and granted by courtesy. Held together by an unexampled concurrence of sentiment, which, is nevertheless subject to change, and which, every secret enemy is endeavoring to dissolve. Our present condition is, legislation without law; wisdom without a plan; a Constitution without a name; and, what is strangely astonishing, perfect independence, contending for dependence. The instance is without a precedent; the case never existed before; and who can tell what may be the event? The property of no man is secure in the present unbraced system of things. The mind of the multitude is left at random, and seeing no fixed object before them, they pursue such as fancy or opinion starts. Nothing is criminal; there is no such thing as treason; wherefore, every one thinks himself at liberty to act as he pleases. The Tories would not have dared to assemble offensively, had they known that their lives, by that act, were forfeited to the laws of the State. A line of distinction should be drawn between English soldiers taken in battle, and inhabitants of America taken in arms. The first are prisoners, but the latter traitors. The one forfeits his liberty, the other his head. . . .

Put us, say some, upon the footing we were on in sixty-three. . . . To be on the footing of sixty-three, it is not sufficient, that the laws only be put on the same state, but that our circumstances, likewise be put on the same state; our burnt and destroyed towns repaired or built up, our private losses made good, our public debts (contracted for defense) discharged; otherwise we shall be millions worse than we were at that enviable period. Such a request, had it been complied with a year ago, would have won the heart and soul of the Continent, but now it is too late. "The Rubicon is passed."

Besides, the taking up arms, merely to enforce the repeal of a pecuniary law, seems as unwarrantable by the divine law, and as repugnant to human feelings, as the taking up arms to enforce the obedience thereto. The object, on either side, does not justify the means; for the lives of men are too valuable, to be cast away on such trifles. It is the violence which is done and threatened to our persons; the destruction of our property by an armed force; the invasion of our country by fire and sword, which conscientiously qualifies the use of arms: And the instant, in which such a mode of defense became necessary, all subjection to Britain ought to have ceased; and the independency of America, should have been considered, as dating its era from, and published, by the first musket that was fired against her. This line is a line of consistency; neither drawn by caprice, nor extended by ambition; but produced by a chain of events, of which the colonies were not the authors.

I shall conclude these remarks, with the following timely and well intended hint. We ought to reflect that there are three different ways, by which an independency may hereafter be effected; and that one of those three, will one day or other, be the fate of America, viz. By the legal voice of the people in Congress; by a military power; or by a mob. It may not always happen that our soldiers are citizens, and the multitude a body of reasonable men; virtue, as I have already remarked, is not hereditary, neither is it perpetual. Should an independency be brought about by the first of those means, we have every opportunity and every encouragement before us, to form the noblest purest constitution on the face of the earth. We have it in our power to begin the world over again. A situation, similar to the present, has not happened since the days of Noah until now. The birthday of a new world is at hand, and a race of men, perhaps as numerous as all Europe contains, are to receive their portion of freedom from the event of a few months. The reflection is awful and in this point of view, how trifling, how ridiculous, do the little paltry cavilings, of a few weak or interested men appear, when weighed against the business of a world. . . .

In short, independence is the only bond that can tie and keep us together. We shall then see our object, and our ears will be legally shut against the schemes of an intriguing, as well as a cruel enemy. We shall then too be on a proper footing to treat with Britain; for there is reason to conclude, that the pride of that court will be less hurt by treating with the American states for terms of peace, than with those she denominates "rebellious subjects," for terms of accommodation. It is our delaying it that encourages her to hope for conquest, and our backwardness tends only to prolong the war. As we have, without any good effect therefrom, withheld our trade to obtain a redress of our grievances, let us now try the alternative, by independently redressing them ourselves, and then offering to open the trade. The mercantile and reasonable part in England will be still with us; because, peace with trade, is preferable to war without it. And if this offer is not accepted, other courts may be applied to. On these grounds I rest the matter. And as no offer hath yet been made to refute the doctrine contained in the former editions of this pamphlet, it is a negative proof, that either the doctrine cannot be refuted, or, that the party in favor of it are too numerous to be opposed. Wherefore instead of gazing at each other with suspicious or doubtful curiosity, let each of us hold out to his neighbor the hearty hand of friendship, and unite in drawing a line, which, like an act of oblivion, shall bury in forgetfulness every former dissension. Let the names of Whig and Tory be extinct; and let none other be heard among us, than those of a good citizen, an open and resolute friend, and a virtuous supporter of the rights of mankind and of the free and independent states of America.

Federalist No. 51 (1788)

Commentary

Alexander Hamilton (1755–1804), James Madison (1751–1836), and John Jay (1745–1829) authored *The Federalist*, or *The Federalist Papers*, a collection of essays designed to help gain ratification of the new federal Constitution. In his continuing effort to identify the right way to maintain a separation of power among the three branches of the federal government (legislative, executive, and judicial), Madison explains in *The Federalist 51* (published 1788) that in "a free government the security for civil rights must be the same as that for religious rights. It consists in the one case in the multiplicity of interests, and in the other in the multiplicity of sects."

He notes that it "is of great importance in a republic not only to guard the society against the oppression of its rulers, but to guard one part of the society against the injustice of the other part. Different interests necessarily exist in different classes of citizens. If a majority be united by a common interest, the rights of the minority will be insecure."

One solution to this problem, he says, is to create "so many separate descriptions of citizens as will render an unjust combination of a majority of the whole very improbable." In other words, Madison sees the structure of the Constitution itself as a safeguard against the tyranny of the majority. The Constitution preserves states as distinct political entities and reserves to them certain powers (the most obvious being equal votes in the Senate and voting by states in the electoral college and for constitutional amendments). Because each state has different interests, Madison says, this form of government will act against "oppressive combinations" that threaten the rights of the minority.

Madison concludes his argument with his belief that "among the great variety of interests, parties, and sects which [the United States] embraces, a coalition of a majority of the whole society could seldom take place on any other principles than those of justice and the general good."

MADISON

To what expedient, then, shall we finally resort, for maintaining in practice the necessary partition of power among the several departments as laid down in the Constitution? The only answer that can be given is that as all these exterior provisions are found to be inadequate the defect must be supplied, by so contriving the interior structure of the government as that its several constituent parts may, by their mutual relations, be the means of keeping each other in their proper places. Without presuming to undertake a full development of this important idea I will hazard a few general observations which may perhaps place it in a clearer light, and enable us to form a more correct judgment of the principles and structure of the government planned by the convention.

In order to lay a due foundation for that separate and distinct exercise of the different powers of government, which to a certain extent is admitted on all hands to be essential to the preservation of liberty, it is evident that each department should have a will of its own; and consequently should be so constituted that the members of each should have as little agency as possible in the appointment of the members of the others. Were this principle rigorously adhered to, it would require that all the appointments for the supreme executive, legislative, and judiciary magistracies should be drawn from the same fountain of authority, the people, through channels having no communication whatever with one another. Perhaps such a plan of constructing the several departments would be less difficult in practice than it may in contemplation appear. Some difficulties, however, and some additional expense would attend the execution of it. Some deviations, therefore, from the principle must be admitted. In the constitution of the judiciary department in particular, it might be inexpedient to insist rigorously on the principle: first, because peculiar qualifications being essential in the members, the primary consideration ought to be to select that mode of choice which best secures these qualifications; second, because the permanent tenure by which the appointments are held in that department must soon destroy all sense of dependence on the authority conferring them.

It is equally evident that the members of each department should be as little dependent as possible on those of the others for the emoluments annexed to their offices. Were the executive magistrate, or the judges, not independent of the legislature in this particular, their independence in every other would be merely nominal.

But the great security against a gradual concentration of the several powers in the same department consists in giving to those who administer each department the necessary constitutional means and personal motives to resist encroachments of the others. The provision for defense must in this, as in all other cases, be made commensurate to the danger of attack. Ambition must be made to counteract ambition. The interest of the man must be connected with the constitutional rights of the place. It may be a reflection on human nature that such devices should be necessary to control the abuses of government. But what is government itself but the greatest of all reflections on human nature? If men were angels, no government would be necessary. If angels were to govern men, neither external nor internal controls on government would be necessary. In framing a government which is to be administered by men over men, the great difficulty lies in this: you must first enable the government to control the governed; and in the next place oblige it to control itself. A dependence on the people is, no doubt, the primary control on the government; but experience has taught mankind the necessity of auxiliary precautions.

This policy of supplying, by opposite and rival interests, the defect of better motives, might be traced through the whole system of human affairs, private as well as public. We see it particularly displayed in all the subordinate distributions of power, where the constant aim is to divide and arrange the several offices in such a manner as that each may be a check on the other—that the private interest of every individual may be a sentinel over the public rights. These inventions of prudence cannot be less requisite in the distribution of the supreme powers of the State.

But it is not possible to give to each department an equal power of self-defense. In republican government, the legislative authority necessarily predominates. The remedy for this inconveniency is to divide the legislature into different branches; and to render them, by different modes of election and different principles of action, as little connected with each other as the nature of their common functions and their common dependence on the society will admit. It may even be necessary to guard against dangerous encroachments by still further precautions. As the weight of the legislative authority requires that it should be thus divided, the weakness of the executive may require, on the other hand, that it should be fortified. An absolute negative on the legislature appears, at first view, to be the natural defense with which the executive magistrate should be armed. But perhaps it would be neither altogether safe nor alone sufficient. On ordinary occasions it might not be exerted with the requisite firmness, and on extraordinary occasions it might be perfidiously abused. May not this defect of an absolute negative be supplied by some qualified connection between this weaker department and the weaker branch of the stronger department, by which the latter may be led to support the constitutional rights of the former, without being too much detached from the rights of its own department?

If the principles on which these observations are founded be just, as I persuade myself they are, and they be applied as a criterion to the several State constitutions, and to the federal Constitution, it will be found that if the latter does not perfectly correspond with them, the former are infinitely less able to bear such a test.

There are, moreover, two considerations particularly applicable to the federal system of America, which place that system in a very interesting point of view.

First. In a single republic, all the power surrendered by the people is submitted to the administration of a single government; and the usurpations are guarded against by a division of the government into distinct and separate departments. In the compound republic of America, the power surrendered by the people is first divided between two distinct governments, and then the portion allotted to each subdivided among distinct and separate departments. Hence a double security arises to the rights of the people. The different governments will control each other, at the same time that each will be controlled by itself.

Second. It is of great importance in a republic not only to guard the society against the oppression of its rulers, but to guard one part of the society against the injustice of the other part. Different interests necessarily exist in different classes of citizens. If a majority be united by a common interest, the rights of the minority will be insecure. There are but two methods of providing against this evil: the one by creating a will in the community independent of the majority—that is, of the society itself; the other, by comprehending in the society so many separate descriptions of citizens as will render an unjust combination of a majority of the whole very improbable, if not impracticable. The first method prevails in all governments possessing an hereditary or self-appointed authority. This, at best, is but a precarious security; because a power independent of the society may as well espouse the unjust views of the major as the rightful interests of the minor party, and may possibly be turned against both parties. The second method will be exemplified in the federal republic of the United States. Whilst all authority in it will be derived from and dependent on the society, the society itself will be broken into so many parts, interests and classes of citizens, that the rights of individuals, or of the minority, will be in little danger from interested combinations of the majority. In a free government the security for civil rights must be the same as that for religious rights. It consists in the one case in the multiplicity of interests, and in the other in the multiplicity of sects. The degree of security in both cases will depend on the number of interests and sects; and this may be presumed to depend on the extent of country and number of people comprehended under the same government. This view of the subject must particularly recommend a proper federal system to all the sincere and considerate friends of republican government, since it shows that in exact proportion as the territory of the Union may be formed into more circumscribed Confederacies, or States, oppressive combinations of a majority will be facilitated, the best security, under the republican forms, for the rights of every class of citizen, will be diminished; and consequently the stability and independence of some member of the government, the only other security, must be proportionally increased. Justice is the end of government. It is the end of civil society. It ever has been and ever will be pursued until it be obtained, or until liberty be lost in the pursuit. In a society under the forms of which the stronger faction can readily unite and oppress the weaker, anarchy may as truly be said to reign as in a state of nature, where the weaker individual is not secured against the violence of the stronger; and as, in the latter state, even the stronger individuals are prompted, by the uncertainty of their condition, to submit to a government which may protect the weak as well as themselves; so, in the former state, will the more powerful factions or parties be gradually induced, by a like motive, to wish for a government which will protect all parties, the weaker as well as the more powerful. It can be little doubted that if the State of Rhode Island was separated from the Confederacy and left to itself, the insecurity of rights under the popular form of government within such narrow limits would be displayed by such reiterated oppressions of factious majorities that some power altogether independent of the people would soon be called for by the voice of the very factions whose misrule had proved the necessity of it. In the extended republic of the United States, and among the great variety of interests, parties, and sects which it embraces, a coalition of a majority of the whole society could seldom take place on any other principles than those of justice and the general good; whilst there being thus less danger to a minor from the will of a major party, there must be less pretext, also, to provide for the security of the former, by introducing into the government a will not dependent on the latter, or, in other words, a will independent of the society itself. It is no less certain than it is important, notwithstanding the contrary opinions which have been entertained, that the larger the society, provided it lie within a practicable sphere, the more duly capable it will be of self-government. And happily for the republican cause, the practicable sphere may be carried to a very great extent by a judicious modification and mixture of the federal principle.

Publius

A

A. Philip Randolph Institute, 4:147

ABC (American Broadcasting Company), 3:90, 4:187

Abenaki Indians, 1:56, 122

Abolitionists, **2:1–3**
  Anthony, Susan B., 2:11
  Douglass, Frederick, 2:48–49
  emancipation, 2:2
  Fourth of July, 1:73
  free blacks, 2:3–4
  history, 2:159–160
  journalism, 2:123
  music, 2:118–119
  Quakers, 1:167, 170, 171, 2.1
  Stanton, Elizabeth Cady, 2:163
  in states, 1:178
  violence and nonviolence, 2:1–2
  and woman's rights movement, 2:187
  See also Slavery; Thirteenth Amendment

Abu Gharib prison abuse, 4:214

Account of the Battle of Lexington, 1:240

Acheson, Dean, 4:8, 118–119, 120, 148, 194, 195

Acheson-Lilienthal Report, 4:8

Achille Lauro hijacking incident, 4:127, 189

ACLU. *See* American Civil Liberties Union (ACLU)

Act Concerning Aliens (1798), 1:236
  See also Alien and Sedition Laws

Adams, Abigail, **1:1–2**, *2*, 1:61–63, 1:157

Adams, Charity, *3:204*

Adams, Charles, *3:40*

Adams, Eddie, *4:191*

Adams, John (composer), 4:127

Adams, John (politician), **1:2–4**, *3*
  and Adams, Abigail, 1:1, 2, 61–63
  Alien and Sedition Laws, 1:4, 2:164
  American Revolution, 1:3
  in art, 1:137
  and *Common Sense* (Paine), 1:33, 35
  Declaration of Independence, 1:3, 49
  diplomacy and leadership, 1:3–4
  early life, 1:3
  family life, 1:61–63
  Federalist Party, 1:66
  Fourth of July, 1:72

and Jefferson, Thomas, 1:3, 4
Massachusetts state constitution, 1:178
Quasi-War, 1:146
as Revolutionary icon, 1:142
slavery, 1:170
and Warren, Mercy Otis, 1:197

Adams, John Quincy, 1:125, 170, 195–196

Adams, Samuel, 1:24, 43, 137, 167, 174, *174*

Addams, Jane, **3:1–2**, *2*
  disarmament and arms control, 3:39
  dissent in World War I, 3:42
  feminism, 3:55
  nonviolence, 4:145–146
  peace movements, 3:137, 138
  women and World War I, 3:202
  World War I, 3:19
  See also Peace movements

"Address to the Nation on the War in Vietnam" (Nixon), 4:256

Advertising and journalism, World War I, 3:86

Advice to the Unemployed in the Great Depression, (Ford) 3:246

Aerial photography, 3:141, 142, 4:27

Aerospace industry, **4:1–3**, *2*, 38, 39, 125
  See also Military-industrial complex; Space race

AFC (America First Committee), 3:43, 63, *80*, 138, 212

Afghanistan invasion, 4:3, 20, 28, 139, 157–158

AFL. *See* American Federation of Labor (AFL)

AFL-CIO, 4:108

African Americans
  American Revolution, 1:121–122, 143, 157–158, 167, 168, 213
  antebellum era, 2:3–4
  arts as weapon, 4:10
  churches, mainstream, 4:25
  Civil Rights movement, 4:32–35, *33*
  Civil War and its aftermath, 2:4–5
  Civil War music, 2:118, 119
  Civil War troops, 2:30
  Civil War veterans, 2:30
  Civilian Conservation Corps, 3:24
  conscription, World War II, 3:34
  in Continental Army, 1:168
  education, 2:54, 55–56, *56*, 70, *71*
  education, Civil War, 2:55
  education prior to Civil War, 2:54, 55
  family life, 2:64

United States Steel, 3:161, 4:107

United States v. Peters (1809), 1:182, 184

United States-Vietnam Relations, 1945-1967. See Pentagon Papers

Uniting and Strengthening America by Providing Appropriate Tools Required to Intercept and Obstruct Terrorism (USA PATRIOT) Act (2001), 4:5, 32, 139–140

Universal Declaration of Human Rights, 4:85

Universal Military Training, 3:145

University of California, 4:77

Unorganized Militia, 3:131

Urban League, 4:34

Urbanization, 2:175–177, *176*

Uris, Leon, 3:98, 4:89, 215

U.S. Agency for International Development (USAID), 4:65

U.S. Agriculture Department, 2:28, 66–67, 3:147

U.S. Air Force
and aerospace industry, 4:1, 3
CIA and espionage, 4:27
RAND (Research and Development) Corporation, 4:192
September 11 attacks, 4:137–138
Strategic Air Command B-52 Stratofortress, *4:2*
women and World War II, 3:204
women integrated into military, 4:212, 213, 214

U.S. Army
442nd Regimental Combat Team, 3:22, 82, *82*
African American troops, 2:59–60
Civil War, 2:30, 104
conscription, World War I, 3:30
conscription, World War II, 3:33
demobilization, World War I, 3:37–38
drugs and Vietnam War, 4:52–53
Indian removal and response, 2:86, 88
Latino military personnel, 4:109
Longbow helicopter, 4:2
McCarthyism, 4:121
medicine, World War II, 3:108
occupation of Confederate South, 2:125–126, *126*
photography, World War I, 3:141
prisoners of war, 3:146
Quartermaster Corps, 3:67, 203
Quasi-War, 1:146
rearmament during New Deal, 3:131–132
recreation, World War I, 3:165
sports, World War I, 3:178
War of 1812, 1:194

women, employment of, 3:207
women and World War I, 3:203
women and World War II, 3:203
World War I, 3:130
Wounded Knee Massacre, 2:182
See also American Legion

U.S. Army Air Corps, 3:28–29, 132, 193

U.S. Army Air Force, 3:142, 180, *180*, 204

U.S. Army Air Force Band, *3:128*

U.S. Army Air Force Orchestra, 3:127

U.S. Army Corps of Engineers, 3:101, *103*, 103 104

U.S. Army Nurse Corps, 3:202, 205, 206, 207, 4:212

U.S. Army Signal Corps
photography, 3:141, 142
technology, 3:102
women, 3:203, 206–207
and World War II, 3:204
York, Alvin Cullum, 3:212

U.S. Army-Navy Munitions Board, 3:145

U.S. Atomic Energy Commission, 4:11–13, *12*
See also H-bomb, decision to build

U.S. Censorship Office, 3:156

U.S. Central Intelligence Agency (CIA)
arts as weapon, 4:10
and espionage, 4:26–28, *27*
Friedan, Betty, 4:67
Hmong, 4:203, 238
Indonesia, 4:145
not part of Homeland Security Department, 4:140
Vietnam War, 4:203
See also U.S. Federal Bureau of Investigation (FBI)

U.S. Civilian Defense Office, 3:167

U.S. Civilian Public Service, 3:34, 43, 44

U.S. Coast Guard, 3:203, 205, 207, 4:212

U.S. Colored Troops Bureau, 2:155

U.S. Commission on the Wartime Relocation and Internment of Civilians, 3:82–83

U.S. Committee on Public Information
Advertising Division, 3:194
Civic and Educational Cooperation Division, 3:150
conscription, World War I, 3:31
Films Division, 3:150, 194
music, World War I, 3:124
patriotism, 3:136
Pictorial Publicity Division, 3:194
propaganda, 3:150–151
visual arts, World War I, 3:194

World War I, 3:12

U.S. Congress
9-11, 4:4
Alien and Sedition Laws, 1:33
Army rearmament during World War II, 3:131
Articles of Confederation, 1:12, 37
Bonus March, 3:192, 193
CIA and espionage, 4:27–28
Constitution, 1:40
Embargo, 1:54
and Federal Bureau of Investigation, 4:60
Gold Star Mothers pilgrimage, 3:67
Great Society, 4:72
habeas corpus, 2:25, 165
human rights, 4:85
Indian removal and response, 2:86, 88
and Johnson, Andrew, 2:93
and Lafayette's tour, 1:103–104
and military, 1:155
military bases, 4:122
music, musicians, and the war on terrorism, 4:127
naval construction and forces, 3:40, 41
Navy funding during interwar years, 3:145
New Deal, 3:131, 132
Operation Desert Storm, 4:18
Pledge of Allegiance, 4:5, 6
preparedness for World War I, 3:48
profiteering, 3:149
Reconstruction, 2:142–143
Truman Doctrine, 4:194–195
War Powers Resolution (1973), 4:205–206

U.S. Continental Army
African Americans, 1:168
camp followers, 1:29–31, *31*
formation, 1:154–155
generals' wives, 1:81–82
Jefferson, Thomas, 1:43
Lafayette, Marie Joseph Paul Yves Roch Gilbert Du Motier, Marquis de, 1:103, *104*
mobilization, 1:120–122
music, 1:129
Sampson, Deborah, 1:163–164
state battalions, 1:179, 179t
veterans' benefits, 1:189 190
Washington, George, 1:43, 44, 154–155, 158–159

U.S. Defense Advisory Committee on Women in the Services, 4:212

U.S. Defense Department
gays in the military, 4:69–70
military bases, 4:122
military families, 4:123, 124
military-industrial complex, 4:125
Office of Economic Adjustment, 4:122

W